OHIO
Real Estate Law

Sixth Edition

Carol K. Irvin, J.D.
James D. Irvin, J.D.

Irvin & Irvin
Attorneys at Law
11401 Willow Hill Dr.
Chesterland, OH 44026

Gorsuch Scarisbrick, Publishers
Scottsdale, Arizona

Caution: It is not the intention of this book to give legal advice concerning any particular real estate transaction or legal matter. Any person who needs legal advice, concerning any real estate matter discussed or referred to in this text, should seek the advice of an attorney.

The publisher makes every reasonable best effort to ensure the accuracy and completeness of the information and answers contained in this book. Due to the ever-changing nature of applicable laws and practices, the reader is cautioned and advised to always consult with the instructor when questions arise. Test answers have been checked for correct correlation with the question answered. If the reader encounters a questionable answer, the reader should always consult the text or the instructor for a more complete answer and analysis of the answer. Should the reader believe that an alternative interpretation of the information contained in this book is possible, he or she is encouraged to consult with the instructor.

Publisher: Gay L. Pauley
Editor: Shari Jo Hehr
Developmental Editor: Katie E. Bradford
Production Editor: Eric Kingsbury
Cover Design: Don Giannatti
Typesetting: Alice Bowman

Gorsuch Scarisbrick, Publishers
8233 Via Paseo del Norte, F-400
Scottsdale, Arizona 85258

10 9 8 7 6 5 4 3 2

ISBN 0-89787-956-2

Printed in the United States of America.

Library of Congress Cataloging-in-Publication Data

Irvin, Carol K.
Ohio real estate law / by Carol K. Irvin, James D. Irvin. — 6th ed.
p. cm.
Includes index.
ISBN 0-89787-956-2 (alk. paper)
1. Vendors and purchasers—Ohio—Outlines, syllabi, etc. 2. Real property—Ohio—Outlines, syllabi, etc. 3. Real estate business—Law and legislation—Ohio—Outlines, syllabi, etc. I. Irvin, James D. II. Title.
KFO126.Z9I78 1996
346.77104'3—dc20
[347.710643] 96-8625
CIP

ABBREVIATED CONTENTS

CONTENTS

10 OHIO REAL ESTATE LICENSE LAW 258

Case Studies

ILLUSTRATIONS & TABLES

PREFACE

Ohio Real Estate Law, Sixth Edition, covers the state and federal laws and rules that a person interested in real estate in Ohio needs to know. Ohio-specific content makes this book unique. However, when federal laws are important, as in cases where federal law prevails over state law, the federal laws are fully discussed. We believe the result is a reliable set of rules and concepts basic to the professional understanding of real estate in Ohio.

Strong emphasis has been placed on making the sixth edition of *Ohio Real Estate Law* a practical guide to applying laws and techniques. Each chapter opens with a "Key Terms" listing. Proper terminology is stressed throughout, with key terms defined at first use and compiled in a glossary at the end of the text for easy reference. True-to-life hypothetical examples as well as Ohio and federal court case studies illustrate and enforce key material. Because law changes so rapidly, we have updated material throughout the text and have added recent court case studies. A "Summary of Content" and "Review Questions" close each chapter, providing students with an opportunity to review chapter material, test and reinforce their understanding of the material, and offer additional perspective.

When we wrote the first edition of this text, our aim was to educate adult students interested in becoming real estate salespeople. Since that time our materials have been used successfully with other groups, from undergraduate students to graduate students, and from entry-level career people to experienced professionals in real estate, finance, law, and investment.

Many of the changes in this edition are based on suggestions we've received from instructors throughout the state and from our own students. We appreciate their help in revising and updating material. We would like to offer special thanks to our reviewers, Lucille Reider, Miami University, and Nicholas Kemock, Lorain County Community College, for their insightful comments on this edition. We would also like to thank Tom Fisher of Southern Ohio College Northeast for his careful review of the manuscript and his suggestions toward improving the text.

Carol Irvin and James Irvin

To the Student

Here are a few suggestions to help you get the most out of using this text.

1. Read each chapter at least twice, and study the figures and exhibits so you can visualize the principles. The first time through, read for general orientation to the subject area, not for complete understanding of every concept discussed. By all means, use the wide page margins for notes, questions, your own diagrams, or whatever will help you grasp the material. Treat the margins as your space and use your notes to question the instructor and other students during class. On the second reading, aim for greater comprehension. Underline or highlight the sentences and paragraphs that seem especially important, but do not overdo it. Be wary of marking everything in the text because this defeats the purpose of highlighting the most important material.
2. Read and review the "Summary of Content" at the end of each chapter to reinforce your learning of the chapter material.
3. Answer all "Review Questions" at the end of each chapter. Check your answers using the answer key. If you answer a question incorrectly, reread the chapter material related to that question. Mistakes at this stage cost you nothing, so it is a good time to make sure you clearly understand the material.
4. Use the Glossary at the end of the text whenever you encounter a legal term of which you are not sure. Sometimes you may know a word (the word *waste*, for example), yet the legal definition of that word and the legal interpretation of that meaning are completely unexpected. The "Key Terms" at the beginning of each chapter are a handy cross reference to the Glossary.
5. Develop an appreciation for the different types of *legal instruments* used in real estate practice. For example, learn to recognize a deed, a listing contract, a purchase contract, a closing statement, a title guarantee, and so forth. In doing so, you will be able to refer to these documents by their specific names rather than "the papers," and you will be recognized as a professional.
6. Carefully read the case studies in each chapter to grasp points of law and to learn how the legal system works. Discuss the cases with your instructor and other students.
7. Finally, after reading the text and completing the course, keep this text as part of your real estate library. In your career, or even in your own investment plans, you will need to know and refer to these real estate terms and concepts on a regular basis.

With these thoughts in mind, we wish you good luck, good learning, and good fortune.

1 BASIC LAW

KEY TERMS

answer
appeals court
arbitration
civil action
common law
complaint
Constitution
counterclaim
criminal litigation
deposition
discovery
interrogatories
judgment
mediation
precedent
pretrial
reply
service of process
settlement
stare decisis
statute
trial court

CERTAINLY AT ONE TIME or another we have yelled out in frustration, "That's unfair and against the law." We stop from saying more because we do not know which law protects us or where to go to get the law enforced. Finding the specific law, and then the correct forum to enforce that law, is where laypeople find themselves at a loss and turn to lawyers for aid. The topics in this chapter aid laypeople's understanding of the entire legal system by covering sources of law, the court structure, and basic civil procedure. This chapter offers a fundamental understanding of the basic law that is most likely to affect typical real estate practitioners.

Sources of Law

Constitutional Law

Law ordinarily regulates society by well-established rules. These rules are created for the most part by the legislature and are enforced by the judiciary. The primary source of American law is the **Constitution.** *Constitutional law is that law as stated in or derived from the United States Constitution or one of the state constitutions.* It is fundamental legislation directly by and from the people who are acting politically in their sovereign capacity. The Constitution distributes powers to the government, yet also reserves rights and liberties for the people. The U. S. Constitution is the supreme law of the land, the foundation of both American law and government.

A state's constitution is inferior and covers only that state, but it covers matters of state and local government that the federal constitution ignores. On those matters it is the ultimate source of law for the people of that state. Thus, the Ohio Constitution is inferior to the U. S. Constitution and covers only the state of Ohio. The Ohio Constitution also covers matters of local and state government that the federal one does not, and on those matters it is the ultimate source of law for Ohioans.

The Constitution establishes the form of government and the absolute rules of law. Anything in conflict with the Constitution falls in deference to the Constitution. The courts will strike down an unconstitutional Ohio statute, for example. Constitutional law is heavily concerned with rights and liberties of persons and property alike. Constitutional law separates the government into three powers: executive, legislative, and judicial. These three branches check and balance one another and achieve a balance of power in government. This separation of powers exists at both federal and state levels.

Administrative Law

The *executive branch* of the government administers and enforces the laws passed by the legislative branch. The head of the executive branch at the federal level is the president; at the state level it is the governor. The executive head appoints *administrative heads* for divisions of the government called *administrative agencies*. An administrative agency is a governmental authority, other than a court and other than a legislative body, that affects rights of private parties through either *adjudication* or *rule making*.

An administrative agency has the authority to make orders, findings, determinations, awards, or assessments having the force and effect of law and subject to judicial review. Administrative agencies formulate regulations and rules as the legislative branch allows. This is called administrative law. Examples of administrative law are, on a federal level, HUD settling discriminatory housing grievances; on a state/Ohio level, the Ohio Real Estate Commission following rules in hearing license suspension cases; and, in local communities, zoning boards reviewing proposed zoning changes.

Legislative Enactment

An act is administrative law if it executes or administers an existing law. An act is legislative enactment, however, when the legislature creates the law. The legislative branch of the government consists of elected leaders. At both the federal and Ohio levels these leaders are called senators and representatives. The senators sit in the U. S. or Ohio Senate; the representatives in the U. S. or Ohio House of Representatives.

To become law, a bill must pass both the House and the Senate and then be signed into law by the president (federal statute) or governor (state statute). If the president or governor will not sign the bill into law (vetoes it), the senators and representatives can pass the bill only by overriding that veto via a vote by a specified majority of their members.

A **statute** is *an act of the legislature declaring, commanding, or prohibiting something.* Statutes are formally published and made part of the organized system of law. Federal statutes are placed collectively by subject matter in a series of books that constitute the United States Code. In Ohio the statutes are in the Ohio Revised Code. The Constitution takes precedence over statutes. The legislature may not pass laws that conflict with the Constitution.

Legislative authority also exists at the local level. Cities exercise their *home rule power,* the power to govern and legislate locally, given under the Ohio Constitution to enact local ordinances. These are local laws that govern the city or village. Ordinances cannot conflict with the U. S. Constitution, the Ohio Constitution, or the Ohio Revised Code. Ordinances are of particular importance as sources of zoning and traffic-control laws.

Judicial Resolution

Legislative enactment looks to the future and changes existing conditions by making new rules to be applied thereafter to all or some part of those subject to its power. By contrast, the *judiciary investigates, declares, and enforces liabilities as it stands on present or past facts and under existing laws.*

The judicial branches of the federal and Ohio governments decide disputes between adversary parties and *interpret laws* pertaining to the dispute. These decisions usually are written opinions called *cases,* which are published and thus are available to judges and lawyers to aid them in future cases. When one case gives an interpretation of a law, that interpretation is **precedent** for future cases. Precedent occurs when a *principle of law,* actually presented to a court of authority for determination, is declared by that court to serve as a rule for future guidance in same or analogous cases. These subsequent cases, involving the same points of law, should follow the earlier decision. This concept is called ***stare decisis,*** also called the doctrine of precedents, and means that we should adhere to decided cases and settled principles and not disturb matters that have been established by judicial determination.

Over a long time, however, courts of authority do have the power to overturn their own precedents because even precedents must adapt to an ever-changing, evolving society. *Stare decisis* exists because it is necessary and desirable for settlement and certainty to develop in a society's legal system. If one court could easily reverse another's interpretation of law, the system would be chaotic and arbitrary. Therefore, *stare decisis* requires that a lower court be bound by a decision of its higher court. For example, an Ohio common pleas court must follow a legal interpretation on the same issue the Ohio Supreme Court made earlier.

A law's relative weakness or strength can be brought out effectively only by judicial interpretation. Laws do not operate in a vacuum; they are part of a dynamic, ever-evolving legal system, activated at its core by the judiciary. The courts decide whether a law is constitutional; usually this is one of the first cases decided on a new statute. If it is constitutional, it can continue.

Common law, also called *case law* and *judge-made law,* is opposite from legislatively passed law. Common law is a *body of law recognized by the judiciary as principles and rules covering government, persons, and property.* Its principles are broad and comprehensive, based on justice, reasoning, and common sense, and all emanate from the judiciary. Rather than deriving its authority from statutes or other written declarations, common law derives from *principles set forth in court decisions.* The principles of common law adapt to change as society progresses. It is not static but, rather, dynamic and growing. Common law also traces back to antiquity, including old usages and customs and the courts' continual reaffirmation of them through to modern times, in their decisions.

Common law is not enacted by the legislature, nor is it kept in any compilation. Whereas statutes cover a given area of the law certainly and specifically, common law tends to embrace universal and general principles. The lawyer doing research to find common law on a subject reads all the cases covering a principle of common law from early dates to the present. Common law covers many of the principles for real estate contracts and estates and interests in land, which we will study in subsequent chapters.

Civil Law Versus Criminal Law

Most real estate law is in the area of civil rather than **criminal litigation. Civil actions,** or *suits,* are all those that are *not criminal.* They are proceedings in a court of justice *by one party against another* for enforcement or protection against a *private wrong* or for redress or prevention of a private wrong. Civil suits include actions both in law and in equity.

Equity is the court's power, using common law, to *grant relief by ordering that an activity be stopped or started.* Law, by contrast, is the court's power to remedy a wrong by a *monetary award.* Equity promotes fairness and justice. When money damages do not adequately compensate an aggrieved party, the court's equity powers are invoked to do substantial justice. The term "equity" means fairness, justness, and right dealing.

Civil suits have the end goal of remedying wrongs done to private persons, whereas criminal suits have the end goal of the government's punishing wrongdoers for evil acts. These criminal wrongdoers pose enough of a threat to government and society that such governmental intervention is considered the only appropriate action.

Criminal law and civil law have important differences, especially in the rights afforded to the parties. Only the most important to real estate salespeople are discussed here. The *standard of proof* in criminal law is that the defendant must be proven guilty beyond a reasonable doubt. The standard of proof for most civil cases, however, is by a preponderance, or greater weight of the evidence. Finding a defendant in a criminal action guilty is far more difficult than finding a defendant in a civil matter not liable, because the civil standard does not require as high a degree of proof.

In criminal actions the defendant has the *right to an attorney.* If the defendant cannot afford one, the court appoints one and the state pays. This is not true of civil cases. Parties to a civil case have the right to be represented by attorneys if they can find and afford them. Thus, real estate salespeople should find out from their brokers what the brokers will pay for in the event of a lawsuit. Most reputable, substantial brokers will pay for a salesperson's legal expenses as long as there is no conflict of interest between them. Many brokers carry errors and omissions insurance, which will pay defense costs if a salesperson (and the broker) is sued. This insurance is discussed more fully in Chapter 9.

A defendant in a criminal case can *refuse to testify,* whereas a defendant in a civil case cannot refuse to testify. Also, people, whether as defendants or witnesses, can refuse to testify about something that will criminally incriminate them. If the testimony would help bring a civil action, but not a criminal one, against them, however, they can be compelled to testify.

Usually a lawyer advises a client not to discuss the case with anyone except the attorney. Communications made to the lawyer are protected under attorney-client privilege. Thus, lawyers cannot divulge anything their clients tell them, no matter what type of case is involved.

Although civil and criminal law are different in other ways, these are not as important for the real estate salesperson to recognize professionally. Generally, the same courts handle both civil and criminal cases. The courts are not different; an individual's rights and the applicable laws constitute the difference between civil and criminal law. The vast majority of real estate salespeople, should the situation arise, would be involved in civil rather than criminal lawsuits. Civil lawsuits, thus, are the central focus of this text.

Court Structure

The judicial system operates through courts—specifically, lower courts and appeals courts. The *lower courts conduct trials,* which conclusively resolve questions of fact by the evidence presented. No other court can substitute different facts. A judge presides over the trial and also can decide the case if a jury is not requested. If a jury is hearing the case, it makes the decision based on the evidence and the judge's instructions. Thus, the jury is considered the trier of fact unless there is no jury, in which case the judge is the trier of fact. The judge at the trial court level also determines any issues of law by applying the facts at hand to the appropriate rules of law.

Appeals courts determine questions of law; *they decide whether the trial court made an error of law or an abuse of discretion.* They do this by examining a complete record of the trial from the lower court. This record contains everything that was said or done in the case. If error is found, or the judge's abuse of his or her discretionary power, the case is reversed, or reversed and remanded. A *remand* means there should be a new trial. If no error or abuse of discretion is found, the appeals, or appellate, court upholds the trial court's decision. A panel of judges decides appellate cases; juries are never used.

Litigants can keep appealing their cases to even higher courts, but only their first appeal is guaranteed to them. It is called their *appeal by right*. Further appeals are discretionary on the part of the specific higher appeals court as to whether to accept or not accept the case.

Two court systems are important to the Ohio real estate salesperson: the Ohio courts and the federal courts. The federal court system is the final authority within its jurisdiction; the state/Ohio court system may not interfere with it. The federal court system, however, can interfere with the state/Ohio court system if the dispute involves the U. S. Constitution. Otherwise, the state/Ohio court system is its own final authority.

Figure 1–1 illustrates a case traveling on appeal through the Ohio and federal court systems. Refer to the figure while you read each of the subsections below.

Trial Courts

Common pleas court, municipal court, and county court are **trial courts** of the state of Ohio. U. S. District Court is the trial court in the federal court system. The trial court is the level where witnesses are subpoenaed to testify and where exhibits are introduced into evidence. This is necessary to let the trial court perform its essential function, that of *deciding issues of fact*. Trial courts may use juries if a party to the suit has requested one.

The most-used court in Ohio is the *common pleas court*. The Ohio Constitution creates one for every county. Common pleas court is one of *general jurisdiction;* that is, it is the proper place to bring a wide variety of cases, both legal and equitable in nature. If money is involved, the law prescribes a minimum amount, but no maximum, that must be involved. Common pleas court determines *equity as well as law cases*.

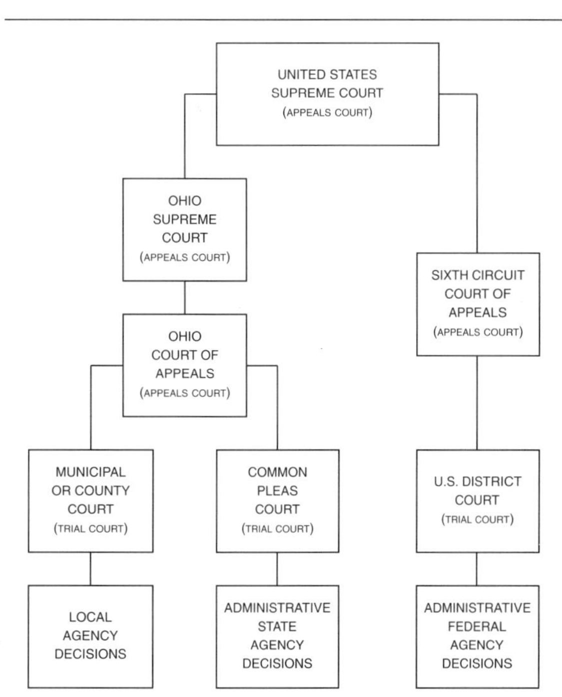

FIGURE 1–1
Path of appeals in Ohio and federal court systems.

Common pleas court also hears *appeals from orders made by administrative agencies*. For example, if a salesperson loses his or her license by order of the Ohio Real Estate Commission, the salesperson may appeal this loss in common pleas court.

The Ohio legislature created *municipal courts* to provide somewhat speedier and less costly trial courts to hear what it considers smaller cases. Municipal court can hear cases up to a maximum dollar amount as prescribed by law. Some municipal courts cover many cities and townships, when population is sparse. Others cover just one city, when population is dense.

County courts were created by statute. They are local courts with limited jurisdiction to hear minor civil cases. Each court's territory is all within a county, not subject to the jurisdiction of any municipal court.

Both municipal and county courts have *limited jurisdiction*. They hear cases concerning limited amounts of money and petty crimes and misdemeanors. These courts help relieve some of the case load pressure from the court of general jurisdiction.

Small claims court is a division within either the municipal or the county court. The parties handle their own cases, which involve small amounts of money and minor legal complaints.

Municipal, county, and common pleas courts hear a number of cases of crucial importance in real estate law. When more than one court has the power to hear the case, the courts are said to have *concurrent jurisdiction*. When only one court has the power to hear the case, that court has *exclusive jurisdiction* and no other court can decide the case. For example, only common pleas court can hear foreclosure suits. Common pleas court and municipal court can have *concurrent jurisdiction*. This occurs when either or both are empowered to determine the case, such as when a real estate broker sues a seller for an unpaid real estate commission. A sample complaint and answer are presented at the end of this chapter.

Common pleas court usually creates separate divisions for a certain type of case within the court structure. These are usually the probate, juvenile, and domestic relations divisions of common pleas court. *Probate court* handles the estates of persons now dead or infirm. If the case involves severe infirmity, the court can appoint a guardian to handle all the property of the infirm person. *Juvenile court* hears any case involving a person under 18 years of age. *Domestic relations court* handles divorces and the attendant disposition of property.

The federal trial court is usually the U. S. District Court. Because it is empowered to hear all kinds of federal cases, most federal cases begin there. These courts usually are found in major urban areas. The federal trial court has jurisdiction to hear a case if it involves a federal legal issue arising out of the Constitution, laws, or treaties of the United States, or in cases of diversity of citizenship—that is, plaintiff and defendant are residents of different states. Diversity of citizenship suits must involve certain threshold amounts of money in controversy as set by federal law.

Courts of Appeals

Intermediate appeals courts are not the highest courts; they are the ones between the highest and the lowest. They exist to lessen the appeal burden on the highest courts. Appeals courts do not have juries; they function to review the record from the trial court to ascertain errors of law or abuse of discretion by the trial court. At this level, evidence is not taken and witnesses and exhibits are not relevant. Both parties to the case file briefs citing legal precedent for the propositions of legal error or abuse being reviewed.

Courts of intermediate appeal exist in both the Ohio and the federal systems. Ohio has only one federal appeals court: the Sixth Circuit Court of Appeals, in Cincinnati. This court hears appeals from U. S. District Court cases from Ohio and other states. The Ohio state court system has Court of Appeal districts, created by the Ohio Constitution. Each Ohio appellate district consists of at least one county. All the appellate courts have multiple judges who together hear and decide cases. These are also the appeals courts wherein the appellants file their appeals by right.

Supreme Courts

There is an Ohio Supreme Court as well as the U. S. Supreme Court. The U. S. Supreme Court can reverse the Ohio Supreme Court, but the Ohio Supreme Court, being a lesser appeals court, cannot reverse or rule contrary to the U. S. Supreme Court.

Supreme courts are concerned primarily with questions of law. They do not have to hear all cases appealed to them; they can reject most cases for review except in a few limited circumstances. Thus, most appellants do not have appeals by right in these courts; these are the discretionary appellate courts.

An important function of supreme courts is to resolve conflicts between their appellate court districts. Thus, if the decisions of two or more Ohio appellate courts are in conflict, the Ohio Supreme Court can resolve the conflict. Likewise, the U. S. Supreme Court can resolve the conflict when two or more federal Circuit Courts of Appeal decisions are in conflict. A decision from the U. S. Supreme Court is binding on all courts within the United States, whereas an Ohio Supreme Court decision is binding upon all courts in Ohio only.

Arbitration and Mediation

Arbitration is a *contractual way of settling disputes.* The parties create their own substitute for a court and a judge, waive all or most appeal processes, and dispense with rules of evidence. Usually a panel of at least three persons acts as arbitrator. These persons usually have some expertise regarding the matter at issue. If it is a business dispute, for example, they are business people. Each side presents its case, in a relaxed fashion, before this panel. Witnesses and exhibits may be used. After each side has presented its case, the panel meets privately and votes upon which side should win. Whoever gets at least two of the votes wins. To be effective, arbitration should be binding; the losing party should not be able to appeal the arbitration results in court.

Two major, longstanding types of arbitration are occupational–professional and private. Members of a group set up *occupational–professional arbitration to resolve disputes between members.* The REALTORS®, the private trade group for brokers and salespersons, has binding arbitration. Its members resolve commission disputes and non-money ethics grievances alike by arbitration. The cost is low and the results are swift. Although REALTORS® bestow the right to use an attorney, many members do not; they personally present their own cases instead. Because the arbitrators are fellow REALTORS®, the method whereby members present their own cases can work well. The optional use of lawyers also contributes to the relatively low cost of arbitration.

Private arbitration usually arises from a contract entered into by two persons. The contract calls for arbitration instead of court, and a private arbitration panel is used. A common example is when a building contractor and a homeowner enter into a contract for a home improvement and each subsequently disputes the other's fulfillment of the contract. A national organization of professional arbitrators, called the American Arbitration Association (AAA), trains arbitrators to resolve this type of private, contractual dispute.

Arbitration, especially the occupational–professional type, can be done inexpensively. Also, it usually is done in a matter of months, at most. These are advantages, but disadvantages exist, too. If the case involves significant legal questions or a large sum of money for the parties, they usually prefer a court. The use of rules of evidence in courts protects the parties, whereas the relaxed rules in arbitration can result in a decision based on improper evidence. Also, if the arbitrators have no legal training, matters other than the merits of the case may unduly sway them.

In Ohio, trial court judges can refer some of their cases to arbitration, using attorneys as the arbitrators. These are cases in which only money is at issue. The sample complaint and answer at the end of this chapter is one that could work as well in the arbitration setting. In judge-referred arbitration, the losing party usually can appeal the results to the assigning judge. The losing party then, at a minimum, must pay all the costs of the concluded arbitration (perhaps a penalty as well) while the judge schedules a trial. Arbitration cannot be used in all cases, such as those in which the title of real property is in dispute. State law and procedure should be consulted on this point.

Mediation is another means of successfully *resolving a dispute short of going to trial.* In mediation, a central person, who often has specialized training, meets with all parties in a filed case. This mediator actively facilitates and negotiates with the parties in a structured fashion, trying to obtain a voluntary settlement from them. If successful, the case will be dismissed.

REALTORS® now also use mediation in their *Homesellers/Homebuyers Dispute Resolution System,* in instances of purchaser and seller disputes with REALTORS®. An approved mediation office is part of this system. The local REALTORS® board functions chiefly to refer the parties in dispute to the approved mediator. The experienced mediator takes over the case and attempts to resolve the dispute short of a lengthy, costly lawsuit. Participating members of REALTORS® incorporate a mediation clause within their purchase contracts stating that the parties agree to mediate any dispute arising from that transaction. If the parties are unsuccessful at mediating the dispute, they are free to pursue arbitration or litigation instead. If the parties are successful at mediating the dispute, they are bound by the results and cannot litigate against one another. Under this plan, mediation is not required for some cases, such as ones involving complex legal issues or criminal law.

Arbitration and mediation are different. One difference is that in arbitration the case is actually tried before the arbitration panel, whereas in mediation the case is not tried at all. Only settlement attempts occur in the mediation process. Another difference is that mediation is a voluntary effort and the parties are not bound by the mediator's decision, whereas arbitration usually binds the parties to the decision as if it were a judgment in a court of law. The trend, which keeps building, is toward increased use of both arbitration and mediation, as alternatives to the courts.

Administrative Agencies

Administrative agencies are not courts. They are *governmental agencies empowered to conduct hearings on areas of the law the agency regulates.* For example, the Ohio Real Estate Commission regulates the license law. Agencies conduct hearings in regard to their limited areas. Agencies may levy a variety of sanctions against any offending party, including private and public letters of reprimand, fines, and suspension or revocation of licenses. At the end of the hearing, the agency renders a decision. This decision usually can be appealed into court. The court may either review the agency's decision or order a complete trial on the merits of the case.

Civil Procedure

This section covers the procedure for a civil lawsuit from start to finish and seeks to acquaint current or future salespeople and brokers with the basics so they can have a fundamental understanding of how a lawsuit is conducted. Unfortunately, because of the overloads in the courts, there may be a one- to five-year wait before a case is heard. This makes it all the more important for practitioners of real estate to understand what their continuing roles are in the litigation process, as well as why attorneys must follow certain procedural steps in their clients' behalf.

Real estate litigation usually is not accepted by lawyers on a contingent fee basis. *Contingent fees* permit lawyers to recover their fees only if they win the case. Then they get a percentage of the money awarded to their clients. If they lose, they are paid nothing. This fee structure is commonly used in personal injury, malpractice, and workers' compensation suits. It is not generally used for real estate litigation; the client instead is billed at an hourly rate regardless of the attorney's success. The plaintiff's (the victim's) attorney frequently uses the contingent fee in fair housing cases.

Settlement

Settlement practice is becoming increasingly common. This involves *offers made by the parties to the lawsuit to settle the dispute for something less in order to avoid trial.* Sometimes settlement negotiations are under way from before the case is filed until the day scheduled for trial. Even if settlement is unsuccessful, no one loses any advantage at trial because of the attempts. As a matter of public policy, which is to encourage out-of-court settlement, settlement offers may not be introduced at trial as evidence of liability.

Juries are never told anything about settlement negotiations. In theory, judges should not be told either, but in practice they often are. Frequently, the judge enters the settlement process prior to trial by conducting a rigorous **pretrial** conference and possibly proposing settlement solutions to the attorneys to present to their clients. Once trial begins, the judge is supposed to disregard settlement attempts in reaching a decision.

The great expense of trial litigation has increased the use of settlement practice. Even if wholly innocent of any wrongdoing, salespersons and brokers should expect their attorneys to explore it as a possible alternative. Paying some amount of money early in the lawsuit may prevent a licensee from having to pay a great deal more money at a later point in the litigation process. This may be of great practical importance to licensees—more important, perhaps, than vigorously litigating their own correctness of action in the subject lawsuit.

The following material on civil procedure does not include administrative agency or criminal procedure, as students will be far less likely to encounter those proceedings in their upcoming real estate careers. An exception is that real estate licensees usually are involved with the administrative agencies of the Division of

Real Estate of the Department of Commerce of the State of Ohio and the Ohio Real Estate Commission. This topic is discussed in detail in Chapter 10, on license law.

Pleadings

Pleadings are legal documents in which the *parties to a lawsuit transmit to each other and to the court the legal wrongs complained of and defenses to those asserted wrongs*. In federal and Ohio courts, the purpose of the pleadings is to give the other party notice of the claims being made against him or her. Short statements of these asserted legal wrongs are all that is necessary. The fact pattern and applicable law controlling the legal wrong need not be set forth except for a few areas of the law, such as fraud or mutual mistake, which usually require specific detail. Figure 1– 2 puts into step format the requirements that both the plaintiff and the defendant must meet to get their pleadings in order.

Service and Summons

All the pleadings must be served upon the opposing party. The term **service of process** means *delivered, received, or somehow put on notice*. The court serves the **complaint,** *the first pleading,* upon the defendant along with the *summons, the official document calling the defendant into that court system for this specific lawsuit*. In federal and Ohio courts, certified mail, return receipt requested, is the preferred method to obtain service of process upon the defendant. Alternatively, personal service can be used. This occurs when the county sheriff personally gives the complaint and summons to the defendant.

Service is important because it proves that a person received proper notice. Without notice, a person is deprived of the constitutional protection of *due process of law*. Improper service is fatal to a case, as it violates a person's fundamental constitutional rights.

FIGURE 1–2 Lawsuit Procedure Chart. This puts into a step format the requirements both plaintiff and defendant usually meet to get their pleadings in order. The need for a responsive pleading is set forth along with the type of service for each stage.

Step No. 1: PLAINTIFF	**Files complaint and:** (A) Court receives original complaint. (B) Defendant receives (by certified mail from the court or in person by the county sheriff) a copy of the complaint.
Step No. 2: DEFENDANT	**Has a set number of days (under Ohio or Federal Rules of Civil Procedure) to either answer or to answer and counterclaim:** (A) Court receives original of answer or answer and counterclaim. (B) Plaintiff receives from defendant (usually by ordinary mail) a copy of answer or answer and counterclaim.
Step No. 3: PLAINTIFF	**Has a set number of days (under Ohio or Federal Rules of Civil Procedure) to reply to counterclaim:** (A) Court receives original of reply. (B) Defendant receives (usually by ordinary mail) a copy of reply.
Step No. 4: PLEADINGS IN ORDER Discovery at either's option until trial	**If settlement between parties has not been reached, case goes:** (A) To pretrial; if still not settled, then, (B) To trial.

Primary Pleadings

The primary pleadings usually needed to get a case ready for trial are the complaint, the answer, the counterclaim and reply, the third-party complaint, and the cross claim. Until these pleadings, as applicable, have been exchanged between the parties, the case cannot progress.

All civil procedures, and thus all the pleadings, in Ohio are governed by the Ohio Rules of Civil Procedure and in federal court by the Federal Rules of Civil Procedure.

Complaint

Plaintiffs file, in the appropriate trial court, their complaints, which set forth the *causes of action against the defendant.* Causes of action are the legal wrongs asserted against the other party, which can be one, a few, or many. *The plaintiff is the person suing; the defendant is the person who is being sued.* The complaint should not attempt to prove the case; short statements of the alleged legal wrongs perpetrated by the defendant are sufficient.

Answer

Defendants must answer the complaint. In their **answer** they can *deny, admit, or admit some and deny the rest of the complaint.* The most common form of answer is a combination of some admissions and the rest a denial. The defendant must answer the complaint within the time frame set forth in the Ohio Rules of Civil Procedure, if sued in an Ohio court. If sued in a federal court, the Federal Rules of Civil Procedure set forth the time limit. If the defendant fails to answer, the plaintiff can ask the court to render a judgment in default against the defendant. Therefore, the plaintiff can win thc case without going to trial.

Counterclaim and reply

The defendant's answer can have within it a **counterclaim.** In the counterclaim the *defendant sues the plaintiff for any legal wrongs* he or she suffered arising out of the same transaction or occurrence that is the subject matter of the complaint. This is called *compulsory counterclaim.*

The defendant also may sue for any claims he or she has against the plaintiff that do not arise out of the same transaction or occurrence that is the subject matter of the complaint. This is called *permissive counterclaim.* When the plaintiff receives the counterclaim, he or she must reply to it. A **reply** resembles an answer; it is called a reply because it is *the plaintiff's, not the defendant's, response.*

Third-party practice

When the *defendant sues another person who has caused his or her liability under the original complaint,* it is called a third-party complaint. A third-party complaint, in layperson's language, is literally saying: "If I am liable to the plaintiff, then that person over there (the third-party defendant) is liable to me." The defendant in the original complaint thus becomes the third-party plaintiff in the third-party complaint. The person he or she sues is the third-party defendant. The third-party defendant must answer. At trial all the issues and persons under both the original and third-party complaint are heard in order to determine liability. Third-party practice is common in real estate litigation. For example, a real estate company negligently fails to disclose information to a purchaser on which the seller directed disclosure, which results in the purchaser's suing the seller in a complaint. The seller can then sue the real estate company in a third-party complaint, as the real estate company is responsible for the seller's liability. The seller also may assert any claims he or she has against other parties that arise out of the same transaction or occurrence that is the subject matter of the lawsuit.

Cross claim

If one party has a *cause of action against another party grouped on the same side of the lawsuit,* that person usually may file a cross claim against the other person. A cross claim resembles a complaint. The essential differences are that a cross claim (a) is between two parties grouped on the same side of the case (both being defendants), (b) is limited to claims arising out of the same transaction or occurrence that is the subject matter of the complaint or counterclaim, or (c) relates to any property that is the subject matter of the litigation.

Discovery

Discovery is a *means of finding out the evidence and testimony of an opposing party or a witness in the lawsuit before trial.* Discovery is begun after the filing of the last responsive pleading, typically the answer or reply. Any party to the suit, defendant or plaintiff, can initiate discovery against the other party. Conversely, any party can wholly elect to forego initiating discovery.

Through discovery, the relative strength of the other side's case can be properly assessed to determine whether settlement or trial is appropriate. Frequently used methods of discovery are oral depositions, written interrogatories, requests for books and records, requests for admissions, and requests for physical inspection.

Deposition

A **deposition** is the *taking of a person's testimony.* One party's attorney calls a witness or a party to the suit for testimony to be given before that attorney and the other party's attorney. One or both attorneys elicit the testimony, usually by asking oral questions of the party or witness. The testimony must be preserved. This usually is done by a court reporter's taking down the testimony. Audiotaping or videotaping may be substituted for the court reporter. A deposition can be done anywhere, but it usually is taken in one of the attorney's offices.

The person who is giving the testimony, either as a witness or a party to the suit, is called the *deponent,* and swears to the testimony he or she is about to give.

If the deposition is being used only for discovery, only the attorney who calls the deponent asks the questions. This attorney has wide latitude in the types of questions he or she can ask. If, however, the deposition is being taken to *perpetuate or preserve testimony,* both attorneys question the deponent in the same manner as they would in a court of law. This latter type of deposition is used when it is feared that the deponent will be unavailable later for trial. Then, at trial, the deposition will be read, or played if videotaped, into evidence before the court.

A salesperson is more likely to be involved in the first type of deposition, used for discovery, than the second, for perpetuating testimony. If the salesperson is elderly or ill or about to move far away, however, he or she might give a deposition to perpetuate the testimony. Depositions have the advantage of face-to-face contact between the deponent and the attorneys. Because the deposition simulates trial, deponents can be assessed properly for credibility, spontaneity, and firmness under questioning.

Sometimes the deponent is required to bring all personal books and records. It is then called a deposition *duces tecum* (bring your papers). During the deposition the examining attorney can question the deponent about these papers, usually marking important papers as exhibits.

Interrogatories

Interrogatories are *written questions served by one party upon another party to the lawsuit.* That other party must answer the questions in writing and return them to the originating party and the court within a prescribed time limit. Interrogatories cannot be used with persons who are witnesses but can be used with other parties to the lawsuit. Through interrogatories, one party can discover what another party can be expected to say or present at the trial. The major disadvantage is that one cannot see how credible, spontaneous, and unshakable the party is in giving testimony.

Interrogatories cannot be used to perpetuate testimony, and they cannot be introduced into evidence at a trial instead of having the party there to testify. They can be used, however, to impeach that party's credibility at trial should one vary one's answers.

Books, records, and entry upon land

Another method of discovery is a motion for production of books and records. The side upon whom this demand is made must *produce specific papers for examination* by the other side. If a deposition is not also requested, no questions will be asked about the papers at the time they are made available to the requesting party. Usually the party making this demand also demands to make copies of any papers. This is allowable.

A party also may want to *enter real property.* At a designated time, place, and date, the requesting party enters the real property for some purpose or purposes, such as inspecting, measuring, testing, or surveying it. The client usually accompanies the attorney to explain or point out the areas relating to the dispute. The attorney usually takes along a still camera or a video camera, or both, to preserve evidence, because real property is subject to change.

Requests for admission

No one should spend time and attorneys' fees battling over indisputable, or easily proven, matters. The request for admission *forces an opposing party to take a position concerning the truth or falsity of a matter that must be proven in the upcoming trial.* Either party using this discovery device may send written statements of admission to the other party regarding any of the following: facts in the case, opinions, genuineness of documents, and application of law to fact. If the party served with these requests denies the admission, he or she must, within a given time, affirmatively state this and for what reasons. If the party remains passive and does nothing, the admission stands; the matter is admitted and will not have to be separately proven in this case's upcoming trial. A litigant using this discovery technique can hone down the matter in controversy and perhaps can settle it.

Requests for admission often are overlooked as a discovery device, but they can be decisive, efficient, and cost-saving. An example is: "The fair market value of 120 Broadway, Metropolis, Ohio, is $67,000 as established by the appraisal of Frank Warner, on July 7, 1994." If the party who is given this request for admission does not affirmatively show the fair market value to be otherwise, it will be deemed $67,000, and no evidence other than this admission will be needed in the case's pending litigation.

Discovery summary

The most likely legal stage for real estate salespeople to get involved in is discovery. Often they are the only people in the real estate company who know firsthand what happened with the opposing party. Salespeople will far more likely be deponents or help answer interrogatories than be called for trial. Therefore, salespeople should keep complete and accurate records of every transaction. They may be asked to produce these for discovery or trial. Also, good records are usually the most helpful tool for refreshing their memories about things that did happen. Credible, steadfast deponents often are predetermined by the quality of records they keep. Further, licensees who keep, in writing in their files, thorough records of everything they said and did in a transaction will be better witnesses at a deposition or during trial, and the records themselves may well be admissible to support the licensees' versions of what transpired.

Motion Practice

Attorneys for either side of the lawsuit may make a variety of motions. The two that the salesperson or broker would most like to have granted against the opposing side are a motion to dismiss and a motion for summary judgment.

Motion to dismiss

A motion to dismiss can be brought for a variety of causes, including lack of jurisdiction, improper venue, and insufficiency of process or service of process. Another ground for raising a motion to dismiss is that the *plaintiff has failed to state in the complaint a cause of action for which the law gives relief.* Thus, if the plaintiff has done no legally recognizable wrong to the defendant, there is no cause of action. Suppose a complaint is brought for fair housing discrimination based on a person's homosexuality. Because the Ohio and federal fair housing laws do not recognize homosexuality as a prohibited basis for housing discrimination, the suit has no basis. Thus, the court grants the motion. When this motion is granted, the lawsuit is over.

Motion for summary judgment

The motion for summary judgment asks the court to give judgment to one party because the *other party can show no genuine issue as to any material fact,* even if everything is favorably weighed in his or her behalf. Practically speaking, this means there is no real evidence to support either the lawsuit or an issue within a lawsuit. Evidence must be presented in these motions to support this proposition; it usually includes documents and affidavits. An *affidavit* is a person's sworn statement giving one's own firsthand knowledge about the matter at issue. Usually ample discovery is needed as part of the documentary evidence to support a motion for summary judgment. If the court grants this motion, the party who made it wins the lawsuit, or wins on that issue within the lawsuit, and the other party loses.

Pretrial

Before trial the court schedules a pretrial conference. All parties to the lawsuit attend, accompanied by their attorneys. Pretrials vary considerably according to the judge. Some judges want, from all the attorneys, lists including the names of all witnesses, all exhibits, admissions made by all parties, and all stipulations. Matters that are admitted or stipulated do not have to be proven in trial. After the pretrial, additional witnesses and evidence cannot be submitted at the trial unless they were undiscoverable at pretrial time. Other judges are relaxed about the pretrial and limit their inquiries to settlement possibilities; if none, they set the case for trial date.

The judge presides over the pretrial and has the attorneys in attendance. Typically pretrials are conducted in the judge's chambers while the parties wait outside, as they are not included in the conference. They must be there, however. A judgment can be rendered against a party for failing to be present. Also, during the conference an attorney may have to leave chambers to consult with his or her client over a just-tendered settlement offer or some point that requires clarification. Witnesses do not attend pretrials because testimony is not taken at them.

Trial

In the trial the facts are essentially told three times. In the *opening statements* the attorneys tell the judge, and jury if called, what will be heard and shown through the forthcoming witnesses and exhibits. Then each side puts witnesses on the witness stand for testimony and presents exhibits into evidence. Finally, in *closing arguments* the attorneys for both sides summarize what the judge or jury just saw and heard and each attorney uses persuasive arguments about why his or her client should be the winning one. Then the judge or jury decides the case. Both sides can waive a jury trial, making the judge the sole decision maker. If the trial has a jury, the judge gives jurors detailed instructions on the questions they should ask themselves in reaching a decision based on what they have seen and heard in court.

The attorneys try the case in court. The salesperson and broker have valuable functions at this level, also. If they present clear, well-documented records, their side of the case is easier for the judge and jury to understand and believe. Some of these records may be used as exhibits introduced as evidence. Others will be needed to adequately refresh the broker's and salesperson's memories for when they testify. Having reviewed the records, the attorney will be able to ask good questions. Examples of these records are the real estate purchase contract, listing contract, and promissory note.

Brokers and salespeople can be witnesses, regardless of whether they are parties to the suit, if they have knowledge of any of the events at issue at the trial. Salespeople and brokers should be wary of questions from the attorney for the party who did not call them as his or her own witness. This opposing attorney has the right to *cross-examine* the witness, and cross-examination gives the attorney wide latitude in asking questions. The questions may be leading and suggestive, but the judge exercises some restraint over cross-examination. Through cross-examination the attorney seeks to destroy the witness's credibility and, in short, make the witness look bad.

The broker or salesperson also has an increased chance of being called upon as an *expert witness* in someone else's case. Expert witnesses are *qualified to give their opinions based on questions in their field of expertise.* Other witnesses may not give opinion testimony. Real estate professionals are experts in the marketability of real property, the state of the real estate marketplace, and the character and type of land development in a neighborhood. In these matters brokers and salespeople are not likely to object to being an expert witness. In real estate malpractice suits, however, one real estate person's testimony is needed as expert testimony to make another real estate person liable. The expert testifies on standards of expected competency in the practice of real estate. Before salespeople agree to testify as expert witnesses in any case, they should secure the broker's permission because of their relationship to the agency.

Judgment and Appeal

The **judgment** is the *decision rendered at the end of a civil trial.* The judgment is in favor of one of the parties and against the other for a certain sum of money. In equity cases, it disallows or allows a specified activity by one of the parties.

This judgment can be appealed to the court of appeals. The broker's function then is to decide whether to pay further for an appellate argument based on an attorney's advice as to how good or poor the case is. Even if the broker does appeal, his or her active function is over. Testimony and exhibits are not used in appeals court. In appeals court only the attorneys argue questions of law before the appellate judges, based on what happened at the trial court level. As a practical matter, most real estate brokers do not take their cases to appellate courts. If the decision will have a long-range ill effect on the business or if the monetary loss is substantial, however, an appeal might be worthwhile.

Sample Lawsuit: Breach of Contract for Real Estate Broker's Commission

This example is of the first stage of the lawsuit.

FOR EXAMPLE

A real estate broker sues a seller for failing to pay his real estate commission. The broker-plaintiff's strongest piece of evidence is his written listing contract, which is attached to his Complaint as "Exhibit A." (See Figures 1–3 and 1–4.) The seller-defendant's strongest defense is that, because the contract is one of an exclusive agency only, he is not subject to the real estate commission for any purchaser he secures through his own efforts. He raises this in point 5 of his Answer (see Figure 1–5). Subsequent discovery on the case also will focus on point 5. Plaintiff-broker should compel the production of defendant-seller's written advertising matter. He also should depose the purchasers so he can question them about how they got together with the seller-defendant.

For fuller understanding of these materials, Chapter 9 addresses the different kinds of listing contracts, including exclusive agency.

CASE STUDY FROM THE OHIO SUPREME COURT

OHIO COUNCIL 8, AFSCME V. OHIO DEPARTMENT OF MENTAL HEALTH 9 Ohio St.3d 139, 459 N.E.2d 220 (1984)

Facts: There were labor contracts between unions and the state agencies; these contracts required that labor grievances be submitted to independent third parties for mediation. After individual labor grievances were mediated, the directors of the state agencies rejected the mediators' determinations, either in whole or in part. The labor contracts did allow for rejection of the mediators' determinations. Ohio Council 8 then brought lawsuits in four counties, asking that the courts enforce the determinations reached by the mediators and not allow the state agency heads to reject those determinations. Ohio Council 8 used Ohio Revised Code Chapter 2711, which contains the arbitration confirmation procedure, to support its position.

Issue: Whether the mediation provisions in the labor contracts are or are not subject to the arbitration confirmation procedure set forth in Ohio Revised Code Chapter 2711.

FIGURE 1–3 Complaint.

IN THE COURT OF COMMON PLEAS
OF
COUNTY, OHIO

ABC Realty Inc. 100 Main Street Anywhere, Ohio Plaintiff	)	Case No. 95-CV-1000
vs.	)	COMPLAINT
John Jones 200 Center Street Anywhere, Ohio Defendant	)	

(1) Plaintiff alleges that it is and has been a licensed Ohio real estate broker since 1970.

(2) Plaintiff alleges that on or about January 1, 1995, it entered into a written exclusive agency listing contract with defendant, attached as Exhibit A, whereby defendant promised to pay plaintiff a seven percent commission if plaintiff secured a purchaser for defendant's real property located at 1200 Broad St. in Anywhere, Ohio.

(3) Plaintiff alleges that on or about January 10, 1995, it directly originated the purchaser for the realty by showing defendant's real property to Mr. and Mrs. John Smith and, further, was the procuring cause of the Smiths' unbroken chain of interest in the aforementioned real property.

(4) Plaintiff alleges that it performed all of its terms under the written, exclusive agency listing contract, attached as Exhibit A, but that the defendant has failed to perform his terms under said contract and is thus in breach of said contract.

(5) Plaintiff alleges that on or about January 11, 1995 defendant entered into a written real estate purchase contract with Mr. and Mrs. Smith containing the same terms as specified to plaintiff in the attached, Exhibit A listing contract.

(6) Plaintiff alleges that defendant conveyed his real property to the Smiths on or about February 10, 1995.

(7) Plaintiff alleges that he has made repeated demand upon defendant for his seven percent commission, which is $4,200 (Four Thousand Two Hundred Dollars).

(8) Plaintiff alleges that defendant has refused to pay his commission and continues to refuse to do so.

WHEREFORE, plaintiff demands judgment against defendant in the amount of $4,200, interest on said sum from February 10, 1995 forward plus costs of this action.

Paula Drake
Paula Drake
Attorney for Plaintiff
100 Union St.
Anywhere, Ohio
(216) 555-2000

FIGURE 1–4 Listing contract.

EXHIBIT A

ABC REALTY INC.
EXCLUSIVE AGENCY LISTING AGREEMENT

In consideration of ABC Realty Inc.'s agreement to use its efforts to secure a purchaser for the subject real property and to list it with the subscribers of the Multiple Listing Service, the owner of said property grants ABC Realty Inc. the exclusive agency right to sell the property for a period of time from January 1, 1995, to March 31, 1995, real property known as 1200 Broad St., Anywhere, Ohio, for the sum of $60,000 gross.

If ABC Realty Inc. is successful in securing a purchaser for the subject property or, if it is sold during the period of exclusive agency to anyone with whom ABC Realty Inc. or any cooperating broker has negotiated during the period of this agreement, the owner agrees to pay ABC Realty Inc. and any cooperating broker a commission of 7% (seven per cent) based upon the price of which the subject property may be sold.

Accepted by: ABC Realty Inc.
100 Main St.
Anywhere, Ohio

By: Ame Hamilton (agent) Date: 1/1/97

The undersigned accepts the terms of the above agreement and acknowledges receipt of a copy of this agreement.

John Jones — 1/1/97
Owner — Date

FIGURE 1–5 Answer.

IN THE COURT OF COMMON PLEAS
OF
COUNTY, OHIO

ABC Realty Inc. Plaintiff	)	Case No. 95-CV-1000
vs.	)	ANSWER
John Jones Defendant	)	

Defendant answers plaintiff's allegations within its Complaint as follows:

(1) He admits Paragraph One.

(2) He admits Paragraph Two.

(3) He denies Paragraph Three.

(4) He denies Paragraph Four.

(5) He admits he entered into a written real estate purchase contract with Mr. and Mrs. Smith for the subject realty but denies that the terms therein were those specified under the Exhibit A, exclusive agency listing contract, defendant having procured the Smiths as purchasers through his own advertising.

(6) He admits Paragraph Six.

(7) He admits Paragraph Seven.

(8) He admits Paragraph Eight.

WHEREFORE, defendant demands that judgment be rendered in his favor and that plaintiff be ordered to pay the costs of this action.

Marian Canfield
Marian Canfield
Attorney for Defendant
200 College St.
Anywhere, Ohio
(216) 729-3000

PROOF OF SERVICE

A copy of the foregoing was mailed by ordinary U.S. mail to plaintiff's attorney, Paula Drake, at 100 Union St., Anywhere, Ohio, on March 30, 1995.

Marian Canfield
Marian Canfield
Attorney for Defendant

Held by the Ohio Supreme Court: Mediation and arbitration represent separate and distinct means of attempting to resolve grievances. Ohio Revised Code Chapter 2711 allows confirmation of awards made in arbitration proceedings only. However, the proceedings that the labor union seeks to enforce do not stem from arbitration but, instead, come from mediation. An examination of the labor contract shows that the third parties were not only labeled as "mediators" but also were supposed to function in an advisory capacity. In addition, either side could reject the advisory opinion for a variety of reasons specifically set forth within the contract. The parties did not agree to be bound by the determinations of mediators. In fact, the contract expressly provides otherwise. Without this critical element of the parties' agreeing to be bound, arbitrations did not take place and, therefore, the provisions of Ohio Revised Code Chapter 2711 cannot be used to confirm the mediators' determinations.

Summary of Content

1. Constitutional law is derived from the United States Constitution and the Ohio Constitution. Constitutional law is the supreme law of the land, and any laws that conflict with the appropriate Constitution would have to defer to that Constitution.
2. Administrative law comes from the executive branch of government and is effectuated by administrative agencies that formulate rules and regulations as allowed by the legislative branch.
3. The legislature enacts laws called statutes, which declare, command, or prohibit something.
4. The judiciary interprets law in actual cases between disputing parties; it establishes precedent to give rules that can be followed in subsequent cases.
5. Civil law is law that is not criminal. It has less of a standard of proof than criminal law, and civil litigants are given fewer rights and protections.
6. Civil law covers both law and equity actions. Law is a court's power to remedy a wrong by a monetary award; equity is a court's power to grant relief by ordering an act to be stopped or started.
7. Federal and Ohio courts alike are structured through lower courts, which hear trials, and appeals courts, which review whether an error of law or abuse of discretion occurred in the lower courts.
8. Trial courts decide issues of fact by using witnesses and exhibits as evidence. The judge applies rules of law to the facts of the case.
9. Appeals courts decide issues of law by reviewing the record and decision from the lower court.
10. Alternatives to using the court system are arbitration and mediation. Arbitration uses a private panel, by agreement of the parties, to reach a decision; mediation is a structured means, using a central negotiator, of reaching a resolution of the dispute.
11. The parties to a case must follow rules of civil procedure in litigating a case. Minimally, pleadings, which state the wrongs complained of and the relief or remedy demanded, are filed with the court and one another by all litigants. These pleadings typically consist of the complaint, answer, counterclaim, and reply.

12. Parties to a lawsuit also may use discovery to uncover evidence for the upcoming trial. The methods typically are: the deposition; interrogatories; production of books, records, and entry upon the land; and requests for admission.
13. Parties to a lawsuit can attempt to win a case without going to trial by using either a motion to dismiss or a motion for summary judgment.
14. Pretrial conferences are held between judge and the litigants to inquire into settlement, limit the matters that will be pursued at trial, and set the date for a trial.
15. A judge or a jury decides a case after hearing opening statements, listening to witnesses, viewing exhibits, and hearing closing arguments.
16. The decision rendered by a judge or jury is called a judgment. Judgments can be appealed to appeals courts.

Review Questions

1. *Stare decisis* makes an Ohio Supreme Court case binding as precedent upon:
   a. a case from another state
   b. a subsequent case decided by the U. S. Supreme Court
   c. a subsequent case decided by an Ohio trial court
   d. all of the above

2. The Ohio Common Pleas Court, as the state trial court of general jurisdiction, usually:
   a. is located in every county
   b. has a high case load
   c. has exclusive jurisdiction over foreclosure suits
   d. all of the above

3. The Ohio Revised Code is written by which branch of the government?
   a. executive
   b. legislative
   c. judicial
   d. none of the above

4. As a source of law, common law is:
   a. not derived from the same source as legislatively passed law
   b. being eradicated throughout the United States
   c. kept in a compilation along with state statutes
   d. all of the above

5. The primary source of law that no other law may conflict with is:
   a. common law
   b. statutory law
   c. constitutional law
   d. ordinances

6. Ohio Real Estate Commission decisions may be first appealed to:
   a. an Ohio court of appeals
   b. the Ohio Supreme Court
   c. a United States district court
   d. an Ohio common pleas court

7. The United States Code is enacted by:
   a. ratification by the states
   b. executive order
   c. the federal Congress
   d. the federal judiciary

8. The causes of action asserted by plaintiffs against the defendants are found in the:
   a. complaint
   b. counterclaim
   c. cross claim
   d. third-party complaint

9. Defendants' response to a complaint, when they do not in turn sue the plaintiffs or a co-defendant is:

   a. reply
   b. answer
   c. cross claim
   d. counterclaim

10. If the defendants wish to sue the plaintiffs, they should:

   a. reply
   b. answer
   c. cross claim
   d. counterclaim

11. An answer is to a complaint as a reply is to a(n):

   a. reply
   b. answer
   c. counterclaim
   d. cross claim

12. Discovery is used:

   a. to perpetuate testimony
   b. to discover the strength of opposing party's claim
   c. to assess a witness's credibility
   d. all of the above

13. Which of the following persons do not attend the pretrial?

   a. witnesses
   b. parties to the case
   c. judge
   d. attorneys for the parties

14. The motion to dismiss is based upon:

   a. failure to have facts to support the case
   b. failure to state a cause of action for which relief can be given
   c. failure to answer the complaint on time
   d. all of the above

15. At trial, the attorneys present the facts through:

   a. exhibits
   b. questions asked of witnesses
   c. properly preserved depositions of unavailable witnesses
   d. all of the above

16. The court's decision after trial on someone's behalf is called:

   a. judgment
   b. certificate of judgment
   c. attachment
   d. garnishment

17. Which of the following can reverse a decision made by the California Supreme Court?

   a. the appropriate federal circuit court of appeals
   b. the U. S. Supreme Court
   c. the Ohio court of appeals
   d. any of the above

18. The judiciary's function is to:

   a. give rule-making power to administrative agencies
   b. enact statutes
   c. amend the constitution
   d. interpret the law

19. The separation of powers in the branches of government is controlled by:

   a. the U. S. Constitution
   b. each state's Code
   c. a specific amendment to the U. S. Constitution
   d. administrative agencies

20. Salespeople's essential function in the litigation process is to:

   a. fully understand each phase of the litigation
   b. supply information based on accurate records of all their transactions
   c. try to be unavailable for depositions to make it harder on the other side
   d. talk to the people on the other side of the case to change their minds

21. This piece of discovery allows one to walk upon the real property at issue in a court case:

   a. motion for physical examination
   b. interrogatories
   c. requests for admission
   d. deposition

22. Which person *could not* be in a trial court case?
    a. plaintiff
    b. defendant
    c. third-party plaintiff
    d. appellant

23. Civil defendants:
    a. have the same rights and protections as criminal defendants
    b. have the right to a lawyer if they can afford one
    c. will be warned that any statements they make can be used against them
    d. can post bond to get out of jail

24. Appellate courts:
    a. listen to voluminous testimony
    b. listen to attorneys' oral arguments
    c. read extensive documentary evidence
    d. empanel juries

25. Concurrent jurisdiction:
    a. means two different courts are hearing cases of similar subject matter
    b. means two different courts have jurisdiction for the same kind of case
    c. is not recognized under Ohio law
    d. has been abolished in Ohio

Answer Key

1. c
2. d
3. b
4. a
5. c
6. d
7. c
8. a
9. b
10. d
11. c
12. d
13. a
14. b
15. d
16. a
17. b
18. d
19. a
20. b
21. a
22. d
23. b
24. b
25. b

2
LAND AS PROPERTY

KEY TERMS

adaptation-to-use test
air rights
annexation/attachment test
appurtenance
attachment, method of
chattel
compensatory damages
emblements
encroach
fixtures
fructus industriales
fructus naturales
improvement
intention test
land
legal description
nuisance
personal property
personalty
property
real property
realty
reasonable person
riparian rights
subsurface rights
tenants' fixtures
trade fixtures
trespass

Real Property and Personal Property

Most people are aware that **real property** and **personal property** are different. Without giving the matter much thought, the average person recognizes the comparatively permanent or fixed quality of real property as contrasted with the flexibility or ease of change that marks personal property.

At the heart of it, movability determines, for most people, whether an item is real property or personal property. Actually, movability is not such a bad test. In fact, the law traditionally applies this very characteristic to determine whether it is dealing with real property or personal property. Think of the word "cattle." Is not a herd of cattle an easily movable, valuable item of property? The word **chattel,** meaning an item of personal property, comes from the word "cattle," and the concept of movability played a large part in selecting that term.

The only problem with the movability test is that it is too limited and lacks the range and sophistication necessary for defining **property** in a modern, complex society. After all, with hydraulics, superhighways, and space-age metals technologies, we are moving things today that no one imagined lifting 50 years ago. For this reason, the law has developed theories and tests going beyond mere movability to indicate **realty** or **personalty.** A detailed discussion of these theories and tests follows.

Land

Throughout this text, we use the term **land** to mean the same thing as *real property, real estate, or realty.* Land is generally thought to be everything from the center of the earth, out through the mass of the earth, continuing past the surface, as described by lines on the surface, up into the atmosphere, above such surface in an expanding geometric form that reflects the surface shape of the property, to infinity. This concept of land is diagrammed in Figure 2–1. Note that the land consists of three components or parts—air rights, surface rights, and subsurface rights.

To actually describe the land, as in the **legal description** on a deed, only the *surface* boundaries of the parcel are referred to. The air rights and the subsurface rights and the rest of the surface rights are *implied by the law* to be included as part of the parcel. For this reason, a parcel of land that is improved by the addition of a residential house is legally described in exactly the same way as a parcel of "raw" or unimproved land. Accordingly, note the language of the following legal description.

> Situated in the City of Lyndhurst, County of Cuyahoga, and State of Ohio: And known as being Sublot No. 4 in a Resubdivision made for The Society for Savings in the City of Lyndhurst of part of Original Euclid Township Lot No. 10, Tract No. 1, as shown by the recorded plat in Volume 100 of Maps, Page 1 of Cuyahoga County Records, and being 25.00 feet front on the Easterly line of South Street, 73.50 feet front on the curved turnout between the said Easterly line of South Street and the Southerly line of Main Street, and extending back 136.43 feet on the Northerly line, which is also the Southerly line of Main Street, 184.78 feet deep on the Southerly line, and being 36.45 feet wide in the rear, as appears by said plat, be the same more or less, but subject to all legal highways.

FIGURE 2–1
Concept of land.

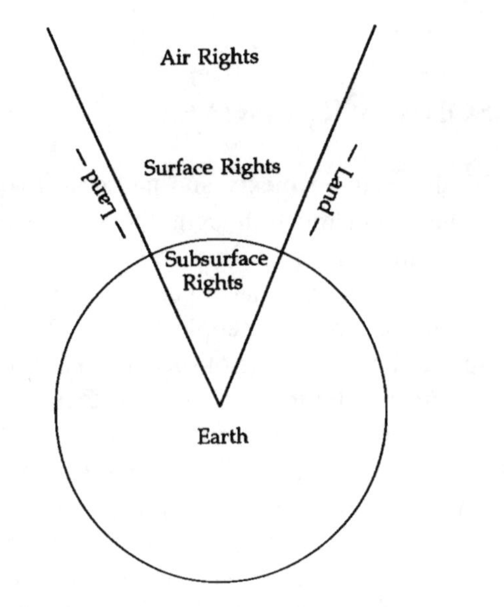

Simply reading this legal description of a parcel of land, one has no way of knowing whether the property has a house on it. If a house rests upon the surface, or if valuable minerals are part of the subsurface, or if important air rights exist, or if harvestable timber grows upon the surface, the purchaser of the "land" described above receives all of these things because they are all part of the land. The standard legal description of a parcel of land is a type of legal shorthand. Leaving most of the parts or components of the land to assumption or implication makes it easy to refer to the land, when necessary, without going into a lot of unnecessary detail.

Land, of course, consists of even more than the tangible, visible building and lot. It also includes appurtenances and attachments. **Attachments** are *things that are attached to the land,* both naturally and by man, and become part of the land. **Appurtenances,** which we will next discuss, are *rights that go along with owning land,* a somewhat intangible element. Students should think of land as a multifaceted item, containing both tangible and intangible components.

APPURTENANCES

Airspace Rights

Early lawmakers, who worked the concept of **air rights** into the total of what real property owners possess when they own land, had no way of perceiving the development of air travel as we know it today. Thus, these lawmakers were easily able to envision an infinite ownership of airspace from the surface of the land to the highest heavens. Although subsurface rights still have this aspect of infinity, air rights ceased having that aspect in the 20th century. The proliferation of air travel rights is responsible for important changes in the airspace component concept of land.

A modern legal definition of land, therefore, limits the airspace component to the *area actually able to be used by the landowner.* Normally, this includes enough airspace to permit raising tall trees or erecting a wind-powered electric generator, a tall ham radio operator's antenna, or even a high-rise apartment complex. Beyond this, present law seems to consider the upper airspaces open for use by aircraft with no duty to compensate the landowner. The trespass and nuisance aspects of airspace rights are discussed further on.

Subsurface Rights

The **subsurface** component of land does extend to infinity, downward vertically into the earth. In owning land, a person also usually owns the subsurface rights as one of the tangible elements of the land. Sometimes, however, a person is interested in owning the subsurface rights only or, conversely, the surface rights while granting another person the subsurface rights.

Oil, gas, minerals, coal, precious metals, and gems are some of the valuable items found in the subsurface component of land. A person might own the right to one of them, for example, by outright *deed* wherein that person has absolute title to, say, the mineral rights of that land. Or an owner might sell the land *except* for the mineral rights, reserving the subsurface use and exploration for himself or herself despite a new owner's right to the rest of the land. A person also might take an oil, gas, or mineral lease on land and thus be a tenant for only that subsurface use of the land. Granting an easement (the lawful use of another's land for a specific purpose) for these subsurface rights is also common. Finally, some mining companies even negotiate for options to explore the subsurface for the possible presence of valuable items. These options are contracts wherein the mining company agrees to pay the owner X dollars for the privilege of exploring the subsurface, and the company pays another price for leasing or buying certain subsurface rights if the exploration results are positive.

Water Rights

Two basic types of land border water: *riparian land,* that which borders a stream or watercourse, and *littoral land,* that which *borders a lake, an ocean, or a sea.* Generally, the rights for both types of land are the same.

In water-rights lawsuits, Ohio follows a **riparian rights** theory: the landowner has the *right to use the water equally* with other riparian landowners. The only requisite is that he or she own land bordering on water. This owner has the right to the ordinary or natural flow of water. If another riparian owner, such as an upstream owner, tries to lessen or cut off the flow of water to a downstream owner (perhaps by damming the water), the downstream owner, applying the riparian theory, can get a court order enjoining (stopping) the upstream owner from interfering with the natural flow of the water (the dam would have to be dismantled).

The practical significance of subsurface, water, or airspace rights for real estate practitioners is that they have to be careful about what representations they make to interested purchasers about the component parts of the real property. An agent should *not* say that the purchaser will have sole use of all of the land and its bordering water, with no one else's interference, when the purchaser actually is subject to an oil and gas lease, is in the flight path of the airport, or has water rights that must be shared with other riparian rights owners.

Chapter 9 discusses in detail the problems that agents encounter in making representations about real estate they are selling. Agents have to treat water/air/subsurface rights much as they do any potential condition or defect in the realty.

ATTACHMENTS

Attachments are both natural and manmade items that become part of the real property. These can be classified as fixtures or as improvements.

Fixtures

A **fixture** is defined as *an item that was once personal property, which became part of the real property.* It is a *man-made attachment* to the real property that is transformed from personalty into realty.

Sometimes an item is so closely related to the real property that there is no question as to the nature of the item. In such cases, a **reasonable person** would clearly recognize the item as real property or a fixture, something having completely lost its character as personal property. Reasonable persons are those who behave as a judge or jury would perceive prudent persons as behaving.

Take for example, a built-in dishwasher. Although the dishwasher was personal property at the time it was purchased at the appliance store, a reasonable person considers it to be realty once incorporated into the realty.

In contrast are items so loosely related to the realty that a reasonable person recognizes them as personalty and things that just happen to be at or on the realty. Pots and pans put into the dishwasher are examples. Certainly the law does not have to provide tests in these instances, but what about the arguable items, those in the gray area? What about the hand-held garage door opener control, the glass fireplace doors, or even the clear plastic toilet bowl seat full of dimes, nickels, and pennies? Legal tests are necessary for items in this gray area because the cost of replacing even some of the most minor items is so high. Even without the cost consideration, though, uncertainty about any aspect of the real estate sales transaction is the last thing anyone needs.

Fixture Tests

The tests for determining whether an item is a fixture have evolved over time.

Annexation/attachment

The **annexation/attachment test** examines the *physical attachment of the item to the realty* or the *annexation or incorporation of the item into the realty.* For a long time this test worked well where the item was either firmly annexed or attached to the realty or was not so annexed or attached. The word *fixture* itself naturally describes something that is well *affixed* to the realty. The dishwasher is an example of an item that qualifies as a fixture under this test, because it is now firmly part of the realty.

The test has its limits, however, and we caution against relying too heavily on it or using it to the exclusion of the other, more modern tests discussed below. It is all too easy to think "fixture" and immediately associate "method of annexation or affixation." Merely attaching an item to real estate does not automatically convert it into being a fixture. Failing to attach an item at all to the real estate could seriously hinder its being considered a fixture, however. The extent and manner of attaching an item vary, of course, with the type of article. One attaches a stove, for example, far differently than attaching bookshelves.

Adaptation to use

The next test developed, the **adaptation-to-use test,** removed many of the limitations of the annexation/attachment test. Together, the two tests can classify just about any questionable item. Applying the adaptation-to-use test, one questions *how well the item is suited to the use to which it is being put.* This is entirely different from asking how well the item is attached or affixed to the realty. An item might be well adapted as to utility but only flimsily attached.

Think of a battery-operated wall clock hung from a nail, fitting into a certain opening in a built-in cabinet and the whole thing harmonizing perfectly with the rest of the built-in lighting fixtures and interior trim of the room. Then imagine the confusion in deciding whether the clock is realty or personalty in the absence of the adaptation test. Not to say that the clock is clearly realty (a fixture), but at least a purchaser could argue that the clock is so well adapted to the realty that, as a fixture, it should pass to the purchaser.

This test also views items as being *constructively annexed.* Even though the items aren't physically attached to the real property, they are so well adapted to it that annexation applies. The modern trend is to increase the importance of this test, especially if it is used in conjunction with the intention test.

Intention

The most recent test, now considered a leading one, usually is referred to as the **intention test.** It goes beyond both of the other tests and allows virtually every questionable item to be tested. It also has potentially uniform application. The test is *objective* rather than subjective; it theoretically rests on concepts everyone shares rather than upon the particular, subjective ideas of the persons involved.

In the intention test, one imagines how a judge or jury would perceive reasonable persons behaving under similar circumstances. The judge or jury thus envisions reasonable persons acting as realty purchasers, seeing the questioned item upon examination of the realty and then asking themselves *what they think sellers intended upon installing the item.* If reasonable purchasers decide that sellers added the item with the intent to devote it to the use and service of the realty in such a way as to increase the serviceability of the whole as a permanent unit of property, they classify the item as a fixture and thus as realty. Or reasonable purchasers decide that the item is personalty, permitting sellers to take the item when they move.

This test does not discard the annexation and adaptation concepts. The same questions of attachment, annexation, and utility are asked. But with the intention test, reasonable purchasers are not limited to just those questions. They may take into account all factors that seem to indicate what sellers intended when installing the item.

Why not simply ask sellers what they intended? Why bother with these hypothetical reasonable purchasers at all? The answer is that sellers who already have taken or plan to take the item invariably say they installed it only temporarily. Purchasers who want the item will argue the reverse. These are subjective arguments, whereas the intention test is objective. This is why hypothetical reasonable purchasers are used. In the absence of an expressed agreement, intention is inferred from the nature of the article itself, the relationship between the interested parties, the way the item is attached, and the purpose for which it is used.

Figure 2–2 presents a vivid example contrasting fixture and non-fixture items.

FIGURE 2–2
Fixture contrasted with non-fixture.

[JACKSON POLLOCK PAINTING HUNG WITH NAILS IN LIVING ROOM OF A RESIDENCE.]

Worth of house: $800,000

Worth of painting: millions

The painting is not a fixture because:

(a) it is not so permanently annexed or attached so as to become one
(b) it is not so adapted to the property that it has become the real property
(c) no reasonable person would intend that an easily removable Jackson Pollock painting would become part of the realty.

House's worth remains at $800,000.

[JACKSON POLLOCK MURAL PAINTED ONTO LIVING ROOM WALL.]

Worth of house: $800,000

Worth of mural: millions

The mural is a fixture because:

(a) it is so permanently annexed and attached so as to become one
(b) it is so adapted to the property as to become one
(c) the person who commissioned the mural must have intended it to be annexed and adapted to the property or he would have commissioned a painting instead.

House's worth is now in the millions. The owner should concentrate on selling the mural to a museum or collector even if it means destroying the house to remove the mural.

Fixtures and the Purchase Agreement

The simplest way to deal with items that may or may not be fixtures is to provide in the purchase agreement for the item either going with the sellers or staying with the purchasers. This has nothing to do with what application of the fixture tests might indicate, however. By specifying in the purchase agreement how the item will be treated, the parties make the disposition of the item a contractual provision—something that must be honored at risk of incurring liability for damages on account of breach of contract. Thus, the status of the article may be determined by agreement between the parties. Whenever possible, salespeople should use the purchase agreement in this way to minimize the chances for misunderstanding.

Ideally, separate agreements are prepared, one for sale of the realty and calling for transfer of title by warranty deed, another for sale of the personalty and calling for transfer of title by bill of sale. By using this technique, items that might fall into the gray area between clearly realty (fixtures) and clearly personalty (non-fixtures) are simply contractually classified by the parties as one or the other and disposed of accordingly. Practically, however, few real estate salespeople use the separate agreements approach; the vast majority uses the one real estate purchase contract to handle the problems with fixtures. Chapter 6 shows how the real estate purchase contract can be used to avoid problems with fixtures.

Fixtures Not Part of the Realty Sale

Another problem in the fixtures area concerns items that clearly are fixtures, but the sellers do not want to sell them. An heirloom dining room cut-glass chandelier provides an example. If the salesperson and the seller discuss how to handle this item at the time the realty is listed for sale (long before a purchaser sees the property and makes an offer to purchase), it does not matter legally whether the item is or is not a fixture. Sellers can decide to sell as much or as little of the realty as they want. If they choose to sell all of the realty except the dining room chandelier, they may do so. Items such as this often are simply noted on the listing agreement, the MLS, or other information source that circulates among the selling brokers.

As long as all salespeople relay this information to all prospective purchasers, everything works out fine. Problems arise when the purchaser knows nothing about the chandelier or does not recall ever having been told anything about it. The purchaser moves in, looks around, sees no chandelier, and immediately calls the broker and threatens the end of the world.

One cure for this situation is a foolproof system of listing information and all salespeople's responsibly using the system. Another method of informing purchasers that a part of the realty is not being sold is to simply hang a tag or paste a strip of tape on the item, bearing an appropriate message. Because a purchaser has the duty to be aware of things a reasonable person would discover after inspecting the property, this approach assures the seller that any purchaser interested in the realty at least has the opportunity to learn about the exception.

Perhaps the best solution is an alternative to the "listing agreement" and the "hang-a-tag" approaches, doing away with the potential uncertainty of the former and the physically and psychologically sloppy effect of the latter. This is what we will call the *removal or replacement* approach, wherein the *sellers remove the item entirely at the time they list the realty for sale.* With this technique, sellers replace the item with a less valuable substitute before purchasers have a chance to see any of the realty.

Before listing the realty, salespeople should examine it, anticipating potential fixture problems. If they thoroughly question the sellers about these items, as well as about items that are clearly personalty or clearly realty, and if they then take appropriate action in the listing, information dissemination, and sales negotiations processes, they are doing all that can be expected to ensure a problem-free transaction.

Tenants' Fixtures

Occasionally a real estate salesperson sells realty that is rented to tenants at the time the purchaser views the realty. In these cases, the salesperson must be more careful than usual to reduce possible misunderstandings about what items of property are included as part of the sale.

We already know that application of the fixture tests to individual items often makes it possible to classify the item as a fixture (realty) or as a chattel (personalty). The term **tenants' fixtures** is misleading, however, causing many people to think that those items are real property merely because they are referred to as fixtures. In fact, tenants' fixtures are considered *personal property owned by the tenant, not real property owned by the landlord.*

The law classifies tenants' fixtures in this way for good reason. The law wants to encourage tenants to improve the properties they rent, even though the tenant may use and possess the property for a relatively short time. By letting tenants take fixtures they pay for, as long as they do so prior to expiration of the tenancy, the law removes a major objection to making relatively permanent additions to the realty. Not only does the tenant get to keep the improvement, but commerce also is stimulated because of the original purchase and installation costs of the items. Usually the tenant must repair any damage that results to the realty from removing the fixtures. Thus, tenants making a domestic use of the premises may remove articles placed by them in or on the realty during their term for their use and enjoyment. *This includes the right to remove items that would have been classed as fixtures had the landowner installed them.*

Tenants' fixtures always include items that would satisfy the fixtures tests. These items could be well affixed to the realty, or well adapted to the use to which they were put. We are not talking about chattels owned by tenants, because these items are clearly personal property and have nothing to do with the realty.

For **trade fixtures**—those used to carry out a business or trade, the law goes directly to the purpose of an item to determine how to treat it. *Articles that are accessory to a business* and that are put on the business premises for that purpose *remain removable property.* They are removable by the business or trade tenant during that tenant's term. Articles that become accessories to the real property and do not peculiarly affect the business, however, become part of the real estate. The trade tenant may not remove these items.

A special agreement between landlord and tenant regarding fixtures supersedes any general rule of law regarding tenants' fixtures. These special terms usually exist within their lease with one another. A residential landlord usually does not like to let tenants install fixtures that they will later remove. Thus, prohibitions against creating domestic tenants' fixtures are common in residential leases. By contrast, commercial leases commonly allow tenants to install trade fixtures. Leasing commercial space would be too difficult if tenants could not install "tools of the trade."

As to the type of transactions in which tenants' fixtures are a factor, trade fixtures, domestic fixtures, and agricultural fixtures are differentiated. The only difference lies in the types of items the different tenants install. For example, a shoemaker installs a heavy-duty sole-stitching machine; this is a trade fixture. A domestic tenant installs bookshelves; these are domestic fixtures. A tenant farmer builds an automatic feeder; this is an agricultural fixture.

Problems for real estate people arise when they show rented properties to potential purchasers and they do not point out the tenants' fixtures. This is more of a problem in commercial than residential leasing because of rental leases' usual prohibition against creating tenants' fixtures. To avoid later legal problems, the salesperson should determine whether the realty is rented, find out exactly which items are tenants' fixtures, and make sure the purchasers know that these items, however much they appear to be a permanent part of the realty, are not to be part of the sale. A list of these items, signed by all parties, is also desirable.

Improvements

An **improvement** is defined as a *valuable addition to real property or major, man-made attachments to the land, which significantly increases its value and goes beyond mere repairs or replacements.* An improvement is intended to enhance the usefulness, the value, or the appearance of the realty; once the improvement has been added, it becomes part of the land. As such, it passes to the purchaser along with the rest of the things that already have been discussed. The most common example of an improvement is a *building* on land.

The other category of man-made attachments, fixtures, are usually small and relatively inexpensive things incorporated into the improvements. For example, if a landowner builds a garage on the surface of the property, the garage is clearly an improvement. If the landowner makes a further addition to the garage, such as adding an electric garage door opener, the garage door opener is (most likely) classified as a fixture, based on the affixation, adaptation, and/or intention tests. Generally a building on land is considered to be both an improvement and real estate. It is legally presumed to be real estate, and the burden of proof is on the party claiming in court that a building is personal property.

Because the range of possible improvements to the land is so vast, and because the legal description of a parcel of land makes no reference to any improvements, prudent purchasers inspect the property to make sure exactly what improvements will be included as part of the sale. In the standard residential transaction, the usual improvements are a house, a garage, a driveway, and sanitary sewer, water, and utility lines. In some cases landowners construct patios, porches, gazebos, fences, swimming pools, garden sheds, and so forth, and often these are permanent improvements. Because some of these things are still portable, however (above-ground swimming pools, for example), purchasers again should exercise caution and make sure that all questionable improvements are itemized in the real estate purchase contract, just as questionable fixtures are listed. A professional real estate salesperson should encourage such action.

When purchasers are buying raw (unimproved) land, they occasionally are confronted with an improvement that may or may not be part of the land. This situation occurs when neither sellers nor purchasers are sure where the property lines are located on the surface. If an old barn, a shed, or even a dwelling house exists near where the parties think property lines are, purchasers should pay for, or convince sellers to pay for, a survey of the property so everyone will know whether the improvement is or is not part of the parcel being sold.

Growing Things

Another type of attachment, growing things, has two subclassifications: (a) ***fructus naturales*** (fruits of nature) and (b) ***fructus industriales*** (fruits of industry). Fruits of nature include wildlife living on the realty, fruit- and nut-bearing trees, the offspring of animals, uncut timber, and a stand of rare wild flowers. These are all considered to be part of the land because they are all capable of continuing to *live and produce without the efforts or the interference of humans.*

Fruits of industry, also called **emblements,** are, by contrast, things that are *produced by the efforts of humans.* Although they used to be considered personal property, the modern trend is to also consider them real property. They become personal property only when harvested, timbered, or otherwise severed or separated from the real property. For example, this year's harvested corn crop is produced by the efforts of people, and it usually is considered personal property. If the corn were still in the field on the stalks, however, it would be considered real property.

A real estate salesperson who sells rural property, sells property rich with the products of nature, or sells agricultural property that is currently under production should separate the personal property from the rest of the land when writing the purchase agreement, so there is no misunderstanding among the parties regarding what is included in the sale and what is not.

TRESPASS AND NUISANCE

If one recognizes that landowners have rights in the subsurface, on the surface, and above the surface, it should come as no surprise to learn that the law protects those landowners' exercise of those rights, regardless of whether they have to do with the subsurface, the surface, or the air. A major legal theory that ensures such protection to landowners is the theory of trespass. **Trespass** can be defined as *some physical invasion or unlawful entry upon real property whereby damages ensuing are direct, not consequential*. The essential idea is that someone without title or right to possess makes entry onto land without consent, permission, or license. The law makes it a *violation of ownership rights for a person to interfere with the land—the subsurface, the surface, and the air—owned by another.* Certainly, most people are aware that trespass rules prohibit them from walking or driving onto the surface of land owned by another. Everyone has seen posted "No Trespassing" signs. To most, these signs convey a clear message to stay off the realty. Legally, the trespass law just as clearly prohibits a person from going into or using the subsurface or airspace of another's realty.

Unless a landowner has valuable minerals, oil, or an important right-of-way as part of the subsurface rights, other persons would not likely ever try to interfere with subsurface rights. But what about the air? As we know, anyone who takes or uses the airspace of another without permission violates ownership rights under trespass law. Imagine a small cherry tree just inside the surface property line of Mr. A's land. If the tree grows in such a way that its branches occupy part of neighbor B's airspace, and it drops overripe fruit and leaves onto B's surface space, technically the tree now trespasses onto B's property. Legally, the tree is said to **encroach** upon B's land. Encroachment is the legal word for *trespassing or intruding onto another's realty.* If the encroachment became serious enough that B believes she has to do something about it, B can initiate a course of action, having the full support of the law, that will result in the removal of all elements of A's property that encroach upon B's.

Does the law place any limits on the extent to which a landowner is protected against trespass? As to the subsurface and the surface, any interference by an outsider would seem to amount to trespass. For example, even a coal mine thousands of feet beneath the surface could not extend into the subsurface of another's land without permission. It would not matter to the law that the landowner neither knew about the trespass nor felt any adverse effects of the subsurface trespass. Any trespass into or onto another's land is deemed to result in damage, and for that reason all trespasses are prohibited.

As long as the trespass is not in the form of an encroachment that would involve great economic waste to tear down (imagine a seven-story building that encroaches three inches onto a neighbor's land) the law supports the landowner. In cases involving such potential economic waste, the courts almost never force demolition of a slightly encroaching building. They come up with some other way to compensate the landowner. Requiring the encroacher to pay the landowner **compensatory damages** is the usual solution.

Distinguishing a trespass from a nuisance is sometimes difficult. A frequently used legal distinction is that, whereas trespass is an invasion of one's interest in exclusive possession of land as by entry upon it, **nuisance** is *interference with one's interest in private use and enjoyment of land that does not require interference with possession.* Figure 2–3 is an illustration differentiating nuisance and trespass.

FIGURE 2–3
Trespass versus nuisance.

Trespass

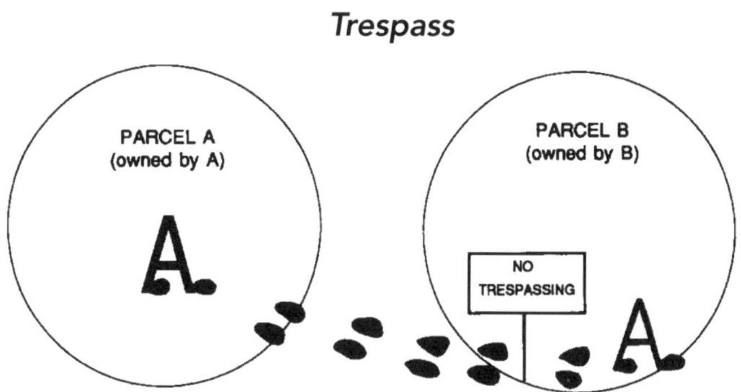

"No trespassing" sign posted by Owner B facing A's realty. Owner A nevertheless enters B's realty. A is *trespassing.*
Note: There can be a valid trespass even without the posted sign.

Nuisance

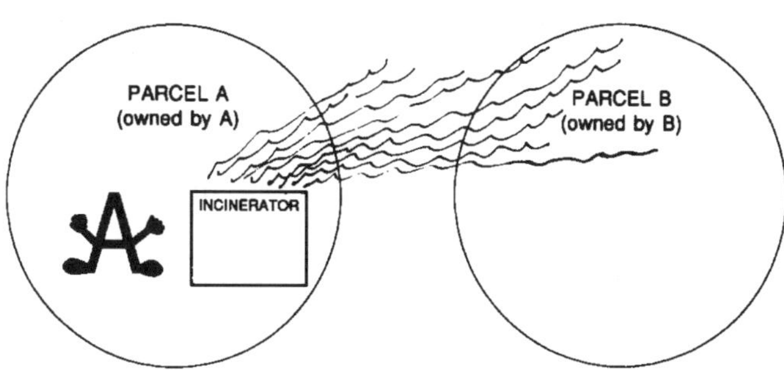

Although A stays on his own realty, the fumes from his use of his incinerator travel onto B's realty, creating a *nuisance.*

Nuisance usually is committed on a parcel of real property different from the parcel affected by the nuisance. It often offends the senses, violates the laws of decency, or obstructs the use of property. For example, one property owner who makes a substance that produces a vile, traveling odor is a nuisance to surrounding residential property owners. This can lead to an actionable nuisance lawsuit. It must be more than an isolated instance, though, because nuisance implies a continuing condition. The reasonable use of realty is usually the standard for measuring whether a nuisance does or does not exist. If victims of nuisance are successful in court, they win money damages or a court-ordered injunction, or both. An injunction commands a party to stop a certain activity. In nuisance law, an *injunction commands offending landowners to cease those acts that are the nuisance*.

As we mentioned earlier, no longer is every pass of an aircraft through the airspace of a landowner considered to be trespass. Technically, of course, it is. Once you view the land as extending into infinity, anything moving into that space without the landowner's permission must be trespassing. The reason for lawmakers' refusal to view aircraft as trespassers stems from powerful considerations of public policy: what is perceived as the best legal solution for the whole of a unit of government, such as the best for all residents of community X. Lawmakers are required to weigh the well-established rights of an individual against the current needs of the community. When public policy prevails, there is no choice but to limit the rights of the individual.

As for the continuing condition of being located near a burgeoning airport, those realty owners do suffer from a nuisance. Public policy, however, must be balanced in evaluating the continuing condition. Often the airport was there first, with the expectation of growing and expanding, which tips the scales of justice to public policy considerations and away from nuisance law. Occasionally a landowner is able to convince a court that aircraft have so interfered with the use of the real estate that, as a practical matter, it is of no value. Various theories, including trespass and nuisance, have been advanced to legally support this position, but in all such cases the facts must show that the aircraft affects the landowner to a far greater extent than normal.

CASE STUDY FROM THE OHIO SUPREME COURT

MASHETER V. BOEHM
37 Ohio St.2d 68, 307 N.E.2d 533 (1974)

Facts: Boehm owned one and one-half acres on which it operated a job-stamping plant for the manufacture of metal components, such as moving parts for machinery. The operation entailed a variety of machinery and equipment, some of which was of such great size and weight that its installation required special foundations, reinforced floors, and similar structural measures. Where such machinery was used, the machine was first installed and allowed to settle, and then a sheltering structure was tailored around it. Of the several structures on Boehm's land, two were erected to house previously installed heavy machinery. Also girders, tracks, and rails were built into the plant structures for moving materials and equipment. This land became subject to appropriation by the Ohio Highway Department; the state decided to "take" the property under its eminent domain powers.

Trial court (Probate court): Virtually all of the above-described property was found to be fixtures, and thus realty instead of personalty. Thus, the Ohio Highway Department was ordered to pay $1,791,465 to Boehm, itemized as follows: land and improvements $83,125; structures $275,000; fixtures $1,433,340. Masheter, Director of the Ohio Highway Department, appealed.

Court of Appeals: Affirmed the lower court's decision. Masheter again appealed.

Issue: At what point will personal property merge with land, or structures on land, appropriated so that it must be deemed part of realty taken and be compensated for in a condemnation award.

Held by the Ohio Supreme Court: Although personal property that has attained fixture status is part of real property taken, personal property, per se, is not taken and therefore is not compensable.

The fact that machinery and equipment is installed with some permanence on land or in a structure as part of an integrated industrial or economic operation will not of itself require that all such items be deemed a part of real property taken in an appropriation proceeding. Such a determination must be made in light of particular facts of each case, taking into account facts such as:

- manner in which annexed to realty
- purpose for which annexation is made
- intention of annexing party to make property part of realty and dedicate it irrevocably to realty for particular use
- degree of difficulty and extent of any economic loss involved in thereafter removing it from realty
- damage to severed property that removal would cause

Reversed and remanded the case to probate court for reconsideration consistent with this opinion. (This means that the Ohio Supreme Court sent this case back to the local probate court, which was to decide the case again, but using the principle set forth above.)

BRENNAMAN V. R.M.I. COMPANY; BECHTEL GROUP, INC.
70 Ohio St.3d 460, 639 N.E.2d 425 (1994)

CASE STUDY FROM THE OHIO SUPREME COURT

Facts: Two workers were killed and one was seriously injured while trying to replace a defective valve in Sodium Handling Area 1100. Suit was brought by their estates against the companies for damages for wrongful death and injuries (in tort law).

An Ohio statute, Ohio Revised Code Section 2305.131, was central to deciding the case. This statute bars such actions against designers and engineers of improvements to real property which are brought more than ten years after completion of the construction services. If the statute applies (if the Handling Area is considered an improvement in real estate), then plaintiffs cannot recover.

Sodium Handling Area 1100 consists of a warehouse-type building with large doors at each end. Railroad tracks run into the building, allowing tank cars to be rolled in for unloading. Unloading is accomplished by connecting the tank car to the plant's piping and storage system. Once the tank car is connected to the piping system, the sodium is heated to a liquid state, pumped out of the car and piped to storage tanks within the facility.

Issue: Whether Sodium Handling Area 1100, the material handling facility, constitutes an improvement to real property. (It is not argued that the production plant is something other than an improvement to real property; the issue is whether one part, the material handling facility, constitutes an improvement. Also, the construction services were rendered more than ten years ago so that is not an issue.)

Held by the Ohio Supreme Court: When determining whether an item is an improvement to real property under the statute a court must look to the enhanced value created when the item is put to its intended use, the level of integration of the item within any manufacturing system, whether the item is an essential component of the system and the item's permanence.

It concluded that Sodium Handling Area 1100 is an improvement to real property and that the statute applies, saying that the facility represents a transportation and storage process essential to the plant's ultimate production goals. As to its permanence, the facility had been in place thirty years prior to the accident. There has been no demonstration of how the facility could be removed from the land on which it sits. It appears that it was and is the intention of R.M.I. and Bechtel that the facility will be in service until it is obsolete or the plant ceases operation.

However, the court concluded that the statute was unconstitutional because it violated the right to a remedy guaranteed by Section 16, Article I of the Ohio Constitution. Thus, the court remanded the case for a new trial.

SUMMARY OF CONTENT

1. Both real property and personal property exist, but they are different things.
2. Movability no longer unqualifiedly defines what is personalty and what is not.
3. Land, or real property, traditionally is defined as everything from the center of the earth, out through the mass of the earth, continuing past the surface, as described by lines on the surface, up into the atmosphere above such surface in an expanding geometric form that reflects the surface shape of the property to infinity. It is synonymously known as real estate or real property.
4. The legal description land refers to only its surface boundaries; all other rights in it are implied.
5. Appurtenances are rights that go along with owning land. These include air, subsurface, and water rights.
6. A more modern definition of land limits the airspace component of the definition of land to airspace that the owner actually could put to use.
7. The landowner also owns the subsurface of the realty but may grant an option, a lease, or an easement in it to another interested party.
8. Riparian rights in water give the landowner the right to use the water equally with other owners.
9. Land also includes items once personalty that are so associated with the land they have lost their personal property characteristics. These items, called attachments, are either natural or man-made items that become part of the realty.
10. Fixtures are one kind of attachment. Property is classified as either a fixture or not, depending upon (a) the nature of the annexation/attachment of the thing to the land, (b) the use to which the thing is put in connection with use of the land, or (c) the objective intention of the landowner who acquired the item and put it to use along with the land.
11. Problems with fixtures in real estate purchase transactions can be eliminated or much reduced by (a) proper use of the purchase agreement, (b) exchange of accurate and complete information between listing/selling brokerages and prospective purchasers, (c) replacement or removal of items prior to listing, and (d) posting of appropriate notices on items to be retained by the seller.
12. Because of the public policy, recognized by law, to encourage tenants to improve the properties they have leased or rented, tenants' fixtures are deemed to be personalty, not realty. Tenants' fixtures include trade, domestic, and agricultural fixtures.
13. Improvements—significantly valuable man-made attachments/additions to the real property that go beyond mere repairs or replacements—are deemed to be part of the land even though they (as with fixtures) are not referred to in the legal description of the land.
14. Attachments that are products of the labors of humans *(fructus industriales)* and products of nature *(fructus naturales)* are considered realty. Only when the item is severed from the realty does it become personalty.
15. When a person enters without permission into or onto the land of another—be it the subsurface, the surface, or the airspace—that entry is considered to be a trespass, and compensable damage is presumed to have occurred. By contrast, nuisance is interference with one's interest in private use and enjoyment of land and does not require interference with possession.

REVIEW QUESTIONS

1. Trees on land become personal property by:
   a. conversion into lumber
   b. sale of land
   c. eminent domain
   d. foreclosure

2. The artists who live next door are burning noxious odors all day long. Legally they are:
   a. maintaining a nuisance
   b. trespassing on the neighbor's realty
   c. acting lawfully if not violating a zoning ordinance
   d. exercising an aesthetic easement right

3. You catch these very same artists sneaking onto your property to remove things to collage onto their work. Legally they are:
   a. maintaining a nuisance
   b. trespassing on your realty
   c. acting lawfully if they are not violating a zoning ordinance
   d. exercising an aesthetic easement right

4. Real property that is considered a fixturc is:
   a. never an item that is capable of being moved
   b. always an item that is both annexed and attached to the realty
   c. not easily, immediately classifiable
   d. so subjective a determination that it rests on each person's perspective of what is personalty and what is realty

5. A legal description shows:
   a. valuable subsurface mineral rights
   b. valuable overhead air rights
   c. an important improvement such as a house
   d. where the realty is located

6. Trespass affects only:
   a. the land itself
   b. the land and its subsurface rights only
   c. the land and air rights only
   d. the land, subsurface, and limited air rights

7. It is *not* a fixture:
   a. built-in appliance
   b. oriental rug
   c. electric garage door opener
   d. electric garage door opener transmitter

8. It *is* a fixture:
   a. mural painted on foyer walls
   b. 9' × 12' painting hung on wall
   c. microwave oven
   d. drapes

9. Tenants' fixtures are considered to be personal property for which of the following reasons:
   a. make it easier to sell rented property
   b. encourage tenants to improve properties while they are still tenants
   c. keep down the cost of fixing up properties after the tenants have vacated the premises
   d. owners shouldn't profit from something they didn't pay for

10. Which of the following is not part of the "land"?
    a. improvements
    b. fixtures
    c. encroachments
    d. *fructus naturales*

11. Sellers most likely would succeed in claiming this item as personal property they could take with them:
    a. their copper pipes in the garage, which carry water to make it usable as a darkroom
    b. their antique Packard sitting on blocks in their garage
    c. their Amish-built cupboards above all of the built-in appliances in the kitchen
    d. their glass chandelier from Venice that has remained hanging in the foyer throughout the real estate transaction without any special notation as to who would receive it

12. Which of the following is most responsible for the limitation of air rights that a landowner today is subject to?
    a. mechanical advances making it ever easier to erect tall buildings
    b. public policy supporting increased air travel
    c. difficulty of policing the air
    d. pollutants in the air

13. How can sellers protect themselves against losing fixtures to purchasers when sellers want to hold onto the items?
    a. make provisions in the purchase agreement
    b. hang a tag on the item
    c. remove the item and replace it with something else
    d. all of the above

14. How can purchasers best assure themselves that they are getting, along with the realty, the items of personalty they want?
    a. test each item on the property to see if it's bolted into place
    b. ask sellers what they're taking with them
    c. provide for them in the realty purchase agreement
    d. personally label each item prior to title transfer

15. Courts are reluctant to force a person to remove a valuable building that encroaches onto the adjacent land of another because of:
    a. policy of the law tending to avoid economic waste
    b. policy of discouraging spurious litigation
    c. principle of practical impossibility
    d. desire to improve the reliability of real property records

16. Real estate salespeople want to handle subsurface, water, and air rights with interested purchasers in the following way:
    a. so thoroughly understand the law that they can fully represent to the purchasers what components will pass as part of the land
    b. make it part of their professional practice to scour county records for any recorded interests in these component parts of land
    c. be careful not to represent the absence or presence of component parts of the land without necessary proof of same rendered by the appropriate experts
    d. all of the above

17. The following act, by persons who do not own any interest, right, or title in the land, is considered a trespass upon that land resulting in a probable damage award to the landowners:
    a. flying over it in their airplane
    b. excavating its soil while searching for a valuable mineral
    c. spewing noxious, traveling odors into the air from their adjacent parcel
    d. passing by it in a boat in the middle of a river that the land borders

18. The following act, by persons who do not own any interest, right, or title in X parcel of land, is considered a nuisance against X landowner, resulting in a probable damage award to X landowner:
    a. flying over X's land in their airplane
    b. excavating X's soil while searching for a valuable mineral
    c. spewing noxious, traveling odors into the air from their own parcel, adjacent to X
    d. passing by X in a boat in the middle of a river that X's land borders

19. Riparian rights landowners:
    a. can dam off owners downstream
    b. have a swimming pool on their realty
    c. have the right to use the water equally with other riparian landowners
    d. if they use the water first, can gain superior rights in it compared to other riparian landowners

20. Appurtenances are rights in realty's:
    a. airspace
    b. subsurface
    c. water rights
    d. all of the above

21. The word *chattel* comes to us from:
    a. cattle
    b. chatelaine
    c. cart
    d. champagne

22. It is an appurtenance to the land:
    a. electric garage door opener
    b. precious metals in the subsurface
    c. a pewter chandelier
    d. an airplane

23. When salespeople see no oil or gas wells, no landing strips, and no water on real property they are selling, they can say to purchasers:
    a. there are no oil and gas leases on the realty
    b. there are no limitations on the air rights
    c. there is nowhere to dock their boat
    d. all of the above

24. Reasonable persons were invented in the law:
    a. to dispose of all legal claims
    b. to eliminate real property cases
    c. to substitute mediation for litigation
    d. to impose an objective standard that a jury can use in determining fixture cases

25. It is a trade fixture:
    a. hog watering trough on a farm
    b. bookshelves in an apartment
    c. a barber's swivel chair, bolted onto the floor
    d. all of the above

ANSWER KEY

1. a
2. a
3. b
4. c
5. d
6. d
7. b
8. a
9. b
10. c
11. b
12. b
13. d
14. c
15. a
16. c
17. b
18. c
19. c
20. d
21. a
22. b
23. c
24. d
25. c

3
ESTATES AND INTERESTS IN LAND

KEY TERMS

community property
curtesy
dominant tenement
dower
easement
easement appurtenant
easement in gross
encumbrance (also called incumbrance)
estate for years
estate from year to year
fee simple absolute
fee simple determinable or conditional
freehold estates
incorporeal rights in land
leasehold estates
license
life estate
nonfreehold estates
periodic tenancy
profit *à prendre*
qualified fees
servient tenement
tenancy at sufferance
tenancy at will
term tenancy

Restrictions in Land Ownership

TO THE AVERAGE PURCHASER, becoming a landowner is synonymous with "making it" financially. One reason purchasers so positively view acquiring interest in land is that they assume that by purchasing land they automatically will be obtaining a real property interest wherein they may rule as "lord of the castle," free from interference by any other person. There is good reason for taking this view, because most purchasers do obtain rights as landowners that are superior to the rights of all others. Purchasers generally assume that they will obtain these rights because it is conventional in the average real estate transaction to pass to the purchaser the "best," or least restricted, title to the land that the law knows how to supply—a fee simple absolute.

As a real estate salesperson, one has to be aware of other, lesser forms of land ownership, such as life estates and fee simple conditionals and even easement rights in another's realty. Because they have value, these interests also can be marketed. As long as salespeople know what sort of an interest they are selling, and as long as purchasers know what they are negotiating for, all is well. Imagine, however, the difficulty when purchasers assume they are obtaining the best title (fee simple absolute) and real estate salespeople assume they are marketing the best title (fee simple absolute), but the sellers do not realize the title they are selling is less than the best (fee simple conditional, life estate, or other). Although such a combination of misunderstandings might seem unlikely, given the advertised expertise of real estate brokers today, they do occasionally happen. This results, in large part, from the inability of the parties to recognize that other, lesser estates and interests in land exist.

Average American real estate purchasers, conditioned to expect that the best estate in land automatically will be theirs once they become landowners, might be surprised to learn that the very estate or interest most common in the United States is rare in other places, such as in many European countries. Even in the U.S. state of Hawaii, conditions exist that make ownership of land by the average person in the least restricted form uncommon. In Hawaii large corporations and powerful individuals hold the major estates in land. Ordinary residents have no more than lesser interests in the land. The situation in much of Europe is similar.

The easiest way to think of the varying degrees of land ownership is in the form of a continuum from least restricted (most common) to most restricted forms of land ownership, as shown in Figure 3–1. At one end of the continuum are freehold estates, the least restricted and, therefore, generally the most desirable forms of land ownership. Next are leasehold estates, commonly considered to be lesser estates in land. Although leasehold estates technically are not real property, they are estates in land. At the other end of the continuum are incorporeal rights in land. These are not interests or estates in land, just bodiless rights in land. Still, they have value and purchasers often desire them and negotiate for them with a vengeance.

Taken together, all components of the continuum (discussed throughout this chapter) span the major estates, interests, and rights in land with which the typical purchaser of real property is concerned. The estates and interests in land are distinguished by the quantity of interest a person has in land. That quantity of interest ranges from just about everything (fee simple absolute) to naked possession (tenancy at sufferance) to borrowing the property (license). The important thing for real estate salespeople is to be constantly aware of exactly what estate, interest, or right they are marketing. Selling a fee simple absolute estate in land is one thing, and marketing a fee simple absolute subject to an oil and gas easement is quite another.

LIMITATIONS AFFECTING ALL ESTATES AND INTERESTS IN LAND

Before defining and fully discussing the many estates and interests referred to in Figure 3–1, we must discuss several factors that affect all estates and interests, from the least restricted to the most restricted. These are the *public and private controls* over the ownership and use of land. We sometimes forget about the importance and the overpowering influence of these factors, usually because we are so used to their presence that we simply assume they are involved. Although public controls over the ownership and use of land are always involved in determining the nature of an estate or interest in land, private controls are present only sometimes.

FIGURE 3–1 Continuum of restrictions in land ownership.

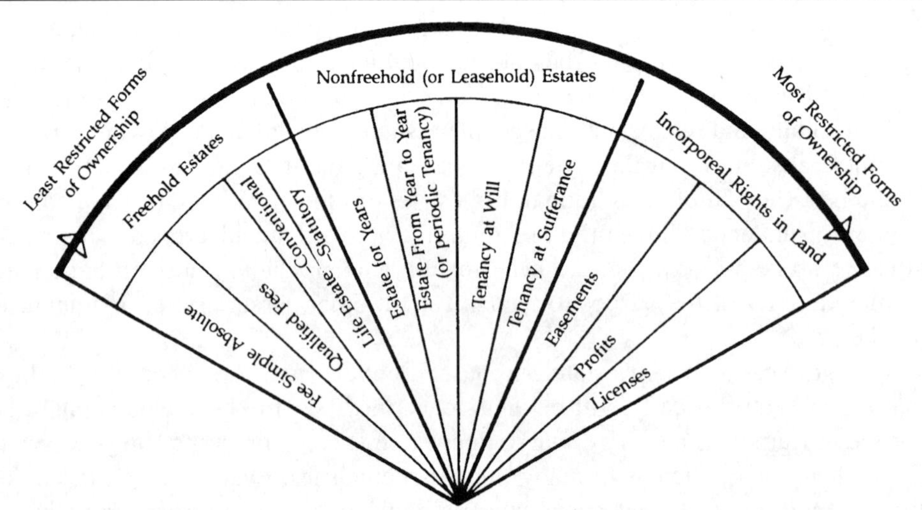

All of the above estates and rights are subject to any of the following as may exist:

Public Controls over Land Ownership/Usage

- Taxation
- Eminent domain
- Escheat

Private Controls over Land Ownership/Usage

- Deed restrictions
- Declarations of restriction
- Restrictions placed by the developer on the plat of a subdivision
- Private agreements among neighboring property owners
- Condominium declarations and bylaws
- Cooperative proprietary leasehold covenants

Public Controls

Our system of land ownership recognizes the overpowering need of the government to control the ownership and use of land to a limited extent. The power to tax, the power to regulate the proper use of land (police power), the power to take private property for public use (eminent domain), and the power to acquire full ownership rights in property if an owner dies without disposing of the property by will or without any heirs (escheat to the state) are governmental powers that take precedence over the rights of all landowners, even the owners of the least restricted form of ownership known to our law—the fee simple absolute freehold estate.

Even though these powers only rarely affect a single parcel of land, it can happen. If so, the landowner has to yield to the rights of the government to exercise those powers. We discuss these powers in greater detail in other sections of this text, but readers should recognize now that such powers can influence all estates and interests. To fully assess the real value of an estate or interest, one must consider the effects of public powers.

Private Controls

Although less frequent a factor than public controls, which are nearly always present to one extent or another (property taxes, for example), private controls can also exist over the ownership and use of land. When they are present, they must be complied with, assuming they are legal.

FOR EXAMPLE

> Assume that a former owner of a parcel of land hated subdivisions with tiny lots. He was a farmer, with a farm 300 acres in size. When he sold his farm to a developer of residential subdivisions, he conditioned the conveyance in this way: He made the purchaser (the builder) promise never to divide the farm into anything less than one-acre homesite lots.
>
> Such a restriction generally has been held to be legal when challenged in the past. As long as land is still relatively plentiful, chances are good that such a restriction will not be "against public policy" and, hence, will continue to be legal and enforceable. The supporting reasoning is that, because the builder knew the conditions of the sale when he negotiated and contracted with the farmer in the first place, neither he nor those who stand in his shoes (purchasers from him) should be able to disregard this private control in the future.

Because private controls take precedence over all estates and interests, interested parties should be aware of their presence or absence from the start of negotiations. These restrictions usually are a matter of public record and thus can be found in the county recorder's office in the county where the real estate is located. A title search and resulting report typically reveal them.

Warning: As will be fully discussed in Chapter 11, prohibitions against selling real estate to minority group members have been declared unconstitutional and thus are unenforceable.

Refer back to Figure 3–1 for a delineation of public control versus private control limitations over estates and interests in land.

FREEHOLD ESTATES

Of uncertain duration, because no one knows when they will end, **freehold estates** are *possessory interests in real property.*

We will first discuss the most common and most important freehold estate, the fee simple absolute.

Fee Simple Absolute

Much of our real property law came to us from Great Britain where, historically, land was owned by the aristocracy. Homeowners, those who owned the building on the land, leased the land from an aristocrat. That system can be found to this very day in Great Britain and parts of Hawaii. The United States, which never had an aristocracy like the one in Europe, developed instead the concept of a person's owning both the lot and the building on it. That person thereby received the highest form of ownership—the fee simple, also known as the fee or the fee simple absolute.

The **fee simple absolute** is the *least restricted and, hence, the most desirable, form of land ownership known to the law; ownership of land by a person is subject only to the public and private controls* set forth above. All other estates, interests, and rights in land are conceptually smaller to start with, and are reduced further in scope by the foregoing governmental and private restraints.

The fee simple absolute is the highest right, title, and interest one can own in land. It is potentially infinite in how long it can last, which is a characteristic of freehold estates. Its duration does not hinge on other events happening, as do the lesser fees. The fee simple absolute also can be passed on by its owner, by conveyance, while still alive, by will, or by the statute of descent and distribution if there is no will, after death. Courts construe conveyances of land to be fee simple absolutes unless a contrary intent is clearly found on the instrument creating the estate in land.

Qualified Fees

Conceptually, **qualified fees** are nearly as broad as the fee simple absolute. In fact, until they end, they have all the same characteristics, permitting the owner to do all of the same things that a fee simple owner could do—possess the land, sell the land or any portion, lease it, improve it, mortgage it, deplete it, alter it, share the ownership of it, and so on. The distinguishing characteristic is that qualified fees are *all capable of ending upon the happening of some already designated event.* They are classified as the fee simple determinable or conditional, the fee simple subject to condition subsequent, and the fee simple subject to executory limitations.

The most common qualified fee is the **fee simple determinable or conditional.** It is *created by an instrument providing that the estate automatically ends upon the happening of a stated event.* The instrument must contain limiting words such as "so long as." A common example of a fee simple determinable is a grant providing "so long as said property is held and used for church purposes and no longer," and then further providing for reversion or forfeiture if the property is used for some other purpose. This means that the church can exert full ownership rights—that is, the rights of a fee simple absolute owner—as long as it uses the property for church purposes.

Although this form of ownership gives the church considerable rights in the land, it involves a loss of full freedom as well. Still, cities, youth groups, nature lovers, and all sorts of other groups have directly benefitted, within the range of the stated limitations, from what often were gifts of real property from people who did not mind parting with the land as long as they knew the land would never be used for anything other than its stated purpose.

If the holder of a fee simple conditional estate tries to use the land contrary to the stated purpose, persons known as *reversioners (persons to whom the residue—what is left—of the freehold estate returns or reverts)* can step in and take the property back. Essentially, the reversioners "stand in the shoes" of the original owner and hold themselves ready to reacquire the original owner's right in the land should the condition be broken.

Another type of qualified fee is the *fee simple subject to condition subsequent.* The instrument creating this fee states that the conveyor or a successor has the power to terminate the estate upon the happening of a given event. This type of fee has no automatic feature.

The third type of qualified fee is the *fee simple subject to executory limitations.* The instrument creating this fee states that, upon the happening of a given event, the interest passes to a *remainder person, someone other than the conveyors or their successors.*

Although the qualified fees and other, even more exotic interests were common under the British system of real property law, they were never as popular with Americans. The British, with their nobility, were committed to tying up land in intricate ways through successive generations to protect their landed aristocracy. Americans who try to tie up property usually resort to trusts instead, as discussed in Chapters 4 and 14. But even trusts have limitations on how long they can be perpetuated. Americans like their land *freely alienable—they can do what they want with their land.* Real estate agents should be aware that the qualified fees exist, even though they will not likely be called upon to market them. If agents do handle qualified fees, these are sufficiently unusual and perilous to warrant everyone being represented by counsel through every step of the transaction. Brokers, purchasers, and sellers all should have their own attorneys to advise them on the dangers of dealing in qualified fees.

Life Estate

The third type of freehold estate, the **life estate,** is of both great and minor importance to the salesperson.

Refer back to Figure 3–1, which shows the entire continuum of estates, interests, and rights in land. It lists two sorts of life estates, conventional and legal. The conventional life estate, though important to some experts such as estate planners, is not something the average real estate practitioner needs to know much about. If purchasers or sellers question the real estate salesperson about the legal ramifications of owning a life estate in the land (the motivation almost always being to avoid estate taxes), the salesperson should refer these persons to an expert who is qualified to answer. For informational purposes only, and to enable the salesperson to recognize what others are talking about when they discuss life estates, the *conventional life estate is to some extent a fee simple absolute ownership of the land limited by the duration of a person's life.* Persons presently in possession of the estate, *life tenants,* may do nearly all of the things that fee simple absolute owners may do, except that *when life tenants die, all of their rights in the land die as well.*

One can appreciate the obvious appeal of the life estate for the do-it-yourself estate planner who, trying to minimize estate taxes, understands that (theoretically at least) the life tenant has no estate in the land as of the moment of death. Of course, the question of taxability to the estate is a far more complex issue, one not determined merely by the type of interest held.

The conventional life estate can be created by deed or by will. An example by deed is: "to A for life, remainder to B." The life estate can exist for A, the person presently in possession of the property, measured by the duration of A's life, or it can be held by C, some other person. In C's case, he or she is able to exert the usual rights in land as long as A is alive. In both cases, A's life is used to measure the duration of the estate (called the measuring life). Upon A's death, the life estate ends, and no matter who is in possession of the land at that time, all rights in the land pass to B, the remainderman (person to whom the remainder of the estate returns).

An important limitation upon life tenants is that they *may not commit waste.* This means that tenants must not permanently diminish the value of the realty. They must do those things reasonable people do in preserving their own realties, such as making ordinary repairs to the realty. An example of waste by a life tenant is extracting all of the sand, gravel, oil, minerals, and other valuable components from the land, or allowing a house to fall into disrepair.

Legal Life Estate (Dower), Curtesy, and Community Property

Virtually all states have some provisions to protect a spouse's interest in his or her husband's or wife's real estate. Dower, curtesy, or community property are the usual protections. In Ohio, there exists another kind of life estate, created by a specific statute, relating to **dower** rights protection. This is the *legal or statutory life estate.* The statute *gives either a husband or a wife rights to a potential one-third life estate in the other spouse's real estate.*

Ohio does not recognize curtesy. **Curtesy** applies to husbands only and generally gives a husband rights to a life estate in the wife's real estate. In Ohio, once a man and woman are married, all real property owned during the marriage is subject to dower rights. These rights apply whether the real property is owned by one or both of the spouses, and it does not matter to the law how the real property came to be owned. The real property could have been purchased by, inherited by, or even given to a person when he or she was single. As soon as this person gets married, the spouse gains dower rights in this real property. If a spouse acquires real property after the marriage, dower rights for the other spouse are the same. If both spouses own the same real property together, each has dower rights in the other spouse's part ownership of the real property.

These dower rights are not immediately exercisable upon creation of the marital status, because they have two aspects or degrees: inchoate (also known as contingent or incomplete) and choate (also known as vested or complete). *Inchoate* dower, in turn, has two elements: marriage, and title or interest in real property subject to dower rights. *Choate* dower requires more. Beyond the marriage, the owner of the freehold real estate has to sell the realty without the spouse's consent, then die and be survived by the other spouse (who, you will recall, never consented to the sale). If all of these elements are present, a choate dower interest is created by the law for the benefit of the surviving spouse, be it husband or wife. The surviving spouse may go to the present owner and assert her (or his) rights to a one-third life tenancy in all real property the deceased spouse sold without the consent of the surviving spouse.

In their real estate transactions, Ohio real estate salespeople encounter spouses with inchoate dower rights. Salespeople must recognize that even inchoate dower rights in real estate so badly cloud the real estate title that the real estate is essentially unmarketable unless they obtain the signatures of both spouses, which releases their right of dower. Salespeople rarely encounter a choate dower problem. When they do, a complex lawsuit usually is involved as well. Salespeople should avoid taking the listing until the choate dower problems are resolved through the legal action.

Inchoate dower rights are extinguished when the person with the rights dies before the marital partner who owns the real property. These dower rights do not pass or transfer to anyone else but instead are completely terminated. Dower typically is considered an inchoate right and is not an estate in land. The following example shows a typical dower problem that a real estate salesperson might encounter.

FOR EXAMPLE

Mr. Anderson has his home listed with XYZ Realty. He is married, but his wife did not sign the listing contract because the property was in Mr. Anderson's name. XYZ presents an offer by purchasers to Mr. Anderson, which he accepts. His wife does not sign the real estate purchase contract either. When Mr. Anderson has an attorney prepare the deed, the attorney asks him if he is married. Mr. Anderson says he is. "But because she doesn't own the realty, what difference does that make?" he and XYZ ask. You may ask the same question. It makes an enormous difference.

Mrs. Anderson has inchoate dower rights in the real estate. She will have to sign the deed along with her husband so she can release her inchoate dower rights. And what if she refuses? Because Mrs. Anderson never signed the listing or real estate purchase contracts, she can refuse to sign the deed and thus refuse to release her inchoate dower rights without being in breach of contract or any other law. No one can sue her. The purchasers can sue Mr. Anderson for breach of the real estate purchase contract, however, as he will be unable to convey the clear title he promised. Purchasers also might sue XYZ for negligence, claiming it had a duty to get Mrs. Anderson's signature on both listing and purchase contracts so she later could be compelled to release her inchoate dower rights on the deed.

Further imagine in this example that Mr. and Mrs. Anderson are locked in the beginnings of a horrendous divorce case, assuring XYZ that Mr. Anderson never will be able to talk his wife into releasing her inchoate dower rights short of the absolute decree of divorce, ending those rights. All of these problems could have been avoided if the real estate salesperson realized from the outset that Mrs. Anderson's release of inchoate dower rights had to be assured throughout every stage of the transaction.

Some states, not Ohio as yet, have community property law instead of dower or curtesy. Community property is statutory law, not common law. The specific provisions, thus, vary from state to state, depending on what each state's legislature has enacted. Generally, **community property** gives either *the husband or the wife a one-half interest in property acquired by the labor of the other spouse during the course of the marriage.*

The concept of community property has an important corollary: *separate property.* This is property owned by the husband or the wife prior to their marriage, or property acquired by the husband or wife during the marriage by will, inheritance, or gift. In a state with community property law, the husband or wife has no claim whatsoever against the other spouse's separate property. Dower, by contrast, gives a husband or wife rights against the other spouse's real property regardless of how or when it came to the spouse who owns it.

There are a few exceptions to the requirement that a spouse release dower, curtesy, or community property rights before a sale can be properly completed. One exception involves a husband and wife who enter into an *ante nuptial agreement* with one another prior to the marriage, providing that certain property owned by the husband, for example, remains the sole and separate property of the husband. Ante nuptial agreements are contracts that determine property rights between the marital partners in a forthcoming marriage. Thus, a husband and wife can set up the ownership of certain real property such that no spouse's release is necessary at the time of sale, because that spouse's interest was dealt with in the ante nuptial agreement. Even in such cases, title companies (who provide the evidence or proof for purchasers that the seller's title is what he or she says it is) typically require a spouse's release at the time of sale, thinking that perhaps the ante nuptial agreement someday may be struck down by a court for one reason or another.

The purpose of dower, curtesy, and community property rights is to protect one spouse from being cheated by the other spouse. The law reasons that real property a married person owns is going to require anything from a minimal (paying taxes on a small lot) to a large (the principal asset of the marriage) sacrifice by both spouses to maintain. When the asset is sold or encumbered, it seems only fair to give both spouses the opportunity to know about and consent to what is going on. Even though a stranger pays money to purchase this land, the law views the rights of a deprived spouse as more important, reasoning further, perhaps, that purchasers could have provided against these kinds of claims by purchasing the appropriate title insurance policy prior to their taking title (discussed thoroughly in Chapter 8).

NONFREEHOLD OR LEASEHOLD ESTATES

The next portion of the Figure 3–1 continuum deals with **nonfreehold,** or **leasehold,** estates. Technically, the law classifies these as personal, not real, property, although they do amount to an estate in land and thus give the tenant important rights in the land. Although there are many types of leasehold estates, taking into account the basic types and the variations created by the parties in response to needs that arise from time to time, most leasehold estates can be characterized as an estate for years (also called a term tenancy), or an estate from year to year (sometimes called a periodic tenancy), or a tenancy at will, or a tenancy at sufferance. All four cases involve both a *lessor* and a *lessee*. The lessor is the landlord (the owner of the freehold estate), and the lessee is the tenant (the owner of the leasehold estate). The tenants/lessees in all leasehold estates have lesser rights in the land than do any of the freeholders.

Recall that holders of freehold life estates are known as life tenants and that life tenants can do anything they want with the land except commit waste. Nonfreeholders also are called tenants and, as such, they must not commit waste either. For *nonfreehold tenants,* however, *waste is defined much more broadly* than it is under the life estate. If nonfreehold tenants rip out the wall-to-wall carpeting, for example, so as to enjoy the wooden floors underneath, they may well be committing waste. By contrast, this usually is not considered waste if done by life tenants. With leasehold estates, the landlord is the one who is concerned that the tenants keep the premises up and do not let the property go to waste. Under the life estate, the remaindermen are the ones who must complain about waste.

The minimal right of every leaseholder is the exclusive possession and use of the leased premises for the duration of the tenancy. Though this might seem a far cry from the extremely broad rights of a fee simple absolute freeholder, often it completely satisfies the needs of the leaseholder/tenant. Many states, including Ohio (as discussed more fully in Chapter 13), have modern landlord-tenant acts giving these leaseholders/tenants fuller rights and protections in residential leaseholds than existed previously under common law. The characteristics that differentiate the various leasehold interests are described next.

Estate for Years

The estate for years, also called a **term tenancy,** is *an interest in land for some definite period, which has a specific beginning and ending date,* such as "commencing on January 1, 1995 and ending June 30, 1996." This tenancy is to last six months exactly. Do not be misled by the word "years" in the phrase "estate for years." In this context, the word years means *any length of time,* as long as the period has fixed starting and ending dates. This tenancy ends upon expiration of the stated term without any action taken by either the lessor or lessee.

Estate from Year to Year

The **estate from year to year** continues for *successive periods of a year or successive periods of a fraction of a year.* Also called a **periodic tenancy,** it differs from the estate for years in one major way: Although this tenancy has a specific commencement date and continues for a set length of time, it renews itself for another identical period unless the parties *notify* one another that the next period will be the final one. There is *no specific ending date.*

Estates from year to year are created by operation of law or by agreement of the parties. A common form of this tenancy extends from month to month (meaning a calendar month) and continues until either party notifies the other, at least one month before the termination date, that the tenancy will cease at the end of the next month. The computation of time for terminating the periodic tenancy is based on the periodic rental date.

Tenancy at Will

The third nonfreehold estate is the **tenancy at will,** whereby the *land and its tenements are let by one to another, to have and to hold at the will of the lessor/owner of the freehold.* These arrangements rarely are created by express agreements. They more commonly arise by implication, both from the way the lessor and lessee have been acting toward one another and the way they act toward the real property.

The tenancy at will sometimes is confused with the periodic tenancy. Under a periodic tenancy, however, one party must notify the other party that termination shall occur at the end of the next period. By contrast, a tenancy at will can end with the expiration of the current term.

Tenancy at Sufferance

In **tenancy at sufferance,** tenants *continue to possess realty after their rights to do so have expired.* A person who has this form of an estate often is described as being "one step above a trespasser." The difference between tenants at sufferance and trespassers are that whereas tenants at sufferance once were rightfully upon the realty (as tenants under an estate for years, for example, now holding over or staying beyond their rightful terms), trespassers never had the right to be upon the land. The phrase "tenancy at sufferance" derives from the idea that the landlord "suffers" or puts up with the tenant remaining upon the realty until the landlord gets around to having the tenant removed. Usually a tenancy at sufferance is created when a tenant holds over.

Although real estate salespeople rarely deal with leasehold estates (unless they specialize in property management), they should understand how the rights of tenants compare with the rights of other estate holders. One misconception regarding the sale of a leased property is that when the property is sold, the sale, in and of itself, ends the rights of any tenants of the realty. This is an incorrect assumption. Salespeople should realize that when they sell a fee simple absolute that is presently subject to an estate for years, the new owner may not "throw out" the tenants until that tenancy expires. The tenants have the right to exclusive possession and use of the property for the duration of the term. As long as tenants pay rent, do not commit waste, follow the terms of the lease, and comply with all pertinent laws affecting tenants, they may remain. These kinds of problems are discussed more fully in Chapter 13.

Incorporeal Rights in Land

The last group of rights is described as **incorporeal rights in land,** that is, *immaterial or intangible rights.* These include easements and licenses, the former being generally permanent and irrevocable, the latter, temporary and revocable. Also included are profits or, more correctly, profits *à prendre* (discussed later). These are imposed upon corporeal, or material or tangible, property.

Easements

An **easement** is a *nonpossessory interest* in another's real property with the *right to use that real property for a particular purpose or limited use.* The last words "for a particular purpose or a limited use" hold the key to the whole concept of easements.

Earlier in this discussion the fee simple absolute freehold estate was described as ownership of land permitting use of the land for any purpose, subject only to the aforementioned governmental limitations and any private restrictions of record. At the opposite end of the rights continuum, the easement use of the land is permitted for a particular purpose or limited use. The land may not be used for virtually any purpose or in an unlimited way as it may be used along the other parts of the continuum. The rights of an easement holder are even more restricted than those of a leasehold tenant, who at least has the right to exclusive possession and use of the realty for broadly described purposes during the term of tenancy. By contrast, the *easement holder is not entitled to either the present or future possession* of the real property subject to the easement.

The law recognizes only two major types of easements, although they may be created in many ways: easements appurtenant and easements in gross. There is only one type of easement appurtenant and two types of easements in gross—commercial and personal.

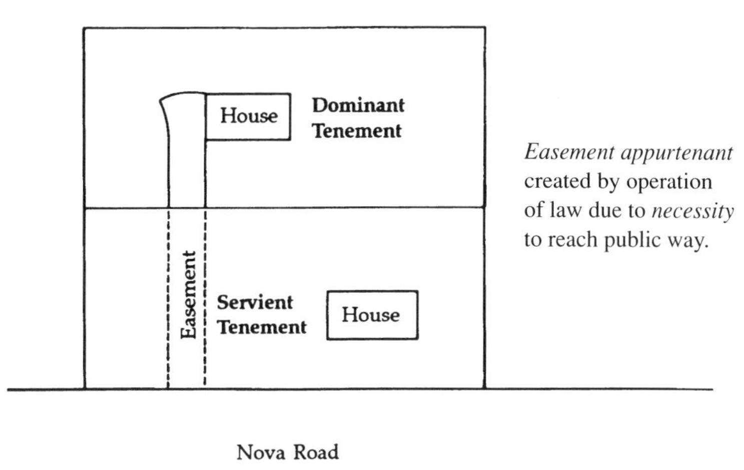

FIGURE 3–2
An easement appurtenant. *Purpose:* For ingress and egress to public way.

Easement appurtenant

An **easement appurtenant** *gives one owner of a parcel of real property the right to use and benefit from another landowner's parcel* of real property. The two tenements or estates involved are called the dominant tenement and the servient tenement. (Tenement is an ancient term signifying land, with all of its accompanying rights.) The **dominant tenement** is *the parcel of land that benefits from, or has the right to use, the easement.* Because it is "appurtenant," the right to use the other parcel accompanies ownership of the dominant tenement. The **servient tenement** (the "other" piece of land) is *subject to the easement* and must put up with the stated use. An easement appurtenant is diagrammed in Figure 3–2.

The important characteristic of all easements appurtenant is that they consist of two separate parcels of land, with one parcel having the right to use the other for some designated purpose. Appurtenant easements are often *created by grant using a deed.* The deed is in writing and is executed with all the requisite formalities required by other deeds (fully discussed in Chapter 5). The person granting the easement by deed must have legal capacity and have title to or an estate in the servient tenement.

Easement in gross

Like easements appurtenant, **easements in gross,** as rights in realty, burden another's parcel of land. Easements in gross differ from easements appurtenant in that they *always consist of just one type of parcel-servient tenements.* There is no dominant tenement. Instead, the thing that dominates, or has the right to use the servient tenement in the easement in gross, is either a *commercial entity or a person.* The former amounts to a commercial easement in gross and the latter, a private easement in gross.

Commercial easements in gross are very common ownership rights in land. They can be held by large utility companies. An electric company, for example, must have the right to enter others' real property to install and service the electrical lines for those realties. The easement in gross gives the electric company this right. The easement in gross covers a great number of servient tenements. Figure 3–3 shows an easement in gross.

Occasionally an individual, instead of some commercial enterprise, has the right to use servient tenements in a particular way. Although cases of *private easements in*

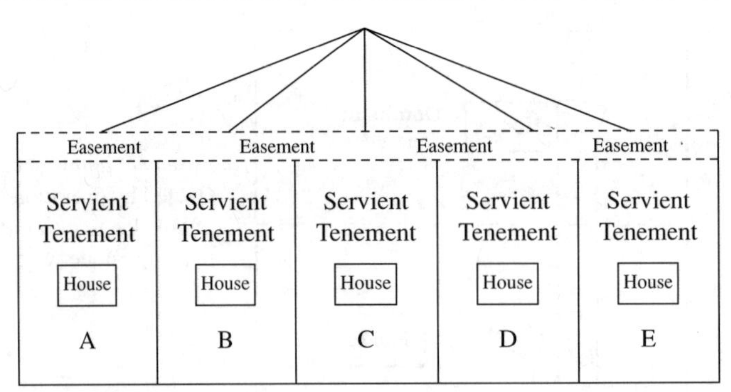

FIGURE 3–3 An easement in gross. *Purpose:* For transmission/delivery/installment/repair of electric utility lines.

gross are not common, they do exist, and as long as the designated person having the rights is alive, the rights continue. An example of a private easement in gross is the right of a hunter to use the lands of several different people for hunting as long as he lives.

Easements in gross often are *created by deed.*

Creation of Easements

Of necessity, by prescription, and by implication the law can create easements when it feels they have some good reason to exist. Upon carefully examining the physical reality of easements, one finds that an easement can be classified as either an easement appurtenant or an easement in gross. The law is simply trying to ensure that land is not tied up in such a way that unreasonable waste will occur.

Because easements are interests in real property, they must be created by a *writing*. (The statute of frauds, discussed in Chapter 6, requires the writing.) That writing is usually the *deed.* This is the easiest and most certain way of creating an easement, and it usually results in the fewest legal problems. Easements are created within deeds themselves in two ways. The first is by expressly *granting* the easement within the deed. For example, X grants to Y, along with parcel Y, an easement to use the driveway on her, X's, land. The second way is by a *reservation* within the deed, wherein the grantors/sellers retain the right to use the parcel they are conveying to another for some particular purpose. For example, A conveys parcel B to B, but reserves the right to use parcel B's driveway. Deeds are thoroughly discussed in Chapter 5, along with specific forms.

In certain situations the law also *implies* an easement from what seems to be the parties' original intent. This occurs when one or more parcels of real estate are granted away from a much bigger tract all owned by one person. An example is when, by necessity, one person must cross another's land to prevent being landlocked; the person has no way (on the surface) to reach a public or private roadway. This is considered an easement appurtenant, implied by operation of law from the dominant tenant's necessity to reach a public road (refer back to Figure 3–2 for an illustration of this point). The second situation in which the law implies an easement is when there has been *prior use*.

FOR EXAMPLE

Three parcels of land, all owned by X, all had use of the same heavy, loadbearing roadway (different from the driveway for ingress and egress that each parcel has). X conveyed parcel A to A and parcel B to B. A and B continued to use the roadway for their heavy loadbearing equipment. X never, by grant or reservation in any deed, gave A or B an easement for use of this roadway. A and B sell their parcels to C and D. X then tries to stop C and D from using the roadway based on there being no easement granted for such use. The law might well support A's and B's positions, saying that the prior use of this roadway created an easement by implication. (This is an easement appurtenant, X being the servient tenement and A and B being the dominant tenements.)

Another easement created by the law to satisfy the need to keep land productive and useful is the *easement by prescription*. Again, analysis of the easement will show it to be one of the two types of easements that we have already described—either an easement appurtenant or an easement in gross. What happens in this case is that the *law grants an easement to persons when they have been using the land as if they were the true owners for a relatively long time*.

FOR EXAMPLE

A uses the roadway on B's land even though A has a roadway that A simply does not like as much. A did not acquire the land from B's owner or a preceding owner (thus, no legitimate claim is possible). A continually uses B's roadway even though A has no right to do so. A does not cease this use at any time, nor does A obtain B's permission to use it. If A keeps this up long enough, A may well acquire an easement to use B's roadway. (This, too, is an easement appurtenant. B is the servient tenement, and A is the dominant tenement.)

A number of people, one after the other, also might use the property in such a way that finally the last person, in an unbroken chain, asserts easement rights created by operation of law. This consecutive process is called *tacking*. The reason for granting people such as these an easement when they are truly no more than trespassers (having no rights to the land) is to encourage people to take an interest in, use, make productive, invest in, and improve their land. Thus, complete strangers who are no more than trespassers are able to acquire valuable rights in land if they go about it in the proper way and keep it up for long enough. In addition, they may be able to acquire even more than easement rights by following this course of action. They may well acquire *complete title* to real estate when they make open, continuous, and adverse use of realty for a set period of time. This is known as *acquiring title by adverse possession,* which we will discuss further in Chapter 5.

Termination of Easements

As to the duration of these two types of easement (appurtenant and in gross), much depends upon the purpose for which the easement was created. If for ingress and egress, the easement could continue indefinitely. If for the purpose of maintaining a garden, by contrast, once the garden is discontinued, the easement also might end, by *abandonment*. An abandonment requires more than the dominant tenant's not using the easement, however. The circumstances should show the tenant's clear intent to wholly abandon the use.

Occasionally the easement is classified from the start as lasting a certain number of years. When that term is up, it ends by *expiration*. A party might negotiate with the easement holder and offer something of sufficient importance to get the easement back, again effectively terminating it by *release*. The release, of course, should be an executed writing, recorded to put the public on notice that there is no longer an easement.

FIGURE 3–4
Merger diagram.

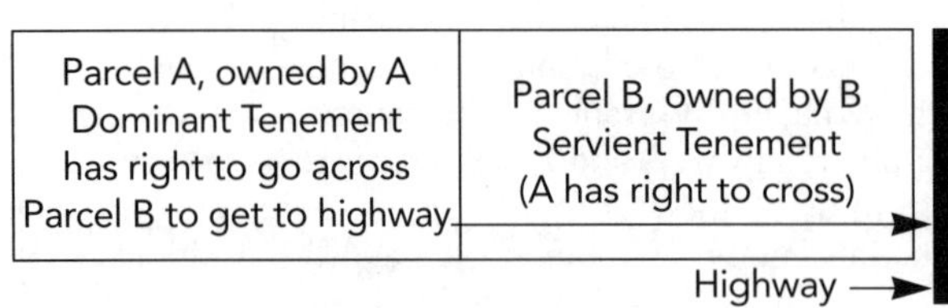

Then, A buys B from B, resulting in:

Parcel A, owned by A A can use parcel A however he wishes	Parcel B, owned by A A can use parcel B however he wishes

There is no longer an easement because of the merger that has taken place.

If the dominant tenement owner becomes the owner of the servient tenement, the easement again is terminated, because the freehold estate thus acquired easily includes all conceivable easement rights along with many other rights. This outcome, called *merger,* is diagrammed in Figure 3–4. Or the government may want to acquire the easement and use its *eminent domain* powers to purchase the easement. (Eminent domain purchases are forced sales to the government, discussed fully in Chapter 12.)

Running with the Land

Easements often are characterized as *running with the land.* This phrase, which applies to easements appurtenant, means that *when the dominant tenement is sold, even though no specific mention of the easement is made, the new owner of the dominant tenement also acquires the easement rights over the servient tenement.* This is consistent with the concept of easement appurtenant, because the easement rights were created to benefit that parcel in the first place. Certainly, if the parcel is sold, all rights that are part of the same parcel pass to the purchaser. Commercial easements in gross also are *alienable;* they can be transmitted or passed on to another. Personal easements in gross, however, are not alienable.

When easements are indicated on recorded deeds, the grantee is presumed by the law to have notice of the easement prior to taking title. Because purchasers agree in most real estate purchase contracts to take the real estate subject to any easements of record, they usually cannot rescind (cancel) the transaction if they discover the easement after entering into the real estate purchase contract but before the closing of that transaction. The result is different, however, if purchasers make it a part of the real estate purchase contract's provisions that they have to approve of any easements that come to light during the title search and, if they do not approve, they can declare the contract voidable. This is the only way to really protect prospective purchasers against any easements that pass with the land and ordinarily are not discovered until the time of the title search.

To rely on sellers' telling either prospective purchasers or realty agents about the existence of these easements is unwise. Sellers often perceive easement information as negative because it may prevent their selling the realty advantageously. Therefore, they might not tell purchasers and realty salespeople about them.

Licenses

A **license** is a *personal, nonassignable, and revocable privilege for one to do an act(s) on the land of another.* A license also is the right to use land for a specific purpose. The fundamental difference between the license and the easement is that whereas *the easement rights are mandatory, the license rights are only permissive.* The person giving the license (licensor) may revoke or cancel these rights at any time. The reason the easement is so permanent and the license is so temporary stems from what happened—what was given and received—when these rights were created. An easement usually involves negotiation; the person giving the easement (the grantor) receives in exchange from the other (the grantee) something the grantor considers to be valuable and to which the grantor would not otherwise be entitled. Often a license results from the licensor giving to the licensee rights to temporarily use the land, and the licensor expects and receives nothing in return from the licensee.

Unfortunately, the test of "receiving something" does not always serve to properly identify the rights transferred. What finally determines the matter is the intention of the parties. Easements usually are created by written documents showing the intention of the parties. An ideal case for proof of a license exists where the parties also signed a written statement providing only temporary and permissive use. Because most licenses are casual and oral, this does not happen often. Termination of licenses is not as involved as termination of easements. Because a license is most often a temporary and completely permissive use from the start, termination can occur whenever the licensor chooses.

As the licensee has no permanent rights, the uncertainty as to duration is entirely consistent. If licensees want greater security, they should negotiate with the landowners for an easement. If a license is coupled with an interest (the licensee stands to lose a valuable property interest negotiated or paid for), it is irrevocable.

FOR EXAMPLE

If Peter sells Paul quarry stones located on his realty and in addition gives Paul the right to use the quarry, Paul's license to enter Peter's land is irrevocable because it is coupled with an interest (Paul's interest in the quarry stones).

Profits (Profits à Prendre)

The last category of incorporeal rights are those known as profits or, technically, ***profits à prendre,*** which are also *nonpossessory rights in real property.* These are similar to easements. Profits go a step beyond easements, however, in that they *permit the holder of the profit not only to use another's land but to take from the land as well.* An example of profit is the right to go across the surface of another's land, to tunnel into that land, and then to take out oil, gas, and minerals. Similarly, the right to move cattle onto another's pasture and then to permit grazing involve a profit. Many landowners accomplish the purpose of a profit through a carefully drafted easement providing for a use of the land that involves some taking from the land.

Estates, Interests, and Rights Versus Encumbrances

All of the above-described estates, interests, and rights in land should not be confused with any of the following, known as encumbrances.

1. Private controls over the use of land (such as deed restrictions).
2. Public controls over the use of land (such as zoning ordinances).
3. Encroachments.
4. Clouds on the title (we are referring to a cloud such as dower rights and not a cloud that might be an easement).
5. Liens.

An **encumbrance** is *anything that hinders, burdens, or limits the value of the land.* It is broad in scope and covers all diminutions to the value of the land, but it may be more fully classified for other purposes. It has been said that all liens are encumbrances but not all encumbrances are liens. This is a correct statement.

FOR EXAMPLE

A mortgage is always a lien, and the mortgage lien is always an encumbrance because it clearly diminishes the value of the estate of land. A deed restriction prohibiting the cutting of timber is not a lien, although it is always an encumbrance, because the restriction clearly diminishes the value of the estate.

Encumbrances are discussed at other points in the text. For now, it is sufficient to know that encumbrances merely reduce the value of the estate, interest, or right, as tarnish dulls the sheen of a silver spoon.

CASE STUDY FROM THE OHIO SUPREME COURT

CENTEL CABLE TELEVISION CO. OF OHIO, INC. V. COOK
58 Ohio St. 3d 8, 567 N.E.2d 1010 (1991)

Facts: The Cooks granted and conveyed to Dayton Power and Light Co. (DP&L) a six-foot-wide easement through their 151.58-acre farm "for a line for the transmission and/or distribution of electric energy thereover, for any and all purposes for which electric energy is now, or may hereafter be used." This easement was made to DP&L, "its successors and assigns forever." DP&L installed utility poles and aboveground electrical lines along the easement.

DP&L entered into a joint use agreement with Centel Cable, and thereafter Centel attached to the DP&L electric utility poles, located on the Cooks' property, a strand of coaxial cable carrying electrical transmission television signals. When Centel tried to enter Cooks' property to repair a broken coaxial cable wire, the Cooks refused entry and 300 Centel customers experienced a longer period of interrupted service. The Cooks subsequently wanted $10,000 damages for Centel's alleged trespass onto their property.

Issues: Whether an easement granted to a utility company may be apportioned and partially assigned to a cable television company in a situation where the grantors were silent regarding their intent to allow apportionment of the easement and where the grantors made no express reservation regarding apportionment.

Held by the Ohio Supreme Court: The easement could be so apportioned and assigned to a cable television company. The stringing of coaxial cable by a cable television company along an easement owned by a public utility constitutes no additional burden to the owner of the servient estate. Further, the transmission of television signals through coaxial cable by a cable television company constitutes a use similar to the transmission of electric energy through a power line by an electric company in accordance with the language of the original granting of the easement. Thus, the Cooks failed in their claim for damages.

NOLLAN V. CALIFORNIA COASTAL COMMISSION 483 US 825, 97 L Ed 2d 677, 107 S Ct 3141 (1987)

CASE STUDY FROM THE U.S. SUPREME COURT

Facts: The Nollans owned a beachfront lot in Ventura County, California. A quarter-mile north of their property, in Faria County Park, was an oceanside public park with a public beach and recreation area. Another public beach area, known locally as "the Cove," lay 1,800 feet south of their lot. A concrete seawall approximately 8 feet high separated the beach portion of the Nollans' property from the rest of the lot. The historic mean high tide line determines the lot's oceanside boundary. In order to build a house on the lot, they were required to obtain a coastal development permit from the California Coastal Commission. On February 25, 1982, they submitted a permit application to the Commission.

The Nollans were informed that their application had been placed on the administrative calendar, and the Commission staff recommended that the permit be granted subject to the condition that they allow the public an easement to pass across a portion of the property bounded by the mean high tide line on one side and their seawall on the other side. This would make it easier for the public to get to Faria County Park and the Cove. The Nollans protested imposition of the condition, but the Commission overruled their objections and granted the permit subject to their recordation of a deed restriction granting the easement. The Nollans filed a petition in the County Superior Court.

California County Superior Court (Trial Court): Held in favor of the Nollans that the permit condition was invalid.

California Court of Appeals: Reversed, ruling that imposition of the condition did not violate the Takings Clause of the Fifth Amendment, as incorporated against the States by the Fourteenth Amendment.

Issue: Whether there was a "taking" of Nollans' property for this beach access easement by the government (California Coastal Commission) without payment of just compensation.

Held by the United States Supreme Court: A permit condition requiring the Nollans to allow persons already on the beach to walk across the property does not serve the supposed purpose of protecting the public's visual access to the beach, or of lowering psychological barriers to access to the beach, or of remedying additional congestion on the beach caused by construction of the new house. Even if the requirement of a public easement could be justified on the ground that the public interest would be served by a continuous strip of publicly accessible beach, the state must pay the owners for such an easement.

(*Note:* Read the *Nollan* case again when you read Chapter 12, which discusses the principles of eminent domain. That way you can put together the concepts of easement rights and eminent domain.)

Summary of Content

1. Freehold estates are the *highest* or least restricted forms of land ownership known to the law, and the fee simple absolute is the best of these.
2. All estates and rights in land are subject to both private and public controls over usage of land.
3. Qualified fees have the same characteristics as the fee simple absolute but are all capable of ending upon the happening of some already designated event.
4. The fee simple conditional, or determinable estate, is essentially a fee simple absolute limited by a stated condition; e.g., . . . "to be used as a boys' camp and for no other purpose."
5. Life estates are either conventional or statutory. The conventional life estate is measured by the life tenant's life and then is passed to another person known as the remainderman.
6. In Ohio, the statutory life estate, known as *dower,* protects a spouse's interest in his wife's or her husband's or real estate.
7. Leasehold estates involve the right to exclusive possession and usage of land for a designated/agreed period of time.
8. Whereas freehold estates are technically real property, leasehold (or nonfreehold) estates are deemed to be personal property even though leaseholds also are classified as *estates in land.*
9. The several types of leasehold estates vary by (a) the length of the exclusive right to possession/use and (b) the duties surrounding notification to the opposite party if termination of the tenancy is desired.
10. An easement is a permanent, irrevocable, usually written right to use land for a specific purpose and no other.
11. An easement appurtenant gives the owner of a parcel of real property (dominant tenement) the right to use and benefit from another landowner's parcel of real property (servient tenement).
12. An easement in gross consists of only servient tenements and a commercial entity or person who dominates and uses servient tenements.
13. Easements of necessity, by prescription, and by implication are ways by which the law can create easements when it believes there is some good reason for them to exist. The resulting easement is either appurtenant or in gross.
14. Some easements continue indefinitely, whereas others can end by abandonment, expiration, release, merger, or eminent domain.
15. An easement *runs with the land* when the dominant tenement is sold; even though no specific mention of the easement is made, the new owner of the dominant tenement also acquires the easement rights over the servient tenement.
16. Licenses are temporary, revocable, usually oral, permissive rights to use land for a specific purpose. Licenses do not run with the land.
17. Profits *à prendre* involve the right to go beyond a mere easement-type right to use the land. Profits permit taking or extracting from the land things of value.
18. An encumbrance is anything that hinders, burdens, or limits the value of the land, such as deed restrictions, encroachments, or zoning ordinances.

REVIEW QUESTIONS

1. A dies and wills his real estate to his surviving spouse for her life and then, upon her death, to B, their son. The estate in land the widow has is:
   a. dower
   b. life estate
   c. fee simple conditional
   d. fee simple absolute

2. Which of the following are remaindermen?
   a. persons who acquire possession of the estate upon death of the life tenant
   b. the government acquiring the property by eminent domain
   c. holders of rights of reverter pursuant to a fee simple conditional
   d. a sublessee taking over the remainder of a tenant's lease

3. An appurtenant easement is not terminated by:
   a. abandonment
   b. purchase of dominant tenement by servient tenement owner
   c. express release
   d. necessity

4. An encumbrance is:
   a. a cloud on the title
   b. a life estate
   c. an easement
   d. a license

5. If an owner sells stones located on her realty to a sculptor, along with the right to use the quarry, the sculptor has a(n):
   a. easement appurtenant
   b. license
   c. license coupled with an interest
   d. easement in gross

6. The farthest degree of estate or interest in land on the continuum from the fee simple absolute is:
   a. fee simple conditional
   b. life estate
   c. estate for years
   d. license

7. The closest degree of estate or interest in land to the fee simple absolute is:
   a. fee simple conditional
   b. easement
   c. estate for years
   d. license

8. Which one of the following is a freehold estate in land?
   a. easement
   b. fee simple absolute
   c. estate for years
   d. tenancy at sufferance

9. Which one of the following is not an estate in land, only the right to use the land for a particular purpose?
   a. easement
   b. fee simple absolute
   c. estate for years
   d. tenancy at sufferance

10. Two parcels of land wherein one parcel has the use of another for a specific purpose is called:
    a. easement in gross
    b. license
    c. easement appurtenant
    d. fee simple determinable

11. An estate in land that has a limitation upon it, such as "to be used for church purposes only," is called:
    a. life tenancy
    b. fee simple
    c. fee simple absolute
    d. fee simple determinable

12. Which of the following can a life estate tenant *not* do to the real property?
    a. improve it
    b. possess it
    c. sell it
    d. commit waste upon it

13. Doctrine giving a husband or wife a potential one-third life estate in the spouse's real property:

    a. dower
    b. curtesy
    c. hybrid of dower and curtesy
    d. community property

14. Which one is not a type of easement, but rather a method of creating an easement?

    a. easement appurtenant
    b. easement by prescription
    c. easement in gross
    d. easement by dower rights creation

15. A leasehold estate commencing on September 1, 1994, and ending on June 30, 1995, is classified as which of the following?

    a. conditional fee
    b. permissive license
    c. estate for years
    d. estate from year to year

16. A leasehold commencing on August 1, 1994, and running for consecutive monthly periods until terminated by at least 30 days' notice is classified as:

    a. tenancy at will
    b. estate for years
    c. monthly fee simple absolute
    d. periodic tenancy

17. Public controls over the ownership and use of land, such as taxes, the power of eminent domain, police power, and escheat, affect which of the following estates and interests in land?

    a. only incorporeal rights in land
    b. only leasehold estates in land
    c. only freehold estates in land
    d. all estates, interests, and rights in land

18. A purchaser of a fee simple absolute estate subject to a leasehold interest with three years yet to run on the lease could *not* do which of the following?

    a. evict the tenants
    b. evict the tenants if they commit waste
    c. collect the rents
    d. sell the fee, subject to the leasehold estate

19. Which one of the following is most valuable (worth the most money)?

    a. freehold fee simple absolute estate
    b. leasehold estate for years
    c. an easement for ingress and egress
    d. impossible to determine as market valuation is not determined solely by the type of estate or interest in land

20. Termination of an easement, whereby the owner of the dominant tenement purchases a fee simple absolute estate in the servient tenement, exemplifies which of the following legal theories?

    a. prescription
    b. necessity
    c. merger
    d. eminent domain

21. If the owner of a fee simple estate conveys a remainder interest in his property and retains the right to use this property so long as he lives, this retained interest would be a(n):

    a. estate for years
    b. life estate
    c. homestead
    d. dower mansion

22. Which one of the following is a future interest as opposed to a present interest in real estate?

    a. life estate
    b. tenancy in common
    c. remainder
    d. fee simple condition

23. If dower is abolished in Ohio, the most likely doctrine to replace it, by statute, is:

    a. curtesy
    b. mansion house
    c. community property
    d. *femme sole* trader

24. The least likely state in which you'll be able to purchase a fee simple absolute is:

    a. Hawaii
    b. Ohio
    c. Florida
    d. California

25. Americans prefer the following way of encumbering property in family lines within a generation or two:

    a. limitations on the fee itself
    b. easements
    c. life estates
    d. trusts

Answer Key

1. b	8. b	15. c	22. c
2. a	9. a	16. d	23. c
3. d	10. c	17. d	24. a
4. a	11. d	18. a	25. d
5. c	12. d	19. d	
6. d	13. a	20. c	
7. a	14. b	21. b	

4
SEVERAL AND JOINT OWNERSHIP

Key Terms

- annual meeting
- articles of incorporation
- beneficiary
- bylaws (condominium)
- common areas
- common assessments
- condominium
- condominium conversion
- cooperative
- cooperative assessment
- corporation
- declaration
- estate (or tenancy) by the entireties
- expandable condominium
- occupancy agreement
- partnership
- percentage interest
- probate court
- proprietary lease
- right of first refusal
- severalty ownership
- statutory survivorship tenancy
- sweetheart contract
- tenancy in common
- trust
- trustee
- trustor
- unit owners' association

Variety in Ownership

NOW THAT WE KNOW what land and its estates and interests are, it is time to discover how people or entities can own it. There are more options than one might think at first glance, and there is *no perfect method* of realty ownership. Each option has its pluses and its minuses.

A threshold issue is whether the real property will be owned by one person or more than one person. From that core determination all other options flow. Any number of people, having any of a great variety of legal and other relationships with one another, can own the same piece of realty at the same time. Not only can realty be owned by a variety of groups of people, but the type of coownership itself also is subject to considerable variation. Essentially, however, *coownership of any sort involves two or more persons who have interests in the same piece of real property.* In this chapter we will explain the different forms of coownership of real property by discussing the various types, which include tenancy in common, Ohio's statutory survivorship tenancy, and estate by the entireties. We expand the discussion to include the special coownership schemes of a cooperative and a condominium. We begin with the direct contrast to coownership, *single ownership,* which is legally referred to as ownership in severalty.

Severalty Ownership

Severalty ownership is *not a form of coownership.* It means *ownership by a single person, either by an entity or a natural person.*

Usually, many people are involved in the entity of a **corporation.** They typically include officers, directors, stockholders, and employees. Nevertheless, the law regards the corporation as a *single, artificial person.* Thus, when a corporation owns realty, it is by ownership in severalty. The stockholders own the corporation through their personal property stock shares. They share in the corporation's profits by dividends and increases in value of their stock. That stock represents their only ownership rights in the corporation and any of its real estate.

Generally, a **partnership** *owns real estate in its name only and, therefore, in severalty.* To achieve this status, the partnership must record its business name certificate in the county of its principal place of business as well as in the county where the real estate is located. Although partners have the right to share in the profits and excess of the partnership, they do not have a right in any portion of the partnership's property, such as a specific piece of real estate.

Both a partnership and a corporation, therefore, involve many people with ownership rights. This makes them related conceptually to coownership of real estate. This is really ownership in severalty, though, because a partnership and a corporation are each regarded as a single entity.

By contrast with the corporation and the partnership, a *natural person* is simply a single human being. When a person owns real estate in his or her name only, that is severalty ownership.

Severalty real estate ownership by a natural person has increased because of the continuing high rate of divorce in our society. In many cases, the resulting single person subsequently holds title to real estate in his or her name alone. If and when such individuals remarry, they may still wish to hold title in their name only, perhaps hopeful that if another divorce results, they can better prove having brought this realty into the marriage as separate property (and therefore, arguably, entitled to retain it). Some of these individuals may even have an ante nuptial agreement with one another that requires them to keep their real and personal property separate, each from the other. Thus, real estate ownership is likely to be in severalty, in only one or the other's name. This is also referred to as *separate property* when the severalty owner is a married person.

A married couple seeking to *lessen liability exposure* can hold the real estate in only one marital partner's name. Thus, a wife who is a surgeon and a husband who is a teacher might choose to hold title in his name only. Then if the wife is sued (more likely, given their respective occupations), the wife's judgment creditors cannot pursue the real estate if she loses the lawsuit.

Widowed people receive title in severalty after taking appropriate steps with their decedent spouse's estate. If and when these people remarry, they often want ownership in severalty (kept in his or her name alone) for the same reasons a divorced person wants it. Nevertheless, dower rights may exist in the real property the spouse of the person with title takes. Such a spouse frequently is asked to sign a quitclaim deed to give up such rights in the realty. Alternatively, if there is a sale to a third person, the spouse can give up dower rights within the deed that conveys title to the third person. By keeping real estate as separate property/owned in severalty, a husband and wife can avoid mingling their respective decedent estates (real and personal property subject to will or inheritance after death) and marital estates (real or personal property involved in a divorce).

Trust Ownership

Real property can be subject to a **trust,** which is a kind of *hybrid creature, straddling the line between coownership and single ownership.* One coownership aspect of the trust is that the *trustee has legal title,* whereas the *beneficiary has equitable title* to the same real property. Having legal title means that one is the actual title holder to the realty; having equitable title means that one is entitled to all the benefits of ownership of that realty. Another coownership aspect of the trust is that potentially more than one person, a real person(s) or an entity(ies), can be designated as the trustee. The trust form of ownership is diagrammed in Figure 4–1.

The trust is a way of using, managing, and controlling real or personal property for another's benefit. The original owner of the property, the **trustor,** gives, transfers, or conveys the real or personal property to another, the **trustee,** who is to use, manage, and control the trust property for the benefit of the **beneficiary.** Written instruments are used in creating any kind of trust. The trustor can create either a *living* or an *inter vivos trust,* which is one that comes into being while the trustor is still alive, or a *testamentary trust,* which is one that comes into being only upon the trustor's death. Either kind of trust is created by transferring legal title to the property to the trustee.

FOR EXAMPLE

An example of a trust is the trustor's delivering a deed to "Samantha Smith, Trustee, the grantee . . . ," with the further limitation that Samantha Smith, Trustee, must hold and use the property for the benefit of a certain beneficiary, Alan Adams, according to the terms and provisions of a written trust document. In such a case, although Samantha Smith, Trustee, holds legal title, Alan Adams has what is known as *equitable title,* meaning that if Samantha Smith, Trustee, fails to follow the terms of the trust, Alan Adams can file an action in court for relief so he can receive the benefits of his justly deserved ownership rights. Samantha, the trustee, is under a *fiduciary obligation* to Alan, as his agent. This means that Samantha can act in Alan's best interests only with utmost loyalty and good faith toward Alan.

The fiduciary obligation is a legal concept that is discussed fully in Chapter 9. Trusts are discussed further in Chapter 14, accompanied by a complete sample of a testamentary trust. All of the topics introduced to this point represent ownership interests in real estate that involve single people, both artificial and real. The remaining topics all involve some aspect of coownership of real estate.

Tenancy in Common

Tenancy in common is not single ownership but, instead, *ownership by two or more persons.* The persons can be real or artificial. They can be human beings, corporations, or partnerships. Tenants in common each have an *undivided fractional interest* in the realty, with each having the *right to use it equally.* Neither has any greater rights in the realty than the other(s). Thus, no one tenant is entitled to exclusive use of any part or all of the real estate.

Upon the death of the first coowner, in a tenancy in common, the deceased coowner's undivided fractional interest in the property passes to his or her heirs, according to the Ohio statute of descent and distribution if the coowner dies without a will. If this coowner has a will, the property passes to those persons who are to receive the decedent's real property according to the terms of that will.

A tenancy in common coowned by a married couple exists in both of the following conveyances:

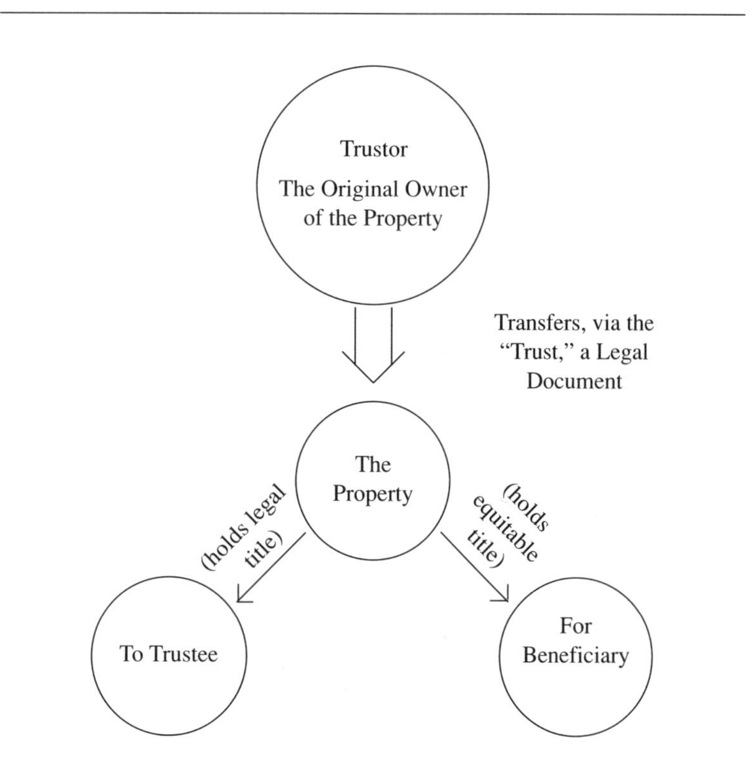

FIGURE 4–1
Trust ownership.

FOR EXAMPLE

George Brown and Mary Brown,
as tenants in common
Grantees . . .

George Brown and Mary Brown,
as tenants in common and not as
joint tenants,
Grantees . . .

George and Mary each own an undivided half of the real estate because there are just the two of them.

A tenancy in common also exists if, instead of George Brown and Mary Brown as grantees, the coowners are John Jones, Alan Adams, Mary Smith, or any number of named coowners. The composition of the group of coowners is subject to great variation. In the case of tenancy in common, virtually any persons or legal entities can together share the ownership of the realty in this way. To determine the percentage of an undivided ownership (one-half, one-third, one-twenty-fifth, and so on), one simply divides the total ownership (1) by the number of listed coowners (2, 3, 25, and so on). The resulting fraction represents the coowner's undivided share.

Instead of the above George Brown and Mary Brown example, a deed might show the coownership to be as follows:

FOR EXAMPLE

John Jones, an undivided one-fourth interest;
Mary Adams, an undivided one-fourth interest;
and Barker Brothers, Inc., an Ohio corporation,
an undivided one-half interest,
Grantees . . .

The number of coowners and the fractional interest of each of these coowners is entirely up to the *agreement of the parties.* The law will not step in to prohibit the creation of any group of coowners, nor will it interfere with the allotted fractional shares, as long as the parties have set forth a clear, complete, and unambiguous plan of coownership.

The major benefit of tenancy in common is that when a tenant in common dies, his or her undivided fractional interest passes to his or her heirs or devisees (persons designated by will).

Using the George Brown and Mary Brown, husband and wife, example, if Mary Brown dies, her undivided one-half interest passes to her heirs or devisees. Thus, if Mary dies leaving a will providing for all her real property to go to her husband, George Brown, then George becomes the sole owner of what was Mary's one-half interest. This occurs, not because of the deed or the statute of descent and distribution but, rather, because of the will.

To acquire an interest by inheritance (via the statute of descent and distribution) or by devise (via a will), a **probate court** must approve the transfer. This cannot be done until the decedent's estate has been administered or probated. The requirement of probate court approval to transfer a deceased tenant-in-common's interest in real property often is perceived as the major potential disadvantage to tenancy in common when the coowners are husband and wife. On the other hand, the true *benefit* of tenancy in common—keeping the realty either in the bloodline of the statute of descent and distribution or making sure certain persons receive the property because of a will—becomes apparent when the tenants in common are other than heirs or devisees, as in the following example.

FOR EXAMPLE

Two college friends, Frank Smith and Robert Akers, wanted to purchase a parcel of land together as an investment. At the time of agreement to purchase this land, both Frank and Robert were single. Ten years after the purchase, Frank died leaving a will. The will provided that all of Frank's property, both personal and real, shall go to his mother, Alice, because Frank never married.

If Frank and Robert owned the land as tenants in common, Frank's one-half interest in the property would go to his mother in accordance with his will. This apparently is exactly what Frank intended, because if he had wanted Robert to become sole owner of the realty, Frank could just as easily have left Robert, in the will, his one-half interest.

Tenancy in common enables coowners to control the exact disposition of their property after death, and the necessity of probate court approval for all transfers virtually guarantees that the deceased coowners' directions will be carried out. Figure 4–2 is a sample deed that conveys a tenancy in common to Frank Smith and Robert Akers.

FIGURE 4–2 Deed showing tenancy-in-common ownership.

WARRANTY DEED, short form, with release of dower — No. 22 (Reprinted 3/87) apco Registered in U.S. Patent and Trademark Office anderson publishing co. cincinnati, ohio 45201

Know All Men by These Presents

That Robert Anderson and Melodie Anderson, husband and wife, Grantors

of Montrose *County, Ohio,*

in consideration of Ten Dollars ($10.00) and other valuable consideration

to us *in hand paid by* Frank Smith and Robert Akers, Grantees as Tenants in Common

whose address is 103 Reindeer Avenue Mayville, Ohio 49972 *do hereby* **Grant, Bargain Sell and Convey** *to the said* Grantees their *heirs and assigns forever, the following described* **Real Estate,**(1)

Situated in the City of Mayville, County of Montrose and State of Ohio: And known as being Sublot No. 97 in the Seltzer Square Company's Mayville Park Overlook Allotment No. 4 of part of Original One Hundred Acre Lots Nos. 283 and 284 as shown by the recorded Plat in Volume 123 of Maps, Page 24 of Montrose County Records, and being 40 feet front on the Northerly side of Reindeer Avenue, and extending back of equal width 100 feet, as appears by said Plat, be the same more or less, but subject to all legal highways,

and all the **Estate, Right, Title and Interest** *of the said grantor*s *in and to said premises;* **To have and to hold** *the same, with all the privileges and appurtenances thereunto belonging, to said grantee* ,their *heirs and assigns forever. And the said* Grantors

do hereby **Covenant and Warrant** *that the title so conveyed is* **Clear, Free and Unincumbered,** *and that* they *will* **Defend** *the same against all lawful claims of all persons whomsoever,* except (a) any mortgage assumed by Grantee, (b) all restrictions, reservations, easements (however created), covenants, and conditions of record, (c) all of the following as do not materially adversely affect the use or value of the property: encroachments, oil, gas and mineral leases, (d) zoning ordinances, if any, and (e) taxes and assessments, both general and special, not currently due and payable.

Prior Instrument Record:

Vol 90-556 Pg 13

(1) Include reference to volume and page of next preceding recorded instrument through which grantor claims title. (R.C. § 319.20.).

In Witness Whereof, *the said* Grantors *and* each of them, individually, *who hereby release their right and expectancy of dower in said premises, have hereunto set their hand*s*, this* 1st *day of* June *in the year A. D. nineteen hundred and* ninety.

Signed and acknowledged in presence of us:

Robert Anderson

Melodie Anderson

State of Ohio, Montrose **County, ss.**

On this 1st *day of* June *, 19* 90 *, before me, a* notary public *in and for said County, personally came* Robert Anderson and Melodie Anderson *the grantor*s *in the foregoing deed, and acknowledged the signing thereof to be* their *voluntary act and deed.*

Witness *my official signature and seal on the day last above mentioned.*

JAMES DONATO IRVIN, Attorney
NOTARY PUBLIC - STATE OF OHIO
My commission has no expiration date.
Section 147.03 R. C.

This instrument was prepared by CAROL K. IRVIN,
Attorney at Law,
11401 Willow Hill
Chesterland, Ohio 44026
(216) 729-1655

Warranty Deed

From
Robert Anderson
and
Melodie Anderson
husband and wife

To
Frank Smith
and
Robert Akers
as Tenants in Common

Transferred 19

County Auditor

Ohio's Statutory Survivorship Tenancy

Ohio offers a **statutory survivorship tenancy** that allows, *upon the death of any one of the tenants, the decedent's interest to pass to the survivor(s).* Figure 4–3 shows a sample Ohio statutory survivorship deed. Upon the death of any one of the tenants, the decedent's interest passes to the survivor(s). The principles of the Ohio statutory survivorship tenancy come from the common law joint tenancy with rights of survivorship, which was developed from case law principles.

Although passing of the real estate occurs automatically by operation of law from the decedent tenant to the survivor(s), the survivor tenant(s) must take one final step. He or she (or they) has to make this change *of record* to put the public on

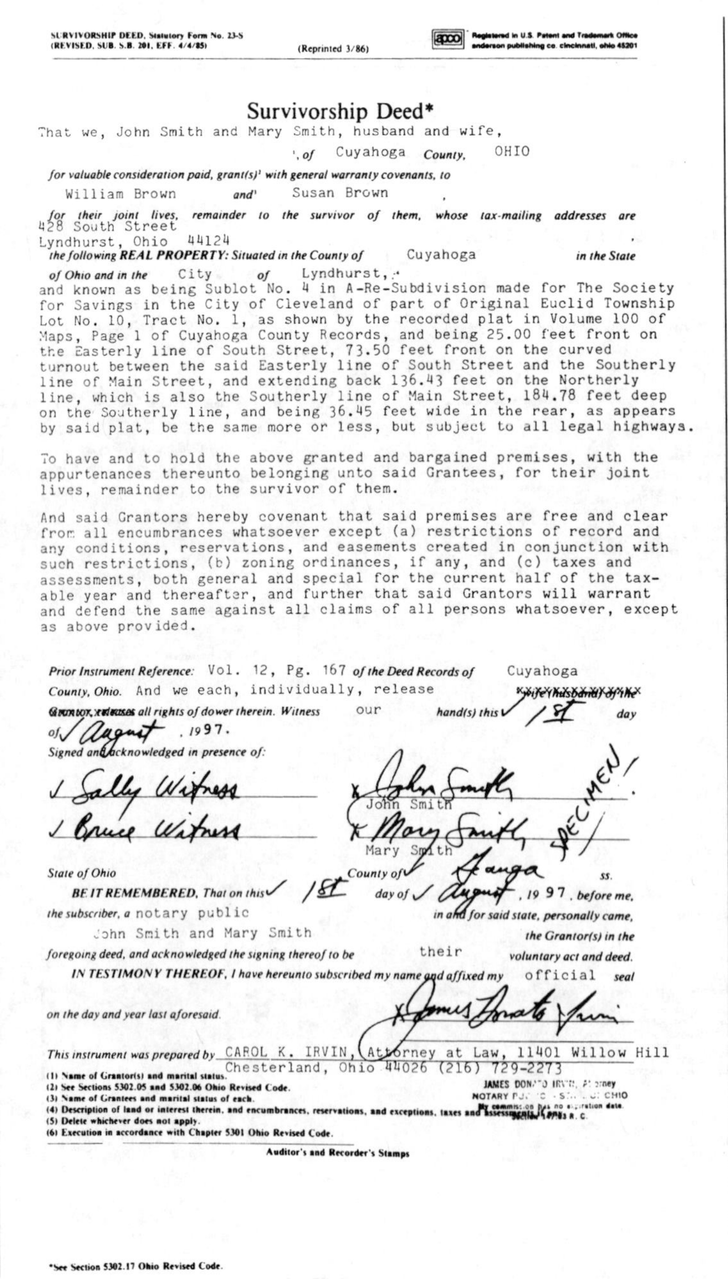

SURVIVORSHIP DEED, Statutory Form No. 23-S
(REVISED, SUB. S.B. 201, EFF. 4/4/85)

(Reprinted 3/86)

apco Registered in U.S. Patent and Trademark Office
anderson publishing co. cincinnati, ohio 45201

Survivorship Deed*

That we, John Smith and Mary Smith, husband and wife, [1], of Cuyahoga County, OHIO

for valuable consideration paid, grant(s)[2] *with general warranty covenants, to* William Brown *and*[5] Susan Brown, *for their joint lives, remainder to the survivor of them, whose tax-mailing addresses are* 428 South Street Lyndhurst, Ohio 44124

the following ***REAL PROPERTY:*** *Situated in the County of* Cuyahoga *in the State of Ohio and in the* City *of* Lyndhurst, [4]
and known as being Sublot No. 4 in A-Re-Subdivision made for The Society for Savings in the City of Cleveland of part of Original Euclid Township Lot No. 10, Tract No. 1, as shown by the recorded plat in Volume 100 of Maps, Page 1 of Cuyahoga County Records, and being 25.00 feet front on the Easterly line of South Street, 73.50 feet front on the curved turnout between the said Easterly line of South Street and the Southerly line of Main Street, and extending back 136.43 feet on the Northerly line, which is also the Southerly line of Main Street, 184.78 feet deep on the Southerly line, and being 36.45 feet wide in the rear, as appears by said plat, be the same more or less, but subject to all legal highways.

To have and to hold the above granted and bargained premises, with the appurtenances thereunto belonging unto said Grantees, for their joint lives, remainder to the survivor of them.

And said Grantors hereby covenant that said premises are free and clear from all encumbrances whatsoever except (a) restrictions of record and any conditions, reservations, and easements created in conjunction with such restrictions, (b) zoning ordinances, if any, and (c) taxes and assessments, both general and special for the current half of the taxable year and thereafter, and further that said Grantors will warrant and defend the same against all claims of all persons whatsoever, except as above provided.

Prior Instrument Reference: Vol. 12, Pg. 167 *of the Deed Records of* Cuyahoga *County, Ohio.* And we each, individually, release ~~wife (husband) of the Grantor, releases~~ *all rights of dower therein. Witness* our *hand(s) this* 1st *day of* August, *19*97.

Signed and acknowledged in presence of:

Sally Witness — John Smith
Bruce Witness — Mary Smith

SPECIMEN

State of Ohio *County of* Geauga *ss.*

BE IT REMEMBERED, *That on this* 1st *day of* August, *19*97, *before me, the subscriber, a* notary public *in and for said state, personally came,* John Smith and Mary Smith *the Grantor(s) in the foregoing deed, and acknowledged the signing thereof to be* their *voluntary act and deed.*

IN TESTIMONY THEREOF, *I have hereunto subscribed my name and affixed my* official *seal on the day and year last aforesaid.*

This instrument was prepared by CAROL K. IRVIN, Attorney at Law, 11401 Willow Hill Chesterland, Ohio 44026 (216) 729-2273

JAMES DONATO IRVIN, Attorney
NOTARY PUBLIC - STATE OF OHIO
My commission has no expiration date.
Section 147.03 R. C.

(1) Name of Grantor(s) and marital status.
(2) See Sections 5302.05 and 5302.06 Ohio Revised Code.
(3) Name of Grantees and marital status of each.
(4) Description of land or interest therein, and encumbrances, reservations, and exceptions, taxes and assessments, if any.
(5) Delete whichever does not apply.
(6) Execution in accordance with Chapter 5301 Ohio Revised Code.

Auditor's and Recorder's Stamps

*See Section 5302.17 Ohio Revised Code.

FIGURE 4–3
Ohio statutory survivorship deed.

notice. The survivor tenant(s) thereafter can freely transfer the real estate without any title problems that may come about in a search of the public records. A title company searches the public records before issuing a title guarantee, assurance, or insurance. This final step must be done if the real estate is to pass its scrutiny. To do so, the survivor presents to the county recorder a certificate of transfer or an affidavit accompanied by a death certificate.

A survivorship tenancy is a form of coownership entirely separate from tenancy in common; it is as legally different from tenancy in common as is possible. Unfortunately, the two are consistently confused, probably because of a misunderstanding of the word *survivorship*. The word *survivor* appears in discussions of both tenancy in common and survivorship tenancies, but the word means different things in each context.

As we mentioned earlier, a tenant in common can direct by will or can leave it up to the statute of descent and distribution to direct the transfer of one's undivided fractional interest to survivors—persons who live beyond the date of death of the tenant in common. But the tenant-in-common idea of devisee or heirs surviving a person is not the kind of survivorship referred to in connection with a survivorship tenancy. In the latter concept, survivorship pertains to those *named coowners on the deed who survive the deceased coowner, not to those devisees or heirs who outlive the decedent.*

Another important difference between the survivorship tenancy and the tenancy in common is that *survivorship tenants all have equal shares in the undivided interests of ownership of the real property.* When we discussed tenancy in common, we learned that the tenants can take different percentage interests in the undivided interests. For example, one tenant can have a one-quarter undivided interest and the other tenant a three-quarter undivided interest. This is not true in survivorship tenancy; all tenants have the same amount of undivided interests.

The Ohio statutory survivorship tenancy has the following characteristics or ramifications:

1. Each of the survivorship tenants has an equal right to share in the use, occupancy, and profits, and each is subject to a proportionate share of the costs related to the ownership and use of the real property subject to the survivorship tenancy.
2. A conveyance from all of the survivorship tenants to any other person, or from all except one of the survivorship tenants to the remaining survivorship tenant, terminates the survivorship tenancy and vests title in the grantee (in severalty).

Figure 4–4 compares the tenancy in common with the Ohio statutory survivorship tenancy.

The increase of those in U. S. society who are in second or third marriages presents a special problem in survivorship tenancies. In the traditional first-marriage situation, a survivorship tenancy can work well because the husband and wife have the same children together and they usually want the real estate to transfer to the children after both of them are dead. Thus, they can hold a survivorship tenancy with one another. Then, after the first one dies, the survivor typically holds the real estate in severalty and provides in his or her will for the real estate to pass to the children upon his or her own death. This plan usually does not work in second and third marriage situations, however, because the marital partners may not share the same children.

FOR EXAMPLE

Jack and Jill, a husband and wife, were each married and divorced prior to this marriage. Jack has three children by his former wife, and Jill has two children by her former husband. If they use Ohio's statutory survivorship form of coownership, one set of children may never participate in this real estate. If Jack dies first, having held title with Jill in the Ohio statutory survivorship form, all interest in the real estate passes automatically to Jill upon Jack's death. Jill draws up a new will after Jack's

FIGURE 4–4 Tenancy in common versus Ohio statutory survivorship tenancy.

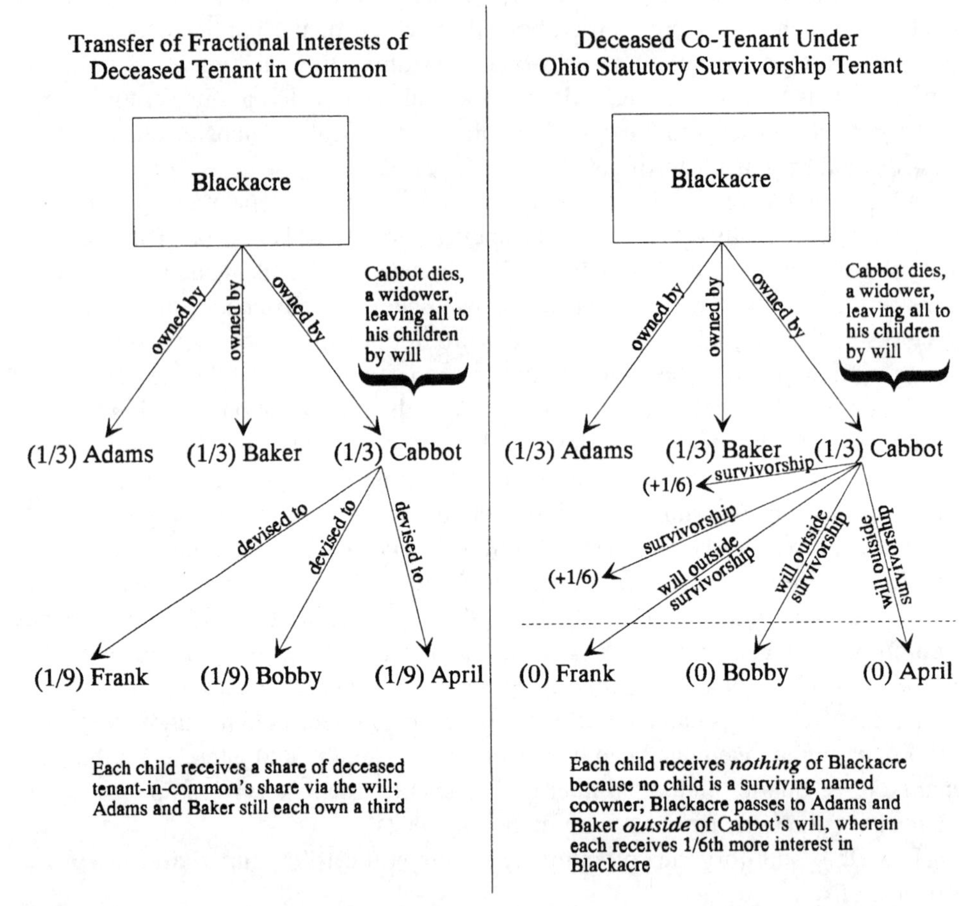

death. In Jill's will she leaves all of her property to her own two children. Jill dies, owning the real estate in severalty. Her two children receive the real estate through Jill's will. Jack's children receive no interest whatsoever in the real estate.

This situation can be avoided if Jack and Jill have a tenancy in common in the real estate instead. Coupled with the tenancy in common, however, should be well-thought-out wills providing for Jack's children to receive his half share of the realty and Jill's children to receive her half. This should be done with the aid of an attorney who is well-versed in estate planning practice, because second and third marriage situations typically involve complex estate planning problems.

With the "graying of America" (an increase in age of the general population), another problem with survivorship tenancies looms on the horizon. Smitten by the idea of avoiding probate court at all costs, some elderly people are making a younger family member a survivorship tenant in the elder person's real property.

FOR EXAMPLE

A woman of age 70 makes her only daughter of age 40 a survivorship tenant with her in her principal place of residence. Her sole reason is that she does not want her daughter to go through the expense and delay of the probate court process when she dies but, instead, to obtain the real estate automatically. What the 70-year-old mother fails to realize, however, is that the moment she creates the survivorship tenancy with her daughter, the daughter becomes coowner and then has full legal rights in the real estate.

Many legal problems can be precipitated thereby—problems far worse and more expensive to handle legally than transferring real estate through the approval of probate court.

FOR EXAMPLE

In Ohio, if the daughter marries, her spouse could obtain dower rights in this real estate. His approval thus would be necessary for any action the mother and daughter might want to make in regard to this realty in the future, such as selling it. Even worse, what if this new husband talks the daughter into selling the real estate even though the mother does not want to sell it? The result could be that the daughter and her husband end up suing the mother to force a sale of the realty. (This is called partition and is discussed in Chapter 7.)

These same problems with the daughter and her new husband could come about if the daughter were a tenant in common with the mother instead of a survivorship tenant. The mother would not likely be motivated to make her daughter a tenant in common, though, because that choice would not avoid having to go through probate court. The safest and best choice for the mother would be to remain the sole owner (in severalty) herself and to leave the daughter the real estate in her will. Although the daughter will have to go through the probate process to obtain title to the real estate, the mother risks none of the potential problems that attend coownership during her own lifetime.

Table 4–1 charts some of the problems connected with using the various forms of ownership.

ESTATE BY THE ENTIRETIES

The Ohio legislature set forth by statute in 1971 a method by which a husband and wife, and only a husband and wife, can establish a form of coownership, known as **estate by the entireties.** Essentially, under this concept, the realty is owned by a single entity, as an "entirety," and that entity is the marriage. Each spouse owns an undivided interest in the entire estate. Further, both the husband and the wife must consent to any sale to a third person(s), and thereafter both convey to a third

TABLE 4–1
Problems associated with various forms of ownership.

STATUTORY SURVIVORSHIP TENANCY	TENANCY IN COMMON	SEVERALTY
1. Can be dangerous for those in second or subsequent marriages, especially if they have children by prior marriages.	1. For most couples in first marriages, the survivorship form is probably better. Can work for those in second or subsequent marriages.	1. Can be the best choice for those who have divorced and remarried (especially for multiple-divorce situations).
2. Can be dangerous for those with ante nuptial contracts when such contracts have different provisions for the real estate.	2. This is as dangerous a choice as a survivorship when an ante nuptial contract has different provisions.	2. Many ante nuptial contracts require real estate to be held in the name of *only* the person who brought it into the marriage.
3. Can be dangerous for adult children and aging parents, especially if the marital situation of either might still change. Also dangerous for minor children and adult parents, as a guardianship will have to be created for the minors in probate court.	3. This is as dangerous a choice as a survivorship form when there are adult children and aging parents, especially with the possibility that the marital situation of either could still change. Also as dangerous for minor children and adult parents.	3. An aged person is often best left holding title in his or her name only, with a guardianship established in probate court, when it becomes necessary, to manage the estate. Likewise, an adult parent usually is better off holding title in his or her name only, without minor children as coowners.

person(s), because the entity (the marriage) owns the real estate. One marital partner alone cannot convey, encumber, or alienate the real estate held in the estate by the entirety. One marital partner always needs the consent of the other partner.

In 1984 the Ohio Supreme Court gave even fuller life to all of the above principles in a precedent-setting case, holding that a creditor could not foreclose on realty coowned by husband and wife in entireties where only one spouse owed the debt. The court upheld the philosophy of the deed itself: Because ownership was shared by husband and wife, neither spouse could dispose of the realty without the consent of the other. This decision was highly favorable to couples holding realty by entireties. As soon as this decision came out, creditors lobbied for repeal of the law, and it was abolished effective April 4, 1985.

This only abolished creating any more estates by the entireties, however. Those already in existence were left perfectly valid after that date. It will take a generation for these estates by the entireties to disappear through sale of the realties, or death or divorce of a spouse. Real estate practitioners, therefore, will be selling real properties owned by estates by the entireties, but they will not be dealing with any purchasers who can use, or request, that form of coownership.

Ohio's statutory survivorship deed form does not protect one coowner against liens placed on the realty by the other coowner's creditors. Only the entireties deed afforded that protection.

The Choice of a Form of Coownership

Many standard real estate form purchase contracts contain the following provision:

> Title shall be taken in the name or names of . . . .

Some of these contracts further ask if a survivorship feature is requested, and the purchasers then can check off "Yes" or "No." Because real estate salespeople are almost always the ones who actually fill in the blanks on these standard-form purchase agreements, they naturally become involved in determining the "how title should be taken" question. We warn that even though this involvement by salespeople might seem perfectly natural, it should be avoided at all costs. As a review of the previously discussed forms of coownership implies, the choice of a particular form of coownership involves knowledge of a great many points of law. The legal knowledge required for a proper choice of a form of coownership is actually greater than one can obtain from studying the information given in this chapter.

We purposely have avoided getting too deeply into the tax and other legal issues raised by the various forms of coownership. This is a subject for specialized lawyers and estate planners. The myths that abound in choice of coownership can have an adverse impact if they are believed and acted upon. An example follows.

FOR EXAMPLE

Bart decides to enter into a survivorship form of coownership with his daughter, Betty. This choice is based upon his real estate salesperson's advising him that he can "avoid the probate court process and, therefore, state and federal estate taxes, too, by using one of the survivorship forms of coownership." What the salesperson and Bart fail to realize is that *probate court proceedings and state and federal estate and gift taxes are two independent and separate matters*. Thus, Bart or Betty may well have to pay any number of taxes regardless of holding this realty in a survivorship form. If this example were between John and his wife, Mary, the taxation consequences could be entirely different, based on their being husband and wife instead of father and daughter. Further, if Bart and Betty are both married, they probably need a legal analysis of the effects of putting their spouses into the survivorship scheme with them, or leaving them out, or all four being tenants in common.

What may seem like a relatively simple problem immediately raises some complex questions that can be answered only by someone who is up-to-the-minute on taxation, probate, and real estate law. Perhaps even more important, these experts can and will assume the responsibility and liability for giving incorrect, outdated, or incomplete advice.

Most purchase agreements require at least 30 days to complete the transaction. This allows the purchaser ample time to obtain the necessary advice and to communicate the choice to the persons who need to know about it: realty agent, seller, deed preparer, and/or lender. The choice of how title should be taken is not a *material term* of the real estate purchase contract; it is not needed to form a valid contract. This is true even though the real estate purchase contract might have a blank for its indication or a check-off for the survivorship feature. One simple, yet effective way of dealing with this is to fill in the blank with the following provisions:

> Purchaser(s) shall supply information about the type of title he/she/they wish to hold prior to title transfer.

The Cooperative

FOR EXAMPLE

> You are attending a large, elegant party in the penthouse suite of what seems to be an apartment building. It has a premium view of the Ohio River. You wander around and hear some interesting conversations going on among other people who also live in this building. One group is talking about a former governor who is applying to "get into" the building. Another group is chortling over the board's recent denial of a nephew who was trying to take over his aunt's unit in the building, even though the nephew had inherited her entire estate upon her death. Finally, you hear another group bemoaning the decision made five years ago to let a well-known sports figure "in" and to subsequently allow him to take over an adjacent unit by knocking out the connecting wall and making the two units into one. The one resulting unit thus becomes incredibly expensive for whomever the board approves as his successor. That is not a concern, however, because other sports figures, equally as rich, are already on a waiting list.

What is this building, and who are these people who stand at the point of entry to keep out the ones they do not consider fit? How can this sort of elitism even be legal?

This entire building, plus the rest of the real estate, is a **cooperative.** One of its chief characteristics is the *high degree of control its board of directors exercises* toward keeping it within a certain master plan. The board of directors represents the corporation. The corporation holds title to the cooperative real estate. Therefore, a cooperative tenant does not possess any deed to the cooperative real estate, including its structure; instead, the corporation possesses the deed. The cooperative corporation owns the cooperative real estate *in severalty,* even though many people have rights and interests in that real property.

Cooperative tenants possess a **proprietary lease,** a *lease coupled with a proprietary stock interest in the corporation* that owns the real estate including the cooperative building. This lease, coupled with an **occupancy agreement** executed by the cooperative corporation, gives the cooperative tenant the right to use and possess his or her own rooms exclusively and the right to use the rest of the cooperative property mutually with the other cooperative tenants.

Cooperative tenants can control the management of, and the resulting cost and quality of, their living arrangements in the building by appropriately *voting their stock rights* in the corporation that holds freehold fee simple absolute title to the building. This latter power of the cooperative tenant—the power that comes from a stock interest in the corporation that owns the cooperative—is the major legal difference between an ordinary leasehold tenant and a cooperative, proprietary leasehold tenant.

Coownership in a cooperative involves the mutual rights of all the cooperative tenants in the shared portions of the cooperative property. These portions are virtually the same areas as the corresponding portions of a similar type of condominium structure or apartment complex—roof, walls, floors, utility lines, hallways, stairways, elevators, parking garage spaces, and so on, in high-rise, multifamily structures.

The law recognizes that the cooperative corporation usually has to place substantial restrictions on the right of the individual to deal freely with his or her property interest in the cooperative. Thus, cooperatives have an extensive set of rules and regulations that the tenants must comply with.

Because the tenants own the cooperative as stockholders, they are the ones who want rules and regulations, not some elusive landlord or developer. Thus, they are more than happy to comply with and enforce them. As stockholders, cooperative tenants do not have to fear annual rent increases as ordinary tenants would. Cooperative tenants instead pay an *assessment,* which covers the *cost of operating and maintaining the entire cooperative.* This **cooperative assessment** also includes the proportionate amount of real estate tax paid by each tenant, as well as any proportionate indebtedness owed on a blanket mortgage (one held on the whole of the cooperative real estate rather than on the individual units). The cooperative tenants/stockholders approve any increase by using their voting rights given to them by their ownership of cooperative stock.

Although in theory a cooperative can be formed for any group of people, as a practical matter this arrangement works best for those on the higher end of the socioeconomic scale who live in sophisticated urban centers. One disadvantage illustrates this point perfectly: the problem with mortgages. Cooperative owners cannot obtain mortgages for their individual units as they can for single-family dwellings and condominium units. Instead, they must participate with all the other cooperative stockholders in a blanket mortgage for the whole of the cooperative. If several stockholders default on this mortgage, it can threaten the whole of the cooperative. This is less of a worry when all the residents are so affluent that they will never need to worry about default. Indeed, many of them may even use cash for their investment.

The pluses also are weighted toward the higher end of the socioeconomic scale. Chief among these is that the *board of directors for the cooperative corporation must approve of any new tenant/stockholder for the cooperative.* No one can assume the lease of the cooperative tenant without board approval. Even if the cooperative interest is inherited, the person who inherits it must gain board approval. Typically, a person who is not within the same socioeconomic class as the rest of the cooperative participants will not gain board approval. This does not mean, however, that cooperatives are exempt from fair housing laws. They may not discriminate on the basis of race, religion, national origin, sex, family status, or handicap. The major forms of discrimination of a cooperative tend to involve a person's affluence, reputation, mode of behavior, and the like. These bases are legal unless they are merely covering up discrimination based on the prohibited factors.

The major legal difference between a condominium (to be discussed next) and a cooperative is this: *In a condominium, the unit owners share ownership of a fee simple absolute, freehold estate, whereas, in a cooperative, the unit owners share ownership of a special type of leasehold estate.* The significant variation between the condominium and the cooperative is that the condominium ownership involves holding title to a freehold estate, whereas cooperative ownership involves holding title to a nonfreehold (or leasehold) estate.

COOPERATIVE	CONDOMINIUM
1. Tenant has leasehold estate.	1. Owner has freehold estate.
2. Tenant obtains stock, a proprietary lease, and an occupancy agreement.	2. Owner obtains a deed showing his or her individual and shared interests of ownership.
3. Board of directors for the cooperative corporation must approve of any new tenant/stockholder for the cooperative. *Warning:* Cooperatives must observe all fair housing laws and cannot fail to approve any new tenant/stockholder because of the prohibited categories of discrimination.	3. At most, a condominium can exercise a right of first refusal by purchasing a unit to keep out a potential condominium property owner. *Warning:* Condominiums must observe all applicable fair housing laws and cannot use a right of first refusal because of any of the prohibited categories of discrimination.

TABLE 4–2 Comparison of cooperative and condominium ownership.

Some people mistakenly assume that the type of building structure is what differentiates a cooperative and a condominium. Both cooperatives and condominiums may use any structure or combination of structures they wish—a single building, town houses, row houses, one structure per unit owner, all of these in combination, and so on. Table 4–2 contrasts the cooperative with the condominium.

THE CONDOMINIUM

Let us return to that cocktail party in the penthouse suite with the view of the Ohio River.

FOR EXAMPLE

> Everything looks exactly the same. The individual suite seems identical, as does everything you had to walk through to get to it: the lobby, the elevator, and the top floor corridor. As you mingle with the guests, who are also residents of this building, however, you hear somewhat different conversations.
>
> This time, the nephew of the recently deceased aunt is in the process of moving into the building. He inherited her entire estate and, as one resident complains, "There was no way of keeping him out." Then you learn, from the next group, that the sports figure just moved in, too. "The association wanted to use its right of first refusal to buy the unit," explains the adjacent-unit neighbor, "but there was no way the association could afford to pay what he could. He went way over market value." Finally, the last group you mingle with is happy, because the former governor, someone they all wanted, did not necessitate their board even having to consider buying the unit on a first-refusal basis to keep him out.

This party was held at a **condominium,** not at a cooperative. At most, a condominium might have a **right of first refusal** to buy an individual unit owner's condominium property, only if this refusal right is not covering up discrimination as prohibited by the fair housing laws. Not every condominium development creates a right of first refusal, however. This kind of right means that the association must be able to *purchase outright* that interest. That is a significant financial commitment that should be used, as a practical matter, sparingly. Compare this with the cooperative, where all the cooperative board has to do is say "no" to keep out a prospective new stockholder/tenant. The cooperative board does not have to buy anything.

Further, this condominium's right of first refusal does not even apply to the nephew who inherited the aunt's condominium property. This is because the condominium association cannot interfere with the *free alienability of land.* The condominium owner owns a fee simple absolute interest in land and, as such an owner, the free alienability of that land cannot be unduly interfered with.

FIGURE 4–5 Diagram of condominium ownership.

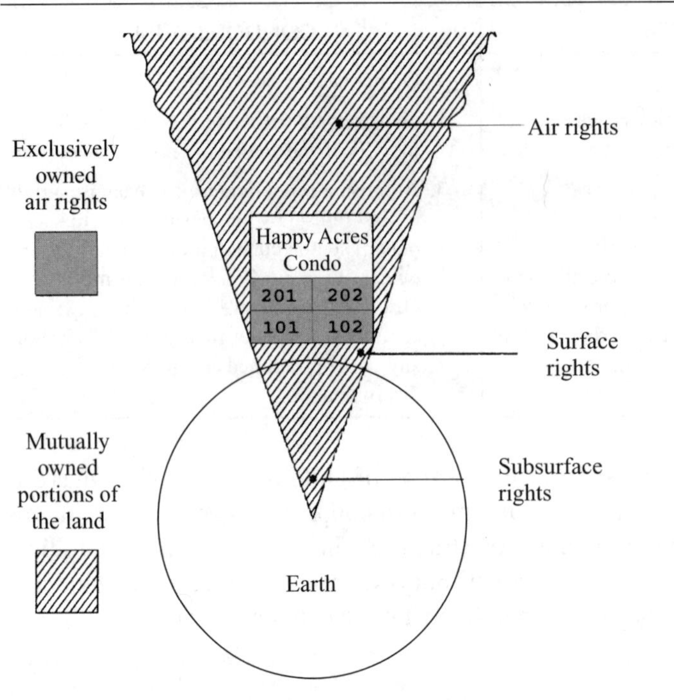

Characteristics of Condominiums

A condominium unit owner has an exclusively owned fee simple absolute estate in a portion of the airspace and a mutually owned fee simple absolute estate in all the rest of what is known as land. This condominium ownership is diagrammed as shown in Figure 4–5. Note that the exclusively owned portion of the land is the airspace designated in the diagram as Units 101, 102, 201, and 202. The mutually owned portion of the land is all the rest: the rest of the building, including floors, walls, ceilings, roof, foundation, and all plumbing and other utility lines within the building; the rest of the surface of the land; the rest of the air rights; and the rest of the subsurface rights.

These mutually owned portions of the condominium are known as the **common areas,** because legally these areas are *owned as a tenancy in common by all the unit owners.* Some condominiums also have *limited common areas,* those *owned in common by all condominium unit owners but serving only a specific condominium unit or structure of units.* These could include things such as parking spaces, garage stalls, balconies, stoops, and equipped laundry rooms.

The only difference between a condominium tenancy in common and the joint ownership kind of tenancy in common is that, in the case of the condominium, some of the land is owned exclusively and other portions of the same land are owned by a group of people. The operative language in a deed to a condominium, for purposes of this discussion of coownership, appears as follows:

FOR EXAMPLE

John Jones,
Grantee,
Situated in the Village of Reminderville, County of Summit and State of Ohio and known as being dwelling Unit 201, as shown by the drawings of Mulberry Hill of Aurora Shores, Condominium Phase A, as shown by Volume 85, Page 18 of Summit County Records and as further described by the Declaration of Condominium Ownership and Bylaws, attached thereto recorded in Volume 5376, Page 106 of Summit County Records, together with an undivided 5.00% interest in and to all the

> Common Areas and Facilities appurtenant to as the same may be amended from time to time, which percentage shall automatically change in accordance with amended Declarations, as the same are filed of record pursuant to the provisions of said Declaration and will attach to the additional common areas and facilities in the percentages set forth in such amended Declarations, which percentages shall automatically be deemed to be conveyed effective on the recording of each such amended Declaration as though conveyed hereby, be the same more or less, but subject to all legal highways.

The above deed refers to only one grantee, John Jones. Yet John Jones is considered to be a tenant in common, or a coowner, as well. Who are his other coowners? They are the other condominium unit owners. John Jones supposedly owns an "undivided 5.00% interest in and to all the Common Areas and Facilities appurtenant to [said Unit]." This fractional interest might lead one to think that Mr. Jones has less rights in the condominium common areas than some of the other unit owners, who might have a greater percentage of ownership in those areas. This is not the case.

Recall that earlier we explained that all tenants in common have equal rights to use the common areas, regardless of their actual undivided fractional interests in the land. Perhaps the reason for this is that the fractional interest of the tenants in common has not yet been apportioned or "divided" during the period of usage and ownership. The fraction indicates what portion of the eventual proceeds of the sale of the land must be paid to each of the coowners. Thus, even though John Jones owns only a 5.00% share of all the common areas, he has the *same right to the use and enjoyment of these areas as any other unit owner.*

Condominiums can be used for residential, commercial, or industrial real estate with the basic legal principles of condominium ownership remaining the same. Water slips as well as land can become condominium property. Most of this discussion, however, focuses on residential condominiums because they dominate the average real estate salesperson's market.

Principles of Condominium Law

Chapter 5311 of the Ohio Revised Code contains a complete statutory scheme covering everything from the condominium's creation to its termination. This section focuses upon those general principles of condominium law.

The declaration

The owner of the condominium (usually also the developer) is the one who creates it. He or she submits the real property to the provisions of Ohio's statutory condominium law by signing and acknowledging the **declaration,** a *legal document that contains the permanent governing principles and constitutional framework for the condominium.* The condominium declaration contains an exhaustive amount of specific information. This includes legal descriptions, percentage of ownership interest in common areas, descriptions and methods of use of both the common areas and the individual units, the procedure for terminating condominium property for a variety of causes, and the purpose of the condominium—whether it is for residential, commercial, or industrial use. The declaration is recorded in the county recorder's office wherein the real estate is located.

Other legal instruments

The owner/developer also submits other legal instruments to the county recorder, usually at the same time as the declaration. These include the drawings, the plat, the plans, and the bylaws of the unit owners' association.

1. The *drawings* show in detail the land, buildings, layout, location, dimensions of the units and common areas, any easements and encroachments, and certification by the surveyor or engineer.

2. The **bylaws** are a *contract* between the unit owners and between the unit owners' association and the unit owners. Bylaws *contain the rules and regulations for the day-to-day affairs and problems of the unit owners' association and provide for flexible administration of condominium property.*

3. A purchaser buys a condominium unit through a *condominium purchase contract.* It closely resembles a standard real estate purchase contract. The variation is that it also covers the common-area aspects of the purchase as well as reference to the condominium documents.

4. The *unit deed* is the legal instrument whereby the condominium developer conveys a unit to a purchaser. The standard real estate deed form is used with additions for the condominium property. These include a letter or number designation of the unit that corresponds to the plat and plans, a statement of the use and restrictions on use, and the percentage of undivided interest the unit has in the common areas. The unit deed also should incorporate, by reference, the declaration, the articles of incorporation, the bylaws, and the condominium plat and plans.

Unit owners' association

Upon becoming an owner of condominium property, one automatically becomes a member of the **unit owners' association.** Conversely, if one is not an owner, one cannot become a member of the association. Because the declaration of the condominium, as well as the bylaws, refers to the unit owners' association, one of the first concerns is how to organize one. The usual selection by the unit owners is to *incorporate the unit owners' association to limit its liability,* just as any other business association uses a corporation for this purpose. The **articles of incorporation** are the principal legal document to bring this about, and give the incorporated association broad powers to meet the owners' needs. The articles also cover membership and voting rights including selection of the board of managers/directors who will govern the incorporated unit owners' association.

Percentage interests

Unit owners derive their voting rights from their **percentage interest** of ownership in the condominium's common areas. At the time of filing the original documents, the owner/developer had to decide how to apportion ownership of the land held in common, the undivided percentage interest ownership of each individual in the common areas.

The developer/owner can use several possible methods for allocating the percentage ownership interests:

1. The *value-to-value* method, which compares the value of the individual unit against the collected value of all units.
2. The *square footage* method, which compares the square footage within the individual unit to all the square footage in all the units in the condominium property.
3. The *par value* method, in which a number of dollars or points are assigned to each unit by the declaration.

The *fractional amount* each unit owner is given also will decide how much of the common assessment each unit owner is to pay. For example, the unit owner with a five-percent interest in the undivided common areas will pay less of an assessment than the unit owner with a seven-percent interest.

Assessments and their collection

Lawsuits have challenged the concept of owing assessments for ownership of the common areas. For example, a unit owner refuses to pay her assessments because she does not use the common swimming pool, tennis court, or bike trail. Her suit fails because her undivided tenant-in-common interest in the common areas makes her liable regardless of her possession or use of them. Payment of common assessments is not optional. By paying the **common assessments,** all of the unit owners *share jointly in the cost of the maintenance, repair, improvement, and operation of the common areas.* The assessment provision imposes upon unit owners a covenant to pay their proportionate share of the common expenses and special assessments for capital improvements.

All sums assessed to any unit for maintenance or improvement of commonly owned properties are *secured by a lien against the unit.* The provisions for assessments usually are found within the bylaws. Condominium expenses and profits are both based upon the percentage of the interest in the common areas by each individual unit owner. The bylaws specify how the individual unit owners are to be assessed and how these assessments are to be collected. Typically, a specific provision within the bylaws provides that no unit owner can avoid the payment of common expenses by waiving his or her right to use some or all of the common areas and facilities. The bylaws usually require the board of directors to prepare a yearly budget with estimated amounts for operating expenses and maintaining a reserve fund of money. The method for collecting assessments from the unit owners may be set forth in either the declaration or the bylaws. If drawn properly the documents contain various penalties for nonpayment of assessments and some means of collecting late assessments. The association can impose a lien upon the unit and its percentage of the common areas in favor of the association for nonpayment and default. In addition, the unit owners' association can accelerate the monthly amount to the annual amount due and owing in the event of a default. If that accelerated figure is not paid, the association possibly can bring a foreclosure action against the delinquent unit owner, if all the appropriate documents allow that result.

Restrictions

Many people who are buying their first condominium do not realize how restrictive a condominium is on use of realty. Most people expect their use of condominium property to not differ significantly from that of their former single-family home. Aside from being a different legal scheme, the condominium is also an entirely different living scheme. Condominiums severely restrict uses on what can be done with the common real property. The following are typically considered valid restrictions in condominiums:

1. No exterior changes, such as painting it a different color.
2. No structural alterations or additions, such as adding a family room.
3. Only common uses of the grass, trees, streams, and so forth. No individual use, such as gardens or flower beds, permitted.
4. No pets, including cats and dogs. (This provision varies considerably from development to development. Many condominiums do allow pets but restrict their size, number, and where one may exercise them.)
5. No rentals to a third party.

Condominium owners have a *free hand only in the interior of their own unit.* Once they leave the interior of their unit, they are heavily regulated on the use of the rest of the real property. This rigid use makes condominium living unpleasant to those who desire freer use of land. Most courts uphold these restrictions. They must

TABLE 4–3 Comparison of single-family and condominium ownership.

SINGLE-FAMILY HOME	CONDOMINIUM
1. Owner owns and possesses all of real estate; no common area ownership because no common areas.	1. Each owner wholly owns and possesses individual unit but owns in common, with all other unit owners, the common areas of real estate.
2. Owner can use all of real estate as he or she sees fit; subject only to zoning and restrictions of record.	2. Each owner cannot use all of real estate personally because of restrictions of declaration of condominium property, including prohibition of individual use of common areas.
3. No payment of assessments for maintenance/repair/improvement of real estate; maintenance, repair, and improvement all done at owner election and cost.	3. Each owner must pay assessments for repair/maintenance and improvement for common areas of condominium property.
4. Owner holds title to whole of real estate either in severalty or in coownership form.	4. Each owners holds title in individual unit either in severalty or form of coownership but holds title to common areas along with all other owners of condominium property.
5. Owner is freely able to sell real estate to others.	5. Owner not as freely able to sell real estate because restrictions in declaration (e.g., cannot sell to be used as rental property).

Note: Neither of the above forms of ownership is "better." Each has its benefits and detriments.

be uniformly and equally enforced, however. If exceptions are made, the courts likely will strike down the restrictions.

Use of condominium common property is not the same thing as use of individual property. *Individual unit owners cannot make individual use of common area space.* As examples, they cannot plant a garden, install a swing, or plant a tree or shrub on common-area property. When individual unit owners make individual use of a common area, they take property that is not their own, and they prohibit cotenants from using the common areas. The courts will prohibit any individual from making an individual use of common property in the condominium. Table 4–3 contrasts the single-family home with the condominium.

Annual meeting

The **annual meeting** of members of the unit owners' association is critically important to all the individuals who own property in the condominium. This is their chance to give input regarding the future handling and cost of operating, maintaining, and repairing the common areas. These considerations have a cost consequence and affect the figures for upcoming assessments. Perhaps the owners will even want to add some amenities, such as tennis courts, which also influence assessments for the future. Also, board members usually are elected at the annual meeting.

The bylaws usually provide that *proper, written notice of the annual meeting* has to be sent to each of the unit owners in advance of the meeting. This notice specifies the date, time, and place of the meeting, and it might also include an agenda. The budget for the fiscal year should either be attached to this notice or be furnished during the meeting. This budget should contain an itemized estimate of the common expenses and an estimated allocation of the common expenses to each owner. The statement also might itemize income and common expenditures authorized for the past year.

The condominium developer

Classically, the developer is the person most disfavored by unit owners of condominium developments. Lawsuits between the two parties are common. Ohio Revised Code

Chapter 5311 placed certain restrictions and duties upon the residential condominium developer to solve recurring problems.

One problem entailed a developer's attempt to control the property by retaining control of the board of managers/directors of the unit owners' association. The solution was to provide that as each percentage of condominium property is sold, the unit owners continue to replace members of the board of managers/directors. When individuals finally own all the units, all members of the board of managers/directors are to be elected by the unit owners' association.

When the developer retained control of the board of managers/directors, **sweetheart contracts** *were another frequent problem. These were long-term contracts for work the developer would grant to various friends and relatives, and the unit owners' association then would be bound to them. For example, the developer's brother might have a 10-year snow-plowing and road-repair contract with the unit owners' association, granted by the developer when he had control of the association. This was solved by the Ohio Revised Code's prohibiting the developer's binding the unit owners' association to long-term management contracts.*

Ohio's Revised Code also requires the developer to disclose to the residential condominium purchaser instruments, warranties, and strict accounting of funds in deposit accounts.

Expandable condominiums

The developer can be allowed to complete the development of the condominium property in phases. **Expandable condominium** means that the *developer can add individual and common-area property to the individual and common area property already in existence.* As the developer adds this property, he or she must *keep the undivided, percentage ownership interests the same.* No condominium owner can end up with more or less undivided percentage interest than before the expansion. For the developer to have the right to expand the condominium, the declaration must state this option.

Conversion condominiums

A **condominium conversion** occurs when *real property formerly operated in another way is submitted, by declaration and other documents, to the county recorder's office as condominium property instead.* The most common conversion is multi-unit rental space changed to condominium.

When developers convert real estate into condominium property, they must make a *disclosure,* a report stating the age and condition of the property and the developer's opinion regarding the useful life of its structural, mechanical, and support systems. Conversion condominium instruments specify that all of the *tenants must be given the option to purchase* their unit and the common areas as condominium property. Further, the tenants must be given *advance, written notice of their duty to vacate. Tenants cannot be ordered to vacate prior to the expiration of their lease.*

Terminating the condominium

The declaration should provide an orderly means for termination of condominium property, specifying those foreseeable circumstances that would result in termination. For example, substantial destruction by fire is grounds for termination. Condominium property terminates when the unit owners unanimously remove the condominium property from the provisions of Ohio Revised Code Chapter 5311 by filing a *certificate of election* with the county recorder. Thereafter, all liens and encumbrances become immediately due and payable, except for taxes and assessments not due. The *unit owners then own the resulting realty in common.* The undivided interest in the realty by each unit owner is the same as the individual's former percentage of ownership in the common areas.

CASE STUDY FROM THE OHIO SUPREME COURT

WAGNER V. GALIPO
50 Ohio St.3d 194, 553 N.E.2d 610 (1990)

Facts: The Wagners obtained a judgment against Charles Galipo for $48,000 in Cuyahoga County Common Pleas Court on September 20, 1983. On the same day, a judgment lien certificate was recorded in Cuyahoga County. At the time, Galipo was the record owner of an undivided half-interest in real property located in Pepper Pike, Ohio. Marilyn Galipo, his wife, owned the remaining half-interest. The following day the Galipos recorded a deed purporting to create in themselves an estate by the entireties (also known as tenancy by the entireties) in the Pepper Pike property. Mr. Galipo claimed to have executed the deed on the morning of September 20, before the judgment lien was filed. The Wagners disputed this, claiming that Mr. Galipo was at the common pleas court and could not have been physically present at the time and place he claimed to have signed the deed. Mr. Galipo made no payments on the lien. The Wagners brought a foreclosure action against the Pepper Pike property, seeking to have it sold to satisfy the debt.

Issue: Whether a valid tenancy by the entireties was created and, if so, whether the tenancy by the entireties resulted from a fraudulent conveyance. (Either an invalid tenancy by the entireties, or a fraudulent conveyance by using a tenancy by the entireties, would allow the Wagners to proceed ahead in their foreclosure action against the real property in Pepper Pike.)

Held by the Ohio Supreme Court: Creation of a tenancy by the entireties is a conveyance and thus may also be a fraudulent conveyance. If the court were to say that creation of an estate by the entireties (or creation of a survivorship tenancy under the current law) could never be a fraudulent conveyance, this would permit a married debtor to avoid both the obligation to his creditors and the operation of Ohio Revised Code Chapter 1336, by placing all of his property into tenancy by the entireties as the Wagners allege Mr. Galipo attempted to do.

In this case there are genuine issues of material fact regarding whether the tenancy by the entireties is valid. The parties disagree on whether Mr. Galipo was physically present at the place and time he purportedly signed the deed. If he was not, the deed was fraudulently executed and the estate was not validly created. Even if otherwise validly created, the estate could be set aside as a fraudulent conveyance if its creation without a fair consideration rendered Mr. Galipo insolvent or if it was created with actual intent to hinder, delay, or defraud either present or future creditors.

The court remanded the case for further proceedings consistent with this opinion. (This means that the trial court had to determine from the known facts whether the estate was ever validly created. If not, the Wagners could proceed ahead against Mr. Galipo, as his realty was not protected from creditors by the estate by the entireties. If there was a validly created estate by the entireties, the trial court could still set that conveyance aside if it decided Mr. Galipo had perpetrated a fraud upon his creditors by the facts surrounding that conveyance. This, too, would permit the Wagners to proceed with their foreclosure action.)

CASE STUDY FROM THE OHIO SUPREME COURT

MCKNIGHT V. BOARD OF DIRECTORS, ANCHOR POINTE BOAT-A-MINIMUM ASSOCIATION, INC.
32 Ohio St.3d 6, 512 N.E.2d 316 (1987)

Facts: On January 1, 1980, a marine condominium was created by recording a Declaration of Condominium Ownership in conformance with Chapter 5311 of the Ohio Revised Code. First Federal Savings and Loan Association of Toledo (First Federal) held the mortgages and security interests in that property, which were in default. Condominium Marine agreed to transfer the Anchor Pointe property to Port

Lawrence Title and Trust Co. as trustee for the benefit of First Federal in lieu of foreclosure. First Federal thus became owner of 362 unsold marine water slips in the Anchor Pointe complex. On March 4, 1984, a meeting of the unit owners' association was called and a board of directors was elected. First Federal cast votes for all members of the nine member board. Six First Federal employees were elected. On February 27, 1985, the board called a special meeting for the purpose of requesting the unit owners to approve a Third Amendment to the Declaration of Condominium Ownership. Following a discussion, the Third Amendment was adopted by 77.15% of the voting power. The Third Amendment enlarged the authority of the board, permitting it to enter into long-term leases of portions of the common areas, including buildings, a restaurant, gas dock, and party store. The plaintiffs, individual owners of the boat slips, filed a complaint for a temporary restraining order, a preliminary and permanent injunction, and a declaratory judgment. They maintained that the Third Amendment was invalid because it was proposed by an improperly elected board of directors. There are special requisites for who may be on the board of directors and in what percentage under the provisions of the Ohio Revised Code. If First Federal was deemed a developer, it had not followed those statutory requisites.

Trial Court Held: First Federal was deemed a developer under Ohio Revised Code Section 5311.01 (T). The board of directors was improperly elected and the Third Amendment was null and void. The board was enjoined from entering into agreements authorized by the Third Amendment.

Court of Appeals Held: Affirmed the Trial Court decision.

Issue: Whether the trial court erred in enjoining the board of directors from entering into agreements authorized by the Third Amendment.

Held by the Ohio Supreme Court: A mortgagee acquiring title to property or other collateral has the right to protect its interests by taking reasonable steps to maintain or preserve the property. However, when the mortgagee performs such acts as to become so intertwined with the promotion and development of the property that it has engaged in the business of the developer, it cannot insulate itself from the duties, constraints, and obligations of the developer pursuant to Ohio Revised Code Chapter 5311. Thus, the board was illegally constituted and the Third Amendment was null and void.

Summary of Content

1. Ownership in severalty is not coownership at all; rather, it is ownership by a single person, either natural (a single human being) or artificial (a corporation or a partnership).
2. The trust is a hybrid creature, straddling the line of both severalty and coownership. Ownership is held in the name of the trustee, yet such ownership is for the benefit of the beneficiary, another person.
3. Coownership involves two or more persons who have interests in the same piece of real property.
4. Tenancy in common is ownership by two or more persons, each of whom has an undivided fractional interest and equal right to use the real estate. Upon death of a tenant in common, his undivided fractional interest in the realty passes to the devisees, if he died with a will; if he died without a will, his fractional interest passes to his heirs.

5. Upon death of an Ohio statutory survivorship tenant, in contrast, her entire undivided fractional interest in the realty passes to the surviving coowner(s) named on the deed.
6. Estate by the entireties is also a survivorship tenancy, between a husband and wife. A creditor cannot foreclose upon an estate by the entireties if only one spouse is the debtor. No estate by the entireties in Ohio could be created after April 4, 1985. Those created before that date are still valid.
7. Although the real estate salesperson should explain to purchasers that various forms of coownership exist, each having radically different legal characteristics, the choice of the best form of coownership for each purchaser(s) involves estate planning, something real estate salespeople are not licensed to do.
8. Probate court proceedings and state and federal estate and gift taxes are two independent and separate matters.
9. A cooperative is a corporation that owns the freehold estate in land and acts through its board of directors. The cooperative tenants own stock in that corporation and use and possess the cooperative property pursuant to a proprietary lease and occupancy agreement.
10. A condominium unit owner has an exclusively owned fee simple absolute estate in a portion of the airspace and a mutually owned fee simple absolute estate in all the rest of what is known as land.
11. Ohio Revised Code Chapter 5311 contains the law on condominiums, covering every aspect, from creation to termination of a condominium.
12. A condominium is created by a declaration, a legal document containing the permanent governing principles and constitutional framework for the condominium.
13. The bylaws of the unit owners' association contain the rules and regulations of the association and provide for administration of the condominium property.
14. Upon becoming an owner of condominium property, one automatically becomes a member of the unit owners' association.
15. Unit owners derive their voting rights from their percentage interest of ownership in the condominium's common areas.
16. Each unit owner pays assessments, based upon his percentage interest in the common areas, to cover his proportionate cost of all common expenses and special assessments for common improvements.
17. Condominiums have extremely restrictive uses of common real property—e.g., no exterior changes, no structural alterations or deletions, and only common uses of grass, trees, streams, and so forth. Individual unit owners cannot make individual use of common-area space.
18. Individual unit owners are given notice of the condominium unit owners' association's annual meeting, which handles the costs of operating, maintaining, and repairing the common areas, plus election of board members.
19. The developer of a residential condominium has the following statutory duties:
    a. As each percentage of condominium property is sold, the unit owners progressively take over the board of managers/directors.
    b. The unit owners' association is not subject to any long-term management contracts entered into prior to its assumption of control.
    c. The developer has to make disclosures of condominium instruments, plus warranties about the subject property, to purchasers.
20. Developers may expand condominiums in phases by adding on more individual and common area property as long as the undivided percentage ownership interest remains the same.

21. A condominium conversion occurs when real property formerly operated in another way (e.g., multi-unit rental space) is submitted by the declaration and other documents to the recorder's office as condominium property instead.
22. The declaration provides for termination of the condominium. In addition, the condominium can terminate when the unit owners remove the condominium from Chapter 5311 of the Ohio Revised Code by filing a certificate of election with the county recorder.

Review Questions

1. A woman and her male companion own real property equally as tenants in common. Each may not:
   a. sell his or her interest without the consent of the other
   b. get married and give a spouse dower rights without the consent of the other
   c. pass his or her interest by will
   d. oust the other from use and possession of the property

2. Paul Jones and Bill Thompson are a gay couple. They may not own real estate together:
   a. in severalty
   b. as tenants in common
   c. as statutory survivorship tenants
   d. as joint tenants with rights of survivorship

3. Paul Jones also has a wife. If Paul dies, she can:
   a. sue Bill for wrongful coownership
   b. take dower rights in this real estate
   c. bring a partition action against Paul for leaving her out
   d. ask a divorce court to take Bill off the title and put her on it in his place

4. Paul and Bill hold their real estate together in statutory survivorship tenancy. Paul dies and leaves no will. Both Bill and Paul's wife survive him.
   a. the real estate passes to Bill
   b. the state statute of intestate distribution cancels out the statutory survivorship tenancy
   c. the surviving spouse has the rights of a leasehold tenant in the real estate
   d. the statutory survivorship tenancy with Bill is invalid because Paul, as a married man, had no legal right to enter into one with anyone but his wife

5. Real estate owned in trust:
   a. cannot be sold until the trust dissolves
   b. involves only minors and incompetents
   c. gives the legal title holder, the trustee, unlimited power to dispose of the real estate
   d. is held in the name of the trustee for the benefit of the beneficiary of the trust

6. Rodney, a married man, and Grace, a single woman, may *not* take ownership in real estate together:
   a. in severalty
   b. as tenants in common
   c. as statutory survivorship tenants
   d. pursuant to a trust they create

7. Rodney and Grace held real estate together as statutory survivorship tenants. Rodney dies, leaving no will.
   a. Grace gets the real estate with no legal problems whatsoever
   b. Rodney's surviving spouse's dower rights vest in that real estate, creating a significant title problem that the spouse can use against Grace
   c. the state statute of intestate distribution cancels out the statutory survivorship ownership
   d. the statutory survivorship tenancy with Grace is invalid because Rodney, as a married man, has no legal right to enter into one with anyone but his wife

8. The person who should select the type of ownership for the purchaser/grantee of the real estate:
   a. real estate salesperson
   b. escrow agent
   c. seller/grantor
   d. purchaser/grantee

9. Which of the following forms of coownership of realty *cannot* be created under current Ohio law?
   a. estate by the entireties
   b. statutory survivorship tenancy
   c. tenancy in common
   d. severalty ownership

10. Two brothers own property equally as tenants in common. Each may *not:*
    a. sell his interest without the consent of the other
    b. get married and give a spouse dower rights without the consent of the other
    c. oust the other from use and possession of the real estate
    d. pass his interest in the real estate by will

11. When a husband and wife take title together today, they always hold title as:
    a. an estate by the entireties
    b. tenants in common
    c. statutory survivorship tenants
    d. insufficient information given to answer question

12. Even though many people are involved in the operation of a normal, medium-sized corporation (for example, as officers, directors, stockholders, employees), realty owned solely by the corporation is owned in which one of the following ways?
    a. statutory survivorship tenancy
    b. ownership in severalty
    c. trust
    d. tenancy in common

13. A trust specifies that when the beneficiary turns 30, the trust dissolves and she receives all the property in the trust. Any realty that comes to her will come to her as:
    a. statutory survivorship tenancy
    b. ownership in severalty
    c. trust
    d. tenancy in common

14. Ann's and Mary's father dies, passing his realty to his second wife, Kim, as his surviving survivorship tenant. Kim dies a year later and leaves the realty to her son. Ann and Mary:
    a. can successfully challenge the will on the basis that they should have been provided for in their stepmother's will
    b. can successfully challenge the survivorship deed that their father held with Kim on the basis that he must not have known its long-range effect
    c. can successfully challenge the constitutionality of the survivorship deed because it happened to have this effect on them
    d. do not appear to have any good legal arguments they can make toward their being entitled to share in that real estate

15. The rules and regulations for administration of the condominium can be found in the:
    a. bylaws
    b. deed
    c. articles of incorporation
    d. restrictions within the declaration

16. Condominium ownership may not lawfully prohibit:
    a. planting a garden behind your unit
    b. using your unit for rentals only, with a different tenant every week
    c. selling a unit to a woman
    d. your installing a deck behind your unit

17. Unlike a condominium, a cooperative:
    a. has a right of first refusal on units
    b. is a high-rise apartment building
    c. is exempt from fair housing laws
    d. gives a tenant/stockholder a proprietary lease, occupancy agreement, and stock in the cooperative corporation instead of a deed

18. The condominium developer:
    a. records the declaration in Columbus
    b. retains control of the board of managers/directors until every unit is sold
    c. cannot bind the unit owners' association to long-term management contracts
    d. can remove himself from any warranty and disclosure provisions upon obtaining the written release of the purchaser

19. A condominium owner usually *cannot* be prohibited from:
    a. planting a garden behind his unit
    b. using the recreational facilities at all times and hours
    c. erecting a bird feeder 30 yards behind his unit
    d. replacing his living room carpet with a wood floor

20. Unlike a cooperative, a condominium:
    a. can prohibit a person from buying one of the units because of race, religion, sex, national origin, handicap, or family status
    b. is a high-rise apartment building
    c. can be located in outlying areas
    d. gives an owner a deed instead of stock and a lease

21. Condominium developments may lawfully prohibit:
    a. selling a unit to a woman
    b. a husband and wife's being coowners
    c. a unit owner's adding on a family room
    d. changing the interior decor of a unit

22. Condominium property owners must:
    a. attend the annual meeting
    b. ratify the bylaws
    c. be members of the unit owners' association
    d. actually use a common area, such as the swimming pool, in order to be assessed for its maintenance and repair

23. The most important, fundamental document for creating a condominium development is the:
    a. declaration
    b. bylaws
    c. articles of incorporation
    d. plat

24. The following is typically recorded at the county recorder's office when the developer is bringing the condominium into being:
    a. declaration
    b. deed for each individual unit owner
    c. disclosures about the condominium
    d. warranties developer provides that run with the land

25. Expandable condominiums allow:
    a. converting present condominium common areas to individual units
    b. individual unit owners to make structural additions to rooms in their units
    c. the developer to add more real property and therefore more condominium individual units and common areas to the development
    d. a residential condominium to expand the use of land to include commercial and industrial

ANSWER KEY

1. d
2. a
3. b
4. a
5. d
6. a
7. b
8. d
9. a
10. c
11. d
12. b
13. b
14. d
15. a
16. c
17. d
18. c
19. d
20. d
21. c
22. c
23. a
24. a
25. c

5 DEEDS

Key Terms

acknowledgment
adverse possession
after-acquired title
attest
auditor's deed
consideration
conveyance
conveyance fee
deed
deed restrictions
dower release
exception
execution
fiduciary deed
general warranty deed
grantee
grantor
legal description ("legal")
limited (or special) warranty deed
quiet title action
quitclaim deed
recording
relation back (doctrine of)
reservation
run with the land
sheriff's deed
title
title company
words of grant or conveyance

The Deed and Transfer of Land Ownership

The Deed and Title to Land

WHAT IS A TITLE? Is a title the same thing as a deed? Can someone have title to real estate without having a deed to prove it? These important questions are related, and understanding the answers is the key to grasping the importance of this entire chapter. Having **title** to land means *being the owner of any of the estates, interests, or rights in land that have value in today's marketplace.* "Being the owners" means that the law will protect and support such persons when they try to exercise any of the powers given to them in their bundle of rights of real estate ownership.

Usually the title holder possesses a **deed,** which is a *document stating that the deed holder is, in fact, the owner.* The deed is also the *legal instrument conveying (transferring) the real property to the owner.* Thus, the deed is the way a landowner acquires ownership rights, whereas title is ownership of real estate.

Title Without a Deed

A person can be the owner of an estate in land without having a deed. One example of this is the *statutory or legal life estate, known as dower.* With dower, a freehold estate in land is created by operation of law to support the public policy that keeps one spouse from stealing from the other. There is no deed.

Another example of achieving an estate in land without a deed is the creation of a fee simple absolute by the legal process known as **adverse possession.** The law requires open, continuous, exclusive, adverse, and notorious usage by the person claiming ownership on account of such factors in order to support a claim of title by adverse possession. This must continue for a long time, 21 years in Ohio.

We already have seen this concept in easements by prescription. Again, no deed exists. Instead, the estate is given form and recognition by the law because a public policy exists to encourage people to make land productive and put it to use, regardless of who may "own" the land according to written documents.

To legitimize their adverse rights in the realty, claimants should bring lawsuits to place their titles on the public record and also gain court approval of their ownership in the real estate. These lawsuits are aptly called **quiet title actions.** If claimants fail to thus settle their rights in the real estate, they may not be able to freely transfer the real estate to successive owners. Successors legitimately fear that they would have to be the ones to bring a quiet title lawsuit to establish valid title that would show up on public records.

FOR EXAMPLE

X moves into an abandoned carriage house on Y's land in Ohio. She occupies it as if she were the true owner, without having Y's permission to so occupy. Y never objects or tries to remove X. After 21 years have passed, X will be considered the owner of the real estate, not Y. X will thus acquire the real estate by adverse possession and not by deed.

Dower and adverse possession are exceptional cases; with dower and adverse possession, title and ownership are deemed to exist because of operation of law. Therefore, a deed is not necessary. Title also can be acquired by operation of law through eminent domain/condemnation proceedings, fully discussed in Chapter 12.

The Deed and Its Recording

In Ohio, there has to be a documentary act to bring about the transfer of land. That document is the deed. Deeds always must be in writing, as required by the statute of frauds, the statute requiring that certain things that exist in the law must be in writing to be valid (fully discussed in Chapter 6). Oral deeds are not legally recognized. Because deeds may not be assigned (one cannot convey by an assignment endorsed on a deed), a new written deed has to be drawn for every transfer of ownership.

At the heart of it, "title" and "ownership" are *intangible;* they are simply words describing the way the law protects those it determines ought to enjoy the rights and powers associated with land ownership. Conversely, the deed is a *tangible;* it is a piece of paper reflecting ownership of land, just as a mirror reflects the object placed before it. Just as the object exists without the mirror, so title and ownership exist without the deed. If this were not the case, every time landowners lose their deeds (by fire, destruction, misplacing, and so forth), they concurrently lose their rights as landowners. This, of course, does not happen. In the usual case, landowners, pursuant to legal process, have another document prepared that will again reflect, or act as tangible evidence, that they are the landowners.

In the typical real estate purchase contract used by real estate salespeople, the deed called for is one that conveys fee simple absolute title with covenants of warranty.

Purchasers-grantees must have the deed recorded. First, they want to be able to prove they hold the title, and if they physically lose the deed, this proof might be difficult. Second, they want to protect their interest in the property against strangers who might claim ownership of the land based on a different deed. Proper **recording** accomplishes both of these goals. An unrecorded deed does not make a deed invalid between the parties themselves. This changes, however, with a subsequent bona fide purchaser for value (one who pays the full purchase price for the realty) as opposed to one who receives realty by gift. A purchaser who has no knowledge of this deed will be able to defeat an unrecorded grantee's rights in the real property and its title if he or she has a valid, recorded deed from the grantor. A defectively executed deed or a void deed will not become valid merely by recording it, though.

Real estate salespeople work only with deeds that are meant to be recorded. The type of closing process used in the transaction usually involves designating a certain person to handle recording of the deed. Not to have a recording of the deed between a seller (grantor) and a purchaser (grantee) who are strangers to one another (typical in real estate companies' transactions) is a serious omission. Because most transactions involve mortgage loans, however, the mortgage lender, at the very least, insists upon recording of the deed as a condition of its granting the loan.

The way the recording process works is that someone (such as an escrow agent) takes the deed to the office of the county recorder located in the same county as the real property described in the deed. That deed later is photocopied into the recorder's records, and the original deed is returned to the grantee. The deed also is entered into the recorder's books, which typically include indexed books of grantors' and grantees' names. These books also might include records that follow the history of each parcel of real estate in the county. As these are public records, anyone can find in the county recorder's office a complete and detailed history of each and every parcel of land in that county. This detailed history often is referred to as the realty's *chain of title.* Any potential grantee has the ability to protect his or her interests in a particular piece of real property by using the county recorder's office. Those who fail to do so take significant risks in owning, and possibly losing, real estate.

Because the deed is such a convenient and accurate way of showing who owns the land, and because transfer of this ownership can be so easily reflected by the creation and the delivery of a new deed, the deed is used in virtually every real estate transaction today. This process of *transferring title by deed,* or alienating real property, is called **conveyance.**

The deed is a straightforward document, as can be observed from Figure 5–1, a reproduction of the standard (or general) warranty deed. We also include, for purposes of comparison, the *statutory form* of the general warranty deed as Figure 5–2. Notice that the statutory form doesn't state all the warranty language found in the nonstatutory form. This is because it refers to, and incorporates by reference, all the warranties listed in the Ohio statute. Both forms of general warranty deed are standardly used in Ohio real estate transactions.

Essential Elements of the Recorded Deed

It is common practice to use a single sheet of paper, front and back, for the deed. If certain formalities are observed, however, a valid deed can have more than one page. The following elements pointed out on Figures 5–1 and 5–2 are necessary in Ohio for the creation of a valid recorded deed.

1. *The grantor must be designated.* A **grantor** is *the person who currently holds title and who will be transferring the title to the grantee.* The "or" in the word *grantor* describes the person who is taking the active, as opposed to the passive, role in the transaction. The grantor is the one who is transferring the title. The "ee" in the word *grantee* characterizes the passive party. The **grantee** *is receiving the title.* This active-passive test always works—the "or" is always doing something, and the "ee" is always receiving something.

If the grantor had, at the time he or she took title, a different name from the name he or she has at the time of conveying to a grantee, the deed should recite both names. Thus, if Mary Smith took title under her previously single name of Mary Doe, the deed should designate her as: "Mary Smith, married, formerly known as Mary Doe, grantor."

2. *The grantee must be designated.* A grantee is the person receiving the title. The grantee is usually, but not always, the same person as the purchaser. A person possibly might purchase real property and put it into someone else's name—as a gift, for example. In this case, the purchaser is not the grantee.

3. *The deed must include a statement that the deed has been given in return for consideration.* **Consideration,** in this context as in others mentioned in this text, means that *something the grantor either wants or deems important is given to him or her by the grantee as an inducement to give the deed.* The usual consideration in real estate transactions is the purchase price, but "love and affection" is a completely adequate consideration to support a gift, for example, of real property from father to son.

Because a deed is an executed contract (discussed more fully in Chapter 6), it usually cannot be attacked for lack of consideration. Between the parties, the words

FIGURE 5–1 Standard (or general) warranty deed.

WARRANTY DEED—No. 102A

The Ohio Legal Blank Co. Cleveland Publishers and Dealers Since 1883

Know all Men by these Presents,

Grantor — **That**, we, John Smith and Mary Smith, husband and wife, the Grantors who claim title by or through instrument, recorded in Volume 1000, Page 10, County Recorder's Office, for the consideration of Ten and no/100 Dollars

Consideration — Dollars ($10.00) and other valuable consideration received to our full satisfaction of

Grantee — William Brown and Susan Brown, the Grantees, whose TAX MAILING ADDRESS will be 428 South Street, Lyndhurst, Ohio 44124 do

Granting Clause — **Give, Grant, Bargain, Sell and Convey** unto the said Grantees, their heirs and assigns, the following described premises, situated in the City of Lyndhurst, County of Cuyahoga and State of Ohio:

Legal Description — and known as being Sublot No. 4 in A-Re-Subdivision made for the Society for Savings in the City of Cleveland of part of Original Euclid Township Lot No. 10, Tract No. 1, as shown by the recorded Plat in Volume 100 of Maps, Page 1 of Cuyahoga County Records, and being 25.00 feet front on the Easterly line of South Street, 73.50 feet front on the curved turnout between the said Easterly line of South Street and the Southerly line of Main Street, and extending back 136.43 feet on the Northerly line, which is also the Southerly line of Main Street, 184.78 feet deep on the Southerly line, and being 36.45 feet wide in the rear, as appears by said Plat, be the same more or less, but subject to all legal highways.

To Have and to Hold the above granted and bargained premises, with the appurtenances thereof, unto the said Grantees, their heirs and assigns forever.

And we, John Smith and Mary Smith, the said Grantors, do for ourselves and our heirs, executors and administrators, covenant with the said Grantees, their heirs and assigns, that at and until the ensealing of these presents, we are well seized of the above described premises, as a good and indefeasible estate in FEE SIMPLE, and have good right to bargain and sell the same in manner and form as above written, and that the same are **free from all incumbrances whatsoever**

Exception Clause — Except restrictions of record and any conditions, reservations, and easements created in conjunction with such restrictions, zoning ordinances, if any, and taxes and assessments, both general and special for the current half of the taxable year and thereafter.

General Warranty Provisions — and that we will **Warrant and Defend** said premises, with the appurtenances thereunto belonging, to the said Grantees, their heirs and assigns, against all lawful claims and demands whatsoever except as stated above.

Dower Release — And for valuable consideration we each, individually, do hereby remise, release and forever quit-claim unto the said Grantees, their heirs and assigns, all our right and expectancy of **Dower** in the above described premises.

In Witness Whereof we have hereunto set our hands, the 1st day of August, in the year of our Lord one thousand nine hundred and ninety-seven.

Execution & Witnessing — Signed and acknowledged in presence of

William Witness — John Smith (John Smith)

Sally Witness — Mary Smith (Mary Smith)

Notarization — **State of Ohio**, Lorain County, ss. Before me, a Notary Public in and for said County and State, personally appeared the above named John Smith and Mary Smith who acknowledged that they did sign the foregoing instrument and that the same is their free act and deed.

In Testimony Whereof, I have hereunto set my hand and official seal, at Chesterland, Ohio this 1st day of August, A. D. 1997.

James Donato Irvin
JAMES DONATO IRVIN, Attorney
NOTARY PUBLIC - STATE OF OHIO
My commission has no expiration date.
Section 147.03 R. C.

Ident. of Deed Preparer — This instrument prepared by:
CAROL K. IRVIN, Attorney at Law
11401 Willow Hill
Chesterland, Ohio 44026
(216) 729-1655

Warranty Deed

John Smith and Mary Smith husband and wife

TO

William Brown and Susan Brown

Transferred ______ 19__

COUNTY AUDITOR

State of Ohio

County of ______ ss

Received for Record on the ______ day of ______ 19__ at ______ o'clock __M. and Recorded ______ 19__ in Deed Book ______ Page ______

COUNTY RECORDER.

Recorders Fee $ ______

This instrument prepared by

FIGURE 5–2
Statutory form of general warranty deed.

Grantor →
Consideration →
Granting Clause →
Grantee →

G E N E R A L   W A R R A N T Y   D E E D

(STATUTORY FORM)

JOHN SMITH and MARY SMITH, Husband and Wife, of Cuyahoga County Ohio, for valuable consideration paid, grant with general warranty covenants, to WILLIAM BROWN and SUSAN BROWN, whose tax mailing address is 428 South Street, Lundhurst, Ohio, the following real property:

Legal Description →

Situated in the City of Lyndhurst, County of Cuyahoga and State of Ohio and known as being Sublot No. 4 in a resubdivision made for The Society for Savings in the City of Lyndhurst of part of Original Euclid Township Lot No. 10, Tract No. 1, as shown by the recorded plat in Volume 100 of Maps, Page 1 of Cuyahoga County Records, and being 25.00 feet front on the Easterly line of South Street, 73.50 feet front on the curved turnout between the said Easterly line of South Street and the Southerly line of Main Street, and extending back 136.43 feet on the Northerly line, which is also the Southerly line of Main Street, 184.78 feet deep on the Southerly line, and being 36.45 feet wide in the rear, as appears by said plat, be the same more or less, but subject to all legal highways.

Exception Clause →

Except for restrictions, conditions, limitations, reservations and easements of record; zoning ordinances, if any, and taxes and assessments, both general and special, for the current half of the taxable year and thereafter.

Prior Instrument Reference: Volume 13200, Page 254 of Cuyahoga County Records of Deeds.

Dower Release →

And we each, individually, hereby release all rights of dower therein.

Witnessing & Execution →

WITNESS our hands this 15th day of February, 1997.

Barry Brown	John Smith JOHN SMITH
Dolly Meadows	Mary Smith MARY SMITH

Notarization →

STATE OF OHIO)
Cuyahoga County) SS:

Before me, a notary public in and for said county and state, personally appeared the above named John Smith and Mary Smith who acknowledged that they did sign foregoing instrument and that the same is their free act and deed.

IN TESTIMONY WHEREOF, I have hereunto set my hand and official seal at Lyndhurst, Ohio this 15th day of February 1997.

James Donato Irvin

this instrument prepared by:
JAMES D. IRVIN - Attorney
11401 Willow Hill Drive
Chesterland, Ohio 44026
(216) 729-2273

JAMES DONATO IRVIN, Attorney
NOTARY PUBLIC - STATE OF OHIO
My commission has no expiration date.
Section 147.03 R. C.

making up consideration within the deed are immaterial. If the deed is challenged by creditors whose rights are affected by the transfer, however, the type of consideration and its amount can be critical.

One type of consideration is *valuable* consideration, which is money, goods, and services in exchange for the real property (called a deed of purchase). The other type of consideration is *good,* which consists of ties of blood, natural love, and affection (called a deed of gift). One must look within the deed for the recital of consideration and its receipt to determine whether a deed is one of purchase or of gift. Deeds of gift are as valid and effective as deeds of purchase. The rights of creditors are different, however.

FOR EXAMPLE

Imagine that an older man, a father, lost a large lawsuit and that most of his assets are tied up in his real estate equity. If the father conveys his realty to his daughter by deed of gift to avoid paying the judgment creditor (winner of the lawsuit), that creditor probably can get the conveyance set aside as a fraud upon him. Had the father sold his realty to a stranger by deed of purchase instead, the creditor would have great difficulty setting aside the conveyance.

Even if the daughter pays some nominal sum, the conveyance probably will still be set aside for fraud. This is because the court may consider the small sum of money inadequate consideration (discussed in full in Chapter 6) for the grantee to be considered a bona fide purchaser for value and entitled to protection. The stranger, by contrast, is regarded as a bona fide purchaser for value, and the conveyance to him is valid. Chapter 1336 of the Ohio Revised Code, the Ohio Uniform Fraudulent Transfer Act, covers and prohibits these kinds of transactions.

The sample deed form in Figure 5–1 shows "for the consideration of Ten Dollars ($10) *and other valuable consideration,*" meaning that in response to payment by the grantee to the grantor of the sum of $10, plus additional money, the grantor is transferring the property. Why not use the actual purchase price? In Ohio, it is customary not to, and perhaps because many purchasers and sellers do not want the whole world to know exactly how much was paid for the real property. Ten dollars, as in Figure 5–1, is nominal consideration, but it is enough to support a legal conveyance in Ohio. The salesperson should be aware that the deed itself, as used in most transactions, may well recite only that consideration exists. Some other deeds, such as auditor's and sheriff's deeds (discussed later in this chapter) actually do state, to the penny, what was paid as consideration to support the transfer.

4. *The deeds must contain appropriate words showing the grantor's intent to convey.* **Words of grant or conveyance,** such as "do hereby give, grant, bargain, sell, and convey," along with words showing the quantity of the estate in land being conveyed, such as a fee simple, clearly identify the deed as a document involving the giving or transferring by someone of something to another person. This element may seem obvious, to the point of being ridiculous, but imagine picking up the document and trying to understand it without these words of grant. Although technical words usually are used, plain words are fine as long as it is understood that the grantor intends to convey. Deeds that are missing words of grant or conveyance do not transfer title to another.

5. *The deed must give a sufficient description of the subject real property.* This is typically the **legal description,** which defines the boundaries of the real property being transferred. This usually is done by making reference to lines drawn upon the surface of the earth, showing the outside edges of the parcel. These lines describe only length and width of the piece of land; the "depth" component is implied, consistent with the concepts explained in Chapter 2. Only in the case of a condominium does the legal description make reference to depth or height, because a unit owner has exclusive ownership of a specific amount of air space (only), and to describe this requires measurements of length, width, and height.

The several methods to describe land are (a) using "metes and bounds," (b) using the governmental (or rectangular) survey, or (c) referring to a particular sublot in a subdivision. Operative deeds must describe the land intended to be conveyed with enough certainty so the land can be located and distinguished from other lands. The courts strive to uphold any description, regardless of method, that shows the true intent of the parties and the true nature and amount of land. If a competent engineer can locate the land from the legal description, that is enough.

The words "be the same more or less," given at the end of the legal description, are commonly used at that point in the deed. They do not make the description indefinite. Instead, they are precautionary, intended to cover expected but relatively unimportant variations.

6. *Another necessary element is signature by the grantor,* or **execution** of the deed by the grantor. By contrast, the grantee does not sign the deed. Beginning real estate salespeople frequently misunderstand this and incorrectly assume the purchasers-grantees must sign the deed. The reason grantees do not sign the deed is that it symbolizes the transfer of something the grantor has (the title) to the grantee. It would make little sense to require grantees to sign deeds showing they consent to receive the property, because they are paying for it in the first place.

Grantors may not sign deeds in blank. If a deed instrument is blank and the grantor signs it, it cannot become valid later by filling in the blank parts. It is a void deed.

Grantors must be of sound mind at the time they sign the deed; that is, they must be able to understand the nature and effect of executing a deed to convey real estate. A grantor's lack of mental capacity renders a deed voidable, and it might be set aside. Challengers to a grantor's capacity face a tough legal battle, however. They must show that the grantor is totally, not just partially, incapacitated. In addition, the law presumes the grantor is sane and the challenger must prove otherwise.

Minors are persons under the age of majority, which in Ohio is age 18. If a minor has an interest in real estate being sold, such an interest usually shows up in one of two ways.

a. *Pursuant to a trust,* in which the minor is the beneficiary and another person is the trustee and title holder. The trustee, therefore, is the grantor who executes the deed for the minor's benefit.
b. *Pursuant to a guardianship* established and administered through the local probate court. Approval of the sale and transfer of title, as being in the best interests of the minor, has to be obtained through probate court. The guardian subsequently executes the appropriate deed as the grantor, acting pursuant to the orders of probate court.

A grantor also may give another person a *power of attorney.* This is created by a written instrument and *authorizes a person to act as his or her agent to the extent indicated in the instrument.* The person who is made this agent is called the *attorney-in-fact.* This should not be confused with an attorney-at-law, because an attorney-in-fact does not have to be an attorney-at-law but can be anyone. The person who gives the power is the principal. If a power of attorney is created properly, the attorney-in-fact is the legal substitute for the grantor. He or she can sign the real estate contracts as well as the deed, as long as the power of attorney grants the power to do so.

Powers of attorney can be revoked at any time. Death of the principal or the attorney-in-fact also terminates it.

Powers of attorney should be signed, attested, and acknowledged, just like the deed. There should be a definite identification of the real estate. The power of attorney should be recorded prior to recording of the deed. A revocation should be recorded as well, because an unrecorded revocation is ineffective against a recorded power of attorney.

7. *Signing of the deed by the grantor must be in the presence of at least two competent witnesses.* This is called **attestation.**

Competency of attesting witnesses means they are able to comprehend that the grantor is signing something called a deed and is doing it of his or her own free will.

Grantees cannot be witnesses to a deed that attempts to convey title to them. Ohio law, however, seems to allow interested persons who may have some personal interest in the transaction (for example, stockholders in a corporation, the corporation being the grantee). It also seems to allow older children to be witnesses, but because deeds may be set aside for reasons such as fraud, misrepresentation, duress, undue influence, and the like, it is common and prudent practice to use only adult witnesses who are disinterested (have no personal stake in the transaction).

8. *The grantor must deliver the deed.* Although this might seem to imply that the grantor must physically hand or personally deliver the deed to the grantee, all that must be done is for the grantor to surrender his or her possession of and control over the deed. Mailing the deed to the grantee is good delivery, even before the grantee actually receives the document. The act of mailing is a surrendering of possession and control sufficient to satisfy the requirement. On the other hand, putting the deed under your pillow when you are on your deathbed and telling your nurse, "If I don't make it through the night, give this deed to my nephew, Morris," and then dying is not considered good delivery. Why? Possession and control over the deed was never given up before the grantor's death. After death, a deed has no power to transfer the title. At such a point, either a person's will or a statute that applies when a person dies without a will (the statute of descent and distribution) directs what should be done with the title to the realty. The deed, never having been delivered, is ignored.

Delivery into escrow is another type of delivery that should be clarified and understood. Real estate transactions in Ohio often involve an *escrow closing,* basically a three-way affair involving buyer, seller, and disinterested escrow agent, the latter in the capacity of "stakeholder." Escrow is much like a one-way street where everyone expects to arrive at the same point with no turning back—the closing or completion of title transfer without the need for a physical meeting of all concerned parties. The escrow agent collects all pertinent documents and funds from the parties during an escrow period, and when all that is agreed to be done has been done, the escrow agent transfers title to the purchaser. Often the purchaser and seller never even see one another; they make their separate deposits to escrow at different times, either personally or by mail. Therefore, either one of the parties might complete his or her portion of the transaction before the other.

This characteristic of an escrow—the ability of one party to do all that was agreed upon before the other party has done so—is particularly valuable when a grantor dies after having placed the deed in escrow but before the deed has been delivered to the grantee. As long as the grantor has done all things necessary to complete the transaction before dying, including getting the deed to the escrow agent, the law considers that delivery has taken place. This doctrine, called **relation back,** considers, in this case only, *delivery to have taken place when the deed was first placed into escrow.* Because escrow is basically irrevocable, or "one-way," this makes sense.

This does not mean that deposit of the deed with an escrow agent is always equivalent to delivery. It is only so in the case of a grantor using an escrow closing who dies after doing his or her part in the transaction but before the title transfers. Because many sellers are wary of signing a deed before receiving their funds from the purchasers, the salesperson should understand the foregoing distinctions so, in the case of an escrow closing, the agent can assure sellers that by signing the deed and delivering it to the escrow agent, they are not transferring title to the purchaser. The escrow agent transfers title only, pursuant to the real estate purchase contract after all that was promised has been done. The rule is that a *deed takes effect upon delivery except in escrow, whereupon it waits for performance of conditions stipulated.* The deed becomes effective upon performance of the condition(s). If no condition is to be performed by the grantee named in the deed, the transaction is not classed as a deed in escrow. The deed, therefore, becomes effective at once.

For the deed to properly convey, grantors must deliver it with the intention that they will sever their rights to control it further. The grantees' intentions must be to assume control of the deed. If the deed's grant is beneficial to the grantees, however, the law presumes they intend to accept the deed. A deed does not gain force and effect if it is recorded but delivery is not accomplished.

9. *Acknowledgment. The grantor's signing of the deed also must be acknowledged.* **Acknowledgment** is the *affirming under oath by the grantor* to the notary public (or someone else having power to administer oaths, such as a judge) *that the signing of the deed was done freely by the grantor and not because of duress or undue influence.* A common way acknowledgment occurs is for the grantor to sign the deed in front of two witnesses, one of whom can be the notary, and then swear orally to the notary that the signing is proper. After the witnessing, the notary signs the document, stamps the deed with information showing his or her commission is still valid, and then seals the deed using a device that forces an insignia onto the paper.

10. *An identification of the deed preparer must be part of the deed.* The deed typically is prepared by an attorney-at-law.

11. *A satisfaction of state and local tax is required.* This is called a **conveyance fee.** Ohio levies a tax on sellers of real estate based on a percentage of the consideration given to support the transfer of title. The local unit of government might assess its own tax as well, in addition to the state tax. In any event, unless the transaction is exempt from taxation (a few are), the tax(es) must be paid before the recorder will accept the deed for recording.

12. *The tax mailing address for the grantee is stated on the face of the deed* so the county auditor knows the correct place to send the tax bills. This address might be different from the subject property's address, such as when the property being conveyed is a vacant lot or an apartment building. The volume and page number of the prior conveyance, where the grantor took title, also should be stated.

All of the foregoing elements are those essential to create a valid recorded deed in Ohio.

Real estate salespeople often hear the phrase "execution of the deed." This means that all acts necessary to make the instrument operative are completed. No transfer of title can take place without an executed deed.

Release of a Spouse's Rights by Deed

Standard deed forms include a clause that reads, "And for valuable consideration, we each, individually, do hereby remise, release and forever quitclaim unto the said Grantees, their heirs and assigns, all our right and expectancy of Dower in the above described premises." This clause, called **dower release,** operates as a giving up, or releasing, of a spouse's inchoate dower interest in the property. Although one can release dower on a separate instrument, such as a quitclaim deed (discussed in full later in this chapter), dower typically is released on the deed. All releases of dower must be executed with the same formalities as the deed itself. The preceding chapter explored dower interest as given to spouses by operation of law. No written document gives these rights, but often the title to realty is held in the name of only one of the spouses. For example, a husband might have inherited property formerly owned by his mother. In this case, when the husband decides to sell the property, the wife has to release her inchoate (incomplete) dower rights in this property her husband owns in fee simple. If the situation were reversed, the outcome would be exactly the same; the husband would have to release his dower rights in the property.

Inchoate rights of dower cannot be transferred separately from the estate in land they pertain to. Thus, in this example, the wife cannot release her inchoate dower rights if the husband is not conveying the fee to a third person grantee. The wife and husband also cannot release their inchoate rights of dower directly to one another. These rules exist because inchoate rights of dower always are released to *extinguish* dower rights, not to transfer dower rights. The grantor of a deed states in writing, at the beginning of the deed, his or her marital status. This is to put the grantee on notice of any potential dower problems. Often title is held in the names of both the husband and the wife. In that event, each has to release dower rights in the other spouse's one-half interest. If the grantor is single or divorced, no release of dower is necessary because there is no spouse. A widowed grantor also needs no dower release because dower ends upon death of the consort. Otherwise, dower becomes a factor and must be released so there are no clouds on the title transferred to the grantee. Table 5–1 summarizes these distinctions.

Exception Clause and Reservations

Another clause reads that the grantor is transferring to the grantee a title that is free and clear of all claims and encumbrances whatsoever, "except . . .," and then follows a lot of language in very small print that most people glance at but few understand. (Turn back to Figure 5–1 and read the exception clause pointed out there, at the bottom.) Although the exception clause does not appear in all deeds, it always appears in the general warranty deed, the most common type of deed used in real estate transactions.

An **exception** is *some part of the estate that is not granted.* It separates a part of that embraced in the realty's description and already existing in the same kind or form. The purpose of the exception clause is to allow the grantor to give a relatively unencumbered title but not a completely unencumbered one. In the usual transaction the grantor cannot give a completely unencumbered title because of the always-present governmental limitations to ownership of land, as discussed in Chapter 3.

TABLE 5–1 Distinctions in dower rights.

TO BE RELEASED BY GRANTOR'S SPOUSE WHEN:	NO DOWER RIGHTS ATTACH WHEN:
1. Grantor is married, either common law or statutory.	1. Grantor is single and has never married.
2. Grantor is widowed and has remarried.	2. Grantor is widowed and has not remarried.
3. Grantor is divorced and has remarried.	3. Grantor is divorced and not remarried (assuming all rights were properly extinguished by divorce proceeding).
4. Grantor is in process of divorcing.	4. Grantor is "married" to "spouse" of same sex as Grantor when a state does not recognize marriages between persons of the same sex. (Ohio is such a state.)
5. Grantor has separated from spouse.	5. Grantor is merely "living together" with opposite-sex person. (Caution: This may have been converted into common law marriage, which is impossible for real estate agent to determine.)
	6. Grantor has valid ante nuptial contract barring spouse from acquiring dower rights in Grantor's real estate.

Taxation and the police power are factors that always exist, and they must be accounted for in the standard transaction. More precisely, both general and special real property taxes are a governmental charge/lien against the realty, and the exercises of police power via zoning, building, and other local ordinances also are limitations affecting the realty. The owner of even a fee simple absolute estate in land is powerless to transfer that estate to another free and clear of such encumbrances, because this owner also holds title subject to these encumbrances. Likewise, fee simple owners cannot transfer completely unencumbered title when either they or some former owner granted or made easements, leases, private controls over the use of land, or even mortgages that were intended to remain effective during and even beyond the period of new ownership.

Therefore, the grantor can create a **reservation,** which is a *limitation reserved to the grantor of some right in the land conveyed,* such as an easement out of the land granted. A reservation must be to the grantor or the person executing the conveyance and not to a stranger. The exception clause, and possibly a reservation as well, acts as a safety valve that basically gives the grantor the needed flexibility to give, if not a completely unencumbered title, at least the best that can be given.

Rescission and Estoppel

Deeds may be *rescinded* (set aside) just as contracts may be set aside. Some of the grounds for rescission of a deed are *fraud, misrepresentation of material fact, concealment, undue influence, duress, insanity, mistake, and minority.* These grounds, discussed in depth in Chapters 6 and 9, apply as fully to deeds as they do to contracts. When a court rescinds a deed, the grantor receives back the real estate, and the grantee receives back the money paid for the real estate. Grantors also can be estopped (prevented from asserting their legal rights) if they have behaved wrongfully, by the doctrine of *estoppel by deed.*

For example, where grantors had no title or defective title and conveyed with covenants of warranty, if they later acquire good title, they will be estopped from benefiting themselves. This **after-acquired title** *benefits the grantee instead, by the estoppel by deed doctrine.* Another example of this doctrine is a case involving a fraudulent conveyance in which the party who perpetrated the fraud later tries to have the deed rescinded. The estoppel doctrine applies, and the conveyance is upheld. The fraudulent party is unsuccessful in getting the deed rescinded.

Deed Restrictions and Restrictions of Record

Grantors/sellers can use deeds to restrict the use of the realty being conveyed. Grantors (sellers/developers) and grantees (purchasers) may *restrict future use of the realty being transferred between them, by their agreement* in what are formally called *restrictive covenants* but more commonly known as **deed restrictions** and restrictions of record. Any landowners can put restrictions in the deed as the grantors when they convey land to a grantee.

Often, landowners who own two adjoining tracts of land, one of which they sell and the other they keep, use deed restrictions. They put restrictions on the lot they sell to protect the one they keep. For example, they might require that the other lot have a structure no closer than 100 feet from their retained lot line, or that no roosters or other agricultural animals be kept on the land. One neighbor also can obtain from another, pursuant to a contract and recorded deed with restrictive covenants, these same kinds of protective restrictions.

The most common way restrictions occur, however, is that a subdivider/developer has a general plan for restricting use of lots in the subdivision. The purpose of the general plan is to keep the subdivision uniform in appearance and to maintain the highest fair market value, usually by allowing only uses that are compatible with reasonable, single-family residential living patterns. This general plan covers all the lots. The purchaser of any lot enforces the restrictions against the purchaser of any other lot. Thus, one lot owner obtains a court order, or injunction, prohibiting other lot owners from using their lots contrary to the restrictions.

Grantors/sellers or grantors/developers put these restrictions on real property(ies) in three ways:

1. They incorporate *identical restrictions in the deed(s)* that they as grantors convey to the grantee(s) who purchases from them.
2. They incorporate the restrictions in the *recorded plat.* (A plat is a detailed drawing and blueprint of all the realty.)
3. They incorporate the restrictions within a *declaration of restrictions,* which they record at the same time as the plat. The deed recites that the land is subject to those recorded restrictions.

Purchasers and real estate salespersons can find all three types in the county recorder's office where the realty is located. (The restrictions in item 1 also can be found within the deed itself.) Whichever way restrictions are put on realty, purchasers have constructive knowledge of them because they are matters of public record. Therefore, purchasers usually cannot complain later that they are being unfairly or illegally stopped from using their land in the restricted way.

Developers also can create *homeowners' associations* within their subdivisions to enforce the restrictions on use of the land. The association is set up as a nonprofit corporation when the subdivision is created. Owners of the lots in the subdivision are members of this association. They pay dues, which can be used to pay for obtaining an injunction. An injunction is sought against a fellow landowner who is not complying with the restrictions, to prohibit this noncompliance. *Most of these restrictions are for the benefit of the development and are reasonable,* such as specifications about minimum square feet in the house, exterior construction, and setbacks; prohibitions against dumping, incinerating, and maintaining nuisances; and prohibitions against using the realty for business purposes.

Racially restrictive deed covenants are totally unenforceable, as we fully discuss in Chapter 11. A realty owner cannot have as a restriction, "realty to be sold only to members of Caucasian race"; the realty must be available to all for purchase. Otherwise restrictions can be highly particular, and nevertheless enforceable. Examples include a deed restriction requiring that only picket or split-rail fences be used (as opposed to chain-link); or that the only animals that may be kept on the land are dogs and cats (not horses and chickens); or that a pond cannot be put on realty (as it will attract too many geese, ducks, and insects); or that any home constructed on the lot must have a minimum of 2,500 square feet; or that brick homes cannot be painted. These have been upheld as valid restrictions. The best policy is for purchasers to be given the opportunity to review these restrictions before purchasing.

Restrictions on the use of realty can be lost in several ways:

1. They have a *time period of expiration.*
2. The lot owners unanimously *vote to discharge them,* or they are discharged by a lesser vote if the restrictions allow less than a unanimous vote.

3. The *neighborhood substantially changes* from one major use to another, such as residential to commercial.
4. The other landowners allow numerous violations of the restrictions; the courts construe this as an *abandonment* and do not enforce the restrictions.
5. The landowners unduly *delay* in stopping another owner from using his or her realty in a prohibited way.

Restrictions are valid as long as they control only the use of land as *reasonable restraints.* If they hinder the free alienability of realty by restricting owners' basic rights to sell their land, they are void. Restrictions give the sellers of real property the right to restrict future use of it in a way they find desirable. In all cases, restrictions become an obligation on all subsequent purchasers of the realty. In this sense, the restrictions **run with the land** because selling the realty does not discharge the restrictions.

The law and the courts generally view restrictive covenants with disfavor. This aversion is overcome when there is evidence showing a general plan, however. If the covenant or restriction is enforced consistently in the same manner throughout the community, it is seen as a reasonably enforced restriction. This aids its being upheld if legally attacked.

Restrictions may prohibit a use that zoning allows. For example, the zoning ordinance allows agricultural animals on the realty, but the restrictions allow only cats and dogs. Owners can keep only cats and dogs on their realty. In this sense, the restriction takes precedence over the zoning. The validity of deed restrictions and constitutionality of a zoning ordinance are independent matters. They usually are decided in two entirely separate legal proceedings. The *presence of deed restrictions has no effect on the zoning.* For example, if deed restrictions limit certain realty to single-family use, that does not prevent the municipality from rezoning that realty for a different use. We discuss zoning in detail in Chapter 12.

Real estate salespersons should not recommend uses that can be made of real property without knowing the zoning code and the restrictions within the deed, plat, or declaration. Even better, they should urge the purchaser to consult an attorney when deed restrictions emerge as a potential problem on a piece of realty being marketed.

Types of Deeds

General Warranty Deed

The most common type of deed is the **general warranty deed,** also known as the *standard warranty deed,* or sometimes just the *warranty deed.* It *conveys all the grantor's right, title, and interest, both legal and beneficial, in and to the real property described.* It should be easy to understand the appeal of the general warranty deed. Through it, grantors promise that they will "warrant and defend," or stand behind, the grantees' complete, untroubled, and uninterrupted use of the property if a problem arises because of something that happens to the title. This protection applies from the beginning of time until the time of transfer of title to the present grantee. (Refer back to Figures 5–1 and 5–2 for samples of both the nonstatutory and statutory general warranty deeds.)

If the general warranty deed sounds like a great guarantee, you are not mistaken. It is about as broad a warranty as the law knows how to create. As long as the grantor makes good on the warranty, the grantees, if they ever have to call upon it, are fully protected against virtually all flaws in the title except for the stated exceptions (discussed just prior to this section) and except for problems caused during the grantee's own ownership and caused by the grantee. In Ohio, *most standard real estate transactions handled by real estate agents result in delivery to the grantee of a recorded general warranty deed.* In addition to the covenant to warrant and defend the realty by the grantor for the benefit of the grantee, general warranty deeds warrant that the grantor has *seisin* (the existence of a right to convey) and a *warranty against encumbrances* (a statement that the property is free and clear of all encumbrances except those found in the exception clause).

Corporations as grantors also use the general warranty deed. The board of directors for the corporation authorizes, in a written resolution, a corporate officer(s) to execute the deed to the grantee. Because corporations do not have spouses, there are no releases of dowers to be obtained, but more than one signature may be needed.

Limited or Special Warranty Deed

In some cases, grantors do not want to give a general warranty deed because of the vast warranty involved, so they use a **limited or special warranty deed.** The only thing special about this deed is that it is especially good for the grantor. Here the *warranty extends only from the time the present grantor takes title until the time title transfers to the present grantee.* Developers often use this type of deed for conveyance of title from themselves to the first owners of the divided plot. Often the developer is incorporated, and thus the corporation is the grantor. Developers usually use limited or special warranty deeds to save money on the insurance against defective title that purchasers usually require in addition to the deed. (More about this insurance appears in Chapter 7.) These limited or special warranty deeds are used occasionally in real estate transactions, so salespeople should know enough about them to realize that when they are negotiating the transfer of such a deed, they are dealing with a nonstandard transaction and ought to request additional assistance from an office manager, a broker, or an attorney.

Quitclaim Deed

A **quitclaim deed** is relatively uncommon in real estate transactions between strangers—the usual situation a real estate salesperson handles when negotiating a sale between an owner and a purchaser. Real estate transactions between strangers also are called *arms-length sales.* Quitclaim deeds, however, are used commonly in other real estate transactions—between husbands and wives getting divorced, for example. This quitclaim deed involves the transfer to one person of the interest of another. The *grantee takes whatever interest the grantor has to pass, be it full title, partial title, or no title at all.* The grantor does not give any warranties or guarantees as to the title of the subject realty, and the grantee takes the estate subject to all existing encumbrances.

Reading some books or articles about the quitclaim deed, a person often gets the impression that it is used exclusively by the gentleman at the bar trying to peddle the Brooklyn Bridge for enough to buy another drink. And the name "quitclaim" often is misspelled, or misunderstood to be some kind of "quick-claim" thing to be used when time is short and desires are unsettled.

Actually, the quitclaim deed is a valuable legal tool, used best upon the advice of an attorney for many transactions when the sole desire is to get rid of, and transfer over to another, whatever interest a certain person has in real estate. In divorce cases, dissolution of marriage cases, probate cases, transfers in the form of gifts (either for the usual reasons or to reduce a person's estate title holders), a simple and complete giving up or "quitting any claim to" rights in the realty at times can do the job. Many of these grantees are not interested in warranties or assurances of good title because they usually know the title is good or, if they do not know it, they are not concerned with it. They just want to remove any interest a spouse or former spouse, for example, might have in the real estate.

The modern quitclaim deed acts very much like a *release,* because it sets free whatever interest the grantor has in the real estate. The quitclaim deed can be an ideal tool, but it must be used with care. An attorney always should be consulted to maximize the chances of coming out with the desired result.

The quitclaim deed is not at all suited to the standard transfer of realty from one stranger to another, because absolutely no warranties or guarantees of any sort are made. The quitclaim deed may actually be considered notice, in and of itself, that there may be title imperfections. Figure 5–3 shows a sample quitclaim deed.

Fiduciary Deed

Also used in standard real estate transactions is the **fiduciary deed.** A *fiduciary is a person or entity placed in a position of high trust or confidence so as to act for another* (or more than one) *and in that person's(s') best interests.* The law requires high duties of care from a person acting in a fiduciary capacity. Because there are many fiduciaries in the law—guardians, trustees, administrators, and executors, for example—any of these persons can use the fiduciary deed when the situation calls for this kind of deed, as contrasted with the general warranty deed.

We mentioned earlier in the chapter, in connection with the requirement of delivery, that deeds serve only to transfer the real property interests of living people. If someone wants title to transfer to another specific person after he or she has died, that result can be easily accomplished by leaving a will directing a named executor (person who acts for the deceased person in carrying out terms of the will) to transfer the property to the second person. For the executor to carry out the deceased person's wishes, he or she has to personally sign some kind of deed, and the type of deed used is the fiduciary deed. The situation is the same in the case of a trustee, a guardian, or the administrator of the estate of a decedent who dies without a will. All these cases use fiduciary deeds because they are the best kind of deed the law can come up with under the circumstances.

The fiduciary deed does not include all of the warranties and guarantees present in the general warranty deed. To require an executor or guardian to personally stand behind the guarantee of complete and uninterrupted ownership of the realty would be unfair when these persons are merely "standing in" for the deceased person or the incompetent.

The ordinary promises and warranties a fiduciary makes usually include the following:

1. That the fiduciary has been properly appointed, qualified, and is acting in the stated fiduciary capacity (as executor, guardian, administrator, and so on).
2. That the fiduciary is authorized to make the sale and transfer of the realty.
3. That the fiduciary has complied with all lawful requirements necessary to bring about the contemplated transfer of property.

Beyond this, the fiduciary makes no warranties. Figure 5–4 shows a fiduciary deed.

FIGURE 5–3 Quitclaim deed.

QUIT-CLAIM DEED—with Dower Clause—No. 89-B

The Ohio Legal Blank Co. Cleveland Publishers and Dealers Since 1883

Know all Men by these Presents

That, I, JOHN R. JONES, Married

, *the Grantor* ,

who claim s *title by or through instrument* , *recorded in Volume* 1022, *Page*715 ,

County Recorder's Office, for the consideration of OTHER GOOD CONSIDERATION and TEN and 00/100------------------------------*Dollars* (*$* 10.00)

received to my *full satisfaction of*

MARY M. JONES, my wife,

the Grantee ,

whose TAX MAILING ADDRESS will be
1234 Happy Dale Drive
Anyville, Ohio 46211

have **Given, Granted, Remised, Released and Forever Quit-Claimed**, *and do by these presents absolutely give, grant, remise, release and forever quit-claim unto the said grantee* , her *heirs and assigns forever, all such right and title as* I , *the said grantor* , *have or ought to have in and to the following described piece or parcel of land, situated in the* Township *of* Anywhere *County of* Somewhere *and State of Ohio:*

and known as being Sublot No. 5-A in Glenn N. Barriball and Franz X. Thruinger's Bell Meadows Subdivision of a part of Original Anywhere Township Lots Nos. 9 and 15, Tract No. 5, as shown by the recorded Plat of said Subdivision in Volume 3 of Maps, Page 50 of Somewhere County Records, be the same more or less, but subject to all legal highways.

To Have and to Hold *the premises aforesaid, with the appurtenances thereunto belonging to the said grantee* , her *heirs and assigns, so that neither the said grantor* , *nor* his *heirs, nor any other persons claiming title through or under* him , *shall or will hereafter claim or demand any right or title to the premises, or any part thereof; but they and every one of them shall by these presents be excluded and forever barred.*

~~*And for valuable consideration*~~

~~*do hereby remise, release and forever quit-claim unto the said grantee* , *heirs and assigns, all right and expectancy of* **Dower** *in the above described premises.*~~

In Witness Whereof, I *have hereunto set* my *hand* , *the* 31st *day of* July , *in the year of our Lord one thousand nine hundred and* ninety-seven.

Signed and acknowledged in presence of

Samuel Smith
Deborah Green

John R. Jones
John R. Jones

State of Ohio, Somewhere *County*, ss. *Before me, a* notary public *in and for said County and State, personally appeared the above named* John R. Jones *who acknowledged that* he *did sign the foregoing instrument and that the same is* his *free act and deed.*

In Testimony Whereof, *I have hereunto set my hand and official seal, at* Anyville, Ohio *this* 31st *day of* July *A. D.* 1997

James Donato Irvin
JAMES DONATO IRVIN, Attorney
NOTARY PUBLIC · STATE OF OHIO
My commission has no expiration date.
Section 147.03 R. C.

CAROL K. IRVIN,
Attorney at Law,
5678 Graphic Rd.
Patrick, Ohio 44078

John R. Jones,
married

TO

Mary M. Jones,
his wife

Transferred ______ 19

COUNTY AUDITOR

State of Ohio

County of ______ ss

Received for Record on the ______ **day of** ______ 19 ______ **at** ______ o'clock ______ M.

and Recorded ______ 19 ______ in **Deed Book** ______ **Page** ______

COUNTY RECORDER

Recorders Fee $ ______

This instrument prepared by:

FIGURE 5–4
Fiduciary deed.

FIDUCIARY DEED, Statutory Form No. 31-S (Reprinted 10/89) apco Registered in U.S. Patent and Trademark Office anderson publishing co. cincinnati, ohio 45201

Deed of Executor, Administrator, Trustee, Guardian, Receiver or Commissioner*

Melodie Anderson, Trustee,

by the power conferred by Gerald Smythe Trust *, and every other power,*
for $107,500 *dollars paid, grants, with fiduciary covenants, to*
Julia Marcourt
whose tax-mailing address is 103 Reindeer Avenue; Mayville, Ohio 49972
the following ***REAL PROPERTY:*** *Situated in the County of* Montrose *in the State of Ohio and in the* City *of* Mayville and known as being Sublot No. 97 in the Seltzer Square Company's Mayville Park Overlook Allotment No. 4 of part of Original One Hundred Acre Lots Nos. 283 and 284, as shown by the recorded Plat in Volume 123 of Maps, Page 24 of Montrose County Records, and being 40 feet front on the Northerly side of Reindeer Avenue, and extending back of equal width 100 feet, as appears by said Plat, be the same more or less, but subject to all legal highways, and also subject to (a) any mortgage assumed by Grantee, (b) all restrictions, reservations, easements (however created), covenants, and conditions of record, (c) all of the following as do not materially adversely affect the use or value of the property: encroachments, oil, gas and mineral leases, (d) zoning ordinances, if any, and (e) taxes and assessments, both general and special, not currently due and payable.

Prior Instrument Reference: Volume 90-550 *Page* 23 *of the Deed Records of* Montrose *County, Ohio.*
Witness my *hand(s) this* 1st *day of* June *, 19*90.
Signed and acknowledged in presence of:

Robert Witness — Melodie Anderson – Tr.
Mary Witness — Melodie Anderson, Trustee

State of Ohio *County of* Montrose *ss.*
BE IT REMEMBERED, *That on this* 1st *day of* June *, 19* 90 *, before me, the subscriber, a* notary public *in and for said state, personally came,* Melodie Anderson, Trustee, *the Grantor(s) in the foregoing deed, and acknowledged the signing thereof to be* her *voluntary act and deed.*
IN TESTIMONY THEREOF, *I have hereunto subscribed my name and affixed my* official *seal on the day and year last aforesaid.*

JAMES DONATO IRVIN, Attorney
NOTARY PUBLIC - STATE OF OHIO
My commission has no expiration date.
Section 147.03 R. C.

James Donato Irvin

This instrument was prepared by CAROL K. IRVIN, Attorney at Law, 11401 Willow Hill Chesterland, Ohio 44026 (216) 729-1655

(1) Executor of the Will of, Administrator of the Estate of, Trustee under, Guardian of, Receiver of, Commissioner.
(2) Description of land or interest therein, and encumbrances, reservations, and exceptions, taxes and assessments if any.
(3) Execution in accordance with Chapter 5301 Ohio Revised Code.

Auditor's and Recorder's Stamps

***See Section 5302.09 Ohio Revised Code.**

Sheriff's and Auditor's Deeds

The **sheriff's deed** and **auditor's deed** might be classified as *public officials' deeds.* Sheriffs and auditors, as public servants, have a broad scope of required activities. Occasionally an *auditor must convey, using a deed when the realty is sold at public auction because back taxes are owed.* Or the *sheriff must convey when realty is sold because a certain lien (or claim), such as a mortgage, is to be satisfied.*

Similar to fiduciary deeds, the sheriff and the auditor do not personally give warranties via the deed. The auditor just gives title free from the tax lien, and the sheriff gives title free from whatever lien is being disposed of by the sale. In all such cases, the deeds simply transfer the title in the best way the law can under the circumstances. The sheriff and the auditor execute the deed only after they have been given an order by the appropriate court to do so. The sheriff and the auditor cannot function without orders from the appropriate court.

The consideration (purchase price) given in return for sheriff's and auditor's deeds is stated accurately, to the penny, at the appropriate place on the deed form. A mere recitation that consideration has been given, as used with the other types of deeds, is not sufficient here. This is because of the general requirement that all public officials reveal exactly what they have done, at all stages of their tasks, so the public can review these activities and easily test them for compliance with all legal requirements.

Figure 5–5 illustrates the continuum from likeliest to unlikeliest deeds a salesperson will handle. Quitclaim deeds are least likely. Residential real estate salespeople see general warranty deeds by far the most often.

Title Companies

By now the student should understand that the intangible bundle of ownership rights that is the realty owner's true title to the land can be reduced to a tangible form by this owner's receiving from a former owner, from a fiduciary, or from a public official a proper deed to the land. In the simplest case, this can be done by a father's quitclaiming his rights in land to his son. Upon delivering the properly executed deed, the son acquires the title. Then what is the purpose of "title" companies? Don't title companies sell titles?

Title companies do not sell titles. They are *privately owned companies, and they sell insurance.*

Suppose someone makes a claim against the grantee after acquiring title caused by some error or event that happened long before this grantee took title. For example, say

FIGURE 5–5 Continuum of deed types handled by real estate people.

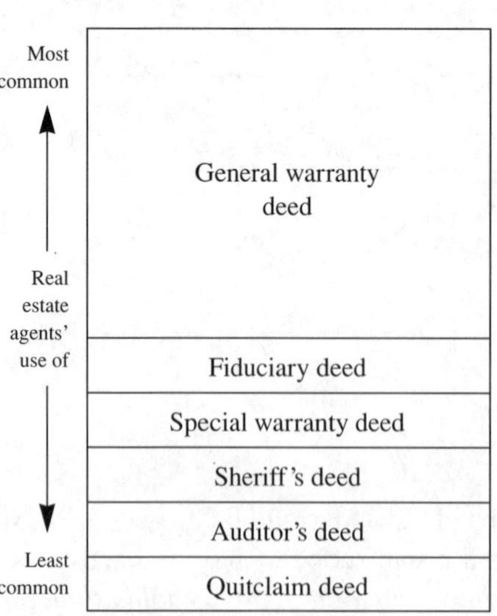

Continuum: This illustration, going from top to bottom, shows the most likely deed forms a real estate salesperson will handle professionally to the least likely.

a spouse never released dower rights but the property is nevertheless sold and conveyed to a grantee. Theoretically, the grantee can demand of the grantor that the grantor make good on the warranty. As long as the grantor can be located and can afford it, the grantee might be able to collect. If the grantor had purchased title insurance from a title company for the benefit of the grantee, however, chances are that the grantor can get the title company to satisfy the claim. As with all types of insurance, the larger the premium, the greater the coverage.

Unfortunately, much title insurance (or "evidence," "further assurance," or "proof" of title) is limited in scope and does not give full protection to the grantee.

We will discuss title evidence in detail in Chapter 8, but for now, the student should understand that the assurance of good title given to the purchaser via an insurance policy is quite a different thing (and strictly optional to the transaction) from the title itself. Different types of title insurance policies that vary in scope of coverage are available.

EMRICK V. MULTICON BUILDERS
57 Ohio St.3d 107, 566 N.E.2d 1189 (1991).

CASE STUDY FROM THE OHIO SUPREME COURT

Facts: The Blendon-Genoa Landowners' Association restricted the subdivision right-of-way, lot sizes, and setback lines of specified property. It also absolutely prohibited any business or activity "obnoxious to a good residence neighborhood," requiring any proposed businesses for the area to obtain the approval of the county zoning board and the approval of the board of the trustees of the Landowners' Association. Signers of the Restriction Contract were landowners in Franklin and Delaware Counties, Ohio. Not all property owners within the designated area signed the Restriction Contract.

These restrictions were recorded in the Franklin County Recorder's office. They were not recorded in the Delaware County Recorder's office, however, until eight months after Multicon bought the subject properties in Delaware County. Multicon bought the properties in Delaware County for the express purpose of building a shopping center and sought rezoning from "rural residential" to "planned community commercial." Both the planning commission and city council approved the rezoning petition.

Thereafter the Landowners' Association filed for declaratory judgment and injunctive relief to prevent Multicon from proceeding with commercial development. The Landowners' Association contended that even though the Restriction Contract had not been timely filed in Delaware County, Multicon had actual knowledge of the restrictions contained therein because of its dealings with restricted property in Franklin County and its knowledge of the Restriction Contract.

Trial Court: Held that unrecorded restrictions were enforceable and enjoined development.

Court of Appeals: Affirmed the trial court's decision.

Issue: Whether Multicon's purchase of properties in the restricted area of Franklin County, combined with its knowledge of the existence of the Restriction Contract, imputes actual knowledge to Multicon that the same restrictions applied to the properties it purchased in Delaware County.

Held by the Ohio Supreme Court: The trial court and court of appeals decisions were reversed. An unrecorded land use restriction is not enforceable against a bona fide purchaser for value unless the purchaser has actual knowledge of the restriction. Although actual knowledge in some instances may be inferred, it may not be imputed to the purchaser on the basis of familiarity with the deed restriction recorded in another county or on the basis of the purchaser's awareness of the bare existence of the document containing the restrictions.

The burden of showing such actual knowledge was upon the Landowners' Association, as well as the burden of showing that Multicon knew the covenants applied to the specific parcels of land purchased in Delaware County. Knowledge that a restriction applies to some lots in a tract does not constitute actual knowledge that those same restrictions apply to other lots within the same tract. The standard that must be met in court is not one of constructive notice but, instead, one of actual knowledge. A "should have known" or "could have known" test is not an appropriate consideration under an actual notice standard. Multicon, therefore, prevailed in this case instead of the Landowners' Association.

CASE STUDY FROM THE OHIO SUPREME COURT

EGGERT V. PULEO
67 Ohio St.3d 78, 616 N.E.2d 195 (1993).

Facts: Puleos originally owned Sublot 37 in Moreland Valley Estates in the village of Moreland Hills which was subject to a deed restriction that stated that the lot's use was limited to private, single-family residential purposes. Puleos wanted a public roadway constructed across Sublot 37 as public access to an adjacent thirty-acre parcel of land they owned. Puleos wished to subdivide that thirty-acre parcel and construct single family residences upon it. The other private landowners in Moreland Valley Estates sued Puleos, asking the court to enjoin (prevent) such a use of Sublot 37. The village of Moreland Hills was eventually brought into this case as a necessary defendant because Sublot 37, after being subjected to applicable platting procedures, had become a public street.

Issue: Can the adjoining landowners prevent the use of Sublot 37 as a public street per their private deed restrictions?

Held by the Ohio Supreme Court: Moreland Hills holds a vested fee interest in Sublot 37. Because a proposed plat was approved and recorded, the fee of the land designated as a public street (Sublot 37) vested in Moreland Hills. A restrictive covenant which may bind private landowners cannot be enforced against a municipal corporation. Additionally, the other landowners may not enforce against Puleos any restrictive covenant applicable to homeowners in Moreland Valley Estates to limit the use of Sublot 37 because Puleos no longer owns Sublot 37.

Summary of Content

1. Title to land is that bundle of ownership rights the law will protect and enforce for the benefit of those it recognizes as having such rights.
2. One can be an owner of an estate in land without having a deed, in the cases of adverse possession and dower.
3. A quiet title lawsuit should be used in adverse possession cases; it places the title on public record and gains court approval of the claimant's ownership in real estate.
4. Although title and ownership involve intangible things, the deed—a simple piece of paper—makes it possible to reduce those intangible property rights to tangible form. As such, the deed clearly indicates to all the world the identity of the owner of those valuable property rights and, further, acts as a convenient and accurate way of transferring those rights to another. Deeds always must be in writing.

5. The elements of a recorded deed that are used in virtually all Ohio real estate transactions handled by real estate agents are:
   - a grantor designated
   - a grantee designated
   - a recitation that consideration has been given supporting the conveyance
   - words of grant (do hereby give, grant, bargain, sell and convey)
   - a legal description of the land being conveyed
   - signature by the grantor before at least two competent, disinterested witnesses
   - delivery either to grantee or, at least, out of the possession and control of the grantor (The doctrine of *relation back* applies to deeds placed in escrow by the grantor. The law considers that delivery has taken place when the grantor dies after depositing his deed into escrow.)
   - acknowledgment by grantor of signing the deed before someone empowered to administer oaths
   - identification of the person who prepared the deed (usually the grantor's attorney)
   - satisfaction of state and local conveyance fees (taxes)
6. Deeds usually state the marital status of the grantor because, if he or she is married, the spouse releases dower rights in that real property within the deed itself. (Sometimes a separate document is used for this release.)
7. The grantor cannot transfer a completely unencumbered title to land because of always-present public controls over land ownership/usage and frequently-present private land ownership controls. The exception clause of the deed allows the grantor to convey the least unencumbered estate that can be conveyed. The grantor also can create a reservation, which is a limitation reserved to the grantor of some right in the land conveyed (e.g., an easement).
8. Deeds may be rescinded for fraud, misrepresentation of material fact, concealment, undue influence, duress, insanity, mistake, and minority.
9. Estoppel by deed prevents grantors from asserting their legal rights if they have behaved wrongfully (e.g., a grantor who makes a fraudulent conveyance).
10. Grantors (sellers/developers) and grantees (purchasers) may restrict the future use of the realty being transferred between them by their agreement. This is private land-use control via the use of deed restrictions and restrictions of record.
11. Any landowner can put restrictions in the deed as the grantor when he or she conveys land to a grantee.
12. Deed restrictions/restrictions of record are recorded in the county recorder's office where the realty is located.
13. A homeowners' association can enforce the restrictions against any homeowner who violates them.
14. Restrictions run with the land; they become an obligation on all subsequent purchasers of the realty.
15. The commonly used types of deeds, each varying in the extent and type of covenants and representations given by the grantor in addition to those absolutely necessary to convey title, are:
    a. general or standard warranty deed, which conveys all the grantor's right, title, and interest in and to the real property. The grantors warrant the grantees' complete, untroubled, and uninterrupted use of the property should a title problem develop.

b. limited or special warranty deed, which warrants the title only from the time the present grantor took title until the time the title transfers to the present grantee.
c. quitclaim deed, which transfers the interest of one person to another without any warranties as to the title of the subject realty.
d. fiduciary deed, which passes title when someone who is other than the grantor and who is in a high position of trust must convey (e.g., the executor of the grantor's estate when the grantor dies). Warranties are limited to the legality of the fiduciary's appointment.
e. sheriff's deeds and auditor's deeds, which are used pursuant to public, court-ordered sales. They convey title without any personal warranties.

16. Title companies do not sell titles to land; rather, they sell insurance, or assurance, that (to the limits of the policy) the grantor's title to the land is as good as she says it is.

REVIEW QUESTIONS

1. A deed is the most commonly used legal instrument for the transfer of:

   a. personal property rights
   b. leasehold estates
   c. freehold estates
   d. licenses

2. Which of the following is not an essential element of a valid deed?

   a. date deed is signed by grantor
   b. legal description
   c. consideration
   d. designation of grantor and grantee

3. Which of the following statements about a quitclaim deed is *not* true?

   a. transfers to the grantee all rights in the property held by the grantor
   b. is a commonly used and valuable legal tool
   c. could transfer title to the Brooklyn Bridge
   d. carries only the limited warranty from the year 1776 until the date of transfer

4. From the grantees' point of view, the worst deed for them (the one that will least protect their interests) is:

   a. grant deed
   b. quitclaim deed
   c. special warranty deed
   d. bargain and sale deed

5. Why would a grantor of a deed indicate marital status within a deed?

   a. because both parties to a deed must always indicate marital status
   b. to place all concerned parties on notice that there either is or is not a spouse's release of dower to be obtained
   c. to eliminate the problem of ex-wives' rights in real estate
   d. to tie into that county's marriage and divorce records

6. Which of the following things does *not* appear in a standard or general warranty deed?

   a. promises by grantor to preserve and protect the property after title transfer
   b. designation of grantor
   c. general warranty clause
   d. legal description

7. Which of the following deeds should be used to transfer the interest of a minor person in real estate?

   a. quitclaim deed
   b. limited warranty deed
   c. general warranty deed
   d. fiduciary's deed

8. Why do purchasers of realty at "arm's length" prefer the general warranty deed?
   a. the grantor and the grantee share the cost
   b. it gives the broadest deed warranty or guarantee known to the law
   c. it is equivalent to a policy of insurance that pays off in case of claims against the title
   d. it is harder to forge

9. From grantors' point of view, the deed that requires no obligations on their part to defend, and thus is the best for them to grant, is a:
   a. quitclaim
   b. general warranty
   c. special warranty
   d. sheriff's

10. A real estate broker can personally sign a deed for his principal, the seller, under which of the following conditions?
   a. if the seller is deceased
   b. if the seller orally tells him to sign
   c. if the broker has the written power of attorney from the seller authorizing such signing
   d. if this is the only way to make sure that title transfers when it is supposed to

11. Oral deeds are valid under which of the following circumstances?
   a. when the seller is too old or too physically ill to write
   b. when the seller is a citizen of a foreign country
   c. to transfer leasehold rights
   d. none of the above

12. Who would be the most likely person to use a special or limited warranty deed?
   a. estate of a deceased person
   b. developer
   c. divorcing spouse
   d. sheriff

13. From grantees' point of view, the deed that best protects their interests is the:
   a. quitclaim
   b. general warranty
   c. special warranty
   d. sheriff's

14. Dower rights usually are released in real estate sales transactions by:
   a. using a deed
   b. using an ante nuptial agreement
   c. using a release of dower rights form
   d. using a community property release form

15. If a grantor dies after delivering a valid, executed deed into escrow:
   a. the transaction must be submitted to probate court
   b. the doctrine of relation back allows the escrow agent to close the transaction using that deed
   c. a fiduciary must be appointed and a new fiduciary deed drawn
   d. the grantor's surviving spouse retains the right to convey title and can do so on another deed form

16. The recording of a warranty deed:
   a. passes the title
   b. insures the title
   c. guarantees the title
   d. gives constructive notice of ownership

17. Title passes to the grantee at the time the deed is:
   a. delivered
   b. recorded
   c. signed
   d. acknowledged

18. From grantors' point of view, the deed that will require the most obligations on their part to defend, and thus is the worst for them to grant, is:
   a. quitclaim
   b. general warranty
   c. special warranty
   d. auditor's

19. Which of the following is an essential element of a valid deed?
   a. a seal on a corporation deed
   b. a date
   c. dower release from a divorced and not remarried grantor
   d. execution from grantor in front of two disinterested witnesses

20. Which of the following deeds conveys the grantor's interest with a guarantee that the grantor has not by any act or omission caused a defect in title, yet does not guarantee against acts or omissions of former owners?
    a. special warranty deed
    b. general warranty deed
    c. quitclaim deed
    d. no deed does this

21. If grantees die shortly after receiving title via a recorded general warranty deed and a defect in title thereafter comes to light:
    a. their heirs and assigns are not protected because the warranties extend only to the grantees
    b. their heirs and assigns are protected because the warranties extend to them as well
    c. the heirs will have to contest the deed in probate court
    d. the grantees will totally control the outcome of this problem

22. Legal descriptions as used in deeds:
    a. are uniformly described in sublot form
    b. must contain metes, bounds, and courses references
    c. must be no longer than one page
    d. vary—there are different methods and lengths

23. Both zoning laws and a deed restriction could prevent this use of land:
    a. painting your house white
    b. traveling on a county road
    c. having a stable with your own horses
    d. writing poetry in your bedroom

24. This deed restriction is *not* enforceable:
    a. the exterior of the house must be painted white
    b. the realty may only be sold to Caucasians
    c. agricultural animals are prohibited
    d. a new structure must be set back 100 feet from the retained lot line

25. Which of the following represent(s) acquisition of title to land when no deed exists tending to prove ownership:
    a. title by adverse possession
    b. title by vested, choate dower interest
    c. title by condemnation (eminent domain) proceedings
    d. all of the above

ANSWER KEY

1. c
2. a
3. d
4. b
5. b
6. a
7. d
8. b
9. a
10. c
11. d
12. b
13. b
14. a
15. b
16. d
17. a
18. b
19. d
20. a
21. b
22. d
23. c
24. b
25. d

6
CONTRACTS

Key Terms

acceptance
accord and satisfaction
anticipatory repudiation
assignment
bilateral contract
breach of contract
capacity
condition
consideration
construction
contract
counteroffer
damages
duress
earnest money
enforceable contract
equitable conversion
express contract
fraud (actual and constructive)
implied contract
impossibility of performance
liquidated damages
minimization of damages
minority (minor)
mitigation of damages
mutual mistake
novation
offer
offeree
offeror
option
parol evidence rule
part performance
promissory estoppel
reformation
rescission
revocation
specific performance
statute of frauds
undue influence
unenforceable contract
unilateral contract
voidable contract
void contract
withdrawal

THE SUCCESS OF REAL ESTATE SALESPEOPLE in the real estate business is determined in large measure by how good they become in negotiating transactions. Their income is derived from successfully negotiating and completing real estate listing and purchase contracts. Therefore, they must look truly professional at this stage; any sign of weakness or incompetency in handling the form contracts and negotiating transactions weakens their persuasiveness with sellers and purchasers.

FOR EXAMPLE

Anne Hamilton, a real estate salesperson, has been working with Phil and Paula for weeks, showing them homes for sale. Finally, Phil and Paula are ready to make an offer on a home. Anne takes them back to her office, where she brings her office manager, Myra, into their conference. She tells Phil and Paula, "Myra's better at filling in these form contracts than I am." Not surprisingly, Phil and Paula thereafter address most of their questions to Myra and not to Anne. Myra is even the one who convinces them that their offer should be another $1,000 higher.

When Myra and Anne take the offer to sellers, the sellers also defer to Myra since Anne also brought Myra to their home when she obtained the listing. Anne likewise told sellers that, "Myra is much better with these form contracts than I am."

If Anne is brand new to the business, her dependence upon Myra is somewhat understandable. Myra, however, should encourage Anne to fill out the form contracts with her assistance rather than taking over the whole process herself. For her own good, Anne also should make every effort to become competent enough to fill in these forms herself within the next week or so.

Further, Anne may lose future business since both purchasers and sellers probably will call Myra when they are next in need of real estate services, because they perceive her as the competent professional. When asked by friends or relatives for a referral, they probably will give Myra's name. (Managers usually continue to accept listings from their own referral base. Occasionally managers also show prospective purchasers specific real properties, but this is not encouraged by many brokers except in emergency situations.)

Excellent real estate practitioners hone their skills in negotiating transactions to a point where they can fill out the form contracts on the hood of a car or on the kitchen table at an open house. They know they must be able to swing into action the moment sellers or purchasers become interested in entering into a real estate transaction. If the resulting document is too messy and too hard to read, the salesperson usually follows up by preparing a neatly typed or handwritten contract in which all terms are legible. The parties sign this new document, which substitutes for the messy one.

If there is any chapter in this text that budding real estate salespersons should spend some extra time on, it is this one. In some other areas, salespersons can and should shift the burden of professional responsibility. They usually can count on sellers' lawyers to prepare deeds, lenders' lawyers to prepare the mortgage deeds, and title companies' lawyers to prepare the documentation for evidence or assurance of title to the subject real property. Contracts, by contrast, place real estate salespersons squarely in the front battle lines with purchasers, sellers, and other real estate practitioners.

This chapter explains the basic principles of contract law and it treats actual real estate contracts in detail. The theory is presented first, in Section I, followed by practical application of this theory, Section II. The practical application material includes forms (a real estate listing contract, a real estate purchase contract, and a promissory note), along with complete explanations. Readers are then referred to the back of the text, where they can practice filling out two form real estate purchase contracts, which they can compare with the correct samples that follow those exercises.

Finally, the "hypothetical situations" at the end of this chapter cover those most frequently encountered by brokers, salespeople, sellers, or purchasers in regard to contracts.

SECTION I

THEORY OF CONTRACT LAW

CONTRACTS DEFINED

A **contract** can be defined as an *agreement between two or more parties that is legally enforceable.* It contains a set of promises that the law gives a remedy for, if breached. The law recognizes the performance of the set of promises within a contract as a duty. Contracts are generally *executory* in nature; the promises must be performed. Something remains to be done by one or both parties. An *executed* contract has been performed by the parties, or all the promises were fulfilled. Contract law for real estate purposes generally is not controlled by statutes but rather by common law, which is found in court decisions. The subject matter of a contract must be legal; an illegal objective defeats an otherwise enforceable contract.

TYPES OF CONTRACTS

Express contracts and implied contracts are different types of contracts. In real estate, the **express contract** is the most commonly used. It is one in which the *parties agree to mutual obligations by words, either orally or in writing.* The real estate purchase, listing, and option contracts are all express and are almost always in writing.

An **implied contract** is one in which the parties exchange no words or promises either in writing or orally, but because of the relationship between the parties and the facts in the case, it is *implied that a contract has been formed.* Although a listing agreement can be an implied contract, this occurs infrequently in real estate. Most brokers insist that listings be in writing since they include promise of the broker's and salesperson's commission. The purchase contract always must be in writing and can never be implied because of the statute of frauds.

Implied contracts are found more commonly in other professionals' practices, such as a doctor who sees patients and then bills them for the consultation. Although no promises are exchanged, patients see the doctor with the knowledge that the doctor works for payment. This analogy works well in a lawyer-client situation, too. To imply a relationship between a real estate broker and purchasers, is difficult, however, as there is a presumption that the broker works for the sellers rather than the purchasers unless there is an express contract with purchasers.

If the real estate broker has a written listing contract with sellers, as is usually the case, it is express. All written contracts are express. If the broker has an oral contract with sellers, it still may be express. For example, sellers say to the broker, "If you sell our house, we'll pay you a commission." The only way an implied contract can come about is if sellers agree to let the broker/salesperson show the realty and the broker/salesperson then brings sellers an offer they wish to accept. By letting the broker/salesperson deal in the realty, a professional relationship develops that ripens into an implied contract. Nevertheless, brokers and salespeople should deal only with written listing contracts because oral contracts, whether express or implied, are difficult to prove in court.

Statute of Frauds

The **statute of frauds** is a doctrine in contract law requiring a *writing to make certain contracts binding*. The writing is not the contract but instead is evidence of the contract. Under the statute of frauds, the writing is also necessary to make the contract enforceable. With an enforceable contract, the parties agree to fulfill the terms of their promises. If one refuses, the other party can sue to force the breaching party to fulfill the promise. By contrast, if an agreement is subject to the statute of frauds but is oral, the injured party cannot sue to enforce it. Thus, any contract for the sale of land or interest in land must be in writing to be an enforceable contract.

The legal basis and necessity for the statute of frauds is to require some of the more important contracts to be in writing, to avoid confusion and litigation, and to lessen the chances for fraudulent conduct between the parties.

Under the statute of frauds, a contract or an option for the purchase and sale of an interest in realty must be in writing by both parties. This also includes an assignment of a contract to sell; a promise to give a mortgage or other lien as security for money; a power of attorney authorizing the person holding it to transfer the principal's realty; a promise to transfer or sign a lease, easement, or rent; and a promise of an equitable interest in land.

The statute of frauds requires that there be a writing including the subject matter of the contract, the identity of the parties, and the essential terms and conditions of the contract. All of these must be described with reasonable clarity. The writing generally can be in any form. In real estate practice, printed form contracts usually are used. Under the statute of frauds, a receipt, an exchange of letters, or a record book is sufficient.

Whatever the form of the writing, it must be signed by the parties, either by their signature or their mark. A *written memorandum* also may satisfy the statute of frauds. This minimally contains a description of the realty, the names of the parties, the essential terms of the sale, and the signatures of the parties. Sometimes the memorandum consists of a series of interrelated writings rather than just one. As a practical matter, though, one entire legal instrument, such as the real estate purchase contract, is used to satisfy the statute of frauds to avoid the many legal problems that could arise (dealt with in this and other chapters).

Today, technology makes possible the use of certain other writings, for example, the FAX (facsimile) machine. A FAX is typically a complete and accurate copy of the original (a duplicate original) and, as such, should satisfy the statute of frauds. Because the FAX is relatively new to the law, however, realty salespersons should follow up the FAX with the signed originals through the mail to any party they cannot deliver the contract to personally. To those they can deliver the contract to personally, they should still deliver signed originals as the safest course. For the ultimate in proof and protection, they may wish to obtain a receipt from the person who receives the documents.

Exceptions to Statute of Frauds

A principal exception to the statute of frauds is that if the contract subject matter is not the transfer of land, it is not within the statute, even though the ultimate purpose is an interest in land, such as with a listing contract.

Another exception to the statute of frauds doctrine is the doctrine of **part performance.** *If the contract has been substantially performed,* it does not have to be in writing. Under the doctrine of part performance, the real estate purchase contract, in special circumstances, can be oral. If, for example, pursuant to an oral real estate purchase contract, purchasers move onto the real property, occupy it, renovate it, or do other positive acts to it, with the sellers' acquiescence, the law can prevent sellers from declaring the contract a nullity because it is oral instead of written. Nevertheless, *payment by purchasers, without anything else, is not enough* to benefit from the part performance doctrine.

Elements of a Valid Contract

Essential elements to the formation of a contract, real estate or otherwise, are the offer, acceptance, and consideration. The offer and acceptance make up the actual agreement, whereas consideration is the mutual exchange of promises or acts of benefit and detriment between the parties that *makes the contract binding.* Legal descriptions are not necessary in any real estate purchase or listing contracts; the street address alone can be used. The real estate listing and purchase contracts do not require witnesses, notarization, or recording. This is generally true of all contracts.

The Agreement

Offer

To reach an agreement to form a contract, the first step is to make an offer. The *persons who make the offer* are called the **offerors.** The *persons to whom the offer is made* are called the **offerees.** The **offer** contains the *offerors' proposed terms for a particular transaction.* In the offer there is a promise by a party to do something or not to do something. This must be something that persons are not already legally bound to do or not to do. An offer, once initiated, is always looking for acceptance. Until it meets that acceptance, there is no agreement.

The courts will not make contracts for the parties. Therefore, the *offer must be definite and specific* in its essential terms, so that each party knows what promises and performances bind him or her. This is usually not a problem in real estate contracts. The purchase contract, for example, must contain a definite price and a description of the subject real property; the listing contract must include specification of the asking price and the real estate commission with its percentage rate. These specifications do away with uncertainty and ambiguity.

Acceptance

Acceptance of the offer *forms an agreement and thus a contract.* Acceptance comes from the offerees, the persons to whom the offer is directed. Offerees must know of the offer at the time they make an acceptance of it. Only persons to whom the offer is made can accept that offer. No other persons can accept the offer on their behalf unless, of course, they have the offerees' power of attorney.

Offerees who are contemplating accepting an offer generally cannot do so by remaining silent. Usually the acceptance must be expressed in words. In real estate contracts they usually are expressed both in words and in writing in the real estate listing and in purchase contracts.

Offerors may specify the way in which the offer must be accepted. For example: "This offer may be accepted only by returning the signed document to offerors through the United States mail. Acceptance is deemed to occur on the date of the postmark."

Counteroffer

The rule of common law is that if offerees change any of the terms of the offer, that is not an acceptance. It is then what is known as a **counteroffer.** Offerees *reject the offer and send back to the persons who initiated the bargaining process a different offer that contains counter proposals.* This commonly occurs in negotiating real estate purchase contracts. With the purchase contract, purchasers typically initiate the offer in writing. Sellers then consider the offer and often change one or more things on it and sign it. Sellers have not accepted that offer but instead have counteroffered on it.

No real estate contract can be formed until there is a *complete meeting of the minds in writing* between the parties. It must be clear, from an examination of the written contract, that the parties intend to be bound to all of its terms. Therefore, realty agents must set forth every element of the agreement in plain, simple language. On every item within the contract, both parties must be in complete written agreement. Customarily, sellers and purchasers initial and date any changed terms on the written real estate purchase contract to show their agreement.

Withdrawal and revocation

Withdrawal means that offerors *take back the offer any time before it has been accepted.* Sometimes the time for expiration of acceptance is expressly stated within the written offer. Without the statement, common law implies a reasonable period of time. For example, if purchasers/offerors insert within the offer in a purchase contract that the offer expires within the next 24 hours, sellers/offerees who accept it at the 25th hour are too late and the contract is not formed. Or sellers at that point have made a counteroffer that then can be sent to the purchasers for acceptance. If purchasers accept, a contract is formed.

If the offerors want to revoke their offer prior to acceptance, they may do so. **Revocation** of that offer becomes *effective when it is received by the offerees,* the persons who would be accepting the offer. If offerees already have accepted the offer, revocation is too late. A contract already has been formed.

Once offerees make a counteroffer to the original offer or reject the offer outright, they lose the power to accept that offer. A common example is of sellers who counteroffer on the purchase contract and thereafter learn that purchasers are not interested in accepting that counteroffer. The sellers no longer can accept the original offer. The offer died when they made the counteroffer.

Inquiries during negotiations

During negotiations, if a party is making inquiries rather than actually changing terms, that is not sufficient to terminate the offer.

FOR EXAMPLE

Upon receiving the counteroffer from sellers, purchasers say to the salesperson, "Would you call the sellers and make absolutely sure that under no circumstances are they willing to leave the draperies?" The salesperson complies, but the sellers say that under no circumstances are they willing to let the draperies be part of the transaction. The salesperson relates this to purchasers who decide "the heck with the draperies" and sign the counteroffer. They merely made an inquiry in the negotiation process; they did not actually change terms of the offer. Therefore, there is no rejection, only an acceptance and, thus, formation of a contract.

Same or implied terms

Sometimes offerees add terms that look like they are new or additional terms (a counteroffer) but really are the same or similar terms as already exist in the offer, or as the law would imply them. This is still an acceptance. For example, the offerees add the following terms: "Subject realty to have good, marketable title." Typically, this phrase is already printed within the real estate purchase contract or the law even implies it because it is so essential. Thus, even though offerees add this term, they are really accepting the offer and not counteroffering upon it. They merely "add" an already existing term.

Death and destruction

Although unusual, if the party who was to accept the offer dies before accepting it, the power to accept terminates. Also, if the realty in question is destroyed before acceptance, the subject matter of the offer is destroyed and, thus, the power to accept is gone. If a contract is formed and a party dies afterwards or if the realty is destroyed, different legal rules apply. This is discussed when we examine form contracts later in this chapter.

Figure 6–1 shows what can happen in trying to form a real estate purchase contract. Purchasers send their offer to sellers, hoping for acceptance. Shortly thereafter, purchasers decide to revoke their offer. If sellers receive the revocation before they accept the offer, the offer dies and no contract is reached. Before they receive the revocation, sellers can either accept the offer or reject it. If they reject it, the offer dies and no contract is ever formed. If they accept it, a contract is formed when the acceptance is put back into the stream of communication.

In Figure 6–2, purchasers again make an offer. They do not follow it with a revocation, however. Sellers may accept or reject the offer, the same as they did in Figure 6–1. They also may make a counteroffer. This counteroffer is sent back to purchasers, who may accept it or reject it. If purchasers reject it, the counteroffer dies and no contract is ever formed. If they accept it, it becomes a binding contract when they put it back into the same stream of communication from which it originated. If consideration also is present, a binding contract is formed. Purchasers also might make a counteroffer with the same results as shown in Figure 6–1.

Figure 6–3 shows the counteroffer and revocation, both sent by sellers. If the revocation reaches the purchasers before acceptance, the counteroffer dies and no contract can be formed. If purchasers accept the counteroffer before they receive revocation and place it back in the same stream of communication to the sellers, a contract is formed. If they reject the counteroffer, it dies and a contract cannot be formed.

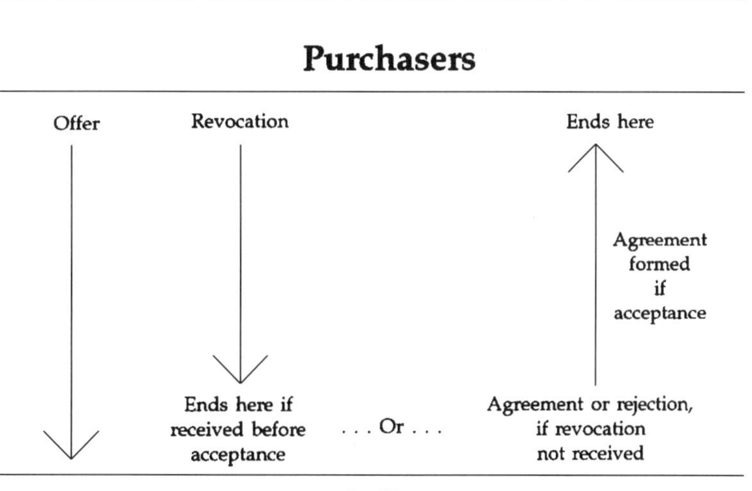

FIGURE 6–1
Forming the real estate purchase contract.

FIGURE 6–2 Counteroffer.

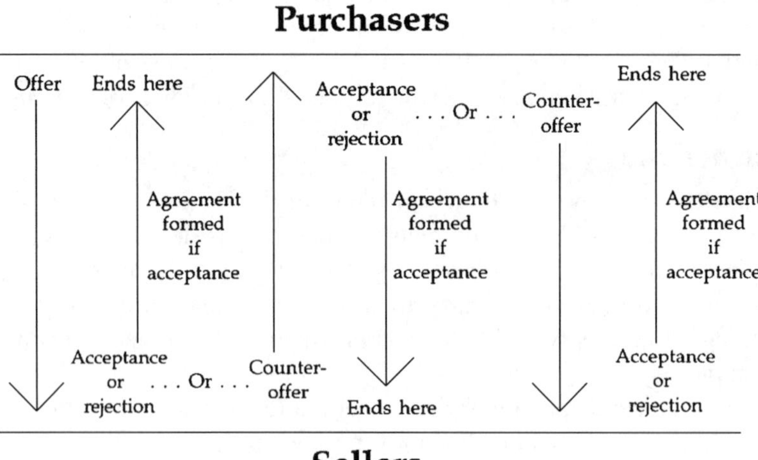

FIGURE 6–3 Counteroffer and revocation.

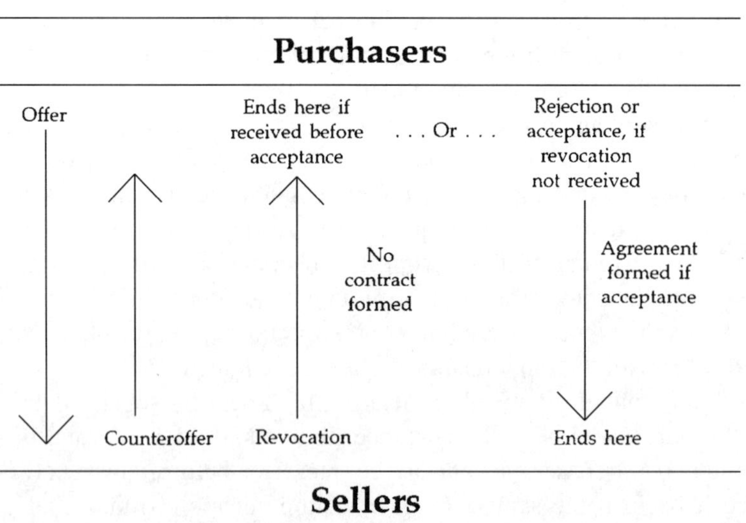

Effectiveness

There must be an expression of the intention to accept an offer by word, sign, writing, or act, communicated or delivered to the persons making the offer (the offerors) or their agent. A private act by offerees, such as merely signing the offer and nothing more, is not sufficient.

Consideration

In addition to offer and acceptance, **consideration** is needed to form a binding contract. Basically, it is the *legal detriment bargained and promised for in exchange for legal benefit, by both parties, either orally or in writing, as required by the statute of frauds*. Table 6–1 shows what consideration is in real estate contracts.

For consideration to be deemed present, both parties to a contract must promise to do something they are not already legally obliged to do, or they must promise to refrain from doing something they are not legally obliged to refrain from doing. If the party is already obliged to do or not do what he or she is promising to do or not do, consideration is not present.

TABLE 6–1 Consideration in real estate contracts.

	LISTING CONTRACT	PURCHASE CONTRACT	OPTION CONTRACT
PARTIES	Sellers and Broker	Sellers and Purchasers	Sellers and Purchasers
CONSIDERATION Benefit	Sellers get benefit of broker's professional service in marketing real property for sale. Get broker to assume overhead expense in marketing real property they were bearing.	Sellers get money for real property.	Sellers get money that purchases do not get refunded.
Benefit	Broker gets listing and thus opportunity to earn commission. Gets a commodity to put within general market. Addition of another commodity helps sell the whole.	Purchasers get real property for money.	Purchasers get time to buy real property at certain price. No one else can buy during this time, and price cannot change.
Detriment	Sellers will owe broker a commission if broker is successful. Lose all or some rights to sell the property by themselves.	Sellers lose real property.	Sellers have real property tied up.
Detriment	Broker must expend money and staff to market real property.	Purchasers must pay for real property by money, mortgage, or combination of both.	Purchasers lose money to get this privilege.
METHOD OF OFFER	By either party. Can be oral.	Usually by purchasers in writing. Also by sellers in writing if counteroffers are made.	Usually by purchasers in writing.
METHOD OF ACCEPTANCE	By either party. Can be oral.	By either party in writing.	Usually by sellers in writing.
USE OF ATTORNEYS	Usually in connection with probating estates or divorce law.	Sometimes; usually at purchaser's demand before presentation of offer. Trend is increased use of attorneys.	Frequently.

FOR EXAMPLE

After the purchase contract has been formed, sellers say to purchasers: "We'll make sure the house isn't abused by our dogs by the time you move in if you give us $500 more." Sellers already are under an obligation, via the real estate purchase contract, to deliver the realty in as good shape as when the contract was formed. Therefore, even if purchasers agree to this demand, it is a void contract because no consideration is given.

Gifts lack this benefit-detriment combination that makes up consideration. Gifts therefore are not enforceable contracts but, instead, are *unenforceable, conditional promises to make a gift*. Persons who promise other persons gifts usually are entitled to change their minds until they have given the gift. There is no lawsuit called breach of a promise to make a gift. Once the donor (gift giver) actually gives the gift to the donee (beneficiary of the gift), the donor may not take it back. Then it has become the property of the donee.

FOR EXAMPLE A promises to give B an acre of his realty. B does not promise A anything in exchange. This is a gift. B has a right to that realty only when it is actually conveyed to her. Likewise, consideration made up of love and affection is not sufficient consideration to form a contract. Thus, if A promises to convey B an acre of realty because he loves her, there is no contract. It is deemed a gift instead, and thus is revocable until actually given.

Adequacy of consideration is not essential toward achieving consideration. The courts say they will not make contracts for the parties and, thus, if the parties make a bad bargain, they are stuck with it. Therefore, *any detriment, no matter how small, usually will do as consideration*. Many agreements begin, for example, with the phrase: "For the sum of $10.00 and other good and valuable consideration, the receipt and sufficiency of which is hereby acknowledged. . . ." This recital is enough for the contract to be deemed to have consideration.

The philosophy of the law of contracts is the freedom to contract—which is why the courts support inadequate consideration. Basically, giving up any legal right, privilege, or immunity constitutes detriment sufficient to be consideration. If purchasers pay too much for a home, for example, they are not excused from performing the contract. The consideration is inadequate, but that is not a defense. The sellers in that instance get the better part of the bargain—more money in exchange for a house worth less than that amount. Although it is unequal, consideration is nonetheless present, and purchasers must perform the binding contract or be in breach of contract.

Sometimes brokers sell a piece of realty within hours of securing a listing contract upon it. Even though these brokers incur no marketing expenses, sellers now owe them an expensive commission. Sellers are bound to perform under the listing contract by paying brokers the commission. Brokers promised to use professional services and assume the expense of marketing the realty. The fact that they actually had to do little or nothing does not invalidate the presence of consideration. The sellers therefore are bound to pay brokers the commission under the binding listing contract. From the brokers' perspective, this commission makes up for other transactions, into which they put considerable labor and expense but that never closed and that never earned them any money. This "luck of the draw" in earning real estate commissions (expecting to win and lose some commissions as part of a day's work) is, after all, still at the very heart of the real estate business.

The only time when inadequacy of consideration might be used to render a contract void is in using arguments that the consideration was so inadequate that what was actually happening in the bargaining process was fraud, undue influence, duress, or mutual mistake (discussed in full toward the end of this chapter). In that instance, inadequacy of consideration is not the legal ground voiding the contract, but merely *evidence* showing those other grounds.

Real estate companies formerly urged their sellers, upon making their counteroffer, to insert within it "irrevocable for a given period of time." But sellers mistakenly assumed that they could not withdraw the counteroffer or accept other purchasers' offers when, in fact, they could. Sellers had not received anything of value or been promised anything of value by purchasers in exchange for this irrevocable privilege, so consideration was missing. Because the consideration was missing, it was really a defective, *void option contract*. Thus, it was improper for brokers or salespersons to urge this type of provision upon their sellers-clients.

Consideration often is called the cement or glue to a contract, because a contract is easily torn apart if a party opposing its validity is shrewd enough to notice the absence of consideration. Conversely, a contract with consideration "sticks" so the party opposing the contract has a hard time voiding it.

Real estate companies in recent years are using *addenda* frequently. For example, purchasers later decide they also want the free-standing stove to be included in the transaction. They and sellers already entered into a binding purchase contract that did not include this stove. When purchasers make this request, if the real estate agent uses a form called an addendum, which merely lists the change and provides for the sellers' and purchasers' signatures plus dates of signing, consideration is missing.

Typical language used in an addendum is likely to be:

> As an addendum to the purchase contract of Ables and Bradys, dated April 25, 1995, for 100 Main Street, Anywhere, Ohio, Bradys, sellers, agree to let purchasers, Ables, keep the free-standing stove currently located in the subject real property.

There is no consideration in this addendum. Thus, it is not a valid, binding contract. Sellers do not have to leave the stove. The contract would have been valid and binding had purchasers *exchanged something* for the stove, such as adding to the above language:

> In consideration of $10 paid to Bradys, and other good and valuable consideration, the receipt and sufficiency of which is hereby acknowledged, Bradys agree that Ables shall keep the stove.

Now there is consideration, and purchasers have the legal right to the stove.

Conditional promises (often called "contingencies") can be sufficient for consideration. These are common in real estate purchase contracts. The parties reach an agreement, but performance is conditional upon some other event occurring. The understanding is that both parties to the contract are committed to its performance, provided that the condition within it can be fulfilled. Two of the more common conditions are approval of financing by a lending institution or receiving money from the sale of other real property. Executed contracts cannot be set aside because they lack consideration, as they are fully performed contracts. By then it is too late to use lack of consideration as a legal argument.

Promissory Estoppel

Promissory estoppel *prevents a wrongdoing party from escaping from performing according to his or her promises because the contract lacks consideration.* Essentially, the wrongdoer made a promise to the other party and intended that promise to be relied upon. And, in fact, it was relied upon by the other party. That act, made upon that reliance, must cause that other party injury.

FOR EXAMPLE

> In an addendum to the purchase contract not supported by consideration (purchaser did not pay for it), the seller, Mary, promises to move out earlier than the date given in the purchase contract. This gives the purchaser, Bill, earlier possession. Bill vacates his premises and lets another assume possession. When his moving van arrives at his new home, ready to unload, Mary refuses to vacate.

The law in this example invokes the doctrine of promissory estoppel to remedy and give relief to Bill so he can move in early or recover damages, or both. This can occur even though Mary's promise is not supported by any consideration.

Earnest Money

Earnest money is a *small portion of the purchase price that purchasers put down in advance at the time they make an offer.* It demonstrates sincerity, that purchasers are in "earnest" to sellers in making their offer. Earnest money is *not necessary to form a valid contract.* The earnest money is not the consideration; the total purchase price is the consideration. Earnest money can be, but does not have to be, part of the purchase price. If earnest money is used, it should be shown and receipted for on the real estate purchase contract. Earnest money should be *taken as a matter of good real estate practice*. It *protects the seller* because that money can become part or all of the damages if purchasers fail to perform or otherwise breach the contract.

Parties and Promises in Real Estate Contracts

Refer back to Table 6–1. It charts the information given next about the parties and promises in the different kinds of real estate contracts.

Real Estate Listing Contract

The *parties to the real estate listing contract are the broker and the sellers.* Salespersons are never parties to the listing contract. The broker and sellers have assumed certain rights, duties, and obligations under this contract. The listing contract is a **bilateral contract** in which *both broker and sellers owe reciprocal, executory obligations to one another. They both promise something*. Specifically, in exchange for giving the broker most or all of the rights to sell their realty, sellers promise the broker that if the broker can secure a purchaser who is ready, willing, and able to purchase, the sellers will pay the broker a commission. At the same time, the broker promises to assume all the expense of marketing the realty and sellers promise the broker a given period of time in which he or she, as their agent, can exclusively (usually) market their real estate.

The broker thus gains another "commodity," which increases his or her share of the real estate marketplace. The broker thereby can generate other business for other listed real properties, and the broker can attract other purchasers and sellers by adding yet another listed real property to his or her roster. (Sellers and purchasers alike are attracted to real estate companies that have impressive listings of offered real properties in newspapers and magazines.)

The seller's capacity should be set forth in the listing contract. It should state whether the seller is the record owner of the property or, instead, is the executor, administrator, guardian, or trustee. If the appropriate court procedures have been followed, the name of the person on the legal description of the property also is the name of the person signing the listing contract. If the names are different, it could indicate that a court procedure was not followed. For example, if an estate was never probated, the decedent's name would show up instead of the executor's. Because this matter has to go to probate court before the property can be listed, the broker will want to postpone taking the listing.

Later on in this chapter, under Section II, we will study an actual form listing contract in detail.

Real Estate Purchase Contract

The *parties to the real estate purchase contract are the sellers and the purchasers.* Neither the broker nor the salesperson is a party to this contract. Only sellers and purchasers ordinarily have rights, obligations, and duties arising from the promises they make to one another in this contract. There is, however, a modern view of the real estate broker as a third party beneficiary to the purchase contract and thereby entitled to recovery rights for a commission from sellers pursuant to the purchase contract. The more conservative and traditional view is that the broker must refer back to the listing contract for commission rights rather than to derive rights from the purchase contract.

The purchase contract is *bilateral because both parties to it promise to do something.* One's promise is given in exchange for the other's promise. Sellers promise to convey clear title for the real property to purchasers in exchange for the purchase price that purchasers promise to pay sellers. Later on in this chapter, under Part II, we will study an actual form purchase contract in detail.

Real Estate Option Contract

Another real estate contract is the **option** contract. An attorney usually prepares an option contract. The *sellers and the purchasers are the parties to an option contract.* Purchasers want to buy time from sellers in which they alone can buy sellers' real property at a stipulated price.

FOR EXAMPLE

> Peter, the purchaser, wants a week during which he alone can purchase Sarah's home for $74,000. So Peter pays Sarah $1,000 for the privilege of having that week to buy the house for $74,000. During that week Sarah cannot accept any other offers, nor can she change the price or other conditions of sale to Peter. She is committed to her position and has to wait for Peter's act or failure to act. Peter exercises his option by accepting the offer to buy the realty for $74,000 from Sarah. Peter probably will accept by signing the purchase contract for the realty (the purchase contract has been prepared for and signed by Sarah) as the method for Peter to exercise his option to purchase. Sometimes it is provided within the option contract that if Peter elects to purchase the realty, the $1,000 (the amount paid for the option right) can be applied to the purchase price. If Peter does not exercise his option, he loses the $1,000 to Sarah and she may freely market and sell the real estate again.

Option contracts are **unilateral contracts.** Only one person makes a promise to induce an act. The seller of real property agrees to sell realty to purchaser only (and not anyone else), if purchaser decides to purchase the realty within a given period of time as set forth in the option contract. Sellers are bound to perform only if purchasers elect to purchase.

The promises within all these contracts are the consideration. A promise for an act (the unilateral contract) is also deemed consideration.

Figure 6–4 charts the optioning process between the seller/optionor and the purchaser/optionee.

ENFORCEABILITY OF CONTRACTS

Contracts are enforceable or unenforceable, voidable or void. In real estate contracts, the most typical types are those that are either enforceable or voidable. An **enforceable contract** is one that is *binding and cannot be broken.* The party that breaches the enforceable contract can be sued by the other party.

A **voidable contract** is one in which *one (or both) party(ies) has the right to disaffirm the contract (notify the other party that he or she is canceling the contract and has the legal right to avoid performing the contract).* The party so electing cannot then be sued for breach of contract. For example, some condition has not been fulfilled or there is a capacity problem (discussed in the next section). Thus, one party can legally declare the contract void and of no further force and effect. Except for a lack of capacity or an incompetency problem, most contracts are voidable *only until they are completely performed* by both parties. Usually, the voidability election ceases after full performance has occurred.

Unenforceable contracts are those that are *missing whatever is required to make them legal.* An example is a real estate purchase contract that has not been made in writing. Because all real estate purchase contracts must be in writing, under the statute of frauds, an oral purchase contract is totally unenforceable.

A **void contract** is *no contract whatsoever; it is a nullity and thus is of no effect.* For example, an essential element of the contract, such as consideration, is missing. Thus, there is no contract. A void contract also occurs when an *illegal purpose* is central to it.

FOR EXAMPLE

If someone sells realty used for illegal drug traffic to another person who wants to use it for that same purpose, the contract is void. If the facts are changed, however, and the purchaser does not know the illegal purpose and intends a legal purpose for the realty, the court probably will uphold the contract as valid and enforceable. If voidable, the court, in the drug example, makes it so only at the election of the innocent purchaser.

Capacity to Contract

Some people cannot enter into a binding contract because they lack the **capacity** to contract, others because they are considered incompetent. A discussion of the usual categories of lack of capacity and of incompetency follows.

FIGURE 6–4
Optioning process.

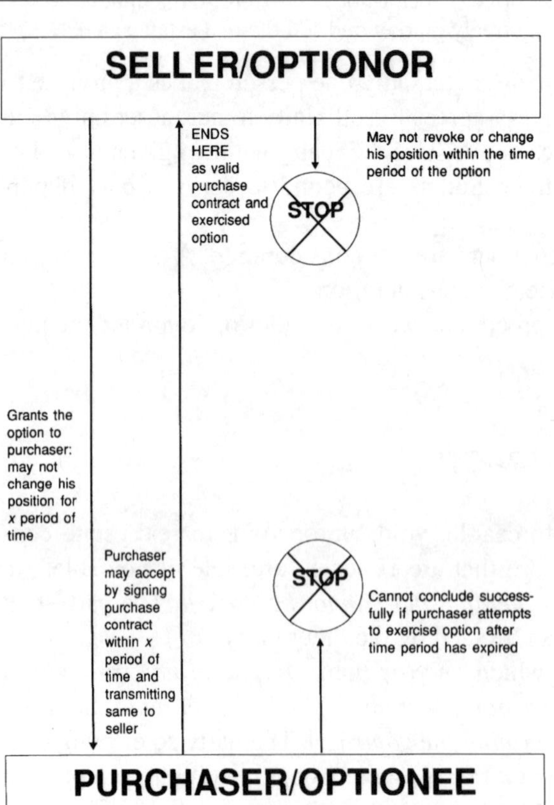

Minors

State law controls what is the age of majority. In Ohio, *age of majority is 18 years.* A person is the age of **minority** until his or her 18th birthday.

A minor can enter into a binding contract. It is the other party entering into the contract with a minor who does so at his or her own peril. This is because the *contract is voidable at the minor's election and not at the election of the other adult party.* Minors exercise their voidability election by disaffirming the contract. They refuse to perform on the contract and surrender their rights under it. Minors may disaffirm their contracts up to a *reasonable period of time* after reaching their age of majority. If they have not disaffirmed after a reasonable period of time upon reaching the age of majority, the contract may be held enforceable against them.

Minors are only occasionally parties to real estate transactions. If minors do have funds or property available to them, these more typically are held in a trust. In that situation, the trustee instead of the minor beneficiary enters as a party into the binding contract. If there is no trust covering a minor, the minor's guardian, as approved by probate court, typically acts as the proper party to any real estate contract.

Mental Infirmity

A contract entered into by a party who is mentally infirm is generally *voidable at the infirm person's option.* If the person has been adjudicated as incompetent or insane, however, and has been committed, with appointment of a court guardian, the *contract is usually totally void.* This is because the insanity or incompetency is a matter of public record, putting all, including the other party, on constructive notice of the infirmity.

Mental incompetency is a more difficult area than minority because the courts treat the contract as voidable if there are grossly inadequate terms acting to the detriment of the mentally infirm party. If the mentally healthy party to the contract does not take unfair advantage of the infirm party and is not able to detect in any reasonable way that the person is infirm, the contract may not be voidable unless the infirm person, through the acts of his or her court-appointed guardian, can restore the other person to his or her status before the transaction takes place. If the person can be reasonably perceived as infirm, the contract is always voidable by the infirm person. Severe mental retardation should be viewed as comparable to mental infirmity.

Only the mentally infirm person, not the competent one, has the election of voidability. These cases are somewhat rare, also. Real estate practitioners, however, should be wary of listing and selling homes for the extremely aged without inquiring with their attorney. Often these people are borderline incompetent and have extreme difficulty understanding what is going on around them. They are much in need of legal advice. To detect incompetency of the nature required by law is hard for a real estate salesperson. Generally, the salesperson should recommend to these persons that they consult the same attorney who prepared their wills about any contracts they wish to enter into.

Chemical Dependency

Some laws are emerging about the capacity of drugged or intoxicated persons to contract. The court cases that make voidable, or declare void, a contract on this basis usually find that these people lack capacity or are incompetent because they are chemically dependent. The nature and severity of the dependency usually must be *sufficient to commit people to a treatment facility and appoint a guardian through probate court.*

Chapter 14 focuses on probate court, guardianship appointments, and trusts.

STANDING

Persons other than those discussed to this point generally have the capacity to contract. They are presumed competent. Such persons entering into a contract become parties to the contract. A person *usually must be a party to a contract before taking any rights or responsibilities under it.* A recent trend within the law is to expand the category of persons who have the right to sue (standing) based on rights derived from an original party to the contract.

PAROL EVIDENCE RULE

The **parol evidence rule** states that *when there is a final and complete writing, a total integration of the parties' agreement or contract, such agreement may not be contradicted or supplemented by evidence of prior agreements or expressions.* The court considers as evidence only the final, written contract.

The parol evidence rule is a *rule of substantive law and evidence,* which becomes applicable whenever there is a written contract. If there is more than one contract, it is the last one, which incorporates all of the parties' intents, that is the controlling one.

The parol evidence rule requires that, when parties put their agreement into writing, all other previous agreements merge into the writing. Therefore, the final, written contract cannot be modified or changed by the previous agreements.

Because of this rigid definition, the parol evidence rule has exceptions. Therefore, if a party can show that the writing is either final but incomplete or complete but not final, the written agreement can be contradicted by prior agreements or expressions and may be supplemented by evidence of consistent additional terms. The parol evidence rule allows any relevant evidence to be introduced if that evidence shows that the agreement was neither final nor complete. The more complete and final the contract appears, the less likely it is that other evidence will be admissible.

The party trying to fight against exclusion of evidence under the parol evidence rule can make other arguments. The court will likely admit parol evidence, for example, if it believes fraud or duress were present in the transaction.

In keeping with the modern trend of the case law, if it strongly appears that the parties' intents are clearly not shown by the contract, the courts tend to allow the introduction of evidence showing what the parties truly intended by their contract. This disregard of the parol evidence rule usually occurs when the written contract is ambiguous or hard to understand.

FOR EXAMPLE

The parol evidence rule might come into play in real estate contracts when the agent or purchaser forgets to place a *financing condition* within the purchase contract, but, upon examining that contract, discovers that there is a dollar figure filled in for the mortgage amount in a *price breakdown clause* and/or it states that the purchaser has so many days to apply for financing. In this instance, a court likely will find the purchase contract ambiguous and thus will allow parol evidence about the contract's being conditioned upon the purchaser securing financing.

CONSTRUCTION OF CONTRACTS

If the terms of a contract are plain and unambiguous, a court does not need to interpret it. The court enforces the contract in its *plain and ordinary sense,* giving it a practical **construction** if possible. It will consider all the surrounding circumstances.

If the court needs to construe the terms of a written contract, it will look primarily for its *makers' intent.* Further, the court will construe the contract *as a whole* rather than try to focus on a single part. A legal or other technical word or phrase will be construed by its legal or technical definition. In real estate contracts, terms such as mortgage, warranty deed, marketable title, and so forth will be defined by their legal definition.

Specific provisions are preferred to general provisions. If written and printed terms within a contract conflict, the written controls. Typewritten provisions are preferred to those printed in a form contract. Any ambiguity in a contract is construed most strongly against the party, or the party's agent, who prepared the contract. Because an ambiguous term placed in the contract by the realty agent can therefore result in an award in damages against the principal (whether that be the seller or the buyer), the realty agent must take extra care to avoid using ambiguous terms in real estate contracts.

Courts favor construing contracts so they are effective and valid, not void. Courts will not use rules of construction to make a contract for the parties, however, if the parties failed to form a contract. Therefore, if the parties failed to include the essential elements or terms of a contract, or if they left essential terms open for future negotiation, the courts will hold that there is no contract. If there is no contract, the court will not have to apply any rules of construction.

CONDITIONS WITHIN CONTRACTS

Conditions are commonly used in form real estate purchase contracts but are not commonly used in the listing contracts. Conditions precedent requires that *an act must take place before a duty of performance of a promise arises.* If the condition is not fulfilled, the contract becomes null and void. Conditions also are referred to as *contingencies* within the real estate business. The following are conditions precedent inserted within many form real estate purchase contracts.

1. A common condition is: "If the purchasers are unable to secure financing, based on a minimum down payment of [insert percentage], then the purchasers are excused from performing this contract." In a good faith attempt to satisfy this condition, purchasers try to obtain financing through a lending institution, using a stated minimum percentage amount as a down payment. (The more down payment there is, the more likely it is that purchasers will obtain financing. This is why it is desirable to have purchasers committed to a minimum but not a maximum; one can use more money as a down payment, but not less.) Purchasers are excused from performing the purchase contract if they are not granted financing at these terms.

2. "If purchasers are unable to secure the proceeds of the sale of their home at [insert address], then they are excused from performing this contract." This condition is used when purchasers have sold their home but have not yet received the funds from the sale (the transaction has not yet closed). If they do not receive the funds from sale of their home, they are excused from performing the contract.

3. "If purchasers are unable to sell their home located at [insert address] within thirty days of the formation of this contract, then purchasers are excused from performing this contract. If other purchasers appear and enter into a binding contract with sellers, then these purchasers have seventy-two hours within which to remove this condition or this contract is null and void." This condition is for purchasers who have not sold their home yet. It gives them a chance, yet is fair to sellers too.

If new purchasers appear, these purchasers have 72 hours to remove the condition. If they can purchase the new home without selling their old home, they remove the condition. Once they remove this condition, however, they must proceed to close the transaction based on the remaining terms of the contract.

4. "If purchasers are unable to secure VA financing, then they are excused from performing this contract." This is used when purchasers can finance the transaction only by using the VA (Veterans Administration) program. They are excused if VA financing cannot be secured.

5. "If purchasers cannot secure FHA financing, then they are excused from performing this contract." This is used when purchasers can finance the transaction only by using the FHA (Federal Housing Authority) program. They are excused if FHA financing cannot be secured.

6. Present-day purchase contracts typically have some condition about inspections being conducted by a professional for the purchasers' benefit. These typically give purchasers the option to terminate the contract if the realty does not pass such an inspection(s). This is dealt with in detail both in the explanation of the Figure 6–6 form real estate purchase agreement and in Chapter 9.

Some conditions that real estate practitioners should avoid are:

1. "If purchasers are unable to secure an interest rate of [insert percentage], then they are excused from performing this contract." This means that if purchasers cannot get a mortgage loan at that rate of interest, they are excused from performing the contract. This can be used acceptably, however, if the percentage ceiling is several percentage digits higher than the rates currently available. Even then, this works best for a fixed interest rate loan. If a variable or adjusted rate is used instead, one has to expand the condition to include caps that the rate can change to.

2. "If purchasers are unable to secure a loan at XYZ Bank, then they are excused from performing this contract." This means that purchasers need to try obtaining financing at only that one particular lending institution. Without a specified lending institution, the law of contracts might require purchasers to apply for a loan at a reasonable number of lending institutions before excusing them from performance.

3. "If the purchasers are unable to obtain acceptable or satisfactory financing, then they are excused from performing this contract." Courts can construe this condition to mean that if purchasers do not like the financing arrangements, regardless of their objective desirability, they can let that failure of condition excuse them from performing the contract. Thus, this contract becomes null and void based on personal dissatisfaction. Sometimes, though, the court imposes the standard of a reasonable person's satisfaction. This clause should not be used because of the uncertainty of its legal interpretation.

4. "If purchasers are unable to terminate their lease without penalty, then they are excused from performing this contract." This means that if the landlord will not excuse the tenants from their lease, or if the landlord requires money for release, that failure of condition excuses purchasers from performing the real estate purchase contract. Most landlords do not excuse tenants from a lease without some monetary penalty. This is too big a loophole in purchasers' behalf.

5. "If the purchaser's spouse does not approve of the subject real property/If the purchaser's parents do not approve of the subject real property, then the purchaser is excused from performing this contract." Again, this is too great a loophole in the purchaser's behalf. Spouses and parents are unlikely to approve of realty about which they have never been consulted. Conditions that go even further than this are so fantastic that a court will say the contract is *illusory; there is no contract at all because the parties really do not intend to be bound.* Thus, sellers cannot condition their acceptance, for example, "upon our later deciding whether we truly want to sell or not."

Conditions weaken any real estate purchase contract. Without conditions, a contract is extremely strong. Therefore, one uses only tightly worded, precise conditions. The law does require, however, that the party seeking to be excused from performance of the contract because he or she cannot fulfill the conditions must have exercised *good faith and diligence* in trying to fulfill them, such as actually making applications for a mortgage loan.

A condition sometimes used by sellers so that the real estate is not tied up for too long is: "If purchasers are unable to secure loan approval within twenty-one banking days, then this contract is null and void." This means that if purchasers have not secured loan approval within that time, the contract is null and void and sellers can put the realty back on the market for sale. When financing is tight, the amount of banking days necessary to secure loan approval should be lengthened to accommodate the tight market.

The conditions discussed so far are all *express* conditions and are provided for by the parties. They are not in any way implied. This is the general way conditions are used in real estate practice.

The most common scenario—using conditions within the form real estate purchase contract—is that purchasers either can or cannot obtain financing, and the property either does or does not pass the inspection(s). Purchasers are excused from performing when they fail to obtain the financing and/or the property fails to pass the inspection(s). Real estate companies ask that both purchasers and sellers sign a mutual release, the terms of which direct who is to receive the earnest money (typically it is purchasers if there has been a good faith attempt to fulfill the conditions).

Impossibility of Performance

Impossibility of performance means that an *unforeseen act makes it impossible for a party to perform one's contractual duty.* This event occurs subsequent to entering into the contract. It *excuses performance* of the contract. The contract is discharged and is ended without any further liability by or against either party.

Impossibility of performance generally covers destruction, deterioration, or unavailability of the subject matter of the contract, which acts as a discharge, or end to, the contract and its obligations. Impossibility of performance can be used only as an excuse in very serious situations. The real estate case law commonly involves destruction of the subject matter as a method of discharge under the doctrine of impossibility of performance. This usually means destruction of the home or structure on the land. Great injustice would take place if destruction—which is good grounds for impossibility of performance—could be done by one of the parties to the contract in order to escape the liability of that contract. Therefore, the courts hold that the *party responsible for the event that makes the performance impossible cannot use the impossibility of performance defense.*

When there are two innocent parties to the contract, who must bear the risk of that destruction? Form real estate purchase contracts usually provide that if substantial damage occurs to the realty, or if a set percentage of loss occurs, purchasers can elect to be excused from performing the contract or, alternatively, receive the proceeds from sellers' insurance and complete the transaction (refer to clause 10 of Figure 6–6).

An *injunction* issued by a court prohibiting performance and a *governmental order* also make performance impossible; these excuse a party from proceeding and performing on a contract. *Death* of one of the parties can excuse performance based on impossibility of performance, but if the contract expressly provides that it binds the heirs, administrators, or assigns of the party, impossibility of performance cannot be used as an excuse for performance. Brokers' form real estate purchase contracts usually do have such a clause (refer to clause 17 of Figure 6–6). This conforms to the general rule of contracts that if *performance is delegable,* excuse of performance under the defense of impossibility of performance will not prevail. The converse is also true; if the contract is for *personal services,* performance is not delegable.

Thus, if it is impossible for a party rendering personal services to perform, performance is excused. For example, if someone commissions an artist to do a specific mural on a commercial building and the artist dies or becomes disabled, performance is excused. The courts generally will not recognize anything short of impossibility of performance as an excuse for not performing on a contract. Therefore, *unforeseen difficulties and increased cost of performance are generally insufficient to constitute impossibility of performance as a ground for excuse.*

Assignment

Contracts usually may be assigned. In **assignment,** *one party to the contract transfers the rights, duties, obligations, and privileges under the contract to some other, third person.* The person who assigns the contract, however, remains liable to the other party in the contract. The person who assigns the contract is called the *assignor.* The one to whom the contract is assigned is called the *assignee.* The assignee is liable for nonperformance to the assignor once he or she accepts the assignment.

Assignments are allowed within contracts unless specifically prohibited. The real estate purchase contract usually mentions that the contract is binding upon assigns. Therefore, assignment is generally *permitted within the real estate purchase contract.*

Novation Versus Accord and Satisfaction

When a *new contract is substituted for an old, preexisting one,* a **novation** occurs. The parties must intend to completely nullify the older contract. The new contract may have the same parties, although a new party may be, and usually is, substituted for an old one. The new contract, if it conforms to all the requisites of a valid, enforceable contract, becomes the controlling contract.

An **accord and satisfaction** *substitutes the performance of new promises to satisfy the obligations of a preexisting contract.* Both parties agree (accord) and are satisfied (they cannot sue) once these new promises are acted upon. An accord and satisfaction also operates as a *settlement* of the preexisting contract, which *releases the parties from the original contract's obligations.*

For example, purchaser and seller may agree to a reduction in purchase price if the general inspection results show expensive repairs to the property are needed. This is written up as an accord and satisfaction to the existing contract and not as a novation (not as a whole new substitute contract).

Breach of Contract

Breach of contract occurs when *one of the parties to the contract fails to perform his or her obligations, so as to materially breach his or her duties, under that contract.* A material breach is something substantial, not slight or trivial, within the contract.

If the party repudiates or fails to perform the contract at the time performance is due, that party is in breach of contract and the other party can then sue him or her. Generally, the party who wishes to perform the contract should *tender performance* (offer to perform) to the other side. If the other party refuses to perform his or her part of the bargain, the contract is breached.

Anticipatory repudiation is an *advance breach of contract.* The breaching party informs the other party that he or she is breaching the contract in advance of performance date, in unambiguous and unequivocal terms. The other party does not then have to wait until the date of performance to institute suit; the second party can sue immediately. If the party *equivocates* before time of performance, there is not an anticipatory repudiation. For example, a party says, "I may not go through with this." That is equivocation, and the nonbreaching party must wait until after the date of performance to sue.

Repudiation and anticipatory repudiation are both breaches of contract. A repudiator can take back the repudiation as long as the other party has not already sued or somehow changed position.

Table 6–2 compares breach of contract with excuse from performance.

Remedies and Relief

Legal remedies and equitable relief are both available through the court in breach-of-contract cases. *Remedies* are **damages,** usually money, and *relief is usually an order of the court* to compel or prohibit an act.

Damages

Compensatory damages are the usual ones allowed by the law in breach-of-contract cases. They are also called *actual* damages. The philosophy of the law is to place the aggrieved party in the same economic position that he or she would have been in but for the breach of contract. If the party would have made profits from the contract, the profits are properly included. The party should be compensated for any losses sustained.

Some compensatory damages commonly awarded in real estate actions are the real estate commission, interest rate differences, title evidence and assurance costs, closing costs, and/or escrow fees, points, additional moving costs, and additional rental costs. When itemized, compensatory damages can sometimes be quite high in breach-of-contract cases.

TABLE 6–2
Breach versus excuse of contract.

BREACH OF CONTRACT	EXCUSED FROM PERFORMANCE
1. Is grounds for lawsuit.	1. Is not grounds for lawsuit.
2. Personal impossibility of performance occurs.	2. Objective impossibility of performance occurs.
3. Purchaser is unable to obtain financing, but no financing condition in contract.	3. Purchaser is unable to obtain financing, and there is financing condition within contract..
4. Condition is not fulfilled due to bad faith.	4. Condition is not fulfilled in good faith.
5. One party refuses to perform because consideration is not adequate.	5. One party refuses to perform because consideration is not present.

Important principles for recovery in breach-of-contract cases were established early in U. S. law. Regarding compensatory damages, the courts have said, ". . . as may fairly and reasonably be considered . . . arising naturally, that is, according to the usual course of things, from such breach of contract itself." And, ". . . such as may reasonably be supposed to have been in the contemplation of both parties at the time they made the contract, as the probable result of the breach of it." Certainly, in every case of breach of contract, the first estimation of damages, as quoted above, is always recoverable. To recover the second type of damage, commonly known as *special* damages, the plaintiff has to be able to prove that both parties contemplated these as a probable consequence of any breach of contract.

In a jury's award of compensatory damages in breach-of-contract actions, they must meet a *standard of certainty;* the damages must be certain both in nature and in regard to causes from which they proceeded. The test is one of reasonable certainty. These are most commonly awarded when lost profits are also involved in the case.

Punitive, or exemplary, damages are not usually allowed in breach-of-contract cases. The philosophy of the law behind them is to punish a malicious or intentional wrongdoer. Punitive damages are allowed in some other areas of the law, such as assault-and-battery cases, but are rarely, if ever, awarded in contract actions, even if the breach is malicious in character. If the malice is fraud, however, a *tort* (civil wrong) has been committed and punitive damages can be awarded on the tort of fraud.

Recovery of the nonbreaching party's *attorneys' fees* from the breaching party usually is not allowed as damages in breach-of-contract cases. This applies to the nonbreaching party's costs of litigating against the breaching party. If the attorneys' fees instead were part of the losses stemming from the breach, such as the attorneys' costs for doing a title search and issuing an opinion about the title, the attorneys' fees would be recoverable as compensatory damages.

Mitigation and minimization of damages

In reference to damage awards, the courts use the terms *mitigation* and *minimization* interchangeably. The law makes a distinction between the two terms, however. **Mitigation of damages** refers to a *reduction in the dollar damage figure* the breaching party owes, because of some extenuating circumstances in favor of the breaching party. **Minimization of damages** refers to a *duty imposed upon the nonbreaching party to prevent the damage figure from going higher,* by exercising reasonable care.

Minimization of damages is what occurs most frequently in a real estate contract problem. The law requires that the party who has suffered from breach of contract not sit idly by and let damages continue to accumulate. This party must make reasonable efforts to keep the monetary amount of damages down. This nonbreaching party has no obligation to incur further expense to minimize damages, however.

FOR EXAMPLE

A common example in real estate purchase contract cases occurs when a purchaser states that she is not going to perform the purchase contract and thereby will fail to close the transaction. The seller sometimes sues the breaching party for money damages. The seller must exercise some caution under the minimization of damages theory, however. Thus, the seller could not sell the house for $30,000 when the breaching party had entered the purchase contract for $90,000 and when it was reasonable to expect a willing purchaser to pay much more than $30,000.

There would appear to be a duty on the part of the seller to put the realty on the market again to minimize damages, even if for a lesser figure. If the seller receives a lesser price on the second arm's-length sale, the court can award the difference between the two sales prices as compensatory damages, even if the breaching purchaser-party paid beyond fair-market value for the real estate.

Liquidated damages

Liquidated damages represents an *amount of money stipulated by the parties within a contract as an amount a breaching party forfeits to the nonbreaching party.* Two questions of critical importance are: Is the figure a penalty instead of liquidated damages? Can the nonbreaching party recover actual damages if he or she keeps the liquidated ones? Neither of these questions is easily answered.

A court will enforce the provision to pay a certain dollar figure as liquidated damages unless the court construes the provision to be a penalty. The modern trend is to construe these provisions as penalties. To rebut this trend, the nonbreaching party proves the amount is liquidated damages by showing that the sum is reasonably proportionate to the loss, that the contract's construction shows the parties intend to settle in that contract the damages that probably would flow from its breach, and that it is hard to fix a dollar amount on the actual damages.

These uncertainties create a problem in the real estate purchase contract, with the retention of the earnest money as liquidated damages in the event of breach of contract by purchasers. The best way to avoid a problem with construing a disallowance of compensatory damages by retaining liquidated damages is to clearly allow the additional recovery of compensatory damages if one party retains the liquidated damages. Perhaps showing a liquidated damage figure as the minimum that compensatory damages would run would also help settle the uncertainties. In addition, an experienced attorney can draft a liquidated damage clause that is enforceable; the broker and the parties can consult counsel regarding this issue.

Equitable conversion and specific performance

From the time of execution forward, the doctrine of **equitable conversion** applies to a real estate purchase contract. This doctrine gives the *purchaser an interest in real property and the seller an interest in personal property.* The purchaser has equitable title, whereas the seller has legal title.

Instead of damages, or in addition to them, the law of contracts allows for the equitable doctrine of **specific performance** to act as relief when a party fails to perform a real estate purchase contract.

FOR EXAMPLE

Sellers of the real property fail to perform the purchase contract by refusing to convey title to purchasers. Purchasers then ask the court to order sellers to specifically perform that contract. The court orders that sellers convey the subject real property to purchasers. If sellers thereafter refuse to convey the realty to purchasers, the court may find sellers in contempt. It then may jail and fine sellers until they convey. Alternatively, the court may issue a decree that can act as a conveyance and thereby pass title to purchasers.

The philosophy behind granting specific performance is that *real property is unique,* and that no amount of monetary damages can ever replace the uniqueness of the real property. Because equity actions always appeal to the court's sense of rightness and fairness, the party bringing the specific performance action (in the example given, purchasers) cannot be guilty of any material wrongdoing. Thus, if purchasers defrauded sellers in some way, for example, in connection with this transaction, purchasers will not be granted the court's equitable relief. Theoretically, specific performance is also available to sellers, but as a practical matter, ordering purchasers to purchase a particular real property is difficult.

A practical advantage of equity (specific performance) over law (damages) is *speed.* When suing for money damages under a breach of contract theory, the plaintiff may wait years on the civil docket for the case to be heard and determined. The philosophy of the courts, however, is that equity should work quickly. Thus, a court may conduct a hearing on specific performance within just one or a few months from filing the suit. At that time, the court will determine only the specific performance issue. If there are damage issues in addition to the specific performance claim, these will be determined at a later time when they come up on the civil docket.

Purchasers also may transfer equitable title interest to another. The equitable interest continues up to the time of transfer of title. Then purchasers receive actual, legal title to the real property and sellers receive personalty, the money paid for the real property.

Rescission

If both parties want to opt out of the contract, they can do so simply by having a *mutual agreement in which they both terminate the contract,* called **rescission.** The consideration making rescission binding on the parties is their mutual surrender of rights under the original agreement. Rescission also takes place when the parties enter into a new contract that substitutes for the old. One party may rescind a contract when the other party does not perform or defaults. If one elects rescission, however, that party cannot sue for breach of contract. The party may choose one but not both. Also, if neither party performs or if both parties abandon the contract, rescission occurs.

Rescission is *also equitable relief granted by the court to remedy actual or constructive fraud,* which is misstatement of a material fact either with or without an intent to do so. We shall use the real estate purchase contract as an example.

FOR EXAMPLE

When purchasers enter into a contract in which sellers were guilty of actual or constructive fraud (e.g., didn't disclose termite infestation of the realty), nonfraudulent purchasers are entitled to have the purchase contract rescinded. The court will void the purchase contract and order restitution, that is, return title to sellers and the purchase funds to purchasers.

As in all equitable doctrines, the party asking the court for the relief by rescission must do so when discovering the grounds for rescission—when the purchasers discover they have been defrauded. Rescission also is available when an undisclosed dual agency has occurred on the part of the realty agent (the agent has represented both purchasers and sellers in a transaction without informing both of same). Rescission is available also when the Ohio Residential Property Disclosure Form is not used correctly. We fully discuss both dual agency and the disclosure form in Chapter 9.

Reformation

Reformation is *making the contract over.* The parties may do this by mutual agreement. Courts sometimes reform contracts, too. For example, the court allows parol evidence because the contract is ambiguous. The court discovers by the parol evidence the intent of the parties, reforms the written instrument, and enforces it accordingly.

FRAUD, DURESS, UNDUE INFLUENCE, MUTUAL MISTAKE

Fraud, duress, undue influence, and mutual mistake are all *grounds for voiding a contract.* The actual cases show that even though one party appears to be agreeing to the contract, the presence of one of these other elements demonstrates that it is *not a free or accurately informed agreement.* These grounds are difficult to prove, and the cases typically reflect severe circumstances.

Actual fraud is *misrepresentation of a material fact, made with an intent to deceive coupled with actual deception, and damage* occurring from a party's reliance on the deception. The fraud should go to the essence, or heart, of the contract and not be on some collateral or minor point instead. **Constructive fraud** has all the same elements *except the intent is missing.* It usually is difficult for plaintiffs to prove that the defrauding party intended to defraud them, so there are more successful cases based in constructive fraud than in actual fraud. With either kind of fraud, the court can rescind the contract and restore everyone to the position they were in before entering into the contract. Fraud and misrepresentation are discussed in detail in Chapter 9.

Undue influence occurs when *one person dominates another,* usually a far weaker person, such as an adult child over an elderly parent. **Duress** means *coercing anyone by threat or force.* The two concepts are closely related and tend to blur in actual sales scenarios. Both are grounds for rescission of the contract by the dominated or coerced party. Undue influence or duress is not a persuasive sales argument, whereas threats made to force a person into a contract are.

Salespersons at times may get caught up in their sales talk and end up spending hours at the offerees' house. A salesperson should avoid particularly prolonged, late-night sit-ins. Salespersons should be especially careful with elderly people, as it takes less to establish a duress or undue influence case with them. Other, younger family members might be encouraged to be present during the presentation of the offer to avoid a later claim of duress.

Mutual mistake also can be grounds to nullify a contract. The parties to the contract each make *an honest mistake about an essential term of the contract.* For example, both parties make a mistake by inserting the wrong real property in the contract. This destroys the requisite meeting of minds, or mutuality of intent, needed for the formation of a contract. Mistake by one party only is not enough, unless the mistake is clearly obvious to the other party as well.

The remedy for fraud, undue influence, duress, and mutual mistake is rescission; the court voids the contract and restores the parties to the positions they were originally in before they entered into the contract. Table 6–3 compares the arguments for upholding contracts and for getting them set aside.

TABLE 6–3 Arguments for upholding contracts and for getting contracts set aside.

ARGUMENTS FOR HAVING CONTRACTS DECLARED VOID, UNENFORCEABLE, OR ELIGIBLE FOR RESCISSION	ARGUMENTS FOR UPHOLDING/ENFORCING CONTRACTS
1. Minority of claiming party.	1. No argument if minority claim is true.
2. Undue influence by other party.	2. Free will of claiming party.
3. Duress by other party.	3. Free will of claiming party.
4. Mutual mistake by both parties.	4. Unilateral mistake by one party.
5. Fraud by other party.	5. Innocent representation by this party.
6. Insanity by claiming party.	6. Some chance for argument if this party couldn't detect insanity and changed his or her position.
7. Undisclosed dual agency of real estate broker.	7. No argument if this can be proven.
8. Objective impossibility of performance.	8. Subjective impossibility of performance.
9. Contract is oral and is within the statute of frauds.	9. Contract has been partly performed.
10. No consideration.	10. Promissory estoppel.

CASE STUDY FROM THE OHIO SUPREME COURT

LATINA V. WOODPATH DEVELOPMENT CO.
57 Ohio St.3d 212, 567 N.E. 2d 262 (1991)

Facts: Home builder Latina was given a right of first refusal by Woodpath Development in its Phase I but not its Phase II developments of residential property in Westlake, Ohio. A right of first refusal is a promise to present offers to buy properties made by third parties to the promisee in order to afford the promisee the opportunity to match the offer. In Woodpath Development Phase III, there was a letter by Woodpath to Latina, in 1984, which said in part, "Woodpath will offer to sell part or all of Phase III to Mr. Latina. . . . Latina shall have the first right to purchase (or refusal to purchase) lots in Phase III. . . ."

Subsequently, Woodpath met with Latina and offered him the opportunity to purchase Phase III lots for $42,000 per lot. Latina countered by offering first $35,000 and then $40,000 for each lot but would go no higher without seeing another builder's offer to purchase at $42,000. Woodpath subsequently accepted another builder's offer for $42,000 per lot without presenting the offer to Latina. Latina sued Woodpath for breach of contract, alleging that Woodpath had given him a right of first refusal on those lots.

Trial Court: Judgment for builder. Developer appealed.

Court of Appeals: Reversed trial court. Builder appealed.

Issue: Whether the 1984 letter from Woodpath to Latina offered a right of first refusal to Latina or, instead, a first opportunity to purchase lots from Woodpath.

Held by the Ohio Supreme Court: The language in the 1984 letter was not ambiguous, that Woodpath offered a "first opportunity to purchase" to Latina, which must be construed by its ordinary meaning. This is different from a right of first refusal to purchase. Woodpath met this obligation by the opportunity it afforded Latina to make an offer at $42,000 in their meeting together.

CASE STUDY FROM THE OHIO SUPREME COURT

REILLEY V. RICHARDS
69 Ohio St.3d 352, 632 N.E.2d 507 (1994).

Facts: Purchaser intended to build his family home on the real property he purchased, which was located at the end of a cul-de-sac. He was not informed before closing that a significant portion of the property was located in a floodplain. Both parties testified at trial that at the time of contracting they were unaware the property was in a floodplain. The builder testified that he would not be able to warrant the building for one year, as is his custom, because it would be located within a floodplain. An engineer testified that more than half the property is in the flood hazard zone. One could not discover that the property was in a floodplain just by looking at it. Purchaser had drafted the contract so that he had a sixty-day escape clause from the contract to satisfy himself that "all soil, engineering, utility and other site related considerations were acceptable." Purchaser voiced no objection during that sixty-day period.

Trial Court: Judged in favor of purchaser on rescission claim.

Court of Appeals: Reversed the trial court; in favor of seller.

Issue: Whether a real estate contract should be rescinded if there is a mutual mistake as to the character of the real estate that was material to the contract and if the complaining party was not negligent in failing to discover the mistake.

Held by the Ohio Supreme Court: That purchaser's and seller's failures to appreciate that significant portion of property was located within a floodplain was mutual mistake that would permit purchaser to rescind the agreement. This was a material term to the contract, i.e., a basic assumption on which the contract was made. The sixty-day escape clause did not mean that the purchaser assumed a duty to discover the floodplain, so he was not negligent. The contract was rescinded.

Section I Summary of Content

1. A contract is an agreement between two or more parties that is legally enforceable.
2. Executory contracts contain promises that still must be performed. Executed contracts are those in which all promises have been performed.
3. Express contracts are those in which the parties agree to mutual obligations by words, either orally or in writing.
4. Implied contracts occur when, by the relationship between the parties and the facts in the case, the law implies that a contract has been formed.
5. The statute of frauds requires some contracts, especially those concerning land, to be in writing. Part performance of an oral contract is an exception to the statute of frauds.
6. The elements necessary to form a valid contract are offer, acceptance, and consideration. The offer and acceptance make up the actual agreement; consideration is the mutual exchange of promises or acts of benefit and detriment between the parties.
7. The first step in forming a contract is for an offeror to propose terms for a particular transaction to an offeree.
8. The next step is for the offeree to accept those terms.
9. A counteroffer occurs when offerees change any of the terms of the offer and send those counter proposals back to the other party as their offer.
10. If a party is making inquiries during negotiations, rather than actually changing terms, that is not sufficient to terminate the offer.
11. When an offeree *adds* terms to an offer, which already exist or are implied within the offer, the offeree has accepted the offer.
12. Death and destruction can terminate the power to accept an offer.

13. An effective acceptance occurs when offerees communicate or deliver acceptance to offerors, or their agent, by word, sign, writing, or act.
14. Consideration is the final element necessary to form a contract. Both parties must promise to do something they are not legally obliged to do, or they must refrain from doing something they are not legally obliged to refrain from doing. Any detriment, no matter how small, usually will do as consideration.
15. Irrevocable counteroffers are usually defective, void option contracts because they are missing consideration.
16. Addenda to previously formed contracts must have their own consideration.
17. Conditional promises can be sufficient for consideration (e.g., approval of financing by a lending institution).
18. Executed contracts cannot be set aside because they lack consideration, as they are fully performed contracts.
19. Promissory estoppel prevents a wrongdoing party from escaping from performing according to his or her promise because the contract lacked consideration. The innocent party must have acted to his or her detriment because of the wrongdoer's promise.
20. Earnest money is a small portion of the purchase price that purchasers put down, in advance, at the time they make an offer, to demonstrate sincerity. It is not consideration, and it is not needed to form a valid contract.
21. All real estate contracts have parties, i.e., those persons bound to perform the promises within the contract.
22. The parties to the listing contract are the broker and the sellers.
23. The listing contract is a bilateral contract in which both brokers and sellers owe reciprocal, executory obligations to one another. They both promise something. The sellers promise to pay the broker a commission in exchange for the sellers' promising the broker a listing of the realty.
24. The parties to a real estate purchase contract are the sellers and the purchasers. It, too, is bilateral because both parties to it promise to do something. The sellers promise to convey title to the realty in exchange for the purchasers' promise to pay them money.
25. The sellers and the purchasers are parties to the real estate option contract. It is a unilateral contract because one person makes a promise to induce an act (i.e., sellers agree to sell their realty to purchasers only if purchasers decide to purchase the realty within the option period of time).
26. Contracts often are categorized by whether they are or are not enforceable.
27. An enforceable contract is binding and cannot be broken.
28. A voidable contract is one in which one party may legally elect to avoid performing the contract.
29. An unenforceable contract is one that is missing whatever is required to make it legal.
30. A void contract is no contract whatsoever.
31. Some people cannot enter into a binding contract because they lack the capacity to contract.
32. Minors can enter into binding contracts but, because they lack capacity, that contract is voidable at the minor's election and not at the election of the other, adult party.

33. A contract entered into by a party who is mentally infirm is generally voidable at the infirm person's option (as exercised by his or her court-appointed guardian).
34. If a person has been adjudicated insane and committed through probate court, or severely chemically dependent and committed through probate court, the contract is usually void.
35. A person usually must be a party to a contract before taking any rights or responsibilities under it.
36. The recent trend is to expand the category of persons who have the right to sue (standing) based on rights derived from an original party to the contract. This gives rights in a contract to persons who are not parties to it.
37. Under the parol evidence rule, when there is a final and complete writing, a total integration of the parties' agreement or contract, such contract may not be contradicted or supplemented by evidence of prior agreements or expressions.
38. If a court needs to interpret a contract, it will use rules of construction. These rules strive to find the true intent of the parties and to uphold the whole contract, not just parts.
39. Conditions within contracts excuse performance when the condition cannot be fulfilled. An act must take place before a duty of performance of a promise arises.
40. Conditions weaken any real estate purchase contract.
41. Objective impossibility of performance of an unforeseen act, which makes performance by anyone in the world, not just a party, impossible, excuses performance of a contract. Personal impossibility, which affects only a party, and foreseen acts are not excuses but breaches of contract.
42. If performance is delegable, excuse of performance, under the impossibility of performance defense, will not prevail. If the contract is for personal services, performance is not delegable and the defense will apply.
43. Rights under a contract can be assigned from one party to another wherein one party transfers his or her rights, duties, and obligations to a third person.
44. Novation occurs when a new contract is substituted for an old, preexisting one.
45. Accord and satisfaction substitutes the performance of new promises to satisfy the obligations of a preexisting contract.
46. Breach of contract arises when a party to a contract does not perform his or her promises under a contract. Anticipatory repudiation is a breach of contract in advance. Both are the basis for lawsuits.
47. Legal damages and equitable relief both are allowed by the courts in breach of contract lawsuits.
48. Compensatory damages are those that place the aggrieved party in the economic position he or she would have been in had the breach of contract not occurred.
49. Mitigation of damages is a reduction in the dollar damage figure owed by the breaching party because of extenuating circumstances. Minimization of damages is a duty imposed upon the nonbreaching party to prevent the damage figure from going higher by exercising reasonable care.
50. Liquidated damages is an amount of money stipulated by the parties within a contract as an amount a breaching party forfeits to the nonbreaching party.
51. The doctrine of equitable conversion applies from the time the real estate purchase contract is executed, giving purchasers an interest in real property and sellers an interest in personal property. Purchasers have equitable title, whereas sellers have legal title.

52. Under the doctrine of equitable conversion, purchasers can use specific performance, an equitable action in which the court can order the contract performed and thus the realty conveyed to purchasers.
53. The court has the power to rescind a contract, restore the parties to their former positions, or reform it (make it over).
54. Fraud, duress, undue influence, and mutual mistake are all legal grounds for rescinding a contract based on extremities of influence and misleading acts.

SECTION II

PRACTICAL MATERIALS

FORM CONTRACTS

As a key part of their function, brokers and salespeople fill in the form real estate listing contract and the purchase contract as well as promissory notes for the earnest money. The form real estate contracts within this chapter show the essential elements that these documents usually contain. The student should be aware, however, that brokers vary in the form contracts they use, as do attorneys. After becoming a practicing real estate salesperson, the student will be reading and handling many different form contracts, not only their own brokers' form contracts. Typically, for example, when an offer is submitted by a broker other than the listing broker, the salesperson for the listing broker then handles the other broker's form real estate purchase contract. That contract might differ somewhat from the listing broker's own contract.

Over a course of time, then, students/agents will become familiar with many form real estate contracts. Typically, learning the first form is the most difficult because everything in it is alien. Once students/agents understand one form well, though, they usually are able to learn other forms more easily. Many of the clauses are the same.

A broker's or salesperson's filling in the blanks within these form contracts usually does not present a problem of practicing law without a license, which is a serious legal offense. Practitioners should limit themselves, as far as is reasonably possible, to filling in the blanks on the printed forms. If purchasers or sellers desire fuller legal assistance or advice, salespeople or brokers should not hesitate to recommend that they seek an attorney's advice.

Listing Contract

Refer to Figure 6–5 when reading this explanation. The *first paragraph* in the sample listing contract recites its consideration: that the real estate company will use its professional skills, including a multiple listing service, in exchange for listing the property with the company. As a gross listing, the broker's commission is computed from the total gross selling price. It also establishes the agency as an exclusive right to sell type; this real estate broker will receive a commission upon sale of this realty, regardless of who procures the sale (discussed further in Chapter 9).

The *second paragraph* pertains entirely to protecting the real estate broker's commission. A seller who rents or exchanges the real property owes the broker a commission on the value of that rental or exchange. The statement about the commission being negotiable and the blank percentage negate complaints about the broker's attempting to price-fix (combine in restraint in trade in violation of federal law, Chapter 9 covers this in full). The salesperson also inserts the percentage rate agreeable to both broker and sellers.

The listing contract also states that if a prospective purchaser sees the real property while it is listed with The Real Estate Company, the sellers will owe The Real

FIGURE 6–5
Sample listing contract.

The Real Estate Company

Exclusive Right to Sell Listing Agreement

In consideration of The Real Estate Company's agreement to use its efforts to secure a purchaser for the subject real property and to list it with the subscribers of the Multiple Listing Service, the owner(s) of said realty grant The Real Estate Company the sole and exclusive right to sell the realty for a period of *(insert no.)* days from *(insert date)* up to and including *(insert date)* real property known as *(insert address)* for the sum of *(insert asking price)* gross, payable to owners in cash or at any price, terms or exchange to which the owner(s) consent.

If the Real Estate Company is successful in securing a purchaser for the subject property, or if it is sold, leased, or rented during the period of the exclusive right to sell, or within *(insert no.)* days thereafter to anyone with whom The Real Estate Company or any cooperating broker have negotiated thereon during the period of this agreement, the owner(s) agree to pay The Real Estate Company and any cooperating broker a commission of *(insert no.)* percent based upon the price of which the subject realty may be sold, leased, exchanged, or rented. The owners are herein advised that real estate companies may not set or "fix" commission rates between or among themselves. Thus, an owner(s) may be able to negotiate the best commission rate by comparing rates between or among real estate companies.

The owner(s) agree to refer to The Real Estate Company all brokers or prospective purchasers who make direct contact and to furnish The Real Estate Company with their names and addresses if known.

In the event of sale, the owner(s) will convey the subject real property by general warranty deed or fiduciary deed with release of dower rights, if any, and will furnish good, sufficient, marketable title.

Accepted by: The Real Estate Company
100 Main Street
Anytown, Ohio
Date:
By: *(real estate agent's signature)*, its agent.

The undersigned accept the terms of the above agreement and acknowledge receipt of a copy of this agreement. The owner(s) understand that the signature of any spouse is required for this agreement, the subsequent real estate purchase contract, and other legal documents, as needed to complete any transaction on the subject realty.

(signature)__________________ *Date* (signature)__________________ *Date*
Owner Owner
Address__________________ Phone__________________

Owner(s) to state capacity:__________________
(record owner; executor; administrator; trustee, guardian, attorney in fact)

Estate Company a commission if the sellers sell the realty to those purchasers, either during the listing period or the designated period thereafter. Prospective purchasers who do not see the realty while it is listed with The Real Estate Company are not within the scope of the listing contract, however.

The *third paragraph* requires that sellers report to The Real Estate Company any brokers or prospective purchasers who contact them directly. All purchasers must go through the broker, because this is an exclusive right-to-sell listing contract. (Sellers retain no right to sell the real property on their own.)

The *fourth paragraph* requires that sellers furnish a general warranty or fiduciary deed conveying marketable title. If sellers are unable to produce such a deed when the broker has an asking price offer, the sellers are in breach of their listing contract and owe the broker a commission. Sellers also are responsible for obtaining their spouses' relinquishment of any dower rights in the real estate, without which marketable title cannot be obtained.

The Real Estate Company is the actual party to the contract. Its name follows the acceptance. The *salesperson signs* after the "By" to signify that he or she is *accepting on behalf of the brokerage as its agent.*

When obtaining a listing from a married couple as sellers, both the husband's and the wife's signatures usually are necessary, even if title is in only one of their names. This is because spouses have dower rights in their husband's or wife's real estate. The signatures of both husband and wife on the listing contract ultimately can be used to force a spouse to relinquish dower in all subsequent documents, such as the real estate purchase contract and deed. If the spouse refuses to so consent, yet has signed the listing contract, that spouse is in breach of the listing contract, which puts the broker in a strong legal position for collecting the commission.

Real Estate Purchase Contract

When reading this explanation, refer to Figure 6–6.

Clause 1 requires the full, correct legal names of the buyer.

Clause 2 stipulates inserting the county of the subject real property. After the phrase "located at," insert the street address. After "and being further described as" a very basic description, such as "a single-family dwelling with attached garage" should be inserted.

The phrase "buyer accepts in its PRESENT CONDITION . . ." is the first mention in this contract that the purchaser is taking this realty in its existing condition, that is, subject to any *existing problems or defects.* (Other clauses in this contract give the purchaser an opportunity to discover defects and give the seller an opportunity to disclose defects or problems that exist in the realty. These clauses are placed in form real estate purchase contracts to eliminate hidden defect and/or fraud and misrepresentation lawsuits that have inundated brokers, as discussed in detail in Chapter 9).

The remainder of this clause covers *fixtures* (real property, which stays with the realty) and *chattels* (personal property, which is subject to removal). This method of treatment makes it easier for a salesperson to include all potentially troublesome items. First, there is a listing of items that almost always stay with the realty. Then, instead of a salesperson's having to specifically insert many items for both purchaser and seller to retain, the salesperson checks off which items are to stay with the realty. If they are not checked off, they do not stay. Furthermore, unless there is an insertion on excepted window treatments, all window treatments stay with the realty. There is also limited space for the agent to insert any chattels or fixtures not covered in this otherwise exhaustive treatment of all the items typically found in today's real properties.

Clause 3, in conjunction with clause 2, shows the *consideration,* or money, the purchaser will pay in exchange for the real property. It also employs a complete *price breakdown* scheme in which the following must be specified: total purchase price, amount of earnest money, balance of the down payment, and the amount of the mortgage loan and a check-off portion for whether it is to be a conventional, an FHA, or a VA mortgage loan. The reason the type of loan is specified is that sellers receive a different amount of proceeds and/or duties based on the type of loan. With an FHA or a VA loan, for example, sellers may have to pay points or make expensive repairs to the real estate, or both. Days also are specifically defined in this clause so there can be no argument as to how the number of days should be calculated.

FIGURE 6–6 Sample purchase contract.

PURCHASE AGREEMENT

EQUAL HOUSING OPPORTUNITY

1-BUYER: The undersigned ____________________
(hereinafter "BUYER") offers to buy the following-described property.

2-PROPERTY: Situated in the ____________ of ____________, County of ____________,
and State of Ohio;
and located at ____________________
and being further described as a ____________________.
Permanent Parcel No. or Tax I.D. No. ____________

The property, which BUYER accepts in its PRESENT CONDITION, except for normal wear and tear before Title Transfer, and except as specifically set forth hereinafter, shall include the land and all appurtenant rights, privileges and easements, (subject to all rights of tenants, if any), and all buildings and fixtures, including without limitation, *all* of the following as are now on the property: electrical, heating, cooling, plumbing and bathroom fixtures; window and door shades, blinds, awnings, screens, storm windows, curtain and drapery fixtures; landscaping; disposals; TV antennas, rotor control units and built-in TV and videotape wiring; smoke alarms; security systems; garage door openers and controls; radiator covers; permanently attached carpeting;
( )ranges and ovens; ( )microwave ovens; ( )dishwashers; ( )refrigerators; ( )window air conditioners;
( )water softeners; ( )gas grills; ( )satellite TV reception systems;

FIREPLACE ( )tools, ( )screens, ( )glass doors, ( )grates; ( )washers, ( )dryers; and all existing window treatments,
EXCEPT these window treatments: ____________________
Also INCLUDED: ____________________
NOT included: ____________________

3-PRICE: For which BUYER shall pay owner of said property (hereinafter "SELLER")----$ ____________
payable as follows:

(A) Earnest Money to be paid to the REAL ESTATE COMPANY, as agent for SELLER, to be deposited upon acceptance of final offer in the REAL ESTATE COMPANY'S Trust Account and credited against the purchase price:

------------( )check ( )note ( )cash--$ ____________
IF A NOTE--TO BE REDEEMED WITHIN FOUR DAYS OF ACCEPTANCE OF CONTRACT.
FURTHER, IT IS AGREED THAT WHEREVER THE WORD "DAYS" APPEARS HEREIN, SUCH SHALL REFER TO CALENDAR DAYS, WITH ALL SUNDAYS AND NATIONAL HOLIDAYS NOT BEING COUNTED.
(B) Remainder of BUYER'S downpayment, to be deposited in escrow
as per paragraph 5. hereinafter---$ ____________
(C) Balance in the form of a Mortgage Loan
------------( )conventional ( )FHA ( )VA ( )OTHER--$ ____________

____

____________________$ ____________

4-FINANCING: This transaction is conditioned upon BUYER obtaining the mortgage loan financing referred to above. BUYER shall make a written application for such financing within ______ days from contract acceptance date and shall obtain a commitment for such loan on or about ____________, 19______. If despite BUYER'S good faith efforts, BUYER cannot obtain such loan commitment, or one for a lesser sum but still acceptable to BUYER, then this Agreement shall be NULL AND VOID and the following shall occur promptly:

BUYER and SELLER shall enter into a written Mutual Release from this transaction, directing the return of the earnest money deposit, or SELLER shall sign an Authorization directing the REAL ESTATE COMPANY to return said earnest money deposit to BUYER. After the execution of same, neither buyer, seller, nor any real estate broker or agent having anything to do with this transaction shall have any liability or obligation to the other(s) stemming from same. (This procedure is referred to hereinafter as "the TERMINATION PROCEDURE.")

5-CLOSING: (choose *one* of the following)

(A) Escrow- All documents, funds, and financial institution commitments for funds necessary to the completion of this transaction shall be placed in escrow with any local Lending Institution, or with any local Title Company on or before ____________,19______ and Title shall transfer to BUYER on or about but not before ____________, 19______;
EXCEPT, if a defect in Title appears, SELLER shall have thirty (30) days after notice to SELLER to remove such defect, and being unable to do so, BUYER may agree to accept Title subject to such defect without any reduction in said purchase price, or may terminate this Agreement and, thereupon, receive the return of all deposits made hereunder, as per the TERMINATION PROCEDURE, set forth in foregoing paragraph 4.

(B) Formal - All documents, funds, and financial institution commitments for funds necessary to the completion of this transaction shall be brought to a formal "sit-down" closing by the parties and their respective representatives and agents to be held at
____________________ Ohio
on the ______ day of ____________, 19______ at ____________ AM/PM, at which time Title shall transfer to BUYER. However, if a defect in Title appears during such attempted closing, SELLER shall have thirty (30) days thereafter to reschedule such closing and to remove such defect, and being unable to do so, BUYER may agree to accept

(continued)

FIGURE 6–6 Continued.

Title subject to such defect, without any reduction in said purchase price, or may terminate this Agreement and, thereupon, receive the return of all deposits made hereunder, as per the TERMINATION PROCEDURE, set forth in foregoing paragraph 4.

6-POSSESSION: SELLER shall deliver possession of the property to BUYER within________days* after the date of Title Transfer,
or on__________________, 19_____, whichever is LATER. The first__________days of said period shall be rental free
and the balance (if any) shall be at $________________ per day, not to exceed__________days, after which time SELLER shall become a tenant at sufferance and subject to eviction. *Days in the case of this paragraph 6., and this paragraph *only*, shall refer to consecutive calendar days, with all Sundays and Holidays being counted.

7-TITLE: SELLER shall convey a marketable title to BUYER by General Warranty Deed and/or Fiduciary Deed, if required, with all dower rights released, free and clear of all liens and encumbrances whatsoever, except (a) any mortgage assumed by BUYER/GRANTEE, (b) all restrictions, reservations, easements (however created), covenants, and conditions of record, (c) all of the following as do not materially and adversely affect the use or value of the property: encroachments, oil, gas and mineral leases, (d) zoning ordinances, if any, and (e) taxes and assessments, both general and special, not currently due and payable.

SELLER shall furnish a Title Guarantee, in the amount of said purchase price, showing record Title to be good in BUYER/GRANTEE, subject to the deed exceptions set forth hereinabove, and any title policy exceptions, to be issued by a Title Company acceptable to SELLER. Should BUYER desire, he may obtain an Owner's Title Insurance Commitment and Policy [ALTA Form B (1970 REV. 10-17-70 & REV. 10-17-84)], or other similar title insurance, so long as he pays the increased premium due because of such additional coverage. If the property is Torrenized, SELLER shall furnish, in lieu of the foregoing, an Owner's Duplicate Certificate of Title, together with a United States Court Search and Tax Search. Where required by ordinance, SELLER shall order a code inspection and shall deposit the results at closing.

8-PRORATIONS: Any of the following as exist -- General taxes, special assessments, Homeowners' Association Fees or other similar fees, city/county or other local charges, and tenant rents -- shall be prorated at closing as of date of Title Transfer. Taxes and assessments shall be prorated based on the latest available tax duplicate. BUYER and SELLER shall prorate and adjust directly any changes in taxes resulting either from a change in valuation and/or tax rate occurring before Title Transfer, or from existing but not yet assessed improvements. Utility charges shall be paid by SELLERS to the date of Title Transfer, or the date of exchange of possession, whichever is LATER; also, the Closing Agent shall withhold the sum of $______________ from SELLER'S proceeds to secure payment of final water and sewer charges, if any, unless SELLER submits proof of payment of such.

9-CHARGES: SELLER shall pay the following costs at closing: (a) cost of title exam and Title Guarantee premium, (b) cost to prepare Deed, (c) amount due to discharge any lien encumbering the property and the cost of recording the cancellation thereof, (d) Real Estate Transfer Tax, (e) cost for inspections and certificates required by public authorities, (f) prorations due BUYER, (g) real estate commissions due brokers, and (h) one-half the closing fee, or the full closing fee should FHA or VA regulations prohibit payment of such by BUYER. If, at time of transfer of utilities to BUYER, a defect is detected in any of the main utility service supply lines on the property, SELLER shall pay all costs for the repair of such, either directly, or at closing.

BUYER shall pay the following costs at closing: (a) cost of filing the Deed for record, (b) one-half of the closing fee (when not prohibited by FHA or VA regulations), (c) any cost incident to BUYER'S obtaining financing, (d) costs of any inspections required by BUYER as conditions of this Agreement, and (e) the additional premium cost for any Title Insurance policy that was provided.

10-DAMAGE: If any buildings or other improvements are damaged or destroyed prior to Title Transfer in excess of ten percent of said purchase price, BUYER may either accept any insurance proceeds payable on account thereof as full compensation therefor, or may terminate this agreement and receive return of all deposits made hereunder. For all damage and destruction valued as less than ten percent of said purchase price, SELLER shall restore the property to its condition as of contract acceptance date.

11-CONDITION OF PROPERTY:

BUYER acknowledges that it has been recommended to him that he engage, at his expense, the services of a professional contractor or building inspector to inspect the property and all improvements to ascertain that the condition of the property is as called for in this Agreement. BUYER further acknowledges that no broker or any agent having anything to do with this transaction has made any verbal, or other statements or representations concerning the property on which BUYER has relied, except as specifically set forth in writing herein. BUYER has examined the property and agrees that the property is being purchased in its present "as is" condition, including any defects that may have been disclosed by SELLER either specifically hereon or by attached addendum. BUYER acknowledges that he has not relied on any representations, warranties or statements whatsoever concerning the property, including without limitation its use or condition, other than as written in this Agreement.

12-SPECIFIC DISCLOSURES: BUYER has relied on the following additional specific disclosures and/or representations in making this Agreement: (IF NONE, WRITE "NONE")

____

Said specific disclosures and/or representations were made by____________________________

13-SELLER'S REPRESENTATIONS: Seller states that he has no knowledge of any hidden or latent defects on the property, including without limitation, any of the following: water seepage; basement foundation or wall wetness (or dampness); bathroom or kitchen leakage; roof leakage; problems with electrical, plumbing, heating, cooling, sewer, septic, well or water systems; structural defects; or faulty major appliances, EXCEPT: (IF NONE, WRITE "NONE")

____

14-INSPECTION CONDITIONS: This Agreement shall be subject to all of the following checked Inspections, which Inspections shall be paid for by BUYER, carried out in good faith by all parties, and completed within the times specified. These Inspections shall be either approved or disapproved by BUYER in writing within said times and if disapproved, this Agreement shall become NULL AND VOID and subject to the TERMINATION PROCEDURE, as set forth in foregoing paragraph 4. (IF NONE, WRITE "NONE")__________

( ) A. GENERAL HOME INSPECTION The property shall be inspected by a general home inspector, construction person, professional property inspector, or other person of BUYER'S choice within_________days from final acceptance hereof.

( ) B. WELL OPERATION AND WELL WATER TEST The well system shall be inspected by a qualified inspector of BUYER'S choice (whose findings would be acceptable to County or other water authorities) for both (1) adequate flow rate and equipment operation and (2) potability, within_________days from final acceptance hereof.

( ) C. SEPTIC SYSTEM INSPECTION The septic or other on-site sanitation system shall be inspected by a qualified inspector of BUYER'S choice (whose findings would be acceptable to County or other sanitary authorities) within_________days from final acceptance hereof. SELLER shall pay the cost of sanitation system *cleaning*, if necessary for Inspection.

( ) D. TERMITE/WOOD-DESTROYING INSECT INSPECTION The property shall be inspected by a licensed pest control inspector of BUYER'S choice within_________days from final acceptance hereof.

NOTE -- Should FHA or VA Regulations prohibit payment by BUYER of the cost of any of the foregoing INSPECTIONS, SELLER shall pay the cost thereof.

WAIVER

Should BUYER fail to have any of the above Inspections completed within the times specified, OR IF BUYER FAILS TO SPECIFICALLY APPROVE OR DISAPPROVE ANY INSPECTIONS WITHIN THE TIMES SPECIFIED, then BUYER shall be deemed to have WAIVED SUCH INSPECTIONS and shall be considered as HAVING ACCEPTED THE PROPERTY ABSOLUTELY AND FINALLY IN ITS PRESENT "AS IS" CONDITION, and neither SELLER nor any real estate broker or agent having anything to do with this transaction shall have any further liability or obligation to BUYER as to such Inspections or Agreement Conditions.

Should the results of any of such Inspections not be satisfactory to BUYER then, within the times specified, BUYER shall notify either SELLER or SELLER'S LISTING BROKERAGE in writing of his specific dissatisfaction, at which point the TERMINATION PROCEDURE set forth in foregoing paragraph 4. shall apply.

15-ADDENDA: This Agreement is subject to the additional terms and conditions as set forth in the attached Addenda, hereby made a part hereof, and described as: ( )AGENCY, ( )HOME SALE, ( )FHA/VA, ( )CONDO, ( )OTHER

16-HOME WARRANTY: ( ) If checked, BUYER shall be provided a limited HOME WARRANTY PLAN issued by the INSURANCE COMPANY. The application service charge of $____________shall be paid by_________ at closing.

17-BINDING AGREEMENT: Acceptance of this Offer, and any attached Addenda, shall create a LEGAL AGREEMENT, BINDING ON BUYER AND SELLER and their heirs, executors, administrators, successors and assigns, and shall contain the ENTIRE AGREEMENT AND UNDERSTANDING of the parties, it being further acknowledged that there are no other conditions, representations, warranties or agreements, expressed or implied, beyond those contained herein. All terms, provisions, covenants, and conditions of this Agreement shall survive Title Transfer of said property to BUYER.

18-BUYER'S OFFER: The undersigned specifically represent(s) that they are of legal age and capacity and are ready, willing and able to purchase the property according to the above terms:

BUYER(S)______________________________/______________________________

ADDRESS/Phone____.

TITLE SHALL BE TAKEN:______________________________(Date)__________

IF TITLE TO BE IN MORE THAN ONE NAME, IS SURVIVORSHIP DEED REQUESTED? ______ (YES or NO)

19-SELLER'S ACCEPTANCE:

The undersigned, being of legal age and capacity, hereby accept(s) the above offer and agree(s) to pay a total commission of

_____percent of said purchase price, payable____percent to the REAL ESTATE COMPANY and_____percent to
______________________________ as the SOLE PROCURING CAUSE(S) of this transaction.

SELLER(S)______________________________/______________________________

ADDRESS/Phone______________________________(Date)__________

20-DEPOSIT RECEIPT: Receipt is hereby acknowledged, as agent for SELLER, of BUYER'S earnest money deposit in the amount specified and in the form described in foregoing paragraph 3.(a), to be held in the REAL ESTATE COMPANY'S trust Account, subject to all terms and provisions of this Agreement.

-------------the REAL ESTATE COMPANY By______________________________(Date)__________

ONCE SIGNED, THIS DOCUMENT BECOMES A LEGALLY-BINDING CONTRACT
IF YOU HAVE QUESTIONS OF LAW, CONSULT AN ATTORNEY LICENSED TO PRACTICE IN OHIO

Clause 4 specifies in detail the buyer's obligations in making a good faith attempt to secure *financing* (satisfy the condition) for this real estate transaction. All that has to be filled in is how long purchasers have to make application(s) for financing and then how much time they have to secure a mortgage loan commitment. The clause also makes the contract null and void if purchasers cannot obtain financing, and it outlines the procedure for return of the purchasers' earnest money.

Clause 5 addresses two types of closing procedure that might be used. The agent is to fill in the applicable data for the closing procedure used in the particular region. With the *escrow closing* (choice A), the agent fills in two different dates. The first date is when all funds and documents must be deposited with the escrow agent, and the second date is the title transfer date. If a *formal closing* is used instead (choice B), the agent specifies where the formal closing is to be held and when.

Sellers also are given 30 days to correct any *title defects* that come to light. Without this provision, if a title problem appears and has to be corrected, the transaction probably will be considered breached by sellers who might miss by a substantial amount the time periods the contract calls for. This is because defects in title usually take more than a few days to correct.

Clause 6 covers *possession.* The agent fills in the appropriate blanks. Possession can be the title transfer date or, alternatively, a certain number of days after title transfer. A specific date is called for because many purchasers and sellers have a "bottom line date"—one by which they must be in or out. This clause also allows purchasers to receive rent. If the agent leaves that blank empty, there will be no rental charge. (For just a short period of time after title transfer, it is customary not to charge rent.) The clause also covers hold-over sellers who will not surrender possession to purchasers/title holders. It makes sellers tenants at sufferance and gives purchasers the speediest way to legally remove sellers, through an eviction action.

Clause 7 gives purchasers the *best kind of title via deed* that grantors can give, the general warranty deed or fiduciary deed. The title is subject only to the exceptions that never can be removed from fee simple absolute estates, such as taxes, zoning restrictions, easements, and so forth. Dower rights also are required to be released.

The second part of clause 7 calls for a *title search* resulting in the issuance to purchasers of a *title guarantee* or, at additional cost to buyers, *title insurance*. Sellers also are required to comply with any local point-of-sale inspections.

Clause 8 is an important *proration* clause. Everything must be prorated up to the date of title transfer. If sellers, for example, have not paid taxes for any of the taxable year and purchasers obtain title four months into the taxable year, purchasers must be credited and sellers debited for the four months. The last available tax duplicate is used for calculating tax prorations. Sometimes the tax duplicate has not been changed but shortly will change to reflect a new valuation on the realty or a change in the tax rate. An example of this is when a home has been constructed on real property, but the real property is still being taxed as if it were raw land. The proration calculation that takes place in closing may, therefore, not be the accurate sum. Thus, the contract calls for purchasers and sellers to directly adjust with one another, after the closing and transfer of title, the correct sum due and owing.

This clause also calls for special assessments to be prorated, and thus purchasers assume them. This is what happens in the vast majority of real estate transactions. If, instead, sellers are required to pay them off, there will have to be a written alteration of this clause.

Another common example of how this proration clause is applied is when the realty is being rented. The rent comes in at the first of the month payable to sellers, and title transfers to purchasers mid-month. In escrow, half that rent must be credited to purchasers and debited to sellers. All utilities are prorated using the title transfer date, too. Prorations also are dealt with in Chapter 8, where we discuss closing procedures in detail.

Clause 9 details what costs purchasers and sellers, respectively, are required to pay at the time the transaction is closed. These are all the *usual and customary charges* that purchasers and sellers incur in typical real estate purchase transactions. Of special note is that sellers are required to pay the broker's real estate commission out of their proceeds at the time of closing. This requirement explains why the real estate profession does not have a collection problem like other professions or businesses do (that is, sellers refusing to pay the commission or delaying payment).

Clause 10 covers the options purchasers have if the subject realty is *damaged* prior to title transfer. Specifically, if greater than 10 percent of the agreed sales price of the realty sustains damage, purchasers may elect to receive insurance proceeds and close the transaction. Alternatively, purchasers may terminate the contract and receive any money back that already was deposited. If the damage is less than 10 percent, sellers must repair the damage before title transfer.

Clauses 11, 12, 13, and 14 deal with potential *defects or problems within the real property subsequently discovered* by purchasers after they own and possess the realty. In recent years buyers have filed a flood of lawsuits against brokers and sellers. We cover this in more detail in Chapter 9, under the topic of fraud and deceit. One of the recommendations we make in that chapter is that brokers aggressively handle the problem, up front, in their purchase contracts. The contract in Figure 6–6 does handle the entire defective realty problem.

The purchasers acknowledge (in clause 11) that they have been warned to engage the services of a *professional inspector* and that they are buying the realty "as is." If anyone has made any representation about the realty, purchasers are further required to list (clause 12) who made such a representation and what it was. Then sellers are required to state (clause 13) whether they have or have not made any representations, or whether they have any knowledge about problems in the realty. This shifts the burden of disclosures to sellers, where it belongs. (If sellers conceal a defect, they typically do not reveal it to the real estate agent either.) Clause 14 gives purchasers an exhaustive *list of professional inspections* that one can elect to have done to the real estate at purchasers' cost. Furthermore, purchasers have the *election to terminate the entire transaction if the inspection(s) yield unsatisfactory results.*

These clauses all culminate in a *waiver,* stating that purchasers accept the realty in its present condition. Present real estate case law does not favor purchasers who are given every opportunity to discover the true condition of a piece of real estate and do nothing thereafter to help themselves.

Clause 15 allows a party or the realty agent to attach any additional terms of the transaction as *addenda* to the purchase contract. The appropriate box is also checked as to the subject matter of the addendum.

Clause 16 has to be filled in if purchasers elect to purchase a *home warranty plan,* which usually covers some but not all problems that come to light in a specific real property.

Clause 17 makes the contract binding upon purchasers and sellers. In addition, the contract is *binding upon their estates or assigns.* If sellers die, for example, their executors are bound to conclude the transaction and convey the property to purchasers. This also reiterates the parol evidence rule in full: that this is the entire agreement and that there are no other terms and agreements apart from this writing.

The *terms and conditions of this contract also survive the closing* and are not merged into the deed that the buyers/grantees receive from the sellers/grantors. Thus, if there is a later lawsuit, all the terms of the purchase contract may be introduced as evidence and may not be barred because they were "merged" into the deed. The deed, which is the last, complete, and final writing, could otherwise bar the use of any prior writings, including the purchase contract, as evidence.

Clause 18 provides for the purchasers *signing the agreement and thereby assenting* to its terms. Purchasers also state, if they then know, *how they wish to take title.* Because the purchasers' form of ownership is not a material term of the transaction, this may be left blank or the agent may insert "information to be later supplied by purchasers."

Clause 19 provides for the *sellers signing the agreement and thereby assenting* to its terms. Sellers also agree to *pay the broker's real estate commission,* the details of which the agent should fill out on the blanks.

Clause 20 allows the real estate salesperson to *evidence receipt, as agent for sellers, of the earnest money deposit.* The salesperson signs and dates the document; the amount and form of deposit is what was set forth in clause 3 of the contract.

Finally, bold language at the end of the contract warns both purchasers and sellers that, once signed, this document becomes a legally binding contract. It urges them to *review it with an attorney* if they have any question of law.

Promissory Note

Promissory notes *often are used as earnest money.* Some real estate brokers prefer using promissory notes because they are legally binding, are easy and safe to store, and can be signed by purchasers in the office or any other place. Other real estate brokers prefer checks, personal, certified, or bank checks. If the offer to purchase is presented in the evening (frequently the case), if a check is used, it typically is a personal one.

The promissory note is a piece of commercial paper, set up like a check (see Figure 6–7). The *purchasers promise to pay a sum of money,* which represents part of the consideration, the purchase price of the realty. If the purchasers are unable to enter into a binding purchase contract, the promissory note is returned to them because there is no need for payment of part of the consideration. The salesperson makes the note payable to the broker, as agent for sellers, so the proper person is paid the money if differences arise between sellers and purchasers and as required by Ohio license law.

FIGURE 6–7
Promissory note.

PROMISSORY NOTE

On demand or no later than September 30, 1997 I/we promise to pay to The Real Estate Company, acting as agents for the seller, $ 1,000 Dollars with interest at 8 percent per annum for a valuable consideration, the receipt and sufficiently of which is hereby acknowledged.

Mr. Buyer

Mrs. Buyer

The salesperson can insert *a date by which purchasers must redeem* the note with a certified or bank check. Alternatively, the salesperson can make it *due on demand,* and whenever the broker demands redemption is the day that purchasers must bring funds or a certified check or a bank check. Under Ohio law, the broker must keep this money in a special account, called the *trust account,* that receives only these earnest money deposits. This account cannot be commingled with the broker's other monies. This practice protects both sellers and purchasers. If purchasers fail to redeem the note, they can be sued for the failure.

Promissory notes are strictly construed in favor of the holder so purchasers are in a less favorable legal position. The only good defense that purchasers can raise is a complete failure of consideration. With a real estate purchase contract, this is either that a *contract was never formed or that a condition within the contract was not fulfilled* so purchasers legitimately can no longer be bound by that contract.

NOTE: Students should now turn to the back of this text, pages 379–396, and fill out the two practice contracts they find there. The correctly filled-out forms follow the practice contracts so students can check their work. (The instructor may wish to have the students complete these exercises during class; alternatively, the exercises may be assigned as outside work. Once the exercises have been completed, students will benefit greatly from a discussion period concerning the contracts, to maximize understanding.)

Hypothetical Situations

During our many years of experience in both the real estate business and the legal profession, we have discovered that the questions asked most frequently by real estate practitioners and licensing candidates pertain to contracts. The following 25 hypothetical situations reflect the questions asked most often.

1. Purchasers submit an offer to sellers in writing through a real estate salesperson. Sellers approve of the price, possession, and escrow period but cross out a sentence giving purchasers the right to keep the rug in the library. Sellers initial where they cross out, and sign at the bottom of the real estate form purchase contract. When sellers hand this back to the agent, what is it? **QUESTION**

   A counteroffer, because there is a term in the contract the parties have not agreed upon. An acceptance must be to all terms within the offer. **ANSWER**

2. In making a counteroffer, the seller writes at the bottom of the form real estate purchase contract, "This is an irrevocable counteroffer, good for 72 hours." The seller then dates and signs it. Another offer comes in 12 hours later. Must the seller wait the 72 hours before accepting this second offer? **QUESTION**

   No. That "irrevocable counteroffer" is a defective option. It is not binding because there is no consideration to support it; the purchaser did not pay the seller for the privilege of having 72 hours in which no one else could purchase the realty. The seller should revoke the counteroffer. He or she then can accept the second offer unless the purchaser already had accepted the counteroffer before receiving the revocation. **ANSWER**

3. Sellers are presented an asking price offer from purchasers through their real estate companies. All the terms within the offer are those that sellers specified within the listing contract. Sellers refuse to accept the offer. Does anyone have a cause of action against sellers? **QUESTION**

ANSWER *The real estate company can sue sellers for its commission, for breach of the listing contract. Purchasers have no rights, as sellers never entered into a contract with them.*

QUESTION 4. Purchasers insert within an offer, "This offer expires at noon on January 15." Sellers sign the offer to signify agreement to its terms at 1:00 p.m. on January 15. What have sellers done?

ANSWER *At best, they have made a counteroffer. The offer died at noon and, thus, could not be accepted. Purchasers are now the ones who can accept or reject the offer sellers are making.*

QUESTION 5. Purchasers insert within an offer, "This offer open for acceptance until August 10." On August 9 they see a home they like better. Can they make an offer on this other home on August 9?

ANSWER *Possibly. An offer can be withdrawn at any time before acceptance. If the offer has not been accepted, they should withdraw it. The language in the offer does not mean that they have to leave that offer open until then. It merely has the offer die on August 10 if it has not been accepted. After purchasers have effectively withdrawn their first offer, they may make an offer on the second home on August 9.*

QUESTION 6. Purchasers submit to sellers a written offer to purchase on sellers' home. Although the purchase price is stated within this offer, no earnest money is specified. Sellers accept the offer in writing. Isn't this a void contract as it is missing consideration?

ANSWER *No. The purchase price in exchange for the real property is the consideration, not the earnest money. Earnest money is not needed to form a valid, enforceable purchase contract. It is a way of protecting sellers by having some of purchasers' money up front if purchasers default.*

QUESTION 7. The real estate purchase contract between purchaser and seller states that the price is $74,000–$78,000; the possession is "two weeks to a month and a half"; the seller must pay "some or all of her taxes up to title transfer." Will a court enforce this contract?

ANSWER *No. Courts will not make contracts for the parties. The terms of a contract must be certain, not ambiguous, and be capable of being performed. The above "contract" fails on all counts.*

QUESTION 8. John Adams, a transferee, is house-hunting. He finds a house he really likes and wants to submit to the seller an offer with a financing condition in it. The real estate salesperson tells him that his wife, Ann, also has to sign the offer to make it legal. John says that Ann is a housewife and has no income to make the mortgage payments. John also has the money for the down payment in an account that is in his name only. The salesperson insists that both husband and wife must sign an offer to purchase real property and that John cannot submit an offer without Ann. Who is right?

ANSWER *John is. One person, who happens to be married, can purchase real property on his or her own. The only relevant point about John being married is that if he needs his wife to secure the down payment or mortgage, she should also sign the offer. Thus, they both would be bound jointly to fulfill the financing condition within the contract. Including John's wife on this offer is really a psychological sales tool, not a legal necessity. Salespeople are easily confused in this area because they are so used to obtaining the signature of a married seller's spouse.*

That is because the seller's spouse usually has dower rights to release. A purchaser's spouse does not have those rights.

9. Our very same John goes ahead and submits an offer with a condition in it stating, "conditioned upon Ann Adams's approval of the real property." Should the seller accept the offer with this condition in it? **QUESTION**

   No. If Ann Adams does not like the house, then John, using failure of condition by her lack of approval, might be able to declare the contract null and void. This is too large a loophole in the purchaser's behalf. **ANSWER**

10. Sam Smith has title to his home in his name only. Sam is married but only he signs the listing contract with the broker and real estate purchase contract with the purchaser. Are these contracts valid? Will Sam be able to perform on them? **QUESTION**

    The contracts are valid because Sam is the owner of the subject realty. In both, however, Sam has pledged to convey title to the realty clear of his spouse's dower rights. As his wife has not signed either the listing contract or the purchase contract, there is no way to legally compel her to release those rights. If she refuses to release these rights, Sam is in breach of both contracts because he cannot transfer a good and sufficient title as both contracts require. **ANSWER**

11. Purchasers cannot secure financing on a home they are bound to purchase pursuant to a written real estate purchase contract. There is no financing condition within the real estate purchase contract. The form contract used recites only the purchase price and does not break down the sum into amount of down payment and amount of mortgage to be secured. Are they in breach of contract? **QUESTION**

    Yes. This is personal impossibility of performance and thus not an excuse for failure to perform. If there had been a financing condition, they would be excused from performance and not be in breach of contract. A financing condition might have been implied or construed into the contract had there been a breakdown clause showing a down payment figure and mortgage figure. **ANSWER**

12. Purchasers present a written offer to purchase sellers' realty. Sellers say they accept it but will sign it later. They never sign it, and purchasers still want the real estate. Do purchasers have a cause of action against sellers? **QUESTION**

    No. Under the statute of frauds, offer and acceptance must be in writing for a real estate purchase contract to come into existence. Sellers never became bound to the contract, as oral acceptance is not sufficient. It is an unenforceable contract. **ANSWER**

13. Sellers unknowingly sell their home for $10,000 less than fair market value. When they discover this, they file an action in court, claiming that their being paid too little is grounds for rescission or reformation of the contract. Will sellers be successful in court? **QUESTION**

    No. Inadequacy of consideration is not a ground for rescinding or reforming a contract. Each party deals with the other at arm's length and at one's own risk in the marketplace. If sellers' real estate broker incorrectly advised them that the sum was fair market value, sellers may have a cause of action in court against the broker for violation of fiduciary duty as sellers' agent—for negligently advising them about their realty's fair market value. This problem is discussed more fully in Chapter 9. **ANSWER**

14. Broker does not have a written listing agreement with sellers. Under an oral listing agreement with sellers, however, she procured a ready, willing, and able **QUESTION**

purchaser for sellers. Sellers refuse to pay broker her commission. Does broker have a cause of action against sellers?

ANSWER *In Ohio, oral listing contracts are recognized as exceptions to (or outside of) the statute of frauds. They are regarded generally as contracts of employment instead of contracts regarding an interest in land. In Ohio, brokers can sue sellers for breach of an oral listing contract. Proving an oral listing contract is difficult, however, usually because of lack of evidence.*

QUESTION 15. Sellers are presented with multiple offers on their real estate. None of them is high enough, though. Thus, they make a written counteroffer on every offer, at a higher price. They send all these counteroffers back, via the real estate brokers, to the prospective purchasers. What can go wrong?

ANSWER *If more than one, or all, accept the counteroffers, the real estate can be sold multiple times. The prospective purchasers should have been told to submit higher bids with (optionally) sellers' orally indicating what they consider a minimum acceptance figure.*

QUESTION 16. Sellers of real estate that has been sold pursuant to a binding purchase contract change their mind and refuse to transfer title to the real estate to purchasers. What relief and remedies are available to purchasers?

ANSWER *Purchasers can sue sellers for specific performance so that the court may compel sellers to convey the real estate to them. If purchasers also lost any money from the sellers' failure to perform, they can sue them for breach of contract and be awarded compensatory damages to cover their loss.*

QUESTION 17. Purchasers and sellers orally agreed, before entering into the written real estate purchase contract, that purchasers could move into the realty before title transfer if their landlord would give them any trouble. Subsequently, when the written purchase contract was formed between them, the writing simply provided, "possession at title transfer." When can purchasers move in if they do have problems with their landlord?

ANSWER *Probably only at title transfer date. The parol evidence rule bars the introduction of oral agreements made before the final, complete writing, which vary or contradict the terms of that writing. All agreements are merged into that final writing. Purchasers may convince a court to apply the promissory estoppel doctrine, however; that is, they can stop sellers from denying the earlier promise they made, because purchasers relied on it to their detriment. If there are no witnesses to the sellers' earlier promise, though, it becomes only the purchasers' word against the sellers' word. That probably is not enough proof to justify a court's applying promissory estoppel.*

QUESTION 18. A 17-year-old enters, as a purchaser, into a binding real estate purchase contract with a 40-year-old seller. The seller changes her mind about selling the realty and tries to void the contract based on the purchaser's lack of capacity to contract since he is a minor. Will the seller succeed?

ANSWER *No. The contract is voidable only at the minor's election, not at the adult's. An adult contracts with a minor at his or her peril.*

QUESTION 19. A 90-year-old woman, about to enter a nursing home as her hardening of the arteries worsens, wants to enter into a listing contract to sell her home with a real estate broker. Should the broker accept?

ANSWER *No. This woman probably is infirm enough to lack the capacity to enter a contract. As her condition is worsening, she probably will lack the capacity to enter* *into a binding real estate purchase contract as well. At her election, she can disaffirm any of these contracts. Thus, the broker should ask her family whether there is a court-appointed guardian or a "durable" power of attorney. If there is, the guardian or the attorney-in-fact is the proper party to enter into both contracts.*

20. Sellers have left town for another state. Their real estate broker receives an offer to purchase their real property. It will take time to send this to the sellers through the mail. Can the broker accept the offer on their behalf to avoid a delay? **QUESTION**

No. An offer can be accepted only by the person to whom it is made. The only legally recognized substitute is a person whom sellers have made their attorney-in-fact by a recorded power of attorney. The broker can accept only if he is the person with the sellers' power of attorney. Also, note the increasing use of FAX machines, using signatures from the purchasers in one location and sellers in another location, which may become the alternative solution to this problem. **ANSWER**

21. Purchasers want time to think over whether to buy the sellers' real estate at the counteroffer figure made to them. During this time, they want assurance that no other person can purchase this real estate. Is there any way they can receive this protection? **QUESTION**

Yes. Purchasers and sellers can enter into an option contract with one another. Purchasers can pay sellers for the privilege of having a set amount of time to consider the counteroffer and accept it. **ANSWER**

22. A condition within the real estate purchase contract states that "loan approval must be obtained within 14 days or this contract is null and void." The 20th day arrives and purchasers have not yet obtained loan approval. Other purchasers, with a better offer, appear. Can sellers declare the first contract null and void? **QUESTION**

Yes. Purchasers failed to fulfill the condition within the contract. Sellers should declare the first contract null and void and then accept the second offer. Sellers must be careful, however, that they have not turned the already allowed late days (from day 14 to day 20) into a waiver of the time requirement and thereby extended the time allowance for purchasers. If purchasers contend there has been a waiver and that sellers have extended the time limit, by the sellers' actions, sellers should consult their attorney before accepting the second offer. **ANSWER**

23. Sellers announce, 30 days before they are supposed to put their deed into escrow, that they are not going to perform the real estate purchase contract. Must purchasers wait the 30 days to see whether sellers put the deed into escrow. Can they sue sellers immediately? **QUESTION**

Under the doctrine of anticipatory repudiation, if one party declares he will not perform in advance of performance date, the other party can sue him immediately for breach of contract. Thus, purchasers can sue sellers immediately. **ANSWER**

24. There is a condition in a written real estate purchase contract stating, "conditioned upon purchasers obtaining conventional financing with a minimum of a third down payment." Purchasers want to be excused from performing this contract based on this condition. What will they have to show? **QUESTION**

Ideally, purchasers should show that they tried to obtain conventional financing at several lending institutions with a third down payment and were turned down by every institution. This demonstrates good faith in trying to fulfill the condition. If they do not try to obtain the loan at any institution, or try using less of a down payment, the condition will not excuse them. **ANSWER**

QUESTION 25. Sellers are presented with two offers. One is $1,000 higher than the other. All other terms are identical in both offers. Do sellers have to accept the higher offer?

ANSWER *No. They can accept whichever they want. There is no doctrine of contract law forcing offerees to accept any particular offer. Other laws might cause sellers trouble, however. For example, if they accept the lower bid because the higher bid was made by a black person, they have violated the fair housing laws, which we discuss fully in Chapter 11. Nevertheless, they have entered into a binding purchase contract with the white, lower-bid purchaser, which probably cannot be set aside.*

REVIEW QUESTIONS

1. Because of the relationship between the parties, the law will find a(n):

   a. express contract
   b. implied contract
   c. quasi contract
   d. defunct contract

2. Inquiries during negotiations:

   a. are really a counteroffer
   b. act as a rejection
   c. do not alter an offer or a counteroffer
   d. act as a withdrawal

3. When purchasers are paying all cash that they have on hand for the real estate, which condition should the salesperson insert in the sales contract?

   a. 14 days for loan approval
   b. cosignature by the purchaser's working wife
   c. sale of the purchaser's own home first
   d. no condition seems necessary

4. The power to withdraw an offer:

   a. rests with the offeree
   b. rests with the offeror
   c. ends after 48 hours
   d. must have a time limit

5. Compensatory damages for breach of the purchase contract by purchasers properly includes to sellers:

   a. the cost of therapy for distress
   b. the cost of a new house
   c. the difference in dollars on a loss they take on the purchase price, as long as sold within a range of fair market value
   d. reasonable attorney's fees

6. When sellers refuse to convey to purchasers, pursuant to a written real estate purchase contract, purchasers may bring an action in specific performance in:

   a. U. S. District Court
   b. Common pleas court
   c. Small claims court
   d. Night court, housing division

7. A real estate purchase contract that is missing this element is so incomplete as to make it invalid and unenforceable:

   a. date purchaser signed it
   b. no reference to title's being of marketable quality
   c. financing condition
   d. amount of purchase price

8. The purchase contract must have:

   a. an offer and acceptance
   b. earnest money payment
   c. notarization
   d. two disinterested witnesses

9. In interpreting the language in a contract, the courts are primarily concerned with:
   a. correct, technical meanings of the words used regardless of whether that is what the parties intended
   b. ordinary and practical meanings of the words used regardless of the high technical level of the document
   c. the actual intention of the parties
   d. coming up with a result that is equally fair to both parties

10. Offers may be terminated by:
    a. acceptance by the offeree
    b. revocation by the offeror
    c. lapse of 24 hours
    d. destruction of the real estate salesperson's automobile

11. Impossibility of performance can be used to justify excuse of performance by a party to a contract when:
    a. personal, subjective impossibility occurs
    b. objective impossibility occurs
    c. performance costs twice as much
    d. the purchaser's wife filing for divorce before closing

12. The parol evidence rule applies:
    a. to an incomplete agreement
    b. to an oral contract
    c. when there is final writing
    d. to listing but not purchase contracts

13. Conditions within a contract generally:
    a. strengthen it
    b. apply to only listing contracts
    c. balance the parol evidence rule
    d. excuse performance if the conditions are not fulfilled

14. An offer can be withdrawn:
    a. at any time prior to acceptance
    b. unless there is a clause stipulating that the offer is open for acceptance until a specified time
    c. only by written notification
    d. by the offeree

15. Consideration within the real estate purchase contract is:
    a. the real property in exchange for the purchase price
    b. earnest money only
    c. a benefit-detriment sustained by one party
    d. the promissory note

16. The statute of frauds requires a writing:
    a. for all contracts
    b. for contracts that involve an interest in real estate
    c. for all contracts covered by the Uniform Commercial Code
    d. for all contracts covered by the U. S. Constitution

17. The real estate purchase and listing contracts are usually:
    a. express
    b. in writing
    c. bilateral
    d. all of the above

18. All people are usually considered to have the capacity to contract unless they:
    a. are in therapy
    b. are members of Al Anon
    c. are minors
    d. are gifted

19. The salesperson is a party to the:
    a. purchase contract
    b. listing contract
    c. option contract
    d. none of the above

20. If the seller defaults on the real estate purchase contract, the purchaser's fastest and best relief is a lawsuit asking for:
    a. money damages at law
    b. specific performance in equity
    c. the court to reform the contract by rewriting it for the parties
    d. punitive damages based on the seller's malicious conduct

21. The most usual condition inserted into the purchase contract covers:
    a. possession
    b. title
    c. financing
    d. chattels

22. Courts construe contracts:
    a. in their most technical sense
    b. so as to make a contract even though the parties have no clear intent and no certain terms
    c. in their plain and ordinary sense
    d. only when they are oral

23. The power to accept an offer:
    a. rests with the offeree
    b. rests with the offeror
    c. automatically ends within 48 hours
    d. must have a time limit

24. The sellers' consideration in the listing contract is:
    a. giving up all or some rights to deal in the property themselves
    b. the certainty that they must pay the commission
    c. the real property
    d. all of the above

25. Damage in excess of 10 percent of the agreed sales price of an $80,000 home, which gives the purchaser an election to opt out of the typical real estate purchase contract, would most likely be:
    a. a broken patio door
    b. a burned and gutted family room
    c. some plumbing problems
    d. burglary of fine art objects

ANSWER KEY

1. b	8. a	15. a	22. c
2. c	9. c	16. b	23. a
3. d	10. b	17. d	24. a
4. b	11. b	18. c	25. b
5. c	12. c	19. d	
6. b	13. d	20. b	
7. d	14. a	21. c	

7 LEGAL ASPECTS OF FINANCE, FORECLOSURE, AND LIENS

KEY TERMS

acceleration clause
assumption of mortgage
auditor's lien
bankruptcy
certificate of judgment
conventional financing
creditor
debtor
deficiency judgment
due-on-sale clause
due-on-transfer clause
ejectment
equitable right to redeem
foreclosure
forfeiture
general lien
involuntary lien
judgment lien
land installment purchase contract
lien theory jurisdiction
mechanic's lien
mortgage deed
mortgagee
mortgagor
partition
promissory note
purchase money mortgage
Regulation Z
special lien
Truth-in-Lending Law
unconventional financing
vendee
vendor
voluntary lien
warranty deed

FOR EXAMPLE

Anne Hamilton has learned how to prepare a written offer to purchase. She is able to do all the negotiating between purchasers and sellers until she ends up with a binding real estate purchase contract for a home. Because there is a financing condition within that contract, Anne knows the purchasers will have to secure a loan to purchase the home.

Although Anne has a role at this stage, it is more limited. This is because *it is solely the purchasers'/borrowers' legal responsibility at this point to apply at a lending institution for mortgage loan financing, to try to fulfill the financing condition within the real estate purchase contract;* of course, Anne may have some suggestions that will aid the purchasers in their quest for desirable financing. Anne knows what to recommend because she is regularly in touch with lenders, keeping up-to-the-minute on their changing terms. Perhaps she and a few other agents in her office share information of this sort, each of them assigned to call and maintain contact with designated area lenders.

After the purchasers have obtained loan approval, the lender presents them with the appropriate legal documentation, which includes a mortgage deed and a promissory note. These are rarely subject to negotiation, so the lender is unlikely to alter any of the terms of the legal instruments prepared by its lawyer. If the purchasers want complete legal advice on their full potential for liability with regard to these instruments, they should take them to a lawyer. Anne, for her part, is familiar enough with the documents to understand that they exist for the purpose of securing the lender's interests in exchange for the loan proceeds. She also knows that the mortgage deed will be recorded to put everyone on notice of its existence. That is likely the extent of her involvement, although she really needs to know the answers to the following questions so she can feel at all times that she is on top of all of her developing transactions. The answers to these questions are contained within this chapter.

1. What are a mortgage deed and a promissory note, and what do they do? (Anne will appear incompetent if she does not know what these legal instruments are and that the excellent security they represent makes possible the modern financing of real estate transactions.)
2. What happens if the borrower defaults on paying the loan that is subject to these legal documents? (If this should happen to any of Anne's purchasers at some time in the future, they may wish to list the realty with Anne for resale to avoid the usually less favorable terms a forced sale will bring them. Knowing this much about the consequences of mortgages will increase Anne's effectiveness as a real estate salesperson.)
3. Can borrowers/purchasers lose everything they have sunk into the realty if they default, or do they get something out of the whole investment they made prior to default? (Anne's knowledge here might help if she is trying to secure a listing to achieve a quick private sale before a forced one is imposed upon the defaulting borrower. Any familiarity she has gained working with the trustees in bankruptcy court can also give her a professional edge in working with such a mortgagor/debtor.)
4. Where did the law come from that created all these rules, and is this one of those areas in which the law is undergoing rapid change? (Although this area of the law has gone through considerable upheaval throughout the centuries, it is presently in a fairly stable state and is not subject to radical changes.)

Terminology

Before we go any further, let us review the terminology used to describe the usual parties to a mortgage transaction (which we will define in the next section, consistent with the rules set forth in other chapters). Again, the person with the "or" suffix is always the one doing something, the active party, whereas the "ee" person is passive, a recipient.

In connection with mortgages, the **mortgagor** is the one *pledging the real property because of the money he or she has borrowed to purchase the real property.* The **mortgagee** is the one *receiving the realty as security for the loan of money to the mortgagor.* The mortgagor is the *borrower* or **debtor,** and the mortgagee is the *lender* or **creditor.** In the usual transaction, then, the purchaser, or buyer, under the purchase agreement is the mortgagor in the mortgage transaction, because the purchaser is the one who is borrowing money to complete the transaction.

Recalling the Chapter 5 discussion on deeds, however, isn't the seller the active party, the grantor, who transfers title to the purchasers? Yes, the seller does take the active role of transferring title to the purchasers via the general warranty deed, but to get that warranty deed from the seller, the purchasers must themselves transfer their interest in the realty to the mortgage loan lender. The purchasers do this by acting as grantors/mortgagors themselves, using a mortgage deed, an entirely separate document from the warranty deed.

To fully appreciate the difference between the mortgage deed and the warranty deed, and also to note the many similarities, the essential components of the warranty deed are reproduced in Figure 7–1 and a common type of mortgage deed is reproduced in Figure 7–2. The **mortgage deed** is essentially a general **warranty deed** coupled with promises to ensure that *the security will be well-maintained and a condition that will conclude the whole transaction upon full payment of the debt.* Finally, the promissory note fits with the mortgage deed as evidence of the understanding of the parties as to the precise terms of the debt.

The Mortgage and the Promissory Note

A mortgage is a *conveyance of an interest in real property, using a written instrument,* usually known as a mortgage deed, which *acts as security for the payment of a debt.* The mortgage is given by the mortgagor to the mortgagee, giving the mortgagee secured rights in the realty. The debt itself is evidenced by a promissory note, an entirely separate document from the mortgage. The **promissory note,** a sample of which is reproduced in Figure 7–3, is a *written legal instrument signed by the borrower for the benefit of the mortgage lender.* The note *creates the debt,* whereas the *mortgage secures payment of that debt.*

Like all legal instruments, the mortgage must contain certain essentials. It must be in writing, under the statute of frauds, because it pledges or conveys title to realty to secure payment of a debt. The instrument must set forth the names of the two interested parties to the mortgage, the mortgagee and the mortgagor. There also must be a legal description of the subject real property, along with language that the mortgage instrument, usually the mortgage deed, is given as the security for a debt of money. The instrument must state the amount of the debt. There is a mortgaging clause stating the mortgagor's intent to mortgage the subject realty to the mortgagee. A *defeasance clause* (which sometimes is a statutory condition) provides that the mortgage lien or mortgage conveyance is defeated in the event the mortgagor completely pays off the debt.

FIGURE 7–1
Sample general warranty deed.

Grantor
Consideration
Granting Clause
Grantee

GENERAL WARRANTY DEED

(STATUTORY FORM)

JOHN SMITH and MARY SMITH, Husband and Wife, of Cuyahoga County Ohio, for valuable consideration paid, grant with general warranty covenants, to WILLIAM BROWN and SUSAN BROWN, whose tax mailing address is 428 South Street, Lundhurst, Ohio, the following real property:

Legal Description

Situated in the City of Lyndhurst, County of Cuyahoga and State of Ohio and known as being Sublot No. 4 in a resubdivision made for The Society for Savings in the City of Lyndhurst of part of Original Euclid Township Lot No. 10, Tract No. 1, as shown by the recorded plat in Volume 100 of Maps, Page 1 of Cuyahoga County Records, and being 25.00 feet front on the Easterly line of South Street, 73.50 feet front on the curved turnout between the said Easterly line of South Street and the Southerly line of Main Street, and extending back 136.43 feet on the Northerly line, which is also the Southerly line of Main Street, 184.78 feet deep on the Southerly line, and being 36.45 feet wide in the rear, as appears by said plat, be the same more or less, but subject to all legal highways.

Exception Clause

Except for restrictions, conditions, limitations, reservations and easements of record; zoning ordinances, if any, and taxes and assessments, both general and special, for the current half of the taxable year and thereafter.

Prior Instrument Reference: Volume 13200, Page 254 of Cuyahoga County Records of Deeds.

Dower Release

And we each, individually, hereby release all rights of dower therein.

Execution & Witnessing

WITNESS our hands this 15th day of February, 1997.

Barry Irvin — John Smith
JOHN SMITH

Dolly Meadows — Mary Smith
MARY SMITH

Notarization

STATE OF OHIO)
Cuyahoga County) SS:

Before me, a notary public in and for said county and state, personally appeared the above named John Smith and Mary Smith who acknowledged that they did sign foregoing instrument and that the same is their free act and deed.

IN TESTIMONY WHEREOF, I have hereunto set my hand and official seal at Lyndhurst, Ohio this 15th day of February, 1997.

James Donato Irvin

this instrument prepared by:
JAMES D. IRVIN - Attorney
11401 Willow Hill Drive
Chesterland, Ohio 44026
(216) 729-2273

JAMES DONATO IRVIN, Attorney
NOTARY PUBLIC - STATE OF OHIO
My commission has no expiration date.
Section 147.03 R.C.

Figure 7–2 shows all of these essentials, along with the requisite signatures, witnessing, and notarization. *Only the mortgagor signs,* or executes, the mortgage deed, because the mortgagor is the one doing the pledging or conveying. The mortgage must be delivered to and accepted by the mortgagee. When all of these requirements are met, there is a valid mortgage.

The promissory note (Figure 7–3), sometimes called the mortgage note when used in conjunction with a mortgage deed, shows that a valid debt exists and contains the terms of the loan along with a promise by the borrower to pay the lender according to those terms. The terms include the total amount of the loan; the interest rate; and when, how, and to whom the loan payments must be made. The borrower signs the note and is personally liable for paying the amount of money set forth in it.

FIGURE 7–2 Sample mortgage deed.

No. 56B (MORTGAGE ASSOCIATION FORM No. 9)—Revised

The Ohio Legal Blank Co. Cleveland
Publishers and Dealers Since 1883

Know All Men by these Presents

That, we, WILLIAM BROWN and SUSAN BROWN, Husband and Wife,

Grantor, *for valuable consideration, receipt whereof is hereby acknowledged, hereby grants, conveys, assigns and transfers to* SUPERIOR SAVINGS & LOAN ASSOC.

Grantee, *(whose address is* 12345 Mayfield Road, South Euclid, Ohio *Ohio), his heirs, personal representatives, successors and assigns, the following described real property, situated in* Cuyahoga *County, Ohio, and known as*

[LEGAL DESCRIPTION]

Also all buildings and improvements now situated or which may be hereafter erected thereon; all elevators, engines, boilers, machinery, equipment, lighting and heating fixtures, appliances, and property of every description forming part thereof or used in connection therewith; all appurtenances now or hereafter pertaining thereto; all rents and profits arising therefrom; all of Grantor's rights under any leases, whether recorded or unrecorded, of all or any part thereof; and all easements, rights and powers relating to all or any part thereof or to the use thereof.

All and singular the rights, easements, titles, issues, powers, estates and property hereby granted, conveyed, assigned and transferred, as aforesaid, are hereinafter sometimes called the "premises."

The premises are sometimes known or designated as

428 South Street, Lyndhurst, Ohio 44124

To Have and to Hold *the premises unto grantee, his heirs, personal representatives, successors and assigns, forever.*

Grantor hereby covenants with grantee that at and until the execution and delivery of this instrument he is seized of the real property hereby granted and conveyed as a good and indefeasible estate in fee simple, is lawfully possessed of the premises, has the lawful right to grant, convey, assign and transfer the same in the manner and form as herein provided, and that the premises are free and clear of all liens, incumbrances and adverse interests whatsoever, or the possibility thereof, except restrictions of record and any conditions, reservations and easements created in conjunction with such restrictions, zoning ordinances, if any, and taxes and assessments for the current half of the taxable year & thereafter

and grantor further covenants with grantee that he will **Warrant and Defend** *the premises to grantee against all lawful claims and demands whatsoever, except those hereinbefore recited.*

And for valuable consideration each of the undersigned does hereby remise, release and forever quitclaim unto the grantee all right and expectancy of dower in the premises.

Whereas, *grantor has executed and delivered to grantee a certain promissory note payable to the order of grantee of even date herewith in the principal amount of*

FIFTY THOUSAND ($50,000.00)- - - - - - - - - - - - - - - - - - *Dollars, due and payable*

and bearing interest at the rate of eight per cent per annum, but providing that so long as all payments of principal and interest are made as they fall due or within ten days thereafter the interest rate shall be reduced to 7-3/4 *per cent per annum;*

And Whereas, *grantor does hereby covenant with grantee, as follows, viz:*

That he will punctually pay and discharge as the same become payable, all taxes, assessments and other governmental charges whatsoever now or hereafter imposed by any public authority upon the premises or any part thereof, or grantee's interest therein, without regard to any law heretofore or hereafter enacted imposing payment of the whole or any part thereof upon grantee;

That he will punctually pay all indebtedness secured, or which purports to be secured, by any lien or incumbrance on the premises to which the lien of grantee on the premises is or may become subordinate, as the same shall become due according to the tenor or terms of the promissory note, notes, or other evidence of the indebtedness secured by such lien or incumbrance, (it being the intention of the parties that any extension of maturity of all or any part of such prior indebtedness, without grantee's consent, shall be deemed a breach of this covenant); and that he will perform all such acts as will preserve and keep valid the lien and priority intended to be created by this instrument;

That he will maintain all buildings and improvements now or hereafter forming part of the premises, in constant repair and working order and in fit condition for their proper use and occupancy;

That, as additional security, he will at all times maintain fire insurance upon all insurable property now or hereafter forming part of the premises, to the full insurable value thereof, which insurance shall be distributed among the buildings and improvements forming part of the premises, if there be more than one, in proportion to their respective values; that all such insurance shall be written in insurance companies satisfactory to the grantee, and the policies shall, by their terms, in form satisfactory to grantee, protect the interest of grantee in the insured property; that he will deliver all such policies to grantee, or, in case such policies shall be deposited with the holder of any prior incumbrance on the premises, then he will deliver to grantee memoranda setting forth the written portions thereof and an irrevocable order to permit grantee to inspect the policies; that in case any building or improvements forming part of the premises are of such character as should, in the judgment of grantee, be insured against casualty other than fire, then grantor will from time to time, on demand of grantee, procure such insurance which shall provide by its terms for the protection of the grantee's interest in the premises, and in such cases, all such policies of additional insurance shall be deposited with grantee; that in case of damage or destruction by fire of any buildings or improvements forming part of the premises all insurance money received by grantee under any such policies, shall, provided grantor shall not at the time be in default in the performance or observance of any of his covenants herein contained, be available for the reconstruction or repair of the buildings or improvements so damaged or destroyed and shall be disbursed upon grantor's written orders accompanied by estimates or certificates of an architect satisfactory to grantee for the payment of labor and materials theretofore performed or used in connection with such repair or reconstruction, provided, however, that no part of said insurance money shall be so available unless and until grantor shall have supplied sufficient additional funds, available solely for the purpose, for repairing or reconstructing the buildings or improvements so damaged or destroyed, free of liens or liability for liens under any mechanic's lien law, to a condition equal to or better than the former condition thereof, and in the event grantor fails to provide such additional funds or to proceed with such repair or reconstruction within a reasonable time, then such insurance money or the unexpended balance thereof, as the case may be, may be applied by grantee on the indebtedness hereby secured;

That grantee may assign parts of or interests in the indebtedness hereby secured, and in any such event any agreements made between grantee and such assignees concerning their relative priorities in the indebtedness and the security shall be binding upon grantor if endorsed upon said note and incorporated in the instrument of assignment and if such assignment be recorded, (it being the intention of the parties that unless such instruments of assignment shall otherwise provide, all assigned parts of or interests in the indebtedness shall be equally and ratably secured hereby);

That grantor hereby acknowledges that the indebtedness hereby secured was incurred in good faith for full value received, and that he has no defenses, set-offs, or counter claims thereto:

That grantee is authorized and empowered to perform all acts which a mortgagee may perform under Section 8321-1 of the General Code of Ohio or any amendments thereof or acts supplementary thereto, for the protection of grantee's interest in the premises;

That in case grantor shall make default in the payment of any indebtedness hereby secured, according to the tenor of said promissory note and the period of grace allowed therein, or according to the provisions hereof, or in case grantor shall fail to perform any one or more of the covenants herein contained on his part to be performed, or in case in any judicial proceeding by a party other than grantee a receiver shall be appointed for grantor or his property on the ground of his failure to pay his debts, or in case in any judicial proceeding by a party other than grantee an order, judgment or decree shall be entered for the sequestration of the premises or any part thereof, or in case grantor shall sell or otherwise dispose of the premises, or any substantial part thereof, and shall fail to cause the party acquiring the same to assume payment of the proportionate amount of the indebtedness hereby secured by separate instrument of assumption and to cause original thereof to be filed with grantee within thirty (30) days thereafter, then and in any such events grantee may at his election declare the entire indebtedness hereby secured to be immediately due and payable, without notice to grantor, (which notice grantor hereby expressly waives) and upon any such declaration the entire indebtedness hereby secured shall be immediately due and payable, anything herein or in said promissory note contained to the contrary notwithstanding;

(continued)

FIGURE 7–2 Continued.

That in case grantor shall fail to pay any taxes, assessments, governmental charges, or principal or interest secured by prior incumbrances or to maintain insurance, as aforesaid, grantee may, if he desires, make good any such default or defaults, and any money advanced by grantee for any such purposes shall be added to the principal debt hereby secured and shall bear interest at the rate of eight per cent per annum from the respective dates of payment, payable quarterly, and shall be secured by the lien of this instrument, as well as by the lien of any prior incumbrances to the benefits of which grantee shall thereby be subrogated; that in case grantee shall pay any such obligation for the payment of which grantor is in default, such payment shall be without prejudice to grantee's right to declare the entire indebtedness hereby secured immediately due and payable as herein provided;

That in the event an action shall be instituted to foreclose grantor's equity of redemption, the Court shall on application of the complainants or their attorneys in such action, ex parte, and without notice appoint a receiver to take immediate possession of, manage and control the premises, notwithstanding that the same or part thereof is occupied by grantor, and collect and receive the rents and profits thereof, and apply the same under the direction of the Court;

That no waiver by grantee of any breach of any covenant of grantor herein contained shall be construed as a waiver of any subsequent breach of the same or any other covenant herein contained;

Now, therefore, the condition of this Deed is:

That if grantor shall punctually pay all indebtedness hereby secured according to the tenor of said promissory note or during period of grace allowed therein and the covenants of grantor herein contained and shall punctually perform the grantor's covenants herein contained, then the grant, conveyance, assignment and transfer hereby evidenced shall become null and void; otherwise the same shall remain in full force and effect.

(Definition) Whenever in this instrument the context so admits, the names of grantor and grantee and the terms "grantor" and "grantee" shall be construed as including the heirs, personal representatives, successors and assigns, as the case may be; and the pronoun as used herein in the third person, singular number and masculine gender, shall be construed as meaning the person, number and gender appropriate to the first designation of the parties.

In Witness Whereof, grantor hereunto affixes his signature this 1st day of September 1997

Signed and acknowledged in the presence of

William Witness — William Brown
WILLIAM BROWN

Sally Witness — Susan Brown
SUSAN BROWN

The State of Ohio, Geauga County } ss.

Before me, a notary public in and for said county, this day personally appeared William Brown and Susan Brown who executed the above instrument and acknowledged that they did sign it and that such signing was their free act and deed and their free act and deed in the capacities indicated by their signatures and designations.

Witness my signature and notarial seal at Chesterland, Ohio, Ohio, this 1st day of September 1997

James Donato Irvin
JAMES DONATO IRVIN, Attorney
NOTARY PUBLIC - STATE OF OHIO
My commission has no expiration date.
Section 147.03 R. C.

Assignment: , Ohio, 19

For value received the undersigned hereby sell , assign , and transfer , unto

all right and title to and interest in the within mortgage and the land and note described therein.

Waiver of Priority:

For valuable consideration, receipt whereof is hereby acknowledged, the undersigned hereby waive the priority of the lien of the within mortgage on the premises therein described in favor of the lien of a certain mortgage from

to

dated 19 , and filed as Document Number in the Office of the Recorder of County, Ohio, intending hereby that the rights of the undersigned under the within mortgage shall be as though the above described mortgage had been executed, acknowledged, delivered and recorded prior to the execution, acknowledgment, delivery and recordation of the within mortgage; all, however, without otherwise affecting the lien of the within mortgage.

Dated at , Ohio, this 19

Witnesses:

Cancellation: , Ohio 19

The conditions of this mortgage have been complied with and the same is hereby satisfied and discharged.

Assumption: , Ohio, 19

Whereas all or part of the premises described in the within mortgage are now owned by the undersigned; and the unpaid principal balance of the debt secured by the within mortgage is $, and interest has been paid thereon to 19 ; and the undersigned requested the holder of the promissory note described in the within mortgage to recognize the undersigned as the principal debtor;

Now, Therefore, for valuable consideration, receipt whereof is hereby acknowledged, the undersigned hereby expressly assume and agree to pay said unpaid principal balance, together with interest thereon from the date last aforesaid, according to the tenor of said promissory note and the terms and provisions of the within mortgage, and, further, hereby agree to keep and perform all covenants and conditions on the part of the grantor to be kept and performed, according to the provisions of the within mortgage and of the promissory note secured thereby, with the same effect as though had been joint maker of said promissory note and joint grantor in said mortgage.

Dated at , Ohio, this 19

Address

Mortgage Deed

WILLIAM BROWN and SUSAN BROWN,
Husband and Wife

TO

SUPER SAVINGS & LOAN ASSOC.
of South Euclid, Ohio

Dated, 19

State of Ohio

County of ss

Received for Record on the
day of 19
at o'clock M.
and Recorded 19 in
Mortgage Book Page

COUNTY RECORDER.

IRVIN & IRVIN, Attorneys
8473 Mayfield Road
Chesterland, Ohio 44026
(216) 729-7239

If a lender wants to make someone a loan and does not require a mortgage as security for payment—simply trusting that the borrower will pay back the loan—the lender can do so. The debt is a personal obligation of the borrower, and the lender is restricted to recovery from the person of the borrower only if the borrower defaults in payment. On the other hand, if the borrower had mortgaged real property for the benefit of the lender, upon default the lender could look for recovery not only to the person of the borrower (via the note) but also to the value of the realty itself (via the mortgage). Thus, *when a loan is secured (in this instance, an amount of money by a piece of realty), the lender has the right to sell the security (the piece of realty) when there is a default by the borrower.* This is the case as long as the debt exists. Conversely, if there is no debt and someone gives another person a mortgage deed, the mortgage deed has no effect because it represents security for repayment of nothing. It is nothing itself.

The promissory note and the mortgage deed together give the lender excellent security that the debt will be paid. The amount of the debt and all charges attendant thereto are clearly set forth as well. Provisions also are made for insurance and preservation of the real property, for guarantee of the loan, for assignment of the right to receive the loan payments, and for avoidance of the entire mortgage upon payment of the debt in full. For these reasons, mortgage deeds, used in tandem with promissory notes, are the most frequently used legal underpinnings in the financing of real estate transactions in Ohio.

FIGURE 7–3 Sample promissory note.

PROMISSORY NOTE

$78,000 February 15, 1997

For value received the undersigned, WILLIAM BROWN and SUSAN BROWN, of 428 South Street; Lyndhurst, Ohio, promise to pay to the order of RELIABLE SAVINGS & LOAN ASSOCIATION, of 83411 Wilson Mills Road; Shaker Heights, Ohio, SEVENTY-EIGHT THOUSAND DOLLARS ($78,000), with interest at the rate of nine percent (9%) per annum, payable NINE HUNDRED EIGHTY-EIGHT and 11/100 DOLLARS ($988.11) per month, commencing February 1, 1997 the principal to be due and payable in full on December 31, 2002 and both principal and interest to be payable at 83411 Wilson Mills Road in Shaker Heights, Ohio 47893 or at any other place hereafter designated by the holder.

Any holder hereof without notice to anyone may declare the entire debt due after forty (40) days continuous default in the payment of any installment of principal or interest or in the performance or observance of any covenant or condition contained in the mortgage securing this note. Upon such declaration the entire debt shall be immediately due and payable.

Overdue installments of interest and principal shall bear interest at the rate of twelve percent (12%) per annum, or at the maximum rate of interest then permitted by law, whichever is least, payable monthly.

This note is secured by a mortgage from the maker or makers to the payee upon premises known or designated as 428 South Street, Lyndhurst, Ohio.

/s/ William Brown
WILLIAM BROWN

/s/ Susan Brown
SUSAN BROWN

Conventional Versus Unconventional Financing

Do not be misled into thinking that "conventional" financing means the kind of financing that most people now use or that it is the present "convention." Perhaps at one time that was the case, but now the word has acquired a particular fixed meaning; it has become a real estate law term like "waste" or "fixture." **Conventional financing** is defined by reference to the nature of the lender's security for the debt. With conventional financing and in the event of default, the *lender can look to the debtor personally on the note and to the realty because of the mortgage deed.* Of course, the "personal security" via the note is not all that comforting to the lender because if things come to default, chances are good that the borrower's personal financial resources are in terrible shape. As a practical matter, then, with conventional financing the *lender's real security is in the realty.* The lender realizes that if there is a default by the borrower, it can force a public sale of that realty and recover the money from the proceeds of the sale.

Unconventional financing gives a lender one additional level of security for repayment of the debt. With unconventional financing, the *United States government, via the FHA (Federal Housing Authority) and the VA (Veterans Administration), provides insurance (in the case of the FHA) or a guarantee (in the case of the VA) to the lender that, should the borrower default, the appropriate government agency will "cover" a certain portion of the outstanding loan balance* by agreeing to insure or guarantee that balance. This gives the lender an additional level of protection against incurring loss from that loan transaction. Not only does the lender have the personal security of the borrower (via the note) and the realty as security (via the mortgage deed), but it also has the provision for payment by the United States government (via the insurance/guarantee) if the borrower defaults.

Foreclosure Legal Proceedings

Foreclosure in the Past

Over the centuries, the basic English law of mortgages, from which current American mortgage laws are derived, has varied in response to the needs and the pressures present in each historical period. Under earlier English law, the courts interpreted a mortgage as a conveyance of real property as security for payment of a debt—as exactly what it appeared to be on its face, a deed. If debtors failed to repay creditors by the date set for repayment, the lenders took over control of the realty. If the debt was for far less than the value of the pledged land, that was the debtors' bad luck. Creditors did not have to pay debtors any amount in compensation. The courts reasoned that the debtors knew the risk they were taking when they mortgaged the realty in the first place so the total forfeiture result upon default should come as no surprise.

But life was never so cut-and-dried as to do justice in every case based on this original interpretation of the mortgage as a simple pledge. Certainly there were cases in which a mortgagor for some good reason was unable to pay off the debt but sometime thereafter did have the full payment, plus interest. Say, for example, a debtor was run over by a cart on the way to make payment and never made it in time. Because a mortgagor in this position would get no relief from the courts of law, which looked no further than the documents (which clearly stated what would happen upon default), troubled mortgagors took their appeals to the king himself, hoping that some exception could be made for them.

Although the king had the power to decide such matters of "conscience" and "justice," clearly matters completely outside the scope of inquiries of the courts of law, he had more than enough to do without hearing appeals from grieving mortgagors. Therefore, he turned over these matters to his high church officials, who were used to dealing with matters of conscience and rightness. In time, the functions of these high church officials solidified into a completely separate system of courts, known as "chancery" or "equity" courts.

Once a mortgagor had lost his realty because of failure to pay by the prescribed date, and after he had convinced the chancellor (chancery official) that justice would be served by letting him redeem his real property, then, upon payment of all amounts owed, plus interest, he got his realty back. As this right to redeem developed in the equity courts, it became known as the **equitable right to redeem.**

Over time, it became easier for defaulting mortgagors to convince the equity officials that redemption would be just. Thus, the right to redeem became recognized as something all mortgagors possessed, regardless of the merit of their reasons for default.

To appreciate the practical significance of the latter development—recognition that all defaulting debtors had the right to redeem their realty by going through equity—consider the uncertainty of the creditor's position. First, the mortgagor defaulted by failing to repay the debt. Then the mortgagee claimed the realty, his security. Finally, some time later, the mortgagor convinced the equity court to let him have the realty back, after paying the mortgagee the entire debt plus interest. The big uncertainty at this stage of development of mortgage law was how long the mortgagee had to hold on to the realty while he waited to see if the mortgagor would try to reclaim it.

The solution to this dilemma came about with the development of an additional procedure called foreclosure. This *early foreclosure procedure amounted to cutting off or closing off the mortgagor's equitable right to redeem the property following default.*

In practice, the equity court set a date up to which time the mortgagor could redeem the property by paying off the debt plus interest. If the mortgagor failed to redeem the realty by the foreclosure date, he was, once and for all and without exception, cut off or foreclosed from later redeeming the realty. Now the mortgagee was in a much stronger position, because he only needed to wait past the foreclosure date to acquire full and permanent ownership rights in the realty. Unfortunately, the mortgagor could still suffer severe hardship if he could not come up with all he owed by the foreclosure date. This kind of foreclosure proceeding is known as *strict foreclosure.*

The great disadvantage of strict foreclosure is its failure to take into account and treat justly the mortgagor who pays off nearly all of the debt before default, then defaults and loses the entire real property and all its accumulated value to the mortgagee.

Foreclosure Today

The courts thereafter adopted the **foreclosure by public sale** approach to rectify the problems with equitable right to redeem. Faced with defaulting mortgagors, the courts now *set a date for the real property to be sold at a public sale, an auction,* *with the realty going to the highest bidder.* The proceeds of the sale are applied against the debt, and if there is any excess of money (as there is if the remaining balance of the debt is small, if the realty is in good condition, and if it brings a fair price at the sale), this excess goes to the mortgagor, who then is released from all claims of the mortgagee.

If the mortgagee also asks for a *personal judgment* on the mortgagor's indebtedness, a **deficiency judgment** can be granted against the mortgagor (if there is a shortfall on the amount still owed the mortgagee after the foreclosure sale). The mortgagee might try to collect on this just as the mortgagee would on any other kind of judgment. If the mortgagor has filed for bankruptcy, however, the deficiency judgment probably will be discharged in the bankruptcy and the mortgagee will be barred from ever collecting it.

Ohio follows the foreclosure by public sale procedure, not the strict foreclosure procedure. It also allows deficiency judgments being granted against mortgagors. Mortgagors have equitable rights to redeem the realty only up to the point that the trial court confirms the sale, which takes place shortly *after* the public sale. From the point of confirmation forward, the mortgagors have no further equitable rights to redeem the property. (This principle is discussed in full in *Ohio Savings Bank v. Ambrose,* one of the case studies at the end of this chapter.)

When a mortgagor defaults under the mortgage deed, the **acceleration clause** in that mortgage (see Figure 7–2) states that in the case of default of payment or other obligations as provided in the mortgage deed, the *whole amount of the note and mortgage becomes due and immediately payable,* not just the one payment or so actually missed. If there were no acceleration clause, only the default amount(s) actually would be owed instead of the entire amount. This would make it impossible, as a practical matter, to sell the realty pursuant to judicial foreclosure sale.

If the mortgagor fails to satisfy this entire remaining balance, thc mortgagcc has the right to bring a foreclosure suit. Usually the mortgagee files suit in the common pleas court in the same county as the real estate, seeking a judicial sale of the mortgaged property—an auction conducted by the county sheriff or court officer or licensed auctioneer (we use the term "sheriff" hereafter for simplicity). Ohio has minimum bid requirements at such an auction, plus appraisal requisites, as set forth in the Ohio Revised Code.

In Ohio, every effort is made to assist the mortgagor in satisfying the mortgagee in one way or another before the realty is sold at auction. If the mortgagor can refinance the property, raise sufficient funds to satisfy the mortgagee using other property, or sell the encumbered realty privately (this is where real estate salespeople come in), all is well. For these reasons, the court does not like to rush through a foreclosure proceeding unless the mortgagor clearly will not be taking advantage of any of these shortcuts to foreclosure. If the mortgagor is still in trouble by the date set for the foreclosure sale, the sheriff, at the direction of the court, auctions off the realty to the highest bidder (as long as the minimum bid requirement is met). Mortgagees can bid upon the realty at the auction, too, and if they are the highest bidder, they are purchasers at the auction.

Following the auction, the sheriff reports back to the court with results of the sale. Real properties that were not sold, either because no one bid or because all bids were below the appraised value minimum bid requirement, are reevaluated by the appraisers and reset for another sale date. The court reviews real properties that were sold. If all is in order, the court confirms the sale. It is at this moment of *confirmation of the sale* that the mortgagor is once and for all cut off—foreclosed—from later redeeming the real property.

The court cannot modify the sale or its terms. It can only confirm the sale or set it aside. The court also makes an order regarding distribution of the proceeds. The sheriff makes a deed to the purchasers at the court's direction after confirmation of sale. This deed transfers all the rights and interests of both mortgagor and mortgagee in the real property to the purchasers. There is no warranty of title in this deed, so the purchasers need to secure the most comprehensive title insurance on the property that they can obtain. Purchasers are in a *caveat emptor* (let the buyer beware) position in regard to this purchase. (The sheriff's deed was discussed fully in Chapter 5.)

Purchasers run additional risks in bidding on properties auctioned at foreclosure sales. For example, they can be held in contempt of court and fined or jailed for (a) failing to pay the necessary deposit when their auction bid is the one accepted or (b) subsequently failing to pay the balance of the purchase price to the sheriff. Purchasers who wish to bid on foreclosure properties should be represented by attorneys because foreclosure sales are much riskier for them than standard real estate transactions between purchasers and sellers.

Sometimes the mortgagor persuades the mortgagee/lender to take a deed from the mortgagor to the realty instead of going through a judicial foreclosure legal proceeding. Stepping outside of the protections and safeguards of these procedures can be hazardous to the lender, as it may not receive the clear and settled title it needs in order to deal in the realty thereafter.

Ohio views the mortgage deed as giving the mortgagee a lien or claim against the real property so that, if necessary, the realty can be sold and as much of the proceeds as required can be applied against the remaining debt. Therefore, *Ohio is known as a* **lien theory jurisdiction** *and operates on the lien theory of the mortgage,* in which the mortgage is viewed as a conveyance to secure the performance of an obligation. If a mortgagee wants possession, it has to bring an **ejectment** action as well. This action *seeks to remove the mortgagor from the realty.* This is separate from the foreclosure action.

As a practical matter, Ohio mortgagees usually file only a foreclosure suit, and not an ejectment suit, because pursuing both foreclosure and ejectment lawsuits poses too many problems. For example, insuring the realty usually becomes more expensive when the mortgagor is removed. Also, renting realty with a pending legal proceeding that is this serious is difficult, especially as the duration of the tenancy is subject to the foreclosure proceeding.

Mortgage Priority

When referring to the type of security that exists for repayment of the loan, real estate borrowers and lenders often mention first, second, or even third mortgages. Legally, however, there is absolutely no difference between a first, second, and third mortgage. The actual language of the mortgage deed is identical in all of them. The designation of first, second, or third mortgages against the realty relates to the sequence in which the mortgages are recorded in the office of the county recorder where the mortgaged real estate is located. This sequence of recording is extremely important. We will explore this concept further in Chapter 8. For now, it is sufficient to realize that a first mortgage is nothing more than a mortgage, any mortgage containing any terms, that happens to be recorded first in the county records as a mortgage lien against the real property. Likewise, a second mortgage is one recorded next in time, and so on.

For a lender, it is vital to have the mortgage lien occupy as high a priority status as possible. *Having high priority status becomes valuable if any lien holder forecloses.* The proceeds of a foreclosure sale usually are applied in the following order: (a) All expenses of forced sale of the realty (court-ordered foreclosure sales typically are fairly expensive); (b) any amounts due for real estate taxes and assessments (these usually are in default as well, so they are often owed); (c) the debt secured by the first mortgage, even if that debt is not in default; (d) the second mortgage debt, and so on, based strictly on time of recording.

It is no wonder that lenders who intend to take back a first mortgage as security carefully scrutinize the county records before doing so to make sure no other mortgage already has been recorded. A mortgagee/lender may even require the mortgagor/borrower to purchase the lender's policy of title insurance to insure the priority of the lender's lien. In a federal bankruptcy discharge, priorities of mortgage liens also are recognized.

Creative Financing

The term *creative financing* is heard when real estate financing becomes tighter (more difficult to obtain) through commercial mortgagees/lenders. Creative financing generally involves some *arrangement directly between purchaser and seller in which all or part of the purchase price is accounted for by the seller's taking back some paper,* usually a purchase money mortgage or a land installment purchase contract, or even purchasers' assumption of sellers' mortgages or purchasers' taking subject to sellers' mortgages. All of these techniques are discussed in this chapter, but let's first discuss some of the ways real estate salespeople negotiate the financing of transactions when the money market tightens and interest rates rise.

The *type of sale that best lends itself to creative financing is one in which the seller owns the realty free and clear.* The drawback is finding a seller who can afford to wait for money. Typically in this type of transaction, the purchaser pays the seller a large enough cash down payment to cover the seller's closing costs, including the real estate broker's commission, with some surplus left over for the seller. The purchaser pays the balance of the purchase price directly to the seller over a period of time. The loan is amortized over a sufficiently long time so the periodic payments (usually monthly) are affordable, and the complete outstanding balance is due in a final, large payment a few years down the line. *The seller simply becomes the lender; no outside lenders are involved.* As security for the loan, the seller usually takes back a purchase money mortgage, or land installment purchase contract, and promissory note. Some of the reasons sellers and purchasers use creative financing techniques follow.

1. The seller has a great need to sell (divorce, finances, job transfer) and is able to dispose of the real property. A sale is deemed to have taken place.

2. The seller is able to earn a fairly high rate of interest on the investment (that is, the difference between the cash down payment and the agreed purchase price). Depending on prevailing rates, a seller might find that the purchaser is willing to guarantee payment of a higher interest rate over a longer period than the seller could obtain, with the same security, if he or she had the cash to invest in the open market.

3. Depending on the numbers, the purchaser might be able to afford to pay the seller an attractive rate but at the same time pay less than a traditional lender would

charge to make the same loan, especially taking into consideration that the seller does not usually demand expensive closing costs and loan qualification fees.

4. The purchaser obtains the considerable advantage of "locking in" the purchase price as of commencement of the transaction. So, if the realty appreciates in value, the purchaser benefits. The purchaser has to pay only the outstanding balance based on the original purchase price, not based on whatever the fair market value of the real property may be as of the final payment day.

5. The purchaser buys some time, so if money becomes available under better terms later, but before the final payment date, the purchaser can simply refinance the debt and pay the seller in full.

6. During a bad time for home loan financing, the seller may not be able to find any better purchaser. By agreeing to sell using a purchase money mortgage or a land installment purchase contract, the seller may be able to get top dollar for the real property, excellent interest during the wait, and if the money supply eases up, perhaps the balance of the purchase price earlier than expected.

Due-on-Sale Clause/Due-on-Transfer Clause

Not every seller is so fortunate as to own real property free and clear. How can a real estate agent creatively finance a sale for this seller? It can be done, but it is more difficult. One of the reasons is the so-called **due-on-sale clause** found in many mortgages. It generally reads:

> Should the mortgagor sell, transfer, change, modify, or otherwise alter the ownership of the land pledged in this mortgage, or any interest therein, without first obtaining the written consent of the mortgagee to such change, then the full outstanding balance owed the mortgagee on account of this transaction shall become immediately due and payable.

If the mortgagors/sellers who are burdened with this clause dispose of mortgaged realty without paying off the mortgage and without obtaining the written consent of the mortgagee/lender, they may have changed the nature of the mortgage loan from a long-term, easy-to-manage affair into a no-more-time, impossible-to-manage nightmare. The lender might now require the mortgagor/seller to pay the entire outstanding balance of the mortgage, using the acceleration clause, on the ground that the mortgagor/seller has violated the due-on-sale clause. The mortgagors/sellers may thus find themselves in a foreclosure action.

In 1982, the U. S. Supreme Court case of *Fidelity Federal Savings and Loan Assn. v. de la Cuesta,* one of the case studies presented at the end of this chapter, upheld the use of due-on-sale clauses by the mortgagee. Ohio case law also indicates that when a mortgagor/homeowner transfers an undivided one-half interest in the real estate to his or her spouse, the **due-on-transfer** is treated the same as the due-on-sale clause; that is, the mortgagee/lender can utilize the acceleration clause against the mortgagor/homeowner. This likewise might lead to a foreclosure action against the mortgagor/homeowner if, as is likely, he or she is unable to pay the entire outstanding mortgage balance to the mortgagee/lender.

Caution: *Not all modern mortgage instruments contain due-on-sale or due-on-transfer clauses.* One has to read the actual mortgage instruments, for each specific mortgage transaction, to ascertain if these clauses do or do not pertain.

The four most commonly used techniques for bringing about a creatively financed real estate transaction are the purchase money mortgage, the land installment purchase contract, assumption of loan and novation, and taking subject to the mortgage.

Purchase Money Mortgage

With a **purchase money mortgage,** instead of receiving all cash, as in the kind of transaction that became standard in the 20th century, the sellers receive some cash and the written, secured promise of the purchasers to pay the balance over a period of time. The *sellers become the mortgagees instead of a commercial lender's taking that role, whereas the purchasers remain in their role of mortgagors.* Typically, the purchasers/mortgagors are required to secure new mortgage loan financing with a commercial lender some years down the road to completely pay off the sellers/mortgagees and discharge the purchase money mortgage.

When using a purchase money mortgage, the purchasers execute a promissory note in favor of the sellers. It is secured by a mortgage on the realty. That loan is subordinate to any existing loan and the purchase money mortgage lien is also behind, in priority, any mortgage lien already existing against the realty. The mortgage deed used in the purchase money mortgage is the same kind of mortgage deed (Figure 7–2) used with a commercial lender. If the purchasers/mortgagors default on the mortgage, the sellers/mortgagees bring a foreclosure lawsuit in common pleas court against the purchasers/mortgagors.

Advantages to the purchasers/mortgagors under a purchase money mortgage are:

1. Fixing the price of the realty at the time of making the purchase money mortgage rather than later, when it must be refinanced with a commercial lender and the property probably will have increased in value.
2. Obtaining more time either to assemble more cash to apply against the purchase price or to take advantage of more affordable financing rates (with the commercial lender), or both.
3. Obtaining the tax advantages of being able to deduct all interest payments made to the sellers/mortgagees, plus all real estate property tax payments, from otherwise taxable income.

Advantages to the sellers/mortgagees are:

1. Selling realty that may have been otherwise unmarketable.
2. Charging a relatively high interest rate, which is applied to a large principal balance, and thereby realizing substantial earnings from the investment.

The chief disadvantages to the purchasers/mortgagors are:

1. Paying more in legal fees for preparation and review of all the documentation necessary to bring about this nonstandard transaction.
2. Coming up with refinancing of the entire transaction some years down the road. If the financing situation does not improve, and they cannot refinance with a commercial lender, they run the risk of defaulting on the purchase money mortgage and thereby going through foreclosure legal procedures.

The chief disadvantages to the sellers/mortgagees are:

1. Paying the legal fees for the considerable documentation that goes along with a purchase money mortgage real estate transaction.

2. The purchasers/mortgagors (possibly) not being as reliable as a purchaser who secures financing through a commercial lender. Thus, the sellers/mortgagees may be courting a higher rate of default with the purchasers/mortgagors. During times when interest rates become truly prohibitive, however, some very credit-worthy purchasers do resort to using purchase money mortgages. The sellers should ask for financial information from potential purchasers/mortgagees, just as a commercial lender would, when they are asked to become the mortgagees. Then they can assess how much risk of default they are taking on. If the purchasers/mortgagors do default, the sellers/mortgagees will have to institute foreclosure legal proceedings against them. These are expensive lawsuits.

Taking all of the above into account, the purchase money mortgage is usually best utilized in tight financing times, when it is difficult for many worthy purchasers to obtain conventional financing through a conventional mortgagee/lender.

Land Installment Purchase Contract

For many years the **land installment purchase contract** (also known as the land contract) was thought to be some kind of shifty, barely legal means for a seller to unload a near-worthless piece of realty on some unsuspecting, uncreditworthy, and equally worthless purchaser. In times of high interest rates and tight financing, the land contract emerges instead as another viable financing alternative. It is one of the most versatile and often-used creative financing techniques in those periods. In some places it goes by the name "contract for deed" or "agreement for deed." *All of these terms refer to a written agreement between the* ***vendor*** *(the land contract seller) and the* ***vendee*** *(the land contract purchaser) providing for payment of the purchase price on an installment basis and, after full payment has been made, providing for the transfer of legal title of the realty to the vendee.* The land contract can be used alone (the usual case) or in combination with any number of other financing techniques.

Because the land contract is a contract, all the requisites for forming a valid contract, as discussed in Chapter 6, are also required for land contracts. The land contract must be in writing because it is within the coverage ("an interest in land") covered by the statute of frauds. Ohio has legislation (Chapter 5313 of the Ohio Revised Code) that specifically requires certain minimums for land installment purchase contracts. These are:

1. The full names and post office address of all parties to the contract.
2. The date when signed by each party.
3. A legal description of the realty conveyed.
4. The contract price of the realty conveyed.
5. Any charges or fees for services that are included in the contract but are separate from the contract price.
6. The amount of the vendee's down payment.
7. The principal balance owed, which is the sum of items (4) and (5) less item (6).
8. The amount and due date of each installment payment.
9. The interest rate on the unpaid balance and the method of computing the rate.
10. A statement of any encumbrances against the realty.
11. A statement requiring the vendor to deliver a deed of general warranty (or an otherwise available deed) upon completion of the contract.

12. A provision that the vendor provide evidence of title in accordance with the prevailing custom in the area where the realty is located.
13. A provision that if the vendor defaults on any mortgage on the realty, the vendee can pay on said mortgage and receive credit for such payment on the land installment contract.
14. A provision that the vendor shall cause a copy of the contract to be recorded.
15. A requirement that the vendee be responsible for payment of taxes, assessments, and other charges against the realty from the date of the contract, unless agreed to the contrary.
16. A statement of any pending order of any public agency against the property.
17. Vendor and vendee each to receive a copy of the land contract.

The land contract also conforms to the formalities required by law for the execution of deeds and mortgages because of the *requirement that it be recorded.* Recording, too, lessens the possibility of the realty's acquiring title problems later. The recording is notice to the public of the vendee's interest in the realty. Without recording, the vendee would have to worry about the vendor's borrowing additional money against the realty. Recording the land contract can prevent the vendor from further encumbering the realty. Other potential lien holders (such as potential mortgagees perhaps later approached by the seller/vendor for a mortgage) thus will be on notice of the vendee's interest, making a potential lien holder reluctant to enter into any transaction with the seller/vendor that uses that realty as security.

Vendees who default on land contracts usually face a legal process called **forfeiture,** which involves *giving up, or forfeiting, to the vendor all of the payments made by vendee up to the point of default, plus restoration of the possession of the premises to the vendor.* A relatively fast, inexpensive, and effective eviction proceeding, known as a *forcible entry and detainer action,* is used with forfeiture. The vendor keeps all payments received from the vendee, whereas the vendee no longer has any right to possession of the premises. Best of all, from the vendors' viewpoint, the real property is restored to them when it may well have appreciated in value. The real property is ready for another sale with no duty by the vendor to compensate the vendee for any lost equity appreciation that might have occurred.

Ohio softens this harsh position for the defaulting vendee by statute. If the vendee defaults after paying a certain percentage toward the agreed sales price, or if the vendee has made land contract payments beyond a set time limit, the vendor cannot evict the vendee and declare that a forfeiture of all land contract payments be made. Rather, the vendor is forced to seek redress solely by the foreclosure proceeding as a mortgagee would in the same circumstances. The foreclosure process is far different (and far more complex, expensive, and lengthy) from the forfeiture process.

Advantages to the vendee under a land installment purchase contract are:

1. Obtaining possession of the realty prior to full payment of the cost of the realty.
2. Fixing the price at the beginning of the period of the land contract rather than later, when the realty might be expected to cost more.
3. Obtaining more time either to assemble more cash to apply against the purchase price or to take advantage of more affordable financing rates, or both.
4. Obtaining the tax advantages, during the whole term of the land contract, of being able to deduct all interest payments made to vendor and all real estate tax payments from otherwise taxable income.

There are also advantages for the vendor:

1. Selling realty that was (usually) otherwise unmarketable.
2. Retaining legal title as security.
3. Being able to charge the vendee a relatively high interest rate and, because this rate is to be applied to a large principal balance, being able to realize substantial earnings from the investment.
4. In many cases, being able to simply evict the vendee from the realty and declare a forfeiture of all payments to date, if the vendee fails to carry out the promises.

Entering into land contracts also has disadvantages. The chief disadvantages to the vendee are:

1. Having to sue for specific performance of the land contract, if the vendor refuses to transfer title, in exactly the same manner as one would under the real estate purchase contract—an expensive undertaking.
2. Incurring the significant expense and time delay of securing title through the probate court process if the vendor dies before transferring title to the vendee.

In both of the above instances, the vendee likely will have to absorb some significant legal fees in addition to other costs.

The chief disadvantages to the vendor lie in:

1. Reliability of the vendee. This person may not be as reliable as a purchaser who buys realty using a conventional mortgage with a mortgage lender. Vendors court higher risk of default by vendees. During times when interest rates become truly prohibitive with mortgagees/lenders, however, some surprisingly creditworthy purchasers are willing to use land contracts.

   The seller/vendor should obtain financial information, such as a credit report and employment verification, from a prospective purchaser/vendee, because the vendee who wants a vendor to "carry this paper" is asking the vendor to be a bank. The vendor, therefore, should act like a bank and require credit information to see whether the prospective vendee is someone who pays his or her bills.
2. The vendor's likelihood of needing the services of a lawyer—greater than in a conventional transaction. The vendor probably will hire a lawyer to draft the land contract and certainly will hire a lawyer to pursue a forfeiture or foreclosure proceeding against a vendee.

For all of the previous factors, the land contract usually is best utilized in tight financing times, when many worthy purchasers have difficulty obtaining conventional financing through a conventional mortgagee/lender.

Figure 7–4 is a sample real estate purchase contract as used by a real estate agent in a land contract transaction. The land contract still has to be prepared using the given terms but, typically, the vendor and vendee prefer that their attorneys prepare and review it for all potential problems. In Ohio, a real estate agent does not fill in the blanks on a land contract, as that is considered practicing law. Instead, a lawyer prepares the land contract. Figure 7–4 follows this conservative approach: The real estate agent fills in the real estate purchase contract that calls for a land contract to subsequently be prepared.

Mortgage Assumption and Novation

In a **mortgage assumption,** the *purchaser pays the difference between the agreed sales price and the amount of the assumed loan by a direct cash payment to the mortgagor/seller, or by a partial cash payment and a purchase money mortgage to*

FIGURE 7–4
Real estate purchase contract used in land contract transaction.

PARTIES/PREMISES

I/We, JOHN SMITH and MARY SMITH, of 428 SOUTH STREET in LYNDHURST, OHIO, hereinafter "Vendor", and I/We, WILLIAM BROWN and SUSAN BROWN, of 10072 CHESTER ROAD in MAPLE HEIGHTS, OHIO, hereinafter "Vendee", in consideration of the promises contained herein do hereby offer to sell and purchase, respectively, the real property located at 428 SOUTH STREET in LYNDHURST Ohio, and being further described as A SINGLE FAMILY FRAME DWELLING WITH TWO-CAR ATTACHED GARAGE, together with all improvements, rights and appurtenances thereunto belonging, including any of the following as may exist thereon: all plumbing, electrical, heating, cooling and air treatment fixtures and appliances; all window and door shades and screens and all storm windows and storm doors; all garage door mechanisms and related controls; all television antennas; all awnings; all landscaping; all curtain and drapery rods; all accessory or supplementary heating devices and TOOL SHED IN REAR YARD, THE FIREPLACE TOOLS AND ACCESSORIES, THE WOODEN WORK BENCH IN THE BASEMENT, THE CLOTHES WASHER and DRYER, AND THE TORO SNOW BLOWER, all of which shall be referred to hereinafter as "the premises".

THE PURCHASE PRICE

Vendee shall pay Vendor as the purchase price for said premises the total sum of EIGHTY-FIVE THOUSAND and 00/100 DOLLARS ($ 85,000.-), payable as follows:

(a) earnest money in the form of A PERSONAL CHECK, paid to VENDOR ....$ 1,000.--

(b) cash, to be deposited in the escrow referred to hereinafter - ~~to be paid at closing~~ (select one) ....$ 9,000.—

(c) balance, to be paid by Vendee to Vendor by land installment purchase agreement, subject to Ohio law, and in a form satisfactory to Vendor and Vendee, and to their respective attorneys, if any, subject to and including at least the following terms: ....$ 75,000.—

(i) A recordable draft of said Land Contract shall be approved by Vendor and Vendee, and by their attorneys, if any, by APRIL 20th, 1997, or this entire transaction shall become null and void and all deposits shall be returned to Vendee immediately, unless both parties agree to an extension of time for preparation and execution of such document. The first draft of such proposed Land Contract shall be prepared and paid for by VENDEE and shall be submitted to the other party for review within twenty days following formation of this Agreement.

(ii) Said balance of $ 75,000.- shall bear interest at the rate of 13 % per year, simple interest, computed MONTHLY, and such sum shall be repaid at the rate of $ 832.08 per MONTH, commencing MAY 1st, 1997, based on an amortization schedule of TWENTY-NINE years.

(iii) The entire remaining balance shall be paid off in full on or before but no later than MAY 1st, 2002 without any additional penalty or charge whatsoever.

(iv) An amortization schedule, marked "Exhibit A," setting forth the foregoing, is attached hereto and is hereby incorporated herein.(strike-if appropriate)

(v) Vendee shall pay Vendor each month, in addition to said payments of principal and interest, one-twelfth of the annual real property tax and special assessment charges levied against Vendor, as may be adjusted by the taxing authority from time to time, which charges, based on the current tax duplicate, would amount to approximately $ 92.50 per month.

(vi) Fire and extended coverage hazard insurance and personal liability coverage shall be maintained at all times during the continuance of said Land Contract, commencing with exchange of possession, subject to the following:

-- both Vendor and Vendee shall be named insureds on all such policies

-- hazard insurance coverage shall be in an amount equal to the full replacement value of all improvements to the premises, adjusted annually on the anniversary of the exchange of possession of the premises

-- hazard insurance loss payments shall be payable to both Vendor and Vendee and shall be used first to repair, replace, or reconstruct all damaged portions of said premises; any excess shall then be divided between Vendor and Vendee based on the percentage Vendee has paid toward the purchase price as of the date of loss or damage, and all payments received by Vendor in this way shall be credited against the principal balance then owed by Vendee by virtue of said Land Contract

-- liability insurance payments shall be payable to or on behalf of either party, as their interest may then appear

-- Vendee shall pay for the full cost of all such insurance coverage and shall provide Vendor either via escrow or at closing, as appropriate, with reliable evidence of the existence and effective date of such insurance coverage

(continued)

FIGURE 7–4 Continued.

-- in the event that Vendor has already mortgaged the premises as of the date of this Agreement, that such mortgage debt will not be paid off as of exchange of possession of the premises, that Vendor's said mortgagee shall have consented to the terms of said Land Contract and that hazard insurance already exists, pursuant to the terms of such mortgage, then in such event Vendor shall and does hereby promise to cooperate with Vendee to do all things necessary to assure that the hazard and personal liability insurance provisions set forth hereinabove shall, nevertheless, be in full force and effect during the entire term of said Land Contract

(vii) The following additional charges shall be made by Vendor of Vendee: - NONE -

(viii) The premises are presently subject to the following encumbrances or pending orders of public agencies: - NONE -

As of the date of recording of said Land Contract, Vendor shall handle the foregoing encumbrances or agency orders in the following way: - NOT APPLY -

Vendor shall in no way further encumber the premises following the date of formation of this Purchase Agreement.

(ix) Upon completion of said Land Contract, Vendor shall deliver or cause to be delivered to Vendee a proper, general warranty deed, or fiduciary deed, if required, conveying marketable title to Vendee, with dower rights, if any, released, free and clear of all liens and encumbrances whatsoever, except restrictions, conditions, limitations and easements of record, zoning ordinances, if any, and taxes and assessments for the current half of the taxable year and thereafter, and except for encumbrances assumed by Vendee or caused by his acts.

(x) Vendor shall also deliver or cause to be delivered to Vendee title evidence in the amount of the purchase price and showing goodness of title, subject to the following:

-- at the time of exchange of possession A TITLE GUARANTEE IN THE AMOUNT OF $85,000.-

and this shall be paid for by VENDOR

-- at the time of title transfer A TITLE GUARANTEE IN THE AMOUNT OF $85,000. (UPDATED)

and this shall be paid for by BOTH PARTIES, EQUALLY

(xi) Should Vendor default, according to the terms of any mortgage that may encumber the property, Vendee shall have the right to make mortgage payments for Vendor during the time of such default, and having made such payments, Vendee shall receive credit from Vendor against Land Contract payments due, in the full amount of all such default payments.

(xii) Said Land Contract shall be executed in duplicate and Vendor shall cause one properly executed, witnessed and notarized copy of said Land Contract to be recorded, at Vendor's expense, within twenty (20) days following execution of the same by both parties.

(xiii) Both parties acknowledge that Ohio law prohibits a vendor from selling real property by land contract when the vendor's mortgage indebtedness against the property is in excess of the principal balance then owed by the vendee to the vendor under said land contract. Further, the parties assert that the transaction set forth herein does not and will not violate that provision of Ohio law.

PRORATIONS

Rentals, utility charges and assumed insurance premium payments or deposits shall be prorated as of exchange of possession of the premises. Real estate taxes and assessments shall be prorated as of FILING OF THE DEED FOR ~~RECORD~~ on the basis of a 365 day year and using the then last-available tax duplicate.

EXCHANGE OF POSSESSION

Vendor shall transfer possession of the premises to Vendee on MAY 1st, 1997, SO LONG AS ALL TERMS OF THIS AGREEMENT HAVE THEN BEEN CARRIED OUT.

CLOSING

Said executed Land Contract and all other funds and documents necessary to the completion of this transaction shall be presented at a formal closing on -NA-, 19____, or shall be deposited in escrow by APRIL 30th, 1997 (select one). If an escrow closing is used, the parties agree to share equally the charge made by the escrow agent for his services. In all events, Vendor shall have thirty (30) days after notice to him to correct any defect in his title as might appear either at or prior to such contemplated closing.

CONDITIONS

This Purchase Agreement is subject to the following conditions. Should such fail to occur, this Agreement shall be deemed to be null and void and any funds theretofore paid or deposited by Vendee shall be immediately and fully returned to Vendee.

(a) Within ten days following formation of this Purchase Agreement, Vendee shall supply Vendor with a credit report or other reasonably reliable evidence of the ability of Vendee to complete this Land Contract purchase in the form and manner set forth herein. Vendor shall have five days after actual receipt of such evidence to either accept or reject Vendee as a proposed debtor. If Vendor rejects Vendee, he shall do so in writing, and having done so, this Purchase Agreement shall become null and void and Vendee shall receive back, immediately, all of his deposited funds. On the other hand, should Vendor find Vendee to be an acceptable credit risk, he shall so state in writing, and this transaction shall move to the next stage; i.e., the preparation of the proposed Land Contract.

(b) - NONE -

ADDITIONAL PROMISES (not being conditions of the Agreement)

The parties also hereby covenant and agree as follows: - NONE -

REAL ESTATE BROKER(s)

The parties acknowledge that RELIABLE REALTY OF LYNDHURST, OHIO is ~~(are)~~ the sole procuring cause of this sale and that no other real estate brokers or salespeople have been involved in any way. Vendor hereby agrees to pay said broker(s) the sum of $ 5,950.- (being -7- % of the purchase price), $ 5,950.- to RELIABLE REALTY and $ -NA- to -NA- and that this is the full amount owed by Vendor as a real estate commission arising on account of this entire transaction.

ENTIRE AGREEMENT

The parties acknowledge that the terms and provisions of this Purchase Agreement represent their full and complete agreement regarding this matter and that they are not in any way relying on any statements, assertions, inducements, representations or other factors that have not been expressly stated herein.

ASSIGNMENT PROHIBITED

It is agreed that Vendee shall not assign, transfer, or otherwise alienate his interest or any portion thereof in this Purchase Agreement or in said Land Contract without first obtaining the written consent of Vendor thereto.

PARTIES BOUND

This Purchase Agreement shall be binding on and shall inure to the benefit of the parties hereto and their respective executors, administrators, other personal representatives, heirs, devisees and to Vendor's assigns. Vendee's assigns shall also be bound, so long as Vendor, or his assigns, shall have first consented to such assignment.

IN WITNESS WHEREOF, the parties have set their hands to - THREE - duplicate copies of this Purchase Agreement, all of which shall be deemed to be originals.

VENDOR: John Smith
Mary Smith
APRIL 1, 1997 (date)

VENDEE: William Brown
Susan Brown
APRIL 1, 1997 (date)

ACKNOWLEDGMENT OF EARNEST MONEY DEPOSIT

Receipt is hereby acknowledged of said $ 1,000 - earnest money deposit, being in the form of A PERSONAL CHECK, which shall be held by me pursuant to the terms of this Agreement.

By: John Smith
APRIL 1, 1997 (date)

NOTE: The foregoing Agreement is a legal document involving burdens and benefits to both parties. If you do not understand it, do not sign it until you have consulted an attorney.

the mortgagor/seller (who will be the mortgagee under the purchase money mortgage to the mortgagor/purchaser) for the difference, or by such a mortgage to account for all of the difference.

Certain mortgage loans are designed to be assumable from the start. FHA and VA loans have long been of this type. Other cases of assumable mortgage loans can be found with some of the mortgage loans that were developed and marketed as alternative mortgage instruments during tight financing times. Some of these shorter-term, flexible interest rate loans were designed specifically to be assumable. In those instances, a purchaser could take over the mortgage loan obligation of the mortgagor/seller without having to obtain the consent of the mortgagee/lender.

Depending upon the type of assumable loan, the mortgagor/seller is either entirely free from responsibility with respect to the original loan obligation, or the mortgagor/seller is only secondarily responsible behind the new, assuming purchaser. The case in which the *mortgagor/seller eliminates all further responsibilities* is not technically a case of assumption, although that term often is applied. More accurately, that is called a *novation,* or an entirely new contract. The case in which the *mortgagor/seller continues to be secondarily responsible,* is a true assumption; here, until a purchaser pays off the mortgagee/lender in full, that mortgagee/lender can still pursue the mortgagor/seller in the event of the purchaser's default. The mortgagor/seller also has the right to sue the purchaser if the purchaser defaults in mortgage loan assumption payments to the mortgagee/lender.

Taking Subject to the Mortgage

Taking "subject to the mortgage" occurs when buyers purchase property subject to the lien of the mortgage that the sellers already have upon it. Essentially those purchasers pay the sellers for their equity in the property. Any interest the purchaser acquires in this property comes behind the interests of the mortgagee/lender and the mortgagor/seller. Usually, if there is a foreclosure and the proceeds from the foreclosure sale are not sufficient, any deficiency judgment responsibility remains the mortgagor's/seller's.

Truth-in-Lending Law

Anyone who is involved in financing real estate transactions or merely in arranging for someone else to provide financing has to know about certain aspects of the **Truth-in-Lending Law** and its interpretation by the Federal Reserve Board, known as **Regulation Z.** This law issued from the Board of Governors of the Federal Reserve System as Title I of the Consumer Credit Protection Act of 1968. It has been updated periodically. The purpose is *to promote the informed use of consumer credit by requiring meaningful disclosures about the loan's term and cost.*

The Truth-in-Lending law is important to real estate brokers and salespersons because of its advertising provisions. Its goal is truthfulness in advertising about available credit terms. If a real estate brokerage advertises specific terms for credit, these terms must be the ones the creditor actually offers on a regular basis.

Truth-in-Lending/Regulation Z also has *triggering terms* in advertising; that is, if an ad contains certain language, other terms must be used in that same ad. Specifically, if the ad states:

- the amount of percentage of any down payment (except if a down payment is not required),
- the number of payments or period of repayment,
- the amount of any payment, and
- the amount of any finance charge,

then the ad must also state:

- the amount of percentage of the down payment,
- the terms of repayment, and
- the "annual percentage rate," using that term and whether the rate is to increase after consummation.

Accordingly, care should be exercised in writing any real estate advertisements that involve financing information.

If real estate brokerages are the entities extending the actual credit in financing real estate transactions, more disclosure duties under this law apply to them.

OTHER (NONFINANCING-BASED) LIENS

So far in this chapter we have discussed in detail the most common lien or claim against realty—the mortgage lien. Most people have to borrow money to purchase realty and lenders want the best security they can get for repayment of those loans (mortgages), so it is no wonder that most real properties are encumbered by mortgage liens. Because the mortgagor has consented to placing the mortgage lien against the realty, that lien is characterized as being a **voluntary or consensual lien.** Likewise, when purchase money mortgages or land installment purchase contracts are used, the liens that result are characterized as voluntary or consensual liens.

There are additional liens or claims against the realty itself, created by law to protect the interest of someone who has dealt with the real property owner and who has a right to some payment. Many of these liens are involuntary. The **involuntary lien,** created by operation of law and without consent, *protects people who have monetary claims against owners of real property.* Mechanics' liens and judgment liens, discussed next, are examples of involuntary liens.

In all situations in which there are liens against realty, *any one of those lien holders can force judicial sale of realty* to generate monetary proceeds to satisfy his or her claim for repayment. Thus, any lien holder usually can bring a foreclosure suit against the owner of realty subject to the lien. The only issue is whether the lien can be satisfied by any parcel of real property owned by an obliged owner or whether it has to be satisfied by a specific parcel of that obliged owner's real estate. If any parcel will do, the lien is a **general lien.** If only a specific parcel can be sold, the lien is a **special lien.**

Mechanic's Lien

The **mechanic's lien** is covered by Chapter 1311 of the Ohio Revised Code. The statutes are quite technical, specific, and detailed, and they are strictly followed by the courts. Mechanics' liens serve as *protection for contractors, subcontractors, materialmen, and laborers (referred to as mechanics) to real property who remain unpaid.* The owner, part owner, or lessee of the real property (referred to as owner) is the one against whom the mechanic's lien is obtained. In obtaining their mechanics' liens, mechanics must be able to show they had a contract with the owner to work upon, supply, or manage construction upon the real property. As *special, involuntary liens,* mechanics' liens apply only to a specific parcel of real estate and are placed without the owner's consent. Mechanics' liens can be *used to force a judicial sale* of the realty to satisfy unpaid claims.

If a piece of real property having a valid mechanic's lien against it is sold, when the time comes to close the transaction, a defect in the title will be found because of that mechanic's lien. Because sellers are given only a short time to clear title defects (30 days under most real estate purchase contracts), they usually are forced to pay off the mechanic's lien so they can give the purchaser clear title and not be in breach of the real estate purchase contract. This is the way real estate agents, sellers, and purchasers typically come across a mechanic's lien problem.

Auditor's Lien

The county auditor is another person who, like the mortgagee and the mechanic, occupies a strong position relative to real property. The **auditor's lien** comes into play if *a real property owner fails to pay local real estate taxes when due, or within the time permitted by law thereafter; the realty can be foreclosed upon and sold by the auditor.* The proceeds are used to pay the delinquent taxes and then all other liens, in order of their priority. The sale/minimum bid procedure is like the sheriff's sale.

The real property tax lien consists of two elements: the general tax lien and the special assessment tax lien. The general lien attaches to the real property and is computed uniformly within each locality of the state based on a rate set by law and applied to a set percentage of the appraised value of the realty. This is why the tax is called general; it applies generally and uniformly throughout the local taxing district.

Special assessments are not the same as general taxes, although they are also liens against the realty. Special assessments arise because certain realties have benefitted from improvements (such as sanitary or storm sewers, sidewalks, street lights, paving, and so forth) and these improvements have not yet been paid for. Because the improvement was put in to benefit only a few real properties, not the whole community, only those few have the duty to pay for the improvement. General tax liens take priority over special assessment liens when funds are paid out of an auditor's sale of the realty; the money is first applied to pay the general taxes in full.

Federal Tax Lien

Coming as a surprise to no one today in this age of significant federal influence in many things, the *federal government can obtain a lien against all realty in the United States owned by persons who owe it money.* These include liens due to failure to pay federal income and estate/gift taxes, plus federal environmental liens. Consistent with the theory of liens as set forth above, if the taxpayer fails or refuses to pay overdue federal taxes, the realty can be sold and the proceeds used to satisfy this obligation.

Ohio Revised Code Sections 317.08 and 319.09 require that notices of liens in favor of the federal government, and certificates of discharge or release of those liens, are to be filed in the county recorder's office of the county where that realty is situated. These provisions simplify the search the title companies must make before they agree to insure or guarantee titles (more fully discussed in Chapter 8).

Judgment Lien

The **judgment lien** that can attach to realty comes about because someone is victorious in a court battle involving a real property owner who loses. The winning party is awarded a judgment, which is a statement signed by the court, that clearly spells out the nature of the claim that the winner of the lawsuit has made against the other. It summarizes the evidence or proof that sustained the winning party's arguments, and the judgment ends by awarding the winning party a sum of money equal to the value of the claim. At this point, the judgment is no more than a piece of paper, signed by a judge, telling the losing party to pay the winning party. The judgment has not yet affected the losing party's real property in any way. The judgment can come about because of any *wrongful or damaging act done by the losing party against the winning party,* such as a breach of contract in a business transaction or personal injuries sustained in an auto collision.

If this winning party, the holder of the judgment, is not able to obtain payment from the losing party, and if the losing party owns real property that the judgment holder knows about, the judgment holder can file a **certificate of judgment** as part of the real property records of the county in which the realty is located. In this way, the judgment holder acquires a lien against the judgment debtor's realty to the extent of the claim. If the losing party owns other real property, the judgment lien holder can file certificates of judgment against that other real estate as well, because the judgment lien is a *general lien.* Once the judgment lien is satisfied, however, any other pieces of real estate with the same judgment lien filed against them have to be discharged from that judgment lien. The right of recovery is not limited to just real property. Because the losing party certainly cannot be characterized as consenting to the judgment lien (if anything, that party is hostile toward paying anything to the winning judgment holder), the judgment lien is characterized as an *involuntary lien.*

The lien holder can initiate an even further course of action, typically a foreclosure suit, which will result in public sale of the realty, the proceeds of which are used to pay off the judgment lien and any other liens. Other liens, however, could well be prior to this judgment lien—such as the mortgage, mechanic's, and, certainly, the tax lien. Proceeds of the sale go to pay off those liens first.

If owners sell their realty subject to a judgment lien, they have to clear off that judgment lien (and any other liens) to convey clear title, as required under the real estate purchase contract. Once again, that purchase contract usually gives them only 30 days to clear up title defects. So, if they cannot pay off the lien(s), they are in breach of that contract. Most sellers in this situation apply as much as is needed of their sales proceeds to pay off all recorded liens so they can perform the real estate purchase contract.

Other Forced Sales of Real Property

Bankruptcy

Bankruptcy is a proceeding in federal court in which individuals, corporations, or partnerships declare themselves bankrupt and request the court to *divide up what assets they have among their creditors* and, in so doing, to terminate any further responsibility of the debtors to pay the creditors. Bankruptcy proceedings involve all of the assets of debtors, not just a particular secured parcel of realty as in foreclosure proceedings. Of course, if debtors own realty and go bankrupt, the realty, as an asset (often the most valuable asset), typically is disposed of along with the other assets pursuant to the bankruptcy rules.

Given the present rules, which permit certain *exemptions* or debtors' holding back from the creditors certain classes of property and certain sums of money, and given that such exemptions are now relatively generous to the debtors, it is often to the debtors' advantage to go bankrupt just as fast as they can. There is a specific federal exemption, worth a set amount of money to the debtors, for the debtors' residential real property. A provision in the federal bankruptcy law permits states to set the limits of the exemptions instead and, if set, requires the federal court to abide by that limit in its proceedings. If the state has set no exemption figure limit, the federal limit is used instead. *By statute, Ohio has its own exemption limits.*

Once a bankruptcy is commenced by filing a petition in federal court, most foreclosure actions against any realty of the debtor are stayed or halted, pending disposition of the debtor's assets.

Stays can be lifted, and the foreclosure case allowed to proceed. Whether the stay against the foreclosure proceeding is lifted depends largely on how much value the real estate has in excess of the mortgage(s) liens plus the value to the debtors/owners of the real property exemptions. The bankruptcy trustee can allow private sales when these circumstances are favorable; that is, when the realty has value in excess of the mortgage liens and/or the debtors qualify for the real property exemptions. The automatic stay probably will remain in effect while the trustee seeks to effect a private sale. Usually trustees use real estate brokers' services and, thus, these cases can be sources of potential listings and sales for real estate agents.

Partition

A final mechanism for getting realty up "on the block" has a name that pretty much carries its heart on its sleeve. **Partition,** refreshingly enough, means exactly what it sounds like it means: *to divide realty into parts or portions based on the relative interests of those who have title to the real property or those who have certain claims against it.* If the owners cannot agree about the division, they must petition common pleas court, asking it to partition the real estate instead.

If the court is able to physically divide the real estate itself into parcels that fit the owners' respective percentage interests, that is the preferred method. This is rarely feasible, though. The more usual result is a public sale, much like a foreclosure sale, with the coowners receiving proceeds from that sale in a ratio commensurate with their ownership interests in the realty.

As with bankruptcies and foreclosures, partition actions are more frequent today, primarily because many single people now live together and take title to their residence in both names. When these individuals break up, they have the problem of dividing up that realty. Because they are unmarried, they do not have the benefit of divorce court proceedings that often involve a court-ordered disposition of realty. If they cannot mutually agree (and they often cannot, as they are "divorcing") on how to dispose of their real property, one or the other of them tends to file an action with common pleas court where their real property is located, asking that the court divide the realty between them according to the rights of each. This is called a partition action, and the particulars are covered by Ohio statutes. Tenants in common and survivorship tenants of any estate in land can be plaintiffs or defendants in a partition action.

A partition action usually requires a public rather than a private sale, and no reference is made for hiring a real estate broker to attempt to procure a private sale,

TABLE 7–1 Comparison of foreclosure, bankruptcy, and partition.

	FORECLOSURE	BANKRUPTCY	PARTITION
Court	Common pleas court.	U.S. District Court.	Common pleas court.
Parties	Mortgagee vs. mortgagor.	Debtor vs. creditors.	Coowner vs. coowner.
Disposition of Realty	Forced sale or possibly private sale if all parties agree and if it occurs before the auction date.	Forced sale or possibly private sale agreed to by debtor and approved by trustee.	Forced sale or possibly private sale agreed to by coowners; rarely, a division of realty into parcels/no sale.
Liens	Paid off to the extent of sale proceeds; mortgagee/borrower might be pursued personally for balance.	Paid off to the extent of sale proceeds (less debtor's exemption); debtor forever discharged from unpaid liens.	If a forced sale, liens paid off to the extent of sale proceeds; coowners might be pursued personally for the balance.

although mutual agreement of the parties and local court practice may permit a private sale. Still, in all cases of partition, several persons in the community with personal knowledge of the value of the real property being partitioned are required, and real estate people with good appraisal skills make ideal candidates for these (paid) positions. A party to the partition suit can elect to purchase the real estate at the appraisal value. If there is no such election, there is a public sale conducted by the sheriff, just like the one for foreclosure. Partition actions continue to be used in the more traditional way, in which any mutual coowners—college friends, joint business venturers, sports enthusiasts, mother and adult child or father and adult child, or any others who have taken title together—cannot agree about disposing of their coowned property and one decides to force the issue by filing a partition action.

Table 7–1 contrasts the essential differences among foreclosure, bankruptcy, and partition actions.

CASE STUDY FROM THE OHIO SUPREME COURT

OHIO SAVINGS BANK V. AMBROSE
56 Ohio St. 3d 53, 563 N.E.2d 1388 (1990)

Facts: On July 6, 1987, Ohio Savings Bank filed a complaint for money, foreclosure, and other equitable relief against Anthony and Mary Lou Ambrose, formerly husband and wife. On January 28, 1988, the trial court found that Anthony Ambrose was in default for failing to respond and that the bank was entitled to $57,629 plus interest. The court ordered that unless the money owed to the bank was paid within three days, the equity of redemption would be foreclosed and the property sold at sheriff's sale. The property was not redeemed within the required time. An order of sale was issued, which indicated by sheriff's return that the property was purchased on April 28, 1988, by Sally Engert. The property had been appraised at $108,000 and conditionally purchased for $80,000.

On April 29, 1988, Mary Lou Ambrose filed a motion to deny confirmation of the sale and to permit her to redeem the property. Mary Lou Ambrose had arranged a private sale that would satisfy the debts to all the lienholders and to that end established a schedule for payment of proceeds from the sale to the lienholders. Pursuant to Ohio Revised Code Section 2329.33, a debtor may redeem the property in question at any time prior to confirmation of the sale. On May 10, 1988, the bank moved to confirm the sale. The trial court continued the confirmation hearing, finding that the defendants were in a position to redeem the property prior to the confirmation of sale.

Trial Court: On May 31, 1988, the trial court set aside sale of the property to Robert and Sally Engert, finding that the property had been redeemed and all liens had been satisfied. In a second judgment entry filed that same day, the court denied the motion to confirm the sale, vacated the sheriff's sale, and ordered that the Engerts' deposit be returned to them with interest. The Engerts appealed both decisions to the court of appeals.

Court of Appeals: Determined that the Engerts were neither parties to the action nor had they filed a motion to intervene in the trial court. In addition, the Engerts had no interest in the property prior to confirmation and their failure to intervene as parties divested them of their capacity to appeal the decision of the trial court. Dismissed the appeal.

Issue: Whether purchasers at a foreclosure sale have a vested interest in property prior to confirmation of the sale by the trial court, so as to establish standing in order to appeal a denial of confirmation.

Held by the Ohio Supreme Court: Purchasers at a foreclosure sale have no vested interest in property prior to confirmation of sale and thus have no standing to appeal when trial court denied confirmation. The primary purpose and goal of a foreclosure sale is to protect the interests of the mortgagor/debtor and at the same time ensure that secured creditors will receive payment for unpaid debts. Permitting purchasers to appeal the denial of confirmation would elevate their position above that of debtors and creditors, the very parties that Ohio Revised Code Chapter 2329 seeks to protect. It would be illogical to grant purchasers, who have no vested interest in the property prior to confirmation, the power to nullify a sale that is more advantageous to the debtor and creditors.

Affirmed the decision of the court of appeals dismissing the appeal.

FIDELITY FEDERAL SAVINGS & LOAN ASSN. V. REGINALD D. DE LA CUESTA 458 US 141, 73 L Ed 2d 664, 102 S Ct 3014 (1982)

CASE STUDY FROM THE U.S. SUPREME COURT

Facts: de la Cuesta and others purchased California real property from those who had borrowed money from Fidelity. As security for the loan, the borrowers had given Fidelity deeds of trust to the property. Each deed of trust contained a due-on-sale clause. Two of the deeds also included a provision stating that the deed was to be governed by the law of the jurisdiction in which the property was located. Fidelity was not notified prior to each person's purchase of property.

When Fidelity learned of the transfers, it gave notice of its intent to enforce the due-on-sale clause. Fidelity expressed a willingness, however, to consent to the transfers if the purchasers agreed to increase the interest rate on the loans secured by the properties to the then-prevailing market rate. Purchasers refused to accept this condition, and Fidelity exercised its option to accelerate the loan. When the loan was not paid, Fidelity instituted a nonjudicial foreclosure (which is used in California) proceeding. Purchasers sued Fidelity in the Superior Court of California for Orange County for declaratory, injunctive, and damages relief against enforcement of the clauses.

California Superior Court: Granted summary judgment against the purchasers by upholding the due-on-sale clause against them.

Court of Appeals, Fourth Appellate District: Reversed on the ground that exercise of the clauses violated California's prohibition of unreasonable restraints on alienation. Struck down due-on-sale clauses.

California Supreme Court: Denied a petition for review.

Issue: Whether the Federal Home Loan Bank Board meant to preempt California's due-on-sale law and, if so, whether that action is within the scope of that board's delegated authority.

United States Supreme Court: Reversed the Court of Appeals and upheld the due-on-sale clause against the purchasers. Held that the Home Owners' Loan Act (HOLA) empowers the Federal Home Loan Bank Board to issue regulations authorizing due-on-sale clauses in the loan contracts of federal savings and loan associations. The board's due-on-sale regulation was meant to preempt conflicting state limitations on the due-on-sale practices of federal savings and loans. HOLA did not simply incorporate existing local loan practices. Rather, Congress delegated to the board broad authority to establish and regulate a uniform system of savings and loan institutions and to establish them with the force of the government behind them. The board had exercised that discretion, regulating comprehensively the operations of these associations, including their lending practices and, specifically, the terms of loan instruments.

CASE STUDY FROM THE OHIO SUPREME COURT

CENTRAL TRUST V. JENSEN
67 Ohio St.3d 140, 616 N.E.2d 873 (1993).

FACTS: Central Trust brought a foreclosure on a mortgage action in Common Pleas Court against Jensen. It obtained both the foreclosure and order of sale. Thereafter, Maxwell successfully bid on the property at public auction for $192,000. He placed $19,200 with the sheriff as his deposit. Maxwell failed to produce the rest of the proceeds of the purchase price within 30 days of the sale, however, so Central Trust obtained an order vacating the sale. Three more public sale attempts were made on the property. For the first two sales, Maxwell received copies of the order of sale. For the third sale, Maxwell did not receive any notice of the sale because it was advertised instead in the *Dayton Daily News*. At the third sale, the property sold for $120,000 to a new buyer. Maxwell received a copy of the court's order confirming the sale. Upon the resale, Central Trust asked the court for Maxwell's $19,200 deposit to cover additional costs and deficiency in price. The court allowed this. Maxwell filed a motion to reconsider the turnover of his deposit, claiming that Central Trust had abandoned its claim against him by failing to notify him of the impending sale.

TRIAL COURT: Overruled Maxwell's motion and let Central Trust keep the $19,200 deposit.

APPEALS COURT: Reversed the trial court, holding that the third sale without actual notice to Maxwell deprived him of due process of law constitutional protection.

ISSUE: Whether a party to a foreclosure action or a person with an interest in the foreclosure sale is entitled to actual notice by mail where his or her address is known, or whether, instead, the Ohio statutory requirement of notice by publication is sufficient to satisfy constitutional due process requirements.

HELD BY THE OHIO SUPREME COURT: That notice by publication given to a party to a foreclosure sale or to a person having an interest therein is insufficient to satisfy due process when the address of that party or interested person is known or easily ascertainable. The requirements of due process do not depend on the technical nature of the proceeding. Nor do they depend on the strength of the interest holder's inkling that its property interest may soon be in jeopardy. The requirements of due process depend instead on the reasonable balance between the property interest sought to be protected and the state's interest in efficiency and finality in proceedings regarding property. When a party's address is known or easily ascertainable and the cost of notice is little more than a first-class stamp, the balance will almost always favor notice by mail over publication. Maxwell received the $19,200 deposit back.

Summary of Content

1. The mortgagor pledges his or her real property to the mortgagee as security for the money the mortgagee has transferred to the mortgagor.
2. The mortgagor is the borrower-debtor; the mortgagee is the lender-creditor.
3. A mortgage is a pledge of real property as security for payment of a debt.
4. The mortgage exists in the form of a deed, which on the face of it transfers title from the mortgagor/grantor/debtor to the mortgagee/grantee/creditor.
5. The debt, for which the mortgage deed is security, exists in the form of a promissory note signed by the borrower for the benefit of the mortgage lender.
6. The mortgage deed is sometimes referred to as a conditional deed; that is, there is a condition to the effect that upon performance of all promises and payment of the debt, the mortgage deed becomes null and void.
7. When a loan is secured (in this instance, an amount of money by a piece of realty), the lender has the right to compel sale of the security (the piece of realty) when there is a default by the borrower.
8. Conventional financing gives the lender the personal security of the debtor through a promissory note and security of the land through a mortgage. In unconventional financing the lender receives one more level of security: insurance or guarantee via the United States government.
9. Strict foreclosure—losing the whole property to the creditor regardless of the amount of the debt—gave way (in most jurisdictions) to foreclosure by judicially ordered public sale (which Ohio uses today). The proceeds of a public sale are applied against the debt, and if there is any excess of money, that excess is paid the mortgagor. The mortgagor is released from all claims of the mortgagee.
10. Ohio allows deficiency judgments; i.e., if there is a shortfall on the amount still owed the mortgagee after the foreclosure sale, the mortgagee can also obtain a personal judgment from the court against the mortgagor and try to collect on it.
11. As a lien theory jurisdiction, Ohio considers the mortgage deed as giving the mortgagee a lien or claim against the real property.
12. A separately but rarely brought ejectment suit by the mortgagee can remove the mortgagor from possession of the real property.
13. The acceleration clause in the mortgage can result in the whole amount of the note and mortgage coming due and payable immediately; there is an auctioning off of the realty at a public sale and application of the proceeds of the sale against that amount.
14. Ohio mortgage foreclosure court actions have this effect: When the court confirms the sale is when the mortgagor is cut off from being able to redeem that real property.
15. The difference between a first mortgage and a second mortgage is the time sequence in which the two mortgages were recorded in the county recorder's office. Those that are recorded first are entitled to receive proceeds from the sale first, and so on down the line.
16. Creative financing is an arrangement directly between purchasers and sellers in which sellers are directly involved in financing the sale of their property.
17. Sellers with mortgages containing due-on-sale clauses might be prohibited from using creative financing techniques.

18. Purchase money mortgages use the standard mortgage deed and note, but the seller is the mortgagee instead of a commercial mortgage lender.
19. Ohio's Code contains detailed provisions of what terms must be contained in land installment purchase contracts. These are written contracts between the seller/vendor and the purchaser/vendee providing for payment of the purchase price on an installment basis and, after full payment has been made, providing for the transfer of legal title of the realty to the purchaser/vendee.
20. Purchasers/vendees who default on a land contract face one of two possible actions: foreclosure or forfeiture. Forfeiture involves the purchasers'/vendees' forfeiting to the seller/vendor all of their payments, plus the premises are restored to the seller/vendor.
21. Some loans are designed to be assumable from the start; i.e., purchaser can take over the mortgage loan obligation of the mortgagor/seller without having to obtain the consent of the mortgagee lender (e.g., FHA and VA loans).
22. Purchasers who take *subject to the mortgage* never personally obligate themselves to pay the amount of the mortgage loan to the mortgagee/lender. Thus, sellers continue making their own mortgage payments while receiving land installment purchase contract payments from their purchasers/vendees.
23. The Truth-in-Lending Law/Regulation Z has important advertising provisions for real estate salespersons and brokers. If certain advertising terms are used, other, specific advertising credit information also must be given so the consumer can see the true situation in the ad.
24. Lienholders can force judicial sale of realty to generate cash to satisfy their claims for repayment.
25. Voluntary liens involve the consent of debtors that a lien be placed against their realty (e.g., mortgage liens).
26. Involuntary liens are created by operation of law to protect those who have monetary claims against real property owners (e.g., mechanics' liens).
27. General liens allow any parcel of an obliged realty owner to be sold; special liens allow the sale of only a specific parcel of real property.
28. Any mechanic who labors or furnishes workers, material or machinery, or manages construction upon any item of the realty, including improvements, pursuant to a contract between the owner and the mechanic, may file a mechanic's lien against that realty for nonpayment. These are special, involuntary liens.
29. If a real property owner fails to pay local real estate taxes when due, or within the time permitted by law thereafter, the realty can be foreclosed upon and sold by the county auditor.
30. The federal government can obtain a lien against all realty in the United States owned by persons who owe it money.
31. Winners of lawsuits not paid by the losers can file a certificate of judgment as part of the real property record of the county in which the realty is located. This is a lien against the judgment debtor's realty that is general and involuntary.
32. Bankruptcy and partition are two other legal proceedings that can result in the forced sale of realty. Bankruptcy is used to divide up assets when debtors seek to terminate responsibility to their creditors. Partition occurs when coowners of realty cannot agree upon its use or disposition and the court determines how to divide it.

REVIEW QUESTIONS

1. Unpaid taxes on real estate become a:
   a. lien
   b. mortgage
   c. judgment
   d. forfeiture

2. A mortgage that has not been recorded:
   a. has no legal effect
   b. is effective against a subsequent purchaser of the real estate
   c. is effective between the parties
   d. puts everyone on notice

3. Making the mortgage deed null and void upon full payment of the debt is an example of operation of the:
   a. consideration clause of the mortgage
   b. condition clause of the mortgage
   c. warranty covenants of the mortgage deed
   d. express warranty of the mortgage deed

4. Which of the following is a lender in a mortgage loan transaction?
   a. mortgagee
   b. mortgagor
   c. land contract vendee
   d. assignee of mortgagor's rights

5. Which of the following is *not* the kind of clause, term, or provision found in a mortgage deed?
   a. promise to pay a real estate broker's commission
   b. reference to the amount borrowed
   c. signature by mortgagor
   d. reference to the specific real estate mortgaged

6. Which of the following statements correctly classifies a mortgage?
   a. loan of money to be used to purchase realty
   b. document that creates personal liability to repay a debt; sometimes called a promissory note
   c. pledge of real property as security for repayment of a debt, which debt is evidenced by a promissory note
   d. public sale that terminates the borrower's equity of redemption

7. Unconventional loan financing involves which of the following types of security to the lender that the loan will be repaid?
   a. personal security of the borrower
   b. security of the land, as pledged via the mortgage
   c. insurance or guarantee of a United States government-related entity as to part of the debt
   d. all of the above

8. A judgment creditor can recover against a judgment debtor by:
   a. using his automatic lien upon realty
   b. converting his judgment to a lien using a certificate of judgment filed against the judgment debtor's real estate
   c. bringing a partition action
   d. all of the above

9. Failure to pay local real property taxes may result in a forced sale of the realty by which of the following?
   a. Internal Revenue Service
   b. county auditor
   c. former spouse of the title holder
   d. adult child of title holder

10. The mortgage deed most closely resembles (but is not identical to) which of the following standard real estate documents?
    a. purchase agreement
    b. escrow instructions
    c. promissory note
    d. warranty deed

11. Which of the following is the *borrower* in a mortgage loan transaction?
    a. land contract vendee
    b. mortgagee
    c. assignee of mortgagee's rights
    d. mortgagor

12. Which two legal documents work together to make possible the financing of most real estate purchases?
    a. escrow instructions and mechanic's lien affidavit
    b. listing and purchase contracts
    c. warranty deed and title insurance policy
    d. promissory note and mortgage deed

13. Bankruptcy, foreclosure, and partition actions all usually have which of the following in common?
    a. can result in a public sale of real property
    b. involve judicial proceedings
    c. might benefit from the efforts of real estate agents to sell the realty before it goes to public sale
    d. all of the above

14. If Ace Savings & Loan Association gives a loan on Monday and takes back a mortgage as security, and Third Bank gives a loan on Wednesday of the same week, taking back a mortgage covering the same realty, what would be the best way for Third Bank to hold a first mortgage as security?
    a. merely look to the date the mortgage deed was signed
    b. argue that the Ace Savings & Loan transaction was fraudulent
    c. record its mortgage before Ace can record its mortgage
    d. forget the whole idea; it is impossible for Third to hold a first mortgage

15. Ultimately, who is responsible for trying to obtain the best financing arrangement possible?
    a. real estate brokerage and its "financing specialists"
    b. lender
    c. borrower
    d. real estate salesperson who sells the property

16. Which of the following is a creative financing technique?
    a. FHA financing
    b. land installment purchase contract
    c. VA financing
    d. mortgage loan granted by a commercial lender

17. A real estate agent in Ohio can fill in the blanks on a:
    a. land installment purchase contract
    b. purchase money mortgage
    c. real estate purchase contract
    d. lease with option to purchase

18. This law has specific disclosure requirements of credit terms in real estate advertisements that refer to financing:
    a. Ohio Revised Code
    b. land installment purchase contract statute
    c. HUD's rules of credit
    d. Truth-in-Lending Law/Regulation Z

19. This does not occur with a land installment purchase contract:
    a. vendor retains title in her name
    b. vendee obtains title before the contract is paid in full
    c. forfeiture or foreclosure can be used as a remedy depending on the circumstances
    d. a conventional, commercial lender is bypassed

20. The due-on-sale clause can be found, when present, in which of the following?
    a. promissory note
    b. purchase agreement
    c. mortgage deed
    d. warranty deed

21. Assumption of the seller's mortgage means:
    a. the purchaser is taking title subject to the mortgage
    b. the purchaser is now primarily liable for payment of the debt secured by the mortgage
    c. the mortgagor/seller is always completely "off the hook" (no longer has to pay the debt)
    d. the mortgagee/lender will be paid twice what is owed

22. Giving up all that has been paid is a characteristic of which of the following?
    a. forfeiture
    b. foreclosure
    c. eviction
    d. forcible entry and detainer

23. When purchaser pays seller the $85,000 purchase price in cash, with seller taking responsibility for paying off the existing mortgage lien, this is a:
    a. purchase money mortgage
    b. taking title subject to present mortgage
    c. mortgage assumption
    d. land contract

24. From the sellers' perspective, the best financing usually is a:
    a. land contract
    b. purchase money mortgage
    c. lease-option
    d. seller not involved; purchaser secures mortgage loan from mortgagee/lender

25. When purchaser pays $20,000 toward the $85,000 purchase price and assumes paying the monthly payments on the existing $65,000 mortgage, this is:
    a. taking of title subject to mortgage
    b. purchase money mortgage
    c. land contract
    d. assumption of present mortgage

ANSWER KEY

1. a
2. c
3. b
4. a
5. a
6. c
7. d
8. b
9. b
10. d
11. d
12. d
13. d
14. c
15. c
16. b
17. c
18. d
19. b
20. c
21. b
22. a
23. b
24. d
25. d

8
THE REAL ESTATE CLOSING AND PROOF OF TITLE

KEY TERMS

abstract of title
attorney's opinion letter
certificate of title
closing statement
escrow closing
formal closing
Marketable Title Act
owner's fee policy of title insurance
prorations
Real Estate Settlement Procedures Act (RESPA)
relation back, doctrine of
seller's affidavit of title
title guarantee
Uniform Settlement Statement

WE HAVE NOW COME to the moment that purchaser, seller, broker, and salesperson have all been waiting for—the closing of the transaction and transfer of title. The real estate closing is a bit like a wedding: Both involve a wait, both lead up to a significant event, and, most important to our present purposes, though both always end up with the expected result, both a wedding and a real estate closing conclude with an amazing variety of ceremonies and procedures. Not only do real estate closing procedures differ widely from state to state, but even within the same state, standard closing techniques can vary so much as to completely baffle an experienced real estate salesperson who has changed locations. It is no wonder that purchasers and sellers moving from or to other states, or even from or to different parts of the same state, are confused when they are faced with radically differing closing procedures.

So that real estate salespeople will understand the basic closing techniques to the extent that they can at least explain to all parties what is happening and what will happen as the parties move through this period, we set forth in this chapter all of the basic closing techniques. In addition, we explain the differences between the many types of "title evidence," another confusing and often misunderstood body of information. Finally, we outline the major functions of the typical county recorder's office as they affect real estate closings.

Role of the Real Estate Salesperson During the Closing

Throughout the text, we emphasize that the role of the real estate salesperson in a typical transaction, and the job for which they are licensed by the state, is to bring real estate sellers and purchasers together and then to create conditions that will lead to formation of a real estate purchase contract between them. Of course, to create such favorable conditions, it helps tremendously for salespeople to know something about the work of the many allied professionals who will also be involved with the transaction: the lenders, insurers, lawyers, construction workers, city and county officials, taxing authorities, and so forth. With this knowledge, real estate salespeople can act as constant, informative, and dependable guides to purchasers and sellers alike as they move through the transaction. Although salespeople never personally perform these other specialized services, the general information can be invaluable. Also, by "riding herd" on the entire transaction, salespeople can reduce to a bare minimum the chances that any of the other parties will fail, neglect, or forget to do any of the things that they are supposed to do. Salespeople who take an active role in this function, as overseer or "whip," often find that fewer of their transactions collapse or are delayed because of sloppy practices.

As to the closing itself, real estate salespeople are much like marriage brokers in that they bring the parties together. After doing this, their personal role is reduced and the closing itself (the "marriage") is performed by another.

Closing Specialists and Types of Closings

Closings take place in two major ways: the formal, "sit-down" closing and the escrow closing. Both procedures are used in Ohio. Local preference generally determines the specific form.

Formal Closing in General

With the **formal closing,** all of the following *people are "players" and attend an actual meeting, the end result of which is to be the transfer of title to the purchasers and the transfer of the net proceeds of the sale to the sellers:* the real estate broker, a representative of the lender, the purchasers and sellers and their attorneys, a representative from the supplier of the title evidence, and, perhaps, the real estate broker's attorney. Often the purchasers' attorney directs (and hosts) the closing.

Escrow Closing in General

The **escrow closing** involves an entirely different procedure, although the end result—transfer of the deed to the purchaser and the net sale proceeds to the seller—is exactly the same. With an escrow closing, *some disinterested third person (having no personal stake in the transaction) is chosen by both purchasers and sellers.* As long as this third person agrees to do so, he or she receives and holds the necessary documents and funds, makes sure that all promises are carried out and all conditions are satisfied, and then transfers the title by the sellers'/grantors' deed to the purchasers/grantees and the net proceeds to the sellers.

The escrow agent is viewed legally as the *agent of both parties,* as well as a *trustee of the funds and documents.* With an escrow closing, purchasers and sellers often never even see one another, as much or all of what has to be done is accomplished through the mail. Escrow agents can be individuals chosen from title companies (suppliers of title evidence), individuals from the escrow departments of lending institutions, lawyers, and occasionally responsible and trusted members of the community who are known to both purchaser and seller.

The escrow closing is an entirely *contractual matter.* A document called "Conditions of Acceptance of Escrow" or "Escrow Instructions," or other-named documents, is executed by all of the parties—sellers, purchasers, and escrow agent. This document and the real estate purchase contract provide a complete working plan of the closing. If the terms of the escrow agreement and the real estate purchase contract are in conflict, the escrow agreement is the one followed (unless the purchase contract has been incorporated into the escrow agreement, in which case parol evidence probably will be necessary to resolve the conflict or ambiguity).

Advantages of the escrow closing are:

1. The parties can do their own share of the required functions at their convenience and never need appear at a place and time set for transfer of title.
2. Fewer specialists need be involved, thus reducing expense.
3. The purchaser and the seller both know that a paid professional expert, the escrow agent, is involved with the transaction, minimizing the chances that the deed will be transferred or the funds disbursed when they should not have been.
4. The law places an extremely high standard of trust, competence, and accountability on escrow agents.

If escrow agents neglect to carry out their duties under the escrow agreement, they can be held liable for any damages that purchasers and sellers suffer. (An Ohio Supreme Court case, *Miles v. Perpetual Savings and Loan,* demonstrates this, in Chapter 9.) Further, because escrow agents are not empowered to perform any acts that the escrow agreement does not authorize, they also can be liable for acting outside the scope of their agency.

Formal/Sit-Down (or Round-Table) Closing in Detail

Many transactions involve the formal/sit-down, or round-table, closing. This involves the following procedure: At the time of closing, all of the persons listed earlier gather at one of their offices, or even at a room in a local courthouse or county administration building. Each of them brings to this scheduled closing his or her portion of all of the documents or funds necessary to complete the transaction or to "close it." If someone is not able to attend the closing or if some document or some act is not completed by that time, the closing can be reset for another time, as long as all parties agree. If time was made "of the essence" of the agreement, however, flexibility is severely limited.

Sellers' role

The sellers (or the sellers' attorney) generally bring the following items to the closing:

1. An *executed deed* of a type called for by the real estate purchase contract (usually a general warranty or fiduciary deed) in a form suitable for recording; that is, it is acknowledged before and executed by a notary public or other official authorized to administer oaths and take acknowledgments.
2. A *document showing that the sellers have title to the real property* (the kinds of evidence of title are dealt with more fully later in this chapter).
3. A *statement from the sellers' mortgage lender* showing exactly *how much is owed* as of the date set for closing (called a payoff statement).
4. A receipt or other evidence showing that current local *real property taxes,* both general and special, *have been paid* up to a certain date.
5. Documents showing the condition of the sellers' *insurance coverage* and showing that premium payments have been made to cover the period through closing.
6. Executed assignments of any *leases* affecting the realty. Also, transfers of security deposits, consents from tenants to the transfer of such security deposits (if required by the lease or rental agreement), a rent roll statement, contracts for rental property services, roof guarantee, trash pickup, pest extermination, lawn and building maintenance, and all payroll records and necessary forms for employees of the sellers/lessors who are to become those of the new building owner.
7. Certificates of *compliance with all applicable local realty inspections and codes,* or, in lieu thereof, agreements signed by purchasers to be responsible for the repairs or modifications as required to bring the realty into compliance with such regulations.
8. *Executed easements* from neighboring realty owners onto whose realty portions of the sellers' realty encroach (for example, overhanging eaves, gutters and downspouts, a common driveway, a garage, or an outbuilding).

9. *Executed quitclaim deeds* from persons whose interests in the realty either do or may amount to clouds on the title.
10. An *affidavit of title* executed and sworn to by the sellers, stating that the sellers have done nothing, nor do they know of anything that has taken place since the completion date of the title examination (which is the same as the date of the real estate purchase contract) that affects or in any way reduces the condition of the title. (For example, sellers swear that any repairs done since signing the real estate purchase contract have been paid for, will be paid for, or will in no way become the purchasers' responsibility.)
11. Evidence of the condition of *utility reserves* and/or charges.
12. In the case of a sale of a *going business involving transfer of personal property,* all documents showing compliance with the *Ohio Bulk Transfer Act,* giving notice to all creditors of the seller of the impending sale of the business and its assets.
13. *Any other documents required* by the real estate purchase contract or by local practice.

This list of things that sellers bring to a formal closing seems extensive, but only a small portion of all transactions requires all of those documents. Most real properties are not rented, and most are not operating businesses. Still, all of those documents may have to be presented at closing from time to time. When the closing is complex, sellers and purchasers both ought to be fully represented by attorneys to ensure that preparation of the documents, their review, and their acceptance are done correctly.

Purchasers' role

Purchasers normally have to do fewer things to complete their portion of the closing. As long as their check is good (usually the check must be a cashier's, certified, or bank check instead of a personal check, so this is not a problem), and as long as the purchasers have satisfied the lender and themselves that they are getting what was contracted for, the purchasers have done their part. Even though the purchasers' role is simpler, from a practical standpoint, it theoretically involves an additional legal step. For purchasers who are not paying all cash (the usual situation), the closing is actually two closings involving two different transactions: (a) the purchasers' mortgage loan transaction and (b) transfer of title from the seller to the purchaser.

Closing the purchasers' mortgage loan transaction. To close the mortgage loan transaction, purchasers need to supply the lender with the following items:

1. *General loan data,* including: completed loan application form, credit check, verification of earnings report, appraisal of the realty, and "spot" survey of the realty.
2. An *executed promissory note* in the amount of the loan.
3. An *executed mortgage deed,* suitable for recording, securing that promissory note.
4. A *mortgagee's policy of title insurance* giving the mortgagee/lender further assurance that the title the purchaser will pledge, via the mortgage, can be so pledged by the purchaser.
5. Evidence that homeowner's or *casualty insurance* has been obtained covering the realty.
6. A *deposit of cash* to cover (a) current interest due on the amount being lent; (b) an insurance premium reserve fund; (c) a similar fund for future real property

taxes; and (d) charges for the services of loan application, credit report, appraisal, spot survey, loan service charges and/or points, preparation of documents (including note and mortgage), recording of deed from seller, and recording of mortgage deed.

Once the mortgage lender is satisfied that purchasers have done all that is necessary to obtain the loan, purchasers have to do the following to acquire title to the realty:

1. Deposit the *proceeds* of the loan.
2. Deposit evidence from the real estate broker that the *earnest money* has been paid and is available to be applied against the purchase price.
3. Deposit the balance of the *down payment.*
4. Deposit *cash* sufficient to pay *additional closing costs,* including (a) amounts due to the seller because of assumption of seller's already-paid-for-insurance (if that has taken place) or because of purchases from seller of other personal property, utility reserves, and so forth, and (b) amounts due to others who have assisted or rendered services to the purchaser (lawyer, termite inspector, engineer, home improvement contractor, and so on).

Consummation of the transaction

When all of the parties have come to the sit-down closing and all of the previously described documents have been prepared, deposits made, and acts completed, the closing can commence. The *sellers* do, or are charged or credited to:

- give *deed* to purchasers.
- receive the *purchase price* from purchasers.
- give *title abstract or certificate of title* to purchasers.
- *assign leases,* security deposits, and all other lease-allied documents to purchasers.
- satisfy their own current *mortgage loan debt.*
- prove that all required local *inspections* and necessary *repairs* have been done.
- give purchasers an *affidavit of title* to cover possible flaws in the title that may have occurred since the final date of the title examination and up to the date of closing.
- pay purchasers for *taxes that are a lien against the real property* and for which the seller is liable but for which taxes have not yet become due and payable.
- pay *real estate broker's commission* if a broker is involved.
- pay to purchasers the portion of *prepaid rents* to which the purchaser is entitled, if any.
- receive payment from purchasers to cover the portion of *prepaid insurance* that purchasers are taking over, if any.
- if purchasers are taking *subject to or are assuming a mortgage,* sellers to receive appropriate *credit* against the mortgage debt.
- receive credit for *fuel reserves* taken over by purchasers.
- pay either utility companies or purchasers all *current utility charges* to date of closing.
- give purchasers all *easements and/or quitclaim deeds* that have been prepared to clear the title.
- pay all *professional and other fees* incurred because of the sale (including fees to record a satisfaction of mortgage, to prepare a new deed, and to pay an attorney).

Concurrently with the foregoing, the purchasers do, and are credited or charged with, the corresponding acts, and in addition to:

- pay all *loan charges,* from application fee through fees required to record mortgage deed.
- pay for *mortgagee's title evidence* (title insurance policy).
- pay for their *own title evidence,* if they require additional assurances beyond the evidence that sellers have provided and if sellers have not agreed to supply and pay for such additional title evidence. (This additional title evidence usually will be an owner's fee policy of title insurance, discussed later in this chapter.)
- pay for their own *professional or other fees* or charges incurred because of the closing.

At this point the closing is complete and the "honeymoon" (the reality of living in real property and meeting the many obligations of that privilege) can begin.

Escrow Closing Compared to Formal Closing

As mentioned earlier in this chapter, although the formal sit-down closing and the escrow closing differ in the mechanics of the closing process, the end result is the same: transfer of the deed to the purchasers and the net sales' proceeds to the sellers. The difference between the two procedures is that in the escrow closing, instead of the parties depositing, reviewing, and exchanging documents face to face, they simply deposit them with the escrow agent, who then completes the transaction according to instructions. If the parties do not do as they have agreed and if the escrow agent therefore is unable to complete the transaction, the agent normally returns all of the documents and funds to the parties who deposited each of them. Under some circumstances, the escrow agent may have to involve both parties in a court action so as to obtain an order of the court as to who should receive which documents and funds.

Escrow agents commonly receive executed deeds from the sellers well before the closing. The deed usually is delivered into escrow by the realty agent. Upon delivery of the deed, the realty agent should obtain a receipt from the escrow agent. In this way the realty agent can avoid liability such as shown in the example.

FOR EXAMPLE After the realty agent delivers the deed into escrow, the purchaser steals the deed out of the escrow file. The purchaser records the deed and then places a large new loan on the realty, pocketing the loan proceeds for himself. The escrow agent subsequently claims that the realty agent gave the deed to the purchaser instead of delivering it into escrow. Thus, the escrow agent shifts liability from herself onto the realty agent. Had the realty agent obtained a receipt for delivering the deed into escrow, the escrow agent, instead of the realty agent would have been liable.

As the end result of the escrow closing and the formal closing is the same, it should come as no surprise to learn that the *specific documents and funds deposited by purchaser and by seller are virtually identical to those required under the formal closing*. One slight difference involves the proof required of the sellers showing that they have good title. Instead of an abstract of title commitment showing good title up to the date of the real estate purchase contract plus a sellers' affidavit to cover the period from the date of the agreement to the date of closing, the escrow agent accepts a title report from a title company that covers right up to the date of closing. Table 8–1 shows the differences between the two major closing procedures.

Doctrine of Relation Back

A unique feature of the escrow closing involves the rule of law known as the **doctrine of relation back** (also discussed in Chapter 5). If the closing is done by escrow, as long as the seller deposits the deed and all other necessary items with the escrow agent before dying, transfer of title can still take place. In this case only, the *deed is deemed by the law to have been delivered to the purchasers when sellers placed it into escrow.* The law, out of justice or necessity, creates a legal fiction to avoid interference with the purpose of the escrow.

This doctrine of relation back also applies to the items the purchasers are supposed to do. As long as the purchasers complete their portion of the transaction by deposits to escrow before dying, title will transfer to the purchasers'/decedents' estate.

Closing Statement

If a single term can strike terror in the heart of virtually every student of real estate law, that term is "closing statement." One fact should dispel a good deal of this terror: *Typically, the real estate salesperson is not the person responsible for filling out the closing statement.* Usually, however, the purchaser and the seller both ask the salesperson at various stages of the transaction what other customary charges each of them will have to pay to complete the transaction. Before reading on, we recommend that readers should again examine the lists of documents and funds required of both parties to close the transaction, as set forth earlier in this chapter. If readers have a clear idea of who must provide what, or who will be charged with what, understanding the closing statement will be easier.

The **closing statement** is nothing more than a *written summary of charges and credits that have arisen because of the transaction.* The purchasers and sellers each have their own separate closing statement. A list of charges (or debits) and credits is prepared, one pertaining to the sellers and one to the purchasers. Often these two separate schedules are completed on a single sheet of paper but the two schedules are not identical. They cannot be, because, if you recall from the above-described list of duties of both parties, in most cases a charge or credit is not shared; it is the responsibility or benefit of either purchasers or sellers. The two schedules are combined on a single sheet of paper merely for convenience and for purposes of comparison.

TABLE 8–1
Differences between the two major closing procedures.

FORMAL (SIT DOWN) CLOSING	ESCROW CLOSING
1. An actual meeting occurs.	1. No actual meeting occurs.
2. The doctrine of relation back does not apply (disadvantage).	2. The doctrine of relation back does apply (advantage).
3. Attorneys routinely represent seller and purchaser (advantage).	3. Seller and purchaser usually are not represented by counsel (disadvantage).
4. There is no central agent with broad powers, such as the escrow agent.	4. An escrow agent is appointed by purchasers and sellers, represents them equally, and does everything to bring the transaction to a close.
5. The closing must take place in person.	5. The entire closing can be done through the mail.

The beginning of a closing statement for sellers and a corresponding beginning closing statement for purchasers would look like Table 8–2. The monetary amounts used are for illustration purposes only.

Closing statements reflect the financial charges and credits that have been agreed to by all the parties. Salespeople will find the closing statement to be a helpful and informative document, exactly what it was intended to be. Fortunately, the great variety of forms used for closing statements has been reduced as a result of RESPA (the Real Estate Settlement Procedures Act, discussed later in this chapter), so at least the form is familiar in most cases.

PRORATIONS

In some cases, paying for an item is not the sole responsibility of either the seller or the purchaser; rather, it is shared by both. This involves **proration,** or *division of the expense, the split being made as of a certain date*. The usual items that are prorated are tenant rents, and real estate taxes. *Tenant rents* are prorated when the sellers have received rents in advance and the advance rentals apply to the time the purchasers will own the realty.

Local real estate taxes are made up of two components: (a) the general tax and (b) the special assessment tax. General real property taxes are always prorated, because they always continue and because neither seller nor purchaser has any choice about paying them. Special assessments are either prorated or not, depending upon the agreement of the parties. A special assessment is a charge made for improvements to a relatively small part of the taxing district. As such, paying for these improvements becomes the sole responsibility of those owners who benefit from the improvement. Because the cost of the special assessment is fixed, it can be paid off all at once at any point during the payment period.

Occasionally purchasers require sellers to pay off in full all special assessments prior to transfer of title to purchasers. In negotiating the transaction, naturally the sellers demand a higher purchase price, because paying off the special assessments often can take thousands of dollars. On the other hand, by assuming repayment of the special assessments, which is what happens when they are prorated along with general taxes, the purchasers can expect to pay less of a purchase price to the sellers, because sellers no longer have to worry about paying for these improvements.

One *standard date* frequently used for prorations is the *date of title transfer* of the subject real property from sellers to purchasers. By agreement, however, the parties may use any date for calculating prorations.

REAL ESTATE SETTLEMENT PROCEDURES ACT (RESPA)

During the 1970s the federal government became involved in many closings by way of legislation known as the **Real Estate Settlement Procedures Act (RESPA).** RESPA, administered by the U. S. Department of Housing and Urban Development (HUD), *applies only to transactions involving first mortgages of residential real estate that are federally related.* Most first mortgage loans are federally related because the lenders are insured by FDIC; the loans are insured by FHA or guaranteed by VA; or they will be sold off to the secondary (federally influenced) money markets. The purpose for which RESPA was enacted was to:

TABLE 8–2
Beginning of a closing statement.

SELLER'S CLOSING STATEMENT

	Charges	Credits
Mortgage Loan	$66,000.00	
Purchase Price		$100,000.00
Real Estate Commission	$7,000.00	
Title Abstract	$175.00	
Preparation of Deed	$45.00	
etc.		

PURCHASER'S CLOSING STATEMENT

	Charges	Credits
Earnest Money		$1,000.00
Balance of Down Payment		$19,000.00
Mortgage Loan		$80,000.00
Purchase Price	$100,000.00	
Loan Fees	$987.00	
Recording of Deed/Mortgage	$10.50	
etc.		

- give purchasers and sellers advance disclosure of closing costs.
- reduce the cost of closings by prohibiting illegal referrals of closing business among specialists in closings and by prohibiting illegal kickbacks and side deals.
- explain to purchasers generally what to expect during the closing transaction.
- prescribe a standard form closing statement to be used in all RESPA closings, again reducing the mystery and uncertainty that often plague closings.

Accordingly, RESPA requires the following in every transaction covered by the act:

1. Every loan applicant must be given a copy of the booklet entitled "Settlement Costs and You," prepared by HUD. This booklet explains the RESPA provisions, describes the standard closing statement, and gives general closing information. The booklet also suggests questions the borrower should ask the lender, such as whether there are late fees, whether a prepayment penalty will apply if there is an earlier payoff, whether there are assumption possibilities (or not) of this mortgage loan; and other questions to which borrowers need answers for their own protection.

2. A *good faith estimation of closing costs* must be given to the borrower at the time of loan application, or within three business days thereafter. These costs need not be exact, although they should be as close as possible to the expected range of costs then current in the area. Some of the items that should be included in this estimation are: appraisal fee, title search fee, loan origination fee, document preparation fee, credit report fee, and other, similar charges. If the lender requires the use of any particular closing agent, it must reveal the nature of its business relationship with that closing agent.

3. The closing statement must be the one known as HUD Form-1, the **Uniform Settlement Statement.** This form is designed to standardize the reporting of all closing credits and charges. It appears as Figure 8–1, along with the cover page. If the purchasers desire to examine the closing statement, they may do so by a request to the closing agent one business day prior to closing.

4. No kickbacks, or payments of fees that have not been earned, are permitted to be paid by one person who profits from the closing to another who has merely referred the work to the first person. This does not apply to fee splitting between real estate brokers because of cooperative sales, multiple listing, or national/international

FIGURE 8–1 Excerpts from HUD guide to settlement costs.

SETTLEMENT COSTS

A **HUD** GUIDE
REVISED EDITION

CONTENTS

INTRODUCTION

PART I

PART II

APPENDIX

U.S. Department of Housing and Urban Development
March 1987

(continued)

FIGURE 8–1 Continued.

U.S. DEPARTMENT OF HOUSING AND URBAN DEVELOPMENT OMB No.2502-0266

A. SETTLEMENT STATEMENT

B. TYPE OF LOAN

1. ☐ FHA 2. ☐ FMHA 3. ☐ CONV. UNINS. 4. ☐ VA 5. ☐ CONV. INS.	6. File Number	7. Loan Number	8. Mortgage Insurance Case Number

C. NOTE: This form is furnished to give you statement of actual settlement costs. Amounts paid to and by the settlement agent are shown. Items marked "(p.o.c.)" were paid outside the closing; they are shown here for informational purposes and are not included in the totals.

D. NAME AND ADDRESS OF BORROWER	E. NAME AND ADDRESS OF SELLER	F. NAME AND ADDRESS OF LENDER

G. PROPERTY LOCATION	H. SETTLEMENT AGENT	
	PLACE OF SETTLEMENT	I. SETTLEMENT DATE rec: cls:

J. SUMMARY OF BORROWER'S TRANSACTION		K. SUMMARY OF SELLER'S TRANSACTION	
100. GROSS AMOUNT DUE FROM BORROWER		400. GROSS AMOUNT DUE TO SELLER	
101. Contract sales price		401. Contract sales price	
102. Personal Property		402. Personal Property	
103. Settlement charges to borrower (line 1400)		403.	
104.		404.	
105.		405.	
ADJUSTMENTS FOR ITEMS PAID BY SELLER IN ADVANCE		ADJUSTMENTS FOR ITEMS PAID BY SELLER IN ADVANCE	
106. City/Town taxes to		406. City/Town taxes to	
107. County taxes to		407. County taxes to	
108. Assessments to		408. Assessments to	
109.		409.	
110.		410.	
111.		411.	
112.		412.	
120. GROSS AMOUNT DUE FROM BORROWER		420. GROSS AMOUNT DUE TO SELLER	
200. AMOUNTS PAID BY OR IN BEHALF OF BORROWER		500. REDUCTIONS IN AMOUNT DUE TO SELLER	
201. Deposit or earnest money		501. Excess Deposit (see instructions)	
202. Principal amount of new loan(s)		502. Settlement charges to seller (line 1400)	
203. Existing loan(s) taken subject to		503. Existing loan(s) taken subject to	
204. Application deposit		504. Payoff of first mortgage loan	
205. Second lien mortgage		505. Payoff of second mortgage loan	
206.		506.	
207.		507.	
208.		508.	
209.		509.	
ADJUSTMENTS FOR ITEMS UNPAID BY SELLER		ADJUSTMENTS FOR ITEMS UNPAID BY SELLER	
210. City/Town taxes to		510. City/Town taxes to	
211. County taxes to		511. County taxes to	
212. Assessments to		512. Assessments to	
213.		513.	
214.		514.	
215.		515.	
216.		516.	
217.		517.	
218.		518.	
219.		519.	
220. TOTAL PAID BY/FOR BORROWER		520. TOTAL REDUCTION AMOUNT DUE SELLER	
300. CASH AT SETTLEMENT FROM OR TO BORROWER		600. CASH AT SETTLEMENT TO OR FROM SELLER	
301. Gross amount due from borrower (line 120)		601. Gross amount due to seller (line 420)	
302. Less amounts paid by/for borrower (line 220)	( )	602. Less reduction amount due seller (line 520)	( )
303. CASH ☐ FROM ☐ TO BORROWER		603. CASH ☐ TO ☐ FROM SELLER	

Buyer ________ Date ________ Seller ________ Date ________

Buyer ________ Date ________ Seller ________ Date ________

Settlement Agent ________ Date ________

Previous Edition is Obsolete
F1061.LMG (7/94)

HUD-1 (07-87) RESPA, HB 4305.2

U.S. DEPARTMENT OF HOUSING AND URBAN DEVELOPMENT
SETTLEMENT STATEMENT
Page 2

L. SETTLEMENT CHARGES	PAID FROM BORROWER'S FUNDS AT SETTLEMENT	PAID FROM SELLER'S FUNDS AT SETTLEMENT
700. TOTAL SALES/BROKER'S COMMISSION(based on price)		
Division of commission (line 700) as follows: $ @ %= $		
701. $ to		
702. $ to		
703. Commission paid at Settlement		
704.		
800. ITEMS PAYABLE IN CONNECTION WITH LOAN		
801. Loan Origination Fee %		
802. Loan Discount %		
803. Appraisal Fee to		
804. Credit Report to		
805. Lender's Inspection Fee		
806. VA Funding Fee to		
807. Assumption Fee		
808. to		
809. Underwriting Fee		
810. Tax Service Fee		
811.		
900. ITEMS REQUIRED BY LENDER TO BE PAID IN ADVANCE		
901. Interest from to @ $ /day		
902. Mortgage Insurance Premium for mos. to		
903. Hazard Insurance Premium for yrs. to		
904. yrs. to		
905.		
1000. RESERVES DEPOSITED WITH LENDER FOR		
1001. Hazard Insurance mos. @ $ /mo.		
1002. Mortgage Insurance mos. @ $ /mo.		
1003. City Property Taxes mos. @ $ /mo.		
1004. County Property Taxes mos. @ $ /mo.		
1005. Annual Assessments mos. @ $ /mo.		
1006. mos. @ $ /mo.		
1007. mos. @ $ /mo.		
1008. mos. @ $ /mo.		
1100. TITLE CHARGES		
1101. Settlement or Closing Fee to		
1102. Abstract or Title Search to		
1103. Title Examination to		
1104. Title Insurance Binder to		
1105. Document Preparation to		
1106. Notary Fees to		
1107. Attorney's Fees to		
(includes above items No.:)		
1108. Title Insurance to		
(includes above items No.:)		
1109. Lender's Coverage $		
1110. Owner's Coverage $		
1111.		
1112.		
1113.		
1200. GOVERNMENT RECORDING AND TRANSFER CHARGES		
1201. Recording Fees: Deed $; Mortgage $; Release $		
1202. City/County tax/stamps: Deed $; Mortgage $		
1203. State tax/stamps: Deed $; Mortgage $		
1204.		
1205.		
1300. ADDITIONAL SETTLEMENT CHARGES		
1301. Survey to		
1302. Pest Inspection to		
1303.		
1304.		
1305.		
1400. TOTAL SETTLEMENT CHARGES (enter on line 103, Section J and line 502, Section K)		

Items marked "(p.o.c.)" were paid outside the closing; they are shown here for information purposes and are not included in the totals.

The Undersigned Acknowledges Receipt of This Settlement Statement and Agrees to the Correctness Thereof.

Buyer ________ Seller ________
SS# ________ SS# ________

Buyer ________ Seller ________
SS# ________ SS# ________

Buyer ________ Date ________
SS# ________

Buyer ________
SS# ________

HUD-1B Settlement Statement
F1006.LMG (7/94)

referral services, or within the brokerage itself, as between broker and salespeople and/or for receiving a fee for actually providing the financing as long as that fact is disclosed (brokers who have in-house financing). Real estate salespeople can violate RESPA, however, if they receive kickbacks from the customer and client referrals they make to lenders, escrow agents, title companies, and the like. For example, if real estate salespeople refer all their sellers to the same title company for their title work, and that title company gives those salespeople a set percentage of its total fee from every referral, this in all likelihood will be a RESPA violation.

For real estate salespeople to make referrals of this nature, however, is totally appropriate. In fact, purchasers and sellers alike often are at a loss as to whom to use for some of these functions. Therefore, salespeople commonly refer purchasers and sellers to lenders, title companies, and even lawyers (for preparation of the deed and attorney's opinion regarding title). As long as the salesperson does not receive a kickback payment, referrals of this sort are fine.

Practitioners should follow carefully the current development and refinement of RESPA law, especially now that more and more "controlled business arrangements" are being created subject to RESPA regulations. Review such changes periodically with your attorney.

Proof of Title and the County Recorder

Throughout this text we refer to "evidence" and "further assurance" and "proof" of title. These things are essential to the operation of real estate transfers today, not because title cannot be transferred without proof or evidence but, rather, because it is conventional today to provide purchasers with something in addition to the deed that will tend to show the sellers' title is as good as they say it is. Delivery of a properly executed deed transfers title. Thus, a purchaser can become owner of the land simply upon receiving the deed from the seller. As long as the purchaser is willing to accept the risk that the seller's title might not be as good as the seller says it is, the purchaser can go ahead and complete the transaction by merely accepting the deed.

Today, however, most purchasers do not want to take the gamble, and even if they did, their lenders, who provide the bulk of the funds, require more. Lenders insist on being assured that sellers' title is as good as they say it is and that no one later will make an adverse claim. To accomplish these ends, several types of title evidence or proofs of good title have been devised, giving purchasers and mortgage lenders further assurance. These types of title evidence vary considerably in the degree of further assurance they supply. As with all forms of assurance or "insurance," the greater the protection, the greater the cost of obtaining it. All of the following function as evidence that sellers' title is as good as sellers say it is:

1. Abstract of title
2. Certificate of title and seller's affidavit of title
3. Attorney's opinion letter
4. Title guarantee
5. Owner's fee policy of title insurance

These forms of title evidence are compared and contrasted in the following discussion.

Abstract of Title

The **abstract of title** is a *long and detailed history of the ownership of the parcel of realty,* often extending as far back as the original owners of the land who received it by grant from the king. Although the title abstract is detailed and thorough, it is no more than a listing of persons who have exercised ownership rights in the realty and whose rights have been reflected in the public records. The examiner searches at the recorder's office, consulting the deed books and index, the mortgage books and index, and any other pertinent books and records, such as judgment and mechanics' liens records, to find this history of ownership.

With the abstract alone as title evidence, a purchaser's quiet possession of and title to the realty can be upset if the person who examines the title (usually, either an employee of a title company or a real estate attorney) negligently overlooks some flaw in the title that appears on the public records or if the flaw in the title exists because of something that cannot become apparent from even the closest examination of the public records. Some examples of flaws are:

- valid but unrecorded documents
- forged documents
- signatures made under duress
- signatures made by incompetents
- signatures made by minors
- ineffective documents because of failure to obtain dower releases in the case of married grantors, when the grantors represent on the face of the deed itself that they are not married
- ineffective documents because of failure to obtain signatures of persons who were mistakenly left out of the probate of a decedent real property owner's estate
- ineffective documents as a result of failure to obtain proper signatures of title holders because of other fiduciaries' mistakes, including mistakes by guardians, executors, administrators, trustees, and other court-appointed persons charged with the duty of holding and transferring titles to real property

For these reasons, and even though the title abstract is often impressively lengthy and detailed, it makes for poor title evidence when used alone.

Certificate of Title and Sellers' Affidavit of Title

A **certificate of title** is the *written result of an examination of the public real property records,* the examination typically going back at least 40 years and showing an unbroken chain of ownership up to and including the date the real estate purchase contract is entered into. Again, and similar to the title abstract procedure, either a title company or a real estate attorney issues the certificate of title. The **seller's affidavit of title** is a *signed, sworn statement made by the seller, representing the condition of the title,* and covering the period from formation of the real estate purchase contract up to and including the date of the present title transfer.

Together, the certificate of title and the seller's affidavit show the chain of title going back at least 40 years from the time of the present title transfer. Forty years is chosen because Ohio's **Marketable Title Act** provides that *if a recorded title shows* *a clear, not flawed "chain" at least 40 years long, it is good,* or "marketable" enough, to be transferred.

The certificate of title, as in the case of the abstract of title, represents only the results of an examination by some person of the public real property records, and the seller's affidavit represents only what the sellers say they have done with the title since the time of forming the real estate purchase contract. Both the certificate of title and the seller's affidavit suffer from the same potential inaccuracies and flaws as the abstract of title does.

Attorney's Opinion Letter

Purchasers could recover from the attorney (or title company) any actual damage sustained by the attorney's (or title company's) negligence. This presents some problems, however.

The **attorney's opinion letter** goes one step beyond both the abstract of title and the certificate of title/seller's affidavit because now a *real estate attorney looks over and renders a legal opinion on the "goodness" of the title.* This opinion is based upon the attorney's review of the results of the title examination—either a review of an abstract of title or a review of a certificate of title/seller's affidavit.

Instead of a mere report of the results of a title examination, the purchaser and mortgage lender are able to rely on the opinion of a specialist in looking at title reports, the attorney. If the attorney renders a poor opinion because of negligence, and if the purchaser suffers an upset in the peaceful enjoyment of the realty because of this negligent examination, the purchaser can look to the attorney for compensation, assuming that the purchaser can prove the attorney is negligent (or malpracticed) in rendering the opinion. The purchaser is financially satisfied only if the attorney can be found and sued, if the attorney is financially solvent enough to cover the large dollar amount of this kind of damage, or if the attorney carries sufficient malpractice insurance to cover this loss. The purchaser, therefore, may not be able to recover from the attorney because the attorney cannot be found or is insolvent or is uninsured.

In addition, if the problem stems from matters the attorney cannot have known about, such as forged documents, the attorney is not even liable to the purchaser, as he or she made no error. The certificate of title presents these same problems. Thus, the attorney's opinion letter is not all that comforting to the purchasers as total proof of title either, given its limitations.

Title Guarantee and Owner's Fee Policy of Title Insurance

The **title guarantee** is used in some sections of Ohio. It is a better form of title evidence than those we have already discussed. A title company or a real estate attorney *examines the public title records,* going back at least 40 years. The title company or attorney, as agent for an insurance company, then issues a title guarantee, *guaranteeing the accuracy of the title examination,* subject to the following limitations:

1. The protection against flaws is limited by the *face amount of the policy,* usually equal to the amount of the purchase price. A single premium payment is made as consideration for issuing of the policy, and coverage extends to the purchaser, the purchaser's legal representatives, and assigns, from the "beginning of time" to the date of title transfer.

2. It covers only flaws that can be revealed by *examining the public records*.
3. It *excludes flaws, liens, limitations, conditions,* and all other encumbrances revealed during the examination.

The big advantage of the title guarantee over the attorney's opinion letter based on either the abstract of title or the certificate of title/seller's affidavit is that with the title guarantee, *negligence need not be proven*. If the issuer of the title guarantee misses something on the public records and the purchaser suffers, regardless of whether the mistake is negligent or otherwise, the title insurer has to "pay off" up to the limit of the policy. Disadvantages to the title guarantee are (a) the small likelihood that the title guarantee will miss anything on the records and (b) the same potential flaws that the abstract of title does not uncover because they cannot be discovered by even the most careful title examination of the public records.

Other sections of Ohio routinely use the **owner's fee policy of title insurance,** which is the *broadest and best form of title evidence*. It can be purchased in all sections of Ohio, and purchasers who want the ultimate in coverage do purchase it. The owner's fee policy of title insurance is the *most expensive* title evidence and is paid with one single premium at the time of closing the real estate transaction. Options for the payment are (a) it can be paid in full by either seller or purchaser or (b) it can be shared by the two. Local custom usually establishes which of them pays and in what proportion, if any.

The title insurance policy gives *all of the protection of a title guarantee and in addition covers problems that cannot be detected by close examination of the public records,* such as deeds by persons allegedly single but secretly married that thus are missing dower releases, deeds executed under expired powers of attorney, forged instruments, signatures of deeds or other documents made under duress or by minor or incompetent persons, and all the other potential problems listed in our discussion of other types of proof of title. It covers defects that exist prior to or when the policy is issued but does not cover defects that come into existence after the policy is issued. Purchasers should definitely obtain an owner's fee policy of title insurance when there has been a multiplicity of ownership on the property or when there has been recent litigation concerning it (divorce, foreclosure, or probate, for example).

Negligence is not an issue for realty owners with fee policies of title insurance. This is because the policies cover the realty owners for loss regardless of third parties' fault and regardless of whether the insurance companies are or are not ever reimbursed by those persons. In addition, the purchasers/beneficiaries of owner's fee policies of title insurance typically can expect the policies to cover the legal fees for defense of the titles, as long as the policies' limits are not exceeded.

An insurance company will issue a title insurance policy to cover only what it considers to be an insurable title to a specific real property. Thus, the insurer insists on receiving an acceptable title exam or abstract of title on the realty before committing itself to issuing the owner's fee policy of title insurance.

Also available to purchasers/soon-to-be realty owners is an extended coverage (ALTA) title insurance policy (also known as a mortgagee's policy). This policy additionally covers title problems that a survey would have revealed.

Title companies are surprisingly flexible in what they will insure. If the price is right, they often issue a policy, or rider, to cover a potential title problem.

A realty agent should use a knowledgeable and experienced escrow officer for these transactions. Escrow officers can identify and assist in solving problems, including potential title problems, and knowing about available title insurance policies that might resolve such problems.

TABLE 8–3 Comparative strength of forms of title evidence.

MOST PROTECTION TO GRANTEE	LESS PROTECTION TO GRANTEE
1. Owner's fee policy of title insurance.	1. Abstract of title.
2. Title guarantee.	2. Seller's affidavit of title.
	3. Attorney's opinion letter.

In a seller-financed transaction (as discussed in Chapter 7) sellers usually carry a note from the purchasers. These purchasers should be required to purchase a lender's policy of title insurance to secure the priority of the seller's lien.

Table 8–3 gives the comparative strength of the various forms of title evidence.

CASE STUDY FROM THE OHIO SUPREME COURT

TOTH V. BERKS TITLE INSURANCE CO. 6 Ohio St. 3d 338, 453 N.E.2d 639 (1983)

Facts: In 1974, Toth purchased two adjacent parcels of property for $300,000. One parcel is within the city of Fairlawn, and the other is within the city of Akron. At the time of purchase, there was no allocation of any portion of the original purchase price between the two parcels of property. Toth purchased a title guarantee from Berks Title Insurance Co. and Berks Title Agency Inc. (Berks) at the same time he purchased the parcels. This title guarantee did not list any setback use restrictions. Toth sold the Fairlawn property for $300,000 to the Akron Credit Bureau and reached an initial agreement with LaFatch whereby LaFatch would purchase the Akron property for $85,000.

LaFatch contacted the Chicago Title Insurance Company to secure a title guarantee on the property. Chicago Title discovered the existence of certain setback use restrictions that had been created by a 1924 deed to Henry H. Camp and expressed again in a recorded 1926 land plat. The title company noted the setback use restrictions would have to be listed as an exception to the title guarantee. Following Chicago Title's report, Berks was asked to issue a title guarantee to LaFatch that would not include the use restrictions listed as an exception. Berks would not issue the title guarantee, as requested, and LaFatch withdrew from the purchase negotiations for the Akron property.

Toth brought suit against Berks for damages payable under the title guarantee he had purchased on the Akron property. Appraisers for both parties appraised the Akron parcel at between $25,000 and $30,000 based upon fair market value with the setback use restrictions listed as an exception to the title guarantee. The transactions that pertained to the Akron property were the 1928 transfer to Anna M. Camp from Henry H. Camp, the 1966 transfer by Anna M. Camp's estate, and the 1974 transfer to Toth. The 1928 deed had no mention of the setback use restrictions. The 1966 deed did contain a specific note that specifically referred to the setback use restrictions that are the center of this controversy.

Trial Court: Entered judgment for Toth for $55,000.

Court of Appeals: Vacated judgment based upon the improper admission of hearsay evidence and remanded case for a new trial.

Trial Court: Again returned a judgment for Toth, but for $35,000.

Court of Appeals: Reversed judgment of trial court and entered judgment for Berks, holding that under the Marketable Title Act, Ohio Revised Code Sections 5301.47 to 5301.56, the setback use restrictions had been extinguished and therefore were not an exception that Berks should have noted on Toth's title guarantee.

Issue: Whether the setback use restrictions were extinguished by the Ohio Marketable Title Act.

Held by the Ohio Supreme Court: The reference in the 1966 deed to the setback use restrictions was specific, not general, and as such, it is an interest or defect that is "inherent in the muniments." Any interest or defect that is referred to specifically in a muniment (documentary evidence of title) within the marketable record title of a parcel of property, as defined by Ohio Revised Code Section 5301.48, is not extinguished by the Ohio Marketable Title Act. Because the setback use restrictions were referred to specifically in the 1966 deed, which is a part of Toth's marketable record title, the court of appeals erred in reversing the final judgment of the trial court. For the foregoing reasons, the judgment of the court of appeals is reversed and the judgment of the trial court is reinstated.

G/GM REAL ESTATE CORPORATION V. SUSSE CHALET MOTOR LODGE OF OHIO, INC.
61 Ohio St.3d 375, 575 N.E.2d 141 (1991)

CASE STUDY FROM THE OHIO SUPREME COURT

Facts: On March 4, 1985, G/GM and Susse signed a contract for a motel and restaurant owned by Susse in Marion, Ohio, at a purchase price of $1,000,000. On July 11, 1985, one day prior to the closing, the Wexford title agency, which G/GM had retained, issued a commitment for title insurance through the First American Title Insurance Company of New York. Schedule B, Section 1 of the commitment contained a list of seven items the title company required to be completed, including No. 6: "Proper affidavit canceling Lease from Susse to Hospitality Systems Ltd., dated June 28, 1979, and recorded on July 27, 1979, in lease Vol. 37, page 903, Marion County Recorder's Office, Marion County, Ohio." The reference was to a "memorandum of lease" that the parties subsequently agreed did not comply with the Ohio statute setting forth the requirements for recording a lease and should have not been accepted for recording.

McGrath, an attorney and president of Wexford, testified at trial that he had discovered the memorandum during his title search the last week of June and conveyed that information to all parties. He also testified that he asked Susse for an affidavit stating that the lease had been canceled for noncompliance with its terms as . . . "just good, prudent underwriting," even though he believed the memorandum presented no risk from a title insurance perspective.

The parties met as scheduled for the closing on July 12, 1985, but the sale did not close. There were additional negotiations on the morning of July 13, but the parties were unable to come to terms on a new agreement. G/GM also had failed to secure financing for the transaction. Susse subsequently sold the motel on September 13, 1985, for $1,050,000—$50,000 more than the price agreed to between G/GM and Susse. G/GM subsequently sued Susse, alleging breach of contract, and Susse counterclaimed.

Court of Common Pleas (Trial Court): Judgment for Susse.

Court of Appeals: Reversed in favor of G/GM.

Issue: Whether the improperly recorded memorandum of lease created an unmarketable title that gave G/GM sufficient cause to not close the transaction with Susse and to rightfully claim Susse had breached the contract.

Held by the Ohio Supreme Court: Reversed the judgment of the court of appeals and reinstated the judgment of the trial court in favor of Susse, stating that (a) improperly recorded memorandum of lease, which had lapsed, did not render title unmarketable and (b) G/GM breached contract by refusing to close based on discovery of previously recorded memorandum of lease.

> The real cloud here was the one employed by G/GM in its attempt to divert attention from its failure to secure financing for the purchase . . . An objection to a title must have some substantive merit in order to defeat a claim for specific performance . . . A title need not be free of any possible defect in order to be marketable, but must be in a condition as would satisfy a buyer of ordinary prudence.

SUMMARY OF CONTENT

1. A formal closing involves an actual meeting of the parties, their attorneys, the lender, the title evidence supplier, and real estate brokers. At this meeting the funds and documents are exchanged with the end result that title is transferred to the purchasers and net sales' proceeds are transferred to the sellers.
2. An escrow closing involves the selection of a disinterested third party, the escrow agent, who receives all funds and documents from the parties and then transfers title. There is no actual meeting of the parties and others with an escrow closing.
3. The escrow closing is a contractual matter whereby a contract often known as Conditions of Acceptance of Escrow or Escrow Instructions sets forth a working plan, along with the purchase contract, of the closing.
4. The sellers are responsible for providing all documents needed to close the transaction at the closing.
5. The purchasers ordinarily have a dual role in closing procedures. They must close their mortgage loan transaction with their lender and then conclude their transaction with the sellers whereby they receive title.
6. A unique feature of the escrow closing is application of the doctrine of relation back. Under this doctrine: If the seller deposits his deed with the escrow agent and thereafter dies before the closing, that deed is deemed by law to have been delivered to the purchaser when the seller placed it in escrow. The escrow closing can, therefore, still take place as scheduled.
7. The real estate salesperson is not typically the person responsible for filling out the closing statement.
8. The closing statement is a written summary of charges or credits that have arisen because of the transaction. The purchasers and the sellers each have their own separate schedules, but usually they are on a single sheet of paper.
9. Some expenses involved in the closing must be prorated (divided between purchasers and sellers) as of a certain point in time.
10. Commonly prorated items include insurance, tenant rents, utility charges, and real estate taxes.
11. Most closing costs, or charges, are not prorated because closing costs are solely the responsibility of either the purchaser or the seller, not both.
12. A standard date used for calculating prorations is the title transfer date.
13. The Real Estate Settlement Procedures Act (RESPA) protects borrowers by requiring lenders to estimate closing costs and by using the Uniform Settlement Statement.
14. RESPA applies only to transactions involving federally related first mortgage loans of residential real estate.

15. Most transactions require that the sellers provide further proof of their good title in addition to the deed. There are different types of this title evidence.
16. An abstract of title is a long, detailed history of ownership of the parcel of realty. With the abstract alone as title evidence, a purchaser's quiet possession of and title to the realty can be upset if the person who examines the title negligently overlooks some flaw in the title that appears in the public records, or if the flaw in the title exists because of something that would not become apparent from even the closest examination of the public records.
17. The certificate of title is the result of an examination of the public records going back the past 40 years, up to the date of the purchase agreement. The seller's affidavit of title is the seller's sworn statement regarding the condition of the title between the date of the purchase agreement and the date of title transfer.
18. Ohio has a Marketable Title Act providing that if a recorded title shows a clear, not flawed chain at least 40 years long, it is good, or marketable enough to be transferred.
19. Both the certificate of title and the seller's affidavit suffer from the same potential inaccuracies and flaws as the abstract does.
20. An attorney's opinion letter is a real estate attorney's written opinion of goodness of title, based on her review of the title exam. The problems with the opinion letter are that even though the purchaser can sue the attorney for any negligent acts, the attorney might be insolvent or uninsured and the attorney is not liable for matters the records would not reveal (e.g., forged documents).
21. The title guarantee is a good form of title evidence. It is an insurance policy covering matters negligently missed during examination of the public records. Negligence need not be proven for the insured realty owner to recover. Disadvantages of the title guarantee are (a) the small likelihood that the title guarantee will miss anything on the record and (b) the same potential flaws that would not be covered by the other forms (flaws that cannot be discovered by even the most careful title examination of the public records).
22. The owner's fee policy of title insurance is the broadest and best form of title evidence because it gives all the protection of a title guarantee and also covers problems that cannot be detected by examining the public records.

Review Questions

1. Which person is present at the escrow closing?
   a. purchaser
   b. escrow agent
   c. seller
   d. real estate agent
2. The following is *not* the purchaser's responsibility in closing:
   a. title guarantee
   b. loan proceeds
   c. executed mortgage deed
   d. executed promissory note
3. The following is the seller's responsibility in closing:
   a. executed mortgage deed
   b. executed promissory note
   c. gross proceeds of sale
   d. title guarantee
4. The following is the real estate broker's responsibility in closing:
   a. proration calculation
   b. completed RESPA form
   c. deposit of earnest money from trust account
   d. closing statement

5. It is this person's responsibility to prepare the closing statement:
   a. real estate salesperson
   b. lender
   c. real estate broker
   d. seller's attorney

6. Owner's fee policy of title insurance:
   a. is less expensive than a title guarantee
   b. does not cover any legal fees
   c. covers problems that could not be detected by a close examination of the public records
   d. is not as good evidence of title as a title guarantee

7. Which person is responsible for compliance with the Real Estate Settlement Procedures Act?
   a. real estate agent
   b. lender
   c. seller
   d. purchaser

8. In selecting an escrow agent for a realty closing, which person should *not* be selected?
   a. commercial lender
   b. title company
   c. attorney-at-law
   d. seller of subject realty

9. Which person is *not* present at the formal closing?
   a. appraiser
   b. purchasers and their attorney
   c. sellers and their attorney
   d. real estate broker

10. Escrow agents are usually which of the following?
    a. real estate brokers
    b. disinterested third parties
    c. purchaser's or seller's attorneys
    d. real estate salespersons

11. The principal item purchasers must bring to the closing is:
    a. purchase price plus closing costs
    b. general warranty deed
    c. evidence of the condition of utility reserves
    d. certificate of compliance with local property inspection

12. A credit to the seller at the closing is:
    a. real estate commission
    b. prepaid insurance purchaser is assuming
    c. current utility charges to date of closing
    d. cost of general warranty deed

13. The doctrine of relation back has the following effect on closings when all documents and funds are in escrow and the seller dies:
    a. closing can move ahead as scheduled
    b. the escrow account is sealed by court order
    c. the seller's will must be read
    d. the closing must be done through probate court

14. Prorations are items paid for by:
    a. purchaser
    b. seller
    c. both purchaser and seller
    d. real estate broker

15. One standard date commonly used for computing prorations is:
    a. date of escrow
    b. title transfer date
    c. date of purchase contract execution
    d. due date for real estate taxes

16. It is *not* a proof of title:
    a. closing statement
    b. attorney's opinion letter
    c. abstract of title
    d. certificate of title/seller's affidavit

17. Which of the following proofs of title protects against flaws that cannot be discovered by a close examination of the public records?
    a. abstract of title
    b. owner's fee policy of title insurance
    c. attorney's opinion letter
    d. certificate of title

18. The title guarantee:
    a. affords more protection than an owner's fee policy of title insurance
    b. affords less protection than an abstract of title
    c. guarantees the accuracy of the title examination
    d. is used throughout the state of Ohio as the preferred form of title evidence

19. The Real Estate Settlement Procedures Act (RESPA) applies to:
    a. land contract transactions
    b. loans made by a lender insured by FDIC
    c. purchase money mortgages
    d. all of the above

20. RESPA was enacted to:
    a. give real estate salespeople advance disclosure of closing costs so they, in turn, disclose them to sellers and purchasers
    b. standardize closing procedures to escrow instead of formal
    c. standardize closing procedures to formal instead of escrow
    d. standardize form closing statements

21. Under most real estate purchase contracts, the following causes a delay in closing the transaction:
    a. purchasers' transfer into town delayed
    b. sellers' new home under construction
    c. defect in title appears
    d. two brokers dispute which is owed the selling commission

22. If real estate subject to a trust is put into an escrow closing:
    a. it can close just like any other real estate transaction
    b. the procedure will change to a formal closing
    c. it won't work as both beneficiary and trustee will have to put in an appearance
    d. RESPA triggers certain formalities for realty held by trust

23. Seller's wife, who did not hold title, dies after both parties to realty transaction deposit all funds and documents into escrow. The following happens as a result:
    a. transaction must be turned over to probate court
    b. transaction now needs approval by purchasers
    c. transaction is nullified
    d. closing can proceed as scheduled

24. Although slightly more expensive, a wise investment for the purchasers/grantees regarding the realty they are purchasing is a(n):
    a. fee policy of title insurance
    b. title guarantee
    c. attorney's opinion letter
    d. abstract of title

25. Real estate salespeople should know how to read:
    a. the federal statute called RESPA
    b. a closing statement
    c. an attorney's opinion of title
    d. a fee policy of title insurance

ANSWER KEY

1. b
2. a
3. d
4. c
5. b
6. c
7. b
8. d
9. a
10. b
11. a
12. b
13. a
14. c
15. b
16. a
17. b
18. c
19. b
20. d
21. c
22. a
23. d
24. a
25. b

9
AGENCY AND LIABILITY

KEY TERMS

actual fraud
agency
antitrust laws
"as is" clause
assumption of the risk
buyer's broker
caveat emptor
client
coexclusive
concealment
constructive fraud
corporation
covenants not to compete
customer
deceit
dual agency
errors and omissions
exclusive agency
exclusive right to sell
fiduciary obligation
finder's fee
fraud
latent defect
misrepresentation
multiple listing
negligence
open listing
opinion
partnership
patent defect
price-fixing
principal
procuring cause
puffing
REALTOR®
rescission
single agency
sole proprietorship
subagency

FOR EXAMPLE

Anne has been doing very well in real estate ever since she learned how to negotiate real estate transactions and then "ride herd" on them right through the closing. As can happen with real estate salespeople, Anne is served with her first lawsuit. A purchaser to whom she sold a home six months ago has sued Anne, her broker, and the seller for selling him realty with a defective well. Anne knew nothing about the well. Furthermore, she cannot believe that the purchaser, someone she liked and thought she had helped greatly, has had the audacity to sue her *when she did nothing wrong!* Because the seller never told her about the well either, she thinks the purchaser should be suing the seller only. (Anne does not realize that lawyers feel duty-bound to sue all relevant parties because a statute of limitations may be about to expire or because they do not know the full extent of each party's liability.)

Receiving this first lawsuit is the moment of truth for most real estate salespeople. Even if their broker and their insurance carrier stand behind them the whole way, footing the entire legal bill and ultimately assuming most or all of the cost of settlement or judgment (the usual case), some salespeople are unable to handle the stress, strain, aggravation, and worry that a lawsuit presents, particularly as lawsuits typically take one to five years to conclude through either trial or settlement. Successful real estate salespeople have been known to leave the real estate profession entirely and enter some other occupation because of this factor alone. Most, however, make it through this difficult time and become avid students of preventive law (offered usually in continuing education courses), focusing their energies on keeping the lawsuits down in number or possibly eliminating them altogether (which requires the added factor of having some luck) by practicing real estate defensively.

This chapter also takes the defensive approach; the topics discussed herein involve some of the most frequently brought lawsuits against real estate salespeople and brokers. Like most other businesses, the real estate business has become highly complex, making the salesperson's task all the more difficult. This chapter has been broken down into two sections to group together certain related subjects. The first section examines the broker and the public; the second section focuses on the internal affairs of real estate brokerage.

SECTION I

The Broker and the Public

Agent and Principal

Agency is the *representation of principals, by others, agents.* Real estate brokers always represent **principals.** Furthermore, salespeople are agents of their principal brokers (brokers are the principals of salespeople) and are subagents to any principals of brokers. Agents call principals **clients,** whereas other parties to a transaction, nonprincipals, are called **customers.** Although both brokers and salespeople are also referred to as real estate agents, or simply agents, the term "agent" describes a specific legal relationship, as will be defined in this chapter; thus, care should be exercised when using the term "agent."

Jury instructions on agency, as a judge might use when giving the jury definitions to aid it in deciding a case, give the *fullest definition* of an agent:

> Agents occupy a position of trust and confidence with respect to their principals and are under obligations to exercise good faith, reasonable diligence and standard skills in the performance of their duties in behalf of, and in following the directions of, their principals. These obligations compel them to discharge their duties with absolute fidelity and loyalty to the interests of their principals; to keep their principals informed with respect to, and to make full disclosure to them of all material facts that affect the subject of their agency; to consult with them on emergency developments, if opportunity exists to do so; to exercise the skill and care standard for such employment in the community; in all respects, to discharge faithfully their duties, so as to protect and serve the best interests of their principals.

The rules of agency in real estate used to be easy to follow. Because brokers entered into *listing contracts* with sellers, brokers and their associate salespeople were *agents of the sellers,* (the principals) and *purchasers were not represented* at all. The rule that purchasers lived by was *caveat emptor* (Latin for "let the buyer beware"); they were out there on their own in the marketplace and no one was looking out for their interests.

As the latter half of the 20th century unfolded, mighty chinks developed in this ***caveat emptor*** rule, in the areas of fraud and misrepresentation of material fact, particularly pertaining to some hidden condition of the property (discussed in detail under "Fraud and Deceit"). Furthermore, real estate agents have had a duty for quite some time now to be ethical and honest in dealings with parties (usually purchasers) whom these real estate agents do not represent. This comes about from agents' status as licensed professionals and from the code of ethics followed in the profession.

In the last decade courts began holding that if purchasers had reason to believe they were being represented along with sellers in the transaction, and it turned out they were not, that was *grounds to rescind* the entire real estate transaction. This was true even if there had been no fraud, misrepresentation, overreaching, self-dealing, or even damage to purchasers in the transaction. It appears that sellers, too, can use this doctrine, called *undisclosed dual agency,* to rescind the transaction. Additional remedies available to the principals are: monetary damages awarded to principals; and/or a refund of the brokers' real estate commissions; and/or loss or suspension of the brokers' and/or salespeople's real estate licenses. In 1996 Ohio changed its license law regarding agency. By state statute (see Chapter 10 for the applicable statutes) it became easier for purchasers to become represented as well as for dual agency to take place. The different agency relationships are described in Figure 9–1(A).

FIGURE 9–1(A) Mandatory disclosure form in Ohio.

AGENCY DISCLOSURE STATEMENT

This disclosure form is being provided to help you make an informed choice regarding the type of relationship you wish to enter into with the real estate agent. It is also intended to help you understand the role of other agents who may be involved in your real estate transaction. For purposes of the form, the term "seller" includes a landlord and the term "buyer" includes a tenant.

When you enter into an agency relationship with a real estate agent, the real estate brokerage with whom the agent is affiliated also becomes your agent. Unless they are appointed to represent you, the other agents in the brokerage are not your agents and do not represent you.

AGENCY RELATIONSHIPS PERMITTED IN OHIO

Seller's Agency: In this type of relationship, the agent and the brokerage owe the seller the duties of loyalty, obedience, confidentiality, accounting, and reasonable skill and care in performing their duties, and any other duties contained in an agency agreement. The agent and brokerage are required to act solely on behalf of the seller's interest to seek the best price and terms for the seller. Finally, a seller's agent and brokerage also have a duty to disclose to the seller all material information obtained from the buyer or from any other source.

Subagency: In this type of relationship, buyer's/sellers may authorize their agent and brokerage to offer subagency to other licensees/brokerages. A subagent also represents the client's interests and has all of the same duties as the client's agent, including a duty of loyalty and confidentiality and a duty to disclose all material facts to the client.

Buyer's Agency: In this type of relationship, a buyer's agent and the brokerage owe the buyer the duties of loyalty, obedience, confidentiality, accounting, and reasonable skill and care in performing their duties and any other duties contained in an agency agreement. The agent and brokerage are required to act solely on behalf of the buyer's interests to seek the best price and terms for the buyer. Finally, a buyer's agent and brokerage also have a duty to disclose to the buyer all material information obtained from the seller or from any other source.

Disclosed Dual Agency: In this type of relationship, one agent may represent both parties in a real estate transaction, **BUT ONLY IF BOTH PARTIES CONSENT**. Disclosed dual agency is most likely to occur when both the buyer and seller are represented by the same agent. **IF THIS HAPPENS, THE BUYER AND SELLER MUST SIGN A SEPARATE DUAL AGENCY DISCLOSURE STATEMENT** that describes the duties and obligations of the dual agent. A dual agent may not disclose any confidential information that would place one party at an advantage over the other party and may not disclose any of the following information without the informed consent of the party to whom the information pertains: **1)** that a buyer is willing to pay more than the price offered; **2)** that a seller is willing to accept less than the asking price; **3)** motivating factors of either party for buying or selling; **4)** that a party will agree to financing terms other than those offered; **5)** repairs or improvements a seller is willing to make as a condition of sale; and **6)** or any concession having an economic impact upon the transaction that either party is willing to make.

Permitted Agency Relationships in an In-Company Transaction: In an in-company transaction where the buyer and seller are both represented as clients by the same brokerage, the following applies: If only one agent is involved in the transaction, that agent represents both the buyer and the seller. The agent and the brokerage are dual agents and cannot disclose confidential information to either client. If two agents are involved in the transaction, you and the other party will be represented by the agent with whom you have each entered into an agency relationship. Each agent will represent the sole interest of his/her client and must not share confidential information with each other. The brokerage is a dual agent. The only exception is if a management level licensee is one of the agents involved in the transaction. In this case, the management level licensee and the brokerage represent both the buyer and seller as dual agents.
The brokerage's role, as a dual agent, is to do the following:

- Objectively supervise the agents involved so they can each fulfill their duties, as outlined above, to each of their clients;
- Assist the parties, in an unbiased manner, to negotiate a contract;
- Assist the parties, in an unbiased manner, to fulfill the terms of any contract.

As a dual agent, the brokerage cannot:

- Advocate or negotiate on behalf of either the buyer or seller;
- Disclose confidential information to any party or any other employee or agent of the brokerage;
- Use confidential information of one party to benefit the other party to the transaction.

(continued)

FIGURE 9–1(A) Continued.

DISCLOSURE OF AGENCY RELATIONSHIP

The following agent ______________________________, and ______________________________
(name of agent) (name of brokerage)
the brokerage with which the agent is affiliated, disclose the following concerning their agency relationship (CHECK APPROPRIATE BOX - ONLY ONE):

- □ They represent the seller as the seller's agent.
- □ They represent the buyer as a buyer's agent.

Disclosure of the potential future agency relationships that could be created: (CHECK APPROPRIATE BOX(ES) THAT APPLY):

- □ They represent the seller as a subagent.
- □ They represent the buyer as a subagent.
- □ The same agent who represents you could potentially represent the other party in a transaction involving you. The agent and brokerage would both be **DUAL AGENTS.** A management level licensee is a dual agent in an in-company transaction.
- □ A different agent in the same brokerage could potentially represent the other party in a transaction involving you. Each agent would represent the interest of their separate client. The brokerage would be a **DUAL AGENT.**

C O N S E N T

BY SIGNING THIS FORM YOU INDICATE YOUR CONSENT TO THE AGENCY RELATIONSHIP DISCLOSED ABOVE. BEFORE YOU CONSENT TO ANY AGENCY RELATIONSHIP, YOU SHOULD FULLY UNDERSTAND THE INFORMATION FOUND ON THE REVERSE SIDE OF THIS FORM. IF YOU DO NOT UNDERSTAND THE INFORMATION CONTAINED ANYWHERE IN THIS FORM, YOU SHOULD CONSULT AN ATTORNEY.

______________________________ ______________________________
Buyer/Tenant Date Seller/Landlord Date

______________________________ ______________________________
Buyer/Tenant Date Seller/Landlord Date

TO BE COMPLETED ONLY IN AN IN-COMPANY TRANSACTION INVOLVING TWO AGENTS

Both buyer and seller **ACKNOWLEDGE AND AGREE** that in a contemplated transaction involving property located at ______________________________, the buyer is represented by ______________________________ and the seller is represented by ______________________________.

YOU DO NOT HAVE TO CONSENT TO DUAL AGENCY. BEFORE YOU CONSENT TO ANY AGENCY RELATIONSHIP, YOU SHOULD FULLY UNDERSTAND THE INFORMATION FOUND ON THE REVERSE SIDE OF THIS FORM. IF YOU DO NOT UNDERSTAND THE INFORMATION CONTAINED ANYWHERE IN THIS FORM, YOU SHOULD CONSULT AN ATTORNEY.

By initialing below **BOTH PARTIES ACKNOWLEDGE AND AGREE** that they are aware that both agents are affiliated with the same brokerage; that each agent will represent the separate interest of their separate client, except if a management level licensee is one of the agents involved in the transaction; that it was previously disclosed that this could occur; and that **THEY CONSENT TO THE BROKERAGE ACTING AS A DUAL AGENT**.

Buyer/Tenant's initials: ______________________________ Date ____________________

Seller/Landlord's initials: ______________________________ Date ____________________

Any questions regarding the role or responsibilities of the brokerage or its agents in Ohio can be
Directed to an attorney or to:
Ohio Division of Real Estate
77 S. High Street 20th Floor
Columbus, Ohio 43266-0547
(614) 466-4100

FIGURE 9–1(B) Mandatory dual agency disclosure form in Ohio.

DUAL AGENCY DISCLOSURE STATEMENT

Seller/Landlord(s):________________ Buyer/Tenant(s):________________
Seller/Landlord(s):________________ Buyer/Tenant(s):________________
Property Involved:________________

For purposes of this form, the term "seller " includes a landlord and the term "buyer" includes a tenant.

DUAL AGENCY: Ohio law permits a real estate agent and brokerage to represent both the seller and buyer in a real estate transaction **AS LONG AS THIS IS DISCLOSED TO BOTH PARTIES AND THEY BOTH AGREE. THIS IS KNOWN AS DUAL AGENCY**. As a dual agent, a real estate agent and brokerage represent two clients whose interests are, or at times could be, different or adverse. For this reason, the dual agent(s) may not be able to advocate on behalf of the client with the same skill and energy the dual agent may have if the agent represents only one client.

This statement discloses that ________________
(Name of brokerage)
and its agent(s)________________
(Name of agent(s))
WILL BE ACTING AS A DUAL AGENT IN THE CONTEMPLATED TRANSACTION INVOLVING THE NAMED PROPERTY.

IT IS UNDERSTOOD AND AGREED BY THE PARTIES THAT **AS A DUAL AGENT**, THE AGENT AND BROKERAGE **SHALL:**

1. Treat both clients honestly;
2. Disclose latent, material defects to the purchaser, if known by the agent or brokerage;
3. Provide information regarding lenders, inspectors and other professionals, if requested;
4. Provide market information available from a property listing service or public records, if requested;
5. Prepare and present all offers and counteroffers at the direction of the parties;
6. Assist both parties in completing the steps necessary to fulfill the terms of any contract, if requested.

IT IS ALSO UNDERSTOOD AND AGREED BY THE PARTIES THAT **AS A DUAL AGENT**, THE AGENT AND BROKERAGE **SHALL NOT:**

1. Disclose information that is confidential, or that would have an adverse effect on one party's position in the transaction, unless such disclosure is authorized by the client or required by law;
2. Advocate or negotiate on behalf of either the buyer or seller;
3. Suggest or recommend specific terms, including price, to be offered, accepted, rejected or countered or disclose the terms or price a buyer is willing to offer or that a seller is willing to accept;
4. Engage in conduct that is contrary to the instructions of either party and may not act in a biased manner on behalf of one party.

MATERIAL RELATIONSHIP: Unless indicated below, neither the agent or the brokerage acting as a dual agent in this contemplated transaction has a material relationship with either buyer or seller. A material relationship would include, any personal, family or business relationship with one of the parties. (If such a relationship does exist, explain):________________

COMPENSATION: Unless indicated as follows, the brokerage will be compensated per the listing agreement:________________

RESPONSIBILITIES OF THE PARTIES: The duties of the agent and brokerage in a real estate transaction do not relieve the Buyer and Seller from the responsibility to protect their own interests. The Buyer and Seller are advised to carefully read all agreements to assure that they adequately express their understanding of the transaction. The agent and brokerage are qualified to advise on real estate matters. **IF LEGAL OR TAX ADVICE IS DESIRED, YOU SHOULD CONSULT THE APPROPRIATE PROFESSIONAL.**

FAIR HOUSING STATEMENT

It is illegal, pursuant to the Ohio Fair Housing Law, Division (H) of Section 4112.02 of the Revised Code and the Federal Fair Housing Law, 42 U.S.C.A. 3601, to refuse to sell, transfer, assign, rent, lease, sublease, or finance housing accommodations, refuse to negotiate for the sale or rental of housing accommodations, or otherwise deny or make unavailable housing accommodations because of race, color, religion, sex, familial status, ancestry, handicap, or national origin; or to so discriminate in advertising the sale or rental of housing, in the financing of housing, or in the provision of real estate brokerage services.

It is also illegal, for profit, to induce or attempt to induce a person to sell or rent a dwelling by representations regarding the entry into the neighborhood of a person or persons belonging to one of the protected classes.

BY SIGNING BELOW, YOU ACKNOWLEDGE THAT YOU HAVE READ AND UNDERSTAND THIS FORM. YOU ARE GIVING YOUR VOLUNTARY, INFORMED CONSENT TO THIS DUAL AGENCY. IF YOU DO NOT AGREE TO THE AGENT AND/OR BROKERAGE ACTING AS A DUAL AGENT, YOU ARE NOT REQUIRED TO CONSENT TO THIS AGREEMENT AND YOU MAY EITHER REQUEST A SEPARATE AGENT IN THE BROKERAGE BE APPOINTED TO REPRESENT YOUR INTERESTS OR YOU MAY TERMINATE YOUR AGENCY RELATIONSHIP AND SEEK REPRESENTATION FROM ANOTHER BROKERAGE. IF YOU CHOOSE TO BE REPRESENTED BY ANOTHER BROKERAGE, HOWEVER, YOU MAY BE OBLIGATED TO PAY A COMMISSION TO THE ABOVE NAMED BROKERAGE. ANY QUESTIONS REGARDING POTENTIAL OBLIGATIONS SHOULD BE DIRECTED TO PERSONAL LEGAL COUNSEL.

Buyer/Tenant	Date	Seller/Landlord	Date
Buyer/Tenant	Date	Seller/Landlord	Date
Licensee	Date	Licensee (if more than one)	Date

Any questions regarding the role or responsibilities of real estate brokers, brokerages, or agents in Ohio can be directed to an attorney or to: The Ohio Division of Real Estate at (614) 466-4100

Next, we will examine the fiduciary obligation the agent owes to the principal, as we discovered in the agency jury instructions, given earlier. The discussion is based upon the situation of sellers, not purchasers, being the principals. Note, however, that purchasers can be the principals in the appropriate circumstances. The fiduciary obligation then is owed to purchasers.

FIDUCIARY OBLIGATION

Brokers and salespeople create an agency relationship with sellers of listed real property at the time sellers enter into listing contracts with brokers. Sellers of listed real property are the principals. As agents of sellers, real estate brokers owe fiduciary obligations to sellers. At a minimum, **fiduciary obligations** require:

- full disclosure and confidentiality.
- no self-dealing.
- loyalty and a high degree of care, trust, and honesty, as to all matters within the scope of the broker's and salesperson's employment.
- obedience.
- accounting.

Fraud, bad faith, concealment of facts, or other breach of trust by real estate agents violates fiduciary obligations. Because salespeople are agents of brokers, they have the same fiduciary obligations to sellers. When brokers opt to represent purchasers instead, purchasers are owed fiduciary obligations instead.

Fiduciary obligations also extend to co-brokerage situations, that is, cooperative sales with other brokers. Therefore, if one brokerage is selling the realty that another brokerage has listed, the first brokerage still might owe the fiduciary obligation to sellers instead of purchasers. Now it is possible, however, to have the listing brokerage represent the sellers as the principals and the selling brokerage to represent the purchasers as the principals.

Real estate agents receive both express and implied powers under the fiduciary obligation. The *express* powers are those clearly given under the listing contract. *Implied* powers are those necessary to carry out the agency duty of selling the realty. For example, the listing contract specifies that agents must use their best efforts to sell the realty. This is an express term. By implication, best efforts include putting a "For Sale" sign on the realty and writing ads and placing them in newspapers. Brokers and their salespeople can forfeit the right to a real estate commission if they violate their fiduciary obligations.

Let's examine each aspect of the fiduciary obligation in depth.

Full Disclosure and Confidentiality

Full disclosure prohibits "freezing" the realty. *Freezing realty is an illegal practice* that occurs when real estate companies hold back other offers when one offer is already being negotiated with sellers. All offers must be presented to sellers; there can be no holding back of other offers. To hold back is a gross violation of the fiduciary obligation. Even if the salesperson thinks an offer is ridiculous, the offer must be communicated to sellers. For example, if a customer wants to submit an offer of $40,000 on a house listed for $100,000, the salesperson or broker must communicate this offer to sellers even though it is ludicrous.

At the opposite end of the spectrum are brokers who tell sellers that their realty is worth an excessive figure. The broker may know that the figure is excessive and the records may confirm it, but the broker suggests this inflated figure because other real estate brokerages are competing for the same realty as a listing. Sellers unfortunately are inclined to give listings to the broker who tells them their realty is worth the highest figure. Ultimately, the broker faces a problem if, as is likely, sellers are unable to sell their realty because of the inflated asking price and perhaps suffer damages because it has been on the market so long with no prospects of a sale. As part of their fiduciary obligations, real estate agents should properly research the selling prices of other comparable real properties in the area, the condition of the real estate market in general, and specifically the market in that area; then agents should advise sellers, in light of that research, on realistic asking prices to quote on specific realties. Merely telling sellers what they may wish to hear is not acting in their best interests and arguably does not fulfill fiduciary obligations.

Full disclosure also requires that real estate agents represent only sellers, and not purchasers, when sellers are their principals. Thus, if purchasers give agents any information relevant to sellers' best interests, agents must disclose this to sellers. For example, if purchasers tell agents they are going to "up their bid" by another thousand dollars if sellers counteroffer, this must be disclosed to sellers. Also, if purchasers tell agents they are going to sell the realty to a third person, agents must disclose this intent to sellers.

Essentially, full disclosure means *communicating everything to principals so they may reach a fully informed decision.* If other prospective purchasers want to see the realty while offers are being presented on it, showings can be done if sellers desire. Secondary (additional) offers also must be presented to sellers, even if another offer has been accepted.

When salespeople have relationships with purchasers, that should be disclosed to sellers. For example, when salespeople show relatives housing, they must disclose to sellers their relationship with purchasers.

Also, real estate agents wanting to purchase realty for themselves or someone who will have any interest in that realty, such as occurs in a partnership, should disclose their licensed status to sellers. Licensees are not permitted to buy realty as undisclosed principals. Therefore, they may not conceal their true identities.

When real estate agents own realty and advertise it for sale, giving their names and home telephone numbers and advertising their properties for sale by owner, they must disclose that they are real estate licensees. This is also true if the property is listed. The disclosure should occur both in the advertising of the realties and in the negotiation of transactions on the realties. If the agents fail to do these things, purchasers later may claim that the agents placed them at a disadvantage in those transactions by allowing nonprofessionals to deal with professionals.

The better view, and the one endorsed by the code of ethics of the National Association of REALTORS®, is that agents are obligated to make special efforts to present true and accurate pictures in both advertising and representation to the public.

A salesperson cannot represent to purchasers that a property can be purchased at less than the listed price. Purchasers should come up with their own opening bid to protect the sellers' interests.

Another violation of fiduciary obligation happens when real estate agents pledge either the whole or part of their commission to the purchasers' purchase of the realty in exchange for a second mortgage or some other right in the realty and the agents do not inform the sellers of their involvement on the other end of the transaction. Minimally, in this type of situation, the agents forfeit their right to a commission; probably violate HUD rules and lending regulations and practices, both civilly and criminally; and possibly owe further damages to the sellers if they suffer any monetary loss as a result of this activity.

Loss of a commission because of a violation of the fiduciary obligation does not depend on whether the principals are or are not injured by the conduct of the agents. The very fact that it happened is enough to forfeit the commission. The only way real estate agents can properly lend a purchaser money or participate in the transaction in any way is to make sure the principals, sellers, are fully advised of agents' activities with nonclients.

Confidentiality is the flip side of full disclosure. Real estate agents must keep secret all the information confided in them by the principals.

FOR EXAMPLE

If agents represent sellers and the sellers say during negotiations of a purchase contract that they will come down another $1,000 in price if the purchasers don't accept their counteroffer, the agents *cannot* repeat this information to purchasers because of the confidentiality owed to the principals, the sellers. Of course, if the example changes to concealment of a material part of the transaction, such as a defective septic system on the property, the agents must disclose that information, as discussed more fully under "Fraud and Deceit" later in this chapter.

Self-Dealing

Self-dealing means *working for yourself as broker or salesperson* instead of your employers, the principals (usually sellers). This also violates the fiduciary obligation. Self-dealing further involves agents' receipt of any benefit at the principals' expense.

FOR EXAMPLE

An example of self-dealing occurs in the *straw-person* situation. A real estate agent wants to buy realty listed with his brokerage but is afraid sellers will not sell if they know he is the purchaser. The agent negotiates the transaction, using someone else's name (the straw-person) as the purchaser when the agent is the actual purchaser. This straw-person takes title to the realty and, after an interval of time, conveys the realty to the agent. If sellers discover this activity, they can maintain a lawsuit in fraud, misrepresentation, and violation of the fiduciary obligation against the agent.

Real estate practitioners cannot deal for themselves and at the same time represent the best interest of their principals, which they are required to do under their fiduciary obligation. Of course, real estate agents do buy real property for themselves. *Practitioners should inform sellers that they are licensed and are buying the realty for themselves.* Thus, they are acting as purchasers and not as agents. By putting sellers on notice of agents' true status, sellers know the relationship has shifted and they must be careful in their dealings with agents, who are now ordinary purchasers.

Loyalty, Trust, and High Duty of Care

Loyalty and trust require that real estate agents communicate fully to principal-sellers and in their best interests. High duty of care requires that, while servicing the realty, agents must do so to the best of their ability. This includes full service of the realty and due care while bringing other persons onto the realty to view for possible purchase.

If real estate agents are negligent in the performance of their jobs, they fail to take the high degree of care required under the fiduciary obligation. *Negligence* (discussed later in this chapter) is the failure to act as a reasonable person would in the same or similar circumstances. One who does not have a fiduciary relationship with another may also be negligent. A negligence claim can be made at any time a duty is owed by one to another and that duty is breached.

When applied to professional competence, negligence is called *malpractice*. As the real estate profession continues to raise its standards of competence, this will become a more common basis for lawsuits, and it will be easier to say what is or is not competent practice.

As the customary represented principals, sellers typically can pursue negligence lawsuits against their real estate agents in the following examples.

1. The agent fills in the form real estate purchase contract between sellers and purchasers so poorly that sellers cannot enforce it against purchasers.
2. Agents fail to tell purchasers some vital information about the realty, which sellers clearly specified to be disclosed, such as a defective septic system. If purchasers sue sellers, sellers in turn may sue the real estate brokerage and its careless agents for negligence.

As a practical matter, the way some negligence claims come about is when the real estate broker first sues the sellers for the commission pursuant to their listing contract with one another. The sellers (having nothing to lose because they already are in court) counterclaim by saying that the brokerage should be denied the commission because the brokerage or its salespeople were negligent or, alternatively, that sellers should be awarded damages because of such negligence.

Obedience

Agents must *obey any of their clients' lawful instructions*. If clients ask agents to follow illegal instructions, agents may disobey. For example, an instruction to show the property only when the dog has been removed by prior arrangement is a lawful command that agents must obey. Not showing the property to black persons, however, violates the fair housing laws and agents cannot follow this instruction without exposing themselves to liability.

Accounting

If principals let *agents handle any money* or other valuables in connection with marketing the property, agents must be careful to strictly account to principals for any dealings. If agents spend principals' money, such as to fix the property when sellers are out of town, agents should keep all receipts and submit them to principals.

Because the fiduciary obligation usually comes about because of the listing contract between sellers and real estate brokers, now is the logical time to review the different types of listing contracts brokers can have with sellers and their respective legal ramifications.

Types of Listings

As defined in Chapter 6, listing agreements are contracts. The parties to listing contracts are sellers of realty and real estate brokers. Brokers promise to try to procure purchasers for realties in exchange for sellers' promises to pay them commissions. Brokers can obtain several different types of listings. Table 9–2 compares the major types of listing agreements.

Exclusive Right to Sell

From real estate brokers' perspectives, the best listing is an **exclusive right to sell** in which *a single brokerage has the authority to procure purchasers for the realty.* With exclusive right to sell listings, no matter who produces the ready, willing, and able purchasers, willing to purchase realty upon sellers' terms, that listing brokerage is entitled to receive the commission. That listing brokerage also has the authority to

TABLE 9–1 Differences in listing contracts.

EXCLUSIVE RIGHT TO SELL	EXCLUSIVE AGENCY	OPEN LISTING
Best form from broker's standpoint (owner has no right to deal in property).	Least desirable form from broker's perspective (owner has right to deal in property plus broker must advertise and place in MLS).	"Mixed bag" form from broker's perspective (has to share with other brokers and owner but no duty to advertise or place in MLS).
Worst form from owner/seller's perspective (no right to deal in property on his/her own by owner).	Most desirable form from owner/seller's perspective (can deal in property on own plus broker will advertise and place in MLS).	"Mixed bag" form from owner/seller's perspective (can deal in property on own but no broker advertising or listing in MLS).
Broker is paid commission from owner/seller regardless of who procures the purchaser for the realty.	Broker is paid commission if he/she or another brokerage procures purchaser for realty.	Broker is paid commission only if he/she procures purchase for realty.
Owner/seller retains no right to sell the realty on his/her own.	Owner retains the right to sell the realty on his/her own, along with a particular broker's right to sell it.	Owner retains the right to sell the realty on his/her own, along with any number of brokers who are given the right to sell it.

let another brokerage procure purchasers. The two brokerages can cooperate, or *co-broke,* in the sale and share the commission. If sellers come up with their own purchasers during the period of the exclusive right-to-sell listing contract, sellers nevertheless will owe the real estate brokerage a commission if purchasers purchase the realty.

Exclusive Agency

An **exclusive agency** listing lets sellers also deal in the realty themselves so if they procure purchasers, they do not owe the listing brokerage a commission, but *only that one brokerage has a listing on the realty.* If that brokerage comes up with the purchaser, it obtains the full commission. If another real estate brokerage procures purchasers, the commission is shared between the two brokerages in a cooperative, or **co-broke,** sale.

Open Listing

An **open listing** means the *realty is available for a number of real estate brokerages to sell.* Not just one real estate brokerage has the listing. Whichever real estate brokerage procures purchasers earns the commission. If sellers sell it themselves, no one is owed a commission. Real estate brokerages usually do not favor open listings.

A problem that can arise with an open listing is when two brokerages secure an open listing from sellers and both come up with purchasers who are ready, willing, and able to buy at sellers' exact selling terms. The two brokerages both can try to recover their commissions from sellers if and when they simultaneously come up with asking price offers and identically situated purchasers. They both might succeed in being owed a commission because they both fulfilled the goal of their employment.

Multiple Listing

Multiple listing (called MLS for multiple listing service) is a way in which *listing brokerages make unilateral* ***subagency*** *offers on a mass basis, to all other members of the MLS.* It is also a marketing service provided to sellers. Each member can co-broke sales with other MLS members on any of these realties. That brokerage at the same time can also *offer compensation to buyers' agents who are members of the MLS and who do not accept the unilateral offer of subagency.* Further, MLS is a way of sharing information among real estate brokerages about the listings each has available.

MLS data typically are placed into a central computer bank that all the member MLS realty companies tie into. Whichever brokerage has the actual listing is paid the commission by the seller. If one of the other MLS brokerages procures purchasers, that brokerage must co-broke with the broker who holds the listing, and they share the commission. MLS membership generally includes an agreement that any member is willing to co-broke (enter into a cooperative sale) with a fellow member.

If the listing contract has any *special agency terms,* these must be disclosed to the MLS at time of submission. For example, if the listing brokerage and sellers agree to a lower commission rate if the listing broker sells the real property, this condition of subagency must be disclosed to the MLS. If not, it can be regarded as an *undisclosed dual commission,* and therefore misrepresentation. Certain MLS systems have been innovative. For example, an MLS computer program allows a listing brokerage to state whether buyers' broker will be compensated on that basis rather than as a subagent of the seller.

Exclusions

Within the listing agreement *exclusions* can be made. For example, if sellers are willing to give broker an exclusive right to sell if broker will grant them an exclusion, the broker may well exclude a third person in the agreement in order to obtain that listing. For example, sellers want to exclude their son from the exclusive right-to-sell agreement, so if their son wants to buy their realty, he may do so directly and, thus, no commission is owed to the real estate broker. Generally real estate brokers establish a cut-off date for exclusions. For example: "Joe Smith excluded from this exclusive right to sell for the first 30 days of the listing."

Coexclusives

Coexclusives are not favored by real estate brokers. **Coexclusive** means that *two brokerages share an exclusive right to sell listing on the realty.* Both brokerages are parties to the listing contract with the sellers. The listing agreement stipulates the commission agreement that will prevail. One possibility is that the brokerage that sells the realty under the coexclusive, either via its own purchasers or a cooperating brokerage that goes through it, gets the whole commission and the other brokerage gets nothing. Another example, seen occasionally, is that the brokerage that secures the sale gets 80 percent of the whole commission and the one who does not gets 20 percent. An essential term within a coexclusive listing is that both brokerages agree to the terms of the coexclusive listing contract and the rate of commission.

Legal problems can easily arise with this type of listing, especially if a third brokerage enters the situation and goes through both real estate companies at different points in negotiations. It then becomes difficult, perhaps impossible, to figure out which brokerages are owed what proportions of the commission. This type of listing is not recommended because of the legal difficulties that can so readily ensue from the confusion and communication problems that usually accompany coexclusive listings.

Procuring Cause

The term **procuring cause** means *producing purchasers ready, willing, and able to buy real estate on sellers' terms.* Real estate agents locate the ultimate purchasers, create an interest in purchasing the realty, and secure written promises (the purchase agreement) from purchasers to purchase the realty. Although highly recommended, agents do not have to show purchasers the realty in order to be the procuring cause of sale.

Procuring cause is the *legal test in Ohio that brokerages must meet to recover commissions from sellers.* They must be able to show *contracts of employment* (any of the listing contracts) in addition to showing they were the procuring cause of sales of realty.

In brokers versus owner lawsuits, legal problems usually arise in open listings, as brokers are assumed to be the procuring cause by either type of exclusive listing. Brokers also must prove that they are licensed as such and so are their salespersons. In addition, brokers must show that they performed services for sellers according to the terms of their listing contracts. The amount or degree of these services is immaterial as long as they were rendered.

One frequently used legal test for determining procuring cause is:

> A cause directly originating a series of events which, without break in their continuity, directly result in the accomplishment of the prime objective of the employment of the broker, producing purchasers ready, willing, and able to buy real estate on the owners' terms.

REALTORS® (brokers and salespeople who belong to the private trade group for real estate licensees) enter into binding arbitration agreements within their boards in which they agree that any *disputes between or among members, over which of them was the procuring cause of a sale, and is thus owed the commission, is subject to binding arbitration by the board.* A panel or board of arbiters hears the case and decides who was the procuring cause and thereby earned the commission. The decision is conclusive. The losing party cannot appeal the decision to a court. A critical element is that agents' efforts, although they need not be the sole cause of the sale, must be the predominating cause to be the procuring cause.

"Ready, willing, and able" are the keys to determining whether procuring cause has occurred and thus whether a real estate commission has been earned. "Able" means financially able to purchase the real property. Purchasers can obtain all funds necessary to close the transaction and transfer title. "Financially able" can be all cash in hand or the ability to secure a mortgage loan. If the real estate purchase contract contains a financing condition that excuses purchasers from performance if they are unable to get a loan, sellers do not owe the broker a commission if purchasers use the condition to excuse themselves from the contract's obligations. Purchasers were not able to purchase, so the broker has not fulfilled the obligation of producing an able purchaser.

"Ready" purchasers are presently capable of closing the transaction. Purchasers will enter into a real estate purchase contract and follow it through to closing.

"Willing" purchasers let the broker negotiate the transaction with sellers as sellers' agent. They also will enter into an enforceable real estate purchase contract to purchase the realty.

"Ready, willing, and able" are terms that overlap in their definitions. Taken together, they mean that purchasers will now do all things necessary to bring the purchase of the realty to a close.

If sellers default on the real estate purchase contract, brokers still are owed a commission because brokers nevertheless produced ready, willing, and able purchasers. For instance, sellers who refuse to execute the deed to the realty are in breach of the listing contract and thus still owe the broker a commission. As another example, the broker brings to the seller purchasers who are willing to purchase at all the terms within the listing contract. Seller refuses purchasers. Seller owes broker a commission because broker fulfilled the duty of producing the purchaser ready, willing, and able to purchase at seller's terms. Also, if sellers cannot consummate the sale because of a *defect in the title,* the broker is still owed the commission for securing ready, willing, and able purchasers.

Unless sellers insert within the listing contract that payment of the commission is conditioned upon *actual consummation* of the real estate purchase contract or *upon payment of the purchase price and transfer of title,* sellers can still owe brokers real estate commissions despite there being no closed transaction. This happens whenever the broker procures purchasers but, before closing, some other event causes the sale to collapse. Standard listing contracts that brokers currently use usually do not contain this type of condition for sellers' protection. Without its insertion, the general rule remains that *brokers can recover real estate commissions by securing ready, willing, and able purchasers regardless of whether the realty sale is or is not actually completed.*

Unauthorized Practice of Law

Brokers and salespeople can practice real estate only, not law, but both need to be familiar with the law to know when matters should be referred to lawyers. Unfortunately, what constitutes the unauthorized practice of law is still a somewhat gray area. Complicating an already murky picture is that *states vary considerably on what is considered practicing law without authorization and what is considered practicing real estate instead.* For example, for real estate agents to fill in land contracts, options, mortgages, and deeds is considered the unauthorized practice of law in some states, including Ohio; in other states those activities are considered permissible conduct for real estate licensees. Even in states where these practices are deemed lawful and appropriate, however, agents must be doing them as *incidents to their real estate practice and not charging a separate fee for them.*

Currently any of the following is considered the unauthorized practice of law by real estate licensees in most states, including Ohio:

1. Giving advice to purchasers or sellers about their potential legal liability (for example, specifically commenting about how a court will interpret a particular clause in a legal instrument, such as a real estate purchase contract, in the event of a future lawsuit).
2. Representing purchasers or sellers in courts or before administrative agencies.
3. Giving specific tax advice to purchasers or sellers.

Virtually all states, including Ohio, consider it entirely appropriate for real estate brokers and salespersons to fill in the blanks on preprinted form real estate listing and real estate purchase contracts. This activity by the agents is not interpreted as practicing law without a license.

A common concern for purchasers is, "If I delay to consult a lawyer, will someone else have bought the realty?" The longer the delay, the more likely it is that someone else will submit an offer. Purchasers can avoid this dilemma by involving their attorneys in the process before finding the specific real property. Agents give purchasers' attorneys copies of the form real estate purchase contract that will be used to make the purchasers' offers. Attorneys can review these contracts before purchasers, their clients, find the real property they wish to purchase. Then, when purchasers are ready to make an offer, they can read to their attorney over the phone the inserts within the form contract that the agent has drafted into the offer. After the attorney approves the inserts, the agent proceeds to present the offer.

This procedure allows purchasers to benefit from legal representation without the danger of losing the realty they want to purchase by a delay in time. Attorneys who review contracts beforehand also may spot problem areas that agents miss, thereby decreasing agents' exposure to liability.

Real estate agents should never discourage either purchasers or sellers from obtaining advice from lawyers. To do so seriously impairs agents' positions if lawsuits about the matter of proposed inquiry later come about.

Fraud and Deceit

Fraud is an *intentional act of falsehood calculated to induce another to rely on it and to part with something of value.* **Deceit** is the *intentionally misleading conduct that gives rise to lawsuits based in fraud.* Most fraud and deceit lawsuits are based in *defect disclosure liability law.* These cases have expanded liability for real estate agents. This area is defined and controlled by Ohio law, found in Ohio court rulings, Ohio legislation and the standards and regulation of Ohio's administrative agencies such as the Ohio Division of Real Estate. National trends have to be watched, too, as state courts, legislative bodies, and administrative agencies watch one another's developments in this expanding body of law as signposts for the future.

Actual Fraud/Constructive Fraud/ Negligence/Duty to Inspect

The earliest view was that, to be liable, real estate agents had to *intentionally make material misrepresentations about hidden or not visible conditions of realties* that caused injury to purchasers. Generally, proving agents' intents was difficult because obtaining evidence about peoples' states of mind is not easy. For example, defendant agents, while testifying, usually do not admit they did an act on purpose (although it did happen for that great fictional lawyer, Perry Mason).

Gradually this early view gave way to a lesser standard of proof. Real estate agents' representations no longer had to be proven as intentional. *Reckless statements or grossly negligent ones* were enough. This was easier to prove in court, with evidence other than what defendant agents were thinking about at the time they made the statements. For example, one could look at the listing information furnished to MLS or the listing contract and at statements about the realty made about it by the sellers. If agents failed to disclose relevant factors, that was sufficient intent. Further, if agents passed along representations that sellers made that they should have had some doubts about themselves, or at least have checked out, they might not be able to defend themselves by claiming they were merely passing on sellers' information.

These developments introduced constructive fraud and negligence into this area of the law. These are easier to prove because defendant agents' actual states of mind are not at issue. **Constructive fraud** occurs whenever the law finds any *breach of duty, trust, or confidence, or taking unfair advantage.* It is often used in cases in which real estate agents have a duty to speak about a material fact (perhaps a latent defect) but fail to do so. By contrast, **negligence** is the *failure to behave as a reasonable real estate professional would in the same or similar circumstances* if there is a duty for such professional to act. This also is called *simple negligence.* By contrast, *gross negligence* denotes a shocking or reckless lack of care by professionals. Increasingly, courts are finding that real estate professionals do have a duty to act. Negligence applies particularly to agents' failing to use reasonable care in obtaining or communicating the information that purchasers rely upon in making the decision to purchase real property.

Ohio has been in the process of gradually following most of these evolving doctrines. It recognizes both actual and constructive fraud, plus gross negligence flowing from brokers/salespeople/sellers to purchasers. But it remains somewhat difficult in Ohio to impute simple negligence between brokers/salespeople/sellers and purchasers, because purchasers are not the represented parties. If purchasers were the represented parties, purchasers may sue brokers and salespeople for any negligence on their parts.

Ohio also does not follow an even more liberal expansion of the law in California. That state imposes upon real estate agents a *statutory duty of inspection* of the realty, or diligence in checking out all aspects of the realty, at the time of taking the listing. If the real estate agents should have been able to discover problems, they are liable for failing to do so and subsequently failing to disclose their existence.

This expansion presents many new problems, however. Real estate agents are not engineers, electricians, surveyors, or any combination of other highly specialized occupations. Moreover, to engraft a duty of inspection followed by disclosure, all for the benefit of purchasers, is problematic when principals are typically the sellers. Fortunately, no state holds real estate agents *strictly liable* for the condition of real property. Under a strict liability approach, if purchasers would subsequently discover any flawed or defective condition, real estate agents would be liable for it, regardless of what they did or did not do or say.

Latent Versus Patent Defects and Matters of Record

The early rule was that conditions had to be **latent defects**—*hidden or concealed and wholly incapable of being discovered by the purchasers when they inspected the premises*. Also, if the defect, condition, or problem was a matter of public record (such as easements, utility connections or rights-of-way, and restrictions on use), purchasers were deemed to have constructive knowledge of them and thus were barred from recovery.

Patent defects are ones that are *discoverable by the purchaser*. These defects still might disqualify purchasers from bringing a lawsuit, but nowadays the defects must be fairly easy for them to discover while making their inspection. If real estate agents comment on patent defects, perhaps remarking that "it's not that bad," they might be liable nonetheless. Furthermore, it is becoming more difficult to make purchasers responsible for knowledge of matters of public record, probably because few really have the skills necessary to find those records.

Real estate agents sometimes still rely on the legal doctrine of purchasers' **assumption of the risk** of the condition of the realty, thus *making purchasers responsible for any conditions that later come to light*. This requires full disclosure to the purchasers of all that is known or suspected about the realty, however, and requires the purchasers' express, written declaration that they are nevertheless assuming all the risks of the realty's condition. This would not work if either the seller or the real estate agent had made any misrepresentations to the purchasers or concealed a defective condition from purchasers.

Ohio is one of a minority of states that still recognize the *caveat emptor* doctrine, although it has limited the application of the doctrine to certain types of situations. Nowadays, purchasers are not necessarily barred from obtaining relief when real estate agents make a false representation of material fact in response to the purchasers' queries, even though that representation is not made fraudulently. The purchasers' duty to inspect may end upon hearing these false representations.

More and more, *real estate agents encourage purchasers to hire experts to inspect the realty* so purchasers will receive professional reports about the realty's condition and then can decide whether to assume the risk of purchasing it. Utilizing a professional home inspector to investigate real property can go a long way toward insulating the agent from liability from defects that the inspector could, or should, have found.

In addition, sellers might engage in **concealment**—deliberately *hiding a condition that real estate agents would have no way of knowing about or no likelihood of discovering*. If sellers never disclose this to the agents, there cannot be a duty to disclose it to the purchasers. In court, the agents then would try to shift all the responsibility and liability onto sellers for the concealed condition. If sellers do not disclose a condition that real estate agents can discover more readily, however, or if sellers even say to purchasers that "only an expert can advise you on this," the agents may not be so successful in shifting all the liability to sellers. For real estate agents to innocently repeat any statements sellers make about the condition of the realty is extremely dangerous.

Keeping all of these evolving trends in mind, let's take a look at some important Ohio cases to better understand this area. The cases themselves are the best guides to how real estate agents can expect to fare in an Ohio court if they are sued for a defective property they list or sell.

TRAVERSE V. LONG
165 Ohio St. 249, 135 N.E.2d 256 (1956)

CASE STUDY FROM THE OHIO SUPREME COURT

Facts: The Traverses, the purchasers, sued the Longs, the sellers, and the Longs' real estate agent, Huxtable, when they subsequently discovered defects in the realty. The evidence showed a considerable area of filled-in land on the north side of the subject property, supported by cribbing in the form of loosely placed railroad ties that had rotted and deteriorated to some extent and were partially covered by a growth of vines, on which filled-in land, a driveway and parking area, leading into a garage, had been constructed. While the Longs owned and occupied the premises, holes of varying sizes developed at the north edge of the driveway and parking area, and these were filled with slag covered with a surfacing material. These repairs were visible.

Huxtable testified that "You (Mr. Traverse) asked me whether I thought that support and so forth was sound. And I suggested that we walk up around that area and you look at it yourself, which you did, which we did together. And I expressed the thought that I thought it was in sound condition because Mr. Long had told me it was."

The Traverses testified there were positive misrepresentations of known material facts to them by Huxtable, on which they relied. The Longs testified that they had made no representations to Huxtable. Huxtable insisted that the Longs had made representations. The Longs contended that any representations Huxtable made were based on his honest opinion and were not willfully false representations with respect to known material facts.

Court of Common Pleas (Trial Court): Judgment for defendants (sellers, the Longs, and their real estate agent, Huxtable).

Court of Appeals: Reversed and remanded (sent back to the lower court for redetermination).

Issue: Whether *caveat emptor* (let the buyer beware) applies to this property so as to bar Traverses from recovering damages for fraud and deceit by the Longs and/or Huxtable.

Held by the Ohio Supreme Court: Reversed the judgment of the Court of Appeals and affirmed the judgment of the trial court, in favor of the Longs and Huxtable. The principle of *caveat emptor* applies to sales of real estate relative to conditions open to observation. Where those conditions are discoverable and Traverses had the opportunity for investigation and determination without concealment or hindrance by the Longs, the Traverses have no just cause for complaint even though there were misstatements and misrepresentations by the Longs (or Huxtable) not so reprehensible in nature as to constitute fraud.

Note: The next two cases are two companion cases, decided together, by the Ohio Supreme Court.

CASE STUDY FROM THE OHIO SUPREME COURT

MILES V. PERPETUAL SAVINGS AND LOAN CO. AND MILES V. MCSWEGIN 58 Ohio St.2d 93, 388 N.E.2d 1364, 58 Ohio St.2d 97, 388 N.E.2d 1367 (1979)

Facts: In 1975, the purchasers, Mr. and Mrs. Cletus T. Miles, inspected the realty with the real estate broker, McSwegin. The property was owned by Maylone. McSwegin represented that the realty was a good, solid home, and that it appeared to be a good buy at the price offered. The Mileses entered into a binding real estate purchase contract, at a purchase price of $25,000, with Maylone through McSwegin's services. Afterwards the Mileses obtained their mortgage loan financing through Perpetual Savings and Loan Company.

Before closing the transaction, Perpetual had a termite inspection done on the realty, which revealed termite infestation. This infestation was disclosed to both McSwegin and Maylone but not to the Mileses. Although McSwegin and Maylone took steps to have the realty treated for termites, with Perpetual paying $460 for treatment and deducting that from Maylone's proceeds, they did not disclose the infestation to the Mileses either. All the Mileses learned, prior to closing, was that a termite inspection had been done for $15, which was shown on their closing statement.

After closing, the Mileses took possession and then discovered the termite infestation. After having an estimate done, they learned that the termite infestation would cost $5,962.50 to repair. They thereafter sued McSwegin, Maylone, and Perpetual.

Trial Court: Judgment was entered on a verdict for the Mileses for $2,500 compensatory damages and $25,000 in exemplary damages against Perpetual Savings and Loan. Judgment was entered against McSwegin for $2,500 compensatory damages in favor of the Mileses. The action against Maylone was dismissed.

Court of Appeals: Affirmed.

Issue: Whether McSwegin and/or Perpetual were under a duty to disclose to the Mileses the termite infestation.

Held by the Ohio Supreme Court: In the case against McSwegin, the court found and held against McSwegin and for the Mileses in the $2,500 compensatory damage award. It noted McSwegin's representation to the Mileses that the house was good and solid. When later McSwegin learned the representation had become subject to material qualification (the termite infestation), McSwegin was then under a duty to disclose the condition and not conceal it instead. *Caveat emptor* did not apply because the presence of the termite infestation was not detectable by the Mileses upon reasonable inspection. It was a latent defect that is an exception to *caveat emptor.*

The court also held against Perpetual and for the Mileses, but using a different line of reasoning. It determined there was a principal-agency relationship, with the Mileses being the principals and Perpetual their agent. Through this agency relationship Perpetual was held duty-bound to disclose material facts relating to the termite infestation. When it did not disclose, it became liable to the Mileses. The court said there was no actual malice by Perpetual and so the court affirmed to the Mileses, and against Perpetual, the $2,500 compensatory damage award but not the $25,000 exemplary damage award.

CASE STUDY FROM THE OHIO SUPREME COURT

LAYMAN V. BINNS
35 Ohio St. 3d 176, 519 N.E.2d 642 (1988)

Facts: The sellers, the Binnses, built a home and, when it was near completion, backfilling caused the cinder block foundation to give way. Thus, the real estate had a bowed basement foundation wall. The Binnses installed special steel I-beams to support the bowed walls. When the Binnses listed the house for sale with a broker, they disclosed this problem. The broker did not include this information when entering data on the realty into the MLS service but did inform sales associates of it. The purchasers, the Laymans, viewed the realty, including the basement, with a cooperating real estate agent. The Binnses did not accompany the Laymans into the basement, nor did they mention the bowed wall to the Laymans. The Laymans saw this condition and asked nothing about it, later saying they simply thought the I-beams were part of the structure. Witnesses who viewed the basement, however, said the defect was highly visible because the basement wall was bulging. Mr. Layman did inquire of Mr. Binns about utility bills and moisture at the east end of the basement. Mr. Binns explained that moisture usually entered the basement during excessive rain in the spring.

The real estate purchase contract that was used recited the standard clauses that "this is the entire agreement and no representations are made other than those in the contract" plus "purchasers rely upon their own inspection to determine the condition and character of the dwelling." The Laymans paid $75,000 for the property. Some time later, when the Laymans tried to sell the property, they discovered that the defective basement wall would cost from $32,000 to $50,000 to remedy.

Trial Court: Judgment for the purchasers, the Laymans. Determined that the structural defect in the wall was known to the Binnses and was not apparent upon inspection to inexperienced persons such as the Laymans. The Binnses had an affirmative duty to call the defect to the Laymans' attention and held that such failure amounted to fraud. Awarded $40,000 in damages to Laymans but declined to assess punitive damages against the Binnses because there was no active concealment of the defect by the Binnses.

Court of Appeals: Affirmed the trial court's judgment.

Issue: Whether recovery is barred by application of the doctrine of *caveat emptor* (let the buyer beware).

Held by the Ohio Supreme Court: Reversed in favor of the Binnses, the sellers. There was nondisclosure that does not rise to the level of fraud because (a) the defect was not latent and could have been detected by adequate inspection and (b) there was no misrepresentation or misstatement of fact made to the Laymans.

> The principle of caveat emptor applies to sales of real estate relative to conditions open to observation. Where those conditions are discoverable and the purchaser has the opportunity for investigation and determination without concealment or hindrance by the vendor, the purchaser has no just cause for complaint, even though there are misstatements and misrepresentations by the vendor not so reprehensible in nature as to constitute fraud . . . . Without the doctrine, nearly every sale would invite litigation instituted by the disappointed buyer. Accordingly, we are not disposed to abolish the doctrine of caveat emptor. A seller of realty is not obligated to reveal all that he or she knows. A duty falls upon the purchasers to make inquiry and examination.

The court concluded that the doctrine of *caveat emptor* precludes recovery in an action by purchasers for a structural defect in real estate when (a) the condition complained of is open to observation or discoverable upon reasonable inspection; (b) purchasers had the unimpeded opportunity to examine the premises; and (c) there is no fraud on the part of sellers.

Puffing

Puffing, also called "dealer's talk," is *not fraud.* Sellers or their agents are expected to *praise realty they are trying to sell.* The law expects purchasers to use ordinary *common sense* to separate puffing from material **misrepresentations** of fact. For example, "This is one of the most beautiful houses ever built," is puffing, whereas "This house has a dry, leak-proof basement" (when it really leaks) is misrepresentation of a material fact amounting to fraud. Generally, the more specific the information is about a given real property, the more likely it will be deemed misrepresentation instead of puffing.

Opinion

It is misrepresentations of fact that are fraudulent, not statements of true personal **opinion,** but it is often difficult to separate the two. Just calling a statement an opinion will not make it so. For example: An agent tells the purchaser, "In my opinion, this realty has the most solid foundation imaginable." It turns out that the house is perched on an eroding cliff and is in danger of sliding into the ravine. The statement is really meant to factually mislead even though preceded by the words, "In my opinion . . . ." The statement is, therefore, fraudulent.

By contrast, imagine the real estate agent saying, "I think the person who designed this home had better aesthetic sense than Frank Lloyd Wright." That statement is a true opinion. Everyone has an aesthetic opinion about what is "beautiful" but aesthetics are rarely, if ever, statements of fact.

"As Is" Purchases

Sometimes agents and sellers try to escape liability by putting **"as is" clauses** into real estate purchase contracts, *to shift the entire burden to purchasers for the condition of real property.* If realty is subsequently discovered to be defective, purchasers theoretically are unable to sue broker or sellers for the problem. The growing trend, however, is to ignore "as is" clauses and nevertheless place the duty of disclosure upon sellers and/or real estate agents.

If, however, sellers and real estate agents truly tell purchasers the exact nature of the realty with its exact defects, holding nothing back, the "as is" clause is totally binding upon purchasers. When homes are sold as "fix-ups" or "handyman's specials," for instance, specific language should be included in the purchase contract disclosing that the subject real property is in need of substantial repair and that this is considered in a reduction of the purchase price.

"As is" clauses are disregarded when sellers or real estate agents use them as ways out of telling purchasers what the law requires them to disclose. Therefore, agents and sellers are still liable for any material misrepresentations about the subject real property that induce purchasers' reliance and injury. They also are liable for concealment, failing to disclose a material, hidden condition of the real property.

Remedies and Relief

Defrauded purchasers ask the court, as soon as they discover the fraud, to *rescind the contract and return the parties to the positions they were in before the fraud occurred.* If the defrauded parties do not quickly ask for **rescission,** though, the law restricts their recovery to damages only. Compensatory damages are awarded in cases of both actual and constructive fraud. These damages restore the injured parties to the positions they would have been in but for the fraud. Punitive damages can be awarded only in cases of actual fraud, in which the philosophy of the law is to punish wrongdoers for intentional, malevolent conduct by making them pay additional money to victims. Either rescission or damages are awarded if the facts of the case warrant, or sometimes both are awarded.

Preventing Lawsuits by the Purchaser

Through the following acts, real estate agents can help shift responsibility and liability to the purchasers, either in whole or in part. This protects agents against future legal action. Agents may need to demonstrate this activity on their part for their defense someday, and if they do, these acts will go a long way toward showing they did everything in their power to disclose the realty's true condition.

1. They urge the purchasers to *thoroughly inspect* all of the real property, both the structures and the land. They let the purchasers run the water from several faucets, try the appliances, inspect the heating and cooling systems, feel the walls in the basement, and look for rust on the furnace. In sum, they let the purchasers do everything that would lead to a reasonable, thorough inspection of the realty. The purchasers should be encouraged to inspect every room, closet, and other structural area, as well as to walk all over the land.
2. They tell the purchasers to have their attorney check the public records at the county recorder's office for easements, restrictions, and assessments. The purchasers, or their attorney, also should check any zoning restrictions. This prevents later misunderstandings over what uses may be made of the realty and by whom.
3. They *should not venture an assessment or professional opinion* about the condition of something within the realty unless they have verified, professional proof. For example, they should not state that the well furnishes plenty of water unless they have in their possession the written statement of the professional who checked the well. The same is true for furnaces, septic systems, and the like. Even then, they should say they are merely repeating that expert's opinion and not stating their own.

   They should not stand behind sellers' representations unless they have independent, professional proof. If sellers want to represent a condition, everyone must clearly understand that sellers, not real estate agents, are making the representation. If agents do know something negative about the realty's condition, silence will not protect them. Once they know of a negative condition, they must reveal the condition to all interested parties. It is all right for real estate agents to acknowledge their lack of expertise and experience in matters that are not the marketing of real estate. They can admit their lack of skills in evaluating structural soundness, purity of water, adequacy of septic tanks, soil erosion, pollutants, and similar concerns. They can recommend that the proper expert be hired for this kind of information and advice.
4. They should urge purchasers to have a *professional inspection* of the realty, especially if sellers are leaving the state or immediate area. A great number of property defect lawsuits occur with these kinds of sellers, and it is difficult to sue persons who are out of state or at a distance. Realizing this, sellers often leave unsuspecting real estate agents and purchasers with an unsound realty. An even better course is to have the inspection option in the form real estate purchase agreement, as shown in Figure 9–2, clauses 11–14.

FIGURE 9–2
Purchase agreement, including inspection clauses.

11-CONDITION OF PROPERTY:

BUYER acknowledges that it has been recommended to him that he engage, at his expense, the services of a professional contractor or building inspector to inspect the property and all improvements to ascertain that the condition of the property is as called for in this Agreement. BUYER further acknowledges that no broker or any agent having anything to do with this transaction has made any verbal, or other statements or representations concerning the property on which BUYER has relied, except as specifically set forth in writing herein. BUYER has examined the property and agrees that the property is being purchased in its present "as is" condition, including any defects that may have been disclosed by SELLER either specifically hereon or by attached addendum. BUYER acknowledges that he has not relied on any representations, warranties or statements whatsoever concerning the property, including without limitation its use or condition, other than as written in this Agreement.

12-SPECIFIC DISCLOSURES: BUYER has relied on the following additional specific disclosures and/or representations in making this Agreement: (IF NONE, WRITE "NONE")

____

Said specific disclosures and/or representations were made by______________________.

13-SELLER'S REPRESENTATIONS: Seller states that he has no knowledge of any hidden or latent defects on the property, including without limitation, any of the following: water seepage; basement foundation or wall wetness (or dampness); bathroom or kitchen leakage; roof leakage; problems with electrical, plumbing, heating, cooling, sewer, septic, well or water systems; structural defects; or faulty major appliances, EXCEPT: (IF NONE, WRITE "NONE")

____

14-INSPECTION CONDITIONS: This Agreement shall be subject to all of the following checked Inspections, which Inspections shall be paid for by BUYER, carried out in good faith by all parties, and completed within the times specified. These Inspections shall be either approved or disapproved by BUYER in writing within said times and if disapproved, this Agreement shall become NULL AND VOID and subject to the TERMINATION PROCEDURE, as set forth in foregoing paragraph 4. (IF NONE, WRITE "NONE")_________

( ) A. GENERAL HOME INSPECTION The property shall be inspected by a general home inspector, construction person, professional property inspector, or other person of BUYER'S choice within_________days from final acceptance hereof.

( ) B. WELL OPERATION AND WELL WATER TEST The well system shall be inspected by a qualified inspector of BUYER'S choice (whose findings would be acceptable to County or other water authorities) for both (1) adequate flow rate and equipment operation and (2) potability, within_________days from final acceptance hereof.

( ) C. SEPTIC SYSTEM INSPECTION The septic or other on-site sanitation system shall be inspected by a qualified inspector of BUYER'S choice (whose findings would be acceptable to County or other sanitary authorities) within_________days from final acceptance hereof. SELLER shall pay the cost of sanitation system *cleaning*, if necessary for Inspection.

( ) D. TERMITE/WOOD-DESTROYING INSECT INSPECTION The property shall be inspected by a licensed pest control inspector of BUYER'S choice within_________days from final acceptance hereof.

NOTE -- Should FHA or VA Regulations prohibit payment by BUYER of the cost of any of the foregoing INSPECTIONS, SELLER shall pay the cost thereof.

WAIVER

Should BUYER fail to have any of the above Inspections completed within the times specified, OR IF BUYER FAILS TO SPECIFICALLY APPROVE OR DISAPPROVE ANY INSPECTIONS WITHIN THE TIMES SPECIFIED, then BUYER shall be deemed to have WAIVED SUCH INSPECTIONS and shall be considered as HAVING ACCEPTED THE PROPERTY ABSOLUTELY AND FINALLY IN ITS PRESENT "AS IS" CONDITION, and neither SELLER nor any real estate broker or agent having anything to do with this transaction shall have any further liability or obligation to BUYER as to such Inspections or Agreement Conditions.

Should the results of any of such Inspections not be satisfactory to BUYER then, within the times specified, BUYER shall notify either SELLER or SELLER'S LISTING BROKERAGE in writing of his specific dissatisfaction, at which point the TERMINATION PROCEDURE set forth in foregoing paragraph 4. shall apply.

If the purchasers consistently refuse to take any of the above, active steps after persistent (and perhaps written) encouragement to do so, the law will be reluctant later to aid them because they seemingly assumed the risk of purchasing a defective, unsound realty. Also, the real estate agents laid an excellent foundation in defense of their own professional competence. Some real estate companies are preventively handling these cases by inserting special, protective language in the listing contract, the real estate purchase contract (as shown in Figure 9–2), or, preferably, both contracts.

A typical clause that might be found in the listing contract is:

> Though we, sellers, are listing our realty for sale in an "as is" condition, we acknowledge herein that we may be held responsible legally by purchasers for our failure to reveal or correct any latent or hidden defect or unsound condition of the realty or its value. We also acknowledge that we are under a duty to inform [The Real Estate Company] of such a defect or condition which minimally includes problems with the well, septic system, basement, plumbing, gas lines, roof, major appliances, heating and cooling systems, sewers, and the like. With these thoughts in mind, we state that the following are problems within our realty which need repair and/or are problems which exist but cannot be repaired: [lines are provided on the form for written inserts by the sellers].

> We further acknowledge that we have a continuing duty after we have signed this agreement to inform both [The Real Estate Company] and any purchasers about any defects or conditions which subsequently develop.
>
> We warrant to [The Real Estate Company] that there are no defects or unsound conditions within our realty other than we have written above, and we agree to indemnify [The Real Estate Company] for any untrue statement(s) made herein.

There are some limitations upon how much these contracts can rescue real estate agents from liability, however. *Regardless of any clause's strength, if misrepresentations or concealment* of material fact are made, it will be *difficult, probably impossible, to remove the agents from liability.*

The real estate agent's newest form of protection is Section 5302.30 of the Ohio Revised Code, which requires that sellers of residential property disclose to purchasers various aspects of their real property's physical condition by using the Residential Property Disclosure Form, Figure 9–3. One purpose of this law is to place the risk of defect disclosure law squarely on the shoulders of purchasers and sellers. If the disclosure form is not furnished until after a purchase contract is formed, the purchasers have the right to rescind the contract. Real estate agents are not to assist the seller in completing the disclosure form. If real estate agents do assist the sellers, they too can be made liable for the inaccuracy of the information disclosed. Real estate agents do have the responsibility of drawing their clients' attention to the required use of this form in their transactions. This law covers property that is improved by a building or other structure that has one-to-four dwelling units. The form is not required for the sale of commercial or industrial properties or unimproved land.

The following residential transactions are exempt from this property disclosure form requirement:

1. court-ordered sales
2. foreclosure actions
3. sale of newly constructed property not previously inhabited
4. transfers between co-owners or transfers made to a family member
5. transfers to or from the state or a governmental entity
6. sales to a tenant who has resided in the property for at least one year prior to purchase
7. transfers by a fiduciary in administration of an estate, guardianship, or trust
8. inherited property where the seller has not occupied the property as a personal residence within one year immediately prior to the sale

Residential Lead-Based Paint Hazard Reduction Act

The U. S. Environmental Protection Agency and the Department of Housing and Urban Development have been charged with the duty to issue a final disclosure rule regarding lead paint hazards, consistent with the Residential Lead-Based Paint Hazard Reduction Act, which was approved by Congress in 1992. (Review this rule carefully with your broker and/or with your broker's legal counsel, so that you will fully comply with it in your practice of real estate.)

Here is a general summary of the Act: In 1992, Congress enacted into law the Residential Lead-Based Paint Hazard Reduction Act (Title X of Public Law

FIGURE 9–3
Mandatory Residential Property Disclosure Form in Ohio.

EFFECTIVE JULY 1993

STATE OF OHIO
DEPARTMENT OF COMMERCE

RESIDENTIAL PROPERTY DISCLOSURE FORM

Pursuant to Ohio Revised Code Section 5302.30
TO BE COMPLETED BY OWNER *(Please Print)*

Property Address: ______________________________

Owners Name(s): ______________________________

Date: ______________________, 19______

Owner ☐ is ☐ is not occupying the property. If owner is occupying the property, since what date ______________

Purpose of Disclosure Form: This is a statement of the condition of the property and of information concerning the property actually known by the owner as required by Ohio Revised Code Section 5302.30. Unless otherwise advised in writing by the owner, the owner, other than having lived at or owning the property, possesses no greater knowledge than that which could be obtained by a careful inspection of the property by a potential purchaser. Unless otherwise advised, owner has not conducted any inspection of generally inaccessible areas of the property. THIS STATEMENT IS NOT A WARRANTY OF ANY KIND BY THE OWNER OR BY ANY AGENT OR SUBAGENT REPRESENTING THE OWNER OF THE PROPERTY. THIS STATEMENT IS NOT A SUBSTITUTE FOR ANY INSPECTIONS. POTENTIAL PURCHASERS ARE ENCOURAGED TO OBTAIN THEIR OWN PROFESSIONAL INSPECTION.

Owner's Statement: The representations contained on this form are made by the owner and are not the representations of the owner's agent or subagent. This form and the representations contained in it are provided by the owner exclusively to potential purchasers in a transfer made by the owner, and are not made to purchasers in any subsequent transfers. The information contained in this disclosure form does not limit the obligation of the owner to disclose an item of information that is required by any other statute or law to be disclosed in the transfer of residential real estate.

Instructions to Owner: (1) Answer ALL questions. (2) Identify any material matters in the property that are actually known. (3) Attach additional pages with your signature if additional space is needed. (4) Complete this form yourself. (5) If some items do not apply to your property, write NA (not applicable). If the item to be disclosed is not within your actual knowledge, indicate Unknown.

THE FOLLOWING STATEMENTS OF THE OWNER ARE BASED ON OWNER'S ACTUAL KNOWLEDGE

A) WATER SUPPLY: The source of water supply to the property is (check appropriate boxes):

☐ Public Water Service ☐ Private Water Service ☐ Well ☐ Holding Tank
☐ Cistern ☐ Spring ☐ Pond ☐ Unknown
☐ Other

If owner knows of any current leaks, backups or other material problems with the water supply system or quality of the water, please describe: ______________________________

B) SEWER SYSTEM: The nature of the sanitary sewer system servicing the property is (check appropriate boxes):

☐ Public Sewer ☐ Private Sewer ☐ Septic Tank ☐ Leach Field
☐ Aeration Tank ☐ Filtration Bed ☐ Unknown
☐ Other ______________________________

If not a public or private sewer, date of last inspection ______________
If owner knows of any current leaks, backups or other material problems with the sewer system servicing the property, please describe:

C) ROOF: Do you know of any current leaks or other material problems with the roof or rain gutters? ☐ Yes ☐ No

If "YES," please describe: ______________________________

If owner knows of any leaks or other material problems with the roof or rain gutters since owning the property (but not longer than the past 5 years), please describe and indicate any repairs completed: ______________________________

D) BASEMENT/CRAWL SPACE: Do you know of any current water leakage, water accumulation, excess dampness or other defects with the basement/crawl space? ☐ Yes ☐ No

If "YES," please describe: ______________________________

If owner knows of any repairs, alterations or modifications to the property or other attempts to control any water or dampness problems in the basement or crawl space since owning the property (but not longer than the past 5 years), please describe: ______________________________

E) STRUCTURAL COMPONENTS (FOUNDATION, FLOORS, INTERIOR AND EXTERIOR WALLS): Do you know of any movement, shifting, deterioration, material cracks (other than visible minor cracks or blemishes) or other material problems with the foundation, floors, or interior/exterior walls? ☐ Yes ☐ No

If "YES," please describe: ______________________________

If you know of any repairs, alterations or modifications to control the cause or effect of any problem identified above, since owning the property (but not longer than the past 5 years), please describe: ______________________________

(Page 1 of 2)

(continued)

FIGURE 9–3
Continued.

If "YES," please describe: ______________________________

For purposes of this section, mechanical systems include electrical, plumbing (pipes), central heating and air conditioning, sump pump, fireplace/chimney, lawn sprinkler, water softener, security system, central vacuum, or other mechanical systems that exist on the property.

G) **WOOD BORING INSECTS/TERMITES:** Do you know of the presence of any wood boring insects/termites in or on the property or any existing damage to the property caused by wood boring insects/termites? ☐ Yes ☐ No

If "YES," please describe: ______________________________

If owner knows of any inspection or treatment for wood boring insects/termites, since owning the property (but not longer than the past 5 years), please describe: ______________________________

H. **PRESENCE OF HAZARDOUS MATERIALS:** Do you have actual knowledge of the presence of any of the below identified hazardous materials on the property?

		Yes	No	Unknown
1)	Lead-Based Paint	☐	☐	☐
2)	Asbestos	☐	☐	☐
3)	Urea-Formaldehyde Foam Insulation	☐	☐	☐
4)	Radon Gas	☐	☐	☐
	4a) IF YES, indicate level of Gas if known ______			
5)	Other toxic substances ______	☐	☐	☐

If the answer to any of the above questions is "YES," please describe: ______________________________

I. **DRAINAGE:** Do you know of any current flooding, drainage, settling or grading problems affecting the property? ☐ Yes ☐ No

If "YES," please describe: ______________________________

If owner knows of any repairs, modifications or alterations to the property or other attempts to control any flooding, drainage, settling or grading problems since owning the property (but not longer than the past 5 years), please describe: ______________________________

J) **CODE VIOLATIONS:** Have you received notice of any building or housing code violations currently affecting the use of the property?
☐ Yes ☐ No

If "YES," please describe: ______________________________

K) **UNDERGROUND STORAGE TANKS/WELLS:** Do you know of any underground storage tanks, oil or natural gas wells (plugged or unplugged), or abandoned water wells on the property? ☐ Yes ☐ No

If "YES," please describe: ______________________________

L) **OTHER KNOWN MATERIAL DEFECTS:** The following are other known material defects currently in or on the property: ______________________________

For purposes of this section, material defects would include any non-observable physical condition existing on the property that could be dangerous to anyone occupying the property or any non-observable physical condition that would inhibit a person's use of the property.

Owner represents that the statements contained in this form are made in good faith based on his/her actual knowledge as of the date signed by the Owner.

OWNER: ______________________ **DATE:** ______________

OWNER: ______________________ **DATE:** ______________

RECEIPT AND ACKNOWLEDGEMENT OF POTENTIAL PURCHASERS

Potential purchasers are advised that the owner has no obligation to update this form but may do so according to Revised Code Section 5302.30(G). Pursuant to Ohio Revised Code Section 5302.30(K), if this form is not provided to you prior to the time you enter into a purchase contract for the property, you may rescind the purchase contract by delivering a signed and dated document of rescission to Owner or Owner's agent, provided the document of rescission is delivered prior to all three of the following dates: 1) the date of closing; 2) 30 days after the Owner accepted your offer; and 3) within 3 business days following your receipt or your agent's receipt of this form or an amendment of this form.

I/WE ACKNOWLEDGE RECEIPT OF A COPY OF THIS DISCLOSURE FORM AND UNDERSTAND THAT THE STATEMENTS ARE MADE BASED ON THE OWNER'S ACTUAL KNOWLEDGE AS OF THE DATE SIGNED BY THE OWNER.

My/Our Signature below does not constitute approval of any disclosed condition as represented herein by the owner.

PURCHASER: ______________________ **DATE:** ______________

PURCHASER: ______________________ **DATE:** ______________

(Page 2 of 2)

102-550). Section 1018 of Title X sets forth the procedures to be followed in disclosing the presence of lead-based paint for sales of *pre-1978 properties.*

In the event of a *sale* of a pre-1978 property, the seller, or the seller's agent must:

1. distribute a federal lead hazard pamphlet;
2. disclose any information (known to the seller or agent) concerning lead paint and/or lead paint hazards on the property; and
3. provide a 10-day, or mutually agreeable, period of time for a lead paint assessment or inspection, before a purchaser becomes obligated to purchase under the contract.

In the event of a *lease* of a pre-1978 property, the lessor, or their agent must:

1. distribute a federal lead hazard pamphlet; and
2. disclose any known lead paint and/or lead paint hazards.

Sales contracts must contain a standard lead warning statement, in large type and on a separate sheet of paper. The warning statement includes an acknowledgement that purchasers must sign to indicate that they have been given the lead pamphlet, have read and understood the warning statement, and have been given an opportunity to have the property tested for lead hazards.

Knowing violations of the Act can subject the seller, lessor, and/or agent to federal criminal and civil penalties and joint and several liability and treble damages in civil lawsuits.

Antitrust Laws

Under the **antitrust laws,** a trade group or members of that trade (for our purposes the "trade" is the real estate industry), *cannot join together for the purposes of group activities that will restrain that trade.* **Price-fixing** of commission rates *already has been held to be in restraint of trade and, thus, illegal.* Brokers, therefore, cannot fix commission rates by having two or more brokers set a commission rate they will not go beneath. Nevertheless, an individual broker can charge any commission rate or fee he or she chooses. For example, "I (my company) charge(s) a six percent commission for the sale of this type of realty" is legal, but "I have to take seven percent because we all have to" is an illegal price-fixing statement, as is, "Broker X and I are the biggest and the best in this area. We've agreed not to undercut one another. So if you want the best, seven percent is what you'll have to pay as a commission rate."

Some analogous statements are also a violation, if they lead to an inference that the broker(s) is engaged in an illegal conspiracy to restrain free trade in the real estate marketplace. Two examples are: "Broker X doesn't even belong to the Board of REALTORS®. How can he call himself a professional?!" and "Broker Y isn't even in the same professional class with us. Everyone knows not to work her listings. She has only part-timers to service those listings without us."

The specific antitrust laws are the Sherman Act, the Clayton Act (15 United States Code Sections 1 to 7, and 12 to 27, respectively) and Title 13 of the Ohio Revised Code. These laws govern trades that operate on various lines of interstate commerce and are combined in a restraint of trade.

Sections 1 and 2 of the Sherman Act are the ones under which the overwhelming majority of lawsuits against real estate brokers are brought in federal court. When using these sections, the plaintiff must show an *effect on interstate commerce* to obtain jurisdiction in federal court and show that the Act has been violated.

The federal government or private persons or entities can be plaintiffs in an antitrust suit. The specific governmental agencies involved are the Justice Department and the Federal Trade Commission, which do terminate some litigation if the defendants are willing to enter into a *consent decree* whereby the real estate defendants consent, by their promise, to stop the offensive activity in the future. Price-fixing was the subject of an early consent decree between the Justice Department and the real estate industry.

Individuals who have been damaged by concerted antitrust activities also can sue, demanding compensation for their damages and penalties (treble, or triple, damages can be assessed) plus termination of the activities that are violations. Antitrust litigation is so complex, time-consuming, and expensive, though, that many individuals are discouraged from bringing suit. Occasionally a state itself will initiate an antitrust suit, through that state's attorney general, on behalf of its citizens who might be injured as a result of violations of its antitrust laws.

Duties to Business Guests on Real Property

Duties are owed to people who are on the real property of another. The highest duty of care is owed to *business guests,* persons on the realty for business purposes. When real estate agents take potential purchasers onto sellers' realties, those purchasers are business guests, and the duty of care includes the sellers' having made a reasonable *inspection of the premises to discover any hazardous conditions.* If, upon making such reasonable inspection of the premises, a hazard is discovered, there is a duty to warn the purchasers about it. If the sellers tell the real estate agents about the hazard and the agents fail to tell the prospective purchasers, who are then injured on the realty, the agents usually will be liable for the injury. Agents should make it their professional habit to question the sellers about hazards located on their listed real properties. Examples of hazards are vicious dogs, broken stairs or railings, falling ceilings, open pits, and the like.

If the sellers or real estate salesperson never made an inspection of the premises and purchasers are injured, the test will be: If a reasonable search of the premises had been made, would the hazard have been discovered? If the answer is yes, the sellers and/or sellers' agent are liable for the damage done to the purchasers.

Real estate agents who are on the realty of sellers, because they are there for business purposes, are also considered business guests. Thus, sellers are liable for any discoverable hazard they fail to warn agents about that injures them.

SECTION II

INTERNAL AFFAIRS OF A BROKERAGE

THE SALESPERSON, THE BROKER'S AGENT

When salespeople list and sell real estate, they act for and represent brokers. Brokers are principals, and salespeople (also known as associates) are the brokers' agents. Because salespeople use real estate skills through brokers, *brokers are responsible for their salespeople.* Salespeople must find out the scope of their own authority from their brokers, as brokers delegate authority to act in the marketplace to their salespeople. The relationship is brought about by their mutual consent, oral or written, and by the brokers' holding salespeople's real estate licenses. *Salespeople owe a fiduciary obligation to their brokers,* exactly the same as the one owed by brokers and salespeople to sellers under a listing contract. Ohio license law, discussed in Chapter 10, defines brokers' and salespeople's functions in detail.

If salespeople *exceed the apparent scope of their authority,* brokers have a cause of action against and could sue them. For example, a salesperson should not reduce or "cut" a commission without first obtaining the broker's consent. Most brokers tell a salesperson that he or she does not have the discretion to reduce a commission from the usual rate the broker charges. "Cutting a commission" is a legal act, but if salespeople have no authority to do so, they nonetheless violate the agency relationship. *Brokers may delegate some of their power to managers.* In Ohio, managers do not have to be licensed brokers, only licensed salespeople. Brokers may give managers greater discretion than individual salespeople have. Thus, if salespeople do not have the authority to take a listing for a 60-day period, for example, they may have to check with the manager to see if the manager has the authority to approve the listing for a 60-day period. Large real estate companies often delegate some degree of their discretion to managers within the branch real estate offices.

Real estate brokerages often outline agency responsibilities between brokers and salespeople in *policy and procedure books* and place them in the branch offices. The salespeople are advised to read this information to find out what they can and cannot do. If salespeople have been told that there is a manual containing salespeople's responsibilities, the salespeople have knowledge of the material and are negligent if they fail to read it. Therefore, salespeople must read these materials and comply with them.

Brokers cannot authorize salespeople to break the law. If a broker asks salespeople to break the law and the salespeople do so, they cannot maintain as a defense that they are doing so under the broker's guidance and authorization. They and the broker *both are liable* for, or deemed guilty of, the illegal conduct.

The agency relationship between broker and salespeople also has *express and implied powers.* Everything stated in the contract between broker and salespeople is an express delegation and thus an express power. For example, securing listings is expressly a power of the salespeople. By implication, the salespeople can do all things necessary to reach the express goal. To secure listings, for example, they can call sellers who are using "For Sale by Owner" signs and write advertisements on listed realties. Many brokers have an express written contract between them and their salespeople. An example of this type of contract is reproduced as Figure 9–4.

Sometimes brokers do not stop a salesperson from doing activities they do not approve of. The salesperson thus *appears to be acting under the agency authority that normally exists* between broker and salespeople. If innocent third parties rely on this activity and assume that salespeople have the authority indicated, the broker later can be *estopped from asserting that the salespeople were acting outside the scope of such authority.*

FOR EXAMPLE

If a broker appears to approve of black purchasers being shown housing only in integrated neighborhoods, that broker may be estopped from later defending himself in a fair housing lawsuit by asserting that the salesperson stepped outside the scope of her granted agency authority. If the salesperson tells the broker, in the presence of the prospective purchasers, that they are seeing houses only in integrated city Z, and if the broker seems to acquiesce to this plan, the prospective purchasers have the right to assume that the salesperson is acting under the authority of that broker. The broker is also liable to the prospective purchasers, not merely the salesperson.

Covenants Not to Compete

Covenants not to compete, common in most sales-related industries, are only recently becoming more commonplace in the real estate field. Brokers expend time, talent, and money to professionally train and develop salespeople who associate with them. A problem some brokers encounter is that after turning salespeople into successful, high-income-producing professionals, the salespeople terminate this association and either work for a competitor or open their own brokerage in the same community. **Covenants not to compete** are contracts, a *broker's way of preventing loss of trained associates.* Some brokers now require a salesperson to enter into this contract before they expend money or the benefits of their experience on the salesperson's professional training.

As in any contract, the factors of offer, acceptance, and consideration must be present. Figure 9–4 contains a covenant not to compete in clause 8. *Brokers offer their professional training in exchange for salespeople's promises that if they terminate association with brokers within a designated time, the salesperson cannot practice real estate within a certain distance or radius of the broker's office for a set period of time.* The courts do not inquire into adequacy of the consideration—how much the training is worth—in determining whether the covenant is or is not enforceable. As long as salespeople receive some benefit, they can be bound by the covenant. The consideration in the contract must be something salespeople receive as a benefit at the time of entering into the contract. This is termed *present consideration.* If a salesperson enters into the contract after receiving the benefit, it is deemed past consideration, which is not sufficient.

Courts generally determine whether the covenant not to compete is "reasonable" under all the circumstances given in a particular case. As a matter of law, under the statute of frauds, these contracts usually do not have to be in writing. As a matter of practice and proof, however, they should be written agreements executed by both brokers and salespeople.

States view these covenants in different ways. Some regularly uphold covenants not to compete; others refuse to uphold them. Ohio tends to uphold covenants not to compete, but the courts typically require an extremely clear contract that brokers have followed in every particular. This is because the contract has a severe economic effect on salespeople. In addition, if brokers require too much time or distance in the contract (say a whole region or state for years, as opposed to a community or few

FIGURE 9–4 Sample broker-salesperson contract.

BROKER-SALESPERSON CONTRACT

THIS AGREEMENT between the undersigned broker and the undersigned salesperson is to be followed by both parties for their mutual benefit under the following terms and conditions:

1. The broker and the salesperson agree to follow the Code of Ethics, Standards of Practice, Advertising Codes, Constitution, and By-laws of the local, state, and national Association of Real Estate Boards and the real estate law of the state.
2. The broker agrees to make available to the salesperson all current open and exclusive listings, and a fair share of the Broker's prospects. The broker will assist the salesperson in his work by advice and instruction including assistance in closing transactions.
3. The broker also agrees to maintain an office properly equipped and provide such advertising as is deemed advisable.
4. After the termination of the contract, the salesperson agrees not to use for any purpose whatsover any prospects, listings, or information gained from the files or the business of this broker. He will return within 3 days all listings and other property belonging to the broker.
5. The salesperson, if recently transferred from another broker, agrees not to solicit listings or prospects of his former broker.
6. The salesperson understands and agrees that all new listings and all prospects secured while with this broker shall remain the broker's property in the event of termination of this contract.
7. The salesperson agrees to use his best efforts to sell, lease, or rent any and all real estate listed with the broker and to solicit additional listings and customers for the broker. The salesperson further agrees to conduct his business and regulate his professional habits so as to maintain rather than diminish the good will and reputation of the broker.

Optional clause used by some brokers.

8. In consideration of the office facilities, equipment, listings, prospects, advice, instuction, past and present training program, and broker's confidential business information and past and present methods provided by broker to the salesperson, the salesperson agrees not to compete with the broker within a radius of ten miles within eighteen months after termination of this contract.
9. Broker and salesperson agree to express no preference based upon race, sex, creed, or national origin in the listing, sale, rental, or showing of property, and mutually understand that such expression of preference is unlawful and may cause the revocation of license of both broker and salesperson.
10. The salesperson agrees to comply with all terms of the Affirmative Marketing Agreement if the broker is a party to it.
11. The broker's full commission as established by the broker's individual commission schedule shall be charged for any service performed. The broker reserves sole discretion to accept a lower rate of commission. All commissions or fees are to be paid to the broker and distributed to the salesperson on the basis of the broker's current commission schedule unless the broker shall have specifically authorized a lower commission rate. If the salesperson takes a lesser commission rate the broker can deduct money from the salesperson's portion of the commission to bring the broker' portion up to the full amount.
12. In no event shall the broker be liable to the salesperson for any commission unless (a) the commission shall have been collected from the party for whom the service was performed and (b) no lawsuit is pending as a result of that transaction.
13. Lawsuits for commissions shall be maintained only in the name of the broker. The salesperson is a subagent only with respect to the clients and customers for whom service is performed. Otherwise he is an independent contractor and not an employee, joint adventurer, or partner of the broker.
14. The broker shall not be liable to the salesperson for any expenses incurred by the salesperson or for any of his acts other than those allowed by the broker in writing. The salesperson has no authority to bind the broker to any promise or representation unless specifically authorized by the broker in a particular transaction.

(continued)

FIGURE 9–4 Continued.

15. Extraordinary expenses which must by necessity be deducted from the commission or are incurred in the collection of, or the attempt to collect, the commission shall be paid by both parties in the same proportion as provided for herein in the division of the commission.
16. No appraisal or placement of a mortgage for a fee shall be made by the salesperson without the consent of the broker.
17. The salesperson shall not accept any fees from either buyer or seller for services rendered on unsuccessful sales without the consent of the broker. In the event the broker consents to such fees, they shall be divided in the manner prescribed in Clause 11 of this agreement.
18. All cash and checks for earnest money payments are to be made payable to the broker. No earnest money payment shall be paid the seller without the written consent of the broker and the purchaser.
19. This contract and the association created hereby may be terminated by either party hereto at any time, by written notice given to the other. The right of the parties to any commission accrued, or earned prior to such notice shall not be lost by the termination of this contract. Any monies owed to the broker shall be deducted from monies due the salesperson.
20. Associate agrees to read and become thoroughly familiar with the broker's current office procedure manual, a written copy of which is on file at the brokers office. This manual and all its updates to termination time shall be a part of this agreement as if fully written herein at length.
21. The salesperson agrees to insure his automobile with public liability insurance with limits of at least $50,000.00 to $200,000.00 and property damage insurance of at least $15,000.00 with a clause inserted naming the broker as coinsured against any and all liability from operation of said vehicle.
22. The salesperson shall not purchase for himself or his immediate family any real estate in the area in which he operates unless he makes known his intention to the broker. The salesperson must list exclusively with the broker his personal residence and all real property in Broker's trading area, but a special commission rate shall apply.
23. Salesperson agrees to belong to the realtor board in the area in which he works, and to remain a member in good standing by always being paid up in his or her dues.
24. Regarding Trade-Ins: salesperson agrees that if he is involved in company trade-ins, that commissions will not be paid until all properties involved have been cleared and all losses, if any, deducted from commissions. The remaining commissions will be divided in the usual manner, and losses beyond the amount of commissions will be borne solely by the company when the salesperson is in a non-participating capacity.

IN WITNESS WHEREOF, the parties hereto have set their hands this__________day of ____________________, 19______, each party hereby acknowledges receipt of a fully executed copy of this agreement.

Signed in the presence of:

____________________ ____________________
BROKER

____________________ ____________________
SALESPERSON

communities for six months to a year and a half), the courts typically strike down the contract as too harsh, because it wholly denies people the ability to earn a living from their profession.

REALTOR® Status

REALTORS® are *licensed brokers or salespeople who are members of specifically designated, private boards of real estate.* They belong to the National Association of REALTORS®, the Ohio Association of REALTORS®, and the local association. Generally, if brokers are REALTORS®, their salespeople are also REALTORS®. The activities of REALTOR® associations are quite diversified, including establishing codes of ethics and professional standards of practice, assembling arbitration panels, lobbying for federal and state legislation beneficial to members, implementing the Affirmative Marketing Agreement (regarding fair housing), and establishing computerized, countywide multiple listing services, to name a few.

Membership in REALTOR® associations is what makes brokers and salespeople REALTORS®; a REALTOR® designation is *not gained just by acquiring a real estate license from the state.* National, state, and local REALTOR® associations are diligent about keeping the term "REALTOR®" as a registered trademark of their members only. REALTOR® organizations bind the members to follow codes of ethics for the good of the public and fellow members. Based on these codes, members can submit grievances to their local Board for arbitration.

Real estate brokers do not have to become REALTORS® to be licensed and operating brokers within the state of Ohio (or any other state). As long as brokers are licensed under Ohio law, they do not have to join any professional organizations to practice real estate. For real estate brokers to completely bypass professional affiliation is somewhat unusual, however.

Business Organizations for Brokerages

Most real estate brokers operate through corporations. A **corporation** is an *artificial person; a fictitious, invisible, intangible entity allowed to be created by law.* The reason real estate brokers incorporate is chiefly to *escape personal liability.* The corporation acts as a shield for the real person, the owner(s) of the corporation. Therefore, only the assets of the corporation can be attached to satisfy a judgment. The owner(s) of the (typical real estate brokerage) corporation usually keep many, or all, of their assets in their names personally. These personal assets cannot be attached to satisfy a judgment against the corporation. A corporation of this nature thus could have few assets. For tax or other purposes, however, some real estate brokerage corporations do elect to keep assets (either or both real and personal property) in the corporate name. Those assets are therefore not shielded.

There is also a trend toward naming both real estate brokers and their salespeople *individually* to lawsuits, in addition to naming the corporation. In these cases, it has to be proven at trial that the brokers/salespeople *stopped acting in their corporate capacity* and acted individually instead. This is called "piercing the corporate shield." If the shield can be pierced, personal liability, as well as corporate liability, is allowed. Courts are reluctant to pierce the corporate shield, however. *Intentional or malicious wrongdoing* has to be demonstrated to make salespeople or brokers personally liable and thus pierce the corporate shield. The most likely area in which this is possible is in cases of **actual fraud.** Also, if brokers/salespeople do a personal act, such as physically assaulting purchasers or sellers, they step out of their corporate function and are personally liable.

If the corporation goes *bankrupt,* the persons who own the corporation do not have to declare bankruptcy as well. They and their personal assets remain intact and preserved, although they lose most or all of the corporate assets in the bankruptcy action. Often, former corporate owners merely form a new corporation to carry on the same, or another, business activity.

Partnerships are not often used as real estate business organizations. The primary reason is that they *do not have the limited personal liability* that the corporation does. The partners can be personally liable. Forming a partnership simply involves two or more people carrying on a profit-oriented business as coowners. Partnerships are not formally organized like corporations, and the tax aspects are very different.

Sole proprietorships are *not formal business organizations* at all. A single person puts up the capital for the business, conducts it, and absorbs all profits and liabilities. The sole proprietor has *no limited liability protection* either; he or she is *personally liable* for any judgments entered against the business. When this single owner uses a business name other than his or her own and is not incorporated, this business is also called *doing business as (dba).*

Errors and Omissions Insurance

Insurance companies provide **errors and omissions** insurance policies, which normally cover both real estate brokers and their salespeople who are careless in their practice of real estate; they *unintentionally neglect or omit to do something they should have done in their practice of real estate.* The policies are similar in coverage no matter who is the carrier.

Most of these policies *do not cover intentional conduct.* Policies typically cover real estate brokers, however, if their salespeople engage in willful misconduct without the brokers' knowledge and consent. For example, the policy usually covers brokers when salespeople violate fair housing laws, if the brokers have no knowledge of their salespeople engaging in a discriminatory practice. The brokers must have made it clear, throughout the brokerage, however, that none of their agents is to violate these laws.

The insurance policy typically covers constructive fraud and negligence by the brokers and their salespeople, because these actions are considered errors and omissions. Actual fraud, by contrast, is not considered an error or omission, as it involves an intentional act. The brokers might be covered for actual fraud, however, if they have no knowledge of actual fraud perpetrated by a salesperson and they had instructed their salespeople that actual fraud is a prohibited practice within the brokerage.

Most policies also include, either partially or totally, *costs for the legal defense* of these cases. *Deductibles* in the policies are much like the ones in automobile insurance. The first $1,000 or $5,000, for example, of loss due to a claim is to be borne by the insured licensee and the insurance company is to pay for the amount of loss in excess of that figure.

Summary of Content

1. Agency is the representation of a client, the principal, by another, the agent.
2. The salesperson is the agent of the broker (the broker is the principal of the salesperson) and is a subagent to any principals of the broker.
3. If purchasers have reason to believe they are being represented along with sellers in the transaction and it turns out they are not, that is grounds to rescind the entire real estate transaction.
4. Disclosed dual agency occurs when a real estate agent represents both purchasers and sellers with both of their knowledge and consent. Undisclosed dual agency occurs when the agent does not tell purchasers and sellers and does not obtain their consents.
5. Single agency occurs when the real estate agent represents only one party to a transaction, either purchaser or seller.
6. Buyer's broker or agent status occurs when purchasers, not sellers, are the represented parties and sometimes they, or someone on their behalf, pays a finder's fee to their real estate agent.
7. The fiduciary obligation is an agency duty the broker and the salesperson owe to their principal, requiring full disclosure, confidentiality, no self-dealing, loyalty, trust, a high degree of care, obedience, and accounting.
8. An exclusive right-to-sell listing contract gives a single broker the authority to procure purchasers for the realty. No matter who produces the ready, willing, and able purchasers, that broker is entitled to receive the commission.
9. An exclusive agency differs from the others in one respect: If sellers come up with purchasers on their own, the broker is not owed a commission.
10. Procuring cause is the legal test the broker and salesperson must meet to recover a commission from owners/sellers. They must be able to show a contract of employment (any listing contract) in addition to their being the procuring cause of the realty's sale.
11. The term "procuring cause" means producing purchasers who are ready, willing, and able to purchase real estate on sellers' terms.
12. Brokers and salespeople must practice real estate and not law. In Ohio, brokers and salespeople may fill in the blanks in the preprinted form real estate listing contract and purchase contract.
13. In Ohio, imposing liability upon sellers, brokers, and salespeople is easier under defect disclosure liability law when the condition is latent (hidden) and incapable of being discovered by purchasers when they inspect the realty. By contrast, it is more difficult to impose liability when the condition is patent (capable of being discovered by ordinary purchasers making a reasonable inspection of the premises).
14. The following elements are necessary to maintain an action for damages in actual fraud for concealing a latent defect: actual concealment of material facts; knowledge of the facts concealed; intent to mislead purchasers into relying on such conduct (or reckless disregard or gross negligence); purchasers' reliance upon the false information; and a resulting injury to purchasers because of this reliance. Constructive fraud has all the same elements but is missing the malicious intent (or reckless disregard or gross negligence).
15. Puffing, an agent's praise of the realty, does not create liability.

16. Agent opinion (usually about aesthetics) does not create liability.
17. The "as is" clause in the real estate purchase contract cannot insulate brokers/salespeople from liability when it is used as a way out of telling purchasers what the law requires them to disclose.
18. Defrauded purchasers can ask a court, as soon as they discover the fraud, to rescind the contract and award them damages.
19. Under antitrust laws, members of the real estate "trade" cannot join together in group activities that will restrain trade, such as price-fixing.
20. Brokers cannot fix commission rates by having two or more brokers set a commission rate that they will not go beneath. An individual broker, however, can charge any commission rate or fee he or she chooses and be in compliance with antitrust laws.
21. Business guests on real property are owed the highest duty of care by its owners or agents, including owners' making a reasonable inspection of the premises so as to disclose hazards to these business guests.
22. When listing and selling real estate, salespeople act for and represent the broker. The broker is the principal, and salespeople are his or her agents.
23. Salespeople, as fiduciaries to their brokers, must stay within the scope of the authority their brokers have delegated to them. They are liable to their brokers if they exceed the apparent scope of their authority.
24. Covenants not to compete are contracts wherein the broker offers professional training, or some other consideration, in exchange for the salesperson's promise that, if the salesperson terminates association with the broker within a designated time, he or she cannot practice real estate within a certain distance or radius of the broker's office for a period of time.
25. REALTORS® are licensed brokers or salespeople who are members of the national, Ohio, and local Association of REALTORS®. A real estate broker does not have to become a REALTOR® to be a licensed and operating broker within the state of Ohio.
26. Most real estate brokers operate through corporations (invisible, intangible entities created under law). They incorporate to escape personal liability.
27. Errors and omissions insurance covers loss caused by realty agents who unintentionally neglect or omit doing something they should have done in their practice of real estate.

REVIEW QUESTIONS

1. To prevent a latent defect lawsuit grounded in fraud and deceit, the real estate salesperson, along with purchasers, should:
   a. try to take apart the well
   b. dig a few feet down around the septic system
   c. walk over the entire parcel of the real estate
   d. remove the floorboards in each room above the basement
2. If real estate brokers accept finder's fees from purchasers and commissions from sellers without telling either one about the other's payment, they have acted as:
   a. agents for sellers
   b. agents for purchasers
   c. undisclosed dual agents, representing both purchasers and sellers
   d. disclosed dual agents, representing both purchasers and sellers

3. Covenants not to compete are contracts between brokers and salespeople:
   a. that are not enforceable in Ohio courts
   b. that prohibit practice in the same geographical area for a certain period of time
   c. that are used in the real estate industry and not any other
   d. that are prohibited from being used by the canons of ethics governing the real estate industry

4. A salesperson tells sellers, while trying to list their home, "We and X Realty have agreed not to undercut one another, and we're the best." The salesperson has just:
   a. violated antitrust laws
   b. broken her covenant not to compete
   c. behaved in a totally lawful fashion
   d. made an error and will be entitled to use her errors and omissions insurance

5. An example of a patent defect is:
   a. a deteriorated driveway with visible repairs
   b. a septic system that is worn out
   c. a house infested by termites
   d. a bad well

6. An example of a latent defect is:
   a. a deteriorated driveway with visible repairs
   b. a deed giving more land than the seller has
   c. peeling, exterior paint
   d. a bad well

7. To maintain a fraud lawsuit for concealment of a latent defect, prospective purchasers should:
   a. waive having any inspections done of the real estate, as have been provided for their protection under the real estate purchase contract
   b. make a reasonable, diligent search of the realty
   c. tour the inside of the home completely but not walk the three-acre parcel it is set on
   d. assume that a defect that anyone could obviously observe on the real estate is something sellers should be expected to fix before closing

8. The REALTOR® status is gained by:
   a. joining the national, Ohio, and local REALTORS® Associations
   b. obtaining a real estate license
   c. earning a college degree in real estate
   d. practicing real estate competently for five years

9. From the broker's perspective, the best listing is:
   a. open listing
   b. exclusive right to sell
   c. exclusive agency
   d. coexclusive

10. An agreement that is *not* a contract of employment between broker and seller is:
    a. open listing
    b. exclusive right to sell
    c. exclusive agency
    d. multiple listing

11. An unauthorized practice of law by real estate salespeople would be:
    a. advising purchasers or sellers about their specific liability problems that could ensue from entering into a specific real estate purchase contract
    b. filling in blanks within a form real estate purchase contract
    c. witnessing a will
    d. notarizing a deed

12. Limited personal liability is an advantage of a:
    a. partnership
    b. corporation
    c. sole proprietorship
    d. all of the above

13. Antitrust laws prohibit:
    a. excessive license regulation by the state
    b. businesses from making excessive profits
    c. price-fixing
    d. private trade groups, such as the REALTORS®, from existing

14. In order to be due their commissions, real estate brokers, having a contractual right to sell sellers' realty, must be:
    a. the procuring cause of the sale
    b. a tangential cause of the sale
    c. the sole cause of the sale
    d. able to show they have shown the subject property once

15. Broker A has an exclusive right-to-sell listing, and a Broker A agent has purchasers submit an offer:
    a. if another offer comes in from another broker, that offer has to wait because Broker A gets first crack at its own listings
    b. if another offer comes in from another salesperson associated with Broker A, that too will be submitted to the owner if it is a higher bid
    c. if another offer comes in from a broker who doesn't even belong to the MLS or the board of REALTORS®, that offer won't be submitted at all
    d. all three of the above answers are violations of the fiduciary obligation and thus a fraud against sellers; they give sellers a cause of action against Broker A

16. Exceeding the apparent scope of authority can be a legal problem between:
    a. broker and salesperson
    b. principal and agent
    c. seller and real estate broker
    d. all of the above

17. Salespeople usually have the authority from their broker to:
    a. obtain a listing
    b. cut a commission rate
    c. take a 30-day listing
    d. cross out clauses in the printed form listing and purchase contracts

18. XYZ Realty Co. has a listing on A's realty. It sells A a realty owned by B, which is listed by EZ Realty, pursuant to a buyer brokerage agreement that XYZ has with A. XYZ represents:
    a. A on both realties
    b. B on the property listed with EZ
    c. both A and B
    d. no one

19. Directly causing a series of events without a break in continuity is the legal test for:
    a. fraud and deceit
    b. procuring cause
    c. fiduciary obligation
    d. agency

20. Errors and omissions insurance covers:
    a. actual fraud
    b. fair housing violations by the real estate broker
    c. income tax evasion
    d. negligence

21. The time salespeople ideally should use to select being the buyers' broker:
    a. just before submitting an offer to purchase
    b. upon first meeting with the buyers
    c. when using the agency disclosure form
    d. when setting up the second showing with the listing broker

22. Ohio's mandatory disclosure form on agency makes the salesperson's job:
    a. harder; more paper work
    b. easier; no one can possibly misunderstand no matter when you use it
    c. harder; no one can understand what it says
    d. easier; makes it harder to sue salesperson for failure to disclose agency relationship

23. Ohio's mandatory Residential Property Disclosure Form:
    a. is the uniform one used throughout the country
    b. helps protect real estate agents from suit
    c. holds the seller strictly liable for defects
    d. puts the purchaser into "caveat emptor"

24. Ohio does not recognize the following doctrine in fraud and deceit law as it pertains to material defects in realty:

    a. strict liability
    b. actual fraud
    c. constructive fraud
    d. assumption of the risk

25. The fiduciary obligation does *not* include this element:

    a. confidentiality
    b. accounting
    c. competitiveness
    d. loyalty

ANSWER KEY

1. c
2. c
3. b
4. a
5. a
6. d
7. b
8. a
9. b
10. d
11. a
12. b
13. c
14. a
15. d
16. d
17. a
18. a
19. b
20. d
21. b
22. d
23. b
24. a
25. c

10
OHIO REAL ESTATE LICENSE LAW

KEY TERMS

agency
ancillary trustee
brokers
client
corporation
Director of (Ohio) Commerce
foreign real estate
limited real estate license
Ohio Association of REALTORS®
Ohio Division of Real Estate
Ohio Real Estate Commission
real estate
Real Estate Recovery Fund
subagency
superintendent
trust account

Note: This chapter contains the major changes to the Ohio Real Estate License Law that were made during 1996. Check with your instructor as to the official *effective date* of the individual changes to this important body of law. Generally, however, note that the *non-agency related* changes to the License Law were effective June 13, 1996, while the agency related changes to the License Law were effective December 13, 1996.

LICENSING LAWS

THE PURPOSE FOR LICENSING real estate salespeople is universal: *to protect the public from those who do not have specialized knowledge and regulated standards of behavior and practice.* The reasoning is that those who fail to meet these requisites likely will commit malpractice in that profession against innocent members of the public. This purpose is the same whenever the state requires licensing of those who practice a given profession or occupation. Doctors, lawyers, dentists, accountants, and a whole host of other occupations typically face state regulation and licensing. For all of these professions, conferring the license is considered a privilege extended to a member of society; it is not a right an individual can demand from society. Because it is a privilege instead of a right, it is subject to withdrawal for many reasons, including any that would tend to hurt the very people who confer it—the individuals who make up that state.

All states require real estate brokers and salespersons to be licensed by the state wherein they practice real estate. The states differ in their requisites for obtaining a license.

This chapter centers on the license law of Ohio only. The material here can be cross-referenced with the actual statutes of Chapter 4735 of the Ohio Revised Code. To Ohio salespersons and brokers, Sections 4735.01 to 4735.99 of the Ohio Revised Code are the most fundamental provisions of the license law. The license law begins with definitions of terms that are used throughout. These definitions must be thoroughly understood to properly interpret the rest of the license law.

DEFINITIONS (OHIO REVISED CODE SECTIONS 4735.01 AND 4735.02)

Real estate **brokers** are defined under the license law by what they do with real estate. These functions include selling, exchanging, purchasing, leasing, negotiating, listing, attempting to list, auctioning, dealing in options, operating buildings the public rents as tenants, advertising oneself as being engaged in these activities, and procuring prospects or negotiating transactions (except mortgage financing) that result in the sale, exchange, or lease of real estate.

Those who sell lots or parcels for builders or others must be licensed brokers and salespersons. People who collect rental information to refer tenants for a fee, as well as those promoting the sale or otherwise dealing in real estate, through listing in a publication issued for that purpose or referring such to brokers, also must be licensed brokers and salespersons. Many brokers in Ohio do incorporate their real estate companies, so it is worth noting that the definition of a broker does specifically include the corporation as well as the partnership and the association.

Brokers receive or will receive *consideration* for services. Consideration is a contractual term that in a business setting usually means money in some form. Usually it is the broker's *real estate commission.* **Real estate** is broadly defined as *including every estate in land excluding cemetery lots.*

Salespersons can perform the same services as brokers, with the exception of receiving or paying out commissions from principals, but they must be associated with brokers and perform the services under brokers' names and authority. This does not mean that salespersons must be employees of the brokers. They may be self-employed yet still associated with the brokers.

The **limited real estate license** applies to brokers and salespersons who *engage only in the sale of cemetery interment rights.* This type of limited practice can exist in corporate, partnership, or individual form.

Foreign real estate is *real estate or any interest in real estate not located in Ohio. Foreign real estate dealers* are defined as the same as brokers except that they deal only in real estate not located in Ohio. *Foreign real estate salespersons* can perform the same services as dealers, but they must be affiliated with dealers and perform under their names and authority.

EXEMPTIONS

One can sell real property without being licensed as real estate brokers or salespersons in four ways:

1. *Owners* selling or dealing in their own real property, including management of the real estate or investment in it. The owner can be a corporation, a partnership, or an association, as well as an individual.

FOR EXAMPLE Persons who own real property and want to sell it put an ad in the paper offering it for sale, and they place a sign outside. The owners find purchasers in this way, and they enter into a real estate purchase contract together. This is all right because the people are practicing real estate on themselves, not under any agency relationship. Licensing regulations only prohibit practicing real estate for other persons.

2. *Court appointed or legally designated persons* can legally replace the owners of the property. They can act as and for the owners, because the owners cannot do so. These people include administrators, executors, guardians, trustees, and receivers.

FOR EXAMPLE An executor is the person designated by will to dispose of the property. The owner is dead; the executor is winding up the estate. The executor may sell the property the same as the owner could, subject to probating the estate.

3. *Public officers* can sell real property in an official capacity. In most instances, this person is a sheriff conducting a sheriff's sale pursuant to a court order.

4. *Attorneys* may practice real estate law and sell property out of an estate. The license to practice law, however, does not confer on attorneys a general license of real estate.

FOR EXAMPLE

If a client asks an attorney to list a property for sale on the market, this probably constitutes the practice of real estate, not law. A difference results, however, if the attorney is executor of that property. If a client asks an attorney to draft the listing or purchase contract on a property, that is properly the practice of law, even though the broker has form contracts of the same.

When a partnership, a corporation, or an association holds a real estate license, any of the following persons must have a valid Ohio real estate license: officer, director, manager, or principal employee. In addition, at least one individual in a corporation, a partnership, or an association must be licensed as a real estate broker.

Physically handicapped licensees are defined as those whose handicaps prevent them from attending a course of classroom instruction that is at least three hours long.

RENTAL LOCATION AGENTS (OHIO REVISED CODE SECTION 4735.021)

One must be a licensed real estate broker or salesperson to act as a rental location agent for another. These licensed brokers and salespeople must enter into written employment contracts with prospective tenants when they act as rental location agents. Express provisions of the contract must include how the listings were obtained, and they must provide a refund clause. Owners of real property must consent before these licensees can refer the prospective tenant to the property.

Collecting rental information and selling it to prospective tenants is actually a referral, as that term is used in defining brokers and salespersons. Therefore, these persons must be licensed.

An individual working with residential real property under the supervision of a broker on a salary or an hourly basis is exempt from licensure if he or she is not negotiating contracts or lease agreements or any other duties associated with this activity. The individual is permitted to show rental property and furnish and receive information, applications, and leases.

OHIO REAL ESTATE COMMISSION (OHIO REVISED CODE SECTIONS 4735.03 AND 4735.04)

The **Ohio Real Estate Commission** currently has *five members, appointed by the governor with the advice and consent of the Ohio Senate*. Four of these members are persons licensed as real estate brokers for at least 10 years immediately preceding the appointment. The fifth member of the Ohio Real Estate Commission, the public member, theoretically acts as the representative of the consuming public. This is a partial response to consumer demands upon all regulatory agencies to let members of the consuming public help regulate an industry. The Ohio Real Estate Commission does not run the division of real estate full-time. That job is given to the Director of Commerce or his appointed civil servant, the superintendent. The superintendent is responsible to the Ohio Real Estate Commission.

Only three of the five commission members can belong to one political party. Three also can be a quorum sufficient for voting purposes. The powers of the Ohio Real Estate Commission make it both a quasi court and a regulatory agency if it elects to do so. A regulatory agency polices a specific industry. It can subpoena, investigate, hear an appeal from an action of the superintendent, promulgate codes of ethics, advise the superintendent about the real estate courses, and give licensees information about their activities and decisions. It also may ask a court for an injunction to stop someone from violating the license law. The Ohio Real Estate Commission administers the education and research fund. It also hears appeals from orders of the superintendent regarding claims against the education and research fund, as well as the real estate recovery fund. Further, the commission directs the superintendent on developing real estate education courses, including the content, scheduling, and offering of these courses.

Fair housing is another vital part of the Ohio Real Estate Commission's duties. It must inform brokers and salespeople about changes in state and federal fair housing laws and relevant cases. Further, it informs brokers and salespeople that they are subject to disciplinary proceedings if they do not obey these new laws, and it furnishes brokers and libraries with booklets on housing and remedies for dissatisfied clients under the Ohio Revised Code. The Ohio Real Estate Commission, or the superintendent, can compel the attendance of witnesses at hearings and the production of documents in the witnesses' possession.

Members' powers are the same as judges of county courts. Thus, they can administer oaths, compel attendance of witnesses, and punish them for refusing to testify. In addition, if a person fails to comply with the foregoing, either the Ohio Real Estate Commission or the superintendent may file an application with any Ohio common pleas court for assistance. Thereafter, the court may subpoena the person or order the production of documents. If the person fails to obey the court, the court has the power to order the person arrested and jailed for contempt of court.

Department of Commerce and Superintendent (Ohio Revised Code Section 4735.05)

The Ohio Real Estate Commission is part of another department, the Department of Commerce. The **Director of Commerce** is *ex officio the executive officer of the Ohio Real Estate Commission.* He or she may act as the head or may delegate that job by appointing a superintendent. If a **superintendent** is appointed, the superintendent *acts as the executive officer of the Ohio Real Estate Commission.* The superintendent is also an employee of the Department of Commerce. The director's power of appointment over the superintendent is limited, though, by restricting the choice of superintendent to one of three names submitted by the Ohio Real Estate Commission. The superintendent serves at the "director's pleasure"; the director can terminate the superintendent at will without consulting the Ohio Real Estate Commission.

The *superintendent, rather than the commission, runs the day-to-day operation of the Division of Real Estate.* The superintendent is a full-time civil servant. The superintendent's broad powers include administering, implementing, and enforcing the license law. Specific duties include investigating cases, including licensee conduct; subpoenaing witnesses in connection with investigations and audits; appointing a hearing officer for proceedings being held in connection with the imposition of disciplinary sanctions under the license law; obtaining injunctions and restraining orders of undesirable activity or suspension proceedings, in connection with the license law, as speedily as can be given by the court's equity powers; and maintaining an investigation and audit unit. The audit unit frequently checks brokers' trust accounts to establish whether earnest monies are kept properly there.

If licensees fail to comply with a subpoena, they can be found in violation of Ohio Revised Code Section 4735.18 and be guilty of misconduct, which may subject them to appropriate disciplinary sanctions. The superintendent's investigators have the right to review the licensees' records only during normal business hours. The superintendent must hold in confidence specific information obtained from complainants and witnesses. The superintendent enforces the provision of the license law that prohibits a lending institution affiliated with a real estate broker from requiring a customer to use or employ the services of the affiliated broker to obtain a mortgage.

Also, the superintendent is administrative head of the Division of Real Estate Appraisers within the Department of Commerce. The **Ohio Division of Real Estate** *processes and screens applicants for the residential and general appraiser classifications.* An individual must be state-certified in one of these two classifications to perform appraisals on federally related transactions that are federally funded loans or may be underwritten by federal entities. There are comprehensive standards for those desiring to become state-certified appraisers. Real estate agents who are not also appraisers may still give an opinion of market value, however, in connection with listing and selling real properties.

Ancillary Trustee

The superintendent also appoints **ancillary trustees.** For example, if a real estate company does not have more than one licensed broker with the firm, *in the case of death or loss of license of the broker, the superintendent appoints an ancillary trustee to wind up the business.* The trustee must meet qualification standards as set by the superintendent. This trustee must be approved by probate court if the broker is dead.

The ancillary trustee's duties are limited to supervising and completing existing contracts and obligations of the broker for whom the ancillary trustee is named. New ventures or obligations cannot be started on behalf of the deceased, revoked, or suspended broker. The ancillary trustee assumes all the duties of a real estate broker to conclude transactions already initiated. Because the appointment of an ancillary trustee ends the company's continuation in business, most corporate brokerages have several brokers on their corporate license to avoid the ancillary trustee appointment.

Investigations, Hearings, and Actions Brought Against Licensees (Ohio Revised Code Section 4735.051)

The *Investigation and Audit Unit investigates the conduct of licensees against whom written complaints have been filed.* The superintendent notifies the licensee of the complaint in writing, describing the acts complained of, and informs the licensee that he will be contacted by an investigator. The superintendent acknowledges all written complaints and holds an *informal meeting,* if both parties request one, with the parties and the investigator present. If both parties are able to reach a settlement at this informal meeting stage, the case can be closed. If a violation of the license law is still outstanding, however, the superintendent can proceed with the case even though the parties are willing to settle.

If the licensee and the complainant can't agree to hold an informal meeting, or do hold one but fail to settle, or if the superintendent finds evidence of a licensee violation, the superintendent orders an investigation of a licensee. The investigator subsequently reports his findings to the superintendent, and the superintendent decides whether there is reasonable and substantial violation of the license law. If there is such evidence, he so notifies the parties and schedules a *formal hearing,* which is conducted by a hearing examiner. If the superintendent decides the evidence is insufficient to justify a formal hearing, he so notifies the complainant and licensee.

Licensees also can enter into a settlement agreement with the superintendent, but the Ohio Real Estate Commission must approve it. *Complainants have the right to ask the Ohio Real Estate Commission to review the superintendent's decision.* If a request for review is filed, the Ohio Real Estate Commission reviews the superintendent's decision at its next regularly scheduled meeting. If it concurs with the superintendent, the complainant and the licensee are so notified. If it reverses, the parties are notified that a formal hearing will be held.

The hearing examiner files a report of his findings of fact and conclusions of law with the Ohio Real Estate Commission, the superintendent, and the parties. The Ohio Real Estate Commission reviews this report at its next regularly scheduled meeting. Thereafter, it decides whether to impose disciplinary sanctions upon the licensee. (Such sanctions may include: license revocation; license suspension; imposition of a fine up to $2,500 per violation; issuance of a public reprimand; and the requirement that the licensee complete additional continuing education course work, which would not count toward the usual C.E. requirements for all licensees.) If financial loss is involved, it advises the complainant, or other affected party, that he or she may apply to the Real Estate Recovery Fund, discussed in full later in this chapter.

The Ohio Civil Rights Commission may also be a complainant, and it is entitled to have its complaint reviewed by the Ohio Real Estate Commission directly. The Ohio Real Estate Commission must maintain a transcript of all of the above proceedings and issue a written opinion. If licensees have lost at this stage, they can use the transcript and opinion to appeal their case to court. The Ohio Real Estate Commission may consider a motion for reconsideration (asking it to change its position) only if the motion is filed prior to expiration of the time to file an appeal under Ohio Revised Code Section 119.12 and if no appeal has been filed.

It is recommended to licensees who become involved in these proceedings under Ohio Revised Code Section 4735.051 that they hire an attorney from the beginning. These are adversary proceedings, and any choice licensees make will affect their initial chances as well as their later appeals of adverse decisions.

An investigation under this section is subject to the *statute of limitations* set forth in Ohio Revised Code Section 4735.32. That section provides that the superintendent may commence an investigation against a licensee only if the complaint is filed within *three years* from the date of the alleged violation. After three years, an investigation is barred and no disciplinary action can be taken against the licensee because of the alleged violation. For this section, an investigation commences upon filing a complaint with the division.

BROKER'S LICENSE (OHIO REVISED CODE SECTIONS 4735.06 AND 4735.07)

Application for the broker's license must be in writing, notarized, and accompanied by a photograph of the applicant. Upon receipt of application by the commission, examination dates are given. Signatures of certain designated persons are required on the application to attest to the applicant's good character and reputation.

Brokerage Business Names

Real estate businesses can be formed on other than an individual basis, although made up of individuals. The people who make up the business enterprise must be licensed brokers. The enterprise is not tested; only the individuals who make up the enterprise are. If the Ohio Real Estate Commission approves the name of an enterprise, it issues the license in the enterprise's name, and the brokers' names appear on that enterprise's license.

A **corporation** is the most illustrative of the name approval situation. Before it can do business the corporation's name must be approved by the Ohio Secretary of State's Department. By law no two corporations in Ohio can have the same name. If a corporation can get its name approved by the Secretary of State, there is usually no trouble with the Ohio Real Estate Commission. It is more sensitive, however, to any word in the corporate name that by its industry usage might be misleading or offensive (for example, Cut Rate Realty, Inc., or Rip Off Realty Company).

When the Ohio Real Estate Commission approves the corporate license for real estate, the brokers for that corporation do not have individual licenses. Instead, their names are placed on the corporation's license.

The proposed name for a business enterprise must be clearly distinguishable from a name any existing real estate brokerage has registered with the Division of Real Estate. The name should be one not likely to mislead the public. If the business name uses a surname, it should be only the surname of one or more of the broker licensees actively associated with the brokerage. A broker's or salesperson's surname should be used only by the real estate company with which he or she is actively and publicly associated. When a brokerage business name cannot be distinguished from another licensee's, the superintendent may approve the name if that licensee files written consent with the Division of Real Estate.

If an individual whose surname appears in the name of a brokerage becomes disqualified as a licensee by revocation, the business name of the brokerage must be changed promptly. That individual's name no longer can be used, nor can he or she receive any income from the brokerage. Only income for services rendered prior to revocation may be paid to such an individual.

"Shadow brokerages" are prohibited. These brokerages occur when real estate brokers put their names on real estate businesses but thereafter are not active in managing those businesses.

Application for Broker's License

Individuals apply to take the exam for becoming a real estate broker. To be eligible, they must pay a fee and must meet certain statutory requisites. Applicants are *tested on subjects covered by the real estate education courses* they are required to take. Applicants for a broker's license must be *honest and truthful*. In addition:

1. Applicants should *not have a criminal record,* although an applicant with a record who can provide the superintendent with proof of rehabilitation may still qualify. To have a record, there must be a conviction. A person who is acquitted does not have a criminal record. A criminal record is either a felony conviction or a conviction of a high misdemeanor. Examples of high misdemeanors are passing bad checks and driving while intoxicated.

2. Applicants must *not have a court judgment against them that establishes violation of any fair housing laws.* Two years after judgment has been rendered, applicants can regain their license if they prove by preponderance of the evidence to the superintendent that they have regained their good reputation and that they will not violate the fair housing laws again.

3. Applicants must *not have any record of violations of the license law,* but again may demonstrate rehabilitation to the superintendent.

4. Applicants must be at least *18 years of age.*

5. The broker(s) the applicant has worked for must sign an *affidavit* stating the following: (a) the applicant *has worked for the broker at least two years of the preceding five years as a full-time agent,* expressly defined as 30 hours per week. The time spent showing and listing homes, negotiating transactions, taking office floor time, and conducting open houses all can be counted to reach the 30 hours; (b) the applicant must have *completed 20 real estate transactions,* accomplished in the applicant's capacity as a licensee. In lieu of the 20 transactions, the license law provides that "equivalent experience," as defined by rules adopted by the Ohio Real Estate Commission, can be used to satisfy the requirement.

6. Within one year of issuance of the broker's license, the broker has to complete a *10-hour licensure course in real estate brokerage.*

7. Depending upon when applicants obtained their salesperson's license, they must meet *substantial educational requirements.* These are listed at length in Section 4735.07 of the Ohio Revised Code.

Nonresident Brokers and Reciprocity (Ohio Revised Code Section 4735.08)

Nonresident brokers and salespeople who come from states where licensing laws are similar may be exempted from taking the broker's exam and may be given their licenses. The Ohio Real Estate Commission, at its discretion, may enter into *reciprocity* agreements. It can *waive examination with other states that have similar licensing requirements and where similar recognition is extended to licensees of Ohio.*

Salesperson's License (Ohio Revised Code Section 4735.09)

A salesperson's license has requirements similar to the broker's license, but there are fewer requirements because it is less of a license. The recommendation of the real estate broker, commonly known as "sponsoring," is required on the application. Sponsoring assures that the applicant has good character and a clean (or rehabilitated) legal record.

The main differences in eligibility for a salesperson's license rather than a broker's license are (a) there is *no requirement for transactions* because until one receives this license, it is illegal for an applicant to have any transactions and (b) *four college courses are required*—Ohio Real Estate Principles and Practices; Ohio Real Estate Law; Finance; and Appraisal. The courses must be given by a degree-granting institution, and within 12 months of obtaining the license, the salesperson must complete a *10-hour post-licensure course dealing with consumer-oriented issues*. (There is a similar requirement for a new broker.) After completing the courses, applicants may be examined at any date given them by the Ohio Real Estate Commission. Brokers' and salespersons' licenses both take effect upon the date when the Ohio Division of Real Estate issues the licenses.

Issuance of License

A *75 percent or better score* is necessary to pass both the broker's and the salesperson's exam. Applicants may take the test any number of times they choose until they pass it.

Limited License (Ohio Revised Code Section 4735.091)

A limited branch of real estate practice covers *cemetery interment rights*. A licensed real estate broker or salesperson must obtain this limited license to deal in cemeteries. Anyone applying for a limited broker or sales license is examined separately on this type of practice.

Regulatory Powers (Ohio Revised Code Section 4735.10)

The Ohio Real Estate Commission has the right to make rules and regulations necessary for implementing all of the license law. Some of its rules are within the license law, but its power is not limited to those. The powers already listed in the license law are:

- the form and manner for filing license applications and for placing a broker's license in escrow
- issuing, renewing, suspending, revoking, and applying other disciplinary sanctions concerning licenses, and setting the manner of conducting hearings
- establishing the standards for courses in continuing education for licensees, which standards shall permit the members of a sponsoring entity to receive a reasonable reduction in the fee charged for the class
- time and form for license exam
- issuing annual certificates for continuing business, with filing of deadlines for renewals staggered throughout the year
- requirements for trust and property management accounts, providing (with respect to property management accounts) that as per a written contract with the owner, a brokerage may exercise signatory authority for withdrawals; also, interest on such accounts shall be payable to the property owner unless otherwise agreed in a written contract

The Ohio Real Estate Commission sets up guidelines for the superintendent in the exercise of certain more potent powers. These include the ancillary trustee appointment, approval of real estate business association names, acceptance or rejection of applications to take the license exam, appointment of hearing examiners, acceptance and rejection of applications to take the foreign real estate dealer and salesperson exams (and waivers of those exams), and qualifying foreign real estate.

FOR EXAMPLE A broker either has the license suspended or fails to keep it current. If the broker reapplies for it within two years of so losing it, the superintendent may waive a reexamination.

Real Estate Recovery Fund (Ohio Revised Code Section 4735.12)

The **Real Estate Recovery Fund** is the current ultimate protection for consumers of services obtained from licensed real estate practitioners. Its monies can be used *to satisfy a court judgment that consumers have obtained against real estate licensees.* The services of the licensees must be those covered within the license law definition of brokers and/or salespersons, however (Section 4735.01).

Excluded from coverage are: actions arising from property management accounts maintained in the name of the property owner, acts that occurred on or before March 4, 1975; a bonding company when not a principal in a real estate transaction; and a person suing for payment of a real estate commission or fee. The conduct triggering application of the recovery fund must be a violation of the license law or the rules adopted under it.

To be eligible to apply for this money's being used to satisfy, wholly or partially, the legal wrongs done to them, the following criteria must be met:

1. Aggrieved persons must obtain a court judgment against the licensee in a case arising out of the rendering of real estate services. If the judgment has nothing to do with a licensee's professional acts, only personal ones, the recovery fund cannot be used. For example, the recovery fund cannot be used to pay a licensee's back child support obligation.
2. No appellate court procedures remain to change the decision against the licensees. The court judgment has to stand irrevocably against the licensees.
3. Persons seeking to recover are not the licensee's spouse or the personal representative of the spouse.
4. Aggrieved persons must pursue their legal remedies against all potentially liable persons and all judgment debtors other than the licensee.
5. Aggrieved persons have to make application for relief from the recovery fund no more than one year after items 1, 2, and 4 have been pursued without success.

Aggrieved persons who meet all the above criteria must apply to an Ohio common pleas court and also file notice of such with the superintendent. The superintendent then replaces the defendant. The superintendent, however, is not bound by any prior compromise or stipulation of the licensee (also now called the judgment debtor).

Actual or compensatory damages are recoverable from the recovery fund, but not punitive damages or interest on the judgment. At his discretion, the superintendent may allow payment of attorney's fees and court costs from the recovery fund.

The ceiling for recovery is *$40,000 per licensee*. That it is made per licensee, not per violation, is noteworthy. Some examples should clarify.

FOR EXAMPLE

> Three licensees defrauded the plaintiff for $120,000. A joint and several judgment is rendered against all three. The aggrieved party can recover $120,000 from the recovery fund if all three licensees are unrecoverable. The result is different, however, if only one licensee is liable for $120,000. Then only $40,000 can be recovered. If there is more than one aggrieved party, all have unsatisfied claims against the licensee, and totaled they are more than $40,000, each party shares in the $40,000 according to the percentage of indebtedness owed them. Distribution is made without any regard to priority.

If the recovery fund is used to satisfy their liability, licensees have to pay stiff penalties. A licensee's license is suspended and cannot be reinstated until the fund is repaid in full plus interest. If the licensee is reinstated, the liability of the fund for him or her is once again $40,000, but the violating transaction has to take place after reinstatement.

If the fund has to pay for the licensee the superintendent becomes the judgment creditor against the licensee. The superintendent may try to collect that money from the licensee in any authorized manner of collecting debts, such as garnishment or attachment.

Licensees who repay the fund do not automatically get their licenses back upon repaying the fund. If another independent ground exists for suspension of license, they can remain suspended.

FOR EXAMPLE

> If a judgment is rendered against licensees for violation of the fair housing laws and they don't pay that judgment, plaintiffs can obtain their money from the recovery fund, assuming they meet all other criteria. If the licensees repay, that does not mean automatic return of the licenses, as violating the civil rights laws is an independent ground for revocation or suspension of real estate licenses.

Usage of License (Ohio Revised Code Sections 4735.11 and 4735.13)

The Ohio Real Estate Commission prescribes the form and size of licenses. The license shows the name and address of each licensee and, on a corporate license, the name and address of each corporate officer. Real estate salespersons' licenses show the name of the broker they are associated with. Licenses of foreign real estate salespersons show the name of the foreign dealer they are associated with. Each license is issued under seal and is signed by the president of the Ohio Real Estate Commission and the superintendent.

Only the broker's or, in lieu, the corporate license must be prominently displayed in the real estate office. The salespeople's licenses must be kept in a place convenient for public inspection, if so requested. Any real estate license authorizes the licensee to do business only from the location specified on the license.

If a *salesperson terminates or is terminated by the broker, the broker must immediately return the license to the superintendent*. The broker must send the Division of Real Estate a copy of the notice of cancellation that he sends to a sales associate whose license is being returned to the division for cancellation. Failure to send this copy can constitute broker misconduct under Ohio Revised Code Section 4735.18. The broker also must notify this salesperson that he or she may apply for reinstatement within two years without having to be reexamined.

If the licensee obtains a criminal record or violates the fair housing laws or a court holds the licensee in violation of the fair housing laws, the superintendent should be notified within 15 days. If the superintendent is informed, there will be a hearing and determination of what, if anything, will happen to the license. If the superintendent is never informed and finds out, the violator's license may be revoked without any proceedings whatsoever.

If the real estate office has a change in location, the superintendent must be notified in order to change the address and to issue new licenses reflecting such.

A broker may deal with the broker's license in alternate ways:

1. *Brokers may deposit their licenses and take out salespersons' licenses,* after applying for such and upon the recommendation of the brokers they want to be salespeople for, and they may do this indefinitely. Brokers who opt for this must inform any salespersons associated with their firms before November 1, after which date the salespeople no longer will be able to place their licenses with those brokers; the salespeople must associate with other brokers.

2. *Brokers may have their licenses put on a corporate, partnership, or association license.* They apply for this, and the business entities mail their licenses to the superintendent, who issues the entities new licenses on which the brokers' names also appear.

3. Brokers for good cause also may *deposit their licenses in escrow with the Ohio Real Estate Commission indefinitely.* They are not able to practice real estate while their brokers' licenses are on deposit, however. Thus, real estate brokers who wish to discontinue having an active place of business without canceling their licenses have this option. Brokers who do this must notify their salespeople, if any, as described in item 1. If brokers or salespersons enter the armed forces, they may deposit their licenses with the Ohio Real Estate Commission until six months after their discharge. If licensees are unable to finish continuing education because of their armed service status, they shall have until 12 months after discharge to complete the continuing education.

Continuation of License (Ohio Revised Code Section 4735.14)

Salespeople can continue in business only as long as brokers continue to hold their licenses. *Brokers file a continuation in business certificate* by the date the Ohio Real Estate Commission has adopted by rule for that licensee (thus staggering this filing deadline date throughout the year). They can possibly gain a 15-day extension from the superintendent if they show good cause. If any license is not continued via filing this certificate, the license is revoked. The superintendent mails the certificates to each broker licensee two months in advance of that broker licensee's filing deadline date.

The Division of Real Estate has a rule protecting salespeople from brokers' noncompliance. Real estate brokers who do not intend to renew the license of any salesperson associated with the firm have to give the salesperson notice thereof in writing on or before November 1, by registered mail with return receipt requested. A copy of the notice should be mailed to the Ohio Real Estate Commission within 10 days after the notice is mailed to the salesperson. Failure to give such notice may be a violation of the license law. No salesperson may transfer a license during the month of December unless he or she can prove undue hardship.

CONTINUING EDUCATION REQUIREMENTS (OHIO REVISED CODE SECTION 4735.141)

Licensees, brokers and salespeople alike, must complete 30 classroom hours of continuing education every three years. Limited licensees and licensees who are 67 years of age or older as of June 13, 1996, will have to complete a total of nine classroom hours of continuing education every three years with courses in fair housing law, "Core Law," and canons of ethics. Licensees have to complete the courses only; they do not have to pass an exam.

The continuing education course can be completed in schools, seminars, and educational institutions approved by the Ohio Real Estate Commission. The courses do not have to be offered at two- or four-year colleges, but they may be offered there. Every 30-hour cycle of continuing education courses must include three hours of fair housing law; three hours of "Core Law," and three hours of ethics.

If licensees do not fulfill the continuing education obligation, licenses are automatically suspended. Licenses cannot be reinstated until the suspended licensees fulfill the continuing education requirements. Two years from date of license suspension, licenses are revoked if the continuing education requirements remain unsatisfied. Licenses still may be regained, however, if the revoked licensees fulfill the continuing education requirements thereafter.

Licensees who have physical disabilities may be eligible for time extensions upon meeting their continuing education requisites, depending upon particular circumstances.

BUSINESS LOCATION, ADVERTISING, AND REGISTRATION (OHIO REVISED CODE SECTION 4735.16)

Brokers must maintain *definite places of business with business signs of the brokerage*. Brokers identify themselves as such in advertising. In an ad, no salesperson's name can ever be more prominent than the broker's. *Licensees who sell real estate that they own must disclose in any advertisement that they are licensed.* If salespersons are not selling the property through their brokers, the brokers' names need not be included but their own names must be.

Licensees must furnish copies of listing contracts or any other contract to the other party after obtaining the other party's signature.

The Division of Real Estate publishes and provides *pamphlets* stating that brokers and salespersons are licensed by the Division of Real Estate and that consumers may get in touch with the division if they have a complaint or an inquiry. Brokers and salespeople must make these pamphlets available to their clients. The division's address and telephone number are included in the pamphlet. These pamphlets also must contain the equal housing logo used by HUD and a statement that discrimination in the practice of real estate is illegal on any of the bases prohibited under state or federal fair housing laws. Brokers also must prominently display in each office a statement with all this information on consumer complaints and fair housing rights.

The broker's license and all licenses the broker holds are recorded with the clerk of courts for the county in which the broker maintains the principal place of business. Each branch office registers its license with the clerk of courts for the county in which it is located.

NONRESIDENTS (OHIO REVISED CODE SECTION 4735.17)

Licenses can be issued to nonresidents of the state, whether individuals or corporations, *if they maintain an active place of business within Ohio and consent to be sued in this state* rather than in their own state. If a suit transpires, the plaintiff must serve the suit on the superintendent. A duplicate copy is sent to the defendants-licensees at their main office address. By signing the consent-to-be-sued form, the nonresident must come into Ohio to defend a lawsuit. This is an advantage to the Ohio plaintiff and a disadvantage to the nonresident broker.

SUSPENSION OR REVOCATION OF LICENSES (OHIO REVISED CODE SECTION 4735.18)

There are numerous causes for the imposition of disciplinary sanctions upon a real estate licensee. *The Ohio Real Estate Commission imposes these sanctions, and the superintendent conducts the investigation.* Upon his own motion, the superintendent may cause an investigation of a licensee. All of the itemized causes for imposition of these disciplinary sanctions within the license law should be known by licensees. The exhaustive grounds for these sanctions' suspension or revocation within the license law include the following:

1. *Intentional torts.* For example, stating that the septic system is brand new and in perfect working order when it is really defective and older is violative as both misrepresentation and false promises.
2. *Principal-agency law violations.* An example is to represent both purchaser's and seller's interests in a transaction in a way that would not be permitted under Ohio real estate license and agency laws. Note some of the particulars of such laws as set forth hereinafter in the discussion of R.C. Sections 4735.51 to 4735.74.
3. *Criminal record or gross negligence.* Any felony conviction or crime of moral turpitude suffices. The crime need not be related either to license law or to practicing real estate.
4. *Violation of any of the fair housing laws* (covered in Chapter 11). There is a limitation that the parties involved in the violation, both victim and licensee, must have been making good faith efforts to purchase, sell, or lease real estate.
5. *Procuring a real estate license for oneself as a broker, or for one's salesperson, by fraud, misrepresentation, or deceit.*
6. *Receiving a commission or any portion thereof when one is not licensed as a salesperson or broker in Ohio.* Brokers and salespeople alike can violate this section. A licensed Ohio broker, however, may pay or receive a commission or referral fee from a licensed broker of another state for the referral of clients or prospects. Two examples are (a) paying a commission to an attorney for referring prospects or listings from an estate practice and (b) paying a commission to a corporation's personnel director for referring transferees. In addition, licensees cannot allow unlicensed persons to act on their behalf when a real estate license is necessary to do that activity (e.g., hold an open house).
7. *Using any group name when not a member of the group.* Examples are using the following names when not a member: REALTOR® ; Century 21® .

8. *Violating any fiduciary relationship to the principal.*
9. *Offering anything of value as an inducement, other than the consideration recited in the purchase contract.* A real estate broker, however, may provide home buyers with discount coupons to a department store for example, if that consideration is stated in the purchase contract. This is valid even though the consideration is between the broker and the purchaser. Also, if the real estate agent reduces the rate of real estate commission to obtain the seller's consent to the purchase contract, that reduction must be recited in the purchase contract as part of the consideration, or this provision is violated.
10. *Brokers' or salespeople's dealing as undisclosed principals* (concealing that they are the true buyers). Brokers or salespeople who want to purchase realty must disclose that they are licensees.
11. *Warranting that realty will appreciate by the time of resale.* For example, giving a written or oral guarantee to the purchaser that the property will increase at a certain percentage or dollar rate per year.
12. *Putting a "For Sale" sign on unlisted property.* Probably the most frequent type of violation involves vacant land, as the owner does not have knowledge of the sign's placement.
13. *Bringing about a transaction by inducing the party to breach a contract with another.* A flagrant example is the real estate agent who induces people to enter into a purchase contract as the purchasers by saying, "Don't worry about breaking your lease as landlords don't bother pursuing them." (Many landlords *do* bother). Another example is a real estate salesperson's advising a prospect to default on one real estate purchase contract to enter into another one.
14. *Brokers' or salespeople's contacting owners who have listed realty with other broker.* If a co-broking broker comes up with an offer on that realty, the broker must present it through the other real estate company and not directly to the owner. Both real estate companies can have their agents present at the actual presentation of the offer, however.
15. *Offering realty for sale when there is no listing agreement.* This is acting as an agent without a principal, which is impossible. A more frequent violation is offering the property for sale under terms different from the ones the seller has authorized. An example is: *advertising that the property is for sale and the sellers are willing to accept VA financing when the sellers actually have told the broker they will accept only conventional financing.*
16. *Deceptive advertising.* An example is listing a school system different from the one the property actually uses. Also, the activity of "double-dipping" is deceptive advertising under the license law. This happens when agents use the same figures twice in advertising. For example, salesperson A is advertised as having sold a million dollars worth of real estate. Checking his actual record, one finds that he counted the same sold property twice (once when listing it and again when selling it, or once when the purchase contract was executed and again when title transferred). Any method of counting the proceeds from the sale of a property more than once is double-dipping, and thus is deceptive advertising and a violation of the license law.
17. *Brokers' keeping something off the books or adding something onto them.* Instead of acting as the middleman, brokers keep money or distribute it to the wrong party.
18. *An unwarranted or unjustified lawsuit.*

19. *Brokers' failure to keep records.* Complete records must be kept, going back three years, including listing contracts, earnest money receipts, offers to purchase and their acceptances, and records and receipts of all funds received as broker on a transaction.
20. *Failure to provide true copies of any contracts to all parties.* For example, the owner of listed property must get a copy of the listing contract. For a purchase contract, the owner as well as the purchaser must receive copies.
21. *Brokers' not maintaining a separate trust account.*The **trust account** must be *noninterest-bearing, and all earnest money and other money to be used in concluding a real estate transaction are deposited into it.* No commingling is allowed; brokers cannot put these monies into other accounts. Brokers must maintain all monies received in their fiduciary capacities in their trust accounts. Money received from a purchaser by a salesperson must be receipted and accepted in the broker's name and placed in the trust account.
    a. Brokers may maintain their own funds in trust accounts only when they are clearly defined as the broker's funds and are used only as a minimum balance requirement or to cover a service charge on the account.
    b. Brokers who manage property for another must maintain separate trust accounts designated as the property management trust account. Such management trust accounts may earn interest, which shall be paid to the property owners on a pro rata basis.
    c. Agents from the division regularly investigate trust accounts; these accounts should not be called escrow accounts.
    d. Sometimes legal problems occur with a sale. The seller and the purchaser both demand the earnest money that was deposited in the broker's trust account. The broker must let a court determine who should receive this money when the parties cannot agree in a written release about which party should receive the money. It is a violation of the license law for the broker to make a determination about which party is the proper and lawfully entitled one to have these earnest money funds.
    e. Earnest money must be promptly (generally within 24–48 hours of receipt) deposited into the trust account. Brokers must keep a record of all trust funds received, including escrow funds, security deposits, and other monies the broker receives.
    f. The purchase contract controls at what stage the earnest money is deposited. If the contract specifies that it is to be upon acceptance of the offer, that is when it is deposited. If it is to be deposited upon making an offer, that is the time to deposit. Further, licensees must keep the sellers informed about any change in status relative to earnest money—for example, if the check bounces or if the note is not redeemed.
22. *Omitting the beginning and end dates of all written agency agreements to which the broker is a party.*
23. *Brokers' or salespeople's not paying lawsuits they lose,*with this limitation: The suit had to arise out of their conduct as real estate licensees. They cannot have unsatisfied judgments outstanding that arose out of a real estate transaction. An exception is when the case is still going through the appeals process and the judgment, therefore, can still be reversed by a higher court.
24. *A broker's or salesperson's not showing an owner where the owner's money has been spent.* This is infrequent, as owners normally advance no monies to

brokers to sell the home. Sometimes, however, an owner out of town authorizes the broker to spend money forwarded to repair the house or put improvements in it. Suppose, for example, the roof is leaking. The owner sends the broker or salesperson money to get it repaired and demands a receipt. The broker or salesperson must send a receipt of the repair done, showing cost. In addition, broker and salesperson both are required to file a statement of expenditures or funds advanced for advertising or promoting the sale of the owner's real estate.

25. *Brokers' not paying salespeople their commissions when in receipt of them.* Of course, if there is a court's attachment order claiming that salesperson's commission, the broker must handle the money as the court directs. Under Ohio law it is valid, for example, to withhold money for child support payments, pursuant to statute and order of the court, and the broker has to follow any court orders to this effect.
26. *Brokers' not notifying salespeople that they are not going to continue to hold the salesperson's license.* This must be done in advance of the deadline for filing by the broker of the continuation in business forms.
27. *Real estate brokers' and salespeople's practicing law on the public.*
28. *A court order of incompetency.* An example is commitment to a mental hospital by court order. This section, however, does not cover licensees receiving psychiatric care on a voluntary basis, whether inpatient or outpatient.
29. Acting *as brokers for corporations, partnerships, or associations* unless licensed as brokers.
30. *Failing to notify the Division of Real Estate of a change in business address.*

If the Ohio Real Estate Commission suspends or revokes a salesperson's license, it also may suspend or revoke the broker's license if the broker knew of the salesperson's acts that violated the license law. The Ohio Real Estate Commission can suspend or revoke the license of a foreign real estate dealer or salesperson for any of the above violations as they pertain to foreign real estate. If it suspends or revokes the foreign salesperson's license, it also may suspend or revoke the foreign dealer's license if the dealer knew of the salesperson's violation(s).

The Ohio Real Estate Commission may wholly or partially suspend imposition of any disciplinary sanctions invoked against a real estate licensee under Ohio Revised Code Section 4735.18. The Commission shall notify the real estate appraiser board of any disciplinary action taken under this section against a licensee who is also a state-certified real estate appraiser. There is a *three-year statute of limitations on any violation of the Ohio license law.*

Practices and Procedures

Record Keeping (Ohio Revised Code Section 4735.19)

The Ohio Real Estate Commission must keep records of its proceedings. If a person appeals an order, that order can be changed or vacated by court order or by the Ohio Real Estate Commission's own volition. An application to it to reverse, vacate, or modify an order must be filed within 15 days after the order is mailed to the party.

Illegal Commissions (Ohio Revised Code Section 4735.20)

No commission can be paid to unlicensed persons. Commissions can be paid to licensed brokers of other states, however. If a broker's license is revoked, the licenses of all the firm's salespeople are suspended. Salespeople then must find new brokers, and their licenses will be reinstated with the new brokers. This provision also applies to foreign real estate dealers and salespersons.

Ability to Maintain Suit (Ohio Revised Code Section 4735.21)

Only a licensed real estate broker or foreign real estate dealer can maintain a legal action to collect a real estate commission. Salespeople cannot handle any money for any of the transactions except by using the broker's name with the broker's consent. A real estate salesperson is able to sue only the broker for a commission or any other money due from a transaction. The salesperson cannot sue a purchaser or a seller; the broker must do so. This provision also applies to foreign real estate dealers and salespersons.

Division of Real Estate Operating Fund (Ohio Revised Code Section 4735.211)

This fund pays for the *operating expenses of the Division of Real Estate*. Because the Division of Real Estate is operated within the Department of Commerce, that department's costs are paid out of this fund for administering the division. The Director of Commerce can transfer funds in excess of what the Division of Real Estate needs to the Education and Research Special Account. All fines imposed under R.C. Section 4735.051 are paid into this fund.

Cemetery Lots (Ohio Revised Code Sections 4735.22, 4735.23)

A person who sells cemetery lots cannot promise or guarantee future profits on resale of that lot. Sales commissions should be fixed by the board of trustees for the cemetery.

Foreign Real Estate (Ohio Revised Code Section 4735.25–4735.30)

Interests in foreign real estate (located outside Ohio) may be sold or negotiated only by those licensed as foreign real estate dealers and their affiliated foreign real estate salespersons. For example, a newspaper ad in Ohio of a timeshare development in Colorado must be handled by foreign real estate licensees.

These licensees have to apply to the Division of Real Estate for the foreign license. They take an examination for this license as well. If the person is already an active Ohio broker and has been for at least two years, however, the exam is waived. An individual desiring a foreign license must not have any felony convictions, convictions of certain other crimes, fair housing violations, or violations of the license law as it applies to foreign licensees. The foreign real estate that the foreign licensee wishes to deal in must be registered with the Division of Real Estate.

Owners selling their own foreign real estate in a single transaction are exempt from the foreign licensing requirements. For example, owners of a single condominium unit in Arizona may advertise that unit for sale in Ohio without being foreign licensees. But owners of an Arizona development with several or more units for sale must be foreign real estate licensees to sell them in Ohio. A violator of these foreign real estate sections of the code is guilty of a fourth-degree felony carrying an additional fine of up to $2,500.

Investigations by Commission or Superintendent (Ohio Revised Code Sections 4735.32)

The Ohio Real Estate Commission or the superintendent may commence an investigation of the possible license law violation by a broker or salesperson within three years from the date of the event in question.

Penalties (Ohio Revised Code Section 4735.99)

Violation of certain sections of the license law are *first-degree criminal misdemeanors.* These are punishable by a maximum of $1,000 and/or six months imprisonment. Those sections cover future profits on cemetery lots; practicing real estate without a real estate license, or a real estate broker's or salesperson's practicing law without an attorney's license; and practicing as a rental location agent without being licensed.

Persons representing themselves at an administrative hearing (or their attorney, if they are represented) should study the Rules of Administrative Procedure. Representation by an attorney is recommended.

New Agency Law Provisions (Ohio Revised Code Sections 4735.51–4735.74)

Definitions (Ohio Revised Code Section 4735.51)

The following terms are defined by this statute:

1. **Agency** and *agency relationship,* as *having to do with a relationship in which a licensee represents another person in a real estate transaction.* Note that this definition does *not* include a licensee who, acting merely as a *facilitator* (a

courier or message-carrier, in effect), would be attempting to bring about a transaction. Thus, the *facilitator* concept is *not* recognized at this time as an acceptable way to conduct real estate brokerage or sales in Ohio.

2. *Agency agreement,* meaning a contract between a client and a licensee contemplating the payment to a broker of valuable consideration for performing any act that requires a real estate license under this chapter.
3. *Agent* and *real estate agent,* meaning one who is licensed to represent another in a real estate transaction.
4. *Affiliated licensee,* meaning a licensed salesperson who is associated with a licensed broker.
5. *Brokerage,* meaning the individual or entity that has been issued a broker's license. *Brokerage* also includes the affiliated licensees who have been assigned management duties that include supervision of licensees whose duties may conflict with those of other affiliated licensees.
6. **Client,** meaning *a person who has entered into an agency relationship with a licensee.*
7. *Confidential information,* meaning all information that a client directs to be kept confidential or that, if disclosed, would have an adverse effect on the client's position in the real estate transaction, except to the extent that the agent and/or brokerage is required by law to disclose such information. As well, *confidential information* would include all information that is required by law to be kept confidential.
8. Dual agency relationship, meaning *any of the dual agency relationships set forth in R.C. Section 4735.70.*
9. *In-company transaction,* meaning a real estate transaction in which the purchaser and the seller are both represented by the same brokerage.
10. *Licensee,* meaning any individual licensed as a real estate broker or salesperson by the Ohio Real Estate Commission, pursuant to this chapter.
11. *Management level licensee,* meaning a licensee who is employed by or affiliated with a real estate broker and who has supervisory responsibility over other licensees employed by or affiliated with that real estate broker.
12. *Purchaser,* meaning one seeking to buy; also, to rent or lease real property.
13. *Real estate transaction,* meaning any act described in or related to R.C. Section 4735.01
14. *Seller,* meaning one seeking to sell; also, to rent or lease real property.
15. **Subagency** and subagency relationship, meaning *an agency relationship in which a licensee acts for another licensee in performing duties for the client of that licensee.*
16. *Timely,* meaning as soon as possible under the particular circumstances.

Types of Agency Relationships Permitted Under This Chapter—Generally (Ohio Revised Code Section 4735.52)

The types of agency relationships permitted in a real estate transaction are determined by the provisions of this chapter. Except to the extent the duties of a real estate agent are specifically set forth in this chapter, or are otherwise modified by agreement, the duties of a real estate agent are determined by the common law.

Types of Agency Relationships Permitted Under This Chapter—Specifically (Ohio Revised Code Section 4735.53)

1. An agency relationship between the licensee and the seller.
2. An agency relationship between the licensee and the purchaser.
3. A dual agency relationship between the licensee and both the seller and the purchaser.
4. A subagency relationship between the licensee and the client of another licensee.

When an agency relationship is formed between a licensee and a client, *both* of the following apply:

1. The brokerage with whom the licensee is affiliated and the management-level licensees in that brokerage who have direct supervisory duties over licensees are also agents of that client; and,
2. Any licensee employed by, or affiliated with, the brokerage who receives confidential information from the agent of the client is also an agent of that client.

Further, except as provided in the foregoing items 1 and 2, another licensee who is affiliated with the same brokerage as the licensee is *not* an agent of that client unless that licensee assisted in establishing the agency relationship or is specifically appointed, with the client's consent, to represent the client.

Finally, a payment or a promise of a payment to a licensee does *not* determine whether an agency relationship has been created between a licensee and a client, or between other licensees in the brokerage with which the licensee is affiliated, and that client.

Requirements of a Written Company Policy Setting Forth Agency Relationships of the Brokerage (Ohio Revised Code Section 4735.54)

Each brokerage shall develop and maintain a written company policy that sets forth the types of agency relationships that members of that brokerage may establish. Such policy shall specifically address whether any dual agency relationships, as defined in this chapter, are permitted. The policy shall also set forth procedures to ensure the protection of confidential information; also, the policy shall comply with, at least, the minimum standards concerning this matter, as promulgated by the Superintendent of Real Estate. Finally, upon request the brokerage shall provide a copy of this policy to each client or prospective client.

Specific Requirements of All Written Agency Agreements (Ohio Revised Code Section 4735.55)

This section details the minimum requirements of all written agency agreements, under this chapter. One such requirement is that each written agency agreement shall contain a place for the licensee and the client to sign and date the contract.

Disclosures to Client Before Performance of Any Agency Duties (Ohio Revised Code Section 4735.56)

Prior to performing any duties in an agency relationship, a licensee shall provide to the licensee's client a *written* disclosure of all of the following:

1. the licensee's company policy regarding cooperation with other licensees, including how compensation will be paid;
2. the permitted types of representation by other licensees of the licensee's brokerage;
3. that a purchaser's agent will represent the purchaser's interests, even though the seller's agent or the seller may compensate that agent;
4. whether the licensee might, at some time during the agency relationship, act as a dual agent, and the options and consequences as would then result;
5. whether another licensee, associated with the licensee's brokerage, might at some time during the agency relationship become the exclusive agent for the other party in the transaction.

Agency Disclosure Statement, from the Superintendent of Real Estate (Ohio Revised Code Section 4735.57)

The Superintendent of Real Estate, with the approval of the Ohio Real Estate Commission, shall develop a comprehensive agency disclosure statement, reflecting the requirements of this Chapter and containing a place for the licensee and the parties to the transaction to sign and date the statement.

Use of the Agency Disclosure Statement with Sellers and Purchasers (Ohio Revised Code Section 4735.58)

A licensee acting as a seller's agent shall provide the agency disclosure statement to the seller *prior to* marketing or showing the seller's property.

A licensee working directly with a purchaser (and regardless of the type of agency relationship) shall provide the agency disclosure statement to the purchaser *prior to* the first of a number of possible events, subject further to additional requirements of notice and consent to agency functions. The main thrust of these provisions is to minimize the possibility that a client will reveal information or act in some way that they would *not* have done, had they known the true agency relationships and potential relationships in advance.

Changes to a Licensee's Representation During a Transaction (Ohio Revised Code Section 4735.59)

If a licensee changes his representation after a written agency disclosure statement has been signed and dated, or after verbal disclosure of the agency relationship, the licensee shall obtain the written consent of his original client to represent another party; also, all persons who had been notified of the original relationship must be notified of this change.

Disclosures by a Licensee Representing the Purchaser (Ohio Revised Code Section 4735.60)

During the first contact by the purchaser's agent with the seller's agent (or if the seller is not represented, during the first contact with the seller) the purchaser's agent must disclose that she represents the purchaser. Further, and if the seller is not represented, the purchaser's agent must disclose, during this first contact, any intentions of seeking compensation from the seller.

Licensees' Giving of False Information (Ohio Revised Code Section 4735.61)

No licensee shall knowingly give false information to any party in a real estate transaction.

Fiduciary Duties to a Client (Ohio Revised Code Section 4735.62)

In representing any client in an agency or subagency relationship, the licensee shall be a fiduciary of the client and shall use the licensee's best efforts to further the interests of his client, including, without limitation, complying with a series of required actions, as set forth in this section.

Promoting the Interest of the Seller-Client (Ohio Revised Code Section 4735.63)

A licensee shall promote the interest of her seller-client by doing *all* of the following:

1. seeking a purchase offer at a price and with terms acceptable to the client, subject to the client's direction as to seeking additional offers;

2. making timely presentation to the client of all purchase offers, even if the property is already sold, leased, or subject to a letter of intent;
3. providing the seller with a copy of any agency disclosure form signed by the purchaser prior to presentation of any offer to the seller.

A licensee does not breach any duty or obligation to her seller-client by showing alternative properties to a prospective purchaser or by acting as an agent or a subagent for other sellers.

Prohibited Actions When Representing the Seller (Ohio Revised Code Section 4735.64)

In representing a seller in an agency relationship, no licensee shall do *either* of the following without the knowledge and consent of the seller:

1. extend an offer of subagency to other licensees; or
2. offer compensation to a broker who represents a purchaser.

Required Duties in Representing the Interests of the Purchaser (Ohio Revised Code Section 4735.65)

When representing a purchaser, the licensee shall do *each* of the following:

1. seek a property at a price and with purchase or lease terms acceptable to the purchaser. The licensee need not seek further purchase or lease possibilities after the purchaser is a party to a contract, unless so directed by the purchaser; and
2. present any purchase or lease offer to the seller or his agent in a timely manner, even if the property is already subject to a contract of sale, lease, or letter of intent to lease.

Prohibited Actions When Representing the Purchaser (Ohio Revised Code Section 4735.66)

In representing a purchaser in an agency relationship, no licensee shall do *either* of the following without the knowledge and consent of the purchaser:

1. extend an offer of subagency to other licensees; or
2. accept compensation from a broker who represents a seller.

Disclosures from Licensees, Sellers, and Purchasers (Ohio Revised Code Section 4735.67)

Requirements are herein set forth as to additional necessary disclosures that must be made by licensees, sellers, and purchasers including the setting forth of some limits to such disclosures. For example, licensees are required to disclose to purchasers all material facts of which they have actual knowledge. Note however, that licensees will be considered to have actual knowledge of a material fact if they have acted in bad faith or with reckless disregard to the truth, as to that fact.

Limitations to Liability for Representations by Clients and Their Licensee-Agents (Ohio Revised Code Section 4735.68)

A licensee is not liable to any party for false information that the licensee's client provided to the licensee, and that the licensee in turn provided to another party, unless the licensee had actual knowledge that the information was false or unless she acted with reckless disregard for the truth.

No cause of action shall arise on behalf of any person against a client for any misrepresentation a licensee made while representing that client unless the client had actual knowledge of the licensee's misrepresentation.

Acts That May Be Performed by Licensees for a Party Who Is Not the Licensee's Client (Ohio Revised Code Section 4735.69)

A licensee may assist a party who is not the licensee's client in a real estate transaction by doing *any* of thc following:

1. providing information regarding lenders, inspectors, attorneys, insurance agents, surveyors, draftspersons, architects, schools, shopping facilities, places of worship, and other similar information;
2. providing market information or other information obtained from a property listing service or public records.

Any licensee who assists a party in this way and who is not the licensee's client does not violate the agency relationship with the client, and providing such services for that party neither forms nor implies any agency relationship with that party.

Dual Agents Defined, for Purposes of this Chapter (Ohio Revised Code Section 4735.70)

The following are dual agents under this chapter:

1. a *licensee* who represents both the purchaser and the seller as clients in the same real estate transaction;
2. a *brokerage* that represents both the purchaser and the seller in the same real estate transaction;
3. a *management-level licensee* who represents a client in an in-company transaction.

Procedures Detailed for Participation in a Dual Agency Relationship (Ohio Revised Code Section 4735.71)

Subject to the provisions of the next paragraph, no licensee or brokerage shall participate in a dual agency relationship unless both the seller and the purchaser have knowledge of the dual representation and consent in writing to such representation on the Dual Agency Disclosure Statement described in R.C. Section 4736.73.

The brokerage shall make the dual agency disclosure to both the seller and the purchaser as soon as practicable after it is determined that such dual agency may exist. The parties to the transaction shall sign and date the Dual Agency Disclosure Statement in a timely manner after it is determined that a dual agency relationship exists. The form must be signed and dated prior to the signing of any offer to purchase or lease.

A brokerage that is a dual agent is not required to obtain the consent of the seller and the purchaser on the dual agency disclosure statement if the seller and purchaser are each represented by a different, nonmanagement-level licensee who is affiliated with the same brokerage and *all* of the following conditions are met:

1. the licensees made disclosures as required under R.C. Sections 4735.56 and 4736.58;
2. the potential for the formation of the dual agency was disclosed to all parties in the Agency Disclosure Statement; and
3. each party consented by initialing, in a timely manner after it was determined that a dual agency relationship existed, the section in the Agency Disclosure Statement that discloses the potential for a dual agency relationship.

No brokerage shall participate in a dual agency relationship unless *each* of the following conditions is met:

1. the brokerage has established a procedure under which licensees, including management-level licensees, who represent one client will *not* have access to and will *not* obtain confidential information concerning any other client of the brokerage involved in the dual agency transaction; and
2. the licensee who is an agent for each client in the dual agency relationship fulfills the licensee's duties exclusively to that client.

Functions of the Brokerage and Management Level Licensees Where a Dual Agency Relationship Exists (Ohio Revised Code Section 4735.72)

The brokerage and management-level licensees in a brokerage in which there is a dual agency relationship shall do *each* of the following:

1. objectively supervise the affiliated licensees in the fulfillment of their duties and obligation to their respective clients;
2. refrain from advocating or negotiating on behalf of either the seller or the purchaser; and
3. refrain from disclosing to any other employee of the brokerage, or any party or client, any confidential information of a client of which the brokerage or

management-level licensee becomes aware, and from utilizing or allowing to be utilized for the benefit of another client any confidential information obtained from a client.

When two nonmanagement-level licensees affiliated with the same brokerage represent separate clients in the same transaction, each affiliated licensee shall do *both* of the following:

1. serve as the agent of only the party in the transaction the licensee agreed to represent; and
2. fulfill the duties owed to the respective client as set forth in this chapter and as agreed in the Agency Agreement.

Nothing in this section prohibits the brokerage or management-level licensees in the brokerage from providing factual, nonconfidential information that presents or suggests objective options or solutions, or assisting the parties in an unbiased manner to negotiate or fulfill the terms of the purchase contract or lease, provided that confidential information of a client is not utilized in any manner in formulating such suggestions or providing such assistance.

Making disclosures that are permitted or required by this chapter does not terminate any agency relationship between a licensee and a client.

If a brokerage determines that confidential information of one client in a dual agency relationship has become known to any licensee employed by or affiliated with the brokerage who is representing the other client in the dual agency relationship, as a result of the failure of the brokerage, its licensees, or its employees to maintain such confidentiality, the brokerage shall do *both* of the following:

1. notify both clients of such fact immediately in writing; and
2. offer to resign representation of both clients.

If either client elects to accept such resignation, the brokerage shall not be entitled to any compensation from that client. If either client does not accept such resignation, the brokerage may continue to represent that client.

A licensee who obtains confidential information concerning another client of the brokerage in a dual agency relationship shall not, under any circumstances, disclose that information to, or use that information for, the benefit of the licensee's client.

A client of a brokerage who is involved in a dual agency relationship may bring an individual action against a brokerage and any licensee who has failed to comply with the procedures for ensuring confidentiality of information (R.C. Section 4735.71[D][1]) to recover actual damages and to rescind an agency agreement with the brokerage.

Creation by the Superintendent of the Dual Agency Disclosure Statement (Ohio Revised Code Section 4735.73)

The Superintendent of Real Estate, with the approval of the Ohio Real Estate Commission, shall establish by rule the Dual Agency Disclosure Statement, which shall specify the duties of an agent in a dual agency relationship pursuant to this chapter. The Dual Agency Disclosure Statement shall contain a place for the licensees and parties to the transaction to sign and date the statement and shall contain sections for the disclosure of *all* of the following:

1. unless confidential, the identity, including names and addresses, of both clients;
2. a description of the real property involved;
3. an explanation of the nature of the dual agency relationship, including a statement that in serving as a dual agent licensees in the brokerage represent two clients whose interests are, or at times could be, different or adverse;
4. a description of the duties the brokerage and its affiliated licensees and employees owe to each client, including the duty of confidentiality;
5. that neither the brokerage nor its affiliated licensees have any material relationship with either client other than incidental to the transaction, or if the brokerage or its affiliated licensees have such a relationship, a disclosure of the nature of the relationship. *Material relationship* is defined as any actually known personal, familial, or business relationship between the brokerage or an affiliated licensee and a client that could impair the ability of the brokerage or affiliated licensee to exercise lawful and independent judgment relative to another client.
6. that as a dual agent, the brokerage cannot engage in conduct that is contrary to the interests or instructions of one party or act in a biased manner on behalf of one party;
7. a section specifying the source of compensation to the real estate broker;
8. that the client does not have to consent to the Dual Agency Agreement, and the options available to the client for representation in the transaction if the client does not consent; and
9. that the consent of the client has been given voluntarily, that the signature indicates informed consent, and that the Dual Agency Disclosure Statement has been read and understood.

Duties of a Licensee to a Client After Performance of All Duties or After Any Contract Has Terminated (Ohio Revised Code Section 4735.74)

Unless otherwise agreed in writing, a licensee owes no further duty to a client after performance of all duties or after any contract has terminated or expired, except for *both* of the following:

1. providing the client with an accounting of all moneys and property relating to the transaction; and
2. keeping confidential all information received during the course of the transaction unless:
   a. the client permits disclosure;
   b. disclosure is required by law or by court order;
   c. the information becomes public from a source other than the licensee;
   d. the information is necessary to prevent a crime the client intends to commit;
   e. disclosure is necessary to defend the brokerage or its licensees against an accusation of wrongful conduct or to establish or defend a claim that a commission is owed on a transaction.

The rest of this section repeals formerly existing sections of the license law; it also amends Section 4735.05.

OHIO DIVISION OF REAL ESTATE AND OHIO ASSOCIATION OF REALTORS®

These two separate entities should not be confused. The Division of Real Estate is a *state agency that every real estate agent must use* because it is the only entity that issues licenses. The Division of Real Estate also enforces and administers the license law; those who hold licenses are always subject to the Division of Real Estate's scrutiny. By contrast, the **Ohio Association of REALTORS®** is a private trade organization that provides professional benefits for its members. These members also bind themselves to standards of conduct by codes within the association. The Ohio Association of REALTORS® does not have the power to remove a real estate license, nor do any of the local affiliates or the National Association of REALTORS® have this power. If these associations do find a member violating the law, however, they have the duty to inform the Division of Real Estate, which in turn will investigate.

RICHARD T. KIKO AGENCY INC., V. OHIO COMMERCE DEPT., REAL ESTATE DIVISION 48 Ohio St.3d 74, 549 N.E.2d 510 (1990)

CASE STUDY FROM THE OHIO SUPREME COURT

Facts: Pursuant to a purchase contract for real estate, the purchaser executed a note to Kiko agency for $3,600. A default provision in the contract stated that if purchaser refused to perform, seller could declare the contract void, and all monies, not in excess of 15 percent of the purchase price, to be forfeited to seller as liquidated damages. The purchasers redeemed their note by depositing the $3,600 check into Kiko's account.

The purchasers couldn't obtain financing. Several months of inactivity followed. Some time later, Kiko withdrew the funds from the trust account and placed the funds in a three-month ready money repurchase agreement with the agency as the owner, earning 6.25 percent interest. On March 20, 1986, Kiko withdrew the entire deposit plus interest. Kiko sent $2,100 to the seller, paid $1,500.42 to the Kiko agency, and paid $23 for a termite inspection. The purchasers were not informed of this activity, nor did they consent to the payments.

Hearing Officer and Ohio Real Estate Commission: Placement of funds in an interest-bearing account and withdrawal and payment without consent of all parties constituted misconduct in violation of Ohio Revised Code Section 4735.18 (F). Kiko's license was suspended for 15 days.

Trial Court: Vacated order of commission's 15-day suspension. Finding no definition of "misconduct" in Ohio Revised Code Title 47, the court concluded that Kiko's good faith acts did not amount to gross negligence, dishonest or illegal dealings, as set forth in Ohio Revised Code Section 4735.18. Consequently, the commission's decision to suspend Kiko's license was arbitrary, unsupported by reliable, probative and/or substantial evidence and contrary to law.

Court of Appeals: Affirmed judgment of trial court.

Issue: Whether the Ohio Real Estate Commission had sufficient reliable, probative, and substantial evidence upon which to order Kiko's broker's license suspended for 15 days.

Held by the Ohio Supreme Court: The order of the Ohio Real Estate Commission was properly made. Kiko's failure to inform or obtain consent from the parties before placing escrowed funds in an interest-bearing account breached both the direct language of the statute and his fiduciary duty to the parties. The superintendent of real estate may investigate real estate licensees' conduct pursuant to Ohio Revised Code Section 4735.18. Further, the Ohio Real Estate Commission is empowered to determine whether certain acts constitute broker misconduct, or not, under Section 4735.18(F). Under this section, misconduct includes unprofessional conduct, or conduct involving any breach of duty prohibited under professional codes of ethics, or conduct contrary to law. Thus, the Code of Ethics, as promulgated by the Ohio Real Estate Commission, is also grounds for professional charges of misconduct.

Summary of Content

1. License laws protect the public and are a privilege conferred upon licensees.
2. Real estate brokers and salespersons are permitted a wide range of activities all pertaining to transactions regarding real property.
3. Some persons can sell real property without being licensed, the most usual being the person who owns the subject realty.
4. The Ohio Real Estate Commission regulates the real estate industry and also functions as a quasi court.
5. The superintendent runs the Division of Real Estate and investigates the conduct of real estate licensees.
6. Ancillary trustees are appointed to wind up the business of brokers who die or lose their licenses due to revocation.
7. To apply for a broker's license, a licensed salesperson must meet substantial experience and educational requirements.
8. A person must meet educational requirements to obtain a salesperson's license.
9. The Real Estate Recovery Fund protects consumers against real estate licensees from whom they cannot collect their judgments, up to $40,000 per licensee.
10. When a salesperson terminates, or is terminated by the broker, the broker must immediately return his or her license to the superintendent.
11. Brokers may deposit their licenses and take out salespersons' licenses.
12. Licensees must complete 30 hours of continuing education every three years.
13. Nonresidents of Ohio may obtain Ohio real estate licenses.
14. There are numerous causes for suspension and revocation of real estate licenses.
15. Foreign real estate is that located outside Ohio, and a licensee must obtain a foreign real estate license to deal in it.
16. The Ohio Division of Real Estate is a state agency, whereas the Ohio Association of REALTORS® is a private trade group.

REVIEW QUESTIONS

1. A broker can be:
   a. a person
   b. a corporation
   c. a partnership
   d. all of the above

2. A salesperson's or broker's license can be suspended or revoked for:
   a. using a trade name for an organization that he/she does not belong to
   b. simple negligence
   c. practicing law by a person who has both an attorney's and a broker's license
   d. earnest money's being maintained in the trust account

3. Which person can sell a cemetery lot?
   a. real estate broker
   b. limited real estate broker
   c. real estate salesperson
   d. foreign real estate dealer

4. The Ohio Real Estate Commission:
   a. personally investigates license violations
   b. handles all daily aspects of real estate licensing
   c. recommends three names for superintendent
   d. is composed of three practicing real estate brokers

5. The superintendent is:
   a. a real estate broker
   b. appointed by the Director of Commerce
   c. an ancillary trustee
   d. head of the Department of Commerce

6. Which is eligible to take the broker's exam?
   a. individual licensed as salesperson
   b. real estate partnership
   c. real estate corporation
   d. any individual who is a resident of Ohio

7. Good character can be established on the salesperson's exam application by having this person sign your application:
   a. your current employer
   b. your business associate
   c. the real estate broker who plans to hold your real estate license and is sponsoring your application
   d. the person at your college who can certify you have passed all your required courses

8. A real estate license can be suspended or revoked for:
   a. voluntary admission to a mental institution
   b. outpatient psychiatric care
   c. commission of a felony
   d. commission of a minor misdemeanor

9. A real estate license can be suspended or revoked for:
   a. misrepresentation and fraud
   b. putting earnest money in the trust account
   c. putting a "For Sale" sign on listed vacant land
   d. salespersons introducing themselves to owners during showings

10. It is a first degree misdemeanor to:
    a. practice law without an attorney's license
    b. practice real estate without a real estate license
    c. act as a rental location agent without having a real estate license
    d. all of the above

11. To use the Real Estate Recovery Fund, the aggrieved party must:
    a. be an attorney of the licensee's
    b. file before the licensee declares bankruptcy
    c. be damaged by a real estate licensee who rendered professional services
    d. have won some sort of civil action against the licensee

12. Appointment of an ancillary trustee takes place when:
    a. one of several brokers for a real estate corporation dies
    b. the sole broker for a real estate company dies
    c. one of several brokers has his/her license revoked
    d. a real estate broker takes time off from work

13. The name of a real estate enterprise:
    a. must be approved by the superintendent
    b. can be a surname
    c. must be approved by the Ohio Secretary of State if a corporation
    d. all of the above

14. The Ohio Real Estate Commission regulates:
    a. the form and manner for filing license applications
    b. the manner of conducting hearings
    c. issuing, suspending, and revoking licenses
    d. all of the above

15. The aggrieved party trying to use the Real Estate Recovery Fund files the claim with:
    a. the licensee
    b. the superintendent
    c. the Ohio Real Estate Commission
    d. the licensee's broker

16. All salesperson's licenses must be:
    a. prominently displayed in the real estate office
    b. held by the broker
    c. renewed every January 2
    d. placed on deposit with the state

17. When a salesperson terminates with one broker and joins another, usually:
    a. the first broker sends the second broker the salesperson's license
    b. the first broker gives the salesperson the license
    c. the first broker sends the license back to the Division of Real Estate
    d. the second broker makes up a new license that this salesperson can use

18. The broker's name must:
    a. appear in any advertising
    b. be accompanied by the salesperson's in any advertisement
    c. only be advertised, never the salesperson's
    d. be followed by a photograph

19. The following presumption occurs under the license law:
    a. that the licensee works for the purchaser
    b. that the licensee is a disclosed dual agent
    c. that the licensee works for the seller
    d. none of the above

20. Reciprocity can be extended to other states' licensees wherein they are extended Ohio licensure without examination, and without other requisites being met, because of:
    a. that state's paying Ohio millions of dollars for the privilege
    b. Ohio's requisites being lower than so many other states
    c. Ohio's being desperately short of real estate licensees
    d. that state's extending the same benefit to Ohio licensees

21. As an individual, your being granted an Ohio real estate license is a:
    a. privilege
    b. constitutional right
    c. statutory right
    d. common law right

22. The executor of an estate runs an ad in a newspaper, attempting to sell a city lot owned by the estate for more than half a million dollars. Can the executor do this without being a licensed broker?
    a. no; properties for sale in excess of $100,000 must be handled by a broker
    b. yes; the executor is exempt from the license law when selling the estate property
    c. yes; city property need not be handled by brokers
    d. no; only brokers may attempt to do what this executor is doing

23. If four Ohio real estate commissioners are licensed real estate brokers, the fifth must:
    a. also be a licensed broker
    b. belong to the same political party as the other three
    c. not be a licensed broker
    d. be an attorney-at-law

24. The one who orders that a licensee be investigated is the:
    a. Ohio Supreme Court
    b. Ohio Real Estate Commission
    c. Director of Commerce
    d. Superintendent

25. The superintendent may commence an investigation against a licensee only if a complaint is filed within this statute of limitations:
    a. 180 days
    b. one year
    c. three years
    d. five years

ANSWER KEY

1. d	8. c	15. b	22. b
2. a	9. a	16. b	23. c
3. b	10. d	17. c	24. d
4. c	11. c	18. a	25. c
5. b	12. b	19. d	
6. a	13. d	20. d	
7. c	14. d	21. a	

11
FAIR HOUSING

KEY TERMS

Affirmative Marketing Agreement
antisolicitation ban
blockbusting
checking
Civil Rights Act of 1866
consent decree
dispersion of minorities
equal access
Fair Housing Act
family status
First Amendment
handicap
HUD
injunction
Ohio Civil Rights Law
redlining
restrictive deed covenants (restrictions of record)
standing
statistical records of business
steering
substantially equivalent
temporary restraining order
testing

FAIR HOUSING LITIGATION IS a seasoned real estate agent's idea of being caught in a waking nightmare. These cases can take years to litigate and can also involve significant monetary damage awards, large attorney's fees awards (to the victim of discrimination), and, sometimes, court orders dictating both broker's and salesperson's future conduct. One can even end up defending oneself against no less an entity than the federal government, with the Federal Bureau of Investigation doing all the government's investigating work. Furthermore, Ohio's real estate license laws include violations of these laws as cause for suspending or revoking real estate licenses. And fair housing cases often receive media attention by television and newspapers. It is thus possible that salespeople who violate these laws will see themselves on their local television station's nightly news, recorded by a minicam during the trial or as they leave the courthouse.

Fair housing laws were *passed to create equal, integrated opportunity in housing*. Segregated residential housing patterns were and remain difficult to break, however. Therefore, fair housing is the most controversial aspect of real estate law the student will study. Real estate salespeople, brokers, sellers, landlords, lenders, appraisers, and insurers all must strive together to follow these laws, as the legal penalties for noncompliance are incredibly severe.

The 1960s was the decade when housing discrimination laws really "took off." Civil rights law had been making steady progress before then, particularly in the precedent-setting U. S. Supreme Court case of *Brown v. Board of Education* in 1954, which abolished the separate but equal doctrine that previously had permitted the legal segregation of blacks from whites in public education. Education, voting, and employment rights were among the legal areas that gained the first civil rights victories. Not surprisingly, housing was next in line—for how could a society give rights to its minorities in all other forms of socioeconomic advancement, yet specifically condone segregated neighborhoods? The answer was simple. Housing's time had come, too, by the 1960s.

Civil Rights Act of 1866 and Jones v. Mayer

The Supreme Court of the United States in 1968 recognized the plight of blacks in the housing market, in the landmark decision of *Jones v. Mayer*. This decision was the dramatic, far-reaching case that opened the door for the ongoing battle to promote open, fair housing throughout the United States. It specifically *prohibited private racial discrimination* in the sale, lease, or transfer of realty and personalty.

The facts of the case were that Mr. and Mrs. Jones had tried to buy realty in Missouri and had been turned down because of racial discrimination. The Supreme Court held that this was illegal. The court based its decision on the **Civil Rights Act of 1866.** This act was enabling legislation attached to the Thirteenth Amendment to the U. S. Constitution, which was the prohibition against slavery. The act covered rights other than housing, so the court in *Jones* concentrated on the specific statute under the Act that covered property rights, Section 1982:

> All citizens of the United States shall have the same right in every State and Territory as is enjoyed by White citizens thereof to inherit, purchase, lease, sell, hold and convey real and personal property.

The words "White citizens" used in the statute limited the scope of this law to discrimination based on race only. In 1987 this changed, however, with the U. S. Supreme Court companion decisions of *Saint Francis College v. Al-Khazraji* and *Shaare Tefila Congregation v. Cobb* (both case studies appear at the end of this chapter). The Supreme Court held that the test of who was a Caucasian (white) or not was to be determined by who would have been considered nonwhite back in 1866, the year Congress enacted the 1866 Civil Rights Act and Section 1982. Using books and documents from that era, the Court said the following were not considered white: Finns, gypsies, Basques, Hebrews, Arabs, Swedes, Norwegians, Germans, Greeks, Italians, Spaniards, Mongolians, Russians, Chinese, and Mexicans.

The court concluded that the 1866 Congress intended to protect identifiable classes of persons subjected to intentional discrimination solely because of their ancestry or ethnic characteristic. Thus, the plaintiff class was significantly opened for Section 1982 litigation. Sex discrimination, handicap, and family status victims, however, still have to rely on the Fair Housing Act. All other protected classes (race, color, creed, national origin) now probably qualify for Section 1982 coverage as well.

Section 1982 covers all real estate and does not limit itself to dwellings. The Supreme Court stated the scope of Section 1982 in *Jones v. Mayer. Only private parties* may enforce Section 1982 by *acting on their own initiative*. It does *not* have federal agencies assisting in its enforcement. The courts have allowed sophisticated relief and remedies using Section 1982, and these are discussed after our coverage of the Fair Housing Act, below.

FAIR HOUSING ACT

The federal **Fair Housing Act,** Title VIII of the Civil Rights Act of 1968, and amended through the years, is a more *comprehensive and modern housing law, establishing, within constitutional limits, the basis for fair housing throughout the United States*. It covers discriminatory practices based on *race, religion, national origin, sex, handicap, and family status*. Comprehensive definitions of persons in the last two classes, plus exemptions, are set forth below.

1. **Family status** is defined as *persons under age 18 living with a parent or guardian*. It also covers: children who are domiciled with designee of the parent(s) having custody (with written permission); women who are pregnant; persons who are in the process of attaining legal custody of a child under age 18. The family status category was specifically aimed at ending discrimination in housing against parents/guardians with children. Exemptions and limitations to the family status category of protection are:
   a. Housing and apartment complexes designed solely (100 percent of occupancy) for senior citizens aged 62 and older are exempt.
   b. Complexes that are at least 80 percent occupied by at least one person aged 55 or older per unit are exempt.
   c. State and local occupancy legislation can still be imposed upon dwellings and apartments, but children count the same for this purpose as an adult. Thus, if state or local occupancy laws allow two adults in an apartment, for example, they also have to allow an adult and a child.
2. An individual with a **handicap** is defined as a person with a *physical or mental impairment that substantially limits one or more major life activities*—for example,

substantial vision loss, limited mobility, serious hearing impairment, emotional illness, mental retardation, terminally ill AIDS patients, and the like. Protection also applies when the handicapped person is one who intends to reside in the dwelling with the buyer or renter or when someone associated with the buyer or renter has a handicap. Individuals with handicaps are given rights to reasonably modify public/common-use areas and the interior of their dwellings to make them accessible. This includes allowing seeing-eye dogs and hearing-ear dogs in "no pet" buildings. In addition, covered multifamily dwellings, first occupied after March 13, 1991, must be designed and constructed to accommodate handicapped individuals.

Exemptions and limitations to the handicapped status are:

a. Current illegal drug users are not considered handicapped, but recovered or recovering drug users, not currently using drugs are eligible.
b. Transvestites do not qualify as being handicapped.
c. There is also an exemption if the handicapped person poses a threat to the health or safety of anyone or poses a risk of substantial physical damage to the property of others. One valid example is an alcoholic who is violent when drunk. An example in which the exemption wouldn't apply is when a landlord is concerned about wheelchair nicks on the property.

The Fair Housing Act covers a broad range of discriminatory practices including the sale, rental, advertising, financing, and provisions of services in housing. There has been broad judicial interpretation of these prohibited practices, such as an interpretation that financing also covers insurance because one is prerequisite to the other.

Sexual harassment is also a violation of the Fair Housing Act. If a landlord, for example, promises to rent premises to a woman if she will engage in sexual acts with him, he is violating the Fair Housing Act.

Constitutional attacks upon both the Fair Housing Act and Section 1982 have failed. Also, plaintiffs need not elect between the two if they are covered by both laws. They can sue using both laws. It has also been held that the Fair Housing Act did not replace Section 1982. They are separate laws with different bases.

Relief and Remedies Under Section 1982 and the Fair Housing Act

Compensatory damages are allowed by the courts under *both Section 1982 and the Fair Housing Act.* These damages restore victims to the position they would have been in had the discriminatory act not occurred. The monetary value of the *real property loss* is a significant element, but *humiliation, embarrassment, loss of civil rights, and loss of self-esteem* are also compensatory damages to the plaintiff that are recognized and compensated by many federal courts.

Punitive damages also can be awarded. These are also money, but the amount is based upon the defendant's level of willful intent. The greater the intent, the greater the amount of money awarded. If the salesperson is the one who willfully discriminates, punitive damages are levied against him or her. To obtain a punitive damages award against the broker as well, the plaintiff–victim has to show that the broker authorized or ratified the salesperson's act. If this cannot be shown, the plaintiff–victim may be restricted to recovering only compensatory damages against the broker, as the principal of the salesperson. Because the broker is usually wealthier than the salesperson, the broker's exact conduct is of crucial importance in the worth of these cases. There is no ceiling on how large the punitive damage awards can be under either Section 1982 or the Fair Housing Act.

Real estate brokers may intervene in fair housing litigation with damage claims of their own. For instance, if sellers of listed realty wrongfully thwart a transaction by racial discrimination and the broker does not aid them, the broker should be able to recover his lost real estate commission from the sellers in court.

Equitable relief is sophisticated in its scope. *Equitable orders of the court* can run many pages in case decisions, requiring specific action or inaction by the defendant real estate broker and salespersons.

Restraining orders are also properly put on homes. This means that owners cannot sell them until the plaintiff–victim is given an opportunity to bid.

If the lawsuit asks only for equitable relief, there is no jury. If money damages are demanded, a jury may be used, upon timely request.

Sometimes the discriminatory activity occurs after a real estate purchase contract has been entered into. Then the court can order *specific performance* of that contract. The best case of this sort is when the owner of the real estate is solely (or also) involved in the discriminatory activity and can be compelled to perform as the other party in the real estate purchase contract.

Attorney's fees also are allowed the prevailing plaintiff under both Section 1982 and the Fair Housing Act.

The Federal Fair Housing Act also has *criminal provisions*. These cover intimidation, coercion, or threats made by brokers, salespeople, owners, landlords, or others who are subject to fair housing laws, against persons trying to obtain their fair housing rights. For example, after a Vietnamese family moves into a home in a white neighborhood, the home is fire-bombed. This is a federal crime. The Federal Bureau of Investigation investigates these crimes upon the victim's making a report. If the perpetrators are caught, they may be indicted, tried, and convicted of this serious federal crime.

Statutory Language of the Fair Housing Act

The Fair Housing Act is a huge piece of legislation. Key, statutory language that real estate agents need to remember in daily professional practice is contained in the following. Discrimination in the sale or rental of housing is:

1. To refuse to sell or rent after the making of a bona fide offer, or to refuse to negotiate for the sale or rental of, or otherwise make unavailable or deny, a dwelling to any person because of race, color, religion, national origin, sex, handicap, or family status.
2. To discriminate against any person in the terms, conditions, or privileges of sale or rental of a dwelling, or in the provision or services of facilities in connection therewith, because of race, color, religion, national origin, sex, handicap, or family status.
3. To make, print, or publish, or cause to be made, printed, or published any notice, statement, or advertisement, with respect to the sale or rental of a dwelling, that indicates any preference, limitation, or discrimination based on race, color, religion, national origin, sex, handicap, or family status, or an intention to make any such preference, limitation, or discrimination.

4. To represent to any person because of race, color, religion, national origin, sex, handicap, or family status that any dwelling is not available for inspection, sale, or rental when such dwelling is in fact so available.
5. For profit, to induce or attempt to induce any person to sell or rent any dwelling by representation regarding the entry or prospective entry into the neighborhood of a person or persons of a particular race, color, religion, national origin, sex, handicap, or family status.

Items 1 through 5 cover the most litigated areas in fair housing, as they cover steering and blockbusting (discussed in detail later in this chapter). The broad scope of Section 1982 also covers steering and blockbusting, but more implicitly. Use of the word "dwelling" in the Fair Housing Act makes commercial and industrial real estate exempt from it. Section 1982, however, covers those kinds of real estate. Vacant land sold for the construction of a dwelling is covered by both laws.

Exemptions to the Fair Housing Act

The Federal Fair Housing Act has a number of exemptions:

1. *Private clubs* that let only their members rent or occupy rooms.
2. *Religious organizations* permitting only members of the same religion to rent or occupy their dwelling units as long as the religion doesn't restrict its membership on the basis of race, color, or national origin.
3. The rental of rooms or units in *owner-occupied dwellings* of four or fewer units; no real estate broker can be used, nor can any discriminatory advertising be used.
4. The *sale or rental of single-family homes by private individual owners* without the use of a broker or public advertising. The owner can own no more than three such homes and may use the exemption only once every 24 months if the owner doesn't occupy the house or isn't classed as the most recent occupant.

Homeowners trying to fit into these exemptions within the Fair Housing Act have some formidable requisites to meet in marketing their house or multi-unit complex. They have to sell that realty without any professional services and without any form of public advertising. About the only way they can fit into the exemption is to put their house for sale on the market by word of mouth alone. Anything else probably destroys the exemption.

An even larger hurdle is that Section 1982 contains no exemptions, and the Ohio Civil Rights Law (discussed below) has fewer exemptions. If any of the above activities are done as an act of discrimination against a person entitled to protection under those laws, that person would sue using those laws instead. Thus, the exemptions are proving to be of no practical problem for plaintiff–victims, who simply use instead these other laws that are available.

Homeowners occasionally try to convince a real estate agent that they are exempt from the fair housing laws. At the time the agent lists the house for sale, the owners say, "Remember, we don't have to sell to blacks because we're selling an owner-occupied dwelling so we're exempt from the fair housing laws." Hopefully, the agent recognizes at once that these owners do not qualify for an exemption for the following reasons: They are using a real estate broker, the broker will use public advertising, and this is racial discrimination, which has no exemptions under Section 1982 and the Ohio Civil Rights Law. The best course for the real estate agent is to act as if there are no exemptions, because the exemptions are largely illusory in ultimate impact.

Department of Housing and Urban Development (HUD)

The Department of Housing and Urban Development, known as **HUD,** is the federal agency that administers the Fair Housing Act. An aggrieved party complainant can alternatively file a complaint with HUD. HUD has the power to *conciliate discrimination cases* and to *refer any pattern and practice* of discrimination cases to the U. S. Attorney General (as explained in detail under the Justice Department subhead). HUD also can *adjudicate and judicially enforce cases that cannot be resolved informally,* including awarding damages and imposing financial penalties in cases where discrimination is found. For HUD to initiate enforcement proceedings, it must find reasonable cause to believe that discrimination has occurred.

A complainant can file simultaneously with HUD and in court. This simultaneous activity frequently puts pressure upon the landlord, owner, real estate broker, or salesperson, especially if the court is disposed toward placing an injunction against the realty, forbidding any activity until HUD has a chance to act.

Table 11–1 compares and contrasts the Fair Housing Act with Section 1982.

State Legislation and the Ohio Civil Rights Law

State civil rights laws are modeled largely after the federal ones. The *state laws and agencies that are as stringent, or even more stringent, than the Federal Fair Housing Act and HUD* usually are deemed **substantially equivalent** to the Federal Fair Housing Act and HUD. Ohio's Civil Rights Act and its Civil Rights Commission are deemed substantially equivalent.

Some states also have county, city, or village fair housing laws, which vary greatly in scope and impact. Local governmental entities in Ohio do have fair housing laws. In effect, then, we are living under *layers of law* in fair housing—federal, state, county, and city fair housing laws.

Chapter 4112 contains the **Ohio Civil Rights Law,** which bars discrimination in housing based upon *race, color, religion, sex, ancestry, national origin, familial status, or handicap.* The law limits its applications to residential property or vacant land and otherwise covers almost all the same bases as the Federal Fair Housing Act. The Ohio law covers sales and rentals of housing and applies to brokers, salespeople, owners, landlords, and lenders. Religious, denominational, private or fraternal organizations have limited exemptions under which they can give preference to their own groups in providing housing.

Generally, asking questions about race, color, religion, sex, ancestry, handicap, or national origin is not allowed in connection with purchasing or leasing residential real property under the Ohio Civil Rights law. If the questions are asked in compliance with a monitoring device under the Civil Rights Law, however, such questions are allowable. Both steering and blockbusting (discussed later in this chapter) are specifically prohibited, as is discrimination in lending. Discrimination in the sale of fire, extended coverage, and homeowner's insurance also is a prohibited practice.

The Ohio Civil Rights Commission (OCRC) is the state agency charged with enforcing the Ohio law. Because Ohio has a substantially equivalent fair housing law, HUD can refer Ohio complaints filed with it to the OCRC. The OCRC can conciliate housing grievances after investigating a complaint. If the OCRC concludes

TABLE 11–1 Comparison of Fair Housing Act and Section 1982.

	FAIR HOUSING ACT	SECTION 1982
Factors	Race, religion, sex, national origin, handicap, family status.	Race only but under new, expansive definition, also covers most national origins and religions.
Age	Modern, from 1968 forward.	Older law, 1866.
Activities Covered	Housing discrimination and advertising, financing, and provisions of services in housing discrimination.	Housing discrimination; some judicial interpretation has extended to some other areas (e.g., financing).
Possible Defendants	Real estate brokers/salespersons, lending institutions, owners, landlords, lenders, appraisers, insurers.	Real estate brokers/salespersons, landlords, owners; possibly lenders and appraisers, and insurers.
Possible Plaintiffs	Individuals, classes, the United States through the Justice Department.	Individuals and classes.
Government Agencies	HUD, Justice.	None.
Damages	Compensatory, punitive.	Compensatory, punitive.
Attorney's Fees	Awarded to plaintiff usually.	Awarded to plaintiff usually.
Equitable Relief	Order of court, temporary restraining order, injunction.	Order of court, temporary restraining order, injunction.
Exemptions	1. A private club that lets only its members rent or occupy rooms. 2. A religious organization permitting only members of same religion to rent or occupy its dwelling units as long as religion doesn't restrict membership on basis of race or national origin. 3. Rental of rooms or units in owner-occupied dwelling of four or fewer units. 4. Sale or rental of single-family homes when occupied and sold by owner without use of broker and public advertising.	None.

that a discriminatory practice probably has been or is being committed, it can seek a temporary or permanent **injunction** or **temporary restraining order** (prohibiting, for example, a house from being sold for a certain amount of time). The OCRC can conduct a hearing and, upon finding a violation of the Ohio law, award to a prevailing complainant compensatory damages, limited punitive damages, and reasonable attorney's fees. This decision may be appealed through the court system. The OCRC can refer matters to the Ohio Attorney General's office to begin court proceedings whenever it believes, with reasonable cause, that protected civil rights are being denied to a person(s).

Alternatively, a complainant can bypass the OCRC and file a civil lawsuit in the court of common pleas. The court has the same remedies to apply as the OCRC does.

As discussed in Chapter 10, violation of fair housing laws is ground for suspension or revocation of an Ohio real estate license.

Restrictive Deed Covenants

Shelley v. Kraemer, the landmark United States Supreme Court case decided in 1948, held that *racially restrictive deed covenants are unenforceable in court.* Prior to this, some neighborhoods had inserted, as a private land-use control, a restriction of record in their deeds that no owner could sell to "non-whites." Until this case, **restrictive deed covenants** were considered legal and enforceable. Whole neighborhoods were, therefore, "protected" from integration. These restrictions are still written in some deeds or in the Volume of Records the deed is cross referenced to. They are of *no legal force and effect.* In trying to follow the restriction, one would be violating the fair housing laws.

Real estate agents who encounter the restrictions should realize that these will not protect them or the owners if they nevertheless discriminate in their handling the disposition of the realty held under that deed. It is easy to envision agents being presented with such a deed by the owner at the time they obtain the listing. The owner perhaps says, "Well, I don't have to follow these fair housing laws you're talking about because of what my deed says." The owner couldn't be more misinformed. The clause within his deed is unenforceable, and agents who proceed to follow the deed instead of the law are subject to liability.

Recorders' offices may affix notices in their Volumes of Deeds and/or Restrictions regarding the inability to enforce these provisions. Some do so already to avoid any charge of discriminatory activity. Many of the old covenants have expired or are about to expire, which will lessen the confusion as well.

Of course, realty currently constructed or being constructed can't have any restrictions that discriminate on any of the prohibited bases: race, religion, national origin, sex, handicap, or family status. If restrictive covenants are used, they violate the fair housing laws.

Specific Offenses and Proving Them

Blockbusting and steering are specific offenses that courts consistently hold to be violations of Section 1982, the Fair Housing Act, and the Ohio Civil Rights Law.

Blockbusting

Blockbusting is a practice whereby *real estate agents prey upon the racial fears of owners of housing in a given area,* or "block." Preying upon the fears of other protected classes of victims—that is, national origin, religion, sex, handicap, and family status—is also illegal. Racial violations, however, are the ones that seem to occur most frequently.

Preying on such fears typically results in "panic selling" in that community. The first white owner, for example, to sell to a minority purchaser usually makes the most money. The last owners to sell make the least. This is stressed by real estate agents who get listings in that area and then sell new homes in nonintegrated neighborhoods to the fleeing whites. The practice has been perpetrated not only by white members of the industry but also by fledgling black companies trying to establish a viable market. This has given rise to instances of brokers buying a house, moving a black family into it, and then using that event with the surrounding neighbors to induce them to sell.

Blockbusting used to be a profitable practice for real estate agents. Specifically, where formerly no potential sale existed, inducing panic-selling produced two potential sales—first, the sale of the home in the neighborhood being integrated and, second, the sale of another home to that fleeing owner in a nonintegrated neighborhood. Real estate agents were not totally to blame for this infamous practice. Owners often were pleased to hear this information, expecting the real estate industry to protect them from their own bigotry. In short, people were eager to play the blockbusting game until it became illegal.

FOR EXAMPLE

A real estate salesperson solicits an owner for the listing on his realty by saying, "I think I can still get you a good price for your house, but you have no time to lose. The neighborhood is changing quickly, and lots of homes are for sale already. You don't want to be the only one left, do you? . . . You've got two kids in the schools here. The schools are mixed now, and there's a lot of tension. You ought to sell now before your kids are in the minority. . . . Crime is up here since the neighborhood changed. You'd better get out of here while you can. You owe it to your family's safety."

In their statements, agents did not necessarily make explicit reference to race; rather, they used common terms alluding to it. The courts have held that this type of language is sufficient to indicate blockbusting, noting that if such sophisticated and subtle forms of discrimination were not violations, the fair housing laws would be meaningless. (This also applies to steering, discussed next.)

For the plaintiff–victim to win in court on a blockbusting case, he or she must prove that the defendant:

1. made an uninvited
2. solicitation to sell or rent a dwelling with a
3. profit motive and with the
4. intent to induce a sale by a
5. statement of solicitation that would convey to a reasonable person under the circumstances the
6. idea that members of a race (or other protected category of person) are or may be entering the neighborhood.

Steering

In a later, subtler development in housing discrimination litigation, **steering,** real estate agents *have made housing unavailable and tried to influence choice of housing based on any of the prohibited categories*. Note that although the most common type of steering involves the prohibited class "race," it can involve any of the prohibited classes, i.e., race, color, religion, sex, ancestry, national origin, familial status, or disability. The realty agents channel prospective buyers to particular neighborhoods based on their fears of neighborhoods being acceptable or not because people in the prohibited categories reside there.

FOR EXAMPLE

The real estate salesperson tells a prospective white purchaser: "You don't want to live in Z suburb. That's a mixed neighborhood. You should look at X and Y neighborhoods. The prices are higher in X and Y, but they're worth it since the neighborhoods are solid and safe." And, to an equally qualified, prospective black buyer, the salesperson says instead: "You don't want to live in X and Y neighborhoods. You'd be the first. You'd be more comfortable in Z, as your own kind are already there. Also, you'll get more house for your money." This example shows steering by trying to influence choice of housing based on race. Although no housing is actually made unavailable to either party, the conduct nonetheless is sufficient to violate the fair housing laws.

The type of steering in which housing is made unavailable follows this pattern: A prospective black purchaser asks the salesperson to see houses in X, Y, and Z suburbs. The agent tells him he has houses available only in Z suburb, the integrated one, when in fact he has housing available in all three.

Steering occurs in rental situations, too. A potential minority tenant may be told the unit is already rented. Or a heavier burden, such as a higher security deposit, is put on that rental applicant so he or she won't qualify. Steering also has been deemed to occur when a real estate company makes a practice of assigning black salespeople to offices within integrated neighborhoods and white salespeople within nonintegrated ones. This is steering even if the salespeople approve of this method of placement. Steering also may be done by advertising homes in a racially changing neighborhood in local newspapers usually bought by blacks only and not advertising those same homes in local newspapers bought by whites.

The best way a real estate salesperson can *avoid steering* charges is by *always shifting the burden of choosing a neighborhood back to prospective purchasers.* They should be shown realty anywhere they ask to be shown, eliminating neighborhoods by their own free will. If they refuse to look at housing in a given neighborhood, there is no fair housing violation.

Salespersons cannot do indirectly what they cannot do directly and still be in compliance with the law. For example, the salesperson cannot advise prospective purchasers to check out the neighborhood for themselves by parking outside a school building at the time it lets out to see what the mix of students is.

Table 11–2 summarizes the basic differences between blockbusting and steering.

Evidence

Violations of steering and blockbusting must be proven by the preponderance of the evidence by the plaintiff–victim against the defendant real estate licensee. Fair

TABLE 11–2 Comparison of blockbusting and steering.

BLOCKBUSTING	STEERING
1. Basis of offense: Realty agents prey upon fears of owners (e.g., obtain listings by racial scare tactics).	1. Basis of offense: Realty agents make housing unavailable or impermissibly influence choice of housing (e.g., show white purchasers one kind of housing and black purchasers another).
2. Case proven by the testimony of owners and, possibly, city officials.	2. Case proven by testimony of testers, both neutral and minority ones.
3. Corroborative testimony by fellow real estate agents who used to work with defendant realty agent.	3. Corroborative testimony by fellow real estate agents who used to work with defendant realty agent.
4. Weapon against blockbusting: A total ban against "For Sale" signs and/or a ban against owner solicitation by realty agents. (*Warning:* May violate the First Amendment.)	4. The presence of "For Sale" signs actually makes it more difficult for a realty agent to steer because would-be purchasers can easily see for themselves what is for sale and what isn't.

housing litigation utilizes three types of evidence: testing, testimony by other salespersons, and the statistical records of business.

Testing

Testing, also called auditing or **checking,** is a *monitoring process for compliance.* The key to discrimination is *inequality of treatment.* For example, a black tester works with the salesperson first, and subsequently a white tester works with the same salesperson. If the salesperson treats the black person differently from the white one, or unfavorably, there is evidence of discrimination. The white tester usually is sent through as a less qualified party, having less income and a less desirable credit rating than the black person, so economic inequality cannot be used as a valid defense. Most plaintiffs' attorneys run a credit check on their minority clients to avoid that defense at trial.

Courts like the "three tester sandwich" as a testing device. The white testers both precede and follow the black tester, to cross-check any inconsistencies in their treatment by real estate licensees, sellers, landlords, lenders, and so forth. Many organizations can afford only two—one white and one black—usually working in pairs as testers. This is sufficient evidence for most courts.

FOR EXAMPLE

> A black tester asks to be shown homes in X, Y, and Z suburbs. Only Z is integrated. The salesperson tells the black that houses are available only in Z. A white tester then is sent to the same salesperson. The white tester is equally or less financially able to purchase the same realty as the black tester. The white tester asks to be shown housing in X, Y, and Z suburbs and is shown housing only in X and Y. Housing has been made unavailable, and thus the fair housing laws have been violated. The testers will be witnesses to the discrimination, attesting to the difference in treatment for black and white prospects.

Sometimes testers are accompanied by another person, such as a "spouse" or a "friend." This is to provide a *corroborative witness* who can verify what happened between the testers and the salesperson.

Real estate agents have brought lawsuits against testers on many bases, including interference with economic relations, trespass, nuisance, implied contract, libel, and unjust enrichment. The courts have upheld testers' activities, however, saying that the fair housing laws cannot be effectively implemented without them. One masquerade the tester uses is to *pose as an out-of-towner,* knowing that agents are more apt to give detailed racial or other prohibited information to people from out-of-town who don't know which neighborhoods are "bad." Also, the testers know the agent is eager to have out-of-towners as prospective purchasers because they are so likely to purchase. The agent thinks this information will earn their trust and make them less likely to stray to another brokerage.

When organizations hire testers, they typically give them standard instructions that will help create a strong plaintiff–victim case and destroy standard defense strategies. These instructions usually tell the testers:

1. Take a witness along (frequently posing as a married couple).
2. Ask leading questions requiring yes or no answers, such as: "Will the owner finance the sale?" (Specific, hard evidence of disparate treatment is needed; i.e., a "yes" answer to one tester and a "no" answer to the other).
3. Don't invite any discussion of race or other prohibited categories (whether an agent's truthful response about these matters is illegal is an open issue, so that situation preferably is avoided).
4. Do not request an application (the agent's asking one tester and not the other to fill out an application is better evidence).

5. Do not sign anything or leave a deposit (because doing so makes the tester perhaps liable for entering into contractual agreements he or she intends not to perform or leads him or her beyond testing and into fraud and misrepresentation).
6. Immediately afterward, write notes of what happened during the test (cases this serious will be lost if the testers, as witnesses, fail to fully and accurately recall).
7. Do not arrive with or start the test within the presence of an actual homeseeker or other tester (a neutral setting is necessary so that no explanation is possible to explain the disparate treatment).

These instructions essentially let the real estate agent do most of the talking and negotiating. If the agent treats the testers disparately under these circumstances, powerful evidence exists that can be used against the salesperson. There is a negotiated agreement between HUD and the National Association of REALTORS®, called the Fair Housing Initiatives Program, in which civil rights organizations are to use these kinds of objective standards in the testing process.

Testimony by salespersons

Testimony by other salespersons, who once worked for the same broker and with the defendant salesperson or broker can provide evidence about the *defendant's past acts of discrimination.* Because of the high competition among salespeople and brokers, this testimony by the competition can be vicious and incriminating. The defendant will counter the testimony by trying to impeach the witness's credibility. This is done by showing bias against the defendant broker/salesperson because of their previous association and the fact that they are now competitors. The courts can and sometimes do overlook the bias and give this type of testimony credence, but not when it stands on its own without any other corroboration.

Statistical records

The **statistical records of business**—the *total record of listings and sales*—is reviewed to see if a pattern of discrimination emerges. For example, if the defendant has sold only to blacks in an integrated area and only to whites in a nonintegrated area, the record will create an inference that the agent has been doing what the plaintiff charges. To be probative evidence, statistics must be coupled with other evidence, typically testing episodes that the defendant failed. The statistical record alone is insufficient; there must be evidence of specific conduct that violates the fair housing laws.

Figure 11–1 is an example of incriminating evidence that could be used against a real estate agent.

Lending Protection

Discrimination in lending is also a violation of the Federal Fair Housing Act and Ohio's Civil Rights Law. Section 1982 has been interpreted as covering denials of real estate financing as well. Lending institutions are the defendants in these cases. The plaintiff is a victim, a member of one of the protected classes. As one example, a black plaintiff claims that funds are being denied because of the plaintiff's race or because of the racial composition of the community.

Redlining is the term used in the courts for the practice by *lending institutions of cutting off funds to an area because of the integrated make-up of the community.* The term came from drawing red lines on maps to show which areas would not be financed. An example of such a map is shown as Figure 11–2.

John and Dora Smithers
100 Anonymous
Anywhere, Ohio
231-5467

John is black and Dora is white. They are open as far as neighborhood but they inspire hostility wherever they go. Operating on the assumption that they will do better in an integrated, liberal neighborhood, I showed them houses solely in Tolerance Hts, as follows:

1) 200 Open mind Trail
Tolerance $90,000
John really liked this one but Dora hated the kitchen. Forget this one.

2) 300 aloof ave.
Tolerance $93,000
There are black neighbors on one side and whites on the other and neither was friendly to Smithers. That iced any interest.

3) 400 Avante Garde
Tolerance $85,000
The house is decorated in all purple & yellow. They both love it & want to put in an $80,000 bid. It figures with this weird couple.

FIGURE 11–1
Entry from salesperson's prospect book as evidence indicates that he or she is not keeping neutral records and is courting trouble with fair housing laws.

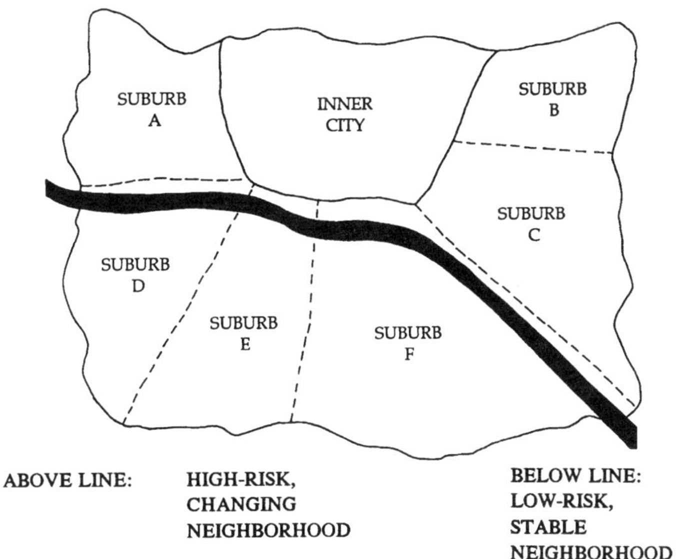

This is an example of how either a lender or insurer may decide, illegally, whether or not to grant loan money or insurance and at what rates. Making and using this type of map is strictly illegal. Real estate brokers and salespeople on occasion have used this type of map with potential buyers. Use of such a map is evidence of steering, a fair housing violation.

The big black line is the "red" line, so named because lenders used red marking pens when marking their maps in this violatory fashion.

FIGURE 11–2
Redlining map.

Lenders' perceptions of neighborhood declines often become *self-fulfilling prophecies*. One example of this is an industry-wide lending decision to withdraw from a certain market. The lenders in this situation typically perceive the integrated neighborhood as a risk and withdraw capital from that neighborhood. Demand then is frustrated by an inadequate supply of loan money. Under this chain of events, the neighborhood inevitably deteriorates. This process by lenders violates all applicable fair housing laws. The fair housing laws also are being linked to *hazard insurance denials* by insurance companies, as an extension of the lending prohibitions. The reasoning is that insurance and financing have a critical relationship, because insurance is a precondition to being granted financing for housing.

Another example of a typical lending-fair housing plaintiff–victim is a *woman* who claims her income is not being weighed the same as a man's comparable income. Real estate agents usually don't mind selling homes to women. Most sex-biased cases are directed more toward lending institutions that make *assumptions of a woman's inability to finance housing*—that she will be unable to secure middle- to upper-level employment and if she becomes pregnant, she will automatically resign her employment. This makes women seem to be a poor risk, and operating under these assumptions is illegal. Further, the lender must consider *alimony and child support* as income for obtaining a loan, as long as the payments are received regularly.

Some landlords illegally discriminate against women by refusing to rent to them. One illegal assumption that landlords make is that single or divorced women are morally loose and therefore undesirable as tenants.

JUSTICE DEPARTMENT

Another federal agency, the Justice Department, also litigates using the Federal Fair Housing Act. One way is that the attorney general in charge of housing is given discretion in determining whether a *pattern or practice of housing discrimination* is being perpetrated. If so, the attorney general can litigate against the offending parties. A single violation is not enough, however. Pattern and practice suits are of two varieties, both of which the Justice Department can pursue: (a) when only one real estate agent has engaged in multiple violations of the act or (b) when more than one real estate agent, in the same general area, have each violated the act (only once per person is enough).

The Justice Department can use only the Federal Fair Housing Act, not Section 1982, for pattern and practice suits. The Federal Bureau of Investigation does the investigative work on these cases, both before and after they are filed in court.

If the Justice Department wins a pattern and practice suit, the court orders the defendant (typically a real estate company, lending institution, or related entity) to do certain acts and refrain from other acts. This is called an *equitable order of the court*. The court will not, however, award money damages to the plaintiff (the Justice Department) in these lawsuits. If the defendant does not obey the court's equitable order, he or she may be found in contempt of court and fined or jailed.

The Justice Department also uses **consent decrees** frequently in these cases. For example, the defendant real estate broker *agrees to a form of conduct* the Justice Department has approved. This becomes an order of the court and the lawsuit is ended. The defendants must follow this order or else they are in contempt of court and subject to fine or imprisonment, or both.

FOR EXAMPLE

The various societies of real estate appraisers entered into a consent decree with the Justice Department. The Justice Department had alleged, in a pattern and practice suit brought under the Federal Fair Housing Act, that the appraisers calculated the fair market value of realty based partially on the changing racial balance within a neighborhood. Thus, if the neighborhood was substantially integrated, it appraised lower than if it were not. Books and manuals the appraisers used also factored the changing racial character of the neighborhood in calculating value. After this consent decree was entered into, appraisers began using neutral factors in appraising realty.

The changing character of a neighborhood cannot be used to lower the value of a piece of realty. Appraisers also now use books and manuals that suggest neutral techniques for conducting an appraisal. Examples of neutral and objective data for appraisals include comparable sales prices, employment stability, marketing time, rent levels, vacancy rates, and level of municipal services. These are all solid economic justifications for a particular pattern of appraisal and, therefore, legal.

A second way the Justice Department can be involved is in individual cases in court, where it can seek civil penalties up to $50,000 for a first offense and $100,000 for a subsequent offense. This comes about when HUD makes a finding of reasonable cause and files a charge. The complainant or respondent may elect to have the case proceed via a civil action in U. S. District Court, whereupon the Attorney General files the action and any aggrieved person is entitled to intervene as a matter of right.

STANDING

Standing is the legal concept of *who has the right to bring suit in court.* The plaintiff must have been injured in some specific way by violation of the law and must seek to protect an interest within the zone of interests to be protected by the fair housing laws.

In fair housing litigation, standing is even more complex. One issue, for example, was whether plaintiffs were barred from suing for racial discrimination if they were white. The answers from the courts have been that plaintiffs can be white but they still have to show injury to themselves by racial discrimination.

The U. S. Supreme Court has broadened standing in cases brought under the Fair Housing Act. White tenants in an apartment complex, for example, were allowed to sue the owner based on the tenants being *denied valuable interracial association.* Also, white testers or white residents could have standing if they could demonstrate that they were denied benefits of an integrated community by the blockbusting and steering that were occurring in their community. Because they were being deprived of interracial association, that was enough to give them standing. Essentially, these kinds of holdings have allowed “citizens’ suits” against real estate companies and other fair housing violators.

FIRST AMENDMENT RIGHTS

The **First Amendment** to the United States Constitution *guarantees freedom of speech, expression, association, and religion.* A vital First Amendment issue for real estate agents is: “What, if anything, can I say about race (or the other prohibited categories) while discussing a real estate transaction?”

Unfortunately, the court cases so far have involved real estate agents going far beyond any reasonable discussion of race or the other prohibited categories. A number of courts have found simple, factual responses by real estate salespeople not to be violations. The danger is in how the response may be interpreted. If it can be interpreted as encouragement to avoid integrated neighborhoods, the response is in violation of the fair housing laws. Therefore, it is recommended to the agent, especially since the U. S. Supreme Court has not directly ruled on this point, that *no discussion of race or other prohibited categories take place between a real estate agent and a prospective purchaser or seller.*

The purchaser's or owner's act of initiating the discussion of race with real estate agents does not insulate agents from liability under the fair housing laws if that initiation "sets them off" on a course of prohibited practices. The courts have held that initiation is not relevant; it is sufficient that the agent participated.

The First Amendment right of free expression was upheld in the U. S. Supreme Court's decision to *strike down community bans on "For Sale" signs,* even though the signs had been banned to prevent panic selling. Thus, real estate signs as commercial speech received First Amendment protection. That case, *Linmark Associates v. Township of Willingboro,* is one of the case studies set forth at the end of this chapter. The court held that prospective homeowners need a *free flow of data* to make their decisions on home selection. Home purchasers have the right to information about which and how many houses are for sale in a community. The court did not say real estate salespeople can give them this information, however.

This case did not make all sign bans unconstitutional, but, to preserve a sign ban, the community has to show that it serves a strong governmental interest. The Supreme Court left open the question of whether a ban would be upheld on a record disclosing a true condition of loss via resegregation and panic sales. The city at issue was not in this condition. A community that is experiencing heavy blockbusting or rapid resegregation would be the most likely to be able to use a sign ban.

Some communities persist in using sign bans even though they do not qualify under U. S. Supreme Court standards. Some cases throughout the country show these communities may be exposing themselves to damage liability. If a community is wrong in its belief that it can ban signs, a real estate company, owner, or other likely plaintiff may win significant money damages in court.

Antisolicitation bans are another important issue in First Amendment versus fair housing cases. This type of ban *prohibits real estate agents from contacting real estate owners, by phone or in person, about selling their realty.* The ban applies even though the real estate agent does not discuss race or any of the other prohibited categories and how these factors may affect the sale of real property.

Typically, the realty owners within such a community must *register their names on a not-to-be-solicited list* maintained by that community. Realty agents can travel to the community hall (or otherwise obtain this information) and scan the list. This can be an oppressive paperwork burden for the agent. Many agents are so discouraged that they decide to call no one in the community—which is precisely what the community was trying to achieve with the ban. If there were no owner registration whatsoever, the ban would seem to violate the First Amendment on its face; a court victory against the ban would be virtually certain.

Presumably owner registration keeps the antisolicitation ban from violating the First Amendment. The community asserts that the ban protects owners' rights to their privacy, while real estate agents argue that this privacy protection is a mere sham, disguising a violation to both the First and Fourteenth Amendments of the U. S. Constitution. (The Fourteenth Amendment to the United States Constitution guarantees equal protection of the laws.) Using the Fourteenth Amendment, therefore, a black real estate broker might argue that the ban's purpose is to prevent blacks from entering the city's housing market by cutting off the black broker's only access to the white real estate market—direct solicitation of the homeowner.

These antisolicitation bans have been struck down in some court cases throughout the country for being overbroad, even with owner registration. The U. S. Supreme Court has not yet rendered a decision on antisolicitation bans. If it does, real estate owners and agents should study the case carefully.

Fair Housing Poster

The *Equal Opportunity in Housing poster is required to be posted in real estate offices.* HUD regulations require such notice of equal housing opportunity. If a broker fails to display the poster, the failure can be considered *prima-facie* evidence of discriminatory practices. Figure 11–3 reproduces the poster that the Ohio Division of Real Estate issues to its licensees.

The poster also must be displayed at the place of business of those engaged in the financing of housing. Model homes and new residential construction sites, too, must display the poster. The poster used by REALTORS® is called the National Association Fair Housing Poster. It has all HUD's public notice information and notice requirements, as well as the code for equal opportunity that the National Association of REALTORS® has developed.

It Is Illegal To Discriminate Against Any Person Because Of Race, Color, Religion, Sex, Ancestry, Handicap, Familial Status, OR National Origin

- **In the sale or rental of housing or residential lots**
- **In advertising the sale or rental of housing**
- **In the financing of housing**
- **In the provision of real estate brokerage services**

Blockbusting is also illegal

The Broker and Sales Associates are licensed by the Division of Real Estate, Ohio Department of Commerce. The Division may be contacted for inquiries and complaints and for information on the Real Estate Recovery Special Account (Section 4735.12 of the Revised Code) as a source of satisfaction for unsatisfied civil judgments against a licensee.

OHIO DEPARTMENT OF COMMERCE
DIVISION OF REAL ESTATE
77 S. High St.
Columbus, Ohio 43266-0547
(614) 466-4100

PROVIDED BY THE OHIO REAL ESTATE COMMISSION

FIGURE 11–3
Fair housing poster.

AFFIRMATIVE ACTION AND THE AFFIRMATIVE MARKETING AGREEMENT

The purpose of affirmative action is to make up for the past wrongs of discrimination by the positive recruitment of minority groups into new and better levels of employment, higher education, and housing. Affirmative action has been around for a long time in employment and higher education, but the first program in housing was the Affirmative Marketing Agreement.

One immediate problem with implementing fair housing and affirmative action in the real estate profession was a conflict over what fair or equal housing really means. The two current interpretations are: (a) fair housing is **equal access** to housing; that a person, *regardless of who or what he or she is, can get housing anywhere and* (b) fair housing is really **dispersion of minorities** equally, that is, a certain *percentage of each group in each neighborhood.* REALTORS® favor the equal access approach, whereas city councils and housing boards prefer the dispersing minorities approach. This conflict of interpretation continues regarding the interpretation of the fair housing laws. *In affirmative action, the REALTORS® have been able to agree with HUD to follow equal access principles pursuant to the Affirmative Marketing Agreement.*

The National Association of REALTORS® entered into an **Affirmative Marketing Agreement** with HUD, *aimed at eliminating fair housing violations* by recruiting local boards of REALTORS® and their member REALTORS® as well. This agreement is still in effect. Those who joined the Affirmative Marketing Agreement were expected to:

- educate their affiliates or associates
- advertise to promote fair housing and equal opportunity in employment to achieve staff integration
- distribute pamphlets on fair housing to clients
- maintain records to monitor compliance and to otherwise act affirmatively to promote fair housing.

HUD sponsored and is a party to the Affirmative Marketing Agreement, its authority stemming from Section 809 of the Federal Fair Housing Law:

> The Secretary of Housing and Urban Development shall call conferences of persons in the housing industry and other interested parties to acquaint them with the provisions of this title and his suggested means of implementing it, and shall endeavor with their advice to work out programs of voluntary compliance and enforcement.

The Affirmative Marketing Agreement can be a useful device for REALTORS® in *defending* fair housing cases. If they are trying to comply with the agreement, a single violation is more easily viewed as an unintentional mistake rather than a violation of the fair housing laws.

The agreement has become broad as it has been renewed through the years. It now provides for program growth within HUD, as well as changes in the housing market, plus it complements HUD's efforts to enforce the Fair Housing Act. There is a more detailed definition of affirmative marketing so that it tries to achieve a condition in which individuals with similar financial resources and interests in the same housing market area have a like range of housing choices available to them regardless of their race, color, religion, sex, national origin, family status, or handicap.

LINMARK ASSOCIATES, INC. V. TOWNSHIP OF WILLINGBORO
431 US 85, 52 L Ed 2d 155, 97 S Ct 1614 (1977)

CASE STUDY FROM THE U. S. SUPREME COURT

Facts: To stop what was perceived as the flight of white homeowners from the Township of Willingboro, New Jersey, a racially integrated community, the township enacted an ordinance prohibiting the posting of "For Sale" signs in the township. The owner of certain real estate in the township and the real estate agent with whom the property had been listed for sale, having been prevented from placing a "For Sale" sign on the property because of the ordinance, brought an action in the United States District Court for the District of New Jersey to obtain declaratory and injunctive relief.

The evidence showed that, from 1970 to 1973, Willingboro's population rose by only 3 percent. More significantly, the white population actually declined by almost 2,000, a drop of more than 5 percent, whereas the non-white population grew by more than 3,000, an increase of approximately 60 percent. By 1973, non-whites constituted 18.2 percent of Willingboro's population.

Testimony from two real estate agents, two members of the Township Council, and three members of the Human Relations Commission showed all of them in agreement that a major cause in the decline in the white population was "panic selling"—the selling by whites who feared that the township was becoming all black and that property values would decline. Witnesses also testified that, in their view, "For Sale" and "Sold" signs were a major catalyst of these fears. One real estate agent testified that the reason 80 percent of the sellers gave for their decision to sell was, "the whole town is for sale, and I don't want to be caught in any bind."

Trial Court (District Court): Held the ordinance unconstitutional. The court said there was no evidence that whites were leaving Willingboro en masse as "For Sale" signs appeared but there was merely an indication that its residents were concerned that there might be a large influx of minority groups moving into Willingboro with the resultant effect of a reduction in property values.

United States Court of Appeals for the Third Circuit: Reversed the trial court's decision and upheld the ordinance, saying that Willingboro was experiencing "incipient" panic selling and that a fear psychology had developed.

Issue: Whether the banning of real estate "For Sale" signs by Willingboro violates the free speech protection of the First Amendment.

Held by the United States Supreme Court: Reversed the Court of Appeals, holding that the ordinance violates the First Amendment, notwithstanding that the ordinance restricts only one method of communication, because it had not been established that the ordinance was needed to assure that the township remained an integrated community, and because, in any event, the ordinance impaired the flow of truthful and legitimate information.

Although in theory sellers remained free to employ a number of different alternatives, in practice realty is not marketed through leaflets, sound trucks, demonstrations, and the like. The options to which sellers realistically are relegated—primarily newspaper advertising and listing with real estate agents—involve more cost and less autonomy than "For Sale" signs, are less likely to reach persons not deliberately seeking sales information, and may be less effective media for communicating the message conveyed by a "For Sale" sign in front of the house to be sold. The alternatives, then, were far from satisfactory.

The Willingboro Township Council acted to prevent its residents from obtaining certain information. That information, which pertains to sales activity in Willingboro, is of vital interest to Willingboro residents, because it may bear on one of the most important decisions they have a right to make: where to live and raise their families. The council sought to restrict the free flow of these data because it fears that otherwise homeowners will make decisions inimical to what the council views as the homeowners' self-interest and the corporate interest of the township: They will choose to leave town.

The council's concern was not with any commercial aspect of "For Sale" signs—with offerors communicating offers to offerees—but instead with the substance of the information communicated to Willingboro citizens. If dissemination of this information can be restricted, every locality in the country can suppress any facts that reflect poorly on the locality, as long as a plausible claim can be made that disclosure would cause the recipients of the information to act "irrationally."

The court said it did not leave Willingboro defenseless in its effort to promote integrated housing. The township remained free to continue the process of education it had already begun. It could give widespread publicity—through "Not for Sale" signs and other methods—to the number of whites remaining in Willingboro. It could create inducements to retain individuals who were considering selling their homes. Despite the importance of achieving the asserted goal of promoting stable, integrated housing, the ordinance could not be upheld on the ground that it promoted an important governmental objective, because it does not appear that the ordinance was needed to achieve that objective and, in any event, the First Amendment disables the township from achieving that objective by restricting the free flow of truthful commercial information.

CLASS DISCUSSION TOPIC

Measure communities that have sign bans in your region against the standards in this case. How do each of those communities compare to the township of Willingboro's fact pattern? Could those communities' sign bans survive a court challenge?

Note: The next two cases were companion cases—related cases decided together by the U. S. Supreme Court.

CASE STUDY FROM THE U. S. SUPREME COURT

SAINT FRANCIS COLLEGE V. MAJID GHAIDAN AL-KHAZRAJI
481 US 604, 95 L Ed 2d 582, 107 S Ct 2022 (1987)

Facts: A United States citizen, born in Iraq and a member of the Muslim faith, was an associate professor at private St. Francis College, located in Pennsylvania. In 1978 the college denied his request for tenure. Subsequently the professor filed a complaint against the college in court. He alleged that the college and its tenure committee violated a statute under the 1866 Civil Rights Act providing that "all persons within the jurisdiction of the United States shall have the same right to make and enforce contracts as is enjoyed by white citizens."

United States District Court, Western District of Pennsylvania: Ruled that an action could be maintained because the complaint alleged denial of tenure because the professor was of Arabian race. Another judge on the court construed the complaint as asserting discrimination on the basis of only national origin and religion and granted summary judgment for the college.

United States Court of Appeals, Third Circuit: Held that, although under current racial classifications Arabs are Caucasians, the professor could maintain his claim under one of the statutes of the 1866 Civil Rights Act.

Issue: Can an Arab-American be entitled to protection under the 1866 Civil Rights Act as a non-white?

Held by the United States Supreme Court: Congress intended to protect from discrimination identifiable classes of persons who are subjected to intentional discrimination solely because of their ancestry or ethnic characteristics, regardless of whether such discrimination would be classified as racial in terms of modern scientific theory. A distinctive physiognomy is not essential for a person to qualify for protection. The professor would be able to make out a case if he could prove he were subject to intentional discrimination based on the fact that he was born an Arab, rather than solely on the place or nation of his origin or his religion.

Elaborating, the court said that the understanding of race in the 19th century was different. All those who might be deemed Caucasian today were not thought to be of the same race at the time the statutes under the 1866 Civil Rights Act became law. Dictionaries and encyclopedias from the 19th century both define race differently than the way it is defined today. Not until the 20th century did dictionaries began referring to the Caucasian, Mongolian, and Negro races or to race as involving divisions of humankind based upon different physical characteristics. Nineteenth-century dictionaries referred to race as "descendants of a common ancestor." Nineteenth-century encyclopedias referred to race in terms of ethnic groups.

SHAARE TEFILA CONGREGATION V. COBB
481 US 615, 95 L Ed 2d 594, 107 S Ct 2019 (1987)

CASE STUDY FROM THE U. S. SUPREME COURT

Facts: The outside walls of a synagogue in Silver Spring, Maryland, were painted with anti-Semitic slogans, phrases, and symbols. The congregation and some individual members brought suit, alleging that the desecrators of the synagogue had violated Section 1982 of the 1866 Civil Rights Act. That Section guarantees all citizens of the United States the same right as is enjoyed by "white citizens" to inherit, purchase, lease, sell, hold, and convey real and personal property.

United States District Court, District of Maryland: Dismissed the claim.

United States Court of Appeals, Fourth Circuit: Held that discrimination against Jews is not racial discrimination and Section 1982 was not intended to apply to situations in which a plaintiff is not a member of a racially distinct group but is merely perceived to be so by defendants.

Issue: Whether Jews are allowed to claim protection, using racial discrimination as their basis, under Section 1982.

Held by the United States Supreme Court: To make out a charge of racial discrimination under Section 1982, it is necessary to allege that defendants were motivated by racial hostility and that such hostility was directed toward the kind of group that Congress intended to protect when it passed the statute. Regardless of whether Jews are considered to be a separate race by modern standards, Jews are not foreclosed from stating a cause of action under Section 1982 against other members of what is considered to be part of the white or Caucasian race, because Jews constituted a group of people that was considered to be a distinct race at the time that Section 1982 was adopted and were hence within the intended protection of the statute. The court referred to the Saint Francis College opinion for its rationale.

CITY OF EDMONDS V. OXFORD HOUSE, INC.
1995 WL 283468 (U.S.) (1995)

CASE STUDY FROM THE U. S. SUPREME COURT

Facts: Oxford House, Inc. operated a group home in a neighborhood zoned for single-family residences in Edmonds, Washington. The group home housed 10 to 12 adults recovering from alcoholism and drug addiction. The City of Edmonds cited the owner and a resident of the house, charging violation of the city's zoning code. The code provides that the occupants of single-family dwelling units must compose a "family." The city code defines family as "persons (without regard to number) related by genetics, adoption, or marriage, or a group of five or fewer unrelated persons."

Oxford House was relying on the Fair Housing Act (FHA), which prohibits discrimination in housing against persons with handicaps. Discrimination covered by the FHA includes refusals to make reasonable accommodations in rules and policies when such accommodations may be necessary to afford the handicapped equal opportunity to use and enjoy a dwelling.

Edmonds sued Oxford House in federal court, seeking a declaration that the FHA does not constrain family definition rule of the city's zoning code. Oxford House countersued under the FHA, charging the city with failure to make a "reasonable accommodation."

District Court: Held that the city's zoning code defining family is exempt from the FHA under 42 U.S.C. Sec. 3607 (b) (1) as a "reasonable restriction regarding the number of occupants permitted to occupy a dwelling."

Court of Appeals for Ninth Circuit: Reversed the District Court, holding that the absolute exemption in Section 3607 (b) (1) is inapplicable.

Issue: Whether a provision in the City of Edmonds' zoning code qualifies for a Section 3607 (b) (1) complete exemption from FHA scrutiny.

Held by the United States Supreme Court: Edmonds' zoning code definition of the term "family" is not a maximum occupancy restriction that is exempt from the FHA under Section 3607 (b) (1).

The defining provision at issue describes who may compose a family unit; it does not proscribe "the maximum number of occupants a dwelling unit may house." The court held that Section 3607 (b) (1) does not exempt prescriptions of the family-defining kind, that is, provisions designed to foster the family character of a neighborhood. Instead, the absolute exemption in 3607 (b) (1) removes from the FHA's scope only total occupancy limits, i.e., numerical ceilings that serve to prevent overcrowding in living quarters. Edmonds' zoning code provision describing who may compose a family is not a maximum occupancy restriction exempt from the FHA under Sec. 3607 (b) (1). It remains for the lower courts to decide whether Edmonds' actions against Oxford House violate the FHA's prohibitions against discrimination set out in Sections 3604 (f) (1) (A) and (f) (3) (B). For the reasons stated, the judgment of the United States Court of Appeals for the Ninth Circuit is affirmed.

HYPOTHETICAL SITUATIONS

QUESTION

1. Out-of-town prospective purchasers come into your real estate office and tell you they want to buy a home five to 10 years old, a colonial, on an acre or more of land, in the $150,000 price range. Are there any potential fair housing problems?

ANSWER

The out-of-town masquerade is a frequent one donned by testers. Therefore, you should concentrate on showing them any available housing that meets any of the criteria they give. As they shift price or other nonracial criteria (or other prohibited categories), show housing anywhere that meets these other criteria. In one case, many testers posed as out-of-towners. The real estate salespersons inevitably gave them detailed analyses about which neighborhoods they should or should not look at based on racial and ethnic criteria. This was usually the first item of conversation between the salespeople and testers. Salespeople even marked maps showing which areas to stay out of because of race.

In all cases your best protection against failing a fair housing "test" is to follow fair housing practices.

2a. A prospect asks you to show him a house or houses for about $100,000 in the most expensive suburb in your area, where the average price for a home is $350,000. The prospect is black. As the salesperson, what should you do? **QUESTION**

b. Same situation, but the prospect is white.

ANSWER *When given the above situation, most real estate salespersons, knowing that homes in the suburb are that high-priced, simply say there is no such thing and let it go at that. Technically that is all right legally, but it is not a very good sales technique or preventive law. To convince purchasers that there is no such thing, and thus win their confidence, it would be better to show them that no such thing exists. This could be done by phone by giving a summation of what is available in that suburb and at what prices. Follow that up with: "Is there any place else you'd consider? I can show you homes anywhere you wish."*

These sentences, preceded by your actions, clearly avoid any steering problems. You've shifted the burden onto the prospective purchasers to pick a neighborhood(s). Your job is to sell them a house wherever they select one. If you're being tested, the tester probably will back off at this point, because you've passed. If bad prospects, they too will back off. The only persons you can be left with are those who want to purchase a home—not a bad situation. In both the situations the answer is that you behave the same toward both black and white prospects.

3. Rodney sells most of his homes by telling owners that they'd better accept the offer from Rodney's customer, as it's the "best you're likely to get, since the neighborhood is going down fast." Another of Rodney's sales tricks is to drive potential purchasers past the school buildings when school lets out so they can "see for yourselves" whether the neighborhood is racially mixed or not. What law(s) is Rodney violating? What can happen to Rodney? **QUESTION**

ANSWER *Rodney is in violation of Section 1982, the Fair Housing Act, the Ohio Civil Rights Law, and the Ohio Real Estate license law. When Rodney worked on the owners, he was blockbusting—trying to induce a sale by preying on the owner's racial prejudices and fears. Whether this practice works on the owner or not is irrelevant. The courts recognize that phrases and practices meaning the same thing as race are violative. "Going down fast" is a classic blockbusting phrase. Rodney's driving past the schools so the purchasers can "see for yourselves" is a classic steering practice. Rodney thereby is encouraging the purchasers to select housing based on racial preferences. The expression "mixed" is recognized as meaning integrated. Rodney can be sued in court, complaints may be filed with HUD, the OCRC can file against him, and he can lose his real estate license after an adjudicatory hearing before the Ohio Real Estate Commission.*

4. It is your real estate company's policy for salespersons to go in person to homes that are advertised "For Sale by Owner." Your purpose is to convince the owner to sell through your realty company. One house that you go to is located in a suburb from which a fair housing suit emanated because so many white people were trying to sell their homes as black families moved into the community. How might your actions be interpreted legally by your going to this house to solicit a listing? **QUESTION**

ANSWER *A "red light" should go off in the salesperson's head when encountering the above situation. That warning should be that this community is already sensitive* *to fair housing violations. The fair housing suit and the reason behind it are the items of information that should warn the salesperson. Although the salesperson's actions here are evidently racially neutral, she should be careful not to use any coded language. For instance, if she says, "You ought to sell now. This house has hit its peak price," it could be inferred that the salesperson is really saying, "Get out while the getting's good."*

The factual situation, however, tells us that the owner already wants to sell, and the salesperson should concentrate on why the owner should use her brokerage rather than another brokerage or the owner's own efforts. Sell your professional skills; do not play on the owner's fears. It would be very easy, with carelessness, to turn this into a blockbuster. If the neighborhood has an antisolicitation ban in effect, check with your broker and attorney before violating the ban. All it takes to violate the ban is to contact the owner. Check the community's registration list, too; if the owner's name is not listed, the ban usually does not apply.

QUESTION 5a. White prospective purchasers come in and ask to see three houses (they have written down the addresses of ones for sale) over in the community of Paradise. The community is integrated, but the prospects have not asked you about the make-up of the community. What do you do?

b. Same situation, but the prospects do ask you about the mix of the community.

c. Same situation, but the prospects are black and Paradise is not integrated. The black prospects do not ask you what the neighborhood is like.

d. Same situation as 3, but the black prospects do ask you what the mix of Paradise is and, furthermore, ask if they will feel safe and acceptable there.

ANSWER *This problem and its three subproblems all require the same action by the salesperson. The salesperson's role does not include giving any information on the racial composition of the neighborhood. Because all purchasers are to be treated alike, do not give this information to any of them. Also, whether they ask for the information or not makes no difference, because the courts generally have held that who initiates the discussion is irrelevant.*

QUESTION 6. Two salespersons present offers on a home listed for sale with Broker D. The offers are identical in price. Salesperson A from Broker B says to the owners, "You should take my offer because my purchasers are white, and the other purchasers are black." Salesperson C from Broker D indeed does have an offer from black purchasers. Salesperson C also listed the home on behalf of Broker D. What should Salesperson C do, if anything?

ANSWER *Salesperson C should tell the owners that Salesperson A may be violating the fair housing laws and that they, too (the owner and Salesperson C), may be violating them to proceed any further. Thus, the owners should accept neither offer until after consulting with their own attorney, after Salesperson C advises Broker D of the violation, after Broker D consults with an attorney, and after the owner's attorney and Broker D's attorney consult with one another.*

QUESTION 7. You are looking over your sales record for the past five years and find that your total sales records show you have sold homes to blacks in only integrated areas and to whites in only nonintegrated areas. You are sued for steering. How can the above be used as evidence against you?

ANSWER *Statistics of your sales record alone usually are not enough for anyone to sue you. They are the weakest evidence but, coupled with testing and damaging testimony of other agents about your past practices, they can lose the case for you. This is because the judge or jury will create an automatic inference: "He must* *be doing what they say he is. His sales record supports it." If the salesperson kept complete records pursuant to the Affirmative Marketing Agreement, however, those records might show the prospects' choosing neighborhoods in this pattern without the salesperson's advice. This is a good defense for the agent.*

Caution: Do not keep racial records on your showings. These have been used against agents in cases because it is claimed they show bias. If you are subject to the Affirmative Marketing Agreement, however, you may be keeping records that show the purchaser's protected class status (or not). It is lawful to use such a form for implementing the Affirmative Marketing Agreement. Also, do not recruit in reverse; that is, do not show blacks in nonintegrated areas only and whites in integrated areas only, as that is also steering. Motive does not count, and probably would be dangerous if it did.

Summary of Content

1. Fair housing laws were passed to create equal, integrated opportunity in housing.
2. The 1968 U. S. Court case of *Jones. v. Mayer* prohibited private racial discrimination in the sale, lease, or transfer of realty and personalty under Section 1982 of the 1866 Civil Rights Act. Later cases enlarged the class of plaintiff–victims by holding that the test of who is white or not was to be determined by who would have been considered non-white back in 1866, the year Congress passed Section 1982.
3. The federal Fair Housing Act, passed in 1968 and liberally amended through the years, is comprehensive and modern legislation establishing the basis for fair housing throughout the United States. It prohibits discrimination in housing based upon a person's race, religion, national origin, sex, handicap, or family status.
4. The Fair Housing Act has some exemptions from its coverage, whereas Section 1982 has no exemptions.
5. The Department of Housing and Urban Development (HUD) administers the Fair Housing Act and adjudicates discrimination cases wherein it has the power to impose financial penalties upon fair housing violators.
6. A plaintiff–victim instead might use the Ohio Civil Rights Law and the Ohio Civil Rights Commission, instead of the Fair Housing Act or HUD, because the Ohio law is deemed substantially equivalent to the federal one.
7. We are living under "layers of law" in fair housing; there are federal, Ohio, and local government fair housing laws in effect.
8. The United States Supreme Court, in *Shelley v. Kraemer,* held that racially restrictive deed covenants are unenforceable in court. Under the fair housing laws, placing restrictive covenants on real property involving any of the prohibited bases of discrimination is unlawful.
9. Compensatory damages—money that will restore the plaintiff–victim to the position he or she would have been in had the discriminatory act not occurred—are allowed under Section 1982, the Fair Housing Act, and the Ohio Civil Rights Law. Attorney's fees can be awarded to the prevailing party. Punitive damages—additional money—might also be allowed if willful intent on the part of the defendant agent/owner/lender/appraiser can be shown.

10. Blockbusting is the illegal, discriminatory practice of real estate agents' preying upon the racial (or other prohibited) fears of owners in a given community or "block." It typically results in panic selling within that community.
11. Steering is the illegal, discriminatory practice in which real estate agents make housing unavailable, as well as try to influence choice of housing, based on any of the prohibited categories (the most common one being race).
12. Steering and blockbusting violations must be proven by preponderance of the evidence by the plaintiff–victim against the defendant real estate agent.
13. Testing is one kind of evidence wherein minority and white persons (or male and female persons, or other prohibited categories) are hired to pose as purchasers. They separately use the services of a real estate salesperson to check whether they are treated differently. If they are, inequality of treatment has occurred, which is the essence of discrimination violations.
14. Another type of evidence is testimony by other real estate licensees, who once worked for the same broker and with the salesperson, about the broker/salesperson-defendants' past acts of discrimination.
15. A final type of evidence is a review of the real estate agent's statistical record of business.
16. Discrimination in lending violates the Fair Housing Act, Section 1982, and the Ohio Civil Rights Law.
17. Redlining is a term used in the courts regarding lending institutions' practice of cutting off funds to a community because of the community's integrated housing.
18. The U. S. Justice Department litigates pattern and practice violations of the Federal Fair Housing Act, enters into consent decrees, and can bring actions on behalf of individuals as authorized by HUD.
19. Standing (who has the right to sue in court) has been interpreted broadly under the fair housing laws. For example, a white plaintiff who has been denied interracial association has standing to sue under the fair housing laws.
20. The First Amendment to the U. S. Constitution guarantees freedom of speech and expression. A serious, unresolved issue revolves around whether and how much a real estate agent's speech can be censored in fair housing situations.
21. The U. S. Supreme Court did strike down a citywide real estate "For Sale" sign ban that restricted the free flow of data and thereby violated the First Amendment.
22. It is unresolved, under the First Amendment, whether antisolicitation bans, as imposed by cities, are or are not constitutional. These bans prohibit real estate licensees from contacting owners about selling their realty.
23. The Equal Opportunity in Housing poster must be posted in real estate offices.
24. REALTORS® believe that fair housing means equal access to housing; that a person, regardless of who or what he or she is, can get housing anywhere. By contrast, city councils, or housing boards, favor the interpretation that fair housing is a dispersion of minorities equally throughout all neighborhoods.
25. In affirmative action, the REALTORS® agreed with HUD to follow equal access principles under the Affirmative Marketing Agreement. The agreement recruited both local boards of REALTORS® and their member REALTORS®. Signatories educate their associates in fair housing, advertise to promote fair housing as well as to attract minorities into entering the profession, distribute fair housing booklets to clients, and maintain in-house records to monitor compliance.

REVIEW QUESTIONS

1. Affirmative Action in housing requires:
   a. that quotas be established in neighborhoods
   b. that black male salespersons be recruited in higher ratios than white female salespersons
   c. that housing be sold to blacks for less money to make up for past wrongs
   d. promoting equal opportunity in housing

2. The landmark U. S. Supreme Court case of 1968 regarding fair housing and racial discrimination is known as:
   a. *Norman v. Bates*
   b. *Jones v. Mayer*
   c. *Black v. Missouri*
   d. *St. Francis College v. Shaare Tefila Congregation*

3. Blockbusting is directed at:
   a. owners
   b. purchasers
   c. real estate companies
   d. real estate agents

4. When real estate licensees contact owners about selling their real properties without observing the community's antisolicitation ban, they are:
   a. steering
   b. checking
   c. redlining
   d. possibly lawfully asserting their First Amendment rights

5. Steering by a real estate agent results in placing purchasers in a community that:
   a. they can afford
   b. they will fit into by race, national origin, sex, religion, family status, or handicap, as judged and selected by the agent
   c. they have requested
   d. is not integrated

6. In its use of steering, a real estate company aims to:
   a. make housing in nonintegrated areas unavailable to blacks
   b. keep blacks in substantially integrated housing
   c. keep values in white neighborhoods stable and high
   d. all of the above

7. When real estate agents show prospective black purchasers homes in only integrated suburbs, they are probably:
   a. steering
   b. blockbusting
   c. redlining
   d. affirmative action recruiting

8. When real estate agents use fear tactics to try to induce people to put their home on the market for sale, they may be guilty of the discriminatory practice known as:
   a. steering
   b. blockbusting
   c. redlining
   d. affirmative action recruiting

9. Women typically encounter their fair housing legal problems with:
   a. real estate salespeople not wanting them in neighborhoods
   b. owners not wanting to sell to them
   c. lenders not wanting to give their income full weight
   d. husbands who don't want them involved in the transactions

10. The Fair Housing Act has this federal agency involved in its administration and enforcement:
    a. Health, Education and Welfare (HEW)
    b. Internal Revenue Service (IRS)
    c. Housing and Urban Development (HUD)
    d. Equal Employment Opportunity Commission (EEOC)

11. If a seller tells a realty agent that he expects her to observe the racial restriction written in his deed, the one stating that he cannot sell to non-whites:
    a. the broker should not accept this listing
    b. there is not a problem until the seller actually turns down an offer from a black purchaser
    c. the seller's deed restrictions make this a lawful activity
    d. this process is lawful because fair housing laws do not pertain to sellers, only to real estate salespeople

12. The Justice Department litigates:
    a. for an individual
    b. as a party plaintiff
    c. against a pattern and practice of discrimination
    d. all of the above

13. Section 1982 covers discrimination based on:
    a. sex
    b. a very expanded interpretation of race
    c. handicap
    d. family status

14. Section 1982 exempts the following persons from suit:
    a. REALTORS® who have entered into the Affirmative Marketing Agreement
    b. owners selling their own homes
    c. landlords renting property that they also live in
    d. none of the above

15. Black resident B of city A sues the city when he finds out it has a policy of maintaining its ratio of 75 percent whites and 25 percent blacks by recruiting prospective purchasers into the city through real estate agents who have agreed to maintain this ratio:
    a. this is reverse steering, which is perfectly legal and B will lose the case
    b. this does not injure B in any way, and he will not have any standing to sue
    c. this stigmatizes B and might give him sufficient standing to sue city A
    d. city A can sue B for trying to ruin the status quo

16. If a seller makes it a condition of granting the listing that the broker tell no one about the listing except those persons the seller can screen beforehand:
    a. there is not a problem until the seller actually screens out a prospective black purchaser
    b. the broker should not accept this listing
    c. if the seller has a deed restriction supporting this screening process, it is a lawful activity
    d. this process is lawful because fair housing laws do not pertain to owners/sellers of real estate, only to real estate agents

17. To avoid steering problems, a real estate salesperson should:
    a. let the prospective purchaser choose the neighborhood
    b. suggest neighborhoods by the make-up of the schools
    c. ask owners in prospective purchaser's presence if any blacks have moved in
    d. call city hall to get a statistical breakdown of racial groups in the neighborhood

18. Evidence used in fair housing cases is:
    a. testing/checking
    b. testimony by formerly associated, fellow agents
    c. statistical sales records of defendant
    d. all of the above

19. The Ohio Civil Rights law does not cover which of the following:
    a. handicapped
    b. homosexual
    c. race
    d. sex

20. The Ohio Civil Rights Law has:
    a. no exemptions like Section 1982
    b. exactly the same exemptions as the Fair Housing Act
    c. its own exemptions, which bear no relationship to any other law
    d. its own exemptions, some of which are the same as the Fair Housing Act's exemptions

21. The Ohio agency directly charged with enforcing the Ohio Civil Rights Law is:
    a. the Ohio Civil Rights Commission
    b. the Department of Commerce
    c. the Ohio Real Estate Commission
    d. the Equal Housing Commission

22. Section 1982 has which of the following exemptions:
    a. no commercial real estate is covered
    b. no industrial real estate is covered
    c. no rental real estate is covered
    d. it contains no exemptions

23. The U. S. Supreme Court case that upheld a "For Sale" sign and struck down a community sign ban is:
    a. *Jones v. Mayer*
    b. *Linmark Associates v. Township of Willingboro*
    c. *Shaare Tefila Congregation v. Cobb*
    d. *Brown v. Board of Education*

24. This person is not covered by the Fair Housing Act, Section 1982, or the Ohio Civil Rights Law:
    a. homosexual
    b. handicapped person
    c. woman
    d. child

25. Appraisers cannot validly use these data on a subject community:
    a. entry of blacks into its population
    b. vacancy rate
    c. physical condition of the property
    d. physical condition of surrounding properties

ANSWER KEY

1. d
2. b
3. a
4. d
5. b
6. d
7. a
8. b
9. c
10. c
11. a
12. d
13. b
14. d
15. c
16. b
17. a
18. d
19. b
20. d
21. a
22. d
23. b
24. a
25. a

12
CONTROL AND REGULATION OF LAND

KEY TERMS

aesthetic reasons
Americans with Disabilities Act
appropriate (take)
conforming use
cumulative zoning
eminent domain
environmental law
exclusionary zoning
exclusive zoning
Fifth Amendment
Fourteenth Amendment
incentive zoning
Interstate Land Sales Full Disclosure Act
National Environmental Policy Act
nonconforming use
Planned Unit Development (PUD)
point-of-sale inspection
police power
property report
pyramid zoning
rezoning
spot zoning
variance
zero lot line
zoning

AT THIS JUNCTURE, after the first 11 chapters, we have covered the matters that real estate salespeople must handle almost daily. We hope the information gained in these chapters will be one of several factors preventing the student from becoming a "court statistic." Some other factors that can make a critical difference are the quality of the training program provided by the broker with whom the salesperson associates and the quality of the continuing education requirements the salesperson will have to meet.

In this chapter and the ones that follow we will cover legal areas the average real estate salesperson will not usually handle daily. From time to time, however, problems arise in these areas, and the salesperson who is informed about these matters may be able to "make that deal" or avoid a lawsuit by having the additional knowledge. Compare and contrast the public controls over land discussed next with previously discussed private controls over land—deed restrictions and restrictions of record in Chapter 5 and condominium and cooperative restrictions in Chapter 4.

ZONING

Zoning is the most common type of land-use control by the public that real estate salespersons will encounter. Generally, local communities have the power to enact legislative controls over the uses that can be made of their land. *Zoning is a local government function,* not a state or federal one, but the enabling legislation that gives local government the power to enact zoning ordinances does come from the state. Ohio's zoning laws are enacted by any one of the state's applicable local government forms: county, village, city or township.

Zoning does not regulate the sale of rights but, rather, the use of land. To be constitutional, zoning must be a reasonable exercise of the community's police power with specific, clear provisions promoting the public health, safety, and general welfare. It must apply equally and in a nondiscriminatory manner to all real property.

If landowners bring a lawsuit against the community, the landowners bear the burden of proving that the community behaved in an arbitrary and unreasonable fashion in formulating its zoning scheme. This standard comes from the equal protection of the law clause in the Fourteenth Amendment to the U. S. Constitution. The courts therefore presume the community's zoning scheme to be a rational one.

Uses of Land

The community designates what each area of land is to be used for. Communities usually prefer, and thus consider, the *highest and best use* of real property to be *single-family residential.* Then, in declining order, come multifamily, light commercial, heavy commercial, light industrial, and heavy industrial. Modern zoning has expanded categories of use so, instead of just "light commercial" there is "commercial office space." Nowadays a community might have 20 categories of zoned uses instead of just four or five. When a city has the categories of, for example, "shopping center district" and "local retail business district," and each of those districts does not allow the other, these classes of use are legal. They can bear a rational relationship to a city's complete, underlying zoning plan and not be arbitrary. Zoning also covers lot size for building, setback requirements, height of buildings, and numerous other controls.

Cumulative Versus Exclusive Zoning

Many communities use the oldest type of zoning scheme: **cumulative zoning** or **pyramid zoning.** This works as follows. If an area that formerly was zoned single-family residential is rezoned multifamily, then both single- and multifamily housing can be built there. If it is then rezoned commercial, then single- and multifamily plus commercial can all be built there. This keeps *expanding until anything from a house to an industrial plant can be put on the same parcel of land.* Essentially, this scheme *recognizes priorities.* In declining order, those priorities are residential, then commercial, and finally industrial.

An **exclusive zoning** plan is better. It looks better, traffic is less, and the community is cohesive. In an exclusive zone, *whatever the area is zoned for is the only use* that can be made of the land. If the area is zoned commercial, then, all that can be put on that land is commercial. If the pyramid concept is used instead, once it is zoned commercial, it can still be used for single- and multifamily residential as well. Table 12–1 contrasts the two major zoning schemes.

Conforming and Nonconforming Uses

Uses of land also are categorized by how they comply with the zoning code. A **conforming use** is one that *complies with the zoning code.* Most realty that real estate salespersons deal in is conforming, and this usually entails no legal problems.

Nonconforming use is *when realty is used in a manner other than that designated in the zoning code.* Nonconforming uses can be lawful, when the realty was zoned in the past for this use but the area since has been rezoned and the realty no longer conforms. An example is a store in an area formerly zoned commercial but now rezoned residential. Under both the Fifth Amendment and the **Fourteenth Amendment** to the U. S. Constitution (due process of law and equal protection of the laws, respectively), it would be unconstitutional to terminate the landowner's

TABLE 12–1 Comparison of cumulative and exclusive zoning.

CUMULATIVE OR PYRAMID ZONING	EXCLUSIVE ZONING
1. Recognizes priorities in zoning designations, with priorities still allowed along with the current zoned use.	1. Whatever the area is zoned for is the only use that can be made of the land.
2. If the land is zoned for commercial use, then single- and multifamily residential (as higher priorities) also are allowed.	2. If the land is zoned for commercial use, then that is the only use that can be developed there.
3. Generally, this is not aesthetically pleasing and can result in a hodge-podge community.	3. Generally, this is aesthetically pleasing, with a cohesive look and use of a community's land.
4. This is a "zoning as you go" approach with no long-range planning by the community.	4. This requires a master plan for decades ahead.
5. Can result in severe traffic problems, especially in communities experiencing rapid growth.	5. Usually results in better traffic control because that has been built into the master plan.

nonconforming use of that realty, because he or she was there both lawfully and first. Nevertheless, it is the *policy of the law to destroy nonconforming uses through gradual elimination*. This is done by requiring the following:

1. The use *cannot be changed* from one nonconforming use to another nonconforming use (for example, changing the store to a restaurant).
2. *Only repairs* and not structural alterations may be done to the realty.
3. If the structure *burns down,* only a conforming use may be built in replacement.
4. If the owners *abandon* the nonconforming use, they cannot continue it at a later time.
5. When a particular use is declared a *nuisance,* it is an unlawful use and no longer a nonconforming use.
6. Through *amortization,* the owner is given a long time (20 years or more) to continue the nonconforming use; at the end of that period, the realty has to be used in conformance with the zoning code.

A city cannot seek to prohibit a mere increase in the volume of business or in proportions of that business as a control over nonconforming uses. A nonconforming use is *not terminated upon the sale, lease, devise, or any other transfer of the land.*

To qualify as a present, valid nonconforming use, a nonconforming use must have been lawful at the time it was established in the past. If it was not permitted by the applicable zoning ordinances when the use was established, it does not constitute a valid, present nonconforming use.

In purchasing a nonconforming-use realty, a purchaser must continually surmount legal obstacles to continue that use, because the law seeks to destroy it. Brokers and salespersons should be aware of the zoning status of any real property they market. If they fail to advise a purchaser that a real property may be a nonconforming use property (when they know the purchaser intends to make structural alterations or expand the business, for example), they may be liable to the purchaser for omission of that material factor. Real estate salespersons also should recommend that the purchaser consult an attorney before entering into a binding real estate purchase contract for a nonconforming-use real property.

Variances

Variances are *conforming uses once they are approved by the zoning board.* They are safer than nonconforming uses because the *law does not seek to destroy them.* Variances usually come about when landowners have a parcel of land they want to use in the same way as zoned, but this realty does not meet some of the requirements. For example, the parcel is zoned single-family residential and that is the use the landowners want to make of the realty, but a minimum of 3 acres is required to build a home there and they have only 2.9 acres. They argue to the zoning board that not to let them build a home there deprives them of any use of the land and imposes an undue hardship upon them.

Generally, landowners are *allowed to deviate from the zoning ordinance if literal compliance would cause practical difficulties or undue hardship. The hardship must be special and peculiar to the particular realty.* It is not special or peculiar if it affects all realties within a zoned district. Realty owners cannot get a variance if they create the hardship or if they are trying to change the essential nature of the zoned district.

Use variances are harder to obtain than variances regarding area requirements. To obtain a variance permitting a commercial use within a residential area is substantially more difficult than to build a home on a 2.9-acre lot when the zoning requires 3 acres. The standard for granting an area variance is usually lower than for a use variance. An area variance requires a *standard of practical difficulties*. A use variance requires a standard of *unnecessary hardship*.

Variances cannot be used to change zoning schemes or to correct errors of judgment in zoning laws. The power to permit a variance does not include the power to alter the character and use of a zoning district. For example, the mere fact that realty can be put to more profitable use does not in itself establish undue hardship if less profitable alternatives are available within the zoning district.

A landowner may apply to the appropriate zoning board for a variance, as can a purchaser who has bought the realty but does not yet have title. Persons merely considering purchasing the realty usually cannot apply for a variance.

Table 12–2 contrasts nonconforming uses and variances.

Spot Zoning and Rezoning

Spot zoning usually occurs *when a community does not rezone a landowner's realty in keeping with all of the rest of the other, surrounding realties.* The community therefore is deemed by the law to have impermissibly singled out and classified realty with no rational basis.

Spot zoning also can be done in other situations. It can evolve from a zoning that works a hardship on the other realty owners. *Extremities* are needed to establish a spot zone argument. For example, the landowners' parcel is zoned single-family residential, yet surrounding the parcel are railroad tracks used by an actively running railroad line, a warehouse, a filling station, and a large road with heavy equipment traffic. The landowners assert that the city has taken the realty without payment in violation of the Fifth Amendment and has arbitrarily and irrationally zoned the property in violation of the Fourteenth Amendment. If they were to build a house, it would be valueless, so they assert that they have been deprived

TABLE 12–2 Comparison of nonconforming use and variance.

NONCONFORMING USE	VARIANCE
1. Realty is used in a manner other than that designated in the zoning code.	1. Realty is used in the same way as zoned but does not meet some of the requirements.
2. Realty in the past was zoned for the use now being made of it.	2. Present deviation from the zoning code is needed because literal compliance causes practical difficulties and/or undue hardship. Past zoning code is not relevant.
3. Policy of the law is to destroy the nonconforming use by gradual elimination.	3. Once granted, a variance becomes a conforming use, and the law seeks to uphold it.
4. Use is not terminated upon the sale, lease, devise, or other transfer of the land.	4. Variance is not terminated upon the sale, lease, devise, or other transfer of the land.
5. Owner cannot switch from one nonconforming use to another nonconforming use.	5. Owner cannot make any nonconforming use of the realty.

FIGURE 12–1
Illegal spot zoning.

Spot Zoning

X — is zoned single-family residential, which does not fit in with the uses made of other surrounding properties, all of which are zoned for commercial or industrial use.

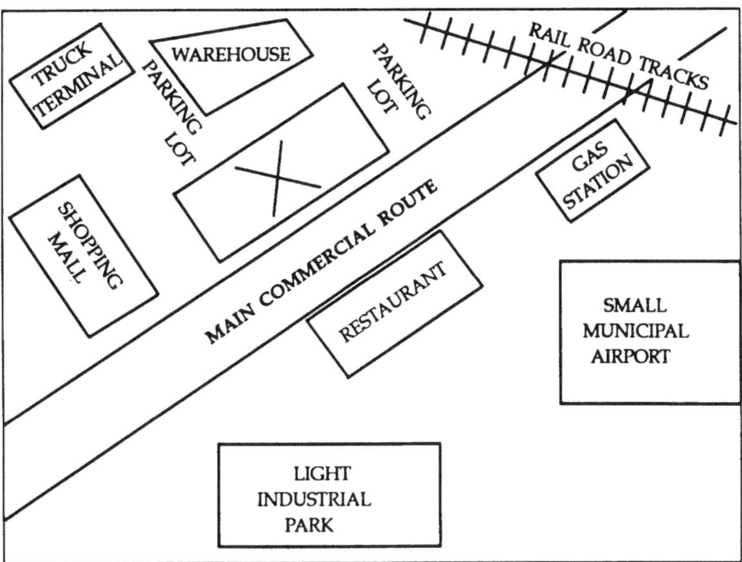

Spot Zoning Chart - This chart shows that the owners of X should probably legally fight the classification of their property as single-family residential. The community has singled them out for treatment that is unconstitutional.

of any use of the real property and that the requirements being imposed are irrational in such a heavy commercial and industrial district. The landowners typically prevail in court and the community will be required to rezone the realty to commercial-industrial.

Landowners subject to spot zoning might alternatively *ask the community to rezone* the real estate from one category to another. This request is practicable only when the proposed **rezoning** fits within the community's overall comprehensive plan for development.

Figure 12–1 is an example of illegal spot zoning.

X is zoned single-family residential, which does not fit with the uses made of surrounding properties, all of which are zoned for commercial or industrial use. The owners probably should legally fight the classification, on the ground that the spot zoning is unconstitutional.

Conditional Zoning

Zoning laws permit uses that benefit the community as a whole but technically are not the uses permitted within that zone. These conditional-use properties can include schools, churches, cemeteries, and even gas stations. The uses are granted subject to certain conditions that prohibit these uses from having certain negative effects on surrounding realties.

Procedure in Zoning Cases

Procedurally, *landowners must exhaust their administrative remedies before challenging a zoning ordinance.* First, they should take the problem to the zoning commission and, if they lose, then to the zoning board of appeals. If the landowners lose the petition before both of these boards, the landowners can file the case in a lower court. On appeal from the authorization or denial of a variance by the city's board of zoning appeals, however, the trial court and the court of appeals are *obliged to affirm the board's action* unless there is evidence that the board's decision was unconstitutional, illegal or arbitrary, capricious, unreasonable, or unsupported by a preponderance of substantial, reliable, and probative evidence. Zoning cases also have been heard in appellate courts, both state and federal, including the U. S. Supreme Court.

Incentive Zoning

Communities want amenities for their residents but often lack the funds to provide them. Some communities offer *inducements to commerce or industry within their zoning scheme* to obtain theaters, plazas, parks, ice rinks, or recreation centers. This is called **incentive zoning.** For example, the city lets a landowner put more stories on a building than the zoning code permits if the owner puts a theater and shopping plaza on the first floor of the building.

Aesthetics

Generally, communities have difficulty zoning for aesthetic, beautifying reasons, alone. **Aesthetic reasons,** *coupled with the goals of protecting realty from impairment and enhancing it instead,* are included within the general welfare provision of the police power, however. For example, expanding a township road by two lanes and coupling it with some aesthetic considerations that will be followed, such as preservation of certain adjoining shrubs and trees, probably will be a legal zoning resolution. In this way, the wedding of police power with aesthetics can result in legal zoning ordinances.

Planned Unit Developments and Zero Lot Lines

Planned Unit Development (PUD) is a product of cluster zoning. The community *permits the structures to cluster together on smaller lots* than called for in the zoning plan, but it *uses greater amounts of land for common areas.* These are areas to be used by all the realty owners.

The PUD developer typically submits comprehensive PUD plans to the zoning or planning commission for its review and approval. PUD is sold as a whole concept to the community as a way of providing attractive, more economical housing. A PUD allows a wide variety of housing ranging from apartment units to single-family houses. PUDs can even combine some nonresidential uses with the residential uses. Each individual owner becomes a member of the PUD's homeowners' association, which regulates use of the common areas. As a member of this association, the homeowner has an interest in and use of the surrounding land. The person has responsibilities as well, including sharing in its maintenance and repair cost. The individual owner remains solely responsible for the repair and maintenance of all individually owned land and structures. The PUD developer records a declaration with the plat that includes restrictions on land use. These restrictions are a comprehensive, general plan covering all of the development.

Zero lot line housing is *a form of planned unit development. Zero lot line owners possess and own exclusively* their housing unit and other realty connected with it and also *share ownership and possession* of common, connected realty with other zero lot line owners. For example, in a zero lot line row house development, all owners exclusively own and possess the interior of their structure and the back and front yards but own in common the exterior roof, fence, and exterior walls shared between units.

Eminent Domain

The federal, state, or local government has the power, known as **eminent domain,** to take landowners' realty from them as long as *that government pays just compensation.* This is an exercise of the government's appropriation powers. The **Fifth Amendment** to the U. S. Constitution requires that the landowner be paid: ". . . Nor shall private property be taken for public use without just compensation." The Ohio Constitution has the same requirement. All the government needs is a *public purpose* to validate taking the realty. The courts have construed public purpose and public use very broadly. A park, a public office building, a highway, and an airport can all be valid public purposes. The government almost always wins if landowners try to challenge the power of the government to take their land.

Another aspect of eminent domain is that landowners, in challenging the zoning of their land, typically claim that the local government (the community) is "taking" their realty by zoning ordinance. Therefore, they conclude, it should have to pay them for the land if it will not let them use it in the way they desire. If the court agrees with the landowner, the zoning law that is acting as a guise for eminent domain is overturned.

Quasi-public bodies, such as railroads and public utility companies, also have eminent domain powers. Eminent domain is a *transfer of title by involuntary alienation; the owner's consent is not necessary.* Because there are different levels of government, there are orders of precedence in eminent domain powers. The federal government takes precedence over the state, and the state over the local.

Eminent domain is a radical way of regulating land, and the salesperson or realty owner encounters it infrequently. If the government does take realty listed for sale through a real estate broker, the broker is paid a commission. Often, the real estate commission is figured into the overall appraisal figure for fair market value.

Often landowners are willing for the government to take the realty, but the landowners simply want more money for it. These are difficult lawsuits for the landowners to maintain, as the government typically has had thorough appraisals. The valuation of real property in eminent domain proceedings is the value of the realty for any and all uses for which it is suited, including the best and most valuable use to which it can lawfully, reasonably, and practically be adapted. When calculating valuation, the date used is whichever of these is earlier: the date of the actual "taking," or appropriation, by the government or the date of trial.

Sometimes an adjacent landowner whose land is not taken by the government wishes it were. Prime examples are a landowner who is not removed for a new airport runway yet now is directly in the flight path of it and a landowner whose land is not taken for a new interstate highway but whose backyard is now edging it. These aggrieved landowners can bring suit claiming under the Fifth Amendment that their land has been taken, too, except not physically. They have lost the quiet enjoyment of the realty, and its value has diminished instead. The courts generally hold against the landowners in these suits, saying that, for there to be a "taking," there must be substantial interference with an owner's dominion over and control of the property.

When the government brings a lawsuit to **appropriate,** or take, land, it is called a *suit in condemnation.* Suits in condemnation are brought in eminent domain actions as well as in suits to close down realty that is not fit or habitable for use. When the landowner is the one who brings the lawsuit against the government, as in the above examples, it is called a suit in *inverse condemnation.* It is inverse because it is the flip side of the government's suing the owner.

Certain complex transactions, such as seller-financed or commercially leased real properties, should contain a contractual provision regarding condemnation proceedings. It should specify who is to receive the proceeds from such a proceeding.

Building and Health Departments

A local building code and a health code are valid exercises of the **police power** to *protect the public health and safety.* Most communities have building departments. They follow a *building code,* which imposes *construction requirements on those desiring to build on land.* Building codes are formulated with considerable concern about the safety of a structure, including fireproofing, stress, exits, stairs, rails, wiring, heating, and so forth.

When landowners want to build, they must comply with zoning ordinances and the building code. They apply for a *building permit* by submitting the plan with specifications to the building department. If it is approved, the owners are issued a permit. Building permits also are *needed for putting additions onto structures.* The building department has an *inspector* who checks the work periodically as the structure goes up. If the inspector is satisfied at completion, he or she issues a *certificate of occupancy* to the owner. Then the building may be used.

Many communities have *ordinances requiring an inspection by the building department of any dwelling sold in that community before title transfer can take place.* These are referred to as **point-of-sale inspections.** Some of these are fairly rigorous, with the inspectors' requiring new wiring, painting, concrete work, or any other fix-up job they spot. The reason communities like these is that values can be maintained for the whole community. The inspections discourage owners from letting a realty get rundown; owners will not be able to sell it unless they fix it. If the salesperson has a listing in a community that requires an inspection before title transfer, this salesperson should have the seller begin work on any needed repairs right from the start of the listing.

Some legal problems have developed with these inspections. They have been held a *proprietary* and not a governmental function. As such, a *municipality cannot go beyond the scope of doing a building inspection for the purpose of discovery and correction of building code violations.* If it does, and thereby intervenes in contracts of sale of such buildings, it can be liable for damages suffered from any inspection that is negligently performed.

Local government also usually has a health department, which can become a critical agency to deal with in the real estate listing and sales setting. For example, before a landowner can begin building, the health department must issue a septic permit if the realty does not connect to a sewer. Septic permits have requirements as to size of the tanks, amount of land necessary, proper location, and so forth.

EXCLUSIONARY ZONING

Many communities seek to keep their housing at a high, affluent level. One way to do this is by *large-lot residential zoning.* A community might rezone, requiring that any new homes be built on a minimum of three acres, for example. The price of the lot alone then can easily be what a home would be on a small lot. Building the home will, of course, be more expensive than the lot. When all the housing in a community becomes affluent, many people cannot afford to live there. The lower and middle classes claim that this is **exclusionary zoning.**

Exclusionary zoning also refers to *keeping out certain uses.* Some communities do not have any zone for multifamily residential or mobile homes. Others exclude industry totally or keep commerce down to a minimum. It is difficult for a court to find exclusionary zoning illegal, because there is *no legal basis, in either the Constitution or in acts of Congress, for attacking economic discrimination alone.* A fundamental right to housing does not yet legally exist. Traditionally, housing in the United States is considered a realistic expectation, not a right. The problem is that the expectation is not being realized by as many people as it once was.

Exclusionary zoning *has sometimes been successfully attacked as constitutionally impermissible racial discrimination,* and racial minority groups have argued successfully that large-lot zoning is donc and maintained to exclude minorities from communities. The arguments are that minority persons are represented disproportionately in the lower income groups and use of land therefore has the discriminatory purpose and effect of excluding the minority persons.

THE INTERSTATE LAND SALES FULL DISCLOSURE ACT

The **Interstate Land Sales Full Disclosure Act,** a 1969 Housing and Urban Development Act (15 U.S.C. 1701) *protects prospective purchasers from land developers who sell lots sight-unseen through interstate commerce.* The act covers purchasers who buy alleged vacation spots that in reality are swamps or deserts. Most of these lots are procured by ads sent personally to prospective purchasers or placed in newspapers or magazines. A condominium unit is a lot covered by this act.

The act covers each purchaser of this land if the developer is selling land through interstate commerce, such as the mail. The *developer must file a Statement of Record with HUD, accompanied by a property report.* Developers must thus file with the government *substantial disclosures about the lots they are selling,* including the names of persons with interests in the lots; a topography description; the state of the title; the condition and price of sale; the availability of water, utilities, and waste disposal; their financial condition; improvements to the lots; and instruments and conveyances affecting the lots.

Developers have the duty of giving to prospective purchasers the information and **property report** they have disclosed to the government. If the developers do not submit the disclosures to purchasers covered by this act, the purchasers have various rights to revoke the contract and recover any money they paid on the lot. The developers must furnish the property report to the purchasers prior to their signing the purchase contract. Purchasers who have not received this information from the developers can sue them in federal district court and receive damages in the amount paid for the lot plus improvements, court costs, and even rescission of the entire transaction. Developers who perpetrate a fraud or misrepresentation upon the purchasers also may be sued by the purchasers under this act.

HUD administrates the act and can initiate action to penalize developers that do not comply. The act has an exhaustive list of exemptions, many of which deal with small- to moderate-sized subdivisions. Other exemptions hinge on the number of sales, or the size of the lot, or the time period in which the building is to be completed, or the land's purpose. These are just a few of the many exemptions to this law.

AMERICANS WITH DISABILITIES ACT

The federal **Americans with Disabilities Act** took effect on January 26, 1992. It *prohibits discrimination against individuals on the basis of disabilities.* A disability is a physical or mental impairment that substantially limits one or more of the major life activities of an individual. This act mandates compliance with stated criteria for people with disabilities by all owners and operators of *public accommodations and commercial facilities,* regardless of size or the number of employees, and by local and state governments. Public accommodations and commercial facilities are to be designed, constructed, and altered in compliance with the accessibility standards of this law.

Public accommodations are facilities operated by private entities whose operations affect commerce. Examples of public accommodations minimally include inn, hotel, motel, restaurant, bar, movie house, theater, concert hall, stadium, auditorium, convention center, retail store, laundromat, bank, terminal, depot, museum, library, gallery, park, zoo, gym, health spa. Public accommodations must remove structural, architectural, and communication barriers in existing facilities where the removal is *readily achievable.* For example, public accommodations must install ramps, put in lower telephones, make curb cuts in sidewalks and entrances, widen doors, install grab bars in toilet stalls, add raised letter markings on elevator control buttons, and remove high-pile, low-density carpeting. A higher standard imposed in the case of new construction or alteration requires that the public accommodation be *readily accessible to and usable by* individuals with disabilities.

Commercial facilities are those whose operations affect commerce and are intended for nonresidential use by a private entity. Although the new construction and alterations provisions are the same for public accommodations and commercial facilities, the other requirements are applicable only to public accommodations.

ENVIRONMENTAL LAW

Federal and state **environmental laws** are in effect *to protect the public from the effects of pollution in the air, land, and water, as well as to conserve our natural resources for the future.* The **National Environmental Policy Act** is a federal law that requires federal agencies to make an *environmental impact statement for actions* *that would significantly impact on the environment,* such as highway construction projects. Private entities also must make the environmental impact statement when their actions require a license from a federal agency or a federal loan. These statements analyze the effect on the environment by going forward with the project. Projects can be halted when the statements are sufficiently adverse.

Under the Clean Air Act, the Environmental Protection Agency (EPA) regulates the emission of air pollutants. Ohio must meet designated clean air standards. The Clean Water Act sets water quality standards with the EPA, prohibiting land uses that discharge pollutants, above a certain threshold level, into lakes or waterways. The Ohio Environmental Protection Agency (OEPA) administers environmental laws in Ohio. To discharge any significant level of pollutants into the air or water, one first must obtain a permit from OEPA. That agency also reviews the federally required environmental impact statements prepared for Ohio projects.

STATE, EX REL. CASALE V. MCLEAN
58 Ohio St. 3d 163, 569 N.E.2d 475 (1991)

CASE STUDY FROM THE OHIO SUPREME COURT

Facts: In 1965 the zoning inspector denied a request to expand a mobile home park because the expansion would enlarge the park by more than 25 percent of the number of parking spaces, in violation of the zoning code. The owners appealed, and the Board of Zoning Appeals granted a variance permitting the addition of 50 new parking pads, stating that literal compliance with the zoning code would work an unnecessary hardship on the mobile home park owners.

The park was sold in 1970 to Casale, and in 1975, when a new zoning inspector was in office, Casale was told that the 1965 variance covered expanding the mobile home parking by 50 pads. In 1987 yet another new zoning inspector, McLean, advised Casale that he would not issue him a zoning certificate permitting the expansion of the park from 54 units to 104 units.

Court of Appeals: Granted Casale a writ of mandamus compelling McLean to issue a zoning certificate in accordance with the 1965 variance.

Issues: (a) Whether the Board of Zoning Appeals acted beyond its authority in granting the variance by its allegedly usurping the legislative functions of the Zoning Commission or Township Board of Trustees; (b) whether the Board acted against the public interest because the mobile home park was surrounded by residential properties.

Held by the Ohio Supreme Court: (a) The board had the authority to grant the variance. Both the township ordinance and the Ohio Revised Code empower the board to issue a variance when not contrary to the public interest, owing to special conditions, and when literal compliance will result in unnecessary hardship; (b) no timely appeal was taken on the basis of surrounding property back in 1965, and thus the matter is *res judicata*—the thing has already been finally decided. Affirmed the holding of the Court of Appeals.

FIRST ENGLISH EVANGELICAL LUTHERAN CHURCH OF GLENDALE V. COUNTY OF LOS ANGELES, CALIFORNIA
482 US 304, 96 L Ed 2d 250, 107 S Ct 2378 (1987)

CASE STUDY FROM THE U. S. SUPREME COURT

Facts: In 1957, the church purchased a 21-acre parcel of land in a canyon along the banks of the Middle Fork of Middle Creek in the Angeles National Forest. The Middle Fork is the natural drainage channel for a watershed area owned by the National Forest Service. Twelve of the acres owned by the church are flat land, and contained a dining hall, two bunkhouses, a caretaker's lodge, an outdoor chapel, and a footbridge across a creek. The church operated on the site a campground, known as "Lutherglen," as a retreat center and a recreational area for handicapped children.

In July 1977, a forest fire denuded the hills upstream from Lutherglen, destroying approximately 3,860 acres of the watershed area and creating a serious flood hazard. Flooding occurred on February 9 and 10, 1978, when a storm dropped 11 inches of rain in the watershed. Runoff from the storm overflowed the banks of Mill Creek, flooding Lutherglen and destroying its buildings.

In response to flooding of the canyon, the county of Los Angeles adopted an ordinance providing that "a person shall not construct, reconstruct, place, or enlarge any building or structure, any portion of which is, or will be, located within the outer boundary lines of the interim flood protection area located in Mill Creek Canyon." The ordinance was effective immediately because the county determined it was "required for the immediate preservation of the public health and safety." The interim flood protection area described by the ordinance included the flat areas on either side of Mill Creek on which Lutherglen had stood. A little more than a month after the ordinance was adopted, the church sued the county for damages.

Superior Court of California (Trial Court): Held that the church could not sue for damages, that the proper method for challenging the ordinance is an action for declaratory relief or for a writ of mandamus.

California Court of Appeals: Affirmed the trial court on the basis of state precedents and noted that the U. S. Supreme Court had not yet ruled whether a state may constitutionally limit the remedy for a taking to nonmonetary relief.

Supreme Court of California: Denied review.

Issue: Whether a temporary governmental taking, instead of a permanent taking, also requires that compensation be paid by the county to the church.

Held by the United States Supreme Court: For the church and against the county as follows:

1. That where a regulation takes all use of a property, the property owner is entitled, under the just compensation clause of the Fifth Amendment, to compensation for the period before the courts finally determine that the regulation effects a "taking" of property.
2. That "temporary" takings, which deny a property owner all use of the property, are not different in kind from permanent takings.
3. That no subsequent action by the government, such as amending or withdrawing the challenged regulation, can relieve the government of the duty to provide compensation for the period during which the taking was effective.
4. That invalidation of the ordinance in question, without payment of fair value for use of the property during the period in which the church was denied such use, would be a constitutionally insufficient remedy.

Reversed and remanded.

CASE STUDY FROM THE OHIO SUPREME COURT

GERIJO, INC. V. CITY OF FAIRFIELD
70 Ohio St.3d 223, 638 N.E.2d 533 (1994)

Facts: Gerijo, Inc. is an Ohio corporation owned by members of the Oliver family. The Olivers have owned the property since the 1870s. The property is 37 acres situated 1,000 feet southwest of State Route 4 in Fairfield, Ohio. Fairfield's land use plan called for a 70:30 ratio between single family and multi-family residential dwellings. The plan also included an intent to confine all industrial development to the area east of Route 4. Up until the last ten years, the property in question was farmed. In the last ten years the land has remained vacant. In its current state, it is an undeveloped area surrounded on three sides by multi-family residential developments. The fourth side is zoned commercially. Although the subject parcel was once zoned as multi-family residential, the city rezoned the area in 1989 as M-1, an Industrial Park District. This is light industrial with the purpose of attracting high-growth and high-tech industries key to the city's economic and tax base. The Oliver family has received offers for multifamily residential use ranging from $30,000 to $70,000 an acre. It has also received one offer for light industrial use at $40,000 per acre. They filed a petition with Fairfield requesting the property be rezoned as multi-family residential use. This allowance would change the Fairfield housing ratio from a 50:50 ratio of single- to multi-family use to a 48:52 ratio of single- to multi-family use when the desired ratio is 70:30. Fairfield rejected this application. Gerijo filed a complaint with Common Pleas court, challenging the constitutionality of the zoning scheme as it related to the subject parcel. Gerijo argued that M-1 zoning prevented the highest and best use of the property and it is arbitrary, confiscatory, unreasonable, and not based on concerns for the public health, safety and morals, and general welfare.

Common Pleas Court: Gerijo failed to prove the M-1 zoning was confiscatory, but the court ultimately invalidated the classification on the grounds that it failed to substantially advance a legitimate government interest.

Court of Appeals: Affirmed the Court of Common Pleas.

Issue: Whether a party attacking a zoning regulation must establish, beyond fair debate, that the zoning classification denies the party an economically viable use of the zoned property without substantially advancing a legitimate interest in the health, safety and welfare of the community.

Held by the Ohio Supreme Court: By repeatedly setting out both economic viability and the advancement of a legitimate governmental interest as two steps of the same test, the court intended to require that a challenging party must prove each element to invalidate the zoning ordinance. Thus, the challenging party must prove that the enactment both (1) deprives the owner of an economically viable use and (2) fails to advance a legitimate governmental interest. Despite Gerijo's arguments in the trial court concerning the confiscatory impact of the zoning ordinance, Gerijo candidly admitted during oral argument before this court that it had not been deprived of the reasonable economic use of its property. Thus, it failed to satisfy the first element of the test. On the second prong, the evidence presented shows that Fairfield rezoned the property to attempt to provide a buffer between the multi-family residential and the commercial section that surround the subject parcel. The city had experienced numerous problems with multi-family dwellings located directly adjacent to retail and commercial uses, especially excessive noise and traffic problems. This did not show that Fairfield was being arbitrary in its classification. Also, the desire to balance the multi-family with the single-family ratio was a legitimate governmental goal to balance types of housing. The zoning classification for the Gerijo property remains light industrial.

Summary of Content

1. Communities have the power to enact legislative controls over the uses that can be made of their land via zoning.
2. Zoning must be a reasonable exercise of the community's police power with specific, clear provisions promoting the public health, safety, and general welfare.

3. Most communities consider that the highest and best use of real property is single-family residential.
4. The oldest zoning scheme is known as cumulative or pyramid zoning, which recognizes priorities.
5. Exclusive zoning requires that whatever the area is zoned for is the only use that can be made of the land.
6. Uses of land also are categorized by how they comply with the zoning code.
7. A conforming use of land is one that complies with the zoning code.
8. A nonconforming use occurs when realty is used in a manner other than that designated in the zoning code.
9. It is the policy of the law to destroy nonconforming uses through gradual elimination.
10. A nonconforming use is not terminated upon the sale, lease, devise, or any other transfer of the land.
11. Variances can be made when a landowner has a parcel of land that he or she wants to use in the same way as zoned; however, this realty does not meet some of the requirements.
12. A variance allows the individual realty owner to deviate from the zoning ordinance where literal compliance would cause practical difficulties or undue hardship that is special and peculiar to the particular realty.
13. Spot zoning occurs when a community does not rezone a landowner's realty in keeping with all the rest of the other, surrounding realties.
14. Procedurally, in challenging a zoning ordinance, landowners must exhaust their administrative remedies before taking the case to court.
15. Incentive zoning occurs when a community offers inducements to commerce or industry within its zoning scheme in order to obtain theaters, plazas, parks, ice rinks, or recreation centers.
16. Aesthetic reasons coupled with the goals of protecting realty from impairment and enhancing it instead are included within the general welfare provision of the police power.
17. Planned Unit Development (PUD) is cluster zoning wherein a community permits the structures to cluster together on smaller lots than called for in the zoning plan but to use greater amounts of land for common areas.
18. Zero lot line housing is a form of planned unit development wherein the owner possesses and owns exclusively his or her housing unit and other realty connected with it and also shares ownership and possession of common, connected realty with other zero lot line owners.
19. The government, pursuant to its eminent domain powers, can take a landowner's realty for a public purpose as long as it pays the landowner just compensation.
20. Eminent domain is a transfer of title by involuntary alienation; the owner's consent is not necessary.
21. When the government brings a lawsuit to take or appropriate land, it is called a suit in condemnation.
22. Most communities have building and health departments that require real properties to meet certain standards.
23. A point-of-sale inspection can be required by a local ordinance mandating an inspection of any dwelling sold in that community before title transfer can take place. These inspections cannot intervene in contracts of sale of such buildings without risking liability for damages.

24. Exclusionary zoning can be attacked as constitutionally impermissible racial discrimination.
25. The Interstate Land Sales Full Disclosure Act protects prospective purchasers from land developers who sell lots sight-unseen through interstate commerce.
26. The Americans with Disabilities Act requires owners of public accommodations and commercial facilities to make their real properties accessible to disabled persons.
27. Federal and state environmental laws are in effect to protect the public from effects of pollution in the air, land, and water, as well as to conserve natural resources for the future.

REVIEW QUESTIONS

1. It is not a valid public purpose for which land can be taken:
   a. state park
   b. amusement park
   c. power plant
   d. interstate highway
2. The building department would *not* be responsible for approving which of the following:
   a. wiring
   b. rails
   c. well
   d. exits
3. The police power of the state must be exercised:
   a. to minimize cost to taxpayers of essential public services
   b. in accordance with rules promulgated by the federal government
   c. to benefit the public health, safety, welfare, and morals
   d. pursuant to written promulgations of the judges of the county's common pleas court
4. Condemnation is required when the government exercises its power of:
   a. escheat
   b. constructive annexation
   c. foreclosure
   d. appropriation by eminent domain
5. Which amendment to the U. S. Constitution is controlling in eminent domain cases?
   a. First Amendment
   b. Fifth Amendment
   c. Fourteenth Amendment
   d. the entire Bill of Rights
6. For just compensation to be owed to a landowner under the Fifth Amendment, there must be:
   a. a permanent taking of the land
   b. a temporary taking of the land
   c. any taking of the land
   d. all of the above
7. Landowners are in the strongest legal position against a community and its zoning scheme when their realty is:
   a. spot-zoned
   b. variant
   c. nonconforming
   d. exclusively zoned
8. The Interstate Land Sales Disclosures Act:
   a. applies only to land in a desert or swamp
   b. is administered by the Consumer Protection Agency
   c. requires that a property report be filed with HUD
   d. all of the above

9. Point-of-sale building inspections:
   a. can be done by a city with complete immunity from liability
   b. can result in the city's being liable for negligence if they intervene in contracts for sale for those buildings
   c. completely assure purchasers of real property that they are getting defect-free property
   d. are so good that the VA and FHA can use these instead of doing their own appraisals

10. The building department approves:
    a. wiring
    b. septic system
    c. sewage problems
    d. all of the above

11. The policy of the law is to destroy, by gradually eliminating:
    a. variant uses
    b. conforming uses
    c. nonconforming uses
    d. all strip malls

12. Incentive zoning can be used for the following:
    a. to stem the rush to southern states from northern ones
    b. to attract new industry
    c. to stimulate culture and recreation
    d. all of the above

13. Exclusive zoning allows:
    a. a single family to still go into an area now zoned light commercial
    b. whatever the area is zoned for is the only use that can be put there
    c. a mushrooming pyramid of uses from single-family to heavy industrial
    d. a community of all residential housing on three acres of land

14. The most likely basis for a court's striking down an exclusionary zoning scheme is:
    a. economic discrimination
    b. racial discrimination
    c. interference with freedom to travel
    d. violation of due process of law

15. The Interstate Land Sales Full Disclosure Act:
    a. applies to all seller-financed properties
    b. applies to housing located in a county other than the purchaser's present place of residence
    c. applies to housing located in another state offered for sale by a developer through interstate commerce
    d. was repealed

16. Eminent domain is a:
    a. private land use control
    b. type of zoning classification
    c. governmental right
    d. freehold interest

17. A community's zoning plan:
    a. must be an exclusive one
    b. is passed pursuant to federal regulations
    c. must be a cumulative one
    d. is presumed rational

18. Even if a lot conforms to the zoning plan, an owner building upon it must:
    a. obtain a building permit
    b. have the health department approve the septic system
    c. get a certificate of occupancy before moving in
    d. all of the above

19. Landowners who attack in court the zoning of their property should be able to show that the present zoning:
    a. is not the best use of the land
    b. is not the most profitable use of the land
    c. is aesthetically displeasing
    d. is so out of character with the surrounding real properties that they will not be able to make any reasonable use of the land

20. A fundamental right to housing for any citizen of the United States can be found:
    a. nowhere, as there is no such fundamental right
    b. in the U. S. Constitution
    c. in the Bill of Rights
    d. in the United States Entitlement Act of 1986

21. The Americans with Disabilities Act took effect in:
    a. 1990
    b. 1992
    c. 1986
    d. 1989

22. A public accommodation is:
    a. a motel
    b. corporate headquarters
    c. single-family housing
    d. an apartment building

23. This law regulates the emission of air pollutants:
    a. No Smoke Act
    b. Emission Free Highway Act
    c. Clean Air Act
    d. Clean Water-to-Air Act

24. This is used to assess adverse effects a project may have on the environment:
    a. containment summary
    b. measuring monitor
    c. assessment report
    d. impact statement

25. When a county prevents a church from "temporarily" making any use of its land, it violates this constitutional amendment:
    a. First
    b. Fourteenth
    c. Fifth
    d. Sixth

Answer Key

1. b
2. c
3. c
4. d
5. b
6. d
7. a
8. c
9. b
10. a
11. c
12. d
13. b
14. b
15. c
16. c
17. d
18. d
19. d
20. a
21. b
22. a
23. c
24. d
25. c

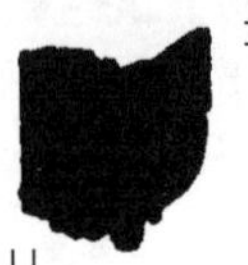

13
LANDLORD–TENANT LAW

KEY TERMS

abandonment
acknowledge
approval clause
assignment
attest
automatic renewal
constructive eviction
conveyance
eviction
forcible entry and detainer
gross lease
ground lease
habitability, warranty of
lease
memorandum of lease
net lease
option to renew
part performance
percentage lease
periodic tenancy
quiet enjoyment, covenant of
reasonable wear and tear
recording
rent
rent depositing
retaliatory eviction
reversion
security deposit
statute of conveyances
statute of frauds
sublease
surrender
waiver
waste, intentional and permissive

LEGAL PROBLEMS RELATING TO landlord–tenant law can arise in the sale of residential real property. A salesperson needs to be aware of these problems to avoid them and the litigation they usually precipitate. Three problems that happen from time to time are the following:

1. A real estate purchase contract closes. The *seller* is supposed to vacate as of closing date but *refuses to vacate at all.* Instead of (or in addition to) suing the seller for breach of the real estate purchase contract, the purchaser might use a forcible entry and detainer action (eviction) to have the sheriff forcibly remove the seller-tenant from the premises. A court hears forcible entry and detainer actions quickly, compared to breach of contract actions.

2. The purchaser is allowed to move into the real estate before title transfer date. When that date comes about, the *purchaser refuses to close* the transaction but *remains in possession* of the premises. This time the seller is the one to use a forcible entry and detainer (eviction) action against the purchaser, instead of (or in addition to) a breach of contract action for the same reason.

3. The real estate company lists a realty that has tenants in possession who have six months left on their lease. The company must carefully inform prospective purchasers that anyone who purchases the realty will *not be able to take possession until the tenants' lease expires*. The purchaser can take title but cannot evict the tenants until the lease expires. Therefore, purchasers will take title subject to the lease provisions. If the company fails to notify the prospective purchasers, the seller and the purchaser may lodge a misrepresentation or negligence claim against the company for misrepresentation and negligence.

Turning to *commercial real estate,* a commercial salesperson might spend a lot of time *negotiating leases* in addition to selling commercial and industrial real estate. Frequently the lease arrangements the salesperson uses are also package deals in which this salesperson must lease a whole mall, and the leases involve the tenants' paying the landlord a percentage from their business receipts. The broker and the salesperson also can be paid from the percentages of the tenants' businesses. This can be profitable, as they usually manage the commercial center or building also.

Property management entails negotiating leases within a large complex of apartments. Property managers typically are salaried employees of large, corporate landlords. They take applications to lease from tenants and have little discretion in changing the terms of the printed form lease. The property managers receive the signed leases and are responsible for receiving and investigating complaints from tenants, collecting and returning security deposits, and itemizing damages a tenant does to a unit. This job is on the lower end of the real estate pay scale. Profits go principally to the landlord.

Landlord–tenant law is also of importance to students who want to become either landlords or tenants themselves. This chapter examines the basics, but consulting an attorney before entering into a lease is advisable. A common mistake landlords make is to go to a legal-blank store, buy a form lease, and use it to lease their realty. This often precipitates involved legal problems because the parties rarely understand the long-range effects of many of the clauses within the form lease without advice from their attorneys.

Fair housing laws also must be observed in selecting a tenant. Landlords can be selective regarding tenants' financial stability and credit worthiness but are not permitted to select tenants based on racial, sexual, ethnic, religious, handicap, or family status preferences, as we learned in Chapter 11.

FUNDAMENTALS OF LEASES

A **lease** is both a *conveyance of an estate or interest in land and a contract between landlord and tenant.* For leasing purposes, the landlord, the realty owner, also is called the *lessor,* and the tenant, the possessor of the premises, is called the *lessee.* Leases also are referred to as *rental agreements.*

As a *contract,* the lease has consideration, mutuality, and exchange of promises between the parties to the lease, the landlord-lessor and tenant-lessee. The required *consideration* is usually the tenant's payment of rent in exchange for possession of the landlord's premises. Promises in the lease, covering the obligations and responsibilities of both landlord and tenant, also are deemed consideration. Because a lease is a contract, it cannot be formed without consideration.

A lease of real property is also a **conveyance** of an estate or interest in land called a *leasehold.* Leasehold estates in land were covered in Chapter 3, which the student should review in conjunction with this chapter. The leasehold tenant has exclusive possession and control of the real property. The landlord has a **reversion,** which means the *real property will return to the landlord at the expiration of the leasehold.*

Anything that creates the relationship of landlord and tenant is called a lease. Therefore, a lease can be either oral or written. To be valid under the **statute of frauds,** however, a *lease for more than a year must be in writing, as must a lease that will expire more than one year after the date the parties agreed to it.* Because of the problems in proving the terms of an oral lease, it is the better practice to put any lease in written form.

The lease must allow the premises to be used only for *legal purposes.* If the lease were to cover an illegal use of the premises, the courts would refuse to enforce it. If it were thereby unenforceable, one party could not hold the other to it. As long as the purpose is legal, the policy of the law is to uphold the lease.

Short-term leases are the primary ones in use today. They cover leaseholds of fewer than 99 years. *Long-term leases* are for 99 or more years, and more typically come about in leasing an industrial plant. *Perpetual leases* are those capable of unending renewal; the courts do not favor these and they can be difficult to have upheld.

In *construing a lease,* words are used in their usual and ordinary meaning as shown by the context in which the words are employed. A court tries to carry out the intentions of the parties as shown by the wording in the lease. If the lease has technical or legal words, as it usually does, the court construes these by their technical definitions unless the lease shows a different intent by landlord and tenant.

The lease should include a *description of the real property* being leased. Leases that are to be recorded must contain the legal description. Complex commercial and industrial leases usually contain the legal description, whereas residential leases often give only the street address. The prime objective of describing the realty within the lease is to lessen the chances for later legal argument between landlord and tenant about what constitutes the leased premises.

Leases should be made only between landlord and tenant who have reached the *age of majority* and are of *sound mind*—the two prerequisites for being considered a person who has the capacity to contract. If either the landlord or the tenant lacks capacity to contract, that person can opt out of the lease without obligation; the other party cannot, if he or she has the capacity to contract.

For a lease to be valid, it must be *signed by the landlord and delivered to and accepted by the tenant.* Because of the contractual aspects of the lease, the preferred rule is to also have the tenant sign the lease. *Some leases must also be recorded,* according to the **statute of conveyances.** Leases that should be recorded are those that are more than three years in duration and those that would last more than three years if an option to renew within the lease were exercised. **Memorandum of the lease** can be recorded rather than the actual lease itself. A memorandum has the names of the parties and the description of the leased property. It does not state the terms of the lease, which sometimes the landlord and the tenant desire to keep private. To record the lease, or memorandum, it must be filed in the county recorder's office, where it becomes a matter of public record. When there is to be a recording, the legal description of the leased premises is required.

Recording the lease *acts as constructive notice to those who subsequently acquire interest in the same land.* If the lease is not recorded, that does not affect the validity between the parties to the lease; the landlord and tenant cannot make the lease voidable by failure to record. But the result might be different when a third party, such as a bona fide purchaser or other tenant, is involved. If a third party acts in good faith, without knowledge of the prior lease, he or she is a bona fide purchaser or tenant. If this third party enters into either a lease or a sale of the same realty, a court might hold that he or she does not have notice of this other lease, because it is not recorded.

Leases for more than three years, and those that would last more than three years if an option to renew within the lease were exercised, must be acknowledged and attested in order to be valid between landlord and tenant. The lease therefore is executed in the presence of two witnesses, who **attest** the signing by also *signing the attestation clause on the lease.* A notary public **acknowledges** the lease by *signing and sealing it* and also can act as one of the witnesses. If the lease is not acknowledged and attested to in this fashion, it is invalid and the court will refuse to enforce it. Either the landlord and tenant could opt out of the lease because it was never properly formed.

Unless prohibited within the lease, a lease may be assigned or sublet. An **assignment** carries the *tenant's entire interest under the lease over to the assignee,* the person to whom the lease is transferred. The assignee becomes liable to the landlord as well as the original tenant, who now is also called the assignor, in case of default on the lease. A **sublease** carries *less than the tenant's entire interest over to the sublessee,* the person receiving the portion of the lease. The original tenant, now also known as the sublessor, is liable to the landlord, not the sublessee, if there is a default. The assignor may take legal action against a defaulting assignee; a sublessor may take legal action against a defaulting sublessee. If the lease prohibits an assignment, the premises still may be sublet; if it prohibits a sublease, it still may be assigned.

In most leases, if landlords do not prohibit subleasing and assignment, they at least reserve the right to approve the sublessee or assignee. An **approval clause** is *acceptable as long as landlords are not arbitrary and unreasonable in withholding approval.* The clause within the lease usually reads, "Landlords' consent, not to be unreasonably withheld, shall first be obtained." Courts do not like unreasonable restraints on transfers of real property, so they strictly scrutinize landlords' reasons for withholding their consent. For example, if landlords withhold their consent because the proposed assignee or sublessee is a divorced person and the landlords think all divorced persons are unstable, the court probably will deem this an unreasonable withholding of landlords' approval. This reason also might violate the fair housing laws under either the family status or the sex category.

If the assignment or sublease is more than a year in duration, it must be in writing to satisfy the statute of frauds. If it is over three years in duration it must be acknowledged and attested to and then should be recorded.

The lease can *restrict the premises for a certain use*. For example, an apartment can be restricted for residential use only, and a shopping center can be restricted to commercial use only.

In summary, a lease should minimally contain the following items:

1. A description of the leased premises.
2. The parties to the lease along with their addresses.
3. The term of the lease with a beginning and end date.
4. A recital of consideration between the parties, which is usually the amount of rent.
5. The purposes for which the premises may and may not be used.
6. The dated signatures of the landlord and the tenant.
7. Preferably in writing, and always in writing if the term is more than a year or the lease will expire more than one year after the parties agree to it.
8. Attestation, acknowledgment, and recording if the term is more than three years or those that would last more than three years if an option to renew within the lease were exercised.

Renewal of Leases

Unless the lease states otherwise, there is no **automatic renewal** of that lease. Many leases today provide for automatic renewals within the terms of the lease. Typically, a clause in the lease states that *the lease will automatically renew for a term of like duration, unless either landlords or tenants notify the other in advance* that they do not want to renew. There might be valid terms, already provided for in the lease, regarding certain escalations, such as increases in rent to be tied into some index of inflation.

Another way renewal is handled within the lease is by **option to renew.** Tenants are given an option to renew their lease term, *either under identical terms or under terms specified in the lease regarding the renewal period,* such as an increase in rent tied into some index of inflation. If the tenants want to exercise their option, they notify the landlord within the period of time stated in the lease. If they fail to exercise their option, the lease does not renew at its expiration.

If there is more than one tenant in the lease, the option to renew can be used only if *all tenants exercise the option* to renew. One tenant's attempt to use the option is really a counteroffer to the landlord, which the landlord may reject. Options are used commonly in commercial leases. In an option, the tenant must affirmatively notify the landlord to obtain a renewal. Under an automatic renewal, the tenant remains passive, or does nothing.

TERMINATION

A tenancy can terminate in a variety of ways. The simplest way is for the term to *expire*. This happens with a tenancy for a fixed term, with no renewal clause, that has specified beginning and ending dates. For example, the leasehold's term begins January 1, 1995, and ends December 31, 1995. There is no renewal clause. The tenancy terminates on December 31, 1995.

The landlord and tenant also can mutually agree to cancel the lease and return to their former positions. In contracts this is called rescission. In landlord–tenant law it is called a **surrender,** because the tenant is surrendering, or giving back, the premises to the landlord.

Tenants can forfeit their rights to the premises by *breaching* the lease. Although this is not popular with the courts, it can happen if tenants are in extreme breach, such as an illegal use of the premises.

Death of the parties will not terminate a leasehold unless a clause within the lease specifies that the tenant's obligations terminate at death. Without that clause, if either the landlord or the tenant dies, the lease becomes binding upon the decedent's estate. Many residential leases have a clause terminating the tenancy upon the death of either the landlord or the tenant. As most commercial leases are between corporations, the clause is not needed because corporations can exist forever.

The tenant also may be evicted. The lawful way for the landlord to proceed on a residential lease is to bring an action for **forcible entry and detainer,** a lawful **eviction** in court *based on the tenant's breach of the lease. The persons most commonly subject to forcible entry and detainer actions are holdover tenants, persons failing to pay rent under an oral tenancy, persons breaching an obligation under their lease, and persons violating the controlled substances (drug) laws.* If the landlord wins a forcible entry and detainer action, the court has the sheriff remove the tenant from the premises if that tenant refuses to go willingly. Most nonresidential landlords also use the forcible entry and detainer procedure, instead of ejecting the tenant on their own, unless their lease gives them the right to summarily eject a tenant. Most commercial and industrial tenants, however, will not agree to an ejectment provision in their leases. Many of these nonresidential landlords also prefer that the sheriff remove the tenants pursuant to court order so as not to risk their own safety or to risk a later lawsuit by those tenants based on alleged damage to their personal property or themselves.

A tenancy also may be terminated by a **constructive eviction.** The law implies that the landlord has evicted the tenants when the *landlords have interfered with the tenants' possession and enjoyment of the premises, compelling the tenants to leave.* To effectively maintain a constructive eviction, the premises usually must be in uninhabitable condition. Continual below-freezing temperatures in the premises, with no effort by the landlord to remedy this lack of heat, is an example of a constructive eviction. If the landlord does not fix the premises, the tenants must relinquish possession in order to assert that there has been a constructive eviction. A constructive eviction operates to the advantage of tenants; it terminates the tenancy with no further obligation on their parts.

A lease also may terminate by **abandonment,** in which the *tenants leave the premises permanently.* The landlord subsequently reenters the premises and resumes control over them.

Tenancy also can terminate upon *destruction* of the premises. Usually the lease has a provision calling for termination of the tenancy upon destruction of the premises that makes them unfit for the intended purpose, much like a constructive eviction. Even without that provision, Ohio law terminates the leasehold when it has been destroyed or severely damaged.

If the landlord *sells* the leased real property, the *tenancy does not terminate*. The purchaser takes the realty subject to the lease. This purchaser becomes the new landlord and can proceed after the tenant for any breach of the lease. The purchaser should notify the tenant of the change in ownership, as otherwise the tenant could validly continue to pay rent to the original landlord. Mortgage deeds usually contain an "Assignment of Rent" clause, which gives a lender the right to direct the tenant to pay rent to it, instead of the landlord, if the landlord is delinquent in his or her mortgage payments.

Notification, when applicable, terminates a tenancy. **Periodic tenancies** *terminate by notification.* The classic month-to-month tenancy requires 30 days' notice, by either landlord or tenant, to terminate the tenancy. Also, automatic renewals are avoided by notifying the landlord at the specified time; only then will the tenancy terminate.

Part Performance

Part performance, discussed in Chapter 6, operates in a similar fashion in landlord–tenant law. If a lease is invalid because it does not conform with either the statute of frauds (a writing) or the statute of conveyances (attestation and acknowledgment), part performance can make it nevertheless an enforceable lease. A court uses its equity powers to enforce the lease. Generally, possession plus improvements by the tenant is considered sufficient part performance for equity relief. Tenants must show that they have detrimentally changed their position and that the parties to the lease cannot return to the position they were in before they entered into the lease. For part performance to be applicable, *intent to make a lease* must be shown. Furthermore, tenants must *accept the lease and follow its terms* as if it were valid. The minimum requirements tenants must meet for enforcement of the equitable doctrine of part performance are that *they must be in possession of the premises, be paying rent, and have made improvements on the realty.*

Payment of Rent

Rent is the *usual consideration tenants pay landlords for their tenancies in the leased premises.* Rent is usually money, but it can also be an exchange of services. Typically rent is paid monthly. If the lease does not specify when rent is to be paid, it is due on the last day of the period. This is unsatisfactory to most landlords, however. Therefore, the lease usually provides that the rent is payable on the first day of the month. With that provision, tenants must pay on the first, not the last day of the month. Destruction of the leased premises suspends the tenants' duty to pay rent.

A frequent problem with rent arises when landlords continually accept rent late. At some later time, landlords may want to rid themselves of the tenants, but by accepting that late rent, the landlords cannot do so. The law will say they waived the right to terminate by receiving the rent too late. Landlords' **waiver** may be discharged, however, by notifying tenants that landlords no longer will accept late rent and that thereafter rent must be paid on the due date. If tenants are late with the next rent payment, landlords have a legal basis for bringing a forcible entry and detainer action (securing a court-ordered eviction) against the tenants.

If landlords have never accepted rent late, they have never waived the right to use that as a ground for termination of the tenancy. If landlords wish to terminate the tenancy, they should not accept late rent and should instead follow the appropriate statutory provisions for forcible entry and detainer.

There does not have to be a lease in order for rent to be due the landlords. For example, if tenants hold over and stay in the premises beyond the terms of the lease, tenants become liable for rent at fair rental value.

Rent should be paid to landlords at the leased premises unless the lease provides otherwise. Most leases do provide otherwise. The most common provision allows payment to be mailed to landlords or a designated agent.

Condition of the Premises

The general rule at common law historically has been for tenants to be in a "buyer beware" position regarding the condition of the premises. They were "stuck" with the premises in the condition they got them. They had to pay their rent regardless of the premises' condition. Fortunately, this doctrine is eroding rapidly throughout the country. Increasingly, states' modern statutes, including Ohio's, place substantial statutory obligations upon residential landlords to keep the premises in a healthy, safe condition. Commercial leaseholds generally do not have this statutory protection. Both residential and commercial leaseholds, however, can take advantage of any applicable *housing and building codes.* If landlords do not maintain the premises in compliance with the housing code and if tenants have notified the landlord of the defects, there can be a breach of an implied warranty to maintain those premises in conformity with the code.

A covenant of **quiet enjoyment** is implied more and more in leases of residential real property. This protects the tenants' right to *undisturbed, peaceful enjoyment and possession of the leasehold.* The following can constitute breach of a covenant of quiet enjoyment: permitting another to enter the premises while tenants are still in possession, letting the premises deteriorate to the extent that it substantially interferes with beneficial enjoyment of the realty, lack of adequate electrical wiring, lack of adequate heat, and lack of structural maintenance.

Also, an implied warranty of **habitability** is applied to residential real estate. Thus, landlords warrant that the realty is *fit to be lived in* and is safe and sanitary for tenants' tenancy. This, too, mandates a certain standard of repair and upkeep by landlords, which did not exist at common law.

Tenants' Possession of the Premises

The lease always must convey to tenants the exclusive possession and control of the leased premises. If it does not, it is not a lease but is instead a revocable license merely to use landlords' realty. While tenants possess the leasehold, they cannot commit **waste** upon it. Tenants cannot let the premises go to "rack and ruin." This waste can be *intentional* (e.g., breaking all the windows) or *permissive* (e.g., not repairing broken windows and letting the elements damage the interior thereby). Waste also can be in the form of making permanent, unauthorized changes on the realty, usually to its detriment. Or waste can be beneficial to the property, such as putting in new wall-to-wall carpeting, but it nevertheless is prohibited.

Landlords might have a statutory right to enter the premises to prevent waste and to seek an injunction or a forcible entry and detainer action in court against tenants. Landlords must carefully follow the Ohio Revised Code's limitations on the right of entry into residential premises. For nonresidential premises, landlords have much broader rights of entry unless the lease itself restricts those rights, and many do.

Tenants have the duty of returning the premises to landlords in *substantially the same condition* as they received them, but they are permitted to commit **reasonable wear and tear** on the realty during their possession. If the carpet requires cleaning and the walls repainting, landlords have to bear that expense as reasonable wear and tear. Generally, anything that needs scrubbing and cleaning, not replacement, is reasonable wear and tear. Table 13–1 contrasts waste with permissible wear and tear.

During tenants' possession of the premises, they must make repairs to keep the realty in the same condition as when they took possession, unless the lease or the Ohio Revised Code places specified repair duties upon landlords instead. In residential leases, many specified repair duties are placed upon landlords pursuant to the Ohio Revised Code. Landlords are usually the ones who have the duty to make *extraordinary repairs*—for example, changing the plumbing from galvanized to copper.

Landlords may recover *money damages* from tenants in court to cover injuries tenants do to the leased premises by waste or failure to repair. These damages will be the monetary difference between the market value of the premises, had it been returned to landlords in the original condition, and its market value in its present, damaged condition. In landlords' action they can show the cost of repairs to establish fair market value of the real estate at the beginning and ending of the lease.

Retaliatory Eviction

Landlords have retaliated against tenants for action the tenants have lawfully taken against them. **Retaliatory eviction** means the *landlords seek to avenge the tenants' action by trying to evict them.* Typically, this involves landlords' violating the building code or health code. The tenants inform the board of health, or other local, appropriate agency, which then takes action against the landlords. In turn, the landlords retaliate against the tenants by raising the rent or trying to evict them. Some landlords have tried to retaliate against tenants who have joined together to bargain with them. The Ohio Revised Code protects tenants from landlords' retaliation in residential premises by providing that landlords may not retaliate against tenants by

TABLE 13–1 Comparison of reasonable wear and tear and waste.

REASONABLE WEAR AND TEAR	INTENTIONAL WASTE	PERMISSIVE WASTE
Landlord needs to steam clean carpet and/or repaint walls when tenant vacates.	Landlord needs to replace floorboards in hardwood flooring and have walls replastered—all because tenant made huge gouges in both.	Landlord needs to have floorboards replaced and walls replastered because tenant never had leaks fixed that damaged both.
Tenant is entitled to return of entire security deposit.	Landlord probably will be able to keep security deposit.	Landlord probably will be able to keep security deposit.
Landlord will not be able to sue tenant for damages.	If security deposit is not large enough, landlord can sue tenant for damages.	If security deposit is not large enough, landlord can sue tenant for damages.

increasing the rent, decreasing services, or bringing or threatening to bring an action for possession of the tenants' premises because of the following:

1. Tenants' complaint to a governmental agency of violation of a building, housing, health, or safety code. The violation should materially affect health and safety.
2. Tenants' complaint to landlords for failure to comply with landlords' obligations under the state code.
3. Joining with other tenants for the purpose of negotiating or dealing collectively with the landlords on any of the terms and conditions of a lease.

If landlords do retaliate against tenants, the *tenants may use the retaliatory action of the landlords as a defense* against the landlords' attempt to evict them, to recover possession of the premises, or to end the lease. In addition, the tenants might recover from the landlords any actual damages together with reasonable attorney's fees. The tenants must prove that the eviction attempt resulted from a retaliatory motive. Tenants, however, must be current in their rent or they won't be able to use the landlords' retaliatory acts as a defense in a forcible entry and detainer suit.

Landlords can increase rent to reflect the cost of improvements made on the premises or to reflect an increase in the costs of operating the premises.

Depositing Rent in Court

Residential tenants have gained relief under the Ohio Revised Code by being allowed to *deposit rent with the court rather than with landlords when landlords are in breach of their statutory duty(ies).* This **rent depositing** occurs when landlords fail to fulfill any obligation imposed by the code or by the lease. Also, the condition of the premises could show that landlords have failed to fulfill their obligations, or a governmental agency could determine that the premises are not in compliance with building, housing, health, or safety codes. These violations are especially pertinent when they might materially affect the health and safety of an occupant.

Tenants give notice in writing to landlords, specifying landlords' noncompliance. This notice is sent to the person or place where rent is normally paid. After landlords receive notice and fail to remedy the condition within a reasonable time, tenants (if current in rent payments) may proceed with any of the following:

1. Deposit all rent that is due and thereafter becomes due to landlords with the clerk of courts of the municipal or county court in which the premises are located.
2. Apply to the court for an order directing landlords to remedy the condition, and simultaneously deposit rent and apply for an order reducing the periodic rent due landlords until such time as landlords remedy the condition. Also, tenants may apply for an order to use the rent deposited in court to remedy the condition. The court may require tenants to deposit rent with the clerk of courts.
3. Terminate the rental agreement.

Rent withholding or depositing has been most commonly used in "slum landlord" situations. Slum landlords rent realty that is in extremely bad shape to poor people. Rent withholding can be used against landlords who have kept the premises in bad condition and thus are in violation of the health and building codes.

The clerk of courts who receives rent deposit money from tenants must follow certain statutory requirements. This is especially important because, as a practical matter, rent deposits usually are made by a large number of tenants acting collectively against landlords. Therefore, a large amount of money may be deposited in court.

Defenses to Rent Deposit

The court orders the release to landlords of rent on deposit with the clerk, less costs, under any one of the following circumstances that landlords have used as a defense:

1. The court finds that landlords have fulfilled their obligations under the code or pursuant to the lease.
2. Landlords have complied with the building, housing, health, or safety codes, or the condition that landlords were notified about has been remedied.
3. Tenants did not comply with the notice requirement for depositing rent.
4. Tenants were not current in rent payments at the time they began rent deposits with the clerk of courts.

If the court discovers that the condition contained in the notice was the result of an act or omission of tenants or that tenants intentionally acted in bad faith, tenants can be held liable for damages caused to landlords and for costs. Reasonable attorney's fees also might be awarded landlords if tenants intentionally act in bad faith.

Partial Release of Rent by Court

While the case between landlords and tenants is pending in court, the clerk can release part of the rent on deposit for payment of periodic interest and/or principal payments due on a mortgage on the premises, insurance premiums for the premises, real estate taxes on the premises, utility services, or repairs and other customary and usual costs of operating the premises as a rental unit. In determining whether to partially release rent for these payments, the court considers the amount of rent landlords receive from other rental units in the same building, costs of operating those units, and costs that may be required to remedy the condition tenants have complained and given notice about. Landlords ask for this relief by filing a motion with the court.

Security Deposits

Most landlords require that tenants put down a **security deposit,** a certain amount of *money, to be held as security for landlords in the event tenants cause damage to the realty.* This amount is usually one month's rent. Ohio law, however, puts no limit on how small or large security deposits can be.

Landlords may not use this money for reasonable wear and tear that tenants cause to the realty. In the past, many landlords abused security deposits. In some cases landlords waited six months or more after the tenancy expired to refund the deposit or they kept part or all of the deposit to cover the cost of cleaning and repainting. These costs are really ordinary wear and tear by the tenants, not damage. Thus, landlords may not deduct for these costs.

Ohio enacted statutes designed to prohibit abuse of the security deposit for residential tenancies. There is a required time limit to refund the security deposit, as well as a required itemization by landlords of any damage done to the premises. Also, interest can be owed on the principal sum of the security deposit by landlords to the tenants.

When the lease ends, any property or money the landlords hold as a security deposit must first be applied to any rent the tenants owe to the landlords. Then landlords apply it toward payment of damages tenants have done to the premises as covered by the Ohio Revised Code or the lease. Any deduction from the security deposit must be itemized, and the landlords must identify the damage in a written notice together with the amount due. Tenants must give landlords a forwarding address in writing to enable landlords to send a written itemization and amount due from the security deposit. If landlords fail to comply with the security deposit return formalities, tenants typically can recover in court money damages plus reasonable attorney's fees.

Personal Injury on the Premises

If landlords know or should know about *hazardous conditions* on the premises at the time they lease them, they have a duty to disclose this hazard to tenants. If they fail to disclose the hazard and either tenants or guests are injured because of it, landlords usually are liable for the injury.

The modern view of tort liability for injuries on leased premises holds landlords liable for any injuries to tenants or guests for a dangerous condition that existed before, or arose after, tenants took possession. To be liable, landlords must fail to use reasonable care to repair the condition and the condition must violate either a duty created by the Ohio Revised Code or an implied warranty of habitability. In nonresidential leases this translates to the landlords' warning the tenant about the danger but not necessarily fixing the dangerous condition. In residential leases, landlords have both the duty to warn about and the duty to repair the dangerous condition. The dangerous condition also should proximately cause the injuries, not merely be a factor.

Apartment buildings have *common areas,* used in common by all the tenants—hallways, stairs, mail room, lobby, driveway, entrances and exits, swimming pools, game rooms, parking garage. Landlords retain control of the common areas and thereby are responsible for using ordinary care to keep these areas in a safe condition. If they fail to do so and tenants or guests are injured, again it is the landlords who are usually liable.

Commercial Leases

Commercial leases cover premises used for a commercial, not a residential, purpose, and the terms of these leases vary. Some call for a fixed monthly amount plus utilities, much like a residential lease. In these **gross leases** landlords *pay all property charges—taxes, mortgage, and insurance.* This is common in the lease of office space for professional purposes, such as doctor's, lawyer's, broker's, and engineer's offices. **Percentage leases** are the most common for commercial retail establishments. These leases require tenants to pay *a fixed monthly rental and, in addition, a percentage from their gross sales.* The rental also could be entirely on a percentage lease basis, with no fixed monthly rental addition. Usually, however, landlords want some guaranteed minimum per month stated in the lease.

Often the commercial real estate broker is paid a commission on a similar percentage basis over the terms of the lease. Any landlords or brokers dealing in a percentage lease or commission set-up are highly particular about tenant quality. They should select only tenants who have a well-established business, heavy volume, and excellent credit rating.

Commercial leases also frequently provide that tenants' rent can be increased or decreased if the real estate taxes or assessments on the realty change. Also, particularly in an inflationary period, many of these leases provide for an increase in the rent to keep even with inflation. Some measure has to be used, and it is typically the cost of living index put out by the government. These adjustments are not usually found in residential leases.

Another variation is that *tenants, rather than landlords, pay all the property charges,* such as taxes, insurance, and mortgage payments. These are called **net leases.** In a specialized form of the net lease, called the **ground lease,** *landlords lease a vacant lot to tenants with the provision that tenants will erect a building.* The term of the ground lease is usually for the life expectancy of the building.

Commercial leases generally are for longer terms than residential ones. Residential leases usually run from one to three years, whereas commercial leases run anywhere from several years to 99.

CASE STUDY FROM THE OHIO SUPREME COURT

MILLER V. RITCHIE
45 Ohio St.3d 222, 543 N.E.2d 1265 (1989)

Facts: The Ritchies rented an apartment in Bethel, Ohio, from Dexter Miller. It was a month-to-month oral tenancy at $200 per month. The Ritchies occupied this unit for more than two years. Throughout their tenancy the real property had serious defects: faulty and dangerous electrical wiring, holes in the floor, inadequate plumbing, and no heating system. The Clermont County Building Inspector had notified Miller that the building was a serious hazard under the Ohio Building Code.

Trial Court: Miller violated the statutory duties owed by landlords under Chapter 5321 of the Ohio Revised Code. Judgment was for the Ritchies for $3,000 plus interest and costs and judgment for Miller in the amount of $800 unpaid rent.

Court of Appeals: Held against Ritchies because they continued to occupy over an extended period of time without pursuing their statutory remedies. The Ritchies were not entitled to damages.

Issues Before the Ohio Supreme Court:

1. Whether the Ritchies waived their right to recover damages by occupying the defective rental premises for more than two years without pursuing statutory remedies.
2. Whether the trial court erred in computing the damages to the Ritchies.

Held by the Ohio Supreme Court:

1. Where a landlord has been placed on notice of a tenant's claim, the tenant's occupancy of defective rental premises over a lengthy period of time does not constitute a waiver of the landlord's duty to maintain the premises as required by Ohio Revised Code 5321.04 or a waiver of the tenant's right to recover for damages resulting from the landlord's breach of duty.
2. Where the landlord breaches a duty to maintain rental property and the tenant does not make repairs, the measure of damages is the difference between the rental value of the property in the defective condition and what it would have been if the property had been maintained.

This case was sent back to the trial court on the second issue only so that the trial court could recalculate damages in accordance with this opinion.

SUMMARY OF CONTENT

1. A lease is both a conveyance of an estate or interest in land called a leasehold and a contract between landlord and tenant.
2. The lease is supported by consideration, which is usually the tenant's payment of rent in exchange for possession of the landlord's premises.
3. To be valid under the statute of frauds, a lease for more than a year must be in writing, as must a lease that will expire more than one year after the date the parties agreed to it.
4. The lease must allow the premises to be used only for legal purposes.
5. Short-term leases (those covering leaseholds of fewer than 99 years) are the primary ones in use today.
6. Legal descriptions are contained in leases that should be recorded.
7. To enter into a lease, landlord and tenant both must have capacity to contract.
8. A valid lease must be signed by the landlord and delivered to and accepted by the tenant. The better view is that the tenant should also sign the lease.
9. Leases for more than three years should be recorded pursuant to the statute of conveyances, as should leases that would last more than three years if an option to renew were exercised.
10. Recording the lease acts as constructive notice to those who subsequently acquire interest in the same land.
11. Leases for more than three years usually must be acknowledged and attested in order to be valid between landlord and tenant, as must those that would last more than three years if an option to renew within the lease were exercised.
12. Unless prohibited within the lease, a lease may be assigned or sublet. Sometimes landlords are given the right to approve of the assignee or sublessee as long as they use reasonable standards.
13. A lease can restrict the premises for a certain use, such as when an apartment is restricted to residential use.
14. A lease can validly renew pursuant to an automatic renewal clause, providing for a term of like duration unless either landlords or tenants notify the other in advance that they do not want to renew.
15. Alternatively, a lease can renew by option; i.e., in the lease, tenants are given an option to renew under like or stated terms, but tenants must notify landlords that they are exercising the option to renew within a period of time stated in the lease.
16. Tenancies can terminate by: expiration, surrender, forfeiture, death, eviction, constructive eviction, abandonment, destruction of the premises, or notification.
17. Forcible entry and detainer suits occur when landlords seek to lawfully eject tenants from the premises using the procedures set forth in the Ohio Revised Code in a court of law.
18. The persons most commonly subject to forcible entry and detainer actions are holdover tenants—persons failing to pay rent under an oral tenancy and persons breaching an obligation under their lease.
19. The law implies that a constructive eviction of the tenant has occurred when there has been such a serious interference with the tenancy that the tenant is compelled to leave the premises.

20. An invalid lease may be enforced if the tenant has partially performed it. Part performance is payment of rent, possession of the premises, and improvements to the property.
21. To rid themselves of a late-rent-paying tenant, landlords must first notify tenant that they will no longer accept late rent. If tenant is late with the next rent payment, landlords have a legal basis for securing a court-ordered eviction of tenants.
22. If landlords do not maintain the premises in compliance with the statutory housing code and tenants have notified landlords of the defects, there can be a breach of an implied warranty to maintain those premises in conformity with the code.
23. A covenant of quiet enjoyment can be implied into residential leases, protecting the tenant's right to undisturbed, peaceful enjoyment and possession of the leasehold.
24. A warranty of habitability also can be implied into residential leases; i.e., that the realty is fit to be lived in and is safe and sanitary for the tenant's tenancy.
25. A tenant cannot commit intentional waste (e.g., breaking the windows) or permissive waste (e.g., not repairing broken windows and letting the elements in) to the leased premises.
26. The tenant has the duty of returning the premises to the landlord in substantially the same condition as received, less reasonable wear and tear.
27. The landlord is responsible for extraordinary repairs, whereas the tenant is responsible for ordinary repairs, unless their lease provides otherwise. Each also must follow repair duties, as set forth in the Ohio Revised Code, which are substantial for residential landlords and tenants.
28. When the landlord tries to evict a tenant of residential premises because the tenant has acted lawfully against the landlord, the law calls this a retaliatory eviction and will not uphold it.
29. Residential tenants can deposit rent with the court rather than with landlords when landlords are in breach of their statutory duty.
30. Landlords can require tenants to pay them a sum of money, held by the landlords, as a security deposit in case any damage is done on the premises. A landlord may not keep this money for ordinary wear and tear and might be required to pay interest on the sum to the residential tenant.
31. The modern view of tort liability for injuries on leased premises holds the landlord liable for any injuries to tenants or guests because of not disclosing a dangerous condition that existed before or arose after the tenant took possession.
32. Landlords are usually liable for any personal injuries that occur in the common areas of their leased properties.
33. In gross commercial leases the landlord pays all property charges—taxes, mortgage, and insurance.
34. In percentage commercial leases, the tenants pay a fixed monthly rental plus a percentage from their gross sales.
35. In net commercial leases, the tenant pays all the property charges.

Review Questions

1. Which of these leases usually should be recorded:
   a. any residential lease
   b. three-year lease
   c. four-year lease
   d. any commercial lease

2. Under the statute of frauds, which of these leases should be in writing:
   a. monthly periodic tenancy
   b. six-month lease
   c. lease for more than a year
   d. one-year lease

3. Which of these leases should be attested and acknowledged:
   a. yearly periodic tenancy
   b. one-year lease
   c. three-year lease
   d. fixed-term tenancy of four years

4. This person receives a leasehold of less than the tenant's entire interest:
   a. sublessee
   b. assignee
   c. tenant with life estate
   d. reversioner

5. The tenant must pay the real estate taxes on the leased real property in which case:
   a. net lease
   b. gross lease
   c. percentage lease
   d. any commercial lease

6. The landlord should pick a tenant with an excellent, large-volume retail business for this lease:
   a. net lease
   b. gross lease
   c. percentage lease
   d. ground lease

7. When tenants leave the premises in a condition in which the walls require repainting and the carpeting requires steam-cleaning, they have committed:
   a. waste
   b. reasonable wear and tear
   c. breach of the duty to repair
   d. nuisance

8. In the situation given in the preceding question, tenants are entitled to:
   a. their entire security deposit
   b. the difference between their security deposit and the cost of cleaning and painting
   c. none of their security deposit
   d. not pay their last month's rent

9. This termination of tenancy should be done pursuant to court order:
   a. notification
   b. abandonment
   c. surrender
   d. forcible entry and detainer

10. This termination is commonly used for periodic tenancies:
    a. notification
    b. destruction
    c. death
    d. sale

11. Residential real estate salespeople will likely experience the following in their practice:
    a. a seller refuses to vacate even though closing and possession dates have passed
    b. a purchaser refuses to close a transaction when he has been given possession prior to title transfer date
    c. purchasers will have to wait for tenant's lease to expire before they can take possession of the realty
    d. all of the above

12. In construing a lease, a court usually:
    a. tries to carry out the intention of the parties as shown in the lease
    b. gives all terms in the lease their most technical definition
    c. does so in terms most favorable to tenants
    d. does so in terms most favorable to landlords

13. If residential tenants are eligible to withhold rent from derelict landlords, they pay their rent to:
    a. the tenants' union
    b. an escrow account maintained by a bank
    c. the clerk of courts
    d. the Housing Commission

14. Residential landlords abuse tenants' security deposits, and may subject themselves to suit, when they:
    a. wait more than a year to refund the security deposit
    b. kept the security deposit to cover the cost of cleaning and repainting
    c. refuse to itemize damage deductions
    d. all of the above

15. An option to renew a lease requires:
    a. notice of exercising the option
    b. silence, which is consent to the option
    c. starting the whole leasing process over
    d. purchasing the real property being leased

16. An automatic renewal clause:
    a. causes the tenant to have an option to renew
    b. will renew for a like term if neither party gives notice
    c. is now invalid for residential leases
    d. is an unconscionable term that courts will not enforce

17. Premises wholly unfit for their intended use terminate as a tenancy by:
    a. abandonment
    b. eviction
    c. constructive eviction
    d. destruction

18. Sellers refuse to vacate their former home after the real estate purchase is closed, even though purchasers now have title. The proper legal action by purchasers is:
    a. specific performance
    b. foreclosure
    c. forcible entry and detainer
    d. quiet title action

19. Landlords usually have the duty to:
    a. disclose hazards they know or should know about at time of leasing
    b. make ordinary repairs
    c. maintain liability insurance on tenants' premises
    d. maintain a strict, moral code in the building

20. What protects tenants' right to undisturbed, peaceful enjoyment and possession of the leasehold?
    a. implied warranty of habitability
    b. covenant of quiet enjoyment
    c. constructive eviction
    d. attestation

21. This person receives a leasehold consisting of the entire interest of the tenant:
    a. sublessee
    b. assignee
    c. tenant with life estate
    d. periodic tenant

22. When a lease expires:
    a. there was an ending date and no renewal occurred
    b. it was a periodic tenancy
    c. it could not have contained an option to renew
    d. the landlord can personally eject the tenants from the premises that very day

23. Landlords' failure to follow the city health code breaches:
    a. covenant of quiet enjoyment
    b. implied warranty of conscionability
    c. covenant of *caveat emptor*
    d. implied warranty of habitability

24. Ohio's landlord–tenant law can be found in the:
    a. Ohio Revised Code
    b. Constitutions
    c. United States Code
    d. Code of Federal Regulations

25. Purchasers move into the realty before title transfer date. They subsequently refuse to close the transaction but remain in possession. In addition to breach of contract, the sellers have an action in:
    a. foreclosure
    b. quiet title
    c. forcible entry and detainer
    d. rent depositing

Answer Key

1. c
2. c
3. d
4. a
5. a
6. c
7. b
8. a
9. d
10. a
11. d
12. a
13. c
14. d
15. a
16. b
17. c
18. c
19. a
20. b
21. b
22. a
23. d
24. a
25. c

14
DECEDENTS' ESTATES

KEY TERMS

administrator
attorney-in-fact
beneficiary
bequest
certificate of transfer
codicils
descent and distribution, statute of
devise
durable power of attorney
escheat
executor
heir
intestate
legacy
power of attorney
probate court
testator
trust
trustee
trustor
ward
will

SOONER OR LATER, real estate salespeople find that they must attempt to list or sell realty owned by the estate of a deceased person (decedent), by a trustee, or by the guardian of a minor. This realty must be put in the hands of some person who has been appointed by the local probate court to manage and sell the realty for the benefit of another person who either will not, or cannot, personally sell the realty. To market these realties most efficiently, salespeople should understand something about the probate court proceedings that affect these sales. Also, because the whole business of probate seems to be shrouded in mystery for most people, the salesperson can help reduce the confusion and uncertainty that are so common with these slightly irregular transactions.

Statute of Descent and Distribution

Ohio has a statute covering to whom, and in what proportion, a decedent's property is to be distributed when the decedent dies **intestate,** or *without leaving a will.* A *person who receives property pursuant to the statute of descent and distribution is called an* **heir.**

The statute of **descent and distribution** covers *persons related by blood or marriage to the decedent.* The decedent's surviving spouse and children are "first in line" to receive property under the statute. If the decedent leaves no children, the surviving spouse receives the entire estate. If there are no children or surviving spouse, the decedent's parents inherit it. Thereafter, the statute covers all the other relatives who might exist by blood or marriage.

If it is discovered that decedents have none of these blood or marriage relations, as designated by the statute, decedents' estates **escheat** to the state. This means that the state *receives all the property in decedents' estates.*

If people have a will, they can leave their property to anyone they choose, including persons or entities not related by blood or marriage. People who know of this escheat provision are more likely to designate a favored charity or other institution than to let the state receive all of their property.

Figure 14–1 is Ohio's descent and distribution statute. It also can be used when the decedent's last will is declared invalid for any reason whatsoever.

FOR EXAMPLE

> The testator, domiciled in Ohio, had two children, Mary and Ann. She survived her spouse, the children's father, by a decade. Testator's last will, made when she was 75 and suffering from the last stages of Alzheimer's, shortly before her death, left her entire estate to Mary and nothing to Ann. Ann probably will contest the will, claiming that her mother was incompetent when she made the will and was subject to undue influence by Mary. She will ask in the will contest that the will be declared invalid and that the statute of descent and distribution be applied instead. If she wins the case (likely), Mary and Ann will share equally in the estate.

Wills

Wills are the *only legally recognized way people can express their desires about how and to whom their real and personal properties are to be distributed after their death.* People who *make wills* are called **testators** (sometimes the term testatrix is used when the person is a woman). Wills take effect only at the moment of testators' deaths. Before death, testators may revoke their wills any number of times and either make new wills or make none at all.

The terminology describing the type of property given by wills differs. **Devises** are *real property.* **Bequests** are *personal property.* **Legacies** are *money.* Testators are not required to separate real property from personal property, or money, under wills. They may lump it all together if they so choose:

FOR EXAMPLE

> I devise and bequeath to my beloved husband, John Doe, all my property of any nature whatsoever.

On the other hand, if the testator wants to separate the property, as in the case of multiple recipients, he or she may do so:

FOR EXAMPLE

> I devise to my beloved wife, Jane Doe, all my real property. To my son, Michael Doe, I bequeath my antique gun collection. To my daughter, Barbara Doe, I leave a legacy of $10,000.

Requirements for Making Valid Wills

Ohio requires the following things to create valid wills:

1. Testators must be possessed of *sound mind and memory* at the time they make their wills.
2. Testators must have reached the *age of majority.*
3. Wills must be in *writing and evidence testamentary intent;* that is, a disposition of property to take effect only at death.
4. Testators must have the necessary *capacity* to make wills; they must understand what wills are and the extent and nature of their property holdings. They must be aware of the existence of those persons who are the natural objects of their bounty, such as a spouse and children.
5. Wills must be *signed by testators at the end.*
6. Wills must be *attested to by at least two witnesses,* who intend to act as witnesses, and sign the wills to validate them. Generally, witnesses sign the wills after seeing testators sign them of their own free accord. Witnesses do not need to read the wills; however, testators must tell witnesses that they are their wills. These witnesses must be competent but *should not be beneficiaries* under the will. In Ohio, if the witnesses are beneficiaries, the wills are considered valid but the witnesses/beneficiaries forfeit their interests under the wills. They are limited instead to receiving what would have come to them as heirs under the statute of descent and distribution.

Devise

When real estate is devised in a will, it is *often encumbered by a mortgage lien.* A devisee commonly assumes that the mortgage will be paid off as a matter of closing out the estate and paying off all testator's debts. Whether this indeed happens or not depends on the exact provision in the will. If the will makes only a general direction to pay the testator's debts, the devisee has no right of exoneration of the mortgage lien. Thus, the devisee obtains the real estate with the mortgage lien. If the will specifically provides a *right of exoneration* for that lien, however, the devisee can

2105.06 Statute of descent and distribution

When a person dies intestate having title or right to any personal property, or to any real estate or inheritance in this state, the personal property shall be distributed, and the real estate or inheritance shall descend and pass in parcenary, except as otherwise provided by law, in the following course:

(A) If there is no surviving spouse, to the children of the intestate or their lineal descendants, per stirpes;

(B) If there is a spouse and one child or its lineal descendants surviving, the first sixty thousand dollars if the spouse is the natural or adoptive parent of the child, or the first twenty thousand dollars if the spouse is not the natural or adoptive parent of the child, plus one-half of the balance of the intestate estate to the spouse and the remainder to the child or his lineal descendants, per stirpes;

(C) If there is a spouse and more than one child or their lineal descendants surviving, the first sixty thousand dollars if the spouse is the natural or adoptive parent of one of the children, or the first twenty thousand dollars if the spouse is the natural or adoptive parent of none of the children, plus one-third of the balance of intestate estate to the spouse and the remainder to the children equally, or to the lineal descendants of any deceased child, per stirpes;

(D) If there are no children or their lineal descendants, then the whole to the surviving spouse;

(E) If there is no spouse and no children or their lineal descendants, to the parents of the intestate equally, or to the surviving parent;

(F) If there is no spouse, no children or their lineal descendants, and no parent surviving, to the brothers and sisters, whether of the whole or of the half blood of the intestate, or their lineal descendants, per stirpes;

(G) If there are no brothers or sisters or their lineal descendants, one half to the paternal grandparents of the intestate equally, or to the survivor of them, and one half to the maternal grandparents of the intestate equally, or to the survivor of them;

(H) If there is no paternal grandparent or no maternal grandparent, one half to the lineal descendants of the deceased grandparents, per stirpes; if there are no such lineal descendants, then to the surviving grandparents or their lineal descendants, per stirpes; if there are no surviving grandparents or their lineal descendants, then to the next of kin of the intestate, provided there shall be no representation among such next of kin;

(I) If there are no next of kin, to stepchildren or their lineal descendants, per stirpes;

(J) If there are no stepchildren or their lineal descendants, escheat to the state.

FIGURE 14–1 Ohio statute of descent and distribution.

compel payment from the estate during its administration. This, of course, is a problem only when more than one person is taking pursuant to the will. If one person is the sole beneficiary under the will, that person will receive all the property and will discharge the testator's debts in the way most advantageous to himself or herself.

Probate court issues a **certificate of transfer** for devised real estate. The certificate gives a description of the realty, along with the testator's and the devisee's names. The certificate is recorded in the county where the subject realty is located.

Exclusions

Generally, testators within their wills can give their property to anyone they choose and also exclude anyone they choose. One important exception is if testators *exclude, or provide too little* (compared to the statute of descent and distribution) *for surviving spouses*. Those spouses then have substantial rights under the Ohio Revised Code to elect against the wills—that is, to follow other property provisions as allowed to them under the Ohio Revised Code.

Testators usually can *exclude from their wills any of their children who have reached the age of majority*. Thus, adult children can be totally excluded from wills and receive no portion of their parents' estates. The term *children,* for purposes of wills and descent and distribution, means the natural or adopted children of testators regardless of children's ages. Stepchildren are not included in this definition.

Revoking or Changing Wills

Testators may revoke wills prior to their death. A typical way testators do this is by making new wills and within them expressly revoking the prior wills. If later wills are inconsistent with earlier wills, the one with the most recent date will take effect. Testators also may revoke their wills by intentionally destroying them or having someone else destroy them at their direction.

Testators can change their wills in two ways: (a) they can revoke their last wills and execute new ones, or (b) they can draw up codicils. **Codicils** are *legal instruments that alter wills without revoking those wills.* The same formalities used in making wills must be used in making codicils. Codicils are generally recommended for making one or two changes to wills but not for making a massive change in the whole thrust of those wills. New wills should be drawn instead in the latter case.

Guardian

Wills should nominate guardians for any minor children of testators. If guardians are not nominated, the probate court will have to appoint them instead. If both parents die simultaneously, this can be a real problem. For example, if the parents have neglected to nominate a guardian, perhaps more than one family member will ask the court to be appointed guardian. Even worse, perhaps no one person will want to act as guardian for all of the children, necessitating that the children be split up among multiple guardians. Testators should ask the persons they desire to be guardians if they will be willing to serve as guardians, because probate court cannot force people to act as guardians.

Probate court appointments of guardians are *also necessary for incompetent adults*—for example, persons who are incapable of handling their own property because of mental infirmity, substance abuse, or confinement to a penal institution. The *person subject to a guardianship,* whether a minor or an incompetent adult, is referred to as the **ward.** Because the guardian will manage all the property, the guardian is the person who must consent to any real estate contracts or conveyances. Guardians legally bind wards as to everything that has been done by guardians within the proper scope of their appointed duties. If guardians do something beyond the authority that the court has given them, those actions will not bind the ward.

So that the probate court can keep tabs on the activities of its appointed guardians, the court requires the guardians to file periodic accounts with the court. These have to be approved before the court will release the guardian from its control.

Ohio law provides for a conservatorship for physically incapacitated adults who are mentally competent. Under this provision, the ward is more involved in the granting, or not granting, of certain powers than is the incompetent adult under a guardianship.

Executor or Administrator

The will also names the executor of the estate (the word executrix is used when the person is a woman). An **executor** is the person who has the *power to dispose of and distribute all the property in the estate after paying off all valid claims against the estate.* The executor can be one of the persons, or the only person, receiving the property in the estate. The executor also can be a person who is receiving no property whatsoever from the estate.

When a decedent dies intestate, probate court appoints a person, the **administrator,** to do generally *the same things an executor does, but pursuant to the statute of descent and distribution instead of the will.* (The term administratrix is used when the administrator is a woman.) The administrator is usually the person most closely related to the decedent, who will take part or all of the estate under the statute of descent and distribution.

Probate Court

Probate court has *exclusive jurisdiction over the dispositions of estates, in hearing and determining cases regarding the validity of wills.* After the testator dies, the will must be filed in probate court. When construing a will, the probate court tries to ascertain the testator's intent. When doing this, the court looks at the will as a whole rather than in parts. It presumes the will is valid unless contrary evidence is presented. This presumption is based on public policy that favors disposition of property by will.

If spouses (or others) put their real and personal property into survivorship methods of coownership, as we discussed at length in Chapter 4, those properties will be outside the jurisdiction of probate court. The surviving coowner will receive that property automatically by that coownership and will not have to put those assets through the probate court process.

Many people confuse the concepts of an estate going through probate court proceedings and an estate having to pay taxes at the federal or state levels. These are actually two independent concerns. If an estate has to go through probate court, it is because that estate has real and/or personal property, either disposed of by will or by the statute of descent and distribution. By contrast, estate tax, on both federal and state levels, is involved with the assets that are subject to estate tax when a death has occurred, and with the class of persons to whom these assets are transferring, as that affects whether an estate tax will or will not be owed. It is entirely possible, of course, that when one dies, the estate will have to be probated and there will be estate taxes due at both the federal and the state levels. It is also possible, however, for many married people to avoid both the probate court process and significant estate tax through advance planning with their attorney.

At times it is advisable to have the estate go through probate court. For example, if minor children are involved, a testamentary trust with a named trustee under the supervision of probate court is usually recommended. This is true particularly if the child (or children) has divorced parents or if both parents were lost simultaneously in a catastrophe.

Will Contest

Wills can be challenged in what is known as a will contest. Fortunately, will contests are not frequent. The ultimate issue in a will contest is *whether the writing produced is the last will or codicil of the testator.* If the testator complied with all the formalities, the usual challenges to the will are that the *testator was of unsound mind or under duress* at the time of making the will or that a *beneficiary exerted undue influence* over the testator in the making of the will. To prove undue influence, a plaintiff has to prove that the testator was susceptible and that the beneficiary had the opportunity to exert influence and did, in fact, exert improper influence, with the resulting will showing the effect of such influence.

FOR EXAMPLE

A testator's children are wholly excluded under the will, and the stepmother-widow receives the entire estate, the stepmother-widow's having exerted undue influence over the testator. Perhaps he was in ill health at the time of making the will and she, while nursing him, had an opportunity to exert influence. If these grounds can be proven in probate court, the will can be set aside and an earlier, unrevoked will or the statute of descent and distribution will be used instead.

Only persons with an interest in a will can contest that will in probate court. In the above example, the testator's children, who were left out of the will but provided for under the statute of descent and distribution, could contest the will. The contesting person must join to the will contest lawsuit the other parties who have an interest in the will. Thus, the parties who necessarily must be joined to a will contest action are the persons designated in the will (the stepmother-widow in the above example), the persons who would inherit under the statute of descent and distribution, and the executor or administrator of the estate.

Power of Attorney (Attorney-in-Fact)

The **power of attorney** is given to *a person named by people to act for them if they physically cannot, or do not feel like acting, for themselves.* The appointee is called an **attorney-in-fact.**

FOR EXAMPLE

A power of attorney could be used if John Smith were going to the state of Washington before necessary real estate closing documents had been prepared and were ready for signature. John could appoint someone, say his wife Mary, to be his attorney-in-fact, using a power of attorney, and Mary could then sign the documents for John. She would sign as:

John Smith

JOHN SMITH, by MARY SMITH,
Attorney-in-Fact

Note that Mary does not sign her own name when she is signing for John as his attorney-in-fact.

A principal can go one step further and create a **durable power of attorney** by adding these words to the document: "This power of attorney shall not be affected by disability of the principal." Thereafter, if the principal becomes disabled, incapacitated, or incompetent, the attorney-in-fact can still use the durable power of attorney validly. If a guardian is thereafter appointed for the principal and the guardian is not the attorney-in-fact, the attorney-in-fact, during continuance of the appointment, accounts to the guardian rather than to the principal. The guardian has the same power the principal would have had, if not incompetent, to revoke all or part of the power and authority of the attorney-in-fact.

An attorney-at-law should prepare the power of attorney. A power of attorney must be *recorded* when the power is used to convey, mortgage, or lease an interest in real estate. Figure 14–2 shows a complete, standard power of attorney.

Power of attorney can have no effect after the death of the person who granted it, because attorneys-in-fact can do only what the person could do if present. Likewise, guardianships terminate with the death of the wards. In both cases the will or the statute of descent and distribution thereafter applies, directing what is to happen to the decedent's property.

Sometimes clients ask salespeople to hold their powers of attorney. This can be risky. Salespeople should refer the matter to their broker. The broker, in turn, should consult with an attorney regarding the potential liability in a licensee's becoming a client's attorney-in-fact.

FOR EXAMPLE

A listing salesperson takes the power of attorney for the seller, who has moved to another state. The listing lingers on the market for many months. With only two weeks left on the listing, the listing salesperson comes up with an offer from one of her last open house prospects. It is $15,000 less than asking price, a sum that the seller has turned down in previous offers. The listing salesperson calls the seller, who advises the salesperson that he has changed his mind and now is agreeable to that sum. He directs the salesperson to accept the offer as his attorney-in-fact. The listing salesperson signs the multiple purchase contracts, gives one to purchasers, and forwards one to the seller.

Upon his receipt of the purchase contract, the seller denies that he consented to the offer. He says that he instructed the salesperson to reject the offer. Claiming conflict of interest, he accuses the salesperson of wrongfully using the power of attorney so as to take advantage of her last chance to earn a commission on his real property. The seller sues the salesperson and the broker for failing to act as his fiduciary and for actual fraud. Purchasers, meanwhile, threaten to sue everyone if no one conveys the real property to them when date of performance comes due on the purchase contract.

This nightmarish scenario could have been avoided entirely if the broker had a policy that salespeople cannot hold powers of attorney for clients because of the risk of conflict of interest. *An attorney always should be consulted in connection with questions about powers of attorney, guardianships, and the sale of real estate,* so that no nasty snags and mistakes materialize to upset an otherwise smooth and efficient transaction.

Table 14–1 compares and contrasts the guardianship, power of attorney, and durable power of attorney.

TRUSTS

When people own property and desire that it be used and managed for the benefit of another, they may well use the legal device called the **trust.** We first discussed this concept in Chapter 4, in regard to one person's holding title and another person's benefiting from that holding. Here, we expand the concept as a *method of estate planning.*

The trust may be one that takes effect while the **trustor,** the *owner of trust property,* is alive, in which case it is called an *inter vivos or living trust.* If the trust is designed to operate after the trustor has died, it is called a *testamentary trust,* because it will operate in conjunction with the will, or testament.

The **trustee** is said to *have legal title to the property,* whereas the **beneficiary** *retains equitable title.* When dealing with real estate, this means that the deed (legal title) is held in the name of the trustee (e.g., to Arnold Adams, Trustee, Grantee), and the beneficiary has the right to go to court to demand that the court do justice (act as an equity or chancery court) and force the trustee to properly manage the property for the beneficiary's best interests.

Ohio has statutes that specify which investments a trustee can make in a beneficiary's best interests. Usually the purchase of a home, for the beneficiary of a trust, is considered one of the best investments the trustee can make. Thus, under one approach the trustee holds legal title to the realty while the beneficiary has the

FIGURE 14–2 Sample durable power of attorney.

DURABLE POWER OF ATTORNEY

I, JOHN SMITH, of CHESTERVILLE, OHIO 44021, hereby appoint ABEL ADAMS, of BRIGHTON OHIO 44023, or if (s)he is unable or unwilling to serve, MABEL ADAMS, of BRIGHTON, OHIO 44023, my Attorney-in-fact, to hold, manage and control all real and personal property now owned and hereafter acquired by or for me, and to do all things (except make health care decisions, which power is separately granted) in the opinion of my Attorney deemed necessary or desirable to protect my interests, including, but not limited to, the following:

(1) To institute, maintain, defend, settle and dismiss legal proceedings;

(2) to collect and compromise debts and claims owed to me;

(3) to pay and compromise debts and claims owed by me;

(4) to endorse and receive payment for checks payable to me, to sign and deliver checks on accounts in my name jointly with another and to withdraw from and deposit to accounts in my name alone and in my name jointly with another;

(5) to sign and perform contracts and written instruments;

(6) to demand and receive interest, dividends and other amounts due me;

(7) to sell, exchange, lease and otherwise dispose of my property (including without limitation, real property, tangible personal property and intangible personal property such as stocks, bonds and other securities) and to execute and deliver deeds, leases, stock and bond powers, assignments and other instruments for such purposes;

(8) to invest and reinvest funds in personal and real property of any kind;

(9) to exercise rights of ownership (including voting rights and granting of proxies) that I may have with regard to securities and other intangible interests;

(10) to borrow money and to renew existing loans for any purpose (including the purchase of securities and other property) at prevailing interest rates, to sign and deliver notes therefor and to secure lenders by pledges or mortgages of my property;

(11) to insure my property and to pay premiums for and cancel policies of insurance;

(12) to execute and deliver releases, discharges and receipts;

(13) to have access to safe deposit boxes rented in my name or that I may enter and to remove the contents thereof and to deposit anything therein;

(14) to employ and discharge attorneys, accountants, investment counsel and other professional advisors and agents;

(15) to act with respect to my federal, state and local taxes for every tax year, including signing and filing returns, receiving refund checks, appearing before agents and tribunals and prosecuting claims for refunds;

(16) to add my property to revocable trusts that I have created and may create and to exercise, with the consent of the trustee of any such trust, rights that I may have to withdraw property from such trusts (hereby releasing the trustee from any liability for giving such consent in the exercise of its best judgment);

(continued)

FIGURE 14–2 Continued.

(17) to open, operate and maintain a securities brokerage account wherein securities of any nature may be bought, sold or traded, on margin or otherwise;

(18) to exercise any right I may have to disclaim as a disclaimant under Section 1339.60 of the Ohio Revised Code or any law of similar import, in compliance with Section 2518 of the Internal Revenue Code, thus granting to my Attorney all authority to disclaim that I may have; and

(19) to make gifts or consent to split gifts (under Internal Revenue Code Section 2513) to my spouse and/or to my lineal descendant(s) in per stirpital shares, including my Attorney, in an amount, with respect to persons other than my spouse, not exceeding $10,000 from me (or, in the case of split gifts, deemed to be from me whether I am the actual donor or the consenting spouse) annually with respect to any one of them, provided, however, that total gifts actually from me rather than by gift-split consent to my Attorney or to anyone to whom he or she owes a legal obligation (including an obligation of support) and which are intended or used for the purpose of fulfilling such obligation shall not exceed $5,000 annually; and

Giving unto my Attorney full power, authority and discretion to do all things required or permitted to be done in carrying out the purposes for which this power is granted as fully as I could do if personally present, with full power of substitution and revocation, hereby ratifying and confirming that which my Attorney or his or her substitute shall lawfully do or cause to be done by virtue hereof. Persons, corporations or partnerships dealing with my Attorney need not inquire into the authority of my Attorney.

I also hereby nominate ____ABEL ADAMS____ to be the guardian of my person and estate if proceedings for the appointment of a guardian of my person, estate or both are commenced hereafter.

I further nominate ____MABEL ADAMS____ as guardian of my person and estate in the event that ____ABEL ADAMS____ does not qualify to serve as guardian or qualifies but thereafter ceases to serve.

I direct that bond be waived for each person nominated as guardian or successor guardian.

This Power of Attorney shall not be affected by disability of the principal or lapse of time. I revoke any prior Power of Attorney which I may have executed, but not the Power of Attorney for Health Care executed by me on this same date.

A photostatic copy of this Power of Attorney, as executed, given by me or my Attorney to any third party shall be conclusive to such third party as to the authority of my Attorney to act for me as provided herein, unless and until such third party shall have received written notice from me or my Attorney of the revocation or limitation of this Power of Attorney.

My Attorney shall be considered "unable or unwilling to serve" if he or she is deceased, adjudged incompetent or has resigned by an instrument in writing delivered to me or the successor Attorney named herein or if his or her personal physician shall have certified to his incapacity in writing.

Such death certificate, certified copy of adjudication, certificate of incapacity or resignation shall be attached hereto and if this Power of Attorney has been recorded, such document shall also be recorded.

(continued)

FIGURE 14–2 Continued.

IN WITNESS WHEREOF, I have signed this Power of Attorney on JULY 02, 19 97.

Witnesses:

Sally Witness
SALLY WITNESS
David Witness
DAVID WITNESS

John Smith
JOHN SMITH

STATE OF OHIO)
) SS:
COUNTY OF Geauga)

Before me, the undersigned, a Notary Public in and for said county and state, personally appeared JOHN SMITH, and the foregoing Power of Attorney was acknowledged before me by (him) (her) as principal on JULY 02, 19 97

James Donato Irvin
Notary Public

JAMES DONATO IRVIN, Attorney
NOTARY PUBLIC - STATE OF OHIO
My commission has no expiration date.
Section 147.03 R. C.

[seal]

This instrument prepared by:
JAMES D. IRVIN
Attorney-at-Law
11401 Willow Hill Drive
Chesterland, Ohio 44026
216/729-3201

beneficial use of the property (lives in it). In another approach, a trustee releases capital to the beneficiary as a down payment to purchase a home or releases capital for the outright purchase of a home. With either of those approaches, the home is actually owned by the beneficiary rather than being in the trustee's name. The actual size of the trust, the trustee's authority under it, and Ohio statutes determine which of these approaches is appropriate.

Many people think that only rich people with lots of property use trusts. This misconception is encouraged by professional trustees—lenders and trust companies—that cannot afford to manage a trust unless the amount of property is large enough to support payment to them of the relatively large management fees they require. Actually, however, the trust is possible for almost anyone who owns property and wants to make sure the property will be used in a certain way.

FOR EXAMPLE

Imagine a young couple with three children, all minors. If both husband and wife are killed in an auto accident, a testamentary trust (a trust within their wills) can operate as follows.

The will nominates an executor to carry out the mechanical functions of probating the estate (making sure the debts of the estate are paid, a primary function of probate). The will also nominates a guardian for the children. (The guardian is responsible to the probate court via filing accounts and bonding, and in this way some control is maintained over the treatment of the children and their property.) The will goes on to nominate a trustee to manage the property pursuant to the specific written directions of the trust provisions. Although a guardianship by law must terminate when the children reach the age of majority (assuming they are otherwise competent at that time), the trust provides for control over the property long after the beneficiary becomes an adult.

Because the trust in this example came about because of a will, probate court continues to oversee the trustee's actions until the trust is terminated. Thus, not only does the trustor give the trustee specific instructions as to property management—far beyond the mere general control of a guardianship—but the trustor also is assured that the trustee obeys for the full duration of the trust.

TABLE 14–1 Comparison of guardianship, power of attorney, and durable power of attorney.

GUARDIANSHIP	POWER OF ATTORNEY	DURABLE POWER OF ATTORNEY
Established through probate court.	No court used; created by properly executed and recorded legal document.	No court used; created by properly executed and recorded legal document.
Used for minors and incompetent or insane persons.	Used for competent, sane adults.	Used for competent, sane adults who become incompetent some time after the durable power of attorney was granted.
Enables the guardian to wholly act for the represented person; will be the one who signs all the legal instruments that attend real estate transactions.	Empowers the attorney-in-fact to wholly act for the principal; will be the one who signs all the legal instruments that attend real estate transactions.	Empowers the attorney-in-fact to wholly act for the principal; will be the one who signs all the legal instruments that attend real estate transactions.
Ends when the ward attains age of majority or when disabled person regains competency; also ends upon the death of the represented person.	Ends upon revocation or death of principal.	Ends upon regaining of competency of principal, coupled with his or her revocation; also ends upon principal's death.

Trustees can be chosen from trusted relatives, friends, family attorneys, and, if the assets of the trust are large enough, from the standard commercial trustees. Virtually anyone with any size estate can apply the trust concept.

Putting It All Together

Figure 14–3 is the reproduction of a Last Will and Testament of a fictitious man named George Morgan. He is married, has one minor child at present, and has an estate worth about $300,000. The will, containing a testamentary trust, gives Mr. Morgan the present knowledge that his property will be managed in the future precisely as he now desires. If he should change his mind tomorrow, next week, or in 10 years, fine, but the document shows that at least Mr. Morgan's present wishes for future usage of his property will be honored.

CASE STUDY FROM THE OHIO SUPREME COURT

CENTRAL TRUST COMPANY OF NORTHERN OHIO V. SMITH
50 Ohio St.3d 133, 553 N.E.2d 265 (1990)

Facts: Testatrix Loretta Smith died testate and her will was admitted to probate in 1964. Central Trust became the trustee under that will. A provision of that trust was that, "One share shall be for the benefit of the children of Ralph Smith, Jr., whether now living or born hereafter, equally, and shall be retained by the trustees." At the time of Loretta Smith's death, her son, Ralph Jr., was alive and had five children. Thereafter, Ralph Jr. divorced and remarried twice, and subsequently adopted Bryan Smith. The final decree of Bryan's adoption was issued by probate court in 1975, when Bryan was 13 years old.

Bryan wrote to the trustee about 1980 or thereafter, claiming to be a beneficiary of the trust. The trustee responded that Bryan was not entitled to any benefits from the trust. After further exchanges between Bryan and the trustee, the trustee filed a declaratory judgment action in 1985, seeking a determination as to whether Bryan Smith was entitled to share in the trust.

Probate Court (Trial Court): Held that the class closed on date of testatrix Loretta Smith's death, so adopted child Bryan Smith was not entitled to a share.

Court of Appeals: Affirmed the trial court's decision.

Issues:

1. Whether Bryan Smith's status as an adopted son of Ralph Jr. excluded him from the class of "the children of Ralph J. Smith, Jr., whether now living or born hereafter."
2. Whether, reasonably construing the terms of this testamentary trust, the period within which new members could be included in this class closed at the time of testatrix Loretta Smith's death, before Bryan became eligible.

Held by Ohio Supreme Court:

1. Child adopted by testatrix's son after death of testatrix was eligible under prior adoption statute to be member of class designated in trust provisions of will as children of testatrix's son.
2. Class in testamentary trust for children of testatrix's son, "whether now living or born hereafter," did not close, and property rights did not vest, at death of testatrix, which occurred before testatrix's son adopted child.

Case reversed and remanded to trial court for further proceedings consistent with this opinion.

FIGURE 14–3
Sample last will and testament.

LAST WILL AND TESTAMENT
OF
GEORGE MORGAN

WITNESSETH: That I, George Morgan, of the City of Smalltown, County of Geauga, and State of Ohio, being mindful of the uncertainties of life and desiring to indicate in due legal form while I am in possession of my faculties what disposition of my estate is to be made after my decease, do now make, publish and declare my Last Will and Testament, in manner and form following, hereby revoking all testamentary powers appointments and dispositions by me heretofore given and made.

ITEM I: I direct that all of my duly presented and allowed debts, funeral expenses and the costs of administration of my estate, be paid out of my estate as soon as practicable after my death. I further direct that my Executrix pay out of my residuary estate, as a general charge thereon, all estate, inheritance or succession taxes that may be assessed by reason of my death, including interest and penalties of such taxes, if any, regardless of whether or not said taxes are assessed against my Executrix, and notwithstanding that some part or all of such taxes may be assessed with respect to property that is not subject to probate administration. In addition, my Executrix may, in her sole discretion, pay out of my domiciliary estate, all or any portion of the costs of ancilliary administration and similar proceedings in other jurisdictions. No part of any payment hereunder shall be deducted from any distribution made from my estate or from any other source, except as to the distribution from my residuary estate, and except as may be required to reimburse my estate for any part of any sum so paid.

ITEM II: All of the rest, residue and remainder of my estate, both real, personal and mixed, of every nature and description and wherever situate, of which I may die seized or possessed, including without limitation, all property acquired by me or to which I may become entitled after the execution of this Will, all property over or concerning which I may have any power of appointment and all property herein attempted to be disposed of, the disposition whereof by reason of lapse or other cause shall fail to take effect, (herein called my residuary estate), I give, devise and bequeath to my beloved wife, Mary Jane Morgan, if living to be her property absolutely and forever.

ITEM III: In the event my wife, Mary Jane Morgan, and I should die as the result of a common accident or catastrophe, or should my wife, Mary Jane Morgan, die within sixty (60) days after my death as a result of a common accident or catastrophe, or any accident or from any cause whatsoever, then for the purpose of this, my Last Will and Testament, our deaths should be construed to be concurrent; in this event, or in the event that my wife, Mary Jane Morgan, should predecease me, I hereby give, devise and bequeath my residuary estate aforesaid to my son, William Morgan and to such other children as may hereafter be born as issue of my marriage to Mary Jane Morgan, share and share alike, to become their property absolutely and forever, subject to the limitations set forth in ITEM IV. hereinafter.

I further direct that in the event any of my children, as aforesaid, shall predecease me, or that his or her death shall be concurrent with my own as hereinabove defined, then I give, devise and bequeath such decedent beneficiary's share of my estate hereunder to the issue of said decedent beneficiary, share and share alike per stirpes; if such decedent beneficiary shall die without issue surviving, then his or her share of my estate hereunder shall pass and I hereby give, devise and bequeath such share to his brothers and sisters, per stirpes as shall survive me at the time of my demise, again subject to the terms set forth in ITEM IV. hereinafter.

(continued)

FIGURE 14–3 Continued.

ITEM IV: Anything herein to the contrary notwithstanding in the event my wife, Mary Jane Morgan, shall have predeceased me or in the event of our concurrent death, as above defined in ITEM III. herein, and in the further event that any of my children, as aforesaid, shall be of minor age at the time of my death, I hereby give, grant and bequeath the shares of my residuary estate to which my said children would otherwise be entitled (hereinafter called "trust shares") to Robert Jones and Jane Jones, as Co-Trustees, (or to the survivor of them) to hold and use such shares upon the following terms and conditions:

A. The Trustees shall divide the assets of my residuary estate (sometimes referred to hereinafter as the Trust Estate) into as many equal shares as there are then living children of mine, counting and treating as one such living child the then living issue of any child of mine who may at that time be deceased leaving such... ...issue, and shall hold one such equal share for the benefit of each of the then living issue, per stirpes, of each deceased child of mine, so that there shall be held for such issue the trust share that would have been held for the benefit of such deceased child of mine and he or she survived. Each share held for the benefit of a child of mine and each share or fraction thereof held for the benefit of one who is the issue of a deceased child of mine shall be administered for tax, distribution and other purposes as a separate and distinct trust estate. Separate books and records shall be kept for each trust estate, but it shall not be necessary that physical division of the assets be made as to each trust.

Anything herein to the contrary notwithstanding, should the trust share held for the benefit of any of my children be exhausted because of extraordinary medical, educational or other legitimate needs of that child, my Trustees shall have the power in the exercise of their discretion to invade all or any part of the trust share of my other children, both income and principal, and to use these funds from my other children's trust shares for the legitimate needs of the child whose own share has already been exhausted.

B. The Trustees shall pay the net income from the trust shares of a child of mine or one who is the issue of a deceased child of mine at least as often as quarter-annually to the Guardian of a child of mine, as hereinafter appointed, or to the Guardian of one who is the issue of a deceased child of mine until such trust beneficiary attains the age of eighteen (18) years.

C. When a child of mine or one who is the issue of a deceased child of mine attains the age of eighteen (18) years, or if at the time that such trust beneficiary's share is apportioned from my trust estate, such beneficiary should be eighteen (18) years of age, the Trustees shall pay the net income from such beneficiary's trust share at least as often as quarter-annually to such beneficiary to become that person's property absolutely and forever.

D. When a child of mine or one who is the issue of a deceased child of mine attains the age of twenty-one (21) years, or if at the time that such trust beneficiary's share is apportioned from my trust estate, such beneficiary should be twenty-one (21) years of age, the Trustee shall distribute free of trust to such beneficiary all of the remaining principal and all of the remaining undistributed income of such beneficiary's trust share to become that person's property absolutely and forever.

E. Notwithstanding any other provision of the Will, so long as a trust share created hereunder for the benefit of any child of mine or the issue of any deceased child of mine is in existence, the Trustees exercising their sole discretion, may pay to or for the benefit of the person for whom such share is held, from time to time, from the principal and/or from the income of the trust share, such amounts as the Trustees shall deem necessary or proper to provide for the health, maintenance, reasonable comfort, and support, and the education (including college and graduate and professional education) of the beneficiary thereof and of his or her spouse and dependents, taking into consideration such beneficiary's desire to purchase a home or to engage in a business or profession and such beneficiary's reasonable prospects of success in such business or profession. In determining whether such discretionary payments shall be made to such beneficiary, the Trustees shall take into consideration all income available to him or her for such purpose.

F. With respect to both principal and income, the interest of any beneficiary of the trust estate or of any trust share created therefrom, shall not be anticipated, alienated, encumbered, or in any other manner assigned by any such beneficiary without the prior written consent of the Trustees, and shall not be subject to any legal process, bankruptcy proceedings or the interferences or control of creditors, spouses, divorced spouses, or others. If for any reason any such interest shall, or except for this provision would vest in or be enjoyed by any person, firm or corporation other... ...than such beneficiary, without the prior written consent of the Trustees having been obtained, then the trust herein expressed concerning such interest shall cease and determine as to such beneficiary, and thereafter the Trustees may pay to such beneficiary, or expend for his health, maintenance, reasonable comfort and support, education and advancement in life, or that of any person dependent upon such one, out of such interest, either principal or income, such sums only as the Trustees, in the Trustees' sole and absolute discretion, shall deem proper, and the Trustees shall retain any unexpended portion of such interest, either principal or income, as part of the principal of the trust estate. Subject to the provisions of the following paragraph, the trust shall terminate upon the death of such beneficiary and the trust estate assets shall be distributed to the persons entitled thereto upon the death of such beneficiary as provided in Paragraph G.

G. In the event that a person for whose benefit the trust estate or a share of the trust estate is held shall die before full distribution to him or her of his or her share of the principal and income thereof, such share of principal and income, including any income therein received by the Trustees from the time of the last income payment and the date of death of such beneficiary, shall be apportioned among and held separately for the benefit of his or her issue per stirpes. If there shall be no such issue, then such share shall be apportioned among and held separately for the benefit of his or her brothers and sisters, share and share alike; provided, however, that if at the time of apportionment a brother or sister of his or her shall be deceased leaving issue surviving, such deceased brother's or sister's share shall be apportioned among and held for the benefit of such deceased brother's or sister's issue per stirpes.

Any share of principal and income of the trust estate, passing by reason of the decease of the beneficiary prior to full distribution of such principal and income, shall thereafter be held, administered and distributed to the succeeding beneficiary or beneficiaries of such share in accordance with the provisions under which such share was held for the original beneficiary thereof; provided, however, that in the event that all children of mine and issue of children of mine shall die before full distribution of the principal and income of all trust shares shall have been made, then upon the death of the last of them to die the principal and income from all such undistributed shares shall be distributed and pass free of trust to the person or persons who would take and in the proportion that he, she or they would take under the laws of descent and distribution of the State of Ohio then in effect if I had owned such trust shares and had then died intestate.

H. Notwithstanding any other provision hereof, the provisions of this Will shall not postpone the vesting of any trust property for more than twenty-one (21) years after the decease of the last survivor of the beneficiaries hereunder in being at the time of my death, and if not previously vested, then immediately prior to the expiration of such period such trust property shall vest in and be distributed to the then beneficiaries hereunder in the same proportions as they are then entitled to

(continued)

FIGURE 14–3 Continued.

receive the current trust income or to have such trust income accumulated on their behalf.

I. My Trustees shall have full powers as are permitted under the laws of the State of Ohio, or in such state as where this Will may be administered, together with all such powers as are hereinafter set forth and as are hereinafter granted to my Executrix.

J. I direct that my said Trustees, as herein designated, shall serve without bond.

ITEM V: In the event that my wife, Mary Jane Morgan, shall have predeceased me or in the event of our concurrent deaths as above defined in ITEM III. hereof, and in the further event that any of my children, as aforesaid, shall be of minor age at the time of my death, I hereby make, nominate and appoint, Robert Jones and... ...Jane Jones, (or the survivor of them), as aforesaid, as Co-Guardians of the person and property of said minor or minors during his, her or their minority.

No bond shall be required of either person hereinabove named as Guardian of my said minor children. My Guardians shall have, in addition to the powers granted to Guardians by law, all of the rights and power granted hereinafter to my Executrix.

ITEM VI: I make, nominate and appoint my beloved wife, Mary Jane Morgan, to be the Executrix of this my Last Will and Testament; in the event that the said Mary Jane Morgan predeceases me, or if she survives me, but is unable or unwilling to serve as Executrix, or if, after undertaking such duties she should die or resign, I make, nominate and appoint Robert Jones and Jane Jones (or the survivor of them), as aforesaid, as successor Co-Executors in her place and stead.

A. I hereby grant to my Executrix full power in her discretion and without any Court order or proceeding to do any and all things necessary to complete the administration of my estate. I hereby grant to my Executrix full power and authority in the settlement of my estate to compromise, compound, adjust and settle any and all claims and demands in favor of or against my estate, upon such terms as she shall deem best.

B. I further grant to my Executrix full power and authority, for any purposes, to sell, dispose of and transfer, at public or private sale, all or any part of my estate, whether real, personal or mixed, upon such terms and at such prices as she may deem best, and to execute and deliver any and all instruments and to do any and all such things which may be necessary to convey title.

C. My Executrix shall have full power and authority to vote, designate and execute proxies, assign or transfer certificates of stock, bonds, or other securities as fully as I could do if living.

D. My Executrix shall have full power and authority to make division of, or distribution of assets in kind, or in money, and partly in kind and partly in money, and to that end, to allot specific property, real or personal, or an undivided interest or interests therein, to beneficiaries hereunder. In the absence of abuse of discretion, the judgment of my Executrix respecting the value of properties or undivided interests therein, for the purpose of such division or distribution shall be binding upon all parties interested in this estate.

E. All of the foregoing powers may be exercised without Court order.

F. No purchaser from, nor lender to my said Executrix need see to the application of any purchase or loan money, but the receipt of my Executrix shall be a complete discharge therefore.

G. No bond shall be required of my Executrix or successor Co-Executors.

H. It is my desire that my Executrix shall not be required to dispose of any property which I shall own at my death; I, therefore, grant to my Executrix the right in her sound discretion to retain unsold during the period of administration of my estate any and all property which I shall own at my death and to continue any business in which I may be interested at the time of my death and to invest assets in such business if my Executrix shall deem it best.

I. My Executrix shall have full power and authority during the period of administration of my estate, and without any Court order, to manage, improve, repair, lease for any term irrespective of duration, rent, sell, exchange, hold, mortgage, control, invest and reinvest any property in my estate, whether real, personal or mixed, in such manner and upon such terms as she shall deem best, irrespective of any... ...statutes of rules or practices of Courts now or hereafter in force limiting the investments of executors, with full power to convert realty into personalty and personalty into realty. My Executrix shall have full power to deposit funds of my estate in a bank, whether or not interest is paid on such deposits.

J. I direct that no inventory or appraisal of any of the assets of my estate be made or taken insofar as the same may be lawfully omitted.

ITEM VII: Where necessary or appropriate to the meaning hereof, the singular shall be deemed to include the plural, the plural to include the singular, the masculine to include the feminine and neuter, the feminine to include the masculine and neuter, and the neuter to include the masculine and feminine.

"Issue", "children" and words of similar purport include persons whose relationship is such by adoption, as well as the issue of such adopted persons, whether such issue be lineal or by adoption. A person in gestation, which person is later born alive, shall be regarded in this Will as a person in being during the period of gestation.

IN WITNESS WHEREOF, I have on this 31st day of January, 1979, set my hand at the end of this instrument of nine (9) pages, which I declare to be my Last Will and Testament.

George Morgan
George Morgan

The foregoing instrument was signed by the said in our presence and was by him to us acknowledged and declared to be his Last Will and Testament, and we, at his request and in his presence, and in the presence of each other, have hereunto set our hands as subscribing witnesses, this 31st day of January, 1979.

Mary Witness residing at 123 Main St. Mytown, OH

Steve Witness residing at 123 Main St. Mytown, OH

SUMMARY OF CONTENT

1. Decedents who die intestate die without leaving wills providing for the distribution of their estates.
2. Statutes of descent and distribution cover who receives decedents' property, and in what proportion, when they die intestate.
3. The statute of descent and distribution covers persons related by blood or marriage to the decedent.
4. Wills are the only legally recognized way people can express their desires about how and to whom their real and personal property is to be distributed after their death.
5. The requirements for making a valid will are: a testator of sound mind and memory who has reached the age of majority; a writing that evidences testamentary intent; a testator with capacity to make a will; a will signed by the testator; and the will attested by two witnesses.
6. When real estate is devised in a will, it often is encumbered by a mortgage lien. If the will specifically provides a right of exoneration for that lien, the devisee can compel payment from the estate during its administration.
7. Devisees receive their real property via a certificate of transfer issued by probate court.
8. If testators exclude surviving spouses from their wills, those spouses often can elect instead to take against the wills from the estates as allowed by the Ohio Revised Code.
9. Testators usually can exclude from their wills any of their children who have reached the age of majority.
10. Wills may be revoked by testators prior to their death.
11. A codicil is a legal instrument that alters the will without revoking that will.
12. The will should nominate a guardian for any minor children of its maker.
13. Probate court appointments of guardians also are necessary for incapacitated adults.
14. An executor (appointed by will) or an administrator (appointed by probate court for intestate distribution) is the person charged with disposing of and distributing all the property in the estate after paying off all valid claims against the estate.
15. Probate court has exclusive jurisdiction over the disposition of estates hearing and determining cases regarding the validity of wills.
16. If spouses (or others) put their real and personal property into survivorship methods of coownership, those properties are outside the jurisdiction of probate court.
17. An estate's going through probate court proceedings is a different matter than an estate's having to pay taxes on either the federal or the state level.
18. Wills can be challenged in what is known as a will contest.
19. The ultimate issue of a will contest is whether the writing produced is or is not the last will or codicil of the testator.
20. The usual challenges to the will are that the testator was of unsound mind, or under duress at the time of making the will, or that a beneficiary exerted undue influence over the testator in the making of the will.

21. Only persons with an interest in a will may contest that will in probate court.
22. Powers of attorney are used by people who name another to act for them if they physically cannot, or do not feel like acting, for themselves. The appointees are called attorneys-in-fact.
23. A durable power of attorney can be created instead. If the principal becomes disabled or incompetent, the durable power of attorney remains in effect, whereas a regular power of attorney does not.
24. Powers of attorney and guardianships both end with the death of the represented person.
25. The trust is used as a method of estate planning.
26. A living trust is one that takes effect while the trustor is still alive.
27. The testamentary trust takes effect after the trustor has died, and it operates in conjunction with a will.

Review Questions

1. The following preferences apply in estate law:
   a. devises are preferred to legacies
   b. legacies are preferred to devises
   c. bequests are preferred to both legacies and devises
   d. none of the above is true

2. A valid will must be made by a testator who is:
   a. of sound mind and memory
   b. possessed of some real property
   c. survived by some living relative
   d. able to read and write

3. The person who is appointed by will to distribute the assets in the estate is called a(n):
   a. administrator
   b. executor
   c. trustor
   d. guardian

4. Disposition of money by a will is a:
   a. testament
   b. bequest
   c. devise
   d. legacy

5. Disposition of real property by a will is a:
   a. testament
   b. bequest
   c. devise
   d. legacy

6. Disposition of personal property by a will is a:
   a. testament
   b. bequest
   c. devise
   d. legacy

7. When a disinherited person, who would have inherited under the statute of descent and distribution, claims the statute should be applied, rather than the will that excluded him, the legal action is called a:
   a. testamentary disposition
   b. competency contest
   c. probate election
   d. will contest

8. If testator had an ante nuptial agreement with his surviving spouse:
   a. the terms of that agreement probably will bind her
   b. she will get the statutory provision for the surviving spouse instead
   c. she can ask the probate court to grant her more, based on need
   d. if one of testator's children dies with him, she gets that child's share as well

9. Your adult parent is presently competent but wants you to handle his affairs. You don't want to encumber yourself with probate court, and you suspect his condition will worsen shortly. The easiest legal tool for you to use is:
   a. a guardianship
   b. a power of attorney
   c. a durable power of attorney
   d. a will

10. A 50-year-old man dies suddenly in a plane crash. His will leaves his surviving spouse everything and his two adult children nothing. The two children can try to elect against the will and probably will take:
    a. all of the estate
    b. half of the estate
    c. one-third of the estate
    d. nothing

11. Used to handle the affairs of an incompetent person:
    a. durable power of attorney
    b. power of attorney
    c. guardianship
    d. both a and c

12. Mother and father die simultaneously in an auto crash, leaving behind three minor children and no will. The children will:
    a. go with their maternal grandparents
    b. go with an adult relative of their choice
    c. be put up for adoption
    d. have a guardian appointed for their care as selected by the probate court judge

13. Sam and Martha are concerned about their son, Homer, age 28, inheriting their $500,000 estate and running through all the assets in a few years, as Homer has never "found himself." Sam and Martha can conserve and manage the assets for Homer by creating a:
    a. will
    b. trust
    c. guardianship
    d. conservatorship

14. You appoint your sister, Mary, as guardian of your children in your will. Mary:
    a. cannot also be the executrix
    b. cannot also be the trustee
    c. cannot also be a beneficiary under the will
    d. can be all of the above

15. Will contests include as named parties to the suit:
    a. persons who would take under the will
    b. persons who would take under the statute of descent and distribution
    c. the executor
    d. all of the above

16. Whenever a person dies, there must be:
    a. a probate court proceeding
    b. filing and payment of a federal estate tax
    c. filing and payment of a state estate tax
    d. There may or may not be a need for any of the above; the individual facts determine what is or is not required

17. A trustee manages trust property only for:
    a. a beneficiary designated by the trustor until the trust ends
    b. incapacitated persons
    c. minors
    d. the time the trustor is still alive

18. The ultimate issue in a will contest is whether:
    a. the probate court has jurisdiction
    b. a jury will hear the case
    c. the writing produced is the last valid will or codicil of the testator
    d. the children or the stepmother will end up with the estate

19. Devisees receive the real estate with the mortgage lien exonerated when:
    a. it is an intestate distribution
    b. the will specifically calls for exoneration of the lien
    c. the will generally provides for testator's debts to be paid
    d. in all of the above instances

20. The proper role of the real estate salesperson in decedents' estates is:
    a. advising customers and clients about how to avoid probate
    b. testifying as an expert witness about any aspect of devises as they apply to estate law
    c. listing real estate for sale that the executor or administrator is empowered to sell
    d. buying up realty as cheaply as possible from those about to die, so as to sell high afterward and build a real estate empire for himself or herself

21. If testator adopts his adult stepchild, B, yet fails to provide for her in his will:
    a. B gets an automatic third of the estate
    b. B can go after the surviving spouse's share
    c. in a will contest, B will be less entitled than testator's natural, adult children
    d. B can contest the will for the portion she'd be entitled to as testator's child under the statute of descent and distribution

22. The following preference applies in estate law:
    a. a complete bypass of probate court
    b. putting all property into survivorship forms of ownership
    c. the use of trusts instead of wills
    d. none of the above three is true

23. An executor distributes assets in the estate according to the provisions in the:
    a. state statute of descent and distribution
    b. trust
    c. will
    d. probate court judge's preferences

24. An administrator distributes assets in the estate according to the provisions in the:
    a. state statute of descent and distribution
    b. trust
    c. will
    d. probate court judge's preferences

25. You appoint your sister Betty as trustee in your testamentary trust. Betty:
    a. cannot also be the executrix of the will
    b. cannot also be the guardian nominated under the will
    c. never could have held your power of attorney
    d. can be all of the above

ANSWER KEY

1. d
2. a
3. b
4. d
5. c
6. b
7. d
8. a
9. c
10. d
11. d
12. d
13. b
14. d
15. d
16. d
17. a
18. c
19. b
20. c
21. d
22. d
23. c
24. a
25. d

PRACTICE PURCHASE AGREEMENTS

PURCHASE AGREEMENT 1

Fill out the blank real estate purchase contract that is included as part of this exercise.

> My name is Mary Smith and I am with you, Anne Hamilton, salesperson for the Real Estate Company. I want to make an offer on one of your company's homes that is listed for sale: 100 Somewhere, Anyville, Ohio, a single-family residential colonial with a two-car attached garage. With me is my husband, John Smith, who also wants to purchase this house. My parents are also with me. Their names are John and Mary Jones. They are giving me a half down payment on the house, up to $70,000. My husband, my parents, and I are all willing to sign the offer as purchasers. The house is listed at $149,900, and we want to make an offer of $120,000. We will give $2,000 in promissory note form as our earnest money. We want a financing condition in which, if we can't get financing with a half down payment within three weeks or so, we are excused from performing the contract.
>
> In addition to the fixtures on the real property, we want the following items: the Oriental rug in the library and the chandelier in the foyer; the microwave oven; the fireplace glass doors, grate, and tools; all the built-in appliances in the kitchen to be included, as well as the refrigerator.
>
> We can put all of our funds into escrow by August 25 and would like the transaction to close then, too. We want to take possession of the house when title transfers.
>
> The real estate has a well instead of city water.
>
> We want the best deed and title protection that the sellers can give us.
>
> We acknowledge that you (Anne Hamilton) have already told us about the slight amount of water that was in the basement in the spring 1989 flooding, which you said the sellers had disclosed to you.
>
> We want the general home and well inspections and can have them done within two weeks.
>
> Since my parents are making the down payment, we've all agreed that title is to be taken in my name alone.
>
> We all will sign the offer.

My name is John Doe. I am the seller, along with my wife, Jane Doe. We do not like parts of this offer, so we are going to make a counteroffer to the Smiths and Joneses. You will make the alterations to their offer that will turn it into our counteroffer.

We want $140,000 as the purchase price.

We are unwilling to let them have the chandelier in the foyer, but they can have the other items.

We cannot vacate on August 25. We need until August 30.

We initial all of our changes on the written form and then sign it as our counteroffer.

You (Anne Hamilton) take this counteroffer back to the purchasers and all the purchasers initial all the changes, signifying their agreement to the Does' terms. You have a completed contract.

EXERCISE 1 Purchase contract.

PURCHASE AGREEMENT

1-BUYER: The undersigned ______________________________
(hereinafter "BUYER") offers to buy the following-described property.

2-PROPERTY: Situated in the ____________ of ____________________, County of ______________, and State of Ohio;
and located at ______________________________
and being further described as a ______________________________.
Permanent Parcel No. or Tax I.D. No. ____________________

The property, which BUYER accepts in its PRESENT CONDITION, except for normal wear and tear before Title Transfer, and except as specifically set forth hereinafter, shall include the land and all appurtenant rights, privileges and easements, (subject to all rights of tenants, if any), and all buildings and fixtures, including without limitation, *all* of the following as are now on the property: electrical, heating, cooling, plumbing and bathroom fixtures; window and door shades, blinds, awnings, screens, storm windows, curtain and drapery fixtures; landscaping; disposals; TV antennas, rotor control units and built-in TV and videotape wiring; smoke alarms; security systems; garage door openers and controls; radiator covers; permanently attached carpeting;
( )ranges and ovens; ( )microwave ovens; ( )dishwashers; ( )refrigerators; ( )window air conditioners;
( )water softeners; ( )gas grills; ( )satellite TV reception systems;
FIREPLACE ( )tools, ( )screens, ( )glass doors, ( )grates; ( )washers, ( )dryers; and all existing window treatments,
EXCEPT these window treatments: ______________________________
Also INCLUDED: ______________________________
NOT included: ______________________________

3-PRICE: For which BUYER shall pay owner of said property (hereinafter "SELLER")----$ ______________
payable as follows:

(A) Earnest Money to be paid to the REAL ESTATE COMPANY, as agent for SELLER, to be deposited upon acceptance of final offer in the REAL ESTATE COMPANY'S Trust Account and credited against the purchase price:
------------( )check ( )note ( )cash--$ ______________
IF A NOTE--TO BE REDEEMED WITHIN FOUR DAYS OF ACCEPTANCE OF CONTRACT.
FURTHER, IT IS AGREED THAT WHEREVER THE WORD "DAYS" APPEARS HEREIN, SUCH SHALL REFER TO CALENDAR DAYS, WITH ALL SUNDAYS AND NATIONAL HOLIDAYS NOT BEING COUNTED.
(B) Remainder of BUYER'S downpayment, to be deposited in escrow
as per paragraph 5. hereinafter--$ ______________
(C) Balance in the form of a Mortgage Loan
------------( )conventional ( )FHA ( )VA ( )OTHER---------------------------------------$ ______________

____
______________________________$ ______________

4-FINANCING: This transaction is conditioned upon BUYER obtaining the mortgage loan financing referred to above. BUYER shall make a written application for such financing within ______ days from contract acceptance date and shall obtain a commitment for such loan on or about ____________________, 19_____. If despite BUYER'S good faith efforts, BUYER cannot obtain such loan commitment, or one for a lesser sum but still acceptable to BUYER, then this Agreement shall be NULL AND VOID and the following shall occur promptly:

BUYER and SELLER shall enter into a written Mutual Release from this transaction, directing the return of the earnest money deposit, or SELLER shall sign an Authorization directing the REAL ESTATE COMPANY to return said earnest money deposit to BUYER. After the execution of same, neither buyer, seller, nor any real estate broker or agent having anything to do with this transaction shall have any liability or obligation to the other(s) stemming from same. (This procedure is referred to hereinafter as "the TERMINATION PROCEDURE.")

5-CLOSING: (choose *one* of the following)

(A) Escrow- All documents, funds, and financial institution commitments for funds necessary to the completion of this transaction shall be placed in escrow with any local Lending Institution, or with any local Title Company on or before ____________, 19_____ and Title shall transfer to BUYER on or about but not before ______________, 19_____; EXCEPT, if a defect in Title appears, SELLER shall have thirty (30) days after notice to SELLER to remove such defect, and being unable to do so, BUYER may agree to accept Title subject to such defect without any reduction in said purchase price, or may terminate this Agreement and, thereupon, receive the return of all deposits made hereunder, as per the TERMINATION PROCEDURE, set forth in foregoing paragraph 4.

(B) Formal - All documents, funds, and financial institution commitments for funds necessary to the completion of this transaction shall be brought to a formal "sit-down" closing by the parties and their respective representatives and agents to be held at
______________________________ Ohio
on the ________ day of ______________, 19____ at __________ AM/PM, at which time Title shall transfer to BUYER. However, if a defect in Title appears during such attempted closing, SELLER shall have thirty (30) days thereafter to reschedule such closing and to remove such defect, and being unable to do so, BUYER may agree to accept

(continued)

EXERCISE 1 Continued.

Title subject to such defect, without any reduction in said purchase price, or may terminate this Agreement and, thereupon, receive the return of all deposits made hereunder, as per the TERMINATION PROCEDURE, set forth in foregoing paragraph 4.

6-POSSESSION: SELLER shall deliver possession of the property to BUYER within_______days* after the date of Title Transfer, or on_________________, 19_____, whichever is LATER. The first__________days of said period shall be rental free and the balance (if any) shall be at $_________________ per day, not to exceed__________days, after which time SELLER shall become a tenant at sufferance and subject to eviction. *Days in the case of this paragraph 6., and this paragraph *only*, shall refer to consecutive calendar days, with all Sundays and Holidays being counted.

7-TITLE: SELLER shall convey a marketable title to BUYER by General Warranty Deed and/or Fiduciary Deed, if required, with all dower rights released, free and clear of all liens and encumbrances whatsoever, except (a) any mortgage assumed by BUYER/GRANTEE, (b) all restrictions, reservations, easements (however created), covenants, and conditions of record, (c) all of the following as do not materially and adversely affect the use or value of the property: encroachments, oil, gas and mineral leases, (d) zoning ordinances, if any, and (e) taxes and assessments, both general and special, not currently due and payable.

SELLER shall furnish a Title Guarantee, in the amount of said purchase price, showing record Title to be good in BUYER/GRANTEE, subject to the deed exceptions set forth hereinabove, and any title policy exceptions, to be issued by a Title Company acceptable to SELLER. Should BUYER desire, he may obtain an Owner's Title Insurance Commitmemt and Policy [ALTA Form B (1970 REV. 10-17-70 & REV. 10-17-84)], or other similar title insurance, so long as he pays the increased premium due because of such additional coverage. If the property is Torrenized, SELLER shall furnish, in lieu of the foregoing, an Owner's Duplicate Certificate of Title, together with a United States Court Search and Tax Search. Where required by ordinance, SELLER shall order a code inspection and shall deposit the results at closing.

8-PRORATIONS: Any of the following as exist -- General taxes, special assessments, Homeowners' Association Fees or other similar fees, city/county or other local charges, and tenant rents -- shall be prorated at closing as of date of Title Transfer. Taxes and assessments shall be prorated based on the latest available tax duplicate. BUYER and SELLER shall prorate and adjust directly any changes in taxes resulting either from a change in valuation and/or tax rate occurring before Title Transfer, or from existing but not yet assessed improvements. Utility charges shall be paid by SELLERS to the date of Title Transfer, or the date of exchange of possession, whichever is LATER; also, the Closing Agent shall withhold the sum of $_____________from SELLER'S proceeds to secure payment of final water and sewer charges, if any, unless SELLER submits proof of payment of such.

9-CHARGES: SELLER shall pay the following costs at closing: (a) cost of title exam and Title Guarantee premium, (b) cost to prepare Deed, (c) amount due to discharge any lien encumbering the property and the cost of recording the cancellation thereof, (d) Real Estate Transfer Tax, (e) cost for inspections and certificates required by public authorities, (f) prorations due BUYER, (g) real estate commissions due brokers, and (h) one-half the closing fee, or the full closing fee should FHA or VA regulations prohibit payment of such by BUYER. If, at time of transfer of utilities to BUYER, a defect is detected in any of the main utility service supply lines on the property, SELLER shall pay all costs for the repair of such, either directly, or at closing.

BUYER shall pay the following costs at closing: (a) cost of filing the Deed for record, (b) one-half of the closing fee (when not prohibited by FHA or VA regulations), (c) any cost incident to BUYER'S obtaining financing, (d) costs of any inspections required by BUYER as conditions of this Agreement, and (e) the additional premium cost for any Title Insurance policy that was provided.

10-DAMAGE: If any buildings or other improvements are damaged or destroyed prior to Title Transfer in excess of ten percent of said purchase price, BUYER may either accept any insurance proceeds payable on account thereof as full compensation therefor, or may terminate this agreement and receive return of all deposits made hereunder. For all damage and destruction valued as less than ten percent of said purchase price, SELLER shall restore the property to its condition as of contract acceptance date.

11-CONDITION OF PROPERTY:

BUYER acknowledges that it has been recommended to him that he engage, at his expense, the services of a professional contractor or building inspector to inspect the property and all improvements to ascertain that the condition of the property is as called for in this Agreement. BUYER further acknowledges that no broker or any agent having anything to do with this transaction has made any verbal, or other statements or representations concerning the property on which BUYER has relied, except as specifically set forth in writing herein. BUYER has examined the property and agrees that the property is being purchased in its present "as is" condition, including any defects that may have been disclosed by SELLER either specifically hereon or by attached addendum. BUYER acknowledges that he has not relied on any representations, warranties or statements whatsoever concerning the property, including without limitation its use or condition, other than as written in this Agreement.

12-SPECIFIC DISCLOSURES: BUYER has relied on the following additional specific disclosures and/or representations in making this Agreement: (IF NONE, WRITE "NONE")

____

Said specific disclosures and/or representations were made by__________________________________.

13-SELLER'S REPRESENTATIONS: Seller states that he has no knowledge of any hidden or latent defects on the property, including without limitation, any of the following: water seepage; basement foundation or wall wetness (or dampness); bathroom or kitchen leakage; roof leakage; problems with electrical, plumbing, heating, cooling, sewer,

(continued)

EXERCISE 1 Continued.

septic, well or water systems; structural defects; or faulty major appliances, EXCEPT: (IF NONE, WRITE "NONE")

____

14-INSPECTION CONDITIONS: This Agreement shall be subject to all of the following checked Inspections, which Inspections shall be paid for by BUYER, carried out in good faith by all parties, and completed within the times specified. These Inspections shall be either approved or disapproved by BUYER in writing within said times and if disapproved, this Agreement shall become NULL AND VOID and subject to the TERMINATION PROCEDURE, as set forth in foregoing paragraph 4. (IF NONE, WRITE "NONE")_________

( ) A. GENERAL HOME INSPECTION The property shall be inspected by a general home inspector, construction person, professional property inspector, or other person of BUYER'S choice within_________days from final acceptance hereof.

( ) B. WELL OPERATION AND WELL WATER TEST The well system shall be inspected by a qualified inspector of BUYER'S choice (whose findings would be acceptable to County or other water authorities) for both (1) adequate flow rate and equipment operation and (2) potability, within_________days from final acceptance hereof.

( ) C. SEPTIC SYSTEM INSPECTION The septic or other on-site sanitation system shall be inspected by a qualified inspector of BUYER'S choice (whose findings would be acceptable to County or other sanitary authorities) within_________days from final acceptance hereof. SELLER shall pay the cost of sanitation system *cleaning,* if necessary for Inspection.

( ) D. TERMITE/WOOD-DESTROYING INSECT INSPECTION The property shall be inspected by a licensed pest control inspector of BUYER'S choice within_________days from final acceptance hereof.

NOTE -- Should FHA or VA Regulations prohibit payment by BUYER of the cost of any of the foregoing INSPECTIONS, SELLER shall pay the cost thereof.

WAIVER

Should BUYER fail to have any of the above Inspections completed within the times specified, OR IF BUYER FAILS TO SPECIFICALLY APPROVE OR DISAPPROVE ANY INSPECTIONS WITHIN THE TIMES SPECIFIED, then BUYER shall be deemed to have WAIVED SUCH INSPECTIONS and shall be considered as HAVING ACCEPTED THE PROPERTY ABSOLUTELY AND FINALLY IN ITS PRESENT "AS IS" CONDITION, and neither SELLER nor any real estate broker or agent having anything to do with this transaction shall have any further liability or obligation to BUYER as to such Inspections or Agreement Conditions.

Should the results of any of such Inspections not be satisfactory to BUYER then, within the times specified, BUYER shall notify either SELLER or SELLER'S LISTING BROKERAGE in writing of his specific dissatisfaction, at which point the TERMINATION PROCEDURE set forth in foregoing paragraph 4. shall apply.

15-ADDENDA: This Agreement is subject to the additional terms and conditions as set forth in the attached Addenda, hereby made a part hereof, and described as: ( )AGENCY, ( )HOME SALE, ( )FHA/VA, ( )CONDO, ( )OTHER

16-HOME WARRANTY: ( ) If checked, BUYER shall be provided a limited HOME WARRANTY PLAN issued by the INSURANCE COMPANY. The application service charge of $____________shall be paid by _________ at closing.

17-BINDING AGREEMENT: Acceptance of this Offer, and any attached Addenda, shall create a LEGAL AGREEMENT, BINDING ON BUYER AND SELLER and their heirs, executors, administrators, successors and assigns, and shall contain the ENTIRE AGREEMENT AND UNDERSTANDING of the parties, it being further acknowleged that there are no other conditions, representations, warranties or agreements, expressed or implied, beyond those contained herein. All terms, provisions, covenants, and conditions of this Agreement shall survive Title Transfer of said property to BUYER.

18-BUYER'S OFFER: The undersigned specifically represent(s) that they are of legal age and capacity and are ready, willing and able to purchase the property according to the above terms:

BUYER(S)______________________________/______________________________

ADDRESS/Phone____.

TITLE SHALL BE TAKEN:______________________________ (Date)__________________

IF TITLE TO BE IN MORE THAN ONE NAME, IS SURVIVORSHIP DEED REQUESTED? ______ (YES or NO)

19-SELLER'S ACCEPTANCE:
The undersigned, being of legal age and capacity, hereby accept(s) the above offer and agree(s) to pay a total commission of

_____percent of said purchase price, payable_____percent to the REAL ESTATE COMPANY and_____percent to ______________________________ as the SOLE PROCURING CAUSE(S) of this transaction.

SELLER(S)______________________________/______________________________

ADDRESS/Phone______________________________ (Date)__________________

20-DEPOSIT RECEIPT: Receipt is hereby acknowledged, as agent for SELLER, of BUYER'S earnest money deposit in the amount specified and in the form described in foregoing paragraph 3.(a), to be held in the REAL ESTATE COMPANY'S trust Account, subject to all terms and provisions of this Agreement.

--------------the REAL ESTATE COMPANY By______________________________ (Date)__________________

ONCE SIGNED, THIS DOCUMENT BECOMES A LEGALLY-BINDING CONTRACT
IF YOU HAVE QUESTIONS OF LAW, CONSULT AN ATTORNEY LICENSED TO PRACTICE IN OHIO

EXERCISE 1 Answer.

PURCHASE AGREEMENT

EQUAL HOUSING OPPORTUNITY

1-BUYER: The undersigned Mary Smith, John Smith, John Jones, Mary Jones (hereinafter "BUYER") offers to buy the following-described property.

2-PROPERTY: Situated in the Village of Any, County of Geauga, and State of Ohio;
and located at 100 Somewhere, Anyville, Ohio, 44026
and being further described as a single-family colonial w/ 2-car attached garage.
Permanent Parcel No. or Tax I.D. No.________

The property, which BUYER accepts in its PRESENT CONDITION, except for normal wear and tear before Title Transfer, and except as specifically set forth hereinafter, shall include the land and all appurtenant rights, privileges and easements, (subject to all rights of tenants, if any), and all buildings and fixtures, including without limitation, *all* of the following as are now on the property: electrical, heating, cooling, plumbing and bathroom fixtures; window and door shades, blinds, awnings, screens, storm windows, curtain and drapery fixtures; landscaping; disposals; TV antennas, rotor control units and built-in TV and videotape wiring; smoke alarms; security systems; garage door openers and controls; radiator covers; permanently attached carpeting;
(X)ranges and ovens; (X)microwave ovens; (X)dishwashers; (X)refrigerators; ( )window air conditioners;
( )water softeners; ( )gas grills; ( )satellite TV reception systems;
FIREPLACE (X)tools, ( )screens, (X)glass doors, (X)grates; ( )washers, ( )dryers; and all existing window treatments,
EXCEPT these window treatments:________
Also INCLUDED: Oriental rug in library, ~~chandelier in foyer~~ JD JD MS JS 7/5/97
NOT included: JJ MJ

3-PRICE: For which BUYER shall pay owner of said property (hereinafter "SELLER")----$ ~~120,000~~ 140,000
payable as follows:

(A) Earnest Money to be paid to the REAL ESTATE COMPANY, as agent for SELLER, to be deposited upon acceptance of final offer in the REAL ESTATE COMPANY'S Trust Account and credited against the purchase price:
------------( )check ( )note ( )cash---------------------------$ 2,000
IF A NOTE--TO BE REDEEMED WITHIN FOUR DAYS OF ACCEPTANCE OF CONTRACT.
FURTHER, IT IS AGREED THAT WHEREVER THE WORD "DAYS" APPEARS HEREIN, SUCH SHALL REFER TO CALENDAR DAYS, WITH ALL SUNDAYS AND NATIONAL HOLIDAYS NOT BEING COUNTED.
(B) Remainder of BUYER'S downpayment, to be deposited in escrow as per paragraph 5. hereinafter---------------$ ~~58,000~~ 68,000
(C) Balance in the form of a Mortgage Loan
------------(X)conventional ( )FHA ( )VA ( )OTHER-----------$ ~~60,000~~ 70,000

Total $ 140,000

JD JD MS JJ MJ 7/5

4-FINANCING: This transaction is conditioned upon BUYER obtaining the mortgage loan financing referred to above. BUYER shall make a written application for such financing within five days from contract acceptance date and shall obtain a commitment for such loan on or about July 26, 19 97. If despite BUYER'S good faith efforts, BUYER cannot obtain such loan commitment, or one for a lesser sum but still acceptable to BUYER, then this Agreement shall be NULL AND VOID and the following shall occur promptly:

BUYER and SELLER shall enter into a written Mutual Release from this transaction, directing the return of the earnest money deposit, or SELLER shall sign an Authorization directing the REAL ESTATE COMPANY to return said earnest money deposit to BUYER. After the execution of same, neither buyer, seller, nor any real estate broker or agent having anything to do with this transaction shall have any liability or obligation to the other(s) stemming from same. (This procedure is referred to hereinafter as "the TERMINATION PROCEDURE.")

5-CLOSING: (choose *one* of the following)

(A) Escrow- All documents, funds, and financial institution commitments for funds necessary to the completion of this transaction shall be placed in escrow with any local Lending Institution, or with any local Title Company on or before August 25, 19 97 and Title shall transfer to BUYER on or about but not before August 25, 19 97; EXCEPT, if a defect in Title appears, SELLER shall have thirty (30) days after notice to SELLER to remove such defect, and being unable to do so, BUYER may agree to accept Title subject to such defect without any reduction in said purchase price, or may terminate this Agreement and, thereupon, receive the return of all deposits made hereunder, as per the TERMINATION PROCEDURE, set forth in foregoing paragraph 4.

(B) Formal - All documents, funds, and financial institution commitments for funds necessary to the completion of this transaction shall be brought to a formal "sit-down" closing by the parties and their respective representatives and agents to be held at
________ Ohio
on the ____ day of ________, 19___ at _____ AM/PM, at which time Title shall transfer to BUYER. However, if a defect in Title appears during such attempted closing, SELLER shall have thirty (30) days thereafter to reschedule such closing and to remove such defect, and being unable to do so, BUYER may agree to accept

(continued)

EXERCISE 1 Answer (continued).

Title subject to such defect, without any reduction in said purchase price, or may terminate this Agreement and, thereupon, receive the return of all deposits made hereunder, as per the TERMINATION PROCEDURE, set forth in foregoing paragraph 4.

6-POSSESSION: SELLER shall deliver possession of the property to BUYER within ~~Ø~~ 5 days* after the date of Title Transfer, or on August ~~25~~ 30, 19 97, whichever is LATER. The first ________ days of said period shall be rental free and the balance (if any) shall be at $________ per day, not to exceed ________ days, after which time SELLER shall become a tenant at sufferance and subject to eviction. *Days in the case of this paragraph 6., and this paragraph *only*, shall refer to consecutive calendar days, with all Sundays and Holidays being counted. JD JD JS BKS JJ MJ 9/5/97

7-TITLE: SELLER shall convey a marketable title to BUYER by General Warranty Deed and/or Fiduciary Deed, if required, with all dower rights released, free and clear of all liens and encumbrances whatsoever, except (a) any mortgage assumed by BUYER/GRANTEE, (b) all restrictions, reservations, easements (however created), covenants, and conditions of record, (c) all of the following as do not materially and adversely affect the use or value of the property: encroachments, oil, gas and mineral leases, (d) zoning ordinances, if any, and (e) taxes and assessments, both general and special, not currently due and payable.

SELLER shall furnish a Title Guarantee, in the amount of said purchase price, showing record Title to be good in BUYER/GRANTEE, subject to the deed exceptions set forth hereinabove, and any title policy exceptions, to be issued by a Title Company acceptable to SELLER. Should BUYER desire, he may obtain an Owner's Title Insurance Commitmemt and Policy [ALTA Form B (1970 REV. 10-17-70 & REV. 10-17-84)], or other similar title insurance, so long as he pays the increased premium due because of such additional coverage. If the property is Torrenized, SELLER shall furnish, in lieu of the foregoing, an Owner's Duplicate Certificate of Title, together with a United States Court Search and Tax Search. Where required by ordinance, SELLER shall order a code inspection and shall deposit the results at closing.

8-PRORATIONS: Any of the following as exist -- General taxes, special assessments, Homeowners' Association Fees or other similar fees, city/county or other local charges, and tenant rents -- shall be prorated at closing as of date of Title Transfer. Taxes and assessments shall be prorated based on the latest available tax duplicate. BUYER and SELLER shall prorate and adjust directly any changes in taxes resulting either from a change in valuation and/or tax rate occurring before Title Transfer, or from existing but not yet assessed improvements. Utility charges shall be paid by SELLERS to the date of Title Transfer, or the date of exchange of possession, whichever is LATER; also, the Closing Agent shall withhold the sum of $________ from SELLER'S proceeds to secure payment of final water and sewer charges, if any, unless SELLER submits proof of payment of such.

9-CHARGES: SELLER shall pay the following costs at closing: (a) cost of title exam and Title Guarantee premium, (b) cost to prepare Deed, (c) amount due to discharge any lien encumbering the property and the cost of recording the cancellation thereof, (d) Real Estate Transfer Tax, (e) cost for inspections and certificates required by public authorities, (f) prorations due BUYER, (g) real estate commissions due brokers, and (h) one-half the closing fee, or the full closing fee should FHA or VA regulations prohibit payment of such by BUYER. If, at time of transfer of utilities to BUYER, a defect is detected in any of the main utility service supply lines on the property, SELLER shall pay all costs for the repair of such, either directly, or at closing.

BUYER shall pay the following costs at closing: (a) cost of filing the Deed for record, (b) one-half of the closing fee (when not prohibited by FHA or VA regulations), (c) any cost incident to BUYER'S obtaining financing, (d) costs of any inspections required by BUYER as conditions of this Agreement, and (e) the additional premium cost for any Title Insurance policy that was provided.

10-DAMAGE: If any buildings or other improvements are damaged or destroyed prior to Title Transfer in excess of ten percent of said purchase price, BUYER may either accept any insurance proceeds payable on account thereof as full compensation therefor, or may terminate this agreement and receive return of all deposits made hereunder. For all damage and destruction valued as less than ten percent of said purchase price, SELLER shall restore the property to its condition as of contract acceptance date.

11-CONDITION OF PROPERTY:

BUYER acknowledges that it has been recommended to him that he engage, at his expense, the services of a professional contractor or building inspector to inspect the property and all improvements to ascertain that the condition of the property is as called for in this Agreement. BUYER further acknowledges that no broker or any agent having anything to do with this transaction has made any verbal, or other statements or representations concerning the property on which BUYER has relied, except as specifically set forth in writing herein. BUYER has examined the property and agrees that the property is being purchased in its present "as is" condition, including any defects that may have been disclosed by SELLER either specifically hereon or by attached addendum. BUYER acknowledges that he has not relied on any representations, warranties or statements whatsoever concerning the property, including without limitation its use or condition, other than as written in this Agreement.

12-SPECIFIC DISCLOSURES: BUYER has relied on the following additional specific disclosures and/or representations in making this Agreement: (IF NONE, WRITE "NONE")

that basement had slight amount of water in Spring 1989 flooding

Said specific disclosures and/or representations were made by real estate agents + seller.

13-SELLER'S REPRESENTATIONS: Seller states that he has no knowledge of any hidden or latent defects on the property, including without limitation, any of the following: water seepage; basement foundation or wall wetness (or dampness); bathroom or kitchen leakage; roof leakage; problems with electrical, plumbing, heating, cooling, sewer,

(continued)

EXERCISE 1 Answer (continued).

septic, well or water systems; structural defects; or faulty major appliances, EXCEPT: (IF NONE, WRITE "NONE") basement had slight amount of water in Spring 1989 flooding

14-INSPECTION CONDITIONS: This Agreement shall be subject to all of the following checked Inspections, which Inspections shall be paid for by BUYER, carried out in good faith by all parties, and completed within the times specified. These Inspections shall be either approved or disapproved by BUYER in writing within said times and if disapproved, this Agreement shall become NULL AND VOID and subject to the TERMINATION PROCEDURE, as set forth in foregoing paragraph 4. (IF NONE, WRITE "NONE")________

(X) A. GENERAL HOME INSPECTION The property shall be inspected by a general home inspector, construction person, professional property inspector, or other person of BUYER'S choice within 14 days from final acceptance hereof.

(X) B. WELL OPERATION AND WELL WATER TEST The well system shall be inspected by a qualified inspector of BUYER'S choice (whose findings would be acceptable to County or other water authorities) for both (1) adequate flow rate and equipment operation and (2) potability, within 14 days from final acceptance hereof.

( ) C. SEPTIC SYSTEM INSPECTION The septic or other on-site sanitation system shall be inspected by a qualified inspector of BUYER'S choice (whose findings would be acceptable to County or other sanitary authorities) within________days from final acceptance hereof. SELLER shall pay the cost of sanitation system *cleaning*, if necessary for Inspection.

( ) D. TERMITE/WOOD-DESTROYING INSECT INSPECTION The property shall be inspected by a licensed pest control inspector of BUYER'S choice within________days from final acceptance hereof.

NOTE -- Should FHA or VA Regulations prohibit payment by BUYER of the cost of any of the foregoing INSPECTIONS, SELLER shall pay the cost thereof.

WAIVER

Should BUYER fail to have any of the above Inspections completed within the times specified, OR IF BUYER FAILS TO SPECIFICALLY APPROVE OR DISAPPROVE ANY INSPECTIONS WITHIN THE TIMES SPECIFIED, then BUYER shall be deemed to have WAIVED SUCH INSPECTIONS and shall be considered as HAVING ACCEPTED THE PROPERTY ABSOLUTELY AND FINALLY IN ITS PRESENT "AS IS" CONDITION, and neither SELLER nor any real estate broker or agent having anything to do with this transaction shall have any further liability or obligation to BUYER as to such Inspections or Agreement Conditions.

Should the results of any of such Inspections not be satisfactory to BUYER then, within the times specified, BUYER shall notify either SELLER or SELLER'S LISTING BROKERAGE in writing of his specific dissatisfaction, at which point the TERMINATION PROCEDURE set forth in foregoing paragraph 4. shall apply.

15-ADDENDA: This Agreement is subject to the additional terms and conditions as set forth in the attached Addenda, hereby made a part hereof, and described as: ( )AGENCY, ( )HOME SALE, ( )FHA/VA, ( )CONDO, ( )OTHER

16-HOME WARRANTY: ( ) If checked, BUYER shall be provided a limited HOME WARRANTY PLAN issued by the INSURANCE COMPANY. The application service charge of $__________shall be paid by________ at closing.

17-BINDING AGREEMENT: Acceptance of this Offer, and any attached Addenda, shall create a LEGAL AGREEMENT, BINDING ON BUYER AND SELLER and their heirs, executors, administrators, successors and assigns, and shall contain the ENTIRE AGREEMENT AND UNDERSTANDING of the parties, it being further acknowleged that there are no other conditions, representations, warranties or agreements, expressed or implied, beyond those contained herein. All terms, provisions, covenants, and conditions of this Agreement shall survive Title Transfer of said property to BUYER.

18-BUYER'S OFFER: The undersigned specifically represent(s) that they are of legal age and capacity and are ready, willing and able to purchase the property according to the above terms:

BUYER(S) Mary Smith John Smith / Mary Jones John Jones

ADDRESS/Phone 100 Nowhere, Anyville Ohio.

TITLE SHALL BE TAKEN: Mary Smith (Date) 7/5/97

IF TITLE TO BE IN MORE THAN ONE NAME, IS SURVIVORSHIP DEED REQUESTED? No (YES or NO)

19-SELLER'S ACCEPTANCE:

The undersigned, being of legal age and capacity, hereby accept(s) the above offer and agree(s) to pay a total commission of

7 percent of said purchase price, payable 7 percent to the REAL ESTATE COMPANY and_____percent to ________________________ as the SOLE PROCURING CAUSE(S) of this transaction.

SELLER(S) John Doe / Jane Doe

ADDRESS/Phone 100 Somewhere, Anyville, Ohio (Date) 7/5/97

20-DEPOSIT RECEIPT: Receipt is hereby acknowledged, as agent for SELLER, of BUYER'S earnest money deposit in the amount specified and in the form described in foregoing paragraph 3.(a), to be held in the REAL ESTATE COMPANY'S trust Account, subject to all terms and provisions of this Agreement.

-------------the REAL ESTATE COMPANY By Anne Hamilton (Date) 7/5/97

ONCE SIGNED, THIS DOCUMENT BECOMES A LEGALLY-BINDING CONTRACT
IF YOU HAVE QUESTIONS OF LAW, CONSULT AN ATTORNEY LICENSED TO PRACTICE IN OHIO

PURCHASE AGREEMENT 2

Fill out the blank real estate purchase contract that accompanies this exercise.

> I am the purchaser, and my name is Linda Lincoln. I am a divorcee. I want to make an offer of $90,000 on a ranch you have listed for sale at $95,000, located at 200 Vista Place, Anyville, Ohio.
>
> We want the following items to be included in the sale: the window air conditioner in the family room; the riding mower; the washer and dryer; the water softener; and the refrigerator, the built-in dishwasher, double oven, and range.
>
> The man I am currently living with, and possibly marrying, is Alan Cunningham. He will also be a purchaser of this home. We will both contribute equally to the down payment and will both apply for the mortgage loan. Alan and I will make a $21,000 down payment on this home. You will have us sign a promissory note in the amount of $2,000 as our earnest money.
>
> We want two conditions included within our offer. First, we need a financing condition providing that if we can't obtain loan approval, then we are excused from performing the contract. Second, that Alan must receive the proceeds from the sale of his condominium at 100 Little Turtle in Anyville or we are likewise excused from performing the contract. Pursuant to Alan's divorce decree with his ex, the sale of their condo splits the proceeds between them. Alan needs those funds for his part of the down payment. We can apply for our financing for Vista Place immediately. You can study the real estate purchase contract on Alan's condominium. It gives all the details of that transaction. You can determine, from both your own knowledge and the purchase contract on the condo, the following: We should have our loan approval by August 1; that we can put our funds and documents into escrow by August 20; and that Vista Place can close by August 25.
>
> We must have possession by August 25, since that is my birthday.
>
> The realty is serviced by a well.
>
> We want the best deed and best title assurance that the seller can furnish. We also want to hold title to the real estate in both of our names but are not sure which is the best way for us to do so. We would like your advice (as Anne Hamilton, our real estate salesperson), on how we should hold title. You have told us that everyone does a survivorship these days to avoid probate so we can go ahead with that.
>
> Alan and I both sign the offer and date it.
>
> ***
>
> I am Rob Ruiz, the seller. The house is in my name alone. I am getting a divorce from my wife, Ruth, but we do not have a final decree as yet. My pending divorce from Ruth is the only disclosure I would like to make to the purchasers. Ruth is not present, of course. I am so happy to be making sure that Ruth will not get a dime out of my real estate that I am agreeable to all the other terms of the offer. Thus, we merely write in the disclosure about Ruth in both clause 12 and 13 on the form, which I initial and date. I sign at the end as well. I realize that my alteration has made this my counteroffer.

You (Anne Hamilton) take this counteroffer back to the purchasers. They both initial the disclosure sections that Rob has changed and give all the papers back to you. You drive back to Rob's and give him his papers. You now have a binding contract on Vista Place. Then, on your ride back to the office, you get a bad feeling about certain things in the whole transaction. What are those things that should be bothering you? (Class discussion is appropriate at this point.)

Class discussion should include the following points:

Anne does have problems with this transaction. The minute Rob told her he was locked in a divorce battle with Ruth, she should have been alerted to a dower problem; that is, that without Ruth's consent, this realty will have a cloud on the title because of Ruth's dower rights. Since Rob and Anne have made this a disclosure on the face of the contract itself, there is even written evidence that Anne was negligent in failing to realize the dower problem she was creating. Although Rob has entered into a binding contract with the Lincoln-Cunningham couple, he will end up breaching that contract if he cannot get Ruth to release her dower rights (a likely prospect). Rob may well end up suing Anne for being negligent as his agent, especially if Lincoln-Cunningham sue him for breach of contract (which they probably will).

Anne's glib answer about the survivorship deed being the choice to elude probate was also bad. This particular couple, with their domestic relations problems, is also the kind who usually should not be thinking survivorship forms of coownership either.

Although Anne quite competently filled out the blank form, her lack of understanding about some of its more serious provisions can get her into a lot of legal trouble. Thus, the student must understand the theory behind the practical materials.

EXERCISE 2 Purchase contract.

PURCHASE AGREEMENT

1-BUYER: The undersigned ______________________________
(hereinafter "BUYER") offers to buy the following-described property.

2-PROPERTY: Situated in the __________ of ________________, County of ______________,
and State of Ohio;
and located at ______________________________
and being further described as a ______________________________.
Permanent Parcel No. or Tax I.D. No. ______________________

The property, which BUYER accepts in its PRESENT CONDITION, except for normal wear and tear before Title Transfer, and except as specifically set forth hereinafter, shall include the land and all appurtenant rights, privileges and easements, (subject to all rights of tenants, if any), and all buildings and fixtures, including without limitation, *all* of the following as are now on the property: electrical, heating, cooling, plumbing and bathroom fixtures; window and door shades, blinds, awnings, screens, storm windows, curtain and drapery fixtures; landscaping; disposals; TV antennas, rotor control units and built-in TV and videotape wiring; smoke alarms; security systems; garage door openers and controls; radiator covers; permanently attached carpeting;
( )ranges and ovens; ( )microwave ovens; ( )dishwashers; ( )refrigerators; ( )window air conditioners;
( )water softeners; ( )gas grills; ( )satellite TV reception systems;
FIREPLACE ( )tools, ( )screens, ( )glass doors, ( )grates; ( )washers, ( )dryers; and all existing window treatments,
EXCEPT these window treatments: ______________________________
Also INCLUDED: ______________________________
NOT included: ______________________________

3-PRICE: For which BUYER shall pay owner of said property (hereinafter "SELLER")----$ ______________
payable as follows:

(A) Earnest Money to be paid to the REAL ESTATE COMPANY, as agent for SELLER, to be deposited upon acceptance of final offer in the REAL ESTATE COMPANY'S Trust Account and credited against the purchase price:

------------( )check ( )note ( )cash--$ ______________
IF A NOTE--TO BE REDEEMED WITHIN FOUR DAYS OF ACCEPTANCE OF CONTRACT.
FURTHER, IT IS AGREED THAT WHEREVER THE WORD "DAYS" APPEARS HEREIN, SUCH SHALL REFER TO CALENDAR DAYS, WITH ALL SUNDAYS AND NATIONAL HOLIDAYS NOT BEING COUNTED.
(B) Remainder of BUYER'S downpayment, to be deposited in escrow
as per paragraph 5. hereinafter--$ ______________
(C) Balance in the form of a Mortgage Loan
------------( )conventional ( )FHA ( )VA ( )OTHER------------------------------$ ______________

____
______________________________$ ______________

4-FINANCING: This transaction is conditioned upon BUYER obtaining the mortgage loan financing referred to above. BUYER shall make a written application for such financing within ______ days from contract acceptance date and shall obtain a commitment for such loan on or about ______________, 19_____. If despite BUYER'S good faith efforts, BUYER cannot obtain such loan commitment, or one for a lesser sum but still acceptable to BUYER, then this Agreement shall be NULL AND VOID and the following shall occur promptly:

BUYER and SELLER shall enter into a written Mutual Release from this transaction, directing the return of the earnest money deposit, or SELLER shall sign an Authorization directing the REAL ESTATE COMPANY to return said earnest money deposit to BUYER. After the execution of same, neither buyer, seller, nor any real estate broker or agent having anything to do with this transaction shall have any liability or obligation to the other(s) stemming from same. (This procedure is referred to hereinafter as "the TERMINATION PROCEDURE.")

5-CLOSING: (choose *one* of the following)

(A) Escrow- All documents, funds, and financial institution commitments for funds necessary to the completion of this transaction shall be placed in escrow with any local Lending Institution, or with any local Title Company on or before ______________, 19_____ and Title shall transfer to BUYER on or about but not before ______________, 19_____; EXCEPT, if a defect in Title appears, SELLER shall have thirty (30) days after notice to SELLER to remove such defect, and being unable to do so, BUYER may agree to accept Title subject to such defect without any reduction in said purchase price, or may terminate this Agreement and, thereupon, receive the return of all deposits made hereunder, as per the TERMINATION PROCEDURE, set forth in foregoing paragraph 4.

(B) Formal - All documents, funds, and financial institution commitments for funds necessary to the completion of this transaction shall be brought to a formal "sit-down" closing by the parties and their respective representatives and agents to be held at
______________________________ Ohio
on the ________ day of ______________, 19____ at ________ AM/PM, at which time Title shall transfer to BUYER. However, if a defect in Title appears during such attempted closing, SELLER shall have thirty (30) days thereafter to reschedule such closing and to remove such defect, and being unable to do so, BUYER may agree to accept

(continued)

EXERCISE 2 Continued.

Title subject to such defect, without any reduction in said purchase price, or may terminate this Agreement and, thereupon, receive the return of all deposits made hereunder, as per the TERMINATION PROCEDURE, set forth in foregoing paragraph 4.

6-POSSESSION: SELLER shall deliver possession of the property to BUYER within_______days* after the date of Title Transfer,
or on________________, 19_____, whichever is LATER. The first__________days of said period shall be rental free and the balance (if any) shall be at $________________ per day, not to exceed__________days, after which time SELLER shall become a tenant at sufferance and subject to eviction. *Days in the case of this paragraph 6., and this paragraph *only*, shall refer to consecutive calendar days, with all Sundays and Holidays being counted.

7-TITLE: SELLER shall convey a marketable title to BUYER by General Warranty Deed and/or Fiduciary Deed, if required, with all dower rights released, free and clear of all liens and encumbrances whatsoever, except (a) any mortgage assumed by BUYER/GRANTEE, (b) all restrictions, reservations, easements (however created), covenants, and conditions of record, (c) all of the following as do not materially and adversely affect the use or value of the property: encroachments, oil, gas and mineral leases, (d) zoning ordinances, if any, and (e) taxes and assessments, both general and special, not currently due and payable.

SELLER shall furnish a Title Guarantee, in the amount of said purchase price, showing record Title to be good in BUYER/GRANTEE, subject to the deed exceptions set forth hereinabove, and any title policy exceptions, to be issued by a Title Company acceptable to SELLER. Should BUYER desire, he may obtain an Owner's Title Insurance Commitmemt and Policy [ALTA Form B (1970 REV. 10-17-70 & REV. 10-17-84)], or other similar title insurance, so long as he pays the increased premium due because of such additional coverage. If the property is Torrenized, SELLER shall furnish, in lieu of the foregoing, an Owner's Duplicate Certificate of Title, together with a United States Court Search and Tax Search. Where required by ordinance, SELLER shall order a code inspection and shall deposit the results at closing.

8-PRORATIONS: Any of the following as exist -- General taxes, special assessments, Homeowners' Association Fees or other similar fees, city/county or other local charges, and tenant rents -- shall be prorated at closing as of date of Title Transfer. Taxes and assessments shall be prorated based on the latest available tax duplicate. BUYER and SELLER shall prorate and adjust directly any changes in taxes resulting either from a change in valuation and/or tax rate occurring before Title Transfer, or from existing but not yet assessed improvements. Utility charges shall be paid by SELLERS to the date of Title Transfer, or the date of exchange of possession, whichever is LATER; also, the Closing Agent shall withhold the sum of $______________from SELLER'S proceeds to secure payment of final water and sewer charges, if any, unless SELLER submits proof of payment of such.

9-CHARGES: SELLER shall pay the following costs at closing: (a) cost of title exam and Title Guarantee premium, (b) cost to prepare Deed, (c) amount due to discharge any lien encumbering the property and the cost of recording the cancellation thereof, (d) Real Estate Transfer Tax, (e) cost for inspections and certificates required by public authorities, (f) prorations due BUYER, (g) real estate commissions due brokers, and (h) one-half the closing fee, or the full closing fee should FHA or VA regulations prohibit payment of such by BUYER. If, at time of transfer of utilities to BUYER, a defect is detected in any of the main utility service supply lines on the property, SELLER shall pay all costs for the repair of such, either directly, or at closing.

BUYER shall pay the following costs at closing: (a) cost of filing the Deed for record, (b) one-half of the closing fee (when not prohibited by FHA or VA regulations), (c) any cost incident to BUYER'S obtaining financing, (d) costs of any inspections required by BUYER as conditions of this Agreement, and (e) the additional premium cost for any Title Insurance policy that was provided.

10-DAMAGE: If any buildings or other improvements are damaged or destroyed prior to Title Transfer in excess of ten percent of said purchase price, BUYER may either accept any insurance proceeds payable on account thereof as full compensation therefor, or may terminate this agreement and receive return of all deposits made hereunder. For all damage and destruction valued as less than ten percent of said purchase price, SELLER shall restore the property to its condition as of contract acceptance date.

11-CONDITION OF PROPERTY:

BUYER acknowledges that it has been recommended to him that he engage, at his expense, the services of a professional contractor or building inspector to inspect the property and all improvements to ascertain that the condition of the property is as called for in this Agreement. BUYER further acknowledges that no broker or any agent having anything to do with this transaction has made any verbal, or other statements or representations concerning the property on which BUYER has relied, except as specifically set forth in writing herein. BUYER has examined the property and agrees that the property is being purchased in its present "as is" condition, including any defects that may have been disclosed by SELLER either specifically hereon or by attached addendum. BUYER acknowledges that he has not relied on any representations, warranties or statements whatsoever concerning the property, including without limitation its use or condition, other than as written in this Agreement.

12-SPECIFIC DISCLOSURES: BUYER has relied on the following additional specific disclosures and/or representations in making this Agreement: (IF NONE, WRITE "NONE")

____

Said specific disclosures and/or representations were made by______________________________________.

13-SELLER'S REPRESENTATIONS: Seller states that he has no knowledge of any hidden or latent defects on the property, including without limitation, any of the following: water seepage; basement foundation or wall wetness (or dampness); bathroom or kitchen leakage; roof leakage; problems with electrical, plumbing, heating, cooling, sewer,

(continued)

EXERCISE 2 Continued.

septic, well or water systems; structural defects; or faulty major appliances, EXCEPT: (IF NONE, WRITE "NONE")

____

14-INSPECTION CONDITIONS: This Agreement shall be subject to all of the following checked Inspections, which Inspections shall be paid for by BUYER, carried out in good faith by all parties, and completed within the times specified. These Inspections shall be either approved or disapproved by BUYER in writing within said times and if disapproved, this Agreement shall become NULL AND VOID and subject to the TERMINATION PROCEDURE, as set forth in foregoing paragraph 4. (IF NONE, WRITE "NONE")_________

( ) A. GENERAL HOME INSPECTION The property shall be inspected by a general home inspector, construction person, professional property inspector, or other person of BUYER'S choice within_________days from final acceptance hereof.

( ) B. WELL OPERATION AND WELL WATER TEST The well system shall be inspected by a qualified inspector of BUYER'S choice (whose findings would be acceptable to County or other water authorities) for both (1) adequate flow rate and equipment operation and (2) potability, within_________days from final acceptance hereof.

( ) C. SEPTIC SYSTEM INSPECTION The septic or other on-site sanitation system shall be inspected by a qualified inspector of BUYER'S choice (whose findings would be acceptable to County or other sanitary authorities) within_________days from final acceptance hereof. SELLER shall pay the cost of sanitation system *cleaning,* if necessary for Inspection.

( ) D. TERMITE/WOOD-DESTROYING INSECT INSPECTION The property shall be inspected by a licensed pest control inspector of BUYER'S choice within_________days from final acceptance hereof.

NOTE -- Should FHA or VA Regulations prohibit payment by BUYER of the cost of any of the foregoing INSPECTIONS, SELLER shall pay the cost thereof.

WAIVER

Should BUYER fail to have any of the above Inspections completed within the times specified, OR IF BUYER FAILS TO SPECIFICALLY APPROVE OR DISAPPROVE ANY INSPECTIONS WITHIN THE TIMES SPECIFIED, then BUYER shall be deemed to have WAIVED SUCH INSPECTIONS and shall be considered as HAVING ACCEPTED THE PROPERTY ABSOLUTELY AND FINALLY IN ITS PRESENT "AS IS" CONDITION, and neither SELLER nor any real estate broker or agent having anything to do with this transaction shall have any further liability or obligation to BUYER as to such Inspections or Agreement Conditions.

Should the results of any of such Inspections not be satisfactory to BUYER then, within the times specified, BUYER shall notify either SELLER or SELLER'S LISTING BROKERAGE in writing of his specific dissatisfaction, at which point the TERMINATION PROCEDURE set forth in foregoing paragraph 4. shall apply.

15-ADDENDA: This Agreement is subject to the additional terms and conditions as set forth in the attached Addenda, hereby made a part hereof, and described as: ( )AGENCY, ( )HOME SALE, ( )FHA/VA, ( )CONDO, ( )OTHER

16-HOME WARRANTY: ( ) If checked, BUYER shall be provided a limited HOME WARRANTY PLAN issued by the INSURANCE COMPANY. The application service charge of $___________shall be paid by ________ at closing.

17-BINDING AGREEMENT: Acceptance of this Offer, and any attached Addenda, shall create a LEGAL AGREEMENT, BINDING ON BUYER AND SELLER and their heirs, executors, administrators, successors and assigns, and shall contain the ENTIRE AGREEMENT AND UNDERSTANDING of the parties, it being further acknowleged that there are no other conditions, representations, warranties or agreements, expressed or implied, beyond those contained herein. All terms, provisions, covenants, and conditions of this Agreement shall survive Title Transfer of said property to BUYER.

18-BUYER'S OFFER: The undersigned specifically represent(s) that they are of legal age and capacity and are ready, willing and able to purchase the property according to the above terms:

BUYER(S)_________________________________/_________________________________

ADDRESS/Phone____.

TITLE SHALL BE TAKEN:_________________________________ (Date)_________________

IF TITLE TO BE IN MORE THAN ONE NAME, IS SURVIVORSHIP DEED REQUESTED? ______ (YES or NO)

19-SELLER'S ACCEPTANCE:

The undersigned, being of legal age and capacity, hereby accept(s) the above offer and agree(s) to pay a total commission of

_____percent of said purchase price, payable____percent to the REAL ESTATE COMPANY and_____percent to _________________________________ as the SOLE PROCURING CAUSE(S) of this transaction.

SELLER(S)_________________________________/_________________________________

ADDRESS/Phone_________________________________ (Date)_________________

20-DEPOSIT RECEIPT: Receipt is hereby acknowledged, as agent for SELLER, of BUYER'S earnest money deposit in the amount specified and in the form described in foregoing paragraph 3.(a), to be held in the REAL ESTATE COMPANY'S trust Account, subject to all terms and provisions of this Agreement.

--------------the REAL ESTATE COMPANY By_________________________________ (Date)_________________

ONCE SIGNED, THIS DOCUMENT BECOMES A LEGALLY-BINDING CONTRACT
IF YOU HAVE QUESTIONS OF LAW, CONSULT AN ATTORNEY LICENSED TO PRACTICE IN OHIO

EXERCISE 2 Answer.

PURCHASE AGREEMENT

EQUAL HOUSING OPPORTUNITY

1-BUYER: The undersigned Linda Lincoln and Alan Cunningham (hereinafter "BUYER") offers to buy the following-described property.

2-PROPERTY: Situated in the Village of Any, County of Geauga, and State of Ohio; and located at 200 Vista Place, Anyville, Ohio 44026 and being further described as a single-family ranch w/2-car attached garage.
Permanent Parcel No. or Tax I.D. No. ______

The property, which BUYER accepts in its PRESENT CONDITION, except for normal wear and tear before Title Transfer, and except as specifically set forth hereinafter, shall include the land and all appurtenant rights, privileges and easements, (subject to all rights of tenants, if any), and all buildings and fixtures, including without limitation, *all* of the following as are now on the property: electrical, heating, cooling, plumbing and bathroom fixtures; window and door shades, blinds, awnings, screens, storm windows, curtain and drapery fixtures; landscaping; disposals; TV antennas, rotor control units and built-in TV and videotape wiring; smoke alarms; security systems; garage door openers and controls; radiator covers; permanently attached carpeting;
(X)ranges and ovens; ( )microwave ovens; (X)dishwashers; (X)refrigerators; (X)window air conditioners; (X)water softeners; ( )gas grills; ( )satellite TV reception systems;
FIREPLACE ( )tools, ( )screens, ( )glass doors, ( )grates; (X)washers, (X)dryers; and all existing window treatments,
EXCEPT these window treatments: ______
Also INCLUDED: the riding mower
NOT included: ______

3-PRICE: For which BUYER shall pay owner of said property (hereinafter "SELLER")---$ 90,000
payable as follows:

(A) Earnest Money to be paid to the REAL ESTATE COMPANY, as agent for SELLER, to be deposited upon acceptance of final offer in the REAL ESTATE COMPANY'S Trust Account and credited against the purchase price:
-----------( )check (X)note ( )cash---$ 2,000
IF A NOTE--TO BE REDEEMED WITHIN FOUR DAYS OF ACCEPTANCE OF CONTRACT.
FURTHER, IT IS AGREED THAT WHEREVER THE WORD "DAYS" APPEARS HEREIN, SUCH SHALL REFER TO CALENDAR DAYS, WITH ALL SUNDAYS AND NATIONAL HOLIDAYS NOT BEING COUNTED.
(B) Remainder of BUYER'S downpayment, to be deposited in escrow as per paragraph 5. hereinafter------------------------------------$ 19,000
(C) Balance in the form of a Mortgage Loan
-----------(X)conventional ( )FHA ( )VA ( )OTHER-------------------$ 69,000
conditional upon purchaser Alan Cunningham's receiving proceeds from sale of his condo, 100 Little Turtle, Anyville, Ohio Total $ 90,000

4-FINANCING: This transaction is conditioned upon BUYER obtaining the mortgage loan financing referred to above. BUYER shall make a written application for such financing within five days from contract acceptance date and shall obtain a commitment for such loan on or about August 1, 19 97. If despite BUYER'S good faith efforts, BUYER cannot obtain such loan commitment, or one for a lesser sum but still acceptable to BUYER, then this Agreement shall be NULL AND VOID and the following shall occur promptly:

BUYER and SELLER shall enter into a written Mutual Release from this transaction, directing the return of the earnest money deposit, or SELLER shall sign an Authorization directing the REAL ESTATE COMPANY to return said earnest money deposit to BUYER. After the execution of same, neither buyer, seller, nor any real estate broker or agent having anything to do with this transaction shall have any liability or obligation to the other(s) stemming from same. (This procedure is referred to hereinafter as "the TERMINATION PROCEDURE.")

5-CLOSING: (choose *one* of the following)

(A) Escrow- All documents, funds, and financial institution commitments for funds necessary to the completion of this transaction shall be placed in escrow with any local Lending Institution, or with any local Title Company on or before August 20, 19 97 and Title shall transfer to BUYER on or about but not before August 25, 19 97; EXCEPT, if a defect in Title appears, SELLER shall have thirty (30) days after notice to SELLER to remove such defect, and being unable to do so, BUYER may agree to accept Title subject to such defect without any reduction in said purchase price, or may terminate this Agreement and, thereupon, receive the return of all deposits made hereunder, as per the TERMINATION PROCEDURE, set forth in foregoing paragraph 4.

(B) Formal - All documents, funds, and financial institution commitments for funds necessary to the completion of this transaction shall be brought to a formal "sit-down" closing by the parties and their respective representatives and agents to be held at
______ Ohio
on the ______ day of ______, 19___ at ______ AM/PM, at which time Title shall transfer to BUYER. However, if a defect in Title appears during such attempted closing, SELLER shall have thirty (30) days thereafter to reschedule such closing and to remove such defect, and being unable to do so, BUYER may agree to accept

(continued)

EXERCISE 2 Answer (continued).

Title subject to such defect, without any reduction in said purchase price, or may terminate this Agreement and, thereupon, receive the return of all deposits made hereunder, as per the TERMINATION PROCEDURE, set forth in foregoing paragraph 4.

6-POSSESSION: SELLER shall deliver possession of the property to BUYER within 0 days* after the date of Title Transfer, or on August 25, 19 97, whichever is LATER. The first ______ days of said period shall be rental free and the balance (if any) shall be at $______ per day, not to exceed ______ days, after which time SELLER shall become a tenant at sufferance and subject to eviction. *Days in the case of this paragraph 6., and this paragraph *only*, shall refer to consecutive calendar days, with all Sundays and Holidays being counted.

7-TITLE: SELLER shall convey a marketable title to BUYER by General Warranty Deed and/or Fiduciary Deed, if required, with all dower rights released, free and clear of all liens and encumbrances whatsoever, except (a) any mortgage assumed by BUYER/GRANTEE, (b) all restrictions, reservations, easements (however created), covenants, and conditions of record, (c) all of the following as do not materially and adversely affect the use or value of the property: encroachments, oil, gas and mineral leases, (d) zoning ordinances, if any, and (e) taxes and assessments, both general and special, not currently due and payable.

SELLER shall furnish a Title Guarantee, in the amount of said purchase price, showing record Title to be good in BUYER/GRANTEE, subject to the deed exceptions set forth hereinabove, and any title policy exceptions, to be issued by a Title Company acceptable to SELLER. Should BUYER desire, he may obtain an Owner's Title Insurance Commitmemt and Policy [ALTA Form B (1970 REV. 10-17-70 & REV. 10-17-84)], or other similar title insurance, so long as he pays the increased premium due because of such additional coverage. If the property is Torrenized, SELLER shall furnish, in lieu of the foregoing, an Owner's Duplicate Certificate of Title, together with a United States Court Search and Tax Search. Where required by ordinance, SELLER shall order a code inspection and shall deposit the results at closing.

8-PRORATIONS: Any of the following as exist -- General taxes, special assessments, Homeowners' Association Fees or other similar fees, city/county or other local charges, and tenant rents -- shall be prorated at closing as of date of Title Transfer. Taxes and assessments shall be prorated based on the latest available tax duplicate. BUYER and SELLER shall prorate and adjust directly any changes in taxes resulting either from a change in valuation and/or tax rate occurring before Title Transfer, or from existing but not yet assessed improvements. Utility charges shall be paid by SELLERS to the date of Title Transfer, or the date of exchange of possession, whichever is LATER; also, the Closing Agent shall withhold the sum of $______ from SELLER'S proceeds to secure payment of final water and sewer charges, if any, unless SELLER submits proof of payment of such.

9-CHARGES: SELLER shall pay the following costs at closing: (a) cost of title exam and Title Guarantee premium, (b) cost to prepare Deed, (c) amount due to discharge any lien encumbering the property and the cost of recording the cancellation thereof, (d) Real Estate Transfer Tax, (e) cost for inspections and certificates required by public authorities, (f) prorations due BUYER, (g) real estate commissions due brokers, and (h) one-half the closing fee, or the full closing fee should FHA or VA regulations prohibit payment of such by BUYER. If, at time of transfer of utilities to BUYER, a defect is detected in any of the main utility service supply lines on the property, SELLER shall pay all costs for the repair of such, either directly, or at closing.

BUYER shall pay the following costs at closing: (a) cost of filing the Deed for record, (b) one-half of the closing fee (when not prohibited by FHA or VA regulations), (c) any cost incident to BUYER'S obtaining financing, (d) costs of any inspections required by BUYER as conditions of this Agreement, and (e) the additional premium cost for any Title Insurance policy that was provided.

10-DAMAGE: If any buildings or other improvements are damaged or destroyed prior to Title Transfer in excess of ten percent of said purchase price, BUYER may either accept any insurance proceeds payable on account thereof as full compensation therefor, or may terminate this agreement and receive return of all deposits made hereunder. For all damage and destruction valued as less than ten percent of said purchase price, SELLER shall restore the property to its condition as of contract acceptance date.

11-CONDITION OF PROPERTY:

BUYER acknowledges that it has been recommended to him that he engage, at his expense, the services of a professional contractor or building inspector to inspect the property and all improvements to ascertain that the condition of the property is as called for in this Agreement. BUYER further acknowledges that no broker or any agent having anything to do with this transaction has made any verbal, or other statements or representations concerning the property on which BUYER has relied, except as specifically set forth in writing herein. BUYER has examined the property and agrees that the property is being purchased in its present "as is" condition, including any defects that may have been disclosed by SELLER either specifically hereon or by attached addendum. BUYER acknowledges that he has not relied on any representations, warranties or statements whatsoever concerning the property, including without limitation its use or condition, other than as written in this Agreement.

12-SPECIFIC DISCLOSURES: BUYER has relied on the following additional specific disclosures and/or representations in making this Agreement: (IF NONE, WRITE "NONE")

Seller is obtaining a divorce from his wife, Ruth Ruiz R.R. L.L.

Said specific disclosures and/or representations were made by real estate agent Anne Hamilton AC 7/5/97

13-SELLER'S REPRESENTATIONS: Seller states that he has no knowledge of any hidden or latent defects on the property, including without limitation, any of the following: water seepage; basement foundation or wall wetness (or dampness); bathroom or kitchen leakage; roof leakage; problems with electrical, plumbing, heating, cooling, sewer,

(continued)

EXERCISE 2 Answer (continued).

7/5/97 RR LL AC

septic, well or water systems; structural defects; or faulty major appliances, EXCEPT: (IF NONE, WRITE "NONE") I am obtaining a divorce from my wife, Ruth Ruiz.

14-INSPECTION CONDITIONS: This Agreement shall be subject to all of the following checked Inspections, which Inspections shall be paid for by BUYER, carried out in good faith by all parties, and completed within the times specified. These Inspections shall be either approved or disapproved by BUYER in writing within said times and if disapproved, this Agreement shall become NULL AND VOID and subject to the TERMINATION PROCEDURE, as set forth in foregoing paragraph 4. (IF NONE, WRITE "NONE")________

( ) A. GENERAL HOME INSPECTION The property shall be inspected by a general home inspector, construction person, professional property inspector, or other person of BUYER'S choice within________days from final acceptance hereof.

( ) B. WELL OPERATION AND WELL WATER TEST The well system shall be inspected by a qualified inspector of BUYER'S choice (whose findings would be acceptable to County or other water authorities) for both (1) adequate flow rate and equipment operation and (2) potability, within________days from final acceptance hereof.

( ) C. SEPTIC SYSTEM INSPECTION The septic or other on-site sanitation system shall be inspected by a qualified inspector of BUYER'S choice (whose findings would be acceptable to County or other sanitary authorities) within________days from final acceptance hereof. SELLER shall pay the cost of sanitation system *cleaning,* if necessary for inspection.

( ) D. TERMITE/WOOD-DESTROYING INSECT INSPECTION The property shall be inspected by a licensed pest control inspector of BUYER'S choice within________days from final acceptance hereof.

NOTE -- Should FHA or VA Regulations prohibit payment by BUYER of the cost of any of the foregoing INSPECTIONS, SELLER shall pay the cost thereof.

WAIVER

Should BUYER fail to have any of the above Inspections completed within the times specified, OR IF BUYER FAILS TO SPECIFICALLY APPROVE OR DISAPPROVE ANY INSPECTIONS WITHIN THE TIMES SPECIFIED, then BUYER shall be deemed to have WAIVED SUCH INSPECTIONS and shall be considered as HAVING ACCEPTED THE PROPERTY ABSOLUTELY AND FINALLY IN ITS PRESENT "AS IS" CONDITION, and neither SELLER nor any real estate broker or agent having anything to do with this transaction shall have any further liability or obligation to BUYER as to such Inspections or Agreement Conditions.

Should the results of any of such Inspections not be satisfactory to BUYER then, within the times specified, BUYER shall notify either SELLER or SELLER'S LISTING BROKERAGE in writing of his specific dissatisfaction, at which point the TERMINATION PROCEDURE set forth in foregoing paragraph 4. shall apply.

15-ADDENDA: This Agreement is subject to the additional terms and conditions as set forth in the attached Addenda, hereby made a part hereof, and described as: ( )AGENCY, ( )HOME SALE, ( )FHA/VA, ( )CONDO, ( )OTHER

16-HOME WARRANTY: ( ) If checked, BUYER shall be provided a limited HOME WARRANTY PLAN issued by the INSURANCE COMPANY. The application service charge of $________shall be paid by________at closing.

17-BINDING AGREEMENT: Acceptance of this Offer, and any attached Addenda, shall create a LEGAL AGREEMENT, BINDING ON BUYER AND SELLER and their heirs, executors, administrators, successors and assigns, and shall contain the ENTIRE AGREEMENT AND UNDERSTANDING of the parties, it being further acknowleged that there are no other conditions, representations, warranties or agreements, expressed or implied, beyond those contained herein. All terms, provisions, covenants, and conditions of this Agreement shall survive Title Transfer of said property to BUYER.

18-BUYER'S OFFER: The undersigned specifically represent(s) that they are of legal age and capacity and are ready, willing and able to purchase the property according to the above terms:

BUYER(S) Linda Lincoln / Alan Cunningham

ADDRESS/Phone 100 Birch Way, Alfa, Ohio

TITLE SHALL BE TAKEN: Linda Lincoln + Alan Cunningham (Date) 7/5/97

IF TITLE TO BE IN MORE THAN ONE NAME, IS SURVIVORSHIP DEED REQUESTED? Yes (YES or NO)

19-SELLER'S ACCEPTANCE:
The undersigned, being of legal age and capacity, hereby accept(s) the above offer and agree(s) to pay a total commission of

7 percent of said purchase price, payable 7 percent to the REAL ESTATE COMPANY and______percent to ________________________ as the SOLE PROCURING CAUSE(S) of this transaction.

SELLER(S) Rob Ruiz /

ADDRESS/Phone 200 Vista Place, Anyville, Ohio (Date) 7/5/97

20-DEPOSIT RECEIPT: Receipt is hereby acknowledged, as agent for SELLER, of BUYER'S earnest money deposit in the amount specified and in the form described in foregoing paragraph 3.(a), to be held in the REAL ESTATE COMPANY'S trust Account, subject to all terms and provisions of this Agreement.

------------the REAL ESTATE COMPANY By Anne Hamilton (Date) 7/5/97

ONCE SIGNED, THIS DOCUMENT BECOMES A LEGALLY-BINDING CONTRACT
IF YOU HAVE QUESTIONS OF LAW, CONSULT AN ATTORNEY LICENSED TO PRACTICE IN OHIO

GLOSSARY

Abandonment Relinquishment of all rights in realty; vacating the realty with no intent to return.

Abatement A decrease or reduction.

Abeyance In expectation of the law; the condition of a freehold when there is no vested owner, such as in a reversion or remainder; the rights are in expectancy.

Abode Place of dwelling.

Abstract of title Summary of the title history to real property including conveyances, liens, and encumbrances.

Abuse of discretion A ground for the appeals court to reverse the decision of a trial court.

Abut Touch or end at other land with no intervening land.

Acceleration Hastening of the vesting of an interest as in land.

Acceleration clause Clause found in mortgages whereby if mortgagor defaults on one payment, he or she becomes in default of the entire amount of the mortgage, not just the sum of the one payment.

Accept Receive with approval; in contracts, the offeree's assent to the offeror's offer.

Access Approach; right of real property owner to come and go from his or her land to adjoining road.

Accord and satisfaction In contracts, one party accepts something other than what was owed him or her and then discharges the other party from any further obligation. This acts as a bar to any later cause of action on the original contract between the parties.

Accretion Gradual growth in the amount of land from natural causes, such as additions in soil to the real property.

Acknowledgment The affirmation, or swearing, by a person before one who is empowered to administer oaths (such as a notary public) that his or her signing of a legal instrument was his or her free act and deed.

Acquisition Becoming the owner of property.

Acre Land containing 43,560 square feet in any shape.

Act of God An occurrence of violent nature without human interference, such as a tornado or other natural disaster.

Actual fraud Occurs when a real estate agent intentionally makes a material misrepresentation about a hidden or not visible condition of the real property that the purchaser relies on and sustains injury because of.

Adaptation-to-use test One of the fixture tests that considers how well suited an item is to the realty.

Addendum Additional term, or a change to a provision(s), of an existing contract that must also contain offer, acceptance, and consideration.

Adjacent Near or close by; not touching.

Adjoining Touching; contiguous.

Administrative law Regulations and rules formulated by administrative agencies as allowed by the legislature.

Administrator Person appointed by probate court having authority to manage estate of deceased person who died intestate; collects assets, pays debts, and distributes residue to rightful heirs from estate.

Ad valorem Tax computation based on fixed percentages of realty's value. Real property taxes are computed ad valorem.

Adverse possession Way to acquire title to realty by state statute requiring open, notorious, hostile, and actual possession against true owner.

Aesthetic zoning A type of zoning, appreciating beauty and quality, that can be lawful when coupled with goals of protecting real estate from impairment.

Affidavit A person's written declaration sworn before a notary public or official empowered to administer oaths.

Affirmative Marketing Agreement A contractual agreement between HUD, boards of REALTORS®, and individual REALTORS®, which promotes equal housing opportunity and equal access to housing.

After-acquired title Good title received by grantors, after they convey, which passes to grantees.

Agency Relationship where one person (agent) acts for another (principal) under that principal's authority.

Air rights The landowner's limited, finite rights to the immediate space above his or her land.

Alienable Freely transferrable.

Alienate Transfer of real property title from one party to another.

Allot To divide real property held before under tenancy in common in rateable portions to each cotenant in his or her severalty share.

Alluvion Increase of earth by force of water's currents or waves done gradually.

Americans with Disabilities Act Requires owners of public accommodations and commercial facilities to make their real properties accessible to persons with disabilities.

Amortization Paying off a mortgage by installments.

Ancillary trustee Person appointed by superintendent to wind up the business of a real estate brokerage.

Annex To attach or join onto something larger.

Annexation/Attachment One of the fixture tests that considers the item's permanent fixation, or not, to the realty.

Annual meeting Yearly meeting of members of the condominium unit owners' association to set amount for upcoming year's common assessments.

Annuity Money paid out on a periodic basis.

Answer Defendant's response, in pleading form, to plaintiff's complaint by denial or a combination of admissions and denials.

Ante nuptial contract Marriage contract; can set forth rights in property, both real and personal, secured for each partner to the forthcoming marriage; contract must be entered into before marriage.

Anticipatory repudiation An unequivocal statement by a party to a contract, before date of performance, that he or she intends to breach the contract and not perform on the anticipated date of performance.

Antisolicitation ban Local law prohibiting real estate agents from contacting real estate owners about selling their real estate.

Antitrust laws Legislation that prohibits combinations in restraint of trade in interstate commerce, such as brokers fixing commission rates between or among themselves.

Apparent authority Scope of agency that appears to have been granted from principal to agent.

Apparent defects Deficiencies discoverable by a reasonable inspection of the realty to be sold; also called patent defects.

Appeals court Determines questions of law whether errors of law or abuse of discretion were made by a lower court.

Appellant Party who appeals a lower court's decision against him or her to a higher court.

Appellee Party against whom an appeal is made.

Apportionment Distribution into proportionate amounts.

Appraisal A professional estimate of the fair market value of real property.

Appraisement The true or fair valuation of realty.

Appraiser certification Control and regulation of real estate appraisers as done by the Ohio Real Estate Commission.

Appropriation of land Setting apart land for a particular purpose, such as public use; eminent domain exercise.

Approval clause Clause in lease whereby landlord has right to approve of assignee or sublessee.

Appurtenance Something belonging to a worthier principal and passes incident to it; adapted to use of realty to which it is connected; appurtenant easement, for example.

Arbitration Determination by panel of arbiters of disputed matter under binding agreement between disputing parties.

Articles of Incorporation Legal papers that form a corporation; sets forth the minimum essentials of doing business in corporate form under state statutory law.

"As Is" clause Clause in real estate purchase contract that attempts to shift the burden of the realty's condition to the purchaser.

Assessed valuation Value of each parcel of real property by which real property tax is computed.

Assessment The adjusted share, for each person from a group of persons, contributed toward achieving some group project, such as a sewer or paved street.

Assignment A transfer from one person to another person of property or rights in property; the assignment of a contract or a lease, for example.

Assumption of mortgage loan A purchaser's taking over primary liability on a seller/mortgagor's mortgage and thereafter making the mortgage payments himself or herself.

Assumption of the risk Doctrine that shifts all risk in a particular transaction to one party (usually the purchaser in real estate transactions).

Attach To take personal property pursuant to a court order, usually to satisfy a judgment.

Attachment, method of One of the fixture tests that considers the item's permanent fixation, or not, to the realty.

Attest To act as a witness for another; to affirm the truth of; for example, the signature of the grantor on a deed.

Attorney-at-law Person licensed by state to practice law on others.

Attorney-in-fact Person authorized to act as agent for another pursuant to power of attorney.

Attorney's opinion letter Legal opinion on the soundness of a title based on the attorney's review of the results of the title examination.

Auction Public sale of land to highest bidder.

Auditor's deed Deed used when real estate is sold at public auction by county auditor because of back taxes owed on realty.

Auditor's lien Lien placed by county auditor on real property when its real estate taxes are in arrears.

Automatic renewal In leases, the extension of a lease for a like period of time; occurs when the parties remain passive per terms of the lease.

Autre vie The life of another; way of measuring a life estate by using another person's life.

Bankruptcy Insolvency; a person who can voluntarily, or involuntarily by action of his or her creditors, have his or her financial assets paid off and liabilities discharged through bankruptcy court proceedings.

Beneficiary The person who holds equitable title to trust property and for whose benefit the trust was created.

Bequest Testator's disposition of personal property by his or her will.

Beyond a reasonable doubt Fully convinced; clearly satisfied; standard of proof used in criminal cases.

Bilateral contract Contract in which both parties are bound to fulfill mutual and reciprocal obligations; mutuality of promise, rights and duties between parties to a contract.

Bind To be under a legal duty or obligation.

Binder Temporary insurance protection that the insurance agent gives by memorandum of agreement until insurance risk can be investigated and policy issued.

Blockbusting A fair housing violation perpetrated by real estate agents against owners wherein racial (or other prohibited categories) fears are preyed upon to obtain a listing and then a sale from the owner. This results in white flight from a neighborhood and eventually resegregates the community with blacks or other minority groups.

Board of Directors/Managers In condominiums, those persons (usually three in number) who are the representatives of all the condominium owners for making decisions affecting the condominium property.

Bona fide Good faith; absence of fraud.

Bond Evidence of indebtedness; legal instrument with money penalty fixed that has to be paid only if the party or parties do not fulfill requirements within that instrument.

Boundary The natural or artificial division of contiguous estates in land.

Breach of contract Legally inexcusable failure to perform any promise within a contract one is a party to.

Broker A person, partnership, association, or corporation licensed by the state to perform specific real estate services under the license law for another in exchange for valuable consideration, which is usually money.

Building code Ordinances or resolutions regulating building construction and enforced by the local government's building department/inspector.

Bundle of legal rights Rights conferred by owning real property, including rights to mortgage, sell, make improvements, lease, and regain possession at the end of a lease.

Burden of proof As a matter of evidence, the duty to affirmatively prove facts in dispute of case; plaintiff carries burden of proof in civil case; burden shifts to defendant once plaintiff has met his or her burden.

Business quest Persons invited onto another's real property for business purposes. They are owed the highest degree of care by landowners and salespeople.

Buyer's broker The real estate agent's representing the buyer and not the seller; the fiduciary obligation is thus owed to the buyer.

Bylaws In condominiums, rules and regulations for the administration of condominium property as a contract between the unit owners as well as between the unit owners' association and the unit owners.

Cancel Abandon or rescind, as in a contract; make a contract void on its face.

Capacity Able to perceive and understand; of sound mind; of age of majority.

Case law Reported cases as a body of jurisprudence; one of the sources of law.

Cash value What property would bring at a private, noninstallment sale; market value.

Cause Bring about.

Caveat emptor Latin for "Let the buyer beware"; the purchaser of real estate's position legally with both the seller and estate agent. It is continually eroding in the law, although less so in Ohio than other states.

Certificate of Judgment Legal instrument enabling judgment holder to file lien against debtor's realty.

Certificate of Occupancy Document issued by building department to owner when his or her structure has passed all building regulations.

Certificate of Sale Document issued by public officer to successful bidder on realty at judicial sale; the certificate entitles the bidder to a deed after the court concludes the sale.

Certificate of Title Following the examination of public records, a written opinion setting forth the condition of the title of real property.

Certificate of Transfer Legal instrument issued by probate court to transfer real property to devisee.

Certiorari Writ or review to a higher court or tribunal.

Chain of title Record showing the successive conveyances for a specific parcel of land from the originating source to the present owner.

Chattel Item of personal property.

Checking *See* testing.

Child A minor; one who is under age 18.

Citation Summons issued to defendant compelling his or her appearance in court.

Cite To refer to the legal authority upholding a proposition of law; usually refers to a case.

Civil action Not criminal; an adversary proceeding for enforcement, declaration, or protection of a private right or to prevent a private wrong; an action to compel payment or redress from private civil wrongs.

Civil Rights Act of 1866 Law prohibiting private racial discrimination; contains Section 1982.

Clause Subdivision within a legal document, such as a contract or deed.

Clear and convincing evidence More than a preponderance but less than a reasonable doubt.

Clear title Good, marketable title free from encumbrances.

Clerk of court Officer of court charged with all clerical court business including records, filing of suit, service of process, and entry of judgment.

Client The person represented by the broker or salesperson.

Closing arguments Each attorney's speech about why his or her client should win, presented after all the evidence in the trial is in.

Closing statement An accounting of all credits and debits to seller and purchaser for sale of real property as done by escrow agent, lending institution, or other agent.

Cloud on title Valid encumbrance affecting title of estate in land such as mortgage or judgment.

Codicil Legal instrument that adds to or changes a will; must meet all the same prerequisites that a will does.

Coexclusive Two real estate companies sharing an exclusive right to sell on a piece of real property.

Commingle In violation of state license law, the broker mixes funds held for purchaser with his or her own funds.

Commission The broker's professional fee, usually a percentage of the sales price, for being the procuring cause of a real property sale; also, the administrative body that regulates and enforces the license law.

Common areas In condominiums, those areas of the condominium property owned by all owners in common and for the use of all, not just certain individuals—for example, greenbelts, landscaping, a pool, clubhouse, bike paths, and other amenities.

Common assessment An amount of money paid by each unit owner in a condominium for the maintenance and repair of common areas. The stipend per owner varies commensurate with their percentage of ownership in condominium property.

Common law Law that derives its authority from principles set forth in court decisions instead of from statutes or other written declarations. Also called case law or judge-made law.

Community property law Statutory provisions that give either the husband or the wife a one-half interest in property acquired by the labor of the other spouse during the course of the marriage.

Compensatory damages Damages that return victim to his or her status *quo ante*.

Competent One who is not incompetent, that is, under 18 years of age, mentally or physically infirm, mentally retarded, or chemically dependent. Severity of condition is needed for categories other than minority.

Complaint The first court pleading, alleging the cause of action within a lawsuit; document that initiates the lawsuit; used in civil law; concise statement giving defendant notice of the causes of action and the relief and remedies demanded by the party filing it.

Compulsory counterclaim A defendant's having to sue the plaintiff for any legal wrongs he or she has suffered arising out of the same transaction or occurrence.

Concealment The seller's and/or real estate agent's hiding a defect in the real estate. This is fraud upon the purchaser.

Concurrent jurisdiction More than one court having the power to hear a case.

Condemnation In real property law, the private owner's realty being taken by the state for a public purpose, for which he or she is paid just compensation; forces sale between owner and condemnor/government.

Condition Qualifier used most frequently in real estate purchase contracts; some event must happen or some act must be performed, after the contract has been formed between the parties, for the contract to be binding; for example, when the financing condition is satisfied, the purchaser is obliged to perform on the contract.

Condominium Form of real estate ownership wherein each owner has an exclusively owned fee-simple absolute estate in a portion of the airspace (typically his or her individual unit) and a mutually owned fee-simple absolute estate in all the rest of what is known as the land (typically the common areas).

Condominium conversion Making realty previously used one way into condominium property pursuant to statutory requisites.

Confirmation of sale The court's affirming sale after public auction; at that moment, debtor/mortgagor's interest in real estate is foreclosed—forever cut off.

Conforming use A use of land that complies with the zoning laws then in effect.

Consent decree Settlement of a lawsuit whereby one agrees to a certain course of conduct for the future pursuant to the order of the court.

Consideration Legal detriment bargained for and promised in exchange for legal benefit for both parties, either orally or in writing when required by the statute of frauds.

Constitution A written instrument for the American people or people of a state, regarded as the absolute law of the land; highest authority of law.

Construction Legal principles about how a court should interpret contracts or other legal instruments.

Constructive eviction A landlord's depriving the tenant of the beneficial enjoyment of the premises, compelling the tenant to vacate.

Constructive fraud Same as actual fraud except it cannot be proven as an intentional act on the part of the perpetrator.

Constructive knowledge or notice Not actual knowledge; rather, knowledge imputed to a person because the facts are a matter of public record.

Contempt of court Failure by a person to comply with the orders of a court; tends to impede the administration of justice; willful disobedience.

Contiguous Close or near; touching.

Contingent Dependent upon an event that may or may not happen.

Contingent legal fee Percentage fee the lawyer is paid if his or her client wins the case; lawyer is paid nothing if client loses the case.

Contract An agreement that is legally enforceable, containing a set of promises that the law gives a remedy for if breached.

Conventional financing Mortgage loan for real property obtained through lending institution. Has two levels of security: borrower personally, through promissory note, and realty through the mortgage deed or deed of trust; not insured through FHA or guaranteed by VA.

Conversion condominium Real property formerly used and operated in another way, which is submitted by declaration and other documents to county recorder's office as condominium property instead.

Conveyance Transfer of title, whether legal or equitable, in land.

Conveyance fee State and/or local, county tax levied upon grantors for passing of real estate.

Cooperative Similar to condominium, but owners own shares of stock in the whole of the cooperative property and reside in their units under an occupancy agreement instead.

Cooperative assessment Each cooperative owner's financial obligation to cover the cost of operating and maintaining the cooperative.

Corporation Artificial person created under state law to conduct a business; when it owns real property, owns it in severalty; acts as a shield for the real person by insulating him or her personally from liability.

Counterclaim The claim made by defendant against the plaintiff either as a claimed amount or a set off; used in civil cases only.

Counteroffer In contracts, an offer; the word counter signifies that the offeree wants to make an offer going back to the original offeror. Now the offeree is the offeror and the offeror, the offeree.

Covenant Any agreement; in real property includes those full agreements of seisin, warranty, further assurance, and quiet enjoyment.

Covenant not to compete A contractual provision between broker and salesperson wherein, in exchange for professional training or other advantages from the broker, the salesperson cannot sell real estate in the broker's area for a given period of time if the salesperson leaves the broker.

Covenant of quiet enjoyment Doctrine requiring landlord to give tenant undisturbed, peaceful enjoyment, and possession of the leasehold.

Covenant running with land Goes with the land; land cannot be separated from or transferred without it.

Creative financing An arrangement directly between purchaser and seller whereby the seller accounts for all or part of the purchase price by "taking back some paper," that is, a land contract or purchase money mortgage.

Creditor Person to whom debtor owes debt; person owed money, usually from business dealing.

Criminal litigation Brought by the government against wrongdoers whose acts pose such a threat to society that governmental intervention and punishment of the wrongdoer are appropriate.

Crossclaim Resembles a complaint but is a pleading a party makes against another party grouped on the same side of the case, such as one codefendant suing the other codefendant.

Cross-examination Examination by the opposing party of a witness at a deposition, calculated to test and weaken the witness's testimony.

Cumulative zoning A zoning scheme wherein, as an area is rezoned, all uses that are higher are included as well.

Curtesy A husband's life estate interest in his wife's real property.

Customer Person who is not represented by broker or salesperson.

Damages Money compensation awarded by court to person who has suffered loss or injury through another person's illegal act; compensatory damages return the person to his or her status *quo ante*, whereas punitive damages award the person money greater than his or her loss to punish the malicious wrongdoer.

DBA Means "doing business as" in referring to a business association operating under a name other than the owner's, which is not incorporated.

Debtor Person who owes a certain sum to his or her creditor.

Deceit Intentional, misleading, fraudulent conduct that gives rise to suit in fraud.

Declaration The legal document that creates the condominium property, filed with the county recorder; remains the controlling document for the condominium property. No other documents may conflict with the Declaration.

Declaratory judgment States parties' rights; court expresses opinion on controversy but does not issue order compelling performance or nonperformance of act.

Decree Judgment from a court using its equity powers under common law; when made between the parties under sanction of the court, called a consent decree.

Dedication In real property, appropriation by the owner of his or her private land for a public use, which use is accepted by the public.

Deed Legal document executed by grantor that conveys realty from him or her to the grantee; must be a written instrument both signed by grantor and delivered to grantee.

Deed of gift Deed that uses good consideration, which is ties of blood, love, or affection in exchange for real property.

Deed of purchase Deed that uses valuable consideration, which is money, goods, or services in exchange for real property.

Deed restrictions Private prohibitions on the use of land found on the deed itself, or by reference to books in recorder's office, which tie into deeds filed there.

Default Failure to perform legal obligation.

Defeasance Instrument that defeats another estate in land or deed; acts to defeat one estate because of performance of condition within deed.

Defeasible Can be undone by occurrence of condition subsequent.

Defendant Person against whom lawsuit is brought; person plaintiff is suing.

Deficiency judgment The balance of indebtedness, as awarded by court, that the debtor/mortgagor owes the mortgagee/creditor; occurs when the price obtained at foreclosure sale is not sufficient to satisfy the mortgage debt obligation.

Delivery Placed within possession and control of another; as in a properly executed deed being absolutely transferred to grantee with the grantor having no power to recall it.

Demand Claim to an award at law or in equity by court.

Depositing rent Law enabling tenant to place rent with clerk of courts rather than paying landlord when landlord is in breach of his or her state's statutory duties.

Deposition The testimony of a witness taken before a person authorized to take oaths wherein such witness can be cross-examined by opposing counsel during discovery or examined and cross-examined by both sides' attorneys in order to perpetuate testimony.

Descent and distribution, statute of Ohio statute covering to whom, and in what proportion, a decedent's property is to be distributed when the decedent dies without leaving a will.

Devise Testator's disposition of real property through his or her will.

Direct examination First questioning of witness, by party who called him or her on merits of case.

Director of Commerce Ex-officio head of division of real estate.

Disability Not legally able to perform act; handicap.

Discovery Litigation techniques for finding out the evidence and testimony of an opposing party or a witness in the lawsuit and/or the contents of books and records and/or the state of real property and/or admissions or denials of facts in controversy; all done prior to the actual trial.

Discrimination Inequality of treatment; making housing unavailable, refusing to sell real property, or creating panic sales based on race, religion, national origin, sex, handicap, or family status.

Dispersion of minorities Fair housing interpretation, usually by cities and their housing boards, that minority group members, especially blacks, should be evenly distributed among all neighborhoods.

Dispossess Take away the right to use real property.

Distribution In probate, dividing and apportioning intestate's estate among legal heirs after payment of debts and expenses under authority of probate court.

Domestic relations court A specialized state court that handles divorce and other marital cases, including attendant disposition of real and personal property.

Domicile Person's permanent home, which he or she always has ultimate intention of returning to.

Dominant tenement Property to which servitude or easement is owed.

Donee Person receiving gift.

Donor Person who gives gift.

Dower A spouse's one-third life estate interest in real property of his or her husband or wife.

Dower release Grantor's spouse releases any right of dower in grantor's conveyance, usually by deed.

Dual agency Real estate agents representing both the seller and the purchaser in a transaction. This is lawful (but not recommended) as long as the dual agency is disclosed to both purchaser and seller and is unlawful if not disclosed to both.

Due care Reasonable care; not negligent.

Due-on-sale/Due-on-transfer clauses Clauses often present in mortgages that give the mortgagee/lender the right to call the entire debt due should the mortgagor/borrower sell, transfer or otherwise change the ownership of the mortgaged realty without first obtaining the mortgagee/lender's consent.

Durable power of attorney A power of attorney that is not affected by any subsequent disability of principal.

Duress Forcing a person against his or her will to perform an act.

Earnest money Money purchasers pay to sellers or their agents, before closing to demonstrate their good faith, which sellers and/or agents can keep as part or all of their damages if purchasers breach the contract.

Easement One person's right to use the land of another for a specific purpose. It is a permanent right, which cannot be terminated unless the person who received these rights agrees to give them up.

Easement appurtenant Easement wherein one owner of a specific parcel of realty has the right to use and benefit from another landowner's parcel of realty.

Easement in gross Right to use realty for a specific purpose, as held by a person or commercial entity.

Egress Access.

Ejectment Thrown out from possession of land.

Emblements Vegetable chattels annually produced by labor.

Eminent domain The taking of private property by the government for public use. It is lawful as long as the owner is paid just compensation.

Encroachment Intruding upon another's real property, such as part of a building that is on another's real property.

Encumbrance Charge or lien against real property existing in someone's favor other than the owner's.

Enforceable contract Refers to a contract that the law will uphold and find a breach of if one party fails to perform.

Environmental law Federal and state laws in effect to protect the public from the effects of pollution in the air, land, and water, as well as to conserve natural resources for the future.

Equal access Fair housing interpretation, usually by real estate licensees and professional affiliates, that a person, regardless of who or what he or she is, can get housing anywhere.

Equal protection of the laws A principle holding that no person is subjected to any greater burden, punishment, or restriction to the courts, liberty, or property than other persons within the same jurisdiction.

Equitable conversion A doctrine giving the purchaser an interest in real property and the seller an interest in personal property from the time of execution of the real estate purchase contract forward.

Equitable right to redeem Mortgagor's right to reclaim the mortgaged realty by payment in full. Ends in Ohio when court issues confirmation of sale via judicial foreclosure.

Equitable title Beneficiary of a trust's interest in property held by trust.

Equity Fairness; justness; relief granted by the courts under well-established equitable principles; used when money damages will not adequately compensate.

Equity of redemption A period of time wherein a former mortgagor can obtain his or her real property back by paying the entire debt, including interest and costs.

Error Mistaken application of law used as grounds for appeal to a higher court.

Errors and omissions Insurance that brokers can carry to cover themselves and their salespersons for negligent or constructively fraudulent activity arising from their performance of real estate services.

Escheat Property reverting to the state when there is no proper heir to inherit.

Escrow Deed or writing delivered by grantor to third person who will subsequently deliver it to grantee upon happening of a certain condition or performance.

Escrow closing Transaction in which disinterested third person is chosen by both seller and purchaser to accept all documents and funds necessary to close real estate purchase. When all terms and conditions have been met, this escrow agent closes the transaction; the purchaser obtains his or her title to the realty and the seller his or her net sales' proceeds.

Estate Interest in land, tenements, or hereditaments; in conveyancing, it means the same as right, title, and interest.

Estate by the entireties Form of coownership of real estate by husband and wife whereupon when one dies, the survivor obtains the real estate by operation of the deed; insulates the realty from creditors when only one spouse is liable to a creditor.

Estate for years Leasehold estate in land for some definite period that has a specific beginning and ending date.

Estate from year to year Leasehold estate in land that continues to renew itself for another identical period unless the parties notify one another that the next period is the final one.

Estoppel Doctrine that prevents one from asserting his or her legal rights because of his or her own wrongful acts.

Et al. Legal abbreviation meaning "and others."

Ethics Moral standards of practice that members of a profession are bound to follow.

Eviction By reentry or legal proceedings, ousting a tenant from his or her possession of land.

Evidence Proof of an issue's truth or falsity, such as documents and testimony.

Exception Clause in purchase contract and deed that specifies parts of estate in land that are not being sold or transferred.

Exclusionary zoning Usually legal, large-lot, residential zoning scheme that keeps out low- to moderate-income persons; also can exclude commerce and industry.

Exclusive agency Listing contract for sale of real estate wherein principal is precluded from dealing through another broker/agent but may still act on his or her own behalf.

Exclusive jurisdiction Occurs when only one court has the power to hear a particular case.

Exclusive right to sell Listing contract for sale of real estate wherein a single broker has authority to procure a purchaser. That broker receives the commission regardless of who procures the purchaser. The principal/seller can deal only through his or her real estate broker.

Exclusive zone In zoning, an area's designation for only one purpose. For example, commercially zoned property can have only commercial real property; residential can have only residential real property.

Executed contract A valid contract that has been performed by the parties.

Execution Writ the court issues to sheriff authorizing him or her to perform some act, such as selling real property.

Execution of deed Completion of all acts necessary to operative effect of instrument, including signing, attestation, acknowledgment, and delivery.

Executor Person appointed by testator through his or her will to carry out directions and dispose of property as set forth in that will.

Executory contract A contract in which the promises have not yet been performed by the parties but only performance remains to be done.

Expandable condominium Condominium in which developer is allowed to add individual and common area property to the individual and common area property already in existence within period of time set by statute.

Expert witnesses Persons with specialized knowledge who are allowed to give their opinions, in their professional fields, as testimony.

Express contract Contract in which the terms have been specifically set forth between the parties, usually in a writing.

Extraordinary repairs Major repairs that landlord remains responsible for, such as changing plumbing from galvanized to copper.

Fair Housing Act Modern fair housing law prohibiting discrimination in housing, lending, and so on, because of race, religion, national origin, sex, handicap, and family status.

Fair Housing Initiatives Program Agreement between HUD and the National Association of REALTORS® for an organized program of testing real estate agents using their mutually agreed-upon standards.

Family status Antidiscriminatory provision under the Fair Housing Act protecting persons under age 18 who live with a parent or guardian, or are pregnant women.

Federal tax lien Lien the federal government has against all real estate in the country when persons owe it money, such as failure to pay income or estate taxes.

Fee simple (absolute) Ownership of land by a person, subject only to public and private controls. The least restricted and most desirable form of ownership.

Fee simple determinable Estate in land that ends automatically upon the happening of a stated event.

FHA Abbreviation for Federal Housing Authority, an agency of the federal government that insures mortgage loans.

Fiduciary deed Deed used when grantor is trustee, executor, or guardian, which contains limited warranties for the grantee.

Fiduciary relationship Agency relationship between broker-salesperson and principal, usually the seller, wherein principal is owed high degree of trust, loyalty, full disclosure, due care, no self-dealing, confidentiality, and accounting.

Fifth Amendment Section of the United States Constitution requiring due process of law and payment of just compensation when government takes private property for public use.

Finder's fee Professional fee paid to broker by purchaser for finding real property for him or her to purchase. This realty usually is not on the market for sale.

First Amendment United States Constitution guarantee of freedom of speech, expression, association, and religion.

First mortgage First lien against the real property determined by its being filed ahead of any others in the county recorder's office.

Fixture An item that was once personal property but has become part of the real property according to the fixture tests, that is, attachment, adaptation to use, and/or objective intent of landowner.

Forcible entry and detainer Through summary legal proceeding, giving possession of land back to the person wrongfully deprived of its possession.

Foreclosure Cutting off the rights of the mortgagor in mortgaged realty by taking and selling the mortgaged real property to satisfy mortgagee's default; usually ends rights of the mortgagor in the real property.

Foreign real estate Real estate outside the state of Ohio.

Forfeiture Loss of a right or interest by failure to perform.

Formal closing Meeting of all persons involved in the closing of a real estate purchase contract who show up in person to complete their tasks. At the end of this actual meeting, the purchaser receives title to the real estate and the seller receives his or her net sales' proceeds.

Fourteenth Amendment Constitutional guarantee of equal protection of the law.

Fraud An intentional act of falsehood calculated to induce another to act in reliance thereon and to part with something of value.

Fraudulent conveyance Transferring realty to another to defraud creditors; prevents creditors' collecting through forced sale of the realty.

Freehold Estate in fee or for life; if a freehold estate, the right of title to land; estate in land of uncertain duration.

Fructus industriales Produced on land by the efforts of people and now considered real property unless harvested.

Fructus naturales Growing things on land that are capable of living and producing without the efforts of people. These are fixtures and remain with the real estate.

General jurisdiction A court's power to hear a wide array of civil and criminal cases.

General lien A lien that can be satisfied by any real property owned by obliged owner.

General tax lien Tax against realty that applies generally and uniformly throughout the local taxing district.

General warranty deed An instrument wherein grantor warrants to protect grantee's right, title, and interest in subject real property against the world.

Gift Owner's parting voluntarily with his or her property without receiving consideration.

Grant Conveyance; transfer of real property by deed.

Grantee Person receiving grant of real property.

Grantor Person making grant of real property.

Gross lease Type of lease whereby lessor pays regular charges upon the real property, such as real estate taxes.

Ground lease Type of net lease in which tenant leases vacant lot and erects the building himself or herself.

Guardian Person legally bound for care, custody, and management of another person and/or another person's property. Usually done for minors and the mentally or physically infirm.

Habendum Clause following granting of the premises in a deed; defines grantee's extent of ownership; begins with "to have and to hold" in deed.

Habitability, implied warranty of In landlord-tenant law, protection for the tenant by requiring that the premises be fit for intended use per housing code. Capable of being resided within.

Handicap Disability qualifying a person for protection under the Fair Housing Act; he or she has a physical or mental impairment that substantially limits one or more major life activities.

Health code Regulations for the public health that affect real property, such as standards for septic systems, enforced by health department.

Heir One who receives an estate or interest in land under the state statute of descent and distribution; person to whom property passes when deceased does not leave will.

Hereditaments Things that can be inherited of real or personal property, including land.

Hold Possess by lawful title; to be the grantee.

Hold over Arrangement whereby tenant keeps possession after expiration of leasehold and landlord agrees by acceptance of rent.

Homeowners' association Organization within a subdivision that is responsible for enforcing restrictions on use of the land.

HUD Abbreviation for the federal government agency Housing and Urban Development, which administers fair housing and other federal real estate laws.

Implied contract An agreement showing intent to form a contract, conduct of parties, and their relationship.

Implied warranty of habitability Doctrine requiring landlord to maintain leased premises in compliance with the housing code.

Impossibility of performance Unforeseen, objective inability by a party to perform a contract because no one could perform it. Performance on contract is then excused. Personal impossibility is not sufficient and person suffering from personal impossibility is in breach of contract.

Improvement Any valuable addition made to real property that goes beyond mere repair or replacements, such as erecting a structure.

Incentive zoning A community's exempting industry or commerce from some zoning requisites if the industry or commerce will include certain amenities for its residents on the property too; for example, more stories on the building in excess of the zoning code in exchange for a theater in the first floor of the building.

Incompetent Not legally able or fit.

Incorporate Create a corporation pursuant to requirements of state law.

Incorporeal rights Intangible rights in realty such as those found in easements and licenses.

Indemnify To pay for a loss or give security to cover a loss.

Ingress Right of entrance.

Injunction A court is using its equity powers to direct a party to a lawsuit to either do an act or refrain from doing some act.

Inquiry during negotiations Asking questions during the offer, counteroffer, and acceptance stages, as opposed to actually making a counteroffer to the offeror.

Installment contract Purchase of real property whereby purchase price is paid by periodic payments rather than in lump sum.

Insurance Contract in which one party compensates the other for a designated loss.

Intention test One of the fixture tests that considers what a reasonable person intended an item to be—realty or personalty.

Interest (1) Having rights in realty; used with terms *estates, right,* and *title;* (2) charge for borrowing money.

Interrogatories Written questions sent from one party to a lawsuit to other party, who must answer them in writing under oath.

Interstate Land Sales Full Disclosure Act Federal law that protects prospective purchasers from land developers who sell lots site unseen through interstate commerce.

Interval ownership Ownership for only a limited period of time in a condominium.

Inter vivos trust Trust that takes effect while the trustor is still alive.

Intestate Person who dies without making a will.

Involuntary Not done by choice or willingly.

Involuntary lien A realty owner's not consenting to a lien being placed against his or her realty.

Judgment Court of law's decision upon the parties' claims within a litigated lawsuit; can be converted into a lien.

Judgment lien Binds the real estate of the judgment debtor; holder can force a sale of realty to satisfy the judgment.

Judiciary System of courts that interpret the law and declare and enforce liability.

Land Soil, earth, permanent fixtures, and everything on, over, or under the surface of the earth.

Land installment purchase contract A real estate purchase contract, drafted in conformance with state law, wherein the seller-vendor accepts installment payments from the purchaser-vendee. Title is conveyed to the vendee only when payments are completed.

Landlord Owner of real property who rents it to another; also called lessor.

Land use The way land can be lawfully utilized, such as agriculturally, residentially, commercially, or industrially.

Latent defect Concealed or hidden defect in or on the real property.

Lease An oral or a written contract between landlord and tenant, which is also a conveyance, wherein the tenant has the exclusive right to possession of the landlord's realty in exchange for the tenant's paying rent to the landlord.

Leasehold Estate in land in which the tenant has the right to occupy real property under a lease.

Lease/option An arrangement in which mortgagor/seller leases the realty to a tenant, who also is given the option to purchase the leased premises.

Legacy Testator's disposition of money by will.

Legal description Written matter that defines the boundaries of realty being transferred; legally recognized description used in deeds and other legal instruments.

Legislature A body of elected leaders who enact laws that govern and regulate society.

Lessee The tenant; rents realty pursuant to a lease with the landlord, the lessor.

Lessor The landlord; owner of realty who gives right to exclusive possession of his or her realty to tenant, pursuant to a lease.

Levy To collect a sum of money or seize property to satisfy an obligation.

Liable To owe; in civil law, the party losing the case now owes legally enforceable obligations, usually money, to the winning party.

License In reference to a real estate license: the right the state gives to qualified persons to become real estate brokers and salespeople. In reference to land use: a mere permissive use of real property owned by another. It is personal to licensee and may be revoked by licensor at any time.

Licensing laws State legislation that regulates the real estate profession so as to protect the public.

Lien A claim or encumbrance placed upon realty for payment of a debt, which makes the realty security for the debt.

Lien theory jurisdiction A state, such as Ohio, that considers the mortgage deed as giving the mortgagee a lien against the realty instead of a transfer of title to the mortgagee.

Life estate Estate in land that is measured by the life tenant's or another person's life.

Life tenant One who has an estate in land that exists as long as his or her life or another designated person's life.

Limited common areas Those areas owned in common by the condominium property owners but for the use of only some of the owners; for example, laundry rooms in each building to be used only by the residents in each building.

Limited jurisdiction Court empowered to determine cases concerning limited amounts of money and petty crimes and misdemeanors.

Limited real estate licensee Broker or salesperson who deals in cemetery interment rights only.

Limited warranty deed Another name used for the special warranty deed.

Liquidated damages An amount of money agreed upon by the parties in a contract about the amount of damages a breaching party forfeits to a nonbreaching party.

Lis pendens Latin for "suit pending." Copy of lawsuit can be recorded along with real property records, which gives notice to the world that there is a lawsuit that may affect the interest in that real property.

Listing An oral or written contract between real estate broker and landowner wherein the landowner agrees to pay the broker a stipulated commission if broker produces a ready, willing, and able purchaser for his or her realty.

Littoral land Land that borders a lake, an ocean, or a sea.

Long-term leases Leaseholds of 99 or more years.

Majority Above the age of minority, which, depending upon state law, is either age 18 or 21. In Ohio it is 18.

Marketable title Good, clear title that is free from defects and thus presents little or no risk of litigation; the necessary title called for in the real estate purchase contract.

Marketable Title Act State law providing that if a recorded title shows a clear, not flawed, chain of title at least 40 years long, that title is good, or marketable enough, to be transferred.

Market value The highest price a willing purchaser will pay to a willing seller.

Mechanic's lien A special, involuntary statutory lien that can be placed on real property by general or subcontractors, laborers, or material suppliers for work done, material supplied or construction managed for a specific piece of real property.

Mediation A structured settlement process utilizing a skilled negotiator working with the parties to a lawsuit.

Meeting of minds Complete agreement between parties to a contract on all its terms.

Memorandum of lease Legal instrument for setting forth the names of the parties and legal description of realty, subject to a lease, which can be recorded instead of the lease itself.

Mental infirmity A person's condition that makes it possible to declare a contract, which he or she is a party to, void or voidable.

Metes and bounds One type of legal description for land that starts at a clearly marked point and goes around the boundaries by distance and direction back to the starting point.

Minimization of damages Duty imposed upon a nonbreaching party to a contract to prevent damage figure from going higher, by requiring him or her to exercise reasonable care.

Minority The age at which a person lacks capacity to contract because he or she has not reached age of majority under his or her state's law (under 18 in Ohio).

Misrepresentation False representation about a factual matter regarding real property being considered for purchase.

Mitigation of damages Doctrine that requires a reduction in the dollar damage figure owed by the breaching party to the nonbreaching party because of extenuating circumstances.

Money judgment Court judgment ordering payment of a specific amount of money rather than ordering that an act be done or not done.

Monument An artificial or natural object used in metes and bounds legal descriptions to establish boundaries for real property.

Mortgage A pledge of real property as security for payment of an obligation; the mortgagee holds this against the mortgagor.

Mortgage deed The legal instrument that creates the mortgage.

Mortgagee The one who receives the mortgage and thus will receive the money payments.

Mortgage lien Lien on the mortgagor's realty securing by the value of the realty the lender's loan proceeds given to the mortgagor.

Mortgagor The one who gives the mortgage and thus will make the mortgage payments; the borrower; usually the person who is the purchaser under the real estate purchase contract and the grantee under the deed.

Motion for books, records, and/or to enter land Discovery device that allows a party to the lawsuit to examine the other party's books and records and/or to enter his or her land for inspection, testing, or filming.

Motion for summary judgment Motion brought by a party in trial court asking for judgment in his or her behalf because, even if everything is weighed favorably in the other party's behalf, he or she still cannot show genuine issue as to any material fact.

Motion to dismiss Motion brought in trial court by the defendant based on lack of jurisdiction, improper venue, insufficiency of process or service of process, or failure by plaintiff to state in its complaint a cause of action for which the law gives relief.

Multiple listing (MLS) A real estate listing arrangement in which a listing broker makes a unilateral subagency offer on a mass basis to all other MLS members; also, method of sharing information among real estate companies about the listings each has available.

Mutual mistake In contracts, a ground for having the contract set aside because both parties made the same mistake about a central aspect of the contract. For example, both parties bargained over the wrong piece of real property.

National Association of REALTORS® The real estate industry's private trade association; its national branch.

Negligence Failure to exercise a reasonable amount of care when owing a duty to another person. For example, a salesperson doesn't research the selling price of comparable realties for the seller when seller has listing contract with that brokerage.

Net lease Lease requiring tenant to pay rent and all costs of maintaining realty, including utilities, taxes, insurance, and repairs.

Net listing A listing contract in which the broker's commission is any and all money above the seller's net sales figure as stipulated.

Nonconforming use A use that once was within the zoning code and no longer is, but is permitted to continue despite the new zoning regulation, to end upon certain, stated events.

Nonfreehold estate A leasehold estate in land.

Note An executed piece of commercial paper acknowledging indebtedness by the signatory and promising payment.

Novation Substituting a new contract or obligation for the old one.

Nuisance An offense to the senses that violates the laws of decency or obstructs the use of realty; interference with one's interest in private use and enjoyment of realty.

Occupancy agreement Contract giving the cooperative tenant the right to solely use and possess his or her unit within the cooperative and mutually share in the rest of the cooperative.

Offer The first step in making a contract, whereby the offeror promises to do something in exchange for something else from the offeree. It is always looking for acceptance.

Offeree Party to whom an offer is made.

Offeror Party who makes an offer.

Ohio Association of REALTORS® Real estate industry's private trade association in Ohio.

Ohio Civil Rights Law Ohio's fair housing law, which is substantially equivalent to the Fair Housing Act.

Ohio Division of Real Estate Administrative agency that regulates brokers and salespeople on a daily basis.

Ohio Real Estate Commission Five-member body appointed by Ohio's governor to regulate real estate in Ohio and oversee the Ohio Division of Real Estate.

Opening statement Each attorney's speech, which opens a trial, about why his or her client should win the case; usually includes summary of the evidence to be presented subsequently.

Open listing A listing contract in which the broker is paid a commission only if he or she, and not another broker or the seller, secures a ready, willing, and able purchaser.

Opinion A stated belief about an aspect of the real estate that cannot factually mislead another, such as a statement about the realty's beauty as made by the real estate salesperson to the purchaser.

Option A contract in which the purchaser pays the seller for the privilege of being the only one, for a certain designated time, who can purchase the seller's realty.

Option to renew lease A lease in which the tenant must affirmatively inform lessor that he or she wishes to extend his or her lease for a like period pursuant to the terms of his or her lease.

Owner's fee policy of title insurance An insurance policy that gives all the protection of a title guarantee plus covers problems that cannot be detected by examining the public records.

Ownership The right to use and possess real property to the exclusion of all others.

Parol evidence rule Rule of law and evidence requiring that when there is a final and complete writing, such agreement may not be contradicted or supplemented by evidence of prior agreements or expressions.

Partition To divide real estate into parts based on the relative interests of those who have title to it; can result in a forced, public sale when real estate cannot be subdivided. Each owner is then paid his or her rateable share afterwards.

Partnership A business enterprise of two or more persons as the proprietors, which does not insulate them from personal liability; when it owns realty, owns it in severalty.

Part performance Doctrine that lifts a contract or lease out of the statute of frauds, which requires a writing, by affirmative conduct that markedly changes the performing party's position.

Party One who is bound by a contract to perform.

Party wall Wall on the boundary line of two adjoining parcels used by the owners of both.

Patent defect A discoverable, not hidden or latent, flaw.

Per *autre vie* A life estate measured by the life of another person rather than the life tenant's life.

Per capita Distribution of estate wherein heirs of different degrees take property on a representative basis.

Percentage interest The proportionate share of the condominium's common areas as are owned by each unit owner of condominium property.

Percentage lease Commercial lease based on the landlord's receiving a portion of the tenant's gross sales on the premises.

Periodic tenancy Lease based on periodic payment, renewal, and termination by year, month, or week.

Permissive counterclaim Defendant's option to sue plaintiff for any claim he or she has against him or her not arising out of the same transaction or occurrence.

Perpetual renewal Leaseholds capable of unending renewal.

Personal property That property that is not real property; movable, not fixed; called chattels.

Personalty Same as personal property or chattels.

Planned unit development (PUD) A development in which many uses of land are for the good of all, usually involving single and multifamily housing, recreation, and limited commerce; an exception to the zoning code wherein the community allows the structures to cluster on less land but the same amount of land, per the zoning code, is used toward the whole of the development.

Plat Recorded land subdivision with identifiable number.

Pleadings Legal documents in which the parties to a lawsuit transmit to each other and to the court the legal wrongs complained of and defenses thereto. Their purpose is to give the other party notice of the claims being made against him or her.

Point-of-sale inspection Ordinance requiring that a structure pass a building inspection before a real estate purchase transaction can close.

Police power The government's basis for regulating the use of land on behalf of the public's health, safety, and welfare.

Power of attorney A legal instrument that gives one person the authority to act for another; an attorney-in-fact, not an attorney-at-law.

Precedent Principle of law declared by a court to serve as a rule for future guidance in same or analogous cases.

Preponderance of the evidence Standard of proof used in civil cases of "more probable than not."

Pretrial Conference scheduled by court before trial, attended by attorneys and parties to lawsuit and presided over by judge.

Price-fixing Two or more brokers agreeing between or among themselves not to take less than a certain agreed commission rate.

Principal (1) Original sum of loan that does not include interest; (2) the person who is represented by another; for example, seller is usually the broker's principal.

Priority Sequential order in filing liens; liens that are filed first take priority over later liens.

Probate court State court that has exclusive jurisdiction over the disposition of estates; hears and determines cases regarding the validity of wills.

Procuring cause Originating a series of events without a break in continuity, which accomplishes the broker's purpose of employment: producing a purchaser ready, willing, and able to purchase realty at seller's terms. Meeting this test entitles the broker to the commission.

Profit *à prendre* Permits one person to use another's realty for a particular purpose and to also remove things from the realty.

Promissory estoppel Doctrine in contract law that prevents a wrongdoing party from escaping performance according to his or her promise because the contract lacked consideration.

Promissory note Legal instrument that creates a debt; used in tandem with both mortgage deeds and real estate purchase contracts.

Property A thing capable of being owned.

Property manager A person who manages properties for an owner, including negotiating leases, collecting rents, repairing, maintaining, and operating the properties.

Property report A report a developer must make available to most purchasers when he or she sells real property in interstate commerce subject to the Interstate Land Sales Full Disclosure Act.

Proprietary lease Cooperative tenant's lease for his or her unit of cooperative real estate, which is coupled with his or her proprietary stock interest in the cooperative.

Proration Clause within real estate purchase contract requiring the seller to pay all taxes, utilities, and charges on the real property up to title transfer date and the purchaser to pay them from that date forward.

Public policy Legal principle favoring acts done for the public good.

Puffing Exaggerated sales talk regarding the positive qualities of real property, which are not misstatements of fact and, thus, not misrepresentation.

Purchase money mortgage Mortgage given by purchaser to seller as part or all of the purchase price of real property.

Pyramid zoning Zoning that permits more than one type of realty use; once a new type of use is permitted, the old uses are retained too. For example, when single-family is enlarged to multifamily and then commercial, all three uses can be built and retained in that zone.

Qualified fee A freehold estate having the same characteristics as a fee simple absolute except it is capable of ending upon the happening of a stated event.

Quiet enjoyment Tenant's right to undisturbed, peaceful enjoyment and possession of the real estate.

Quiet title Court action to remove defects in the title to real property so that good, marketable title can be obtained; court approval of an adverse claimant's becoming the true owner of the realty.

Quitclaim deed A deed in which grantor conveys whatever interest he or she has in real estate without making any warranties to grantee.

Race A non-white person as defined in the discrimination laws. For Section 1982 litigation in fair housing, race has been expanded to mean those persons not considered white in the year 1866.

Ratification Approval of another's act that, when done, was not authorized.

Real estate Land and its improvements and fixtures.

Real Estate Recovery Fund Money set aside in a special account and used to pay real estate consumers for damages sustained to them by a real estate licensee.

Real Estate Settlement Procedures Act (RESPA) Federal law that gives both sellers and purchasers advance disclosure of closing costs; reduces the costs of closing by prohibiting illegal referrals and kickbacks; gives purchasers specific information about closing, and prescribes a standard form to be used as the closing statement.

Real property Land with its fixtures and improvements and bundle of rights.

REALTOR® A trade name for a member of the National Association of REALTORS® and its state and local affiliates.

Realty Land with its fixtures and improvements.

Reasonable person A concept used by the law to measure right and wrong conduct. Reasonable persons are those who behave as a judge or jury would perceive prudent persons as behaving.

Reasonable wear and tear The deterioration a tenant is allowed to commit to the leased premises; the opposite of waste.

Recording Filing or entering a legal instrument in the county recorder's office that causes it to become a public record giving constructive notice of its existence to the world.

Recourse Right to proceed legally against prior property owner.

Rectangular survey Federal government system of accurate land survey and description using baselines and principal meridians.

Redlining Lending institutions' denying mortgage loan money, or lending it but under stricter terms, because the neighborhood of realties is experiencing racial transition.

Reformation Correction of a legal instrument when, by fraud or mutual mistake, it fails to reflect the intent of the parties.

Regulation Z Interpretation of the Truth-in-Lending Law by the Federal Reserve Board.

Rejection In contracts, the offeree's turning down the offer.

Relation back, doctrine of Legal fiction whereby deed placed in escrow by grantor, who subsequently dies before closing, is deemed to have been delivered to grantee.

Release clause As used in the real estate purchase contract, a clause that frees up the seller to proceed with a second purchaser if the first has not removed a condition.

Release of lien Freeing property from liens against it.

Relief What equity allows a wronged party to recover, usually an act compelled or stopped. For example, when the seller refuses to convey title, the court can force him or her to convey by specific performance.

Remainder The estate left at the termination of a prior estate in land, such as a fee simple left after the end of a life estate.

Remedies What the law allows a person subjected to a certain legal wrong to recover, typically in damages. For example, breach of contract allows the wronged party to recover money in the form of compensatory damages.

Rent Consideration in a lease or rental agreement, which is usually a money payment made by the tenant to the landlord in exchange for the tenant's exclusive use and possession of the premises.

Rent depositing Process whereby tenants can deposit rent in court to compel landlord to bring premises up to the standards of the Ohio Revised Code.

Reply A plaintiff's responsive pleading to a defendant's counterclaim; does the same thing for the plaintiff that the answer does for the defendant.

Requests for admission Discovery device that forces a party to a lawsuit to take a position of truth or falsity regarding an evidentiary matter for the upcoming trial.

Rescission Canceling the contract or deed and restoring the parties to their former positions because of fraud, mutual mistake, or other serious wrongdoing.

Reservation Limitation reserved to the grantor of some right in the conveyed realty, such as an easement.

Restraining order Equitable relief, as ordered by court, prohibiting an activity.

Restrictions of record Limitations on how real property can be used by private control set forth on a deed, a plat, or a declaration of restrictions, as recorded in the county recorder's office.

Retaliatory eviction Prohibited practice of landlord seeking to evict tenant after tenant has tried to get landlord to comply with the health or building codes by reporting landlord to authorities.

Reversion The estate in land that returns to the grantor or his or her heirs at the termination of the grantee's estate in land.

Revocation In contracts, the offeror's canceling his or her offer before the offeree has accepted.

Rezoning Changing land from one category of use to another.

Right of first refusal The right to purchase property, or not, before another can proceed to purchase it.

Right-of-way Easement where one has the right to cross or go over the land of another.

Riparian land Land that borders a stream or watercourse.

Riparian rights Landowner's right to the ordinary or natural flow of water that borders his or her real property.

Run with the land Rights in land passing from owner to subsequent owner of real property.

Section 1982 Fair housing law passed as part of the Civil Rights Act of 1866 prohibiting private, racial discrimination in housing. It has a very broad definition of race.

Security deposit Deposit of money by tenant to secure his or her compliance under rental agreement and/or act as security for landlord in the event the tenant damages the realty.

Security interest A property interest, such as real estate, which a creditor can look to for satisfaction when the borrower does not repay.

Seisin Possession by titled owner of real property.

Self-dealing A real estate agent/broker's working for his or her own best interests rather than his or her principal's best interests, in violation of the fiduciary obligation he or she owes the principal.

Seller's affidavit of title A signed, sworn statement made by the seller, representing the condition of the title.

Separate property Real and/or personal property owned by the husband or wife prior to marriage or acquired during marriage by will, inheritance, or gift. The other spouse cannot claim separate property as community property.

Service of process Delivering or somehow putting a defendant on notice that he or she is being sued, so as to give him or her the constitutionally protected due process of law rights.

Servient tenement Land subject to an easement right of another parcel of land, called the dominant tenement.

Setback A zoning restriction stating how far from the lot line a structure must be.

Settlement An agreement by the parties to a lawsuit to each take something less than each desires so as to avoid pursuing the case to trial or beyond.

Severalty ownership One person, real or artificial, owning real property alone and not in coownership.

Sheriff's deed The type of deed given when the realty is sold by the sheriff pursuant to a court order to satisfy a judgment, such as from mortgage lien.

Sign ban Local law prohibiting real estate agents and sellers from posting "For Sale" and other signs on their listed realties.

Single agency Relationship in which the real estate agent/broker represents only one party to a transaction, either the purchaser or the seller.

Site An improved or improvable piece of land usually suitable for building.

Sole proprietorship Business organization wherein the owner simply puts up capital, conducts the business, and absorbs all profit, loss, and liability from that business.

Special assessment Tax levied against specific parcels of real estate for benefits those realties will directly receive, such as sewers, paved streets, street lights.

Special lien A lien that can be satisfied by only a specific parcel of realty of obliged owner.

Special warranty deed A deed in which the grantor warrants only against defects that occurred during his or her ownership and not those that occurred before.

Specific performance An equity court action ordering completion of the real estate purchase contract in which the seller has to convey title to the purchaser and the purchaser has to pay for the realty.

Spot zoning A community's singling out a piece of real property for a use that bears no rational relationship to what surrounding realties are used for.

Standard of proof The degree of evidence needed in a particular type of case. In civil cases, plaintiff needs to prevail by a preponderance of evidence; in criminal cases, defendant needs to be proven guilty beyond a reasonable doubt.

Standing The ability of a person to sue based on whether the law deems he or she has been injured in an ascertainable way by the violation of a certain law.

Stare decisis Legal doctrine that applies when a court declares that a principle of law, as decided in an earlier case(s), serves as precedent and is to be followed by other courts in similar or analogous cases.

Statement of record A substantial disclosure form that a developer must file with HUD pursuant to the Interstate Land Sales Full Disclosure Act.

Statistical records of business Evidence used in fair housing case wherein broker's records show pattern of sales and listings that violate the laws.

Statute Written law, enacted by state or federal legislature, that declares, commands, or prohibits some act.

Statute of conveyances Requires recording of certain real property instruments.

Statute of frauds Requires certain contracts to be in writing, such as the real estate purchase contract, or else they are unenforceable.

Statute of limitations The length of time one has to sue another after which a lawsuit can never be brought.

Statutory lien A lien on real property placed by state or federal statute, such as a local tax lien or an IRS lien.

Statutory survivorship tenancy A way under state statute for two or more persons to hold title to real estate with one another; upon the death of any one of the tenants, the decedent's interest passes to the survivor(s).

Steering Illegal practice in which a real estate licensee makes housing unavailable or tries to influence choice of housing by racial, religious, ethnic, sexual, handicap, or family status factors.

Straw person One who acts in a transaction as if he or she were a principal party but is instead merely standing in for the real party, who is someone else.

Strict liability Being liable to another for a particular condition despite no intent to deceive or even any negligent conduct.

Subagent One who is the agent of another who is an agent in a principal-agent relationship. This person has all the same agency duties.

Subcontractor One who does work on or furnishes material for real property per the order of the general contractor; materialmen or laborer.

Subdivision Tract of land divided into streets, homesites, and improvements by the owner as shown by the recorded plat.

Subject to mortgage A purchaser is obligating himself or herself to take the realty subject to the mortgage but not assuming primary liability to the lender/mortgagee for that mortgage. All payments are made by the purchaser to seller/mortgagor only.

Sublease The tenant leases a portion of his or her term to another.

Subordination Agreement to make one's rights secondary to another's; a reduction in priority of rights.

Subpoena A written, legal command to appear in court to testify.

Subrogation Legal substitution of one creditor for another with the substitute receiving all the legal rights of the original.

Substantially equivalent In fair housing law this means that state law and/or a state agency are about the same as the Fair Housing Act and HUD.

Subsurface rights Land ownership rights beneath the surface that extend to infinity.

Summons Document served by a court upon a defendant summoning, or calling, him or her into court.

Superintendent of Real Estate Executive officer of the Ohio Real Estate Commission who runs the Ohio Division of Real Estate on a daily basis.

Supreme Court Highest appeals court.

Surrender Cancellation of lease by lessor's and lessee's mutual consent.

Survey System of measuring land to formulate a legal description showing how much land there is and where it is located.

Survivorship Type of ownership where one coowner receives another coowner's interest upon the other's death.

Sweetheart contracts Long-term contracts the condominium developer entered into with his or her friends and relatives that were binding on the condominium unit owners' association even after the developer had lost control. These are now expressly outlawed by statute in Ohio.

Temporary restraining order Order of court which, for a limited period of time, prohibits certain activity.

Tenancy at sufferance Lessee who occupies leasehold without any legal right to do so after his or her tenancy has expired.

Tenancy at will Lessee who possesses leasehold until the lessor terminates the tenancy.

Tenancy in common Coownership of real property by two or more persons with undivided shares; ownership passes by devise or descent instead of by survivorship.

Tenant The person in possession of real property by right or title with the owner's permission.

Tenants' fixtures Items that are considered fixtures but are nonetheless removable by tenant at the end of his or her term.

Tenement Permanent holding of property.

Term tenancy Periodic tenancy.

Testamentary intent In wills, a showing that a disposition of property is to take effect only at death.

Testamentary trust Trust that takes effect upon trustor's death.

Testate One who dies possessed of a will.

Testator One who makes a will.

Testing In fair housing, this is a way to monitor compliance by using (usually) a black person and a white person to pose as prospective purchasers with real estate agents to ascertain whether minority people are treated differently from nonminority people when trying to lease or sell real property. Also called auditing or checking, this is used as evidence in trials of fair housing cases.

Third-party practice Occurs when the defendant sues another person who has caused his or her liability under the original complaint.

Time is of the essence A phrase that makes the element of time the most critical, vital part of a contract.

Title Outward evidence of the right to possession or ownership of realty.

Title companies Privately owned firms that sell insurance regarding defects that may exist in the title to real property.

Title defect A flaw in the title that allows claims by another upon the owner's right to title, possession, and ownership of realty.

Title guarantee An insurance policy issued by a title company guaranteeing accuracy of the title examination subject to certain limitations, one of which is flaws that cannot be revealed by examination of public records.

Title insurance Insurance obtained by owner from title company, which protects owner against loss arising from defect in realty's title, including flaws that are not revealed by examination of public records.

Title search Examination of public records to elicit any information that has bearing on which person has the right to title, possession, and ownership of real property.

Topography Shape of the land.

Tort A civil wrong, such as fraud, misrepresentation, negligence.

Tract A piece of land; a lot.

Trade fixtures Objects that are fixtures under the fixtures' tests, which are put in by a business tenant; the tenant has the right to remove them at the end of the tenancy.

Trespass Some physical invasion or unlawful entry upon real property whereby damages ensuing are direct and not consequential; one without title or right to possess entering onto land without consent, permission, or license.

Trespasser A person wrongfully on the realty of another.

Trial court Lower court wherein issues of fact are decided by judge or jury and judgment is rendered.

Trust Real and/or personal property held by one person for the benefit of another.

Trust account A special, noninterest-bearing account in which a broker holds money, usually the earnest money deposits.

Trustee A person who holds and manages real and personal property for another's benefit.

Trustor A person who creates a trust for the use of his or her real and/or personal property.

Truth-in-Lending Law Federal legislation requiring meaningful disclosure of the terms of credit by a creditor to a prospective debtor. Triggered for real estate agents by their advertisements offering credit or arranging of credit by the real estate brokerage.

Unauthorized practice of law Unlawful activity that occurs when brokers/agents practice law instead of real estate upon their clients and customers.

Unconscionable clause Clause in contract or lease that is so overly harsh to one party that a court can refuse to enforce it.

Unconventional financing In addition to the security of note and mortgage, the security of insurance by FHA or guarantee by VA.

Undisclosed principal In contracts, a party to a contract that is not known to the other party.

Undue influence A ground for setting aside a contract or will when one party has been pressured into the contract or will by the other party, especially if the party being pressured suffers from a disability.

Unenforceable contract One in which neither party can force the other legally to perform.

Uniform Settlement Statement Standard form Closing statement, used pursuant to RESPA.

Unilateral contract A contract in which one party makes a promise in exchange for an act done by the other party.

Unit In condominiums, the apartment or house within the condominium property that only the unit owner owns, not all condominium property owners.

United States District Court Federal trial court found in different geographical locations throughout the country.

Unit owner In condominiums, one who has common ownership interest in the condominium property with all other condominium owners and an individual interest in his or her own unit.

Unit owners' association In condominiums, an organization to which all owners of condominium property belong. It meets annually, elects a board of managers/directors, and administrates the condominium property.

Use One of the many ways real property can be developed and then utilized; for example, residentially, commercially, industrially.

Valid contract One that is binding and enforceable; one party can legally force the other party to perform.

VA loan A mortgage loan secured through a lending institution and guaranteed by the Veterans Administration.

Valuation The price a piece of real property is worth.

Variance A use of land that is permitted, even though it is not in strict compliance with the zoning code, because of undue hardship or practical difficulties.

Vendee The purchaser of real property.

Vendor The seller of real property.

Vest Give an immediate right to enjoyment to property.

Voidable contract One that is capable of disaffirmance by either party; potentially one party can opt out of performance.

Void contract One lacking essential elements necessary for formation; of no legal force and effect.

Voluntary lien Lien placed against realty to which the owner has consented, as in a mortgage lien.

Waiver Renouncement of a legal right.

Ward Person who is subject to a guardianship in probate court.

Warranty Grantor's assurance of protection of grantee's right and title to real property.

Warranty deed A deed with the greatest protection as the grantor warrants good, marketable title that he or she will stand behind.

Waste Life tenant's wrongful, permanent diminishment of the value of the realty. For nonlife tenants, there are two categories of waste: (1) intentional waste, such as breaking all the windows, and (2) permissive waste, such as not repairing broken windows.

Will A written, witnessed legal instrument that sets forth testator's property distribution.

Will contest Probate court proceeding to determine whether the writing produced is the last will or codicil of the testator.

Withdrawal in contracts An offeror's taking back his or her offer if it is not accepted.

Words of conveyance Language that follows the consideration in the deed instrument, stating the grantor's intent to convey or transfer the real property.

Writ of execution Legal instrument authorizing officer of the court to carry out order of the court.

Zero lot line The concept whereby owner possesses and owns exclusively his or her housing unit and other real property connected with it and also shares ownership and possession of common, connected real property with other zero lot line owners.

Zoning Ordinances or resolutions passed by the local government, pursuant to its police powers, which regulate how land is to be used in specific areas.

INDEX